LIVING ⊞ LITURGY™

LIVING ✠ LITURGY™

Spirituality, Celebration, and Catechesis for Sundays and Solemnities

Year A • 2023

Jessie Bazan
Chris de Silva
Verna Holyhead, SGS
Jessica Mannen Kimmet
Victoria McBride

LITURGICAL PRESS
Collegeville, Minnesota

www.litpress.org

Cover design by Monica Bokinskie. Art by Ruberval Monteiro da Silva, OSB.

Published with the approval of the Committee on Divine Worship, United States Conference of Catholic Bishops.

ISSN 1547-089X

ISBN 978-0-8146-6608-1   ISBN 978-0-8146-6634-0 (ebook)

CONTENTS

Jessie Bazan helps Christians explore their life callings in her work with the Collegeville Institute for Ecumenical and Cultural Research. She is editor and coauthor of *Dear Joan Chittister: Conversations with Women in the Church* (Twenty-Third Publications) and a regular columnist for *U.S. Catholic* magazine. Her work has also appeared in the *National Catholic Reporter* and on *Catholic Women Preach*. She holds a master of divinity from Saint John's School of Theology and Seminary.

Chris de Silva is a widely published composer of sacred music whose music appears in hymnals and compilations throughout the world. A native of Singapore, he currently resides in Los Angeles where he serves as music minister on the campus ministry team at Loyola Marymount University. Chris holds a bachelor of music in music composition and film scoring from the University of Southern California Thornton School of Music, a master of arts in pastoral theology from Loyola Marymount University, and a doctor of ministry from Candler School of Theology at Emory University.

Verna Holyhead, SGS (1933–2011), Australian Sister of the Good Samaritan of the Order of St. Benedict, wrote with an emphasis on biblical scholarship, liturgical insight, and pastoral challenge. She was the author of the three-volume collection *Welcoming the Word in Year A, B,* and *C,* published by Liturgical Press.

Jessica Mannen Kimmet is a freelance writer and liturgical musician. Formerly a full-time college campus minister, she now spends her days overseeing a domestic church and the growth of her three young sons. Originally from Oregon, she has spent most of her adult life in the Midwest, with the exception of two years of ministry in Wexford, Ireland. She holds a BA in theology and music theory and a master of divinity, both from the University of Notre Dame.

Victoria (Vickey) McBride is the director of campus ministry at Saint Martin de Porres High School (Cristo Rey) in Cleveland, Ohio. Prior to working at Saint Martin, she lived and worked in Brownsville, Texas, as a teacher in the Alliance for Catholic Education, earning her master of education degree from the University of Notre Dame. She contributed to *Five Minutes with the Saints: More Spiritual Nourishment for Busy Teachers,* a book of meditations published by Ave Maria Press in 2014. She serves as a music minister for her parish, Saint Patrick Parish, and as director of the Saint Martin de Porres Gospel Choir.

PREFACE

Introduction

As a premier Catholic publisher, Liturgical Press remains committed to offering liturgical, spiritual, and scriptural resources rooted in the Benedictine tradition. While these resources have changed and developed over the years, the commitment to sound theology and best pastoral practice remains a hallmark of our mission and ministry. *Living Liturgy*™ is one of our most loved and widely used incarnations of this commitment.

Living Liturgy™ will always help people prepare for liturgy and live a liturgical spirituality—a way of living that is rooted in liturgy. The paschal mystery is the central focus of liturgy, of the gospels, and of this volume. *Living Liturgy*™ is more than a title. Rather, "living liturgy" is a commitment to a relationship with Jesus Christ, embodied in our everyday actions and interactions.

We hope this edition of *Living Liturgy*™ will continue to facilitate this relationship, making liturgical spirituality a lived reality.

Authors

As always, we are extremely proud of our team of *Living Liturgy*™ authors. Jessie Bazan, Chris de Silva, Verna Holyhead, SGS (1933–2011), Jessica Mannen Kimmet, and Victoria (Vickey) McBride write at the intersection of theology and pastoral reality, bringing their rich and varied experiences of "living liturgy" to this work. We know that you will find these contributions to be prayerful, practical, and relevant to our church and world today.

Artwork

This edition features stunning original artwork from Ruberval Monteiro da Silva, OSB. Fr. Ruberval, a native of Brazil, resides in the Benedictine community of Sant'Anselmo in Rome. His colorful mosaics grace the walls of churches around the world, and we are excited to once again include his work in *Living Liturgy*™.

SEASON OF ADVENT

SPIRITUALITY

GOSPEL ACCLAMATION
Ps 85:8

R⁊. Alleluia, alleluia.
Show us, Lord, your love;
and grant us your salvation.
R⁊. Alleluia, alleluia.

Gospel

Matt 24:37-44; L1A

Jesus said to his disciples:
"As it was in the days of Noah,
    so it will be at the coming of
        the Son of Man.
In those days before the flood,
    they were eating and
        drinking,
    marrying and giving in
        marriage,
    up to the day that Noah en-
        tered the ark.
They did not know until the
    flood came and carried
        them all away.
So will it be also at the coming
    of the Son of Man.
Two men will be out in the
    field;
    one will be taken, and one will be
        left.
Two women will be grinding at the mill;
    one will be taken, and one will be
        left.
Therefore, stay awake!
For you do not know on which day your
    Lord will come.
Be sure of this: if the master of the
    house
    had known the hour of night when
        the thief was coming,
    he would have stayed awake
    and not let his house be broken into.
So too, you also must be prepared,
    for at an hour you do not expect, the
        Son of Man will come."

Reflecting on the Gospel

At the beginning of the liturgical year, the church tries to make us more attentive to, hopeful about, and prepared for the moment of the great advent of God: the second coming of Christ, when human and cosmic history will have run its course and the timeless, eternal kingdom is fully established. God will come to us, but we also must make our pilgrimage to God.

In the gospel reading for today's Mass, Jesus warns his disciples that they are not to be like the people of Noah's generation, who were so immersed in the ordinary and everyday that they were unaware of the flood of evil that was gradually encroaching on their lives. But this does not mean that we go into a pious retreat from life's everyday demands. As the gospel tells us by its own imagery, the fields still have to be plowed, the flour still ground at the mill, but work or leisure or human relationships cannot be so all consuming that we are not alert and committed to the coming of God into our lives.

One of the problems of the early church was that because of the expectation that Jesus's second coming (or *parousía*, "appearance") at the end of human history was just around the corner, Christians might as well do nothing except wait for it—or try to calculate its arrival. This temptation continues to surface in our own time despite repeated and excused failures! Such passivity is the opposite of the active, discerning vigilance that makes us alert and committed to the daily possibilities of establishing the rule of God in our own life and in the world around us. Pope John XXIII once remarked that if he knew the world was about to end, he would tell the citizens of Vatican City to look busy!—busy with God's work for the kingdom.

In the two mini-parables that Jesus tells today, the men working in the field or the women at the mill are outwardly no different, but one is ready for the kingdom, the other is not. For Matthew, readiness consists in nothing "rapturous," but in doing the work of God in the spirit of the Beatitudes (Matt 5:1-12) and the parable of the Last Judgment (Matt 25:31-46). In another daring image, Jesus compares his coming as Son of Man to a burglary. Any prudent householder who expects to be burgled is on the alert to thwart the robbery. We are to be alert for the day when Jesus will break into our lives—not to thwart him, but to allow ourselves to be "stolen" for heaven.

Jesus will come definitively to each one of us at our own individual end time, which will be our death. For the whole of creation, it will be the *eschaton*, the "end time" not so much *of* the world but *for* the world. Individually and cosmically, this will be a new birth, as unimaginable and yet so much more hugely real than the world that awaited us when we were born from our mother's womb.

Preparing to Proclaim

Key words and phrases: "[S]tay awake! . . . you also must be prepared."

To the point: Even for those of us who believe in observing Advent before Christmas, the secular world's insistence on rushing to the latter can form our expectations. When Advent begins, we come to Mass ready for flickering flame, for slowly growing light, for tidings of comfort and joy. But this gospel snaps us back to reality: it is not Christmas yet. What is described here is rather scary and unsettling. The image of people being suddenly taken away is uncomfortable; the idea of being left behind doesn't sound great either. All this reminds us that our God is a God of surprises. For most of us, God's surprising work will be much more ordinary than vanishing neighbors, but we are still called to stay aware of God's presence and open to the unexpected ways God moves in our hearts and in our world.

Psalmist Preparation

This is a pilgrimage song, one that invites participation in the festal journey to Jerusalem. This trip was an obligation but is here received as a joy. Does your attendance and ministry at liturgy feel more like an obligation or a joy to you? What might be keeping you from the sort of joy the psalmist expresses here? As you prepare this psalm, pray for all who will attend Mass this week only out of obligation. Thank God for their presence; sometimes, going through the motions is a way of witnessing to love as a virtue when feelings of joy are escaping us.

Making Connections

Between the readings: Compared to the gospel, the first reading offers a more comforting and joyful vision of the end times. There is unity and inclusion rather than division; all are called to be part of the lasting peace God envisions for us. The psalmist echoes the joy of the nations streaming toward Jerusalem as he, too, heads there on pilgrimage and prays for its peace. The second reading gives us practical ways to "stay awake," through moral conduct and union with Christ.

To experience: "Staying awake" means remaining attentive to how small choices build into robust lives of faith. It means cultivating awareness of God's ongoing presence in the mundane realities of our lives. It means turning our attention toward the things that really matter and turning away from things that are distracting. Advent might be an invitation to shake off the stupor of binge watching and social media scrolling and to enter into the fully vibrant lives that God wants for us.

Homily Points

• Jesus urges the disciples to prepare. The Son of Man will come—but they know not the time nor the place. Mystery abounds in matters of faith, then and now. God reveals Godself to creation over and over, yet we can never know it all. God is too big, too powerful, too mysterious. How, then, are we to prepare? Like the disciples, we are not expected to solve the mystery. Instead, we are instructed to be present, to pay attention, to awe at the gift of God alive all over.

• What does it feel like to be spiritually awake? Think of a time when your mind, body, and spirit felt awake and present to the divine. What spiritual practices helped you get to that place? Advent is a season of preparation, a time to try new—or resurrect old—spiritual practices that help us wake up to our faith. Pick a practice that works for you: meditate on the daily readings; light a candle; sit in silence.

• The prophet Isaiah paints a vision of God who makes Godself known in bigger and bolder ways. The Lord establishes a house on the highest mountain. People of all nations converge to learn God's holy ways and to walk in the divine light.

Model Penitential Act

Presider: In today's gospel, Jesus urges his disciples to stay awake and prepare for the coming of the Son of Man. For those times we have fallen asleep to Christ's presence in the world, let us ask for mercy . . . *[pause]*

> Lord Jesus, you are the Son of God: Lord, have mercy.
>
> Christ Jesus, you are the Son of Man: Christ, have mercy.
>
> Lord Jesus, you assure us of your presence among us, always: Lord, have mercy.

Model Universal Prayer (Prayer of the Faithful)

Presider: Jesus tells his disciples to stay awake. Heeding his call, let us offer our prayers and petitions.

Response: Lord, hear our prayer.

Enliven the church as we begin a new liturgical year, may the mystery of God energize our hearts through each season . . .

Rouse leaders of all nations, may God call them to work for greater unity and peace . . .

Comfort all who suffer from mental health issues, may the light of the Lord shine in their darkness . . .

Inspire all gathered here, may God stimulate our spiritual lives and the practices that sustain them . . .

Presider: Gracious God, you illumine the way forward for all of creation. Hear our prayers that we might prepare faithfully for the coming of your Son. We ask this through Christ our Lord. **Amen.**

Liturgy and Music

Intentional Ministry: This liturgical year begins with Psalm 122, which reminds us of the importance of pilgrimage. It encourages us to think of what hopes and goals we might set for the upcoming journey. Within the psalm the words of Isaiah echo through—"May peace be within your walls, / prosperity in your buildings." What goals could we set for our music programs to flourish and prosper? Perhaps a goal of being intentional in ministry. A simple start would be to recognize the importance of a good choir rehearsal outline. Entering into a practice without adequate preparation distracts all from entering into prayer and experiencing God's work revealed in music. Careful attention should be paid to developing a musicality that is shaped by a liturgical sensibility. Good rehearsal technique will be one way to foster such musical and liturgical thinking and development.

Beyond the task of getting the notes right, root the beginning and ending of each rehearsal in prayer. Make time to read the coming Sunday's gospel reading or highlight the psalm text to give deeper context to music making. Bring awareness to the ministerial presence that each member holds for each other and to the larger parish community. Respect each other's time and be grateful for each gift. With praise and thanksgiving, we enter the gates of a new liturgical year of service to the people of God.

COLLECT

Let us pray.

Pause for silent prayer

Grant your faithful, we pray, almighty God,
the resolve to run forth to meet your Christ
with righteous deeds at his coming,
so that, gathered at his right hand,
they may be worthy to possess the heavenly Kingdom.
Through our Lord Jesus Christ, your Son,
who lives and reigns with you in the unity of the Holy Spirit,
God, for ever and ever. **Amen.**

FIRST READING

Isa 2:1-5

This is what Isaiah, son of Amoz,
    saw concerning Judah and Jerusalem.
    In days to come,
    the mountain of the LORD's house
        shall be established as the highest mountain
        and raised above the hills.
    All nations shall stream toward it;
        many peoples shall come and say:
    "Come, let us climb the LORD's mountain,
        to the house of the God of Jacob,
    that he may instruct us in his ways,
        and we may walk in his paths."
    For from Zion shall go forth instruction,
        and the word of the LORD from Jerusalem.
    He shall judge between the nations,
        and impose terms on many peoples.
    They shall beat their swords into plowshares
        and their spears into pruning hooks;
    one nation shall not raise the sword against another,
        nor shall they train for war again.
    O house of Jacob, come,
        let us walk in the light of the LORD!

RESPONSORIAL PSALM

Ps 122:1-2, 3-4, 4-5, 6-7, 8-9

R︶. Let us go rejoicing to the house of the Lord.

I rejoiced because they said to me,
  "We will go up to the house of the LORD."
And now we have set foot
  within your gates, O Jerusalem.

R︶. Let us go rejoicing to the house of the Lord.

Jerusalem, built as a city
  with compact unity.
To it the tribes go up,
  the tribes of the LORD.

R︶. Let us go rejoicing to the house of the Lord.

According to the decree for Israel,
  to give thanks to the name of the LORD.
In it are set up judgment seats,
  seats for the house of David.

R︶. Let us go rejoicing to the house of the Lord.

Pray for the peace of Jerusalem!
  May those who love you prosper!
May peace be within your walls,
  prosperity in your buildings.

R︶. Let us go rejoicing to the house of the Lord.

Because of my brothers and friends
  I will say, "Peace be within you!"
Because of the house of the LORD, our God,
  I will pray for your good.

R︶. Let us go rejoicing to the house of the Lord.

SECOND READING

Rom 13:11-14

Brothers and sisters:
You know the time;
  it is the hour now for you to awake from
    sleep.
For our salvation is nearer now than when
    we first believed;
  the night is advanced, the day is at
    hand.
Let us then throw off the works of
    darkness
  and put on the armor of light;
  let us conduct ourselves properly as in
    the day,
  not in orgies and drunkenness,
  not in promiscuity and lust,
  not in rivalry and jealousy.
But put on the Lord Jesus Christ,
  and make no provision for the desires
    of the flesh.

Living Liturgy

A Community of Belonging: The songs and prayers we plant in our hearts and sow in our minds should inspire us toward imagining a welcome space, a space made holy by God and those we serve. Throughout this liturgical year, when we desire shared space and community, the Spirit leads us to discern what it means for music and liturgy to deepen our belonging, enliven our believing and inspire our becoming. During this Advent season we ask the question: What does it mean to be a community of belonging?

During this time of Advent preparation, we try to quiet ourselves amid the busyness of peak retail season to look into our hearts and reflect on this liturgical season in unison with our worship community. Recognizing that the Son of Man will come at an hour that we do not expect, we prepare holy space and take seriously the words of Isaiah as "[a]ll nations stream toward . . . the mountain of the LORD's house." Isaiah calls for unity, beating swords into plowshares, turning spears into pruning hooks. How will we bring people together during this season of Advent waiting? In our waiting and preparing, will we listen for what is missing within our prayer and our music repertoire?

Palestinian-American poet Naomi Shihab Nye paints a picture of a community of belonging in her poem "Gate A-4." She reflects on shared space where simple acts of kindness bring strangers into a blessed world of belonging to each other. At Gate A-4 she encounters unity within the sharing of sugar cookies amid diverse people and cultures. In some way we are reminded of the sacramental nature of our faith tradition—prayer and ritual in unity with this world as we glimpse a world that is to come. What kind of journey will we go on with our choirs and worship communities this new liturgical year?

PROMPTS FOR FAITH-SHARING

• Both the first and second reading contain light imagery. Where in your life do you need God's illumining light?

• The psalm calls us to joy in liturgy and in God's presence. Is anything keeping you from this joy?

• How do you feel reading the gospel's description of Jesus's coming? How could you invite God into any anxiety you may be feeling?

✝ SPIRITUALITY

GOSPEL ACCLAMATION
Luke 3:4, 6

℟. Alleluia, alleluia.
Prepare the way of the Lord, make straight his paths:
all flesh shall see the salvation of God.
℟. Alleluia, alleluia.

Gospel   Matt 3:1-12; L4A

John the Baptist appeared, preaching in the desert of Judea
and saying, "Repent, for the kingdom of heaven is at hand!"
It was of him that the prophet Isaiah had spoken when he said:
A voice of one crying out in the desert,
Prepare the way of the LORD,
make straight his paths.
John wore clothing made of camel's hair
and had a leather belt around his waist.
His food was locusts and wild honey.
At that time Jerusalem, all Judea,
and the whole region around the Jordan
were going out to him
and were being baptized by him in the Jordan River
as they acknowledged their sins.

When he saw many of the Pharisees and Sadducees
coming to his baptism, he said to them, "You brood of vipers!
Who warned you to flee from the coming wrath?
Produce good fruit as evidence of your repentance.
And do not presume to say to yourselves, 'We have Abraham as our father.'
For I tell you,
God can raise up children to Abraham from these stones.

Continued in Appendix A, p. 259.

Reflecting on the Gospel

During Advent, one strong voice that tries to rouse us to the demands of our discipleship is that of John the Baptist. He comes from the wilderness—the privileged place of covenant making and the dangerous environment of temptation to covenant breaking—eager to share what he has learned there.

In "those days" of new beginnings, the Spirit thrusts John the Baptist onto the banks of the Jordan River to be Israel's awakener to what God will do in and through Jesus. Sharpened in wisdom and words by his desert experience, John cuts his way through hypocrisy and sinfulness, and offers to the Jordan crowd his baptism of repentance.

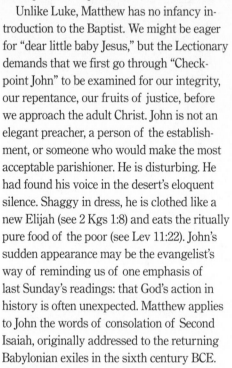

Unlike Luke, Matthew has no infancy introduction to the Baptist. We might be eager for "dear little baby Jesus," but the Lectionary demands that we first go through "Checkpoint John" to be examined for our integrity, our repentance, our fruits of justice, before we approach the adult Christ. John is not an elegant preacher, a person of the establishment, or someone who would make the most acceptable parishioner. He is disturbing. He had found his voice in the desert's eloquent silence. Shaggy in dress, he is clothed like a new Elijah (see 2 Kgs 1:8) and eats the ritually pure food of the poor (see Lev 11:22). John's sudden appearance may be the evangelist's way of reminding us of one emphasis of last Sunday's readings: that God's action in history is often unexpected. Matthew applies to John the words of consolation of Second Isaiah, originally addressed to the returning Babylonian exiles in the sixth century BCE.

But whereas Isaiah dreamed of God cutting a smooth way home through the wilderness for his people, in today's gospel it is the Baptist's strident and fiery words that blaze a trail for the coming of God-with-us in Christ. The wilderness is not just the physical place in which the Baptist preaches; it is also the barren places of our hearts in which a trail of repentance needs to be cut.

It was at the Jordan River that the Hebrews came out of their wilderness wandering and crossed through the waters into the Promised Land. Over twelve hundred years later, the Baptist calls their descendants into the waters for another transition, another entry into the promises of God. If, in retrospect, the calendar year that we'll soon finish seems to have been something of a desert wandering—personally, politically, socially, and ecclesially—Advent is a call to new hope and conversion to Christ. The biblical meaning of "repentance" to which John summons us is much more than just "being sorry." It implies a radical change in our attitudes and matters of the heart, a total transformation of our priorities, the beginning and end of everything in us that is not God.

Sunday after Sunday during Advent, we light a candle on the Advent wreath: a fragile flame that reminds us that in these weeks we are preparing to renew the welcome into our lives of the vulnerable One who was announced by a star rising in the darkness and a song echoing through the night.

Preparing to Proclaim

Key words and phrases: "Repent, for the kingdom of heaven is at hand."

To the point: This week's gospel introduces one of Advent's main characters: John the Baptist. And he is treated as a character here, given a more vivid description than many biblical figures. We are meant to picture him; we know what he wears and what he eats. He is rough. He is unkempt. He is blunt. He is, in a word, weird. And yet, people are drawn to him, listening to his preaching and going to be baptized. Throughout the Advent and Christmas seasons, we hear stories of God coming in ways we didn't expect, from this bizarre desert preacher to a literal infant born into poverty. In John the Baptist, holiness could have been overlooked because of his oddities. But the season insists on reminding us to keep our eyes open to the truth that God often comes disguised in interruption and inconvenience.

Psalmist Preparation

We often associate the word "justice" with criminal justice, with those who do wrong being made to pay some kind of retribution for their offenses. Justice involves people getting what they deserve. In this psalm, we see that the heart of justice is indeed about people getting their due, but what they are owed not as wrongdoers but as beloved children of God. The justice with which this King is concerned is justice that protects the poor, recognizing the dignity of all who seem lowly by our worldly standards. This is a justice that brings "profound peace." Rest in the alliteration and imagery of that phrase; there's a powerful depth to it. Try praying with this line this week, inviting your own heart into the profundity of the peace God promises.

Making Connections

Between the readings: Again, a harsh-sounding gospel is paired with an Old Testament prophecy of lush comfort. At the same time, though, it echoes the gospel's promise that Jesus is not coming to bring peace alone; those who are unrepentantly wicked or ruthless should be afraid of his coming. The second reading affirms that Christ's coming is for all; it is not our background or origin that matters but our choice to follow Jesus.

To experience: Recognizing that God works through the interruptions of our lives is an ongoing challenge. Very often we are tempted to think we know best, especially if we have included God in our discernment and the making of our plans. But our plans—even the ones that seem good and holy—are up for interruption. Convenience is not a prerequisite for how God works. Prophets often appear in our midst in weird and inconvenient ways. They are there for a reason; they interrupt our too-small ways of understanding God. How often do we overlook prophets in our midst?

Homily Points

• Imagine a world in which the words of God through the prophet Isaiah ring true: "There shall be no harm or ruin on all my holy mountain." Imagine living this way *now*. Many days, our world seems far from God's vision of peace and justice: Black people lie dying in the streets, refugees flee violence only to be turned away at the border, young people face bullying online. There is much work to be done to end harm and ruin. We need the prayer for endurance and encouragement from today's second reading. The work of justice is grueling and slow. It can take years to see the wolves and lambs of our time graze together—if we ever see it at all. Yet, imbued with the spirit of the Lord, we are called to keep working toward God's glorious vision.

• John the Baptist displays a wildness that we would do well to embrace this Advent season. The Christian way is rarely neat and tidy. The Spirit of God blows where it wills, wildly with no constraints. Enlivened by this Spirit, how can you tap into your wild side this Advent? What would it look like for you to drop the things constraining you from loving God with your whole heart?

• The image of a root appears in the first reading and the gospel. The writers of Scripture often draw on images of plants to signify spiritual growth and connectedness to Christ. As we prepare for the birth of Christ, reflect on the roots of your faith. Who or what keeps you grounded?

Model Penitential Act

Presider: In today's gospel, John the Baptist tells the people, "Repent, for the kingdom of heaven is at hand!" Calling to mind the need for repentance in our own lives, let us ask our gracious God for forgiveness . . . *[pause]*

Lord Jesus, you came to save the sinner: Lord, have mercy.

Christ Jesus, you preach a message of mercy: Christ, have mercy.

Lord Jesus, you believe in the goodness of all creation: Lord, have mercy.

Model Universal Prayer (Prayer of the Faithful)

Presider: Trusting that the spirit of the Lord is always with us, we bring our needs before God.

Response: Lord, hear our prayer.

Connect pastoral leaders, that they may know the spirit of counsel . . .

Inspire prophets of our time, that they may know the spirit of wisdom . . .

Heal members of family who are at odds with each other, that they may know the spirit of understanding . . .

Fortify those who seek justice for our communities, that they may know the spirit of strength . . .

Presider: God of heaven and earth, you sent your spirit to dwell with us and guide us in the ways of justice and faithfulness. Hear our prayers that we might stay rooted in your way. We ask this through Christ our Lord. **Amen.**

Liturgy and Music

A Simpler Arrangement: During this time of Advent, the General Instruction of the Roman Missal recommends that the use of musical instruments "should be marked by a moderation suited to the character of this time of year, without expressing in anticipation the full joy of the Nativity of the Lord" (GIRM 313). One way to think about this recommendation is to imagine different arrangements of the community's songs and hymns, perhaps simpler arrangements.

To highlight the penitential nature of the season, consider connecting the penitential act with the gathering song. Take the form C setting and weave the tune of the entrance processional into the three tropes. This setting may be sung metrically or in chant form.

Honor the diversity of the parish community and prepare to celebrate the full voice of the assembly during this season of waiting. Build a wider circle of belonging by anticipating your parish's Latinx community's tradition of *Las Posadas*, a reenactment of the Holy Family's pilgrimage from Nazareth to Bethlehem, with singing one piece taken from that traditional celebration. Sing the piece simply, in unison. Justice and peace cannot fully flourish unless we extend a broader embrace to the whole assembly as we sing and "think in harmony with one another," glorifying God.

COLLECT

Let us pray.

Pause for silent prayer

Almighty and merciful God,
may no earthly undertaking hinder those
who set out in haste to meet your Son,
but may our learning of heavenly wisdom
gain us admittance to his company.
Who lives and reigns with you in the unity
of the Holy Spirit,
God, for ever and ever. **Amen.**

FIRST READING

Isa 11:1-10

On that day, a shoot shall sprout from the
stump of Jesse,
and from his roots a bud shall blossom.
The spirit of the LORD shall rest upon him:
a spirit of wisdom and of
understanding,
a spirit of counsel and of strength,
a spirit of knowledge and of fear of the
LORD,
and his delight shall be the fear of the
LORD.
Not by appearance shall he judge,
nor by hearsay shall he decide,
but he shall judge the poor with justice,
and decide aright for the land's afflicted.
He shall strike the ruthless with the rod of
his mouth,
and with the breath of his lips he shall
slay the wicked.
Justice shall be the band around his waist,
and faithfulness a belt upon his hips.
Then the wolf shall be a guest of the
lamb,
and the leopard shall lie down with the
kid;
the calf and the young lion shall browse
together,
with a little child to guide them.
The cow and the bear shall be neighbors,
together their young shall rest;
the lion shall eat hay like the ox.
The baby shall play by the cobra's den,
and the child lay his hand on the adder's
lair.
There shall be no harm or ruin on all my
holy mountain;
for the earth shall be filled with
knowledge of the LORD,
as water covers the sea.
On that day, the root of Jesse,
set up as a signal for the nations,
the Gentiles shall seek out,
for his dwelling shall be glorious.

RESPONSORIAL PSALM
Ps 72:1-2, 7-8, 12-13, 17

℟. (cf. 7) Justice shall flourish in his time,
and fullness of peace for ever.

O God, with your judgment endow the
       king,
   and with your justice, the king's son;
he shall govern your people with justice
   and your afflicted ones with judgment.

℟. Justice shall flourish in his time, and
fullness of peace for ever.

Justice shall flower in his days,
   and profound peace, till the moon be no
       more.
May he rule from sea to sea,
   and from the River to the ends of the
       earth.

℟. Justice shall flourish in his time, and
fullness of peace for ever.

For he shall rescue the poor when he cries
       out,
   and the afflicted when he has no one to
       help him.
He shall have pity for the lowly and the
       poor;
   the lives of the poor he shall save.

℟. Justice shall flourish in his time, and
fullness of peace for ever.

May his name be blessed forever;
   as long as the sun his name shall
       remain.
In him shall all the tribes of the earth be
       blessed;
   all the nations shall proclaim his
       happiness.

℟. Justice shall flourish in his time, and
fullness of peace for ever.

SECOND READING
Rom 15:4-9

Brothers and sisters:
Whatever was written previously was
       written for our instruction,
   that by endurance and by the
       encouragement of the Scriptures
we might have hope.
May the God of endurance and
       encouragement
   grant you to think in harmony with one
       another,
   in keeping with Christ Jesus,
   that with one accord you may with one
       voice
   glorify the God and Father of our Lord
       Jesus Christ.

Continued in Appendix A, p. 259.

Living Liturgy

Justice Shall Flourish: In this season of preparation, John the Baptist reminds us to look deep into our lives in search of the things that distract us from bringing peace and justice into the world. Repentance requires a shaking up of the regular, daily routine of how we choose to belong to God and to each other in harmony. The penitential nature of the Advent season engages our greater awareness; it draws us away from the regular and challenges us to risk making changes to our normal pattern. The changes we choose to make ought to lead us closer to the kingdom of God that Isaiah describes, a peaceable kingdom where justice will flourish. How will our liturgical celebrations prepare this way to peace? How might they be brave enough to elevate justice?

The artwork of John August Swanson provides gentle reminders that these pathways to peace are taken in small steps. In his serigraph painting, *Psalm 85*, psalm texts of justice and peace meld into a farming scene as characters go about their daily tasks of planting and harvesting. Swanson's delicate serigraph work shows us that with each tiny touch of the artist's hand, through a long process, a beautiful scene comes together. With any Swanson art piece, the more attention you pay, the more you see. Sowing peace and justice into our hearts and into the world requires small changes or shifts in our daily routine. Repentance urges us to step out of ourselves and into community, paying attention to the little details that we have overlooked, tending the blind spots, and sharpening our vision to see God's kingdom that is already here. Within John the Baptist's call to repent, we discover an invitation to shift our hearts back to God, to reflect on what it means to do things a little differently, and to share space that will deepen our communal identity of inclusive belonging.

PROMPTS FOR FAITH-SHARING

• The gospel describes John's eccentricities with some detail. Who or what in your life do you write off as odd? How might God be present to you through them?

• Paul names God as "the God of endurance and encouragement." Where do you need endurance and encouragement this season? How can your community help?

• The psalm speaks of rescuing the poor; how can you be part of God's work of supporting those who live in poverty this Advent?

GOSPEL ACCLAMATION
cf. Luke 1:28

R̸. Alleluia, alleluia.
Hail, Mary, full of grace, the Lord is with you;
blessed are you among women.
R̸. Alleluia, alleluia.

Gospel Luke 1:26-38; L689

The angel Gabriel was sent from God
  to a town of Galilee called Nazareth,
  to a virgin betrothed to a man named
    Joseph,
  of the house of David,
  and the virgin's name was Mary.
And coming to her, he said,
  "Hail, full of grace! The Lord is with
    you."
But she was greatly troubled at what
    was said
  and pondered what sort of greeting
    this might be.
Then the angel said to her,
  "Do not be afraid, Mary,
  for you have found favor with God.
Behold, you will conceive in your womb
    and bear a son,
  and you shall name him Jesus.

Continued in Appendix A, p. 259.

See Appendix A, pp. 259–260, for the other readings.

Reflecting on the Gospel

This solemnity commemorates the fact that Mary was conceived without original sin. However, the gospel reading we hear tells of the moment when Mary learns that she will conceive and bear Jesus, the Son of God. This reading reveals why Mary was born with her particular sinless character.

What does it mean to be full of grace? What does it mean for the Lord to be with you? It may be deeply affirming and dignifying, but it also magnifies the heightened gravity of one's existence. It is intimidating to be told that the God who created the universe and all that dwells within it sees you—chooses *you.* Few people experience such a clear unveiling of their vocation as Mary did when the angel told her that she would bear a son who would be called "Son of the Most High." So perhaps it is understandable why Mary's initial reaction was to be "greatly troubled." What are the implications of this call for Mary's life? How can she even comprehend and consent to this calling? What can this story teach us about responding to the significant invitations we are issued in our lives?

It is true that we are sometimes baited into traps and snares by sweet, complimentary words. When one receives such a grand invitation, one must first determine if she trusts the messenger. How does Mary assess the trustworthiness of the messenger or the truth of the message?

An authentic invitation could be one where the invited person is not being asked to walk alone. When she asks how this could possibly come to pass, the angel tells Mary that the Holy Spirit would come upon her and that the power of the Most High would overshadow her. Mary was not asked to bring forth this miracle alone. She would be accompanied and strengthened by the power of God. To do the work of God means that we must be strong enough to employ the gifts with which we have been bestowed while also being humble enough to allow God to work within us.

The angel reassures Mary a second time by informing her that God had also blessed her cousin Elizabeth with a child even though she was thought to be barren. Through this, God not only demonstrates what is thought to be impossible but also provides testimony that would speak to Mary's heart. The witness and example of someone we love and trust goes a long way in shoring up our faith and fidelity to new and scary paths.

As we navigate the deep waters and crossroads we encounter in our lives, we can look upon them with the eyes of Mary. We can look for signs and symbols that indicate that God is speaking to us and attempting to stay close to us. We can look to those who have come before us for the wisdom and witness they have to offer. When we notice these things, we can trust that the voice we hear is indeed the voice of God, and like Mary, we can respond with a trust-filled "yes."

Preparing to Proclaim

Key words and phrases: "May it be done to me according to your word."

To the point: When reflecting on the familiar annunciation story, we often emphasize Mary's obedience. In artistic renderings of this scene, she is often portrayed as docile or meek. And Mary's obedience is important here; her willingness to take on what God was asking of her changes the world. But it is not mere docility at play; God invites her into partnership and participation in God's work of salvation. She possesses full agency here; she consents to God's plan and takes on the huge, life-changing risk of pregnancy and parenthood, made even riskier for being outside the bounds of marriage in her time and place. Her obedience is not one of fear or unquestioning servility; she in fact points out to an angel that what he has suggested is impossible. Rather, this obedience is one rooted in courageously generous love for the one who loved her first.

Model Penitential Act

Presider: On today's Solemnity of the Immaculate Conception of the Blessed Virgin Mary, we honor Mary, mother of Christ and mother of the church, who was born without the stains of sin. Trusting in her intercession, let us lay our sins before the Lord . . . *[pause]*

Lord Jesus, you are the Son of God: Lord, have mercy.
Christ Jesus, you are the son of Mary: Christ, have mercy.
Lord Jesus, you will come again to redeem your people: Lord, have mercy.

Model Universal Prayer (Prayer of the Faithful)

Presider: Through the intercession of the Blessed Virgin Mary, we give voice to our prayers and petitions.

Response: Lord, hear our prayer.

Attune our senses to God's callings within us and within the church . . .

Bless all women called to national and local leadership . . .

Envelop in your love couples struggling to conceive and single people longing to be parents . . .

Foster a culture of consent in our local communities . . .

Presider: God of all wisdom, you created Mary free from sin and gave her the strength and courage to say yes to birthing your Son into the world. Listen to our prayers and grace us with the faithfulness to follow your callings in our lives. We ask this through Christ our Lord. **Amen.**

Living Liturgy

Collaborative Community: Mary of Nazareth's example of ready discipleship paves our path to imagine collaborative ministry. The willingness of the Blessed Mother to consider the angel's words and openly answer "yes" gives us ways to continue to think of how various groups in the parish community might collaborate with each other to celebrate this feast day. Each group's culture honors a particular image of Mary. Take delight in including each tradition, collaborating in the same way the immaculate conception of Mary points to Joachim and Anna working closely together with God. In our music and liturgy today, we think about what discipleship means in terms of stepping out of the ordinary to collaborate.

FOR REFLECTION

• How do you feel about God's will for your life? Is it scary to think of missing it? How could you receive it as an invitation made in love?

• The second reading speaks of our adoption as children of God. What does it mean to you to be part of God's family?

COLLECT
Let us pray.

Pause for silent prayer

O God, who by the Immaculate Conception of
    the Blessed Virgin
prepared a worthy dwelling for your Son,
grant, we pray,
that, as you preserved her from every stain
by virtue of the Death of your Son, which you
    foresaw,
so, through her intercession,
we, too, may be cleansed and admitted to your
    presence.
Through our Lord Jesus Christ, your Son,
who lives and reigns with you in the unity of
    the Holy Spirit,
God, for ever and ever. **Amen.**

Homily Points

• The readings for today's solemnity prove dialogue with the divine is possible. Adam, Eve, and Mary each have direct conversations with God. They hear God's words and respond with words of their own that God clearly understands. Our experiences of dialoguing with the divine will likely never be as clear—at least in this life—but, through prayer, we can converse with our Creator. God longs to be in dialogue with us. We can share our honest emotions and questions with God. We can listen for God's response in a variety of holy avenues, including texts of Scripture, words from faithful friends, and in the natural world.

• On this day when we honor the Immaculate Conception of Mary, let us celebrate moments of conception in our own lives: the realization of dreams, the bud of a big idea, or perhaps even the very beginning of a child's life. Let us also be sensitive to the many among us who struggle to conceive: those who find it impossible to dream amid depression, those whose big ideas fall flat in the face of racism, and those struggling with infertility.

• Consent is crucial when it comes to the conception of a child—including the Son of God. God does not force Mary to carry God's son. God asks for Mary's consent, which she offers. So many aspects of this conception are unique, but consent should be part of every conception.

✠ SPIRITUALITY

GOSPEL ACCLAMATION
Isa 61:1 (cited in Luke 4:18)

℞. Alleluia, alleluia.
The Spirit of the Lord is upon me,
because he has anointed me
to bring glad tidings to the poor.
℞. Alleluia, alleluia.

Gospel   Matt 11:2-11; L7A

When John the Baptist heard in
    prison of the works of the
    Christ,
  he sent his disciples to Jesus
      with this question,
  "Are you the one who is to come,
  or should we look for another?"
Jesus said to them in reply,
  "Go and tell John what you hear
      and see:
  the blind regain their sight,
  the lame walk,
  lepers are cleansed,
  the deaf hear,
  the dead are raised,
  and the poor have the good news
      proclaimed to them.
And blessed is the one who takes
    no offense at me."

As they were going off,
  Jesus began to speak to the crowds about
      John,
  "What did you go out to the desert to see?
  A reed swayed by the wind?
  Then what did you go out to see?
  Someone dressed in fine clothing?
  Those who wear fine clothing are in royal
      palaces.
  Then why did you go out? To see a prophet?
  Yes, I tell you, and more than a prophet.
  This is the one about whom it is written:
      Behold, I am sending my messenger
          ahead of you;
      he will prepare your way before you.
  Amen, I say to you,
      among those born of women
      there has been none greater than John
          the Baptist;
      yet the least in the kingdom of heaven is
          greater than he."

Reflecting on the Gospel

It is the experience of many prison chaplains that when prisoners are on death row, they frequently—and understandably—ask life-and-death questions that would never have occurred to them before. Almost two thousand years ago, Matthew describes the poignant questions that John asks of Jesus through the messengers he has sent to him from Herod's prison. Doubts breed in loneliness and darkness, and they take John a long way from his confident self whom we met on Jordan's banks in last Sunday's gospel. With desperate hope, John sends his disciples with the question: "Are you the one who is to come, or should we look for another?"

Jesus's response echoes the Baptist's own convictions that we heard him voice last week: it is by their fruits that men or women of the kingdom are recognized. Jesus reminds John's messengers about the fruits of his own ministry: Jesus has harvested the blind who see again, the lame who now dance for joy, the lepers who can again kiss their loved ones, the deaf who are startled by a birdsong, the dead who are raised to life. Take this good news to John, says Jesus.

As the Baptist's disciples depart, Jesus turns to the crowd to praise John in terms that would make an excellent Advent review of life for us. John was not a vacillating crowd-pleaser, not a reed that bends in the wind of public opinion. He was not a compromiser, not a well-dressed and powerful "in-group" person, not a political entrepreneur or someone welcome at prestigious places like Herod's palace. Where John did end up was in Herod's prison, and there he would lose his head, but never his heart, to that king's lack of integrity and fear of losing face. John's heart had been lost long ago to Jesus, and no doubt the message sent back to him in prison confirmed John in his love and offered him the truth that the way to deep faith so often goes through deep doubt. Do we, at least to some degree, measure up to such praise—or blame?

The prophets had strong faith in the transformation that God could work in the barren wilderness (the physical and the spiritual ones), and throughout the weeks of Advent in Year A, Isaiah sings and dreams of the transformation that God's coming will work. Just as Israel came through the long wilderness wandering to enter into the Promised Land, so God will again lead his people out of the desert of apathy and despair. Creation will be healed, and the wasteland of human disabilities, fears, disappointments, and oppression will blossom into joy when watered by God's grace. Isaiah is speaking from experience; he has been through humiliation, slavery, and exile, but he assures us that we must keep on dreaming—not as people of the night who wake to find their dreams are fleeting and insubstantial, but as dangerous daytime dreamers who act with open eyes, unsealed ears, and embodied resolve to make their dreams of the reign of God a reality. John the Baptist was such a dangerous, practical dreamer.

Preparing to Proclaim

Key words and phrases: "Go and tell John what you hear and see."

To the point: In this gospel, Jesus instructs John's disciples to serve as witnesses. Witnesses are people who have seen something firsthand and who share what they have seen for the benefit of those who could not be there. Their presence at the scene of what's happening gives their testimony a certain privilege. Witnesses are important; we trust what they say. Jesus instructs these witnesses in what they are to say: most elements are familiar aspects of ancient prophecies, but he throws a twist in at the end. He brings healing not only for those who are blind, lame, deaf, or ill; he restores to life even those who have died. Jesus is the fulfillment of the Old Testament prophecies, but he is also something completely new. The work Jesus is beginning is beyond anyone's wildest hopes or imaginings.

Psalmist Preparation

The psalm contains all the dramatic tension of Advent: God's verbs are all in present tense, affirming who God is and what God does. And yet the response still cries out to God, pleading that God come and save us. God is here already; the fullest realization of God's promises is yet to be seen. As you prepare this psalm, think of one way you have witnessed God's work in your life, as well as one area where you still need Christ's coming. Keep these in mind as you proclaim this psalm to a congregation full of people with stories just like yours, full of both joys and sorrows, abundance and lack.

Making Connections

Between the readings: The future tense of the first reading transforms into present tense in the gospel. With Jesus's coming, the blind *do* see, the deaf *do* hear, here and now. Jesus's presence is effecting healing and change as his earthly ministry begins. It is still effecting healing now as his presence continues with us in countless harder-to-see ways. And yet Advent is also our season of waiting; the second reading reminds us that we are still waiting for Christ's healing work to be accomplished in its fullness. The transformation of our world has yet to be complete.

To experience: We don't often see the grand miracles that Jesus enumerates here, but we, too, are called to witness to God's work of healing and giving life. Jesus usually slips in quietly, blessing us with subtle strength and slow growth that we might fail to notice. Very often in our lives, we have to train our eyes to see it.

Homily Points

• Today's Mass for the third Sunday of Advent begins with a profound call: rejoice. Darkness cloaks our earth during these short winter days—and still, now is the time to seek joy. Christian joy is not always bright and cheery. Take John the Baptist who sits in prison or Jesus who dies a painful death on the cross. These pillars of our faith know suffering—and they persist anyway. They hope anyway. Believe in God's great power to save, they dare to be joyful. May we do the same.

• From his prison cell, John voices an honest question to Jesus: "Are you the one who is to come, or should we look for another?" The greatest of all the prophets models how to live "faith seeking understanding"—in the words of St. Anselm. Sometimes, we think of questions as a sign of faithlessness or weakness. But would anyone dare accuse John the Baptist of lacking faith or strength? The birth of Christ—the Son of God and Son of Man—is deeply mysterious. By bringing our honest questions to prayer, we can dive further into the greatest mystery of our faith. What questions do you carry this Advent season?

• God removes disabilities in Isaiah's version of the coming kingdom. As we sit with the prophet's words, let us be mindful of the various ways people experience disabilities today. Some may receive Isaiah's words as relief after much bodily pain and suffering. Others who embrace their disabilities may receive Isaiah's message with skepticism: Am I not already created in God's image exactly as I am? Ultimately, Isaiah preaches a message of liberation and wholeness for all of creation. May we honor the many diverse ways God leads us into salvation.

✝ CELEBRATION

Model Penitential Act

Presider: In today's gospel, John the Baptist asks Jesus, "Are you the one who is to come?" Indeed, we know now that Christ is the one who came to save us and take away all our sins. Together, let us acknowledge those sins and ask for mercy . . . *[pause]*

Lord Jesus, you came to heal all creation: Lord have mercy.

Christ Jesus, you come to bring joy in our darkness: Christ, have mercy.

Lord Jesus, you will come again to proclaim good news to the poor: Lord, have mercy.

Model Universal Prayer (Prayer of the Faithful)

Presider: Jesus tells John's disciples to "tell what you hear and see." Let us answer Christ's command by voicing our prayers and petitions.

Response: Lord, hear our prayer.

Animate the church, that it may inspire joy in people across the world . . .

Humble leaders of all nations, that they may ask thoughtful questions to seek greater understanding of the needs of the people entrusted to their care . . .

Comfort people in prison, that they may know the love of God and care of communities . . .

Continue to call forth the gifts of people with disabilities in our community, that we may all strive toward liberation together . . .

Presider: Merciful God, you always answer when we call. Receive these prayers and petitions offered by your people gathered here today. We ask this through Christ our Lord. **Amen.**

Liturgy and Music

Familiar and Unfamiliar: The work of music ministry is never done. It is an ongoing process of encountering the beauty of God both in the familiar and in the unknown. Aware of this, challenge yourself to move outside the more familiar Advent repertoire. One might find familiarity in the text and tune of "O Come, O Come, Emmanuel" or the chant "*Conditor Alme Siderum.*" Another might hold close a contemporary setting of the Isaiah reading or the gospel passage. If you are familiar with these songs, try something else. "Be strong, fear not! / Here is your God." Learn an unfamiliar piece that challenges you to find God's beauty in diversity.

For communities that celebrate the Filipino tradition of *Simbang Gabi,* a novena of dawn Masses leading up to Christmas, this Sunday would be the time for choirs to learn a piece from that tradition and share it with the rest of the parish community—perhaps as instrumental piece or choral prelude. This Sunday is the day before the feast of Our Lady of Guadalupe. Here's another opportunity to step into the seemingly unfamiliar and sing a Marian piece bilingually in English and Spanish.

This Sunday, we bring the word *Gaudete* (rejoice) to the center of our music making. The musical feel for today's celebration should move toward a more joyous character in tempo and tone. Let these words of Isaiah echo through your liturgy and music preparation—the desert will exult, the steppe will rejoice, they will bloom with abundant flowers, rejoice with joyful song!

COLLECT

Let us pray.

Pause for silent prayer

O God, who see how your people
faithfully await the feast of the Lord's
Nativity,
enable us, we pray,
to attain the joys of so great a salvation
and to celebrate them always
with solemn worship and glad rejoicing.
Through our Lord Jesus Christ, your Son,
who lives and reigns with you in the unity
of the Holy Spirit,
God, for ever and ever. **Amen.**

FIRST READING
Isa 35:1-6a, 10

The desert and the parched land will
exult;
the steppe will rejoice and bloom.
They will bloom with abundant flowers,
and rejoice with joyful song.
The glory of Lebanon will be given to
them,
the splendor of Carmel and Sharon;
they will see the glory of the LORD,
the splendor of our God.
Strengthen the hands that are feeble,
make firm the knees that are weak,
say to those whose hearts are frightened:
Be strong, fear not!
Here is your God,
he comes with vindication;
with divine recompense
he comes to save you.
Then will the eyes of the blind be opened,
the ears of the deaf be cleared;
then will the lame leap like a stag,
then the tongue of the mute will sing.

Those whom the LORD has ransomed will
return
and enter Zion singing,
crowned with everlasting joy;
they will meet with joy and gladness,
sorrow and mourning will flee.

 *CATECHESIS*

RESPONSORIAL PSALM
Ps 146:6-7, 8-9, 9-10

R∕. (cf. Isaiah 35:4) Lord, come and save us.
   or:
R∕. Alleluia.

The Lord God keeps faith forever,
   secures justice for the oppressed,
   gives food to the hungry.
The Lord sets captives free.

R∕. Lord, come and save us.
   or:
R∕. Alleluia.

The Lord gives sight to the blind;
   the Lord raises up those who were
      bowed down.
The Lord loves the just;
   the Lord protects strangers.

R∕. Lord, come and save us.
   or:
R∕. Alleluia.

The fatherless and the widow he sustains,
   but the way of the wicked he thwarts.
The Lord shall reign forever;
   your God, O Zion, through all
      generations.

R∕. Lord, come and save us.
   or:
R∕. Alleluia.

SECOND READING
Jas 5:7-10

Be patient, brothers and sisters,
   until the coming of the Lord.
See how the farmer waits for the precious
      fruit of the earth,
   being patient with it
   until it receives the early and the late
      rains.
You too must be patient.
Make your hearts firm,
   because the coming of the Lord is at
      hand.
Do not complain, brothers and sisters,
      about one another,
   that you may not be judged.
Behold, the Judge is standing before the
      gates.
Take as an example of hardship and
      patience, brothers and sisters,
   the prophets who spoke in the name of
      the Lord.

Living Liturgy

Encounter Joy: Take some time during this season of preparation to think of the things that bring you the most joy—moments that make your soul sing, conversations that revive your spirit, situations that grant hope that saves us. Pope Francis reminds us in his encyclical, *Evangelii Gaudium*, that "the joy of the gospel fills the hearts and lives of all who encounter Jesus" (EG 1). On this Gaudete Sunday, we are reminded of the encounter and experience of the presence of Jesus in the blind, lame, leper, deaf, dead, and poor. Francis's call beckons us to an understanding of the joy of salvation rooted in encounter with Christ in the other. Look out for signs of joy, for signs of life and of the saving action of God in our daily routine. Locate these saving actions in the present moment and in our shared spaces.

Pierre Teilhard de Chardin insists: "Above all, trust in the slow work of God." Perhaps we could swap in a word—*rejoice* in the slow work of God. While we await the coming of the Lord, rejoice in the present and patient waiting. Embrace a patient trust in God. Why wait to find joy when we could rejoice now in our waiting? The psalmist praises the trustworthy God who cares for the helpless, with the refrain taken from the Isaiah reading, turning it into a plea: You, the God who cares for the weak, save us; come now! And yet we are aware that God has already saved us. A deep encounter with Christ dwells in these moments of quiet certainty and uncertainty, when we open up ourselves to trusting God through the despair and distress that threaten our lives. In our world, through the realities of homelessness and food insecurity that exist in so many cities, we both praise our faithful God for the little we have and plead for God to come quickly and save us.

PROMPTS FOR FAITH-SHARING

• Jesus tells John's followers to witness to Jesus's work; if you were asked to give an account of what you have seen, what would you say? Where in your life have you witnessed God's healing work?

• The second reading is all about patience; where do you need patience in your life?

• How can we train our eyes to see God at work in the ordinary things of our lives?

DECEMBER 11, 2022
THIRD SUNDAY OF ADVENT

GOSPEL ACCLAMATION
cf. Luke 1:28

R⁊. Alleluia, alleluia.
Blessed are you, holy Virgin Mary, deserving of
    all praise;
from you rose the sun of justice, Christ our God.
R⁊. Alleluia, alleluia.

Gospel   Luke 1:26-38; L690A

The angel Gabriel was sent from God
    to a town of Galilee called Nazareth,
    to a virgin betrothed to a man named
        Joseph,
    of the house of David,
    and the virgin's name was Mary.
And coming to her, he said,
    "Hail, full of grace! The Lord is with
        you."
But she was greatly troubled at what was
        said
    and pondered what sort of greeting
        this might be.
Then the angel said to her,
    "Do not be afraid, Mary,
    for you have found favor with God.
Behold, you will conceive in your womb
        and bear a son,
    and you shall name him Jesus.

Continued in Appendix A, p. 261.

See Appendix A, p. 261, for the other readings.

Reflecting on the Gospel

Earlier in the Gospel of Luke, we hear about the angel Gabriel announcing God's plan for Mary to conceive and bring Jesus Christ into the world. Mary, not only full of grace, but also full of trust, declares herself the handmaiden of the Lord and agrees to partner with God in the fulfillment of this mission.

How brave one must be to embark upon such a path without knowing where exactly it will lead! How remarkable the balance of humility and faith that enables one to take each mysterious step on that path and believe it will lead safely to God's ordained destination. This is why Elizabeth felt her son, the infant John, leap in her womb when she first greeted Mary. This is why she declared, "Blessed are you who believed that what was spoken to you by the Lord would be fulfilled" (Luke 1:45). Blessed indeed are the ones who have the faith to trust in the plans that God writes on their hearts.

Juan Diego modeled this faith in 1531 when, after encountering the Virgin Mary on a hill in Tepeyac, he went to the bishop to share Mary's request that a chapel be erected where believers could visit and pray for her intercession. Juan Diego believed in the truth of his encounter with the Blessed Virgin; however, the bishop asked for a sign before he allowed himself to believe in the apparition. Mary, out of an abundance of humility, provided signs that helped the faithful recognize her presence—a miraculous healing of Juan Diego's uncle, flowers unseasonably in bloom on the Tepeyac hill, an image of the Virgin Mary on Juan Diego's tilma (cloak). The parallels between Juan Diego and Mary are clear: they are both humble in social status, both are given paradigm-shifting messages to deliver, and both put their faith in the truth of those messages. Mary would deliver a message of salvation for all humankind in the form of her son, Jesus. In the case of Juan Diego, Mary's apparition demonstrated God's continuous desire to reach out to the lowly (in this case the indigenous communities of sixteenth-century Mexico) and bend a compassionate ear toward their concerns. In every land and in every time period, God will choose the lowly ones for partnership and will bestow upon all people comfort and care.

Mary's visit to Elizabeth during their pregnancies was but the first instance of Christ meeting us wherever we find ourselves. The story of Juan Diego and Our Lady of Guadalupe, along with other Marian apparitions endorsed by the church, are reminders to the faithful that God continues to seek us out. They are also reminders that we are all called to listen deeply for God's word. In listening deeply to the truth that resides in our hearts, we see that God has a plan for all beings to live peacefully and harmoniously in union with him. We need to also listen for the truth that sometimes comes from unexpected messengers. Blessed are we when we truly hear those messages and put our faith in them.

Preparing to Proclaim

Key words and phrases: "[N]othing will be impossible for God."

To the point: In many ways, the annunciation story mirrors the Guadalupe story. There is an unexpected heavenly appearance to a poor, insignificant person. After an initial moment of fear and disbelief, God gives a special mission as well as assurance of heavenly accompaniment in completing it. Both stories culminate in courage; both Mary and Juan Diego say a "yes" that allows God to enter in and disrupt the usual way of the world. In Nazareth we see Mary at the beginning of her story. At Tepeyac, we see that her work is not complete; she continues to partner with God in bringing love and wholeness and beauty to the world.

Model Penitential Act

Presider: On today's feast of Our Lady of Guadalupe, we honor the spirit of God at work in the world. For those times we have failed to notice the divine among us, let us ask God for mercy and forgiveness . . . *[pause]*

Lord Jesus, you are the Son of God: Lord, have mercy.

Christ Jesus, you are the son of Mary: Christ, have mercy.

Lord Jesus, you will strengthen the faith of all believers: Lord, have mercy.

Model Universal Prayer (Prayer of the Faithful)

Presider: Through the intercession of Our Lady of Guadalupe, let us make our prayers and petitions known to God.

Response: Lord, hear our prayer.

Bless the church on this feast of its patroness, that it may help people know the love and mercy of God . . .

Foster a spirit of respect within public authorities, that they may listen closely to the spirit at work within people who are poor and marginalized . . .

Free peoples oppressed by colonization, that they may live into their God-given humanity . . .

Deepen the devotional lives of this community, that our prayers may lead us ever closer to Christ . . .

Presider: Almighty God, you filled St. Juan Diego with hope at the sight of Our Lady of Guadalupe. Receive the prayers we offer you this day and fill us with the hope of your spirit among us. We ask this through Christ our Lord. **Amen.**

Living Liturgy

Mantle of Care: Our Lady of Guadalupe appears as an Indigenous woman dressed in traditional Aztec clothing. Mary's mantle always shields the poor and the vulnerable. During the 1960s farm worker movement in California led by activist Cesar Chavez, the image of Guadalupe played a central role in bringing together people of all faiths through rallies and pilgrimages that brought attention to the unfair treatment of laborers. Poverty, oppression, and injustice still pervade our country today. During this feast day, we venerate Mary as symbol of unity and follow her example of being the one who unites all God's children. In music and liturgy, we reflect on how the Blessed Mother shows us true Christian identity in actively pursuing charitable deeds toward one another.

COLLECT

Let us pray.

Pause for silent prayer

O God, Father of mercies,
who placed your people under the singular protection
of your Son's most holy Mother,
grant that all who invoke the Blessed Virgin of Guadalupe,
may seek with ever more lively faith
the progress of peoples in the ways of justice and of peace.
Through our Lord Jesus Christ, your Son,
who lives and reigns with you in the unity of the Holy Spirit,
God, for ever and ever. **Amen.**

FOR REFLECTION

• How might God be calling you to be a bearer of Christ to the world this Advent?

• At Tepeyac, Mary tells Juan Diego to put her words into his heart, echoing her own practice of pondering in her heart the divine things she encountered. What might God be inviting you to put in your own heart this Advent season?

Homily Points

• The story of Mary, the Mother of God, appearing to Juan Diego on a Mexican hillside reminds us that heaven and earth are not so far away from each other after all. Our deceased loved ones, the great saints of the church, and Christ's very self continue to dwell with us. We can call upon their spirits for guidance and support.

• Today's feast celebrates the gifts of indigenous peoples to the Catholic faith. It is an appropriate time for our community to consider our relationships to indigenous peoples and how we might nurture an ever-deepening respect of native spiritualities.

✠ SPIRITUALITY

GOSPEL ACCLAMATION
Matt 1:23

℟. Alleluia, alleluia.
The virgin shall conceive, and bear a son,
and they shall name him Emmanuel.
℟. Alleluia, alleluia.

Gospel

Matt 1:18-24; L10A

This is how the birth of Jesus
    Christ came about.
When his mother Mary was be-
    trothed to Joseph,
    but before they lived together,
    she was found with child
        through the Holy Spirit.
Joseph her husband, since he
    was a righteous man,
    yet unwilling to expose her to
        shame,
    decided to divorce her quietly.
Such was his intention when,
    behold,
the angel of the Lord appeared
        to him in a dream and said,
"Joseph, son of David,
do not be afraid to take Mary
        your wife into your home.
For it is through the Holy Spirit
    that this child has been conceived in
        her.
She will bear a son and you are to
    name him Jesus,
    because he will save his people from
        their sins."
All this took place to fulfill what the
    Lord had said through the prophet:
*Behold, the virgin shall conceive
        and bear a son,
and they shall name him
        Emmanuel,*
    which means "God is with us."
When Joseph awoke,
    he did as the angel of the Lord had
        commanded him
    and took his wife into his home.

Reflecting on the Gospel

Once betrothed to Joseph, Mary was truly his wife, not a pregnant, unwed teenager, as some well-meaning homilists preach. Betrothal was, by Jewish law, the first stage of marriage, a legal agreement that bestowed on the couple the status of man and wife. Further proof that the betrothed were married are the facts that betrothal could be terminated only by death (after which the remaining spouse was considered widowed) or by the man divorcing his wife. Any infidelity on the woman's part during betrothal was regarded as adultery. The strong honor code of the Middle Eastern world demanded that no man could take possession of what belonged to another, including a child in the womb who had been conceived by another man. Joseph had his dreams of married life, but then comes the nightmare, and the painful human agony of a just man torn between his loyalty to the Jewish Torah (law) and his love for Mary—pregnant, but not by him and therefore considered an adulteress who could possibly be stoned, or at least subjected to public humiliation (see Deut 22:23-24).

But Matthew describes Joseph as a just man, who plans to make some attempt to reconcile steadfast love and law. With deep unease in his soul, perhaps remembering the prophets' call for "loyalty . . . , not sacrifice" (Hos 6:6), Joseph decides to divorce Mary quietly to spare her as much public shame as possible. Such an attitude is an overture to the mercy that Jesus will show in his interpretation of the Law (see Matt 9:13, 23:23) and surely a reminder to the church of all ages to listen to the echo of the prophetic words.

In a dream, a messenger of God tells Joseph not to fear what he cannot understand, not to disown the mystery but enter into it. Joseph wakes up and succeeds where we often fail: he does something about his dream. Obedient to God's word, he responds for the first of many times "as the angel of the Lord had commanded." This biblical dreamer is also a person of action. Joseph offers the hospitality of his love and lineage to Mary and to the stranger-child whom she carries in her womb. He is the radically blessed poor man, ready to surrender the right to choose a name for the child, and generously offering to Jesus, he who saves, a paternity not of his own flesh. What onlookers might consider a scandal, Joseph and Mary believe is the action of the Holy Spirit, who continues to do "scandalous" things in our midst.

Joseph is cast by Matthew along the lines of another Joseph, the patriarch of Genesis, who was also a man of dreams (Gen 37, 40) and a man of God's providence (Gen 45:1-15). Out of the granaries of Egypt over which he was the Pharaoh's chief steward, Joseph cared for his family in a time of famine, despite their poor treatment of him as a young man (Gen 37:15-36). The Joseph of the gospel also cares unobtrusively for his family, stewarding the Grain and the Bread that continues to feed our hunger at every eucharistic assembly.

Preparing to Proclaim

Key words and phrases: "[T]hey shall name him Emmanuel, which means 'God is with us.'"

To the point: Here we have Joseph's side of the story—mostly a story about being left out of a very big decision. Joseph's exclusion is challenging and confusing for him, but it is important; it affirms that Jesus's origins are not natural but supernatural. There is no human father responsible for this son. He is the Son of God, and at the same time, son of Mary, fully human. He enters into human life with all its greatness and littleness, all its joys and sorrows. He is God with us, Emmanuel. He shares in our human experience, even in neediness. And although he was left out of the main event, Joseph does have a decision to make here, and he chooses radical hospitality for the stranger in need that is God in disguise. He accepts this woman into his home and her child as his own. Jesus will even share Joseph's lineage; it is through his foster father that he is a descendant of David.

Psalmist Preparation

In our final week of preparation for Christmas, we call on the Lord to finally enter—to enter our world, our history, our hearts. As you prepare this psalm, think of one specific way you hope the Lord will enter your life in the coming season. Hold that intention close as you proclaim the earnest plea of the psalm. Pray also that you and all gathered this week will have their eyes opened to all the ways that God has already entered and is continually entering our lives, often in unseen or unrecognized ways.

Making Connections

Between the readings: Isaiah's prophecy is so extraordinary that it is not recognized as a sign when it finally occurs in Mary; the presumption is that this virgin's conception is not God's work but a very ordinary moment of human sin and weakness. Our Advent theme continues: this is a God who defies expectations and comes in ways for which we are not ready. In the second reading, Paul packs a lot of theology into the opening of his letter, echoing the idea of Christ's dual origin: fully human, fully divine.

To experience: Have you ever asked for a sign from God? God does work through signs at times, but they are very rarely the signs we would have chosen. Often, God works in places we never would have thought to look. Advent is about training our eyes, about paying attention, about noticing what once we would have ignored—the panhandler, the criminal, the child—and learning to see God there.

Homily Points

• Through the prophet Isaiah, the Lord tells Ahaz to ask for a sign in today's first reading. God longs for Ahaz, king of Judah, to remain faithful. The people of Judah faced great suffering at this time as the threats of war and government overthrow loomed large. God wants Ahaz and the people to keep their trust in the divine strong. God offers the child Emmanuel as a sign to affirm: "God is with us." God also longs for our faithfulness and trust. These practices take time. To continue deepening our relationship with God, we need not be nervous to ask God for a sign of the divine presence truly with us.

• Joseph trusts in God's outrageous plan for his family despite every reason to give up. A virgin impregnated by the Holy Spirit is going to give birth to the savior of the world? God asks Joseph to believe in the most far-fetched reality—and to buck societal expectations for marriage and family life. God asks big things of Joseph. God asks big things of us too. How can we ready our hearts so that, when the time comes, we, too, can answer God's call?

• Familiar stories accompany us in the days leading up to Christmas. Let us listen with fresh perspectives and awe at the miracles being proclaimed: the Savior is born into *this* world; his mother, Mary, conceived through the power of the *Holy Spirit*; Joseph heard *God's messenger* speaking in his dreams. It is often said these late December days are a magical time of year. But what happened with Mary and Joseph is no illusion. Let us marvel at God's goodness as we approach the birth of Christ.

Model Penitential Act

Presider: As we approach the birth of Christ, let us reflect on the many ways we encounter the Son of God in the world today. Let us also call to mind the times we have failed to honor God's presence and ask for mercy . . . *[pause]*

Lord Jesus, you were born into this world out of love for us: Lord, have mercy.

Christ Jesus, you are with us now: Christ, have mercy.

Lord Jesus, you will always be with us: Lord, have mercy.

Model Universal Prayer (Prayer of the Faithful)

Presider: Trusting in Emmanuel—God with us—let us offer our prayers and petitions.

Response: Lord, hear our prayer.

Deepen the dreams of your people, that together the church may imagine a more just world and work to bring it to reality . . .

Rouse the faith of political leaders, that they may work in tandem with God for the betterment of our communities . . .

Relieve the anguish of those suffering from family divisions, that the Spirit of the Lord may inspire healing . . .

Reveal yourself to all of us gathered here, that in this season of celebration we might take time to awe at God's goodness all around . . .

Presider: Almighty God, you sent your only Son into the world to save us. As we draw closer to the birth of Christ, may our hearts fill with trust and wonder at your great love for us. We ask this through Christ our Lord. **Amen.**

Liturgy and Music

God Is with Us: The Christ Child is about to be born. The psalmist proclaims: "Let the Lord enter; he is king of glory." Have we done enough to prepare for this coming day? The paradox of the incarnation is set before us. God's message of deliverance from sin and death is carried by a child. The almighty God comes hidden in the body of an infant, in our own flesh, truly God-with-us.

How might our music selections reflect this rich balance of Christian praise to the almighty and Christian concern for the lowly ones? Is there room in our repertoire to encourage reflection on the self-emptying of Christ today and in the Christmas season?

Choosing a common entrance processional or antiphon sung throughout this season is one way of tying in the messages of John the Baptist and Isaiah heard over these past weeks as the community continues the pilgrimage toward Bethlehem. It also encourages a deeper reflection on the text and the rich imagery of the season. If you haven't programmed it in this year, schedule it for next Advent.

Finally, as we prepare the liturgical environment for the Christmas season, bear in mind this guideline from the document of the United States Conference of Catholic Bishops (USCCB), *Built of Living Stones: Art, Architecture, and Worship*: decorations are to "draw people to the true nature of the mystery being celebrated rather than being ends in themselves" (124). Will these decorations distract from worship and our contemplation of the mystery of power and powerlessness?

COLLECT

Let us pray.

Pause for silent prayer

Pour forth, we beseech you, O Lord,
your grace into our hearts,
that we, to whom the Incarnation of Christ
    your Son
was made known by the message of an
    Angel,
may by his Passion and Cross
be brought to the glory of his
    Resurrection.
Who lives and reigns with you in the unity
    of the Holy Spirit,
God, for ever and ever. **Amen.**

FIRST READING
Isa 7:10-14

The LORD spoke to Ahaz, saying:
    Ask for a sign from the LORD, your God;
    let it be deep as the netherworld, or high
        as the sky!
But Ahaz answered,
    "I will not ask! I will not tempt the
        LORD!"
Then Isaiah said:
    Listen, O house of David!
Is it not enough for you to weary people,
    must you also weary my God?
Therefore the Lord himself will give you
        this sign:
    the virgin shall conceive, and bear a
        son,
    and shall name him Emmanuel.

RESPONSORIAL PSALM
Ps 24:1-2, 3-4, 5-6

℟. (7c and 10b) Let the Lord enter; he is king of glory.

The LORD's are the earth and its fullness;
   the world and those who dwell in it.
For he founded it upon the seas
   and established it upon the rivers.

℟. Let the Lord enter; he is king of glory.

Who can ascend the mountain of the
   LORD?
   or who may stand in his holy place?
One whose hands are sinless, whose heart
   is clean,
   who desires not what is vain.

℟. Let the Lord enter; he is king of glory.

He shall receive a blessing from the LORD,
   a reward from God his savior.
Such is the race that seeks for him,
   that seeks the face of the God of Jacob.

℟. Let the Lord enter; he is king of glory.

SECOND READING
Rom 1:1-7

Paul, a slave of Christ Jesus,
   called to be an apostle and set apart for
      the gospel of God,
   which he promised previously through
      his prophets in the holy Scriptures,
the gospel about his Son, descended from
      David according to the flesh,
   but established as Son of God in power
   according to the Spirit of holiness
   through resurrection from the dead,
      Jesus Christ our Lord.
Through him we have received the grace
      of apostleship,
   to bring about the obedience of faith,
   for the sake of his name, among all the
      Gentiles,
   among whom are you also, who are
      called to belong to Jesus Christ;
   to all the beloved of God in Rome, called
      to be holy.
Grace to you and peace from God our
      Father
   and the Lord Jesus Christ.

Living Liturgy

A Silent Companion in Joseph: For the Northern Hemisphere, this week bears its darkest days as the earth approaches the winter solstice. Yet hope lies hidden between these days of darkness and unwavering light, of busy time and silent reflection. Our Advent waiting gradually brightens, much like the fourth candle in the wreath illumines hope for the journey ahead. The Northern Hemisphere tilts back toward the Sun. God's movement in our lives never ceases.

One of Christina Rosetti's Advent poems, "Earth Grown Old," brims with mystery and movement. Rosetti presents an Advent reflection on the uncertainties of life and on waiting for God's promise and redemption. The poem yields more questions and reveals a struggle of human knowing and unknowing. Might there be a "fire unfelt" within, an unnoticed spark inside that fuels deeper contemplation or perhaps bursts forth with active healing and hope?

The angel in Matthew's Gospel today appears to Joseph with such mystery and movement. God's love manifested in Joseph embodies faithful action and close accompaniment of Mary and the baby growing inside her. As liturgical ministers, we, too, accompany our communities through these final days of Advent. Joseph's example teaches us how to balance the exterior world with inner light, both in big and small ways. From the ancient church the "O" antiphons of Advent offer additional perspective (whether we sing them this week or earlier in the season) and illuminate pathways of renewal leading us onward to Bethlehem—O Wisdom, O Leader of the House of Israel, O Root of Jesse's Stem, O Key of David, O Radiant Dawn, O King of All Nations, O Emmanuel.

PROMPTS FOR FAITH-SHARING

• Where have you noticed God this Advent?

• Where might God have been present in ways you failed to recognize?

• What hopes for your faith journey do you bring into the Christmas season?

• How will you receive hospitality during the upcoming holidays? How could you practice hospitality?

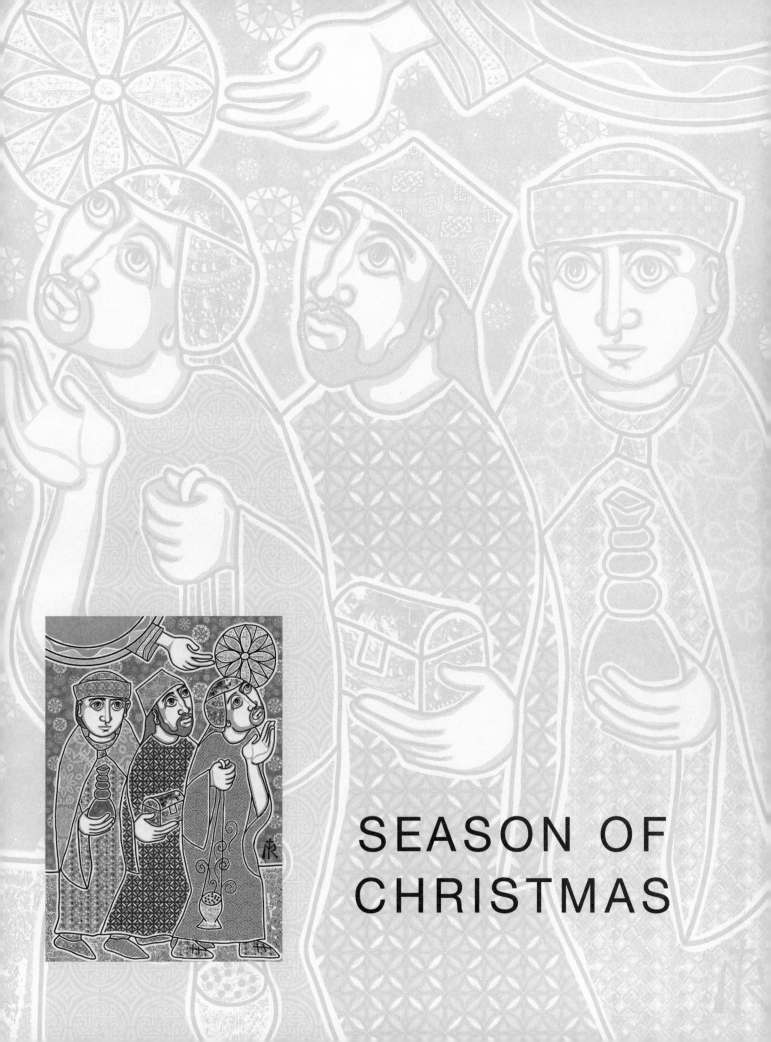

SEASON OF
CHRISTMAS

"The Christmas story is a challenge for us
to break out of the duality
of sacred time and secular time;
to recognize that all moments are ripe
with sacramentality, with miracle potential."

✚ SPIRITUALITY

The Vigil Mass

GOSPEL ACCLAMATION

R⒎ Alleluia, alleluia.
Tomorrow the wickedness of the earth will be
    destroyed:
the Savior of the world will reign over us.
R⒎ Alleluia, alleluia.

Gospel

Matt 1:1-25; L13ABC

The book of the genealogy of Jesus
    Christ,
    the son of David, the son of
        Abraham.

Abraham became the father of Isaac,
    Isaac the father of Jacob,
    Jacob the father of Judah and his
        brothers.
Judah became the father of Perez and
        Zerah,
    whose mother was Tamar.
Perez became the father of Hezron,
    Hezron the father of Ram,
    Ram the father of Amminadab.
Amminadab became the father of
        Nahshon,
    Nahshon the father of Salmon,
    Salmon the father of Boaz,
    whose mother was Rahab.
Boaz became the father of Obed,
    whose mother was Ruth.
Obed became the father of Jesse,
    Jesse the father of David the king.

David became the father of Solomon,
    whose mother had been the wife of
        Uriah.
Solomon became the father of
        Rehoboam,
    Rehoboam the father of Abijah,
    Abijah the father of Asaph.

Continued in Appendix A, p. 262, or
Matt 1:18-25 in Appendix A, p. 262.

See Appendix A, p. 263, for the other readings.

Reflecting on the Gospel

At the beginning of the Gospel of Matthew, the writer provides a genealogy that traces the lineage of Jesus Christ. This was for the benefit of Jewish audiences at the time so that they might be able to recognize how this figure, the Christ, did indeed represent the fulfillment of God's promise to the people of Israel. What meaning can today's readers take from this passage?

When we read the names in this genealogy, some of them may be very familiar to us and others are probably less familiar. Although we may not be deeply familiar with every name and every story included in this litany, we are assured that they are included because they are significant to the unfolding of salvation history. Regardless of their deeds or accolades, their foibles and failures, the individuals included are all significant because they are the stepping stones that led us to Jesus Christ. Each person had a part to play, a contribution to make.

If we are gathered with extended family or friends on this night, perhaps we can also recount the stories in our own histories that led up to this point. Who are the ancestors that took a leap of faith by moving to a new land or embarking on a new vocation or career? Which of our forebears nurtured the family line by taking on the essential role of caretaker? Which matriarchs and patriarchs kept our families strong by preserving the pictures, stories, and traditions?

In his keynote address at the 2017 Ignatian Family Teach-In for Social Justice, Fr. Bryan Massingale, SJ, used the image of a relay race to describe how he understands his role in bringing about God's kingdom: "I will probably never get across the finish line but that's not my role in the race. . . . It's not up to me necessarily to cross the finish line, but if I don't run my race as well as I can, then those who come after me can't do what they need to do." It is difficult to hold both the humility and the bravery that this image evokes. The work is not ours to finish, but it is our duty to do our part to the best of our ability. To remain faithful to this charge, it can be helpful to look back on the stories of those who came before us. It is important to remember that we are not the first to undertake this work and we will not be the last. When we fall short, we can take solace in remembering that God's grace will continue to work to make a way, to bring the divine plans to fruition.

Tonight as we recall and prepare our hearts for the coming of Emmanuel, God with us, we can also offer up a prayer of gratitude for all of the models of faith who faithfully ran their leg of the race and passed the baton until the Christ Child was able to enter the world. We can honor the members of our family whose successes, failures, and faithful attempts have brought us to the present day. And we can ask ourselves: What is our part to play in this leg of the relay race?

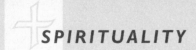

SPIRITUALITY

Mass at Midnight

GOSPEL ACCLAMATION
Luke 2:10-11

R⁄. Alleluia, alleluia.
I proclaim to you good news of great joy:
today a Savior is born for us,
Christ the Lord.
R⁄. Alleluia, alleluia.

Gospel

Luke 2:1-14; L14ABC

**In those days a decree went out from
Caesar Augustus
that the whole world should be
enrolled.
This was the first enrollment,
when Quirinius was governor of
Syria.
So all went to be enrolled, each to his
own town.
And Joseph too went up from Galilee
from the town of Nazareth
to Judea, to the city of David that is
called Bethlehem,
because he was of the house and
family of David,
to be enrolled with Mary, his betrothed, who was with child.
While they were there,
the time came for her to have her
child,
and she gave birth to her firstborn
son.**

Continued in Appendix A, p. 264.

See Appendix A, p. 264, for the other readings.

Reflecting on the Gospel

On this night, we hear the story of Christ's birth from the Gospel of Luke. It begins with Mary and Joseph traveling to Bethlehem to be counted for the census, in accordance with the decree from Caesar Augustus. Mary, though she is heavy with child, is not exempt from this civil duty and must make the arduous journey. It is in the midst of fulfilling this duty that her time comes to give birth to the Christ Child. The timing was neither ideal nor negotiable. The birth of the Messiah could not even be postponed or delayed while suitable accommodations were secured. No, the Son of God would be born in a stable near livestock, wrapped in swaddling clothes, and laid in a humble manger.

We are reminded that God is prepared to do miraculous things in the midst of our everyday lives, whether or not we are prepared for them. In other words, God's time will always have the final say. God's timing, though ultimately for our benefit, will not be dictated by our readiness.

We often think about holidays like Christmas as times when we are especially primed to embrace a spirit of wonder and awe. Indeed, rituals, holidays, and feasts are important parts of the human experience. It is during these special celebrations that we gather from far and wide with the people we love, tell important stories about who we are, and focus our hearts on the deeper, intangible values that matter most to us. These special days heighten our awareness of the divine. They offer us the opportunity to step out of our everyday routines and turn toward God in a special way.

This gospel story, however, could be seen as a challenge for us to break out of the duality of sacred time and secular time; to recognize that all moments are ripe with sacramentality, with miracle potential. The shepherds in the field had no idea that they were working on the first Christmas. The angels appeared above, singing "Glory to God in the highest" and notified the shepherds that something monumental had occurred. At that moment, the shepherds had an important choice to make. They could embrace and listen to the message of the angels or they could dismiss it.

When we experience interruptions to our day-to-day routines, how do we respond? Is it with a spirit of openness, with the hopeful outlook that perhaps there is a message meant for us in the disruption? It is difficult to live in a way that leaves us fully open to whatever each moment presents. Sometimes love and duty require us to tend to our work and our routines with a single-minded dedication and focus. There are times, however, when we need to be jolted out of those routines so that we can remember the sacredness and divine potential of each moment. This Christmas narrative serves as a reminder that the most significant gifts could arrive at seemingly insignificant (or inconvenient) times.

✠ SPIRITUALITY

Mass at Dawn

GOSPEL ACCLAMATION
Luke 2:14

℟. Alleluia, alleluia.
Glory to God in the highest,
and on earth peace to those
on whom his favor rests.
℟. Alleluia, alleluia.

Gospel

Luke 2:15-20; L15ABC

When the angels went away from them
    to heaven,
    the shepherds said to one another,
    "Let us go, then, to Bethlehem
    to see this thing that has taken place,
    which the Lord has made known to
        us."
So they went in haste and found Mary
    and Joseph,
    and the infant lying in the manger.
When they saw this,
    they made known the message
    that had been told them about this
        child.
All who heard it were amazed
    by what had been told them by the
        shepherds.
And Mary kept all these things,
    reflecting on them in her heart.
Then the shepherds returned,
    glorifying and praising God
    for all they had heard and seen,
    just as it had been told to them.

See Appendix A, p. 265, for the other readings.

Reflecting on the Gospel

At last, the day has arrived! The long-foretold promise has finally come to pass. Jesus Christ, the Lord and Savior, has been born! The angels proclaim this joyful news to the shepherds tending their flock, and the shepherds respond with curiosity and wonder: "Let us go, then, to Bethlehem to see this thing that has taken place."

While the angels proclaim the good news with words and songs, the shepherds also proclaim through their journeying. Not only did they go to find the infant, but the writer of the gospel tells us that they went "in haste." Once they arrive, they tell Mary and Joseph about the inspiring words that compelled them to come and find the Christ Child. The shepherds demonstrate for us one important way that love can be made manifest. For what is the beginning of love if not curiosity, if not a willingness to go and witness the beloved?

Let us go and see. Let us go in haste.

It is not enough that Jesus Christ took on human flesh and came to earth if we never seek him out. Our knowledge of and our relationship with Jesus only grows and strengthens the more we pursue him through our words and our actions. After all, Jesus's incarnation is yet another divine invitation rather than a command. God's power is manifest in God's ability and willingness to meet each person wherever he or she may be. However, God's goodness manifests in God patiently waiting for us to turn and receive him. As we celebrate the birth of our Lord Jesus Christ, how can we seek Jesus more intentionally? Where in our lives can we look to see hope being born anew? If we follow the example of the shepherds and take the journey to seek out Jesus, who knows what miracles we will discover?

We can also proclaim God's glory by following Mary's example. In Luke's Gospel, we hear that upon hearing the message from the shepherds, "Mary kept all these things, reflecting on them in her heart." Although Mary had some idea of the significance of Jesus's birth because of the angel Gabriel's message, she could not understand the full implications that his birth would have on her life and the whole world. I imagine that when the shepherds arrived, full of eagerness to see the baby Jesus, Mary felt surprised and awestruck. What could it mean that her child, born in such humble circumstances, touched the hearts of these shepherds so much that they were moved to come and seek him out? What could this mean for how Jesus would touch others throughout his life?

Sometimes, we feel in our hearts the significance of our encounters with God before we understand it in our minds. There are many aspects of our faith that cannot be intellectualized. As we celebrate this Christmas season, we would do well to sit and ponder the mysteries that God presents to us. This, too, is a way of proclaiming the good news. Let us sit with God's words and allow them to permeate our hearts. Even when we cannot decipher their full meaning, they can help us to look at our lives and our world with new eyes—perhaps with God's eyes.

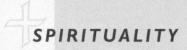

Mass during the Day

GOSPEL ACCLAMATION

℟. Alleluia, alleluia.
A holy day has dawned upon us.
Come, you nations, and adore the Lord.
For today a great light has come upon the earth.
℟. Alleluia, alleluia.

Gospel

John 1:1-18; L16ABC

In the beginning was the Word,
    and the Word was with God,
    and the Word was God.
He was in the beginning with God.
All things came to be through him,
    and without him nothing came to be.
What came to be through him was life,
    and this life was the light of the human
        race;
the light shines in the darkness,
    and the darkness has not overcome it.

A man named John was sent from God.
He came for testimony, to testify to the
        light,
    so that all might believe through him.
He was not the light,
    but came to testify to the light.
The true light, which enlightens everyone,
    was coming into the world.
    He was in the world,
        and the world came to be through him,
        but the world did not know him.
    He came to what was his own,
        but his own people did not accept him.

But to those who did accept him
    he gave power to become children of
        God,
    to those who believe in his name,
    who were born not by natural
        generation
    nor by human choice nor by a man's
        decision
    but of God.

*Continued in Appendix A, p. 265, or
John 1:1-5, 9-14 in Appendix A, p. 265.*

See Appendix A, p. 266, for the other readings.

Reflecting on the Gospel

Many teachers know that one of the most effective ways to teach a new concept or skill is to give students opportunities to practice using the concept or performing the skill. While there are things that can be learned by reading, listening, and observing, many people find that experience is the most effective teacher. Musicians acquire the agility and virtuosity to play their instruments by practicing musical pieces that demand increasing amounts of agility and virtuosity. Soccer goalies learn how to defend the goal by finding the nerve to throw their body in front of the fast-approaching ball in real time.

In this reading from the Gospel of John, the author describes the mystical movement of the Word—the way in which God and the Word cocreated the universe, and the way in which God then sent the Word to become incarnate and one with us. The Word had always existed and was glimpsed through the beauty of creation and through God's teachings revealed in Scripture. If the essential question for this lesson is, "What is the purpose of our lives?" then perhaps God teaches us the answer through the act of sending his only Son, Jesus Christ. On this miraculous Christmas Day, we celebrate how "the Word became flesh and made his dwelling among us." We celebrate how God's teaching and revelatory work shifted from telling and showing into doing.

Jesus came into the world so that we might encounter God in real time and find our joy and purpose in that union. God has made it explicitly clear that the final destiny for all humankind is union with God. We have read and heard this truth in the stories of salvation history told throughout the Old Testament. We observed God showing over and over again how he is willing to extend himself to us when we are most in need. And now we are invited to actively experience and interact with God through the person of Jesus Christ. How, on this holy Christmas Day, might we be invited to actively experience and interact with God?

Perhaps one way is to ask ourselves the question, "Who is Jesus Christ to us?" Jesus comes with a message of renewal and fullness of life for all people, but each person may be drawn to enter into that mystery through a different doorway. Does Jesus represent hope to us? Does he represent compassion? Is he justice for the oppressed? What in the story of Jesus's life and teachings resonates with our spirits and how can we engage with it more fully in our day-to-day lives? Where are the opportunities for us to put on and practice the values Jesus represents for us—in our professional work? Within our significant relationships? In our spiritual practices?

We, as humans, learn most by doing. And so perhaps we can learn to follow Christ into our ultimate destiny of union with God by doing the things that Jesus showed us how to do, by intentionally embracing the parts of our lives where Jesus feels most tangible to us. May we seek to actively encounter and embrace the Word, not just on this day, but every day of our lives.

Model Penitential Act

Presider: Today we celebrate the great gift of God's presence born among us in Jesus Christ. As we begin our worship, let us ask for mercy for the times we have turned away from God . . . *[pause]*

Lord Jesus, you are Emmanuel, God with us: Lord, have mercy.
Christ Jesus, you are the Word made flesh: Christ have mercy.
Lord Jesus, you are the Prince of Peace: Lord, have mercy.

Model Universal Prayer (Prayer of the Faithful)

Presider: Mary birthed the Son of God into this world to intercede for us. Let us offer our prayers and petitions.

Response: Lord, hear our prayer.

Deepen the joy of your church during this Christmas season, that our celebrations of Christ's birth may draw us closer to you . . .

Embrace all of creation in the saving love of Christ, that through his birth we may come to know everlasting life . . .

Comfort all who are alone this holiday season, that they may know of God's great love for them . . .

Open the hearts of those gathered here to your holy interruptions, that like the shepherds we may revel in what the Lord has made known to us . . .

Presider: God of Glory, you sent your only Son into our hurting world to strengthen and save your beloved creation. Receive the prayers we voice aloud and those we hold in the silence of our hearts. We ask this through Christ our Lord. **Amen.**

Living Liturgy

The Work of Christmas: The day we have been waiting and preparing for has arrived. Amid joy and excitement in the Christmas air, we hear today that our eyes have been opened to the light of the newborn Christ. We learn that how we engage in seeing things and how we develop our sight are central components of experiencing the birth of Jesus. The psalmist proclaims that the earth has *seen* the saving power of God, Isaiah cries out that "[t]he LORD has bared his holy arm / in the *sight* of all the nations," and in John's Gospel, we *saw* his glory in the Word that became flesh and dwelled among us.

The gospel message today is one of mystery, of God becoming human and dwelling among us. It is hard to imagine a depiction of the nativity scene without the angels and shepherds, yet today we are challenged to do just that, to see beyond the story of shepherds and angels and enter into the mystery of the incarnation. We are asked in our various liturgical ministries to behold God's saving power as God dwells among us.

Theologian and civil rights leader Howard Thurman encourages those in Christian leadership to spend time with the core message of Christmas in his poem "The Work of Christmas." What happens when the angel song fades away, when shepherds go back to their flocks, when kings return home? Thurman insists that the true work of Christmas then begins in healing the broken, rebuilding relationships, finding the lost, and making music in the heart. Indeed, as we make music, sing, pray, and celebrate the birth of our Savior, we also look deeply into what it means to allow Christ to be born again in us and what it means to recognize and reflect the light of Christ within us, for the splendor of God lives among us!

FOR REFLECTION

• Jesus, the Word of God, entered fully into human life. Do you find this hard to believe? What parts of your life feel distant from how you understand Jesus's earthly experience?

• Are you feeling the joy of Christmas this season? Why or why not? How can your church community offer support if you are not in a place to share the joy of the season?

Homily Points

• The shepherds drop everything to go and see the Christ Child—the one whom the Lord revealed. Imagine how different their lives would have been had they stayed in the fields, deciding that they were "too busy" to change course. Our God is a God of interruptions. God works in unexpected ways and in unexpected times. In the busyness of this Christmas season, let us be open to holy interruptions.

• Holiness appears in the messy realties of daily life. God's messengers appear to the shepherds in the fields. Mary and Joseph experience the most sacred night of their lives inside a stable meant for barn animals. The gospel writer leaves out the exact details of Mary's delivery, but we can be sure it was messy and painful like every other human birth. Nativity sets and Christmas cards often depict a pristine manger scene—likely a far cry from that night's realities. Holiness is not clean and tidy. Instead, God meets us in the mess.

SPIRITUALITY

GOSPEL ACCLAMATION
Heb 1:1-2

R̀. Alleluia, alleluia.
In the past God spoke to our ancestors through
    the prophets;
in these last days, he has spoken to us through
    the Son.
R̀. Alleluia, alleluia.

Gospel

Luke 2:16-21; L18ABC

The shepherds went in haste to
    Bethlehem and found Mary
    and Joseph,
  and the infant lying in the manger.
When they saw this,
  they made known the message
    that had been told them about this
    child.
All who heard it were amazed
  by what had been told them by the
    shepherds.
And Mary kept all these things,
  reflecting on them in her heart.
Then the shepherds returned,
  glorifying and praising God
  for all they had heard and seen,
  just as it had been told to them.

When eight days were completed for
    his circumcision,
  he was named Jesus, the name given
    him by the angel
  before he was conceived in the womb.

Reflecting on the Gospel

The last verse of today's gospel reading is significant, as it proclaims the circumcision and naming of the child Jesus. That Mary and Joseph are obedient to the Jewish Torah is part of Luke's good news. The rite of circumcision, celebrated eight days after birth, is called the "covenant of circumcision" and marks the male child's formal entry into the covenantal Jewish community (see Gen 17:10-11). Every circumcision is a call to Abraham's seed to renew the covenant, but in Jesus, the rite cuts the deepest: the covenant that is made in his flesh will

one day be poured out not only in a drop of foreskin blood, but in the tortured flesh of the Son of Man and of God, crucified for the world's salvation.

At circumcision the child is also named, and Jesus is given the name that was announced to Mary before his conception (Luke 1:31): "Jesus" (or Joshua), meaning "savior." It is not just an external ritual but a matter of identity, a marking of the heart (see Jer 4:6). For present-day parents, what they call their child is important: will it be a family name, one discovered by poring over the baby name reference book, or perhaps that of the latest celebrity? The naming of the Jewish child within the circumcision rite is a significant life-cycle event, for the name links the child to past generations and expresses hope for the future. After the Shoah, many European Jews gave their child the name of a parent or dear relative who had perished in the Holocaust, for in such naming the memory of the dead person is symbolically "born again into the world." Jesus, Savior, is a name for all generations, for the salvation of all. Although we do not know the words of the first-century rite, the prayer that accompanies the Jewish child's naming asks: "May his heart be wide open to comprehend your holy will, that he may learn and teach, keep and fulfill your laws." Jesus would do this most faithfully. We who are named Christians are given our deepest identity by our baptism into Christ. After his resurrection, the early church repeatedly preached and worked miracles "in the name of Jesus," that is, in the power of his personal presence in the Spirit (e.g., Acts 3:6, 4:7-12).

January 1 has also been designated as the day on which the church prays for world peace, and the Solemnity of Mary focuses our gaze on her silent wonder as she contemplates her child, trying to put together the significance of what had happened in the past nine months, dreaming about what the future might hold. In all the gospels, Mary remains a woman wrapped in silence throughout Jesus's preaching, death, and resurrection. After the resurrection, Luke will place Mary at the heart of the community of disciples, still the silent mother, drawing around her the new family of Jesus. It is the peace of Christ that we hope and pray for at the beginning of a New Year: peace in our own hearts and in our families, in our church and in our world.

Preparing to Proclaim
Key words and phrases: "[R]eflecting . . . in her heart."

To the point: This gospel is an active one; the shepherds go in haste and then turn around to share what they have seen. The story is dynamic, full of praise and proclamation of the good news. Mary, though, contrasts with this action. She is, perhaps, somewhat cocooned in her postpartum experience; mothers of newborns often enclose themselves with their infants for a while as they focus on breastfeeding, diapering, and soothing. Her reaction to the great things she is witnessing is different from that of the shepherds. Rather than hastening out to share the news, she keeps these things in her heart, reflecting on and pondering all that she has seen. Others are rightfully celebrating the amazing thing that has happened, and she is quietness in the midst of all this. Both these responses are good. Both are necessary. All of us are called to both at different points in our lifelong journeys of encountering Jesus.

Psalmist Preparation
This psalm includes the words that God gives to Aaron to use as a blessing. You are blessing the congregation as you sing them. At the same time, you are also *part* of the assembly, singing not "May God bless *you*" but "May God bless *us*." As you prepare this psalm, reflect on your dual role at Mass. You are a full member of the congregation, a full participant in the liturgy, *and* you are a leader among the congregation, called forth for a particular role because of your particular gifts. Do you identify with one of these roles more easily than the other?

Making Connections
Between the readings: The words with which Aaron blesses the Israelites are fulfilled in the gospel. Now that God is incarnate, God has a face—a literal one. It is shining on us as God-made-flesh takes in the fullness of the human condition and transforms it into something greater. The second reading reminds us that we share in Jesus's status as a child of God; all of us, through him, have received the privilege of calling God our Father.

To experience: The shepherds work with animals; they know mangers. A contemporary equivalent to this scene would be an office worker visiting someone else's office and finding that someone has given birth on a desk. The extraordinary has entered the very mundane, the very ordinary. God has really truly entered into *this* life. *Our* life. And God remains with us, here and now, present in our midst.

Homily Points
• As we embark on a new year, let us pause to reflect on the many blessings God bestowed upon us this past year. How did the Lord bless you? When did you feel the warmth of the Lord's face shining upon you? Where did you experience the Lord's graciousness, kindness, and peace? Strengthened by these memories of God's great love for us, may we enter this new year with renewed hope.

• Today we celebrate the Blessed Virgin Mary, Mother of God. We have heard it said, "Jesus is the reason for the season." Indeed, this is true—and, it is well worth remembering that Jesus does not come into his world without the hard labor of his mother. Mary said a brave "yes" to the angel's extraordinary request to bear God's son. After months of pregnancy, Mary can now wrap the fruits of her faith in swaddling clothes and lay him in a manger. Our world will never be the same.

• A group of shepherds met the baby Jesus shortly after his birth. They announced the angelic message. They glorified and praised God for all to see. Of all the people to play such a crucial role in the Christmas narrative—why shepherds? They spent their days drenched in dirt doing work many considered to be undignified. Shepherds were part of society's lowest class. This is exactly why God chose them for such an important role. Our God lifts up the lowly. Our God believes in the value of all people—and challenges us to believe the same. Who are the shepherds in our pews? In our neighborhood? In the world?

Model Penitential Act

Presider: Today's gospel takes us into an intimate moment with Mary, who, after giving birth to the Son of God and greeting a group of shepherds, pauses to reflect on all that is stirring in her heart. Let us now also take a moment to pause and call to mind our need for God's mercy . . . *[pause]*

Lord Jesus, you were conceived in Mary's womb: Lord, have mercy.

Christ Jesus, you came into this world with Mary's mighty push: Christ, have mercy.

Lord Jesus, you grew up under Mary's loving care: Lord, have mercy.

Model Universal Prayer (Prayer of the Faithful)

Presider: Guided by the motherly love of Mary, we have the courage to place our needs before God.

Response: Lord, hear our prayer.

Imbue all the baptized with the boldness, wisdom, and contemplative spirit of Mary, Mother of God . . .

Inspire government leaders to create policies and laws that uphold the dignity of all people . . .

Lighten the load of those who enter the new year with fear or trepidation . . .

Grace our local community with blessings in this new year, particularly those who have lost hope . . .

Presider: Loving God, you sent your Spirit to be with Mary as she gave birth to your only Son. Bless us with the presence of your Spirit as we begin a new year. Like Mary, may we draw close to you in reflection and prayer. We ask this through Christ our Lord. **Amen.**

Liturgy and Music

Upside Down: This solemnity of Mary marks the eighth day after Christmas and completes the octave of Christmas. One day is not enough to fully experience the new life found in Christ born of Mary. Within these eight days of jubilee, we contemplate joy and the world-changing event of Jesus's birth. Mary's *Magnificat* maps out a way for this radical way of change to begin and provides a lens through which we view the world upside down. This song of praise reflects God's closeness to the ones the world forgets, showing God's holiness manifested in justice. What lies on the other side of abusive power, arrogance, might, selfishness and greed? Mary carries the answer.

COLLECT

Let us pray.

Pause for silent prayer

O God, who through the fruitful virginity
of Blessed Mary
bestowed on the human race
the grace of eternal salvation,
grant, we pray,
that we may experience the intercession
of her,
through whom we were found worthy
to receive the author of life,
our Lord Jesus Christ, your Son.
Who lives and reigns with you in the unity
of the Holy Spirit,
God, for ever and ever. **Amen.**

FIRST READING
Num 6:22-27

The LORD said to Moses:
"Speak to Aaron and his sons and tell
them:
This is how you shall bless the
Israelites.
Say to them:
The LORD bless you and keep you!
The LORD let his face shine upon
you, and be gracious to you!
The LORD look upon you kindly and
give you peace!
So shall they invoke my name upon the
Israelites,
and I will bless them."

RESPONSORIAL PSALM
Ps 67:2-3, 5, 6, 8

R̸. (2a) May God bless us in his mercy.

May God have pity on us and bless us;
    may he let his face shine upon us.
So may your way be known upon earth;
    among all nations, your salvation.

R̸. May God bless us in his mercy.

May the nations be glad and exult
    because you rule the peoples in equity;
    the nations on the earth you guide.

R̸. May God bless us in his mercy.

May the peoples praise you, O God;
    may all the peoples praise you!
May God bless us,
    and may all the ends of the earth fear
      him!

R̸. May God bless us in his mercy.

SECOND READING
Gal 4:4-7

Brothers and sisters:
When the fullness of time had come, God
    sent his Son,
    born of a woman, born under the law,
    to ransom those under the law,
    so that we might receive adoption as
      sons.
As proof that you are sons,
    God sent the Spirit of his Son into our
      hearts,
    crying out, "Abba, Father!"
So you are no longer a slave but a son,
    and if a son then also an heir, through
      God.

Living Liturgy
Carrying the Word of God to the World: *The Annunciation*, a painting by Henry Ossawa Tanner (1859–1937) found in the Philadelphia Museum of Art, captures an unconventional image of the moment when the angel Gabriel announces to Mary that she will bear the Son of God. Tanner, the son of a minister in the African Methodist Episcopal Church, painted this work after a trip to Egypt and Palestine. His experience of the people, culture, architecture, and light of the Holy Land is reflected in this painting. Mary is shown as an adolescent dressed in rumpled Middle Eastern peasant clothing, without halo or other holy attributes. Gabriel appears as a shaft of light. The scene richly captures multiple moments of trust and doubt, of worry and certainty. Tanner paints the young face of Mary gazing quietly up toward the light, curiously contemplating what it means to be God-bearer—an intimate relationship with God in saying "yes" to the angel. We, too, might ask what it means for us to take on this responsibility of bearing God. Do we realize the close connection we have with God and the mission of Jesus? Mary's role in the life of Jesus becomes our role in Jesus's mission and life as well. May we continually follow Mary's example of carrying the word of God to the world.

PROMPTS FOR FAITH-SHARING

• Do you identify more with the hasty evangelization of the shepherds or Mary's quiet pondering?

• Where do you need God's face to shine in your life? What questions need answers? What dark corners need illumination?

• Do you feel confident in calling God your Father? What holds you back from a relationship of childlike trust with God?

✢ SPIRITUALITY

GOSPEL ACCLAMATION
Matt 2:2

℟. Alleluia, alleluia.
We saw his star at its rising
and have come to do him homage.
℟. Alleluia, alleluia.

Gospel

Matt 2:1-12; L20ABC

**When Jesus was born in Bethlehem
of Judea,
   in the days of King Herod,
   behold, magi from the east ar-
      rived in Jerusalem, saying,
"Where is the newborn king of the
   Jews?
We saw his star at its rising
   and have come to do him
      homage."
When King Herod heard this,
   he was greatly troubled,
   and all Jerusalem with him.
Assembling all the chief priests and
   the scribes of the people,
   he inquired of them where the
      Christ was to be born.
They said to him, "In Bethlehem of
   Judea,
   for thus it has been written through the
      prophet:
     And you, Bethlehem, land of Judah,
     are by no means least among the
       rulers of Judah;
     since from you shall come a ruler,
     who is to shepherd my people
      Israel."
Then Herod called the magi secretly
   and ascertained from them the time of
      the star's appearance.
He sent them to Bethlehem and said,
   "Go and search diligently for the child.
When you have found him, bring me
   word,
   that I too may go and do him homage."**

Continued in Appendix A, p. 266.

Continued in Appendix A, p. 266.

Reflecting on the Gospel

Today is a feast of gospel reversals. Herod had taken the title of "king of the Jews" to himself and perverted it by his ambitious grasp for power. In contrast, Jesus was born a powerless king of the Jews, the title that will be ironically nailed to the humble throne of his cross. Historical controversies aside, the magi thrill our imagination and bring wonder and excitement to the faith-filled search for Jesus that is the focus of every disciple's journey through life. The

magi are the surprising, seeing ones, guided to Jerusalem by their own drive to seek wisdom and by nature's partial revelation in the star that rises in the east. In that city they learn where they will find the child from the special revelation of God's word and wisdom to Israel. They see through the hypocritical protestations of Herod's wish to go to pay homage himself to the newborn child. Herod and his coterie are blind; they have access to the wisdom of the Scriptures, but they refuse to see the meaning of what the prophets wrote. Herod is frantic at the possible risk to his power, while the magi, aristocratic scholars from abroad, are almost naively willing to take risks and add to their scholarly wisdom the wisdom of the Hebrew Scriptures in their search for the royal child. In the wolfish company of Herod and his cohorts, Matthew sees the magi as witnesses to the later call for all disciples to be "shrewd as serpents and simple as doves" (Matt 10:16).

The beauty of this imaginative narrative encourages us to what poetry encourages us: to keen listening, to silent reflection, to transcendence of the ordinary by giving it our full attention. A star, a baby with its mother, human and holy words can lead us with the magi into and beyond the mystery of Christ in silent homage. In our Christmas creches, the magi may seem "odd men out" in the humble company of Mary, Joseph, and the child. But with their fine gifts and opulent robes they do belong there, for they are symbolic of every nation on earth that, in the words of the responsorial Psalm 72, we pray will come to adore God and participate in a kingdom of justice and peace that only God can establish, especially for the poor and needy of the earth.

As we gaze on the magi and hear their story, are we mindful of strangers who come to our own place, not in rich robes but usually in the poverty of contemporary seekers and stargazers: the refugees and asylum seekers from many nations, those tired of hypocrisy and disillusioned about political power-mongering, the young who want a star that is worth following to rise in their lives, even though the journey may be difficult, the old and middle-aged who still dream of something more to enlighten them? And do we not all, at some time, feel ourselves to be strangers and foreigners seeking to belong to a true home (see Eph 2:19) that will be the new Jerusalem?

Preparing to Proclaim
Key words and phrases: "We saw."

To the point: The magi see a new star and are the very few who see and correctly interpret its meaning. They saw the star because they were paying attention; they were scholars who studied the stars. When they started their study, the magi could not have imagined themselves bearing witness to such a hugely unique event. Only once in history will this happen. The birth of Jesus changes the universe in ways far more significant than the appearance of a new celestial body. For the magi, a lifetime of cultivating knowledge and attentiveness culminated in this exceptional moment. They were called to come pay homage to a newborn king. For us, too, our interests and skills can become places of encounter with the God who made all things and who gave us the talents we have.

Psalmist Preparation
Happy tongue twister Sunday! Be proactive in practicing "Tarshish and the Isles" and "nations shall serve" before they trip you up. Note also that this psalm does not just affirm that God is to get worldwide adoration; it also gives a reason that God deserves this. It is God's just and compassionate treatment of the poor and lowly that earns our praise. As part of your preparation with this psalm, could you find a way to participate in bringing about justice for those who are poor? Look for an opportunity for solidarity this week, knowing that God is especially present with those who are afflicted.

Making Connections
Between the readings: The gospel has a clear fulfillment of the first reading's prophecy; the magi from faraway lands are following light to Jerusalem. But there is a dark turn; Herod's wicked jealousy makes Jerusalem an unsafe place even for the newborn king, and the magi must move on to Bethlehem as their ultimate destination. Isaiah's prophecy has yet to be achieved in its fullness. Even still, the magi rejoice at what the star reveals to them; even if the story is not yet complete, this is a moment of God's word being fulfilled.

To experience: The magi found signs of God's saving work in their study of astronomy, an interest and talent that was itself a gift from God. God endows us with an astonishing variety of passions and gifts, and all of these can reveal God to the world in different ways. The fact that our interests vary is precisely why we are given each other; we each reveal a different facet of God's infinite goodness and beauty.

Homily Points
• The prophet Isaiah calls upon the Israelites to rise up and shine in today's first reading. It is not an easy task for people worn and weary after years of exile. The Israelites lived in darkness for so long. Isaiah's vision of the glory to come may seem farfetched—yet, if this season of Christmas has taught us anything, it is that nothing is impossible for God. The divine light can—and will—transform even the darkest corners and thickest clouds. God's glory persists. God's glory engulfs the beloved people. God's glory shines bright for all to see.

• Who is God calling you to be in this new year? The Epiphany story points to the many ways God calls each one of us. Like the magi, we may experience a major moment of clarity when God's calling shines as brightly as a star in the night sky. More likely, we will experience God's callings in the midst of our everyday lives just as the magi did, in the fields of our homes, schools, and workplaces. How will you respond?

• The Epiphany story draws our attention to divine revelation in and among creation. A star leads the magi to Jerusalem. After meeting with Herod, the magi follow that same star to the child Jesus. The guiding star glowed in the night sky as a sign of the divine presence. Creation offers the same direction to us today. Gaze up into the night sky tonight. Revel in the magnitude of stars shining against the darkness. Listen to God speaking through the natural world.

Model Penitential Act

Presider: In today's gospel, the magi follow the guidance of God. For those times we have turned away from God's guidance, let us ask for forgiveness . . . *[pause]*

Lord Jesus, you came into this world out of love for creation: Lord, have mercy.

Christ Jesus, you come into our lives to show us the way: Christ, have mercy.

Lord Jesus, you will come again to bring peace to all: Lord, have mercy.

Model Universal Prayer (Prayer of the Faithful)

Presider: As we journey closer to Christ, let us entrust the needs of our community and the needs of the world to God.

Response: Lord, hear our prayer.

Incline the ears of the baptized to listen to your callings in the midst of our daily lives . . .

Avert the efforts of government officials who, like King Herod, seek to harm the lowly in their communities . . .

Grant safety and good health to travelers, particularly those whose journey takes them into dangerous or uncertain spaces . . .

Shine your divine light onto all of those in our community who feel lost in the shadows of darkness . . .

Presider: Creator God, you journey with each of us just as you journeyed with the magi, drawing us closer to your beloved Son. Receive these prayers, that we may be beacons of hope in the darkness. We ask this through Christ our Lord. **Amen.**

Liturgy and Music

Every Nation on Earth: Today the psalmist proclaims that every nation on earth comes to rejoice. There are many different celebrations of Epiphany around the world—from Spain, Mexico, and many Latin American countries to Greek Orthodox celebrations in Bulgaria and Australia. Each country has gifted the world with its own song. As we consider gift-giving today, how might we not only share our own gifts in music ministry but unwrap the gifts of intercultural song?

Here are three examples. The first is a Cuban piece, "*Tres Guajiros,*" that describes three peasants offering their gifts to the newborn King in juxtaposition to the magi's journey and presentation of treasures to the Christ Child. The peasants offer gifts of "land, labor and love," the gifts of creation. Tony Alonso and Peter Kolar share a lovely arrangement from GIA Publications. Next, consider this engaging text by Chris Shelton, "Bright Star, Where Are You Leading?" set to a little-known French carol, also available from GIA. The first stanza is written from the perspective of the magi. The following two stanzas include us as we journey with the three wise ones, pondering our way through the shadows. Last, this simple Korean melody by Un-yung La, "Lovely Star in the Sky," gives us an opportunity to contemplate the mystery of the Epiphany sky. Use this lovely melody as an instrumental prelude. With these three pieces, we find opportunities not only to follow Christ's light but also to proclaim to every nation on earth that, in Christ, God has revealed the promise of salvation.

COLLECT

Let us pray.

Pause for silent prayer

O God, who on this day
revealed your Only Begotten Son to the
    nations
by the guidance of a star,
grant in your mercy
that we, who know you already by faith,
may be brought to behold the beauty of
    your sublime glory.
Through our Lord Jesus Christ, your Son,
who lives and reigns with you in the unity
    of the Holy Spirit,
God, for ever and ever. Amen.

FIRST READING
Isa 60:1-6

Rise up in splendor, Jerusalem! Your light
        has come,
    the glory of the Lord shines upon you.
See, darkness covers the earth,
    and thick clouds cover the peoples;
but upon you the LORD shines,
    and over you appears his glory.
Nations shall walk by your light,
    and kings by your shining radiance.
Raise your eyes and look about;
    they all gather and come to you:
your sons come from afar,
    and your daughters in the arms of their
        nurses.

Then you shall be radiant at what you see,
    your heart shall throb and overflow,
for the riches of the sea shall be emptied
        out before you,
    the wealth of nations shall be brought
        to you.
Caravans of camels shall fill you,
    dromedaries from Midian and Ephah;
all from Sheba shall come
    bearing gold and frankincense,
    and proclaiming the praises of the LORD.

RESPONSORIAL PSALM

Ps 72:1-2, 7-8, 10-11, 12-13

℟. (cf. 11) Lord, every nation on earth will
adore you.

O God, with your judgment endow the
king,
and with your justice, the king's son;
he shall govern your people with justice
and your afflicted ones with judgment.

℟. Lord, every nation on earth will adore
you.

Justice shall flower in his days,
and profound peace, till the moon be no
more.
May he rule from sea to sea,
and from the River to the ends of the
earth.

℟. Lord, every nation on earth will adore
you.

The kings of Tarshish and the Isles shall
offer gifts;
the kings of Arabia and Seba shall
bring tribute.
All kings shall pay him homage,
all nations shall serve him.

℟. Lord, every nation on earth will adore
you.

For he shall rescue the poor when he cries
out,
and the afflicted when he has no one to
help him.
He shall have pity for the lowly and the
poor;
the lives of the poor he shall save.

℟. Lord, every nation on earth will adore
you.

SECOND READING

Eph 3:2-3a, 5-6

Brothers and sisters:
You have heard of the stewardship of
God's grace
that was given to me for your benefit,
namely, that the mystery was made
known to me by revelation.
It was not made known to people in other
generations
as it has now been revealed
to his holy apostles and prophets by the
Spirit:
that the Gentiles are coheirs, members
of the same body,
and copartners in the promise in Christ
Jesus through the gospel.

Living Liturgy

Setting Out on a New Journey: While the church celebrates Epiphany today, in many Latin American countries, *El Día de Los Reyes* (Three Kings' Day) is celebrated on January 6. This is the twelfth day of Christmas and is marked by gift-giving, mirroring the gifts of gold, frankincense, and myrrh brought to the Christ Child by the three wise men. Some celebrations begin the evening before and include parades of decorative floats and people dressed in costumes of kings bearing gifts. We take some time today to think about what gifts we bring into our own ministry and how we share these gifts with the church, the Body of Christ.

In a 2021 Epiphany homily, Pope Francis tells the faithful that "[w]e need to learn ever better how to contemplate the Lord." He highlights three key phrases in his sermon: "to lift up our eyes," "to set out on a journey," and "to see." As we contemplate the day, how might we offer our gifts in liturgical ministry to foster these three actions of lifting eyes, journeying, and seeing? Francis urges believers to lift eyes in hope and trust in God, to begin journeys of experience and learning, and to see beyond appearances toward things visible and invisible.

As we begin the year, consider inviting parishioners to "set out on a new journey" to offer their gifts to one another within the parish community. Help them see beyond monetary gifts and recognize that gift-giving includes time in ministry, seeing the light of Christ in each other, shining for each other. Lifting up our eyes to the light of the star that guides us to Jesus requires our surrender and complete trust in God. We may not know the way, but we trust that God points us in the right direction. Epiphany is not an event of an ancient time—it is a manifestation of finding God and God's presence within ourselves and in our own community of faith.

PROMPTS FOR FAITH-SHARING

• How can you cultivate attentiveness in your own life?

• Where do you miss the signs of God's presence and action?

• How can our own interests and skills reveal God to ourselves and others?

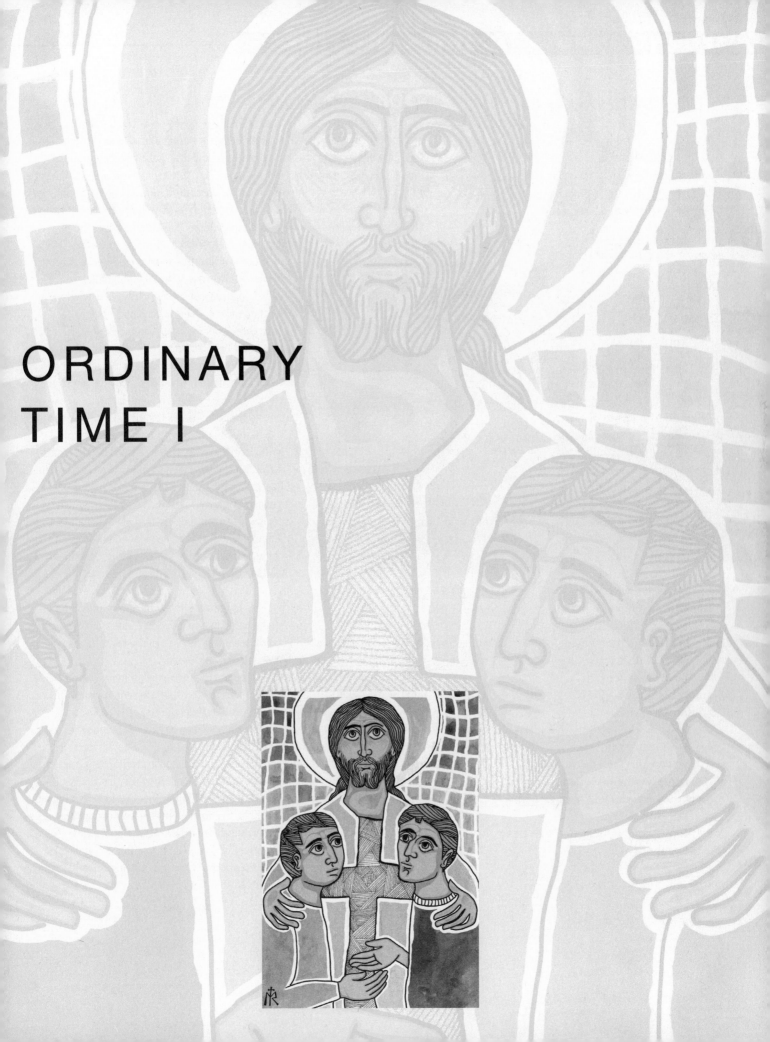

ORDINARY
TIME I

✝ SPIRITUALITY

GOSPEL ACCLAMATION
John 1:14a, 12a

R̸. Alleluia, alleluia.
The Word of God became flesh and dwelt
    among us.
To those who accepted him,
he gave power to become children of
    God.
R̸. Alleluia, alleluia.

Gospel

John 1:29-34; L64A

John the Baptist saw Jesus
    coming toward him and
    said,
  "Behold, the Lamb of God,
    who takes away the sin
    of the world.
He is the one of whom I said,
  'A man is coming after me
    who ranks ahead of me
    because he existed before
    me.'
I did not know him,
  but the reason why I came
    baptizing with water
  was that he might be made
    known to Israel."
John testified further, saying,
  "I saw the Spirit come down like a
    dove from heaven
  and remain upon him.
I did not know him,
  but the one who sent me to baptize
    with water told me,
  'On whomever you see the Spirit
    come down and remain,
  he is the one who will baptize with
    the Holy Spirit.'
Now I have seen and testified that he is
    the Son of God."

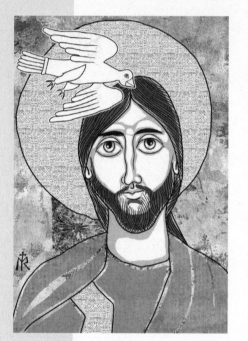

Reflecting on the Gospel

The readings for this Sunday are rather like a hinged door. The Lectionary pushes it open to allow us to gaze backward at the significant figure of John the Baptist, who points to the One we have celebrated as coming among us in the flesh in the Advent and Christmas seasons. And these same readings also direct our gaze forward to our ongoing call to be servants of God among the nations for the long haul of Ordinary Time. The number of Sundays between the Baptism of the Lord (also called the First Sunday in Ordinary Time) and the First Sunday of Lent varies each year, depending on the date on which Lent commences.

What is stressed in today's readings is appropriate as we move out of festal high points: we are called, in all seasons, every day, to live what we are by the grace of God: chosen and gifted people.

In the gospel we meet John the Baptist, who also knew his place in salvation history. He sees Jesus coming toward him and points him out as "the Lamb of God, who takes away the sin of the world." Those listening to John, including those sent from the Pharisees (John 1:24), would be sensitive to the Hebrew biblical, cultic, and liturgical symbol of the lamb, which recalled both the messianic Suffering Servant tradition (Isa 53:7) and the Passover lamb (Exod 12:1-13) in the history of Israel's deliverance. Gathered as a eucharistic assembly, we affirm our faith in the One to whom John pointed, who is coming to us not on the Jordan's banks but as the center of our liturgy: the Lamb of God who, by his life, death, and resurrection, has taken away the sin of the world. The gospel refers to "sin," to the collective brokenness and sinfulness of the world, not to individual sins, and to the collective social and structural evil that will be arrayed against Jesus by his enemies. As human beings we have solidarity in this sin.

The evangelist introduces us to John the Baptist in his prologue (John 1:6-9) because the vision of the prologue is what we hear John is sent to proclaim: Jesus as the preexistent Word, the Spiritfilled one, the Son of God. Today's reading suggests that John recognized Jesus when he came to John for baptism, unreported in this gospel. At Jesus's baptism, explains the Baptist, the Holy Spirit descended on him and still remains with him. John the Baptist's mission was always to point to Jesus, never to himself. The last words that the Baptist speaks later in the Fourth Gospel sum up his calling: "He must increase; I must decrease" (John 3:30). Our discipleship, too, without possessiveness, without blocking the view of Jesus, must point others to the One who is "coming toward" them. We all need the humility of John the Baptist that recognizes that when we are acting prophetically, it is not our cause, our actions, our self-image, but God's about which we are witnessing.

Preparing to Proclaim

Key words and phrases: "Behold, the Lamb of God, who takes away the sin of the world."

To the point: John the Baptist had a central role during Advent; as we move on to Ordinary Time, he reminds us often that he is not the main character. In this gospel he cedes the stage to Jesus, who is beginning his active ministry. In one last testimony, he reminds us of the prophecies we heard during Advent and recounts the baptism of Jesus. He's been saying all along that he's not the real deal; here he steps aside for this one who ranks ahead of him. John also gives us the line we hear before Communion at every Mass: "Behold the Lamb of God, who takes away the sin of the world." Blessed are we who are called to the supper of this Lamb. May we join with John in bearing witness to the one we encounter there.

Psalmist Preparation

We hear this psalm at some big moments in the church year; it is often associated with Mary and proclaimed in conjunction with the annunciation story. But it is also a fitting way to start this new segment of the liturgical calendar. Here, at the beginning of Ordinary Time, we place ourselves in the presence of God; we assume a posture of listening; and we state our intention to live as God wants. As you prepare to proclaim this psalm, think about how God's will has unfolded in your life thus far, and how it is still revealing itself.

Making Connections

Between the readings: It is easy to see foreshadowing of John the Baptist in Isaiah's reference to himself as one "formed as [God's] servant from the womb." After all, we see John's first moment of action when he leaps in Elizabeth's womb, recognizing Jesus in joy even before either of their faces was visible. The second reading is also about callings, both Paul's particular calling as an apostle and the universal call to holiness that his entire audience—including us—shares.

To experience: There will be a lot of light imagery in the coming weeks; this week is about becoming light for others. For those of us in the Northern Hemisphere, this echoes the slow but sure lengthening of days we see in the early months of the year (while in the southern half of the world, these light images can serve as reassurance as days begin to grow shorter).

Homily Points

• John makes Jesus's identity known from the very beginning. The famed Christmas gospel describes Jesus in all his glory: Word made flesh, Son of God, light of the world. Today's gospel introduces a new title for Jesus that does not feel so merry and bright: Lamb of God. John's title evokes an image of Jesus as a weak, wobbly animal who will one day be slaughtered in sacrifice. Is this really the one we are to behold? Indeed, this is the way our almighty God chose to come into this world—not crowned in jewels or heading up armies, but as a little baby, a sacrificial lamb who will one day give up his very life out of love for us.

• John the Baptist kept a watchful eye out for a sign of God's presence. In a moment of awesome wonder, the great prophet saw the Spirit come down upon Jesus "like a dove from heaven." John the Baptist testifies in today's gospel about a particular experience of seeing the Spirit, and in doing so, he paves a way for all disciples to pay attention to God's Spirit alive in the world. As you go about your daily lives this week, consider: Where or in whom are you encountering the Spirit of God? What characteristics does the Spirit embody? What lessons will you take away?

• Today's readings paint a portrait of discipleship. God calls disciples to be servant leaders who shine the light of God's good news to the ends of the earth. God calls disciples to lives of holiness in communion with all other believers. Further, John the Baptist exemplifies traits of discipleship like humility and attentiveness.

Model Penitential Act

Presider: Jesus Christ, the Lamb of God, came to take away the sin of the world. At the start of this Eucharist, let us ask for his mercy and forgiveness . . . *[pause]*

Lord Jesus, you are the Lamb of God: Lord, have mercy.

Christ Jesus, you sacrifice yourself for your beloved people: Christ, have mercy.

Lord Jesus, you will draw us together into eternal life: Lord, have mercy.

Model Universal Prayer (Prayer of the Faithful)

Presider: John the Baptist testified that Jesus is indeed the Son of God. Let us offer our prayers as testimony to the divine presence among us.

Response: Lord, hear our prayer.

Kindle the love of your Spirit in the hearts of all people preparing for baptism . . .

Cultivate a spirit of humility within government officials and other civic and religious leaders . . .

Send relief to people experiencing hunger or homelessness . . .

Reward the many sacrifices offered lovingly by the caregivers in our community . . .

Presider: Almighty God, you sent your beloved Son into the world to take away all our sins. Through the guidance of your Spirit, strengthen the discipleship efforts of all who believe in you. We ask this through Christ our Lord. **Amen.**

Liturgy and Music

Room for God: As leaders of worship, we have a great desire to prepare well for our Sunday prayer. The psalmist cries out, "Here am I, Lord; I come to do your will." Yes, we are ready and eager to do God's will with enthusiasm, to act with our best intentions and our most comprehensive training. Yet, the cry of the psalmist, while personal, leaves room for God to be in charge, for God to "put a new song into my mouth." God is the primary actor, God initiates.

What response do we have then in our liturgical music ministry? Are we in the habit of leaving room for God in our practice and preparation for liturgy? For example, when thinking of texts to sing, do we privilege our own voice over the voice of God? Leaving room for God sometimes means that we should take up less space. So often we tend to control the liturgy with our own set of personal desires or imagined rules. Allow prayer to be God's prayer. Invite God to initiate and to fill in the gaps of our uncertainty.

We must remain intentional with our prayer. Pray over the Sunday's readings. Encourage a different choir member to lead prayer each week before and/or after rehearsal. Rotate prayer leaders among vocal sections of the group. Consider arranging prayer partners. Allow God to place a new song in our mouths this new year.

COLLECT

Let us pray.

Pause for silent prayer

Almighty ever-living God,
who govern all things,
both in heaven and on earth,
mercifully hear the pleading of your
    people
and bestow your peace on our times.
Through our Lord Jesus Christ, your Son,
who lives and reigns with you in the unity
    of the Holy Spirit,
God, for ever and ever. **Amen.**

FIRST READING

Isa 49:3, 5-6

The LORD said to me: You are my servant,
    Israel, through whom I show my glory.
Now the LORD has spoken
    who formed me as his servant from the
        womb,
that Jacob may be brought back to him
    and Israel gathered to him;
and I am made glorious in the sight of the
    LORD,
    and my God is now my strength!
It is too little, the LORD says, for you to be
    my servant,
    to raise up the tribes of Jacob,
    and restore the survivors of Israel;
I will make you a light to the nations,
    that my salvation may reach to the ends
        of the earth.

RESPONSORIAL PSALM

Ps 40:2, 4, 7-8, 8-9, 10

℟. (8a and 9a) Here am I, Lord; I come to do your will.

I have waited, waited for the LORD,
  and he stooped toward me and heard
    my cry.
And he put a new song into my mouth,
  a hymn to our God.

℟. Here am I, Lord; I come to do your will.

Sacrifice or offering you wished not,
  but ears open to obedience you gave me.
Holocausts or sin-offerings you sought not;
  then said I, "Behold I come."

℟. Here am I, Lord; I come to do your will.

"In the written scroll it is prescribed for
    me,
to do your will, O my God, is my delight,
  and your law is within my heart!"

℟. Here am I, Lord; I come to do your will.

I announced your justice in the vast
    assembly;
  I did not restrain my lips, as you, O
    LORD, know.

℟. Here am I, Lord; I come to do your will.

SECOND READING

1 Cor 1:1-3

Paul, called to be an apostle of Christ
    Jesus by the will of God,
  and Sosthenes our brother,
  to the church of God that is in Corinth,
  to you who have been sanctified in
    Christ Jesus,
  called to be holy,
  with all those everywhere who call upon
    the name of our Lord
  Jesus Christ, their Lord and ours.
Grace to you and peace from God our
    Father
  and the Lord Jesus Christ.

Living Liturgy

Becoming Witnesses: Today we are called to witness Christ, which is no ordinary undertaking. There is a beautiful tapestry by John Nava hung over the baptismal font at the Cathedral of Our Lady of the Angels in Los Angeles. What is captivating about this piece of art is its simultaneous simplicity and grandeur depicting the baptism of Jesus. The simple image is one of John the Baptist (facing the viewer) pouring water on the bowed head of Jesus whose back is to the viewer. The central tapestry of this five-paneled monochromatic work is profoundly ordinary in its portrayal of the sacrament yet the message of mission and identity that it proclaims is far from ordinary.

Baptismal identity is not only about a conversion to Christ but a witnessing to the world in the light of Christ. Baptism sends us out to claim our identity as Christians who imitate Christ as light to the nations. Christian witness first requires the humility of Christ. We bow to whatever God calls us to. God has chosen us. Witness does not always involve grand gesture but can be simple acts. Teresa of Calcutta's witness to the poorest of the poor in Calcutta reminds us that little by little the work of God gets done through us, inspiring the saying: "We can do no great things, only small things with great love."

These days of ordinary time ought to be filled with extraordinary witness. The "ordinary" only refers to the ordering of weeks between the seasons of Advent and Christmas, Lent and Easter. It does not refer to a diminished quality of the liturgy. And so, we recognize the importance of our everyday actions in witnessing our Christian faith with joy and humility.

PROMPTS FOR FAITH-SHARING

• How might you imitate John the Baptist's mission of making Jesus known?

• What are some of the moments of calling you've experienced in your life? How did you identify God's voice?

• When we think of "God's will" we often focus on big decisions like our state in life and our career. But God's will is more often lived out in the small, ordinary choices we make every day. Where might God be calling you to greater holiness amidst the mundane realities of your life?

✠ SPIRITUALITY

GOSPEL ACCLAMATION
cf. Matt 4:23

℞. Alleluia, alleluia.
Jesus proclaimed the Gospel of the kingdom
and cured every disease among the people.
℞. Alleluia, alleluia.

Gospel   Matt 4:12-23; L67A

When Jesus heard that John had been
    arrested,
  he withdrew to Galilee.
He left Nazareth and went to live in Caper-
    naum by the sea,
  in the region of Zebulun and Naphtali,
  that what had been said through Isaiah
    the prophet
  might be fulfilled:
    Land of Zebulun and land of Naphtali,
      the way to the sea, beyond the
        Jordan,
      Galilee of the Gentiles,
    the people who sit in darkness have
      seen a great light,
    on those dwelling in a land overshad-
      owed by death
      light has arisen.
From that time on, Jesus began to preach
    and say,
  "Repent, for the kingdom of heaven is at
    hand."

As he was walking by the Sea of Galilee, he
    saw two brothers,
  Simon who is called Peter, and his
    brother Andrew,
  casting a net into the sea; they were
    fishermen.
He said to them,
  "Come after me, and I will make you fish-
    ers of men."
At once they left their nets and followed
    him.
He walked along from there and saw two
    other brothers,
  James, the son of Zebedee, and his
    brother John.

Continued in Appendix A, p. 267, or
Matt 4:12-17 *in Appendix A, p. 267.*

Reflecting on the Gospel

Quoting lines from Isaiah, Matthew proclaims the public appearance of Jesus and his call to repentance, to radical conversion of heart and life for the sake of the kingdom, as the great light that dawns over the land.

Jesus begins to call those who are willing to allow him to rule over their hearts and so spread the reigning presence of God and "make disciples of all nations" (Matt 28:19). His first call is to four fishermen at the Sea of Galilee,

a place of a thriving fishing industry and located on international trade routes, at a sufficient distance from Jerusalem. Significantly, Jesus's first call is to people who have something to leave behind, not to poor men who might jump at the chance of following Jesus to better themselves. He sees the brothers, Peter and Andrew, casting their nets into the lake, not indulging in a more leisurely hook-and-line type of fishing. Casting nets is a labor-intensive job, demanding strength, long hours, unpredictable results, knowledge of what fish to keep and what to toss back (see Matt 4:18-22), and persistent dedication. To such men comes Jesus's invitation to follow him and use all their skills in a different kind of fishing: fishing for people. We are not told if there had been any previous contact between Jesus and these fishermen, nor is their obedient response elaborated. What Matthew wants to stress is the initiative and the personal impact of Jesus, and Peter's and Andrew's readiness to follow him immediately.

Jesus then moves on to call two other brothers, James and John. In this first call of two pairs of brothers, there's a hint of the "brotherliness" (and "sisterliness") in the following of Jesus that will be not only of blood ties, but also of the Spirit. James and John are intent on other skills that are necessary for fishing: mending nets that, along with their boats, need to be kept in good repair. Jesus calls, and these two also respond to him. None of these first disciples can stay put. Peter and Andrew leave what appears to be their own established business; James and John disrupt accepted social conventions by leaving their father's business and family ties. Their apprenticeship begins with hearing Jesus teach in the synagogues throughout Galilee and proclaim the good news of the kingdom. Messiah of the word and deed, he also heals the sick. These are all ministries in which the community of disciples will also be involved, in Jesus's name.

No matter our own lifestyle or social situation, as disciples of Jesus we are all called at various times to leave something behind so that we can follow him. We, too, cannot stay put in an immature understanding of Jesus, cannot remain in enterprises that contradict our baptismal calling, or accept social structures that are contrary to the gospel ethic of love and respect for human dignity. Each of us has to name for ourselves, in our own time and place, how we radically turn our hearts to following Jesus.

Preparing to Proclaim

Key words and phrases: "Come after me, and I will make you fishers of men."

To the point: Three verbs at the end of the gospel summarize Jesus's ministry: teaching, proclaiming, curing. This gives us a preview of his years of active work; this is what we can expect of Jesus's ministry. Names are also important in this gospel: these place names remind us that Jesus's ministry took place in the real world, in a place with a history and a people. New characters are also identified by name: Simon who is called Peter, his brother Andrew; James and John, the sons of Zebedee. These are real people in real places. They have family ties and daily tasks. And Jesus calls them by name. He comes to them right where they are, in all the realness and fullness of their lives, and he calls them to something greater.

Psalmist Preparation

We can imagine the fishermen singing this psalm as they accept Jesus's call; they have identified him as their light and so their fear is cast out as they whole-heartedly choose to follow him. It's okay if you are not able to sing it so whole-heartedly; for most of us the choice to follow Jesus comes gradually, building up through small choices rather than being a once-and-for-all deal. There is much to fear in this world, many reasons to hesitate in giving over our hearts and lives. As you prepare the psalm this week, try to bring your fears and anxieties to Jesus. Know that he sees them, and you, with the utmost love. He does not leave you alone with your fears.

Making Connections

Between the readings: The beginning of Jesus's preaching is the fulfillment of Isaiah's prophecy: Jesus himself is the great light for those who are dwelling in darkness. This must have been evident to Simon, Andrew, James, and John; Jesus's invitation is an odd interruption in their daily work, but they find themselves compelled to drop everything, leave their livelihoods and families behind, and follow him.

To experience: For the apostles called in this gospel, following Jesus meant giving up the concrete realities of their lives and careers and communities. We are given the specific place names of these events to remind us that they are real. They affect real, specific, complex people with stories and families. For us, too, specific places form part of our story. Some serve as homes and comforts; others are special places of brief encounter with God. Some places become places to settle; others are left behind. God is present in all of them, working in each of our specific contexts.

Homily Points

• Jesus calls the disciples in pairs—a powerful reminder that discipleship happens in community. Each of us brings particular gifts, but those gifts are not meant to be siloed. Christ calls each of us to follow him in communion with fellow believers, just as he did with Simon, Andrew, James, and John. Together, we can further Christ's work of proclaiming the gospel to the ends of the earth.

• Jesus calls the disciples in ordinary moments—a valuable reminder for this time between the end of Christmas and the start of Lent. It can be easy to discount the daily calls when we compare our experiences to popular seasonal stories from Scripture. An angel never appeared to me. Jesus never transfigured atop a mountain as I stood there watching. Am I still called? Indeed, Jesus utters the command "follow me" in the places we live and work. Each ordinary day offers the chance to put down our nets and follow him.

• Last week we heard John the Baptist's account of Jesus's baptism. Today's gospel from Matthew brings us to the beginning of Jesus's public ministry. He calls disciples, teaches, preaches, and cures all over Galilee. We will hear more detailed stories of Jesus's activity in the coming weeks. He certainly kept busy! However, let us not miss the very first action Jesus takes in today's gospel: he withdraws. Upon hearing that John had been arrested, Jesus withdraws to Galilee. The gospel writer does not detail what Jesus did during his time away, but if it is like other instances, we can imagine Jesus spending time in quiet prayer to the Father. This too is an important act of ministry.

Model Penitential Act

Presider: Jesus begins his public ministry with a summons: "Repent, for the kingdom of heaven is at hand." For the times we have failed to heed his call, let us ask for mercy . . . *[pause]*

Lord Jesus, you fulfill what the prophets foretold: Lord, have mercy.

Christ Jesus, you notice the good in each of us: Christ, have mercy.

Lord Jesus, you call us to follow you: Lord, have mercy.

Model Universal Prayer (Prayer of the Faithful)

Presider: Confident that God hears our prayers, let us place our needs before the Lord.

Response: Lord, hear our prayer.

Enlighten all ministers who are preaching the good news of Jesus Christ today . . .

Foster a spirit of repentance among all people in need of healing . . .

Deepen the bonds of unity and respect among Christians of all traditions . . .

Awaken the call to discipleship in the ordinary lives of each of us gathered here . . .

Presider: God of blessing, you promised a great light for the people who sit in darkness. Receive our prayers that we too might be beacons of light for the church and the world. We ask this through Christ our Lord. **Amen.**

Liturgy and Music

Music Accompaniment: At one parish that I ministered at some time ago, the English choir and the Spanish choir sat across the aisle and sang only in English and Spanish respectively. There were few opportunities to learn each other's music and to sing each other's songs. Many parishes have since come a long way from those days making progress in integrating bilingual and perhaps trilingual parish choirs. But we must also keep our focus on the music accompaniment of these choirs. Music directors and those that are at the front of leading music must carefully study the elements, rhythms, and instrumentations that shape cultural idioms within each piece. Besides understanding language and proper pronunciation, knowing how to articulate the variety of rhythms and styles from each tradition and culture must be honored. Listen to recordings and emulate what you hear. Resist rearranging the piece to suit your taste. For example, if there is no need for piano accompaniment of a certain style, refrain from playing or adding a piano part. Most of the time, a synthesizer part would enhance the arrangement, but it is important to know the idiomatic expressions of each style, sometimes more nuanced and less florid than we might think.

COLLECT

Let us pray.

Pause for silent prayer

Almighty ever-living God,
direct our actions according to your good
　　pleasure,
that in the name of your beloved Son
we may abound in good works.
Through our Lord Jesus Christ, your Son,
who lives and reigns with you in the unity
　　of the Holy Spirit,
God, for ever and ever. **Amen.**

FIRST READING

Isa 8:23–9:3

First the LORD degraded the land of
　　Zebulun
　　and the land of Naphtali;
　　but in the end he has glorified the
　　　　seaward road,
　　the land west of the Jordan,
　　the District of the Gentiles.

Anguish has taken wing, dispelled is
　　darkness:
　　for there is no gloom where but now
　　　　there was distress.
The people who walked in darkness
　　have seen a great light;
upon those who dwelt in the land of
　　gloom
　　a light has shone.
You have brought them abundant joy
　　and great rejoicing,
as they rejoice before you as at the
　　harvest,
　　as people make merry when dividing
　　　　spoils.
For the yoke that burdened them,
　　the pole on their shoulder,
and the rod of their taskmaster
　　you have smashed, as on the day of
　　　　Midian.

RESPONSORIAL PSALM

Ps 27:1, 4, 13-14

R̂. (1a) The Lord is my light and my salvation.

The LORD is my light and my salvation;
  whom should I fear?
The LORD is my life's refuge;
  of whom should I be afraid?

R̂. The Lord is my light and my salvation.

One thing I ask of the LORD;
  this I seek:
to dwell in the house of the LORD
  all the days of my life,
that I may gaze on the loveliness of the
  LORD
  and contemplate his temple.

R̂. The Lord is my light and my salvation.

I believe that I shall see the bounty of the
  LORD
  in the land of the living.
Wait for the LORD with courage;
  be stouthearted, and wait for the LORD.

R̂. The Lord is my light and my salvation.

SECOND READING

1 Cor 1:10-13, 17

I urge you, brothers and sisters, in the
    name of our Lord Jesus Christ,
  that all of you agree in what you say,
  and that there be no divisions among
    you,
  but that you be united in the same mind
    and in the same purpose.
For it has been reported to me about you,
    my brothers and sisters,
  by Chloe's people, that there are
    rivalries among you.
I mean that each of you is saying,
  "I belong to Paul," or "I belong to
    Apollos,"
  or "I belong to Cephas," or "I belong to
    Christ."
Is Christ divided?
Was Paul crucified for you?
Or were you baptized in the name of Paul?
For Christ did not send me to baptize but
    to preach the gospel,
  and not with the wisdom of human
    eloquence,
  so that the cross of Christ might not be
    emptied of its meaning.

Living Liturgy

Becoming One: In his 2019 apostolic letter *Aperuit Illis* (AI; *motu proprio*), Pope Francis established that this Sunday in Ordinary Time would be devoted to the celebration, study, and dissemination of the word of God. This year it falls within the Week of Prayer for Christian Unity. In light of today's Scripture, we discern how discipleship leads to active belonging. As leaders, we reflect deeply on what it means, within our music making and liturgy preparation, to follow Christ, to belong to each other, and to become one. Francis explains that the celebration has "ecumenical value" and that the Scriptures point listeners and believers "to authentic and firm unity" (AI 3). Francis's vision is a broad one, a full embrace of those who identify as Christian.

In the letter, Francis refers to table fellowship in the Emmaus journey story and the "unbreakable bond between sacred Scripture and the Eucharist," in which from the one table, both word of God and body of Christ are equally vital in making things possible to see ourselves "as part of one another" (AI 8). Are we able to identify with the different groups within our worship communities, to know that all are united in Christ? What steps might we take to become part of one another? The challenge of a community of believers that actively seeks Christian unity is one that transforms hearts to listen to sacred Scripture and then "to practice mercy."

Pope Francis insists that God's word "has the power to open our eyes and to enable us to renounce a stifling and barren individualism and instead to embark on a new path of sharing and solidarity" (AI 13). Let us be faithful disciples who practice our ministerial vocations with sharing mercy and love each day, who study sacred Scripture with open eyes to see possibilities of shedding our individualistic nature, and who participate in the Eucharist with open hearts to know that compassionate welcome and inclusion lead us to authentic unity.

PROMPTS FOR FAITH-SHARING

• What have you been called to give up to follow Jesus? Do you find these sacrifices easy or hard?

• This gospel is full of place names, reminding us that Jesus's ministry happened in a real place. Reflect on the places of your life, those you have called home and those you have left behind. How have they formed you into the disciple you are today?

• For most of us, Jesus calls us to follow him not by leaving behind our families and daily tasks but in the context of those very things. How can you live Christ's call to follow him in the midst of your real life?

JANUARY 22, 2023
THIRD SUNDAY IN ORDINARY TIME

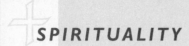

✝ SPIRITUALITY

GOSPEL ACCLAMATION
Matt 5:12a

℞. Alleluia, alleluia.
Rejoice and be glad;
your reward will be great in heaven.
℞. Alleluia, alleluia.

Gospel

Matt 5:1-12a; L70A

When Jesus saw the crowds, he
    went up the mountain,
  and after he had sat down, his
    disciples came to him.
He began to teach them, saying:
  "Blessed are the poor in spirit,
    for theirs is the kingdom of
      heaven.
  Blessed are they who mourn,
    for they will be comforted.
  Blessed are the meek,
    for they will inherit the
      land.
  Blessed are they who
    hunger and thirst for
      righteousness,
    for they will be satisfied.
  Blessed are the merciful,
    for they will be shown mercy.
  Blessed are the clean of heart,
    for they will see God.
  Blessed are the peacemakers,
    for they will be called children of
      God.
  Blessed are they who are persecuted
    for the sake of righteousness,
    for theirs is the kingdom of
      heaven.
  Blessed are you when they insult you
    and persecute you
    and utter every kind of evil against
      you falsely because of me.
  Rejoice and be glad,
    for your reward will be great in
      heaven."

Reflecting on the Gospel

Vargas is an illiterate carpenter living on a garbage dump in Venezuela. All around him the land has been devastated by pollution. Eking out a bare living by his carpentry, he also paints pictures bursting with life: green trees laden with fruit, brilliant birds soaring into a clear, unpolluted blue sky, animals frolicking joyfully. Nobody around him can afford to buy his paintings, but that doesn't worry Vargas. He's a prophet who paints not the world that he knows but the world that he hopes for and believes in.

The crowd that is described at the end of Matthew's fourth chapter is rather like the "garbage-dump people" among whom Vargas lives. They were the ones who had come to Jesus hoping for a cure from physical and mental illnesses, and his healing compassion had reached out to them. That did not mean that their physical, social, and spiritual disadvantages disappeared overnight, but it did mean that they glimpsed in and through Jesus another world of possibilities. It is these people who gather with Jesus on a mountain, where he will give the first of the five great discourses in Matthew's Gospel. In both the Old and New Testaments, the mountain is a privileged place of revelation. Not only can we physically see farther and need to breathe more deeply, but for Jesus, as for Moses when he received the Torah, it is a symbolic place of wider spiritual vision, of looking at this world, certainly, but also at the kingdom of heaven and the possibilities of the reign of God over physical, social, and spiritual realities.

Sitting down in the posture of a rabbinic teacher, Jesus calls his disciples to himself. The crowd is certainly not excluded from what Jesus is saying, but his disciples are at the heart of the people to whom they are called to minister. As we heard last week, only four disciples have been called so far, so it is not the Twelve but the community of disciples, the church to which we belong, that Jesus is addressing in this gospel. Our eyes need to look out and be directed by Jesus's words to the wider "mountain view"—not just to those more immediately around us, but also to our larger society and world.

The radical significance of what we refer to as "the Beatitudes" can be diluted and sanitized by familiarity. Christian intuition is right to recognize the importance of this text as a program of identity and action for Jesus's disciples, but this has often made it a lifesaving raft to which we cling when unable to think of what gospel passage to use, for example, at a funeral, wedding, or school Mass. "Let's have the Beatitudes" seems safe. In fact, this gospel is dangerous, more like a high-powered motorboat that carries us into deep waters of discipleship. In the Germany of the 1930s, Dietrich Bonhoeffer wrote passionately that the Beatitudes are nothing about good behavior; rather, they are an absolute demand that brought a disciple before the face of the living God and the cost of the life, death, and resurrection of Jesus.

Preparing to Proclaim

Key words and phrases: "Rejoice and be glad, for your reward will be great in heaven."

To the point: When hashtags started becoming popular on social media, the hashtag "blessed" quickly turned sarcastic. It is used most often to make fun of the few who do use it sincerely, because it seems that they are often those who habitually overshare or who attribute their life's luxuries to the blessing of God. We know, deep down, that having pretty, Instagramable things is not actually a sign of God's blessing. Here, Jesus also turns around what "blessed" means, but he does it in all sincerity. He affirms that those who practice hard spiritual disciplines, whose lives may not appear "blessed" in an earthly sense, are in fact those favored by God. Jesus reminds us that what we see is not always the truth of the matter; God is up to something greater than that which we can perceive.

Psalmist Preparation

In this psalm, we hear an affirmation of the gospel's message that God's values are not our own. God's efforts—God's preferential love—are for those who are oppressed, imprisoned, and estranged, those who would be seen as lesser in most societies. As you prepare this psalm, consider your own role in cultures of oppression and injustice. Are there systemic sins from which you have benefited? How might you work to do away with them? Keep these in mind as you proclaim the psalm this week, knowing that the ongoing, tiresome work of fighting off injustice is what puts us on God's side.

Making Connections

Between the readings: In the first reading, righteous people are instructed to seek humility. This is a funny command, because it seems that in this life humility often finds us without us trying. We make mistakes often and our very human condition reminds us not to think too highly of ourselves. Humility doesn't always feel good, but it is the thing that saves us; it is another one of the many reversals that Jesus preaches. The second reading affirms God's reversal of human values. Those whom the world considers foolish, weak, and lowly are chosen and called by God.

To experience: We know that God's values are not our own; we hear this repeatedly in Scripture. But, saturated in a culture that values other things, we forget very easily. We put our time and attention into gathering money and security and social capital, even when we know this is not what Jesus asks of us. Consider the Beatitudes this week and how God might be using them to invite you into letting go of one of these false values.

Homily Points

• We all know Jesus's Sermon on the Mount. The Beatitudes are scripted and framed in parish halls across the world. But the Beatitudes can't be relegated to some familiar, lofty statements about the Christian life. Jesus calls serious bluff on what society values most: wealth, power, prestige. He flips the tables on who is truly blessed: the poor, the persecuted, the peacemakers. Jesus preaches a radical sermon that should jar us to action. The Beatitudes aren't meant to just be looked at—they are meant to be lived.

• Jesus names many types of blessed people in today's gospel. Let us call to mind holy people who fall into each category—the mourners in our pews, the advocates thirsting for righteousness in our streets, the persecuted crossing the southern border. By recalling names, faces, and stories, we bring to life in flesh and bone the teachings of Jesus.

• Humility is a theme threading through today's readings. Zephaniah implores the humble of the earth to "seek justice, seek humility." St. Paul proclaims that God "chose the weak of the world." Jesus himself blesses the meek. What does it look like to take on a posture of humility in today's world? Aren't the meek and lowly at risk of being exploited or abused? The power dynamics that riddle communities today will be no more in the kingdom of God—for our God is a God of justice. God's ways *will* prevail, no matter how far off it seems now. The call to act humbly challenges us to trust in God's almighty power.

Model Penitential Act

Presider: In his letter to the Corinthians, St. Paul exhorts the community to "[c]onsider your own calling, brothers and sisters." For the times when we have not lived up to our callings to follow Christ, let us ask for pardon and mercy . . . *[pause]*

> Lord Jesus, you bless your chosen people: Lord, have mercy.
> Christ Jesus, you call on us to rejoice and be glad: Christ, have mercy.
> Lord Jesus, you promise our reward will be great in heaven: Lord, have mercy.

Model Universal Prayer (Prayer of the Faithful)

Presider: With confidence in Christ Jesus and his teachings, let us offer our prayers and petitions.

Response: Lord, hear our prayer.

Cultivate spirits of meekness and mercy within all members of the baptized . . .

Satisfy those who hunger and thirst for righteousness across the globe . . .

Comfort those who mourn and those who face insults and persecution because of their faith . . .

Call forth peacemakers within our local communities . . .

Presider: God of all blessings, you teach us the way to eternal life. Hear our prayers that we might come to embody your lessons in the world today. We ask this through Christ our Lord. **Amen.**

Liturgy and Music

Full Range of Emotion: The psalm text today provides excellent formational material for training new psalmists or for rekindling the ministerial presence of veteran cantors. The psalm opens with a brave declaration of God's faithfulness to the helpless. As part of spiritual and musical preparation, reflect on how to bravely proclaim this beatitude. What might it take to understand the courage required to acknowledge that perhaps we might be the "oppressed" and "bowed down," and that our hope lies completely in God? How do we proclaim this news with humility from such a place of honor, the ambo?

The psalm challenges us to surrender to God. Spend time exploring and understanding this notion of surrender in music making, especially how to interpret it in the proclamation of the psalm this Sunday. As a rule, psalmists should take home a copy of the psalm to review before coming to Mass. There will only be limited time before Mass to refine such interpretations amid other fine-tuning proceedings.

Let this be a starting point for cantors of the psalm to develop an attitude of intentionality toward engaging with psalm texts to express the full range of emotion that these ancient sacred songs offer us.

COLLECT

Let us pray.

Pause for silent prayer

Grant us, Lord our God,
that we may honor you with all our mind,
and love everyone in truth of heart.
Through our Lord Jesus Christ, your Son,
who lives and reigns with you in the unity
of the Holy Spirit,
God, for ever and ever. **Amen.**

FIRST READING
Zeph 2:3; 3:12-13

Seek the LORD, all you humble of the earth,
  who have observed his law;
seek justice, seek humility;
  perhaps you may be sheltered
  on the day of the LORD's anger.

But I will leave as a remnant in your midst
  a people humble and lowly,
who shall take refuge in the name of
    the LORD:
  the remnant of Israel.
They shall do no wrong
  and speak no lies;
nor shall there be found in their mouths
  a deceitful tongue;
they shall pasture and couch their flocks
  with none to disturb them.

RESPONSORIAL PSALM
Ps 146:6-7, 8-9, 9-10

℟. (Matt 5:3) Blessed are the poor in spirit;
the kingdom of heaven is theirs!
    or:
℟. Alleluia.

The LORD keeps faith forever,
  secures justice for the oppressed,
  gives food to the hungry.
The LORD sets captives free.

℟. Blessed are the poor in spirit; the kingdom of heaven is theirs!
    or:
℟. Alleluia.

The Lord gives sight to the blind;
    the Lord raises up those who were
        bowed down.
The Lord loves the just;
    the Lord protects strangers.

R︆. Blessed are the poor in spirit; the kingdom of heaven is theirs!
    or:
R︆. Alleluia.

The fatherless and the widow the Lord
    sustains,
    but the way of the wicked he thwarts.
The Lord shall reign forever;
    your God, O Zion, through all
        generations.
Alleluia.

R︆. Blessed are the poor in spirit; the kingdom of heaven is theirs!
    or:
R︆. Alleluia.

SECOND READING

1 Cor 1:26-31

Consider your own calling, brothers and
    sisters.
Not many of you were wise by human
    standards,
    not many were powerful,
    not many were of noble birth.
Rather, God chose the foolish of the world
    to shame the wise,
    and God chose the weak of the world to
        shame the strong,
    and God chose the lowly and despised
        of the world,
    those who count for nothing,
    to reduce to nothing those who are
        something,
    so that no human being might boast
        before God.
It is due to him that you are in Christ
    Jesus,
    who became for us wisdom from God,
    as well as righteousness, sanctification,
        and redemption,
    so that, as it is written,
"Whoever boasts, should boast in the
    Lord."

Living Liturgy

Speaking Up: A narrative of radical reversal characterizes the message of Jesus today. Those who are of least account in this world can anticipate the highest places in God's kingdom. However, this high place only comes with full participation in God. Those who have no need of God may miss the experience of God. As individuals, we fail to fulfill the characteristics of some or all the blessings poured forth from the beatitudes, but we are blessed nonetheless by the character of the entire community around us.

Contemplating the beatitudes with the movements of peace and justice, I choose to highlight the second beatitude: "Blessed are they who mourn, for they will be comforted."

Collective mourning of the evils of the world urges us as liturgical ministers to question the ways in which we respond with healing action. Do we mourn in silence? Or should we perhaps speak up more against societal ills, challenging the status quo much like Jesus did? Without partisan politics, one could truly discern the message of reversal enshrined within each beatitude. Blessed are the peacemakers!

In addition, personal mourning of our own failings ought to lead to a deeper self-reflective call to action which sets in motion a resilience that comes from the mourning season, a resilience to speak up. From sorrow to joy, the beatitudes shape Christ within us. Amid our failings we struggle to imitate Christ and to know Christ through experience. English mystic Julian of Norwich, through her illness, sorrow, and pain, spoke prophetically of God's motherly love. At a time when misogyny was pervasive and the tradition of female subordination was powerful, Julian had a strong belief that her voice was important. This is an excerpt of her writing from the *Revelations of Divine Love*: "But because I am a woman, ought I therefore to believe that I should not tell you of the goodness of God, when I saw at that same time that it is his will that it be known?"

PROMPTS FOR FAITH-SHARING

• When is a time that you chose humility? What was that like? Can you think of a time when humility found you despite your best efforts?

• Can you name one false value in your life? How can you turn your attention away from that?

• Take a close look at all the Beatitudes from the gospel. Can you find one that sounds like an invitation, an area God might be calling you to grow?

✝ SPIRITUALITY

GOSPEL ACCLAMATION
John 8:12

℟. Alleluia, alleluia.
I am the light of the world, says the
   Lord;
whoever follows me will have the light
   of life.
℟. Alleluia, alleluia.

Gospel

Matt 5:13-16; L73A

Jesus said to his disciples:
   "You are the salt of the earth.
But if salt loses its taste, with
   what can it be seasoned?
It is no longer good for anything
   but to be thrown out and tram-
      pled underfoot.
You are the light of the world.
A city set on a mountain cannot
   be hidden.
Nor do they light a lamp and
   then put it under a bushel
      basket;
   it is set on a lampstand,
   where it gives light to all in the
      house.
Just so, your light must shine before
   others,
   that they may see your good deeds
   and glorify your heavenly Father."

Reflecting on the Gospel

Disciples who live the Beatitudes that we heard proclaimed last Sunday are salt and light, says Jesus, in the continuation of the Sermon on the Mount. He says it directly, forcefully: "*You are . . .*" Good teacher that he is, Jesus compares discipleship with these two things that were familiar to and essential for his listeners.

For the people of Jesus's day, salt had great importance, both socially and religiously. Some of its uses persist today. It was a food preservative and a food seasoning. Adding salt to food made it tastier, while adding it to incense preserved its fragrance and holiness (see Exod 30:35). Newborn babies were rubbed with salt in the belief that this was good for their health and could also have some symbolic religious significance of preservation and incorruptibility. Salt was applied to the skin to heal wounds. It was used in covenantmaking rituals as a symbol of the fidelity to or "preserving" of the covenant (Num 18:19; 2 Chr 13:5). To describe people's speech as "seasoned with salt" (Col 4:6) was to suggest that their words were "tasty"—wise and graciously witty. Although some salt is needed for fertile soil, an excess is harmful, and so in a symbolic gesture of judgment, those who razed a city might scatter or "sow" it with salt (Judg 9:45) to express the hope that nothing would grow there again (Jer 17:6).

When Jesus calls his disciples "the salt of the earth," he is suggesting by this metaphor that they have a responsibility for savoring the world with God's love, making it more to "God's taste" (see 2 Kgs 2:19-22), healing its wounds. What is the contemporary corruption that we need to name and challenge so that our Christian "saltiness" contributes to humanity, society, our church, and our planet being preserved, healed, and enabled for the kingdom of God in Christ? Salt is not sweet and sugary, and neither can our Christian discipleship be. Put salt on a sore spot and it stings as well as heals.

The other comparison that Jesus makes is to light. Disciples *are* the light of the world, as the ritual of baptism declares by the presentation of the burning candle. Like salt, so with fire: both exist not for themselves, but to give taste, warmth, or illumination to something beyond themselves. Not the powerful Roman Empire of the first century or the superpower of any age, but life lived according to the Beatitudes is what will give light to the world. This is to be a communal endeavor, as obvious as a well-lighted city on a hilltop.

Just as salt is used to make food tasty, so a lamp was lit in the one-roomed house of most of Jesus's listeners in order to illuminate the whole living space. Disciples who are salt and light do not draw attention to themselves, but to God. They declare that, through their commitment to the way of life to which Jesus calls his disciples and his sustaining grace, the reign of God is coming into our world.

Preparing to Proclaim

Key words and phrases: "[Y]ou are the light of the world."

To the point: This week, our light imagery shifts a bit. We've been hearing for weeks about God being light for those who walk in darkness. Here, Jesus tells us that we, too, can become light for others. Our participation in God's will—in enacting justice and compassion—allows us to also participate in the beauty of God. We don't create anything new here; the light is not our own. Rather, we reflect God's light out to the world, amplifying it and making it more visible. We spread God's goodness to corners it may not have reached. We see this image clearly at baptism, when a light from the paschal candle is handed to the newly baptized. We are charged with carrying Christ's light into the world wherever we go, thus giving others reason to glorify God.

Psalmist Preparation

This psalm echoes the imagery of both gospel and first reading; people who act in justice and generosity are both recipients and conduits of God's very own light. The psalm adds an element of trust, as well; the just one described here is also characterized by steadfastness and trust in God. As you prepare this psalm, think about opportunities you might have to further enact God's justice and goodness in the world. Pray that all in the congregation will act on their own opportunities so that your community might become a beaming source of light for others.

Making Connections

Between the readings: The first reading shares the light imagery of the gospel, and gives us more explicit instructions for becoming light to the world. We are to provide food, shelter, and clothing for those in need. In readings of the previous weeks, this has been identified as God's work, as God's special area of interest. When we perform these deeds, we participate in God's preferential love for those who are poor. And we share in the beauty that God is continuously bestowing on the world in God's infinite generosity.

To experience: Performing works of mercy does not always look or feel good. This work is very often thankless, unglamorous, and inconvenient. The light we become is not the literal kind others can see; it takes practiced eyes of faith to see this sort of light. God reassures us, though, that these good deeds are beautiful in God's eyes and are worthy of our time.

Homily Points

• God created us in the image of Christ, the light of the world. We are made to shine brightly. Too often, forces of sin and evil try to act as bushel baskets. Racism, patriarchy, colonialism—these are just a few oppressive systems attempting to extinguish the flames of many. What are the bushel baskets in your life? These baskets can seem so sturdy. Thankfully, our light—the light of Christ—is even stronger. Try to cover it up and the basket itself will soon be engulfed in holy flames. Nothing will ever defeat the light of the world.

• The prophet Isaiah connects works of mercy—like feeding the hungry and clothing the naked—with the breaking forth of light. These acts of loving service for a neighbor are beacons of divine light in an often-dark world. Each time we give of our resources, our time, or our very selves, the light of the Lord breaks forth like the dawn. The Lord remains with us, fanning our flames and answering our calls with a resounding: "Here I am!"

• Jesus draws on the images of salt and light to call his disciples to lives of service. Neither element exists just for itself. Salt helps people taste. Light helps people see. How are you being of service to others this week? In what way could you help strengthen someone's sense of the divine?

Model Penitential Act

Presider: Jesus teaches his disciples to "shine before others" so that all may come to know the glory of God. For the times we have hidden our light, let us ask the Lord for strength and mercy . . . *[pause]*

Lord Jesus, you call us to be salt of the earth: Lord, have mercy.

Christ Jesus, you call us to be light for the world: Christ, have mercy.

Lord Jesus, you call us to glorify God: Lord, have mercy.

Model Universal Prayer (Prayer of the Faithful)

Presider: Guided by our mysterious and all-powerful God, let us give voice to our prayers and petitions.

Response: Lord, hear our prayer.

Fan the flames of our baptismal light within all members of the church . . .

Inspire leaders of nations to share bread with the hungry and clothe the naked . . .

Relieve the burdens of people who are oppressed or homeless . . .

Grant the courage to shine brightly to all gathered here . . .

Presider: God of justice, you created each one of us with the abilities to be salt for the earth and light for the world. With your calling comes great responsibility. Receive our prayers that we may continue to grow more into the people you call us to be. We ask this through Christ our Lord. **Amen.**

Liturgy and Music

Preparing for Lent: We are three and a half weeks away from Ash Wednesday and the season of Lent. By this time a seasonal schedule of songs should already be prepared and rehearsals for Lenten music should begin this coming week. Set aside enough time for cantors and choir members to learn and pray the new Lenten repertoire in their hearts. Embodied singing will always help the assembly pray better. Allow the assembly to familiarize themselves with the new songs over these next few weeks.

Find creative ways for introducing the new Lent music selections to the assembly—as choral prelude or during the preparation of the altar and gifts. If singing Lenten text in Ordinary Time is preventing you from introducing these songs ahead of time, try playing the piece instrumentally to give the assembly a sense of the melody line.

Be conservative with the number of songs you choose to introduce during this season. When a sense of familiarity accompanies the assembly's prayer in well-known songs, there will be less distraction from prayer. However, if you haven't updated the community's repertoire in a long while, do some research for there is an abundance of beautiful contemporary Lenten songs as well as fresh arrangements of traditional hymns available.

COLLECT

Let us pray.

Pause for silent prayer

Keep your family safe, O Lord, with
    unfailing care,
that, relying solely on the hope of
    heavenly grace,
they may be defended always by your
    protection.
Through our Lord Jesus Christ, your Son,
who lives and reigns with you in the unity
    of the Holy Spirit,
God, for ever and ever. **Amen.**

FIRST READING

Isa 58:7-10

Thus says the LORD:
    Share your bread with the hungry,
        shelter the oppressed and the homeless;
    clothe the naked when you see them,
        and do not turn your back on your
            own.
    Then your light shall break forth like
        the dawn,
        and your wound shall quickly be
            healed;
    your vindication shall go before you,
        and the glory of the LORD shall be
            your rear guard.
    Then you shall call, and the LORD will
        answer,
        you shall cry for help, and he will say:
            Here I am!
    If you remove from your midst
        oppression, false accusation and
            malicious speech;
    if you bestow your bread on the hungry
        and satisfy the afflicted;
    then light shall rise for you in the
        darkness,
        and the gloom shall become for you
            like midday.

RESPONSORIAL PSALM
Ps 112:4-5, 6-7, 8-9

R̶/. (4a) The just man is a light in darkness to the upright.
> or:

R̶/. Alleluia.

Light shines through the darkness for the
> upright;
> he is gracious and merciful and just.
Well for the man who is gracious and
> lends,
> who conducts his affairs with justice.

R̶/. The just man is a light in darkness to
the upright.
> or:

R̶/. Alleluia.

He shall never be moved;
> the just one shall be in everlasting
> remembrance.
An evil report he shall not fear;
> his heart is firm, trusting in the LORD.

R̶/. The just man is a light in darkness to
the upright.
> or:

R̶/. Alleluia.

His heart is steadfast; he shall not fear.
> Lavishly he gives to the poor;
his justice shall endure forever;
> his horn shall be exalted in glory.

R̶/. The just man is a light in darkness to
the upright.
> or:

R̶/. Alleluia.

SECOND READING
1 Cor 2:1-5

When I came to you, brothers and sisters,
> proclaiming the mystery of God,
> I did not come with sublimity of words
> > or of wisdom.
For I resolved to know nothing while I was
> with you
> except Jesus Christ, and him crucified.
I came to you in weakness and fear and
> much trembling,
> and my message and my proclamation
> were not with persuasive words of
> > wisdom,
> but with a demonstration of Spirit and
> > power,
> so that your faith might rest not on
> > human wisdom
> but on the power of God.

Living Liturgy

The Traveling Onion: The onion exists for other things or for other people, not for itself. To explain, I draw from Palestinian-American poet Naomi Shihab Nye's poem "The Traveling Onion" this beautiful metaphor of the onion to reflect on our continuing work in ministry. She introduces a brief history of the onion from *Better Living Cookbook* outlining the onion's journey from India to Egypt, Greece, Italy, the rest of Europe, and into her stew. She describes how much work goes into preparing the onion, yet when diners comment about the meal, the onion is rarely mentioned. The onion disappears "[f]or the sake of others."

Akin to salt and light, the onion is there to enhance what's already around it. You might say that salt, light, and the onion have properties that make change for the better when used in the right proportions. The pilgrim onion on the journey seeks to make things better.

When we seek to make things better in our liturgy, what steps do we take to allow the liturgy to be the focus? How much of ourselves do we pour in? What steps do we take to play more of a supporting role in preparing for liturgy and during the liturgy itself?

I think Nye's poem challenges leaders of worship to consider discipleship as a disappearing act. To be good followers of Christ involved in various ministries in the parish community, we must become more supportive of our parishioners and liturgical ministers without drawing unnecessary attention to ourselves in ways that distract from the ultimate goal—inclusive, communal prayer. When we take a step back into prayer, the Word and the Eucharist then become focal points of our Sunday worship. Practicing this disappearing act takes a selfless heart. It's not about being recognized for all the work that you do in ministry, it's about how much the work has brought people to recognize God.

PROMPTS FOR FAITH-SHARING

• Reflect on a time when you were in need and someone responded to that need with generosity. How were they God's light for you?

• Can you think of a time when you had the opportunity to be God's light for someone else? How did you respond to the invitation?

• How can you stay committed to works of mercy and justice when our earthly eyes do not always see the rewarding beauty that God promises in these readings?

✦ SPIRITUALITY

GOSPEL ACCLAMATION
cf. Matt 11:25

℟. Alleluia, alleluia.
Blessed are you, Father, Lord of heaven and
    earth;
you have revealed to little ones the mysteries
    of the kingdom.
℟. Alleluia, alleluia.

Gospel   Matt 5:17-37; L76A

Jesus said to his disciples:
    "Do not think that I have come to abol-
        ish the law or the prophets.
I have come not to abolish but to fulfill.
Amen, I say to you, until heaven and earth
        pass away,
    not the smallest letter or the smallest
        part of a letter
    will pass from the law,
    until all things have taken place.
Therefore, whoever breaks one of the
        least of these commandments
    and teaches others to do so
    will be called least in the kingdom of
        heaven.
But whoever obeys and teaches these
        commandments
    will be called greatest in the kingdom
        of heaven.
I tell you, unless your righteousness
        surpasses
    that of the scribes and Pharisees,
    you will not enter the kingdom of heaven.

"You have heard that it was said to your
        ancestors,
    You shall not kill; and whoever kills will
        be liable to judgment.
But I say to you,
    whoever is angry with his brother
    will be liable to judgment;
    and whoever says to his brother, 'Raqa,'
    will be answerable to the Sanhedrin;
    and whoever says, 'You fool,'
    will be liable to fiery Gehenna.

Continued in Appendix A, p. 267, or
Matt 5:20-22a, 27-28, 33-34a, 37 in Appendix A,
p. 267.

Reflecting on the Gospel

The church has always insisted upon the inseparability of the Old Testament and New Testament. Today's gospel offers us an example of "rereading" the Old Testament, the Scriptures that nourished the faith and discernment of Jesus.

As he says, Jesus does not come to abolish the Law or the Prophets but to carry forward to its fulfillment the movement of transcending, interiorizing, stripping away empty externals and legalistic minutiae that had distorted God's revelation. Some of the scribes and Pharisees, the Scripture scholars and lay leaders of their day, bore responsibility for this when they were so arrogantly sure of their interpretation that they could see no farther than their own narrow point of view. The Pharisees had a fierce dedication to carrying out God's will, but this could lead them to place unattainable burdens on others and themselves, with the consequence that their own failures might result in hypocritical and vehement cover-ups. We also need to remember that the gospel writers were well aware that neither of these groups is historically self-contained. In every Christian community, there are also "scribes and Pharisees": learned but self-serving people, and hypocrites whose external religious masks can hide an irreligious heart.

So Jesus focuses not so much on the evils of murder, adultery, or lying, but on the way these take root in the human heart. In other words, he proposes a radical reinterpretation of the teaching. We can look askance at the end point of the continuum of evil and yet not recognize the subtle and dangerous first point when we begin to orient our lives in that direction. Anger, hostility, and insults do not belong in the Christian community, for these are the seedbed of the sin of murder that destroys God's sacred gift of life to another human being.

Sexuality also is a gift from God and not to be abused. Jesus names male lusting for and oppressive attitudes toward women as adultery in the heart (see Job 31:1). Sexual drives cannot dominate a person's life but need to be integrated into a life which is lived according to gospel values. To show the seriousness of this, Jesus uses the literary device (not literal advice!) of exaggeration, the plucking out of an eye or the cutting off of a hand, which is to be preferred to the mutilating effect of unbridled sexual abuse. Jesus is critical of the easy divorce, based on self-interest, that men could often obtain from their wives. Biblical scholars debate what the sexual irregularity (what Matthew calls *porneia*) was that made divorce permissible. The contemporary status of divorced people in today's church and the most pastoral way of ministering to them is still one of our most pressing questions and quests.

Jesus shares the Hebrew horror at the abuse of calling on God to bolster the claims of a false oath (see Lev 19:12). There should be such integrity and truthfulness in the Christian community that there is no need to bring God into the situation as an additional and "reliable" witness to the too-much protesting. A straightforward "yes" or "no," with no oath-taking at all, should be sufficient.

Preparing to Proclaim

Key words and phrases: "Let your 'Yes' mean 'Yes,' and your 'No' mean 'No.'"

To the point: This gospel can feel damning and demanding. Jesus affirms that the commands of Mosaic Law still stand, and also reveals that by-the-book obedience to them is not enough. Righteousness is not just a checklist we can tick off; it is, unfortunately, not a measurable accomplishment. The orientation of our hearts matters more than the externals of our actions. This is challenging. But really, Jesus is issuing a loving invitation. He is calling us to health and wholeness as we live out God's Law. Changing our hearts is hard to measure, but it helps us more than it helps anyone else. Leaving behind sinful actions is one thing, but when we are able to move past the anger and lust that motivate such actions we are able to live in fuller freedom and joy.

Psalmist Preparation

The psalm states briefly and explicitly what the other readings get at more obliquely: "Open my eyes, that I may consider / the wonders of your law." God's commands sometimes feel like a drudgery because of the consequences of sin, but they are in fact a gift, a gracious revelation that enables us to live whole-heartedly aligned with Christ. As you prepare and proclaim this psalm, consider which moral teachings of the church you struggle with or have struggled with. If we trust that God always wills our good, how might God help you understand these teachings not as an obligation to drudgery but as an invitation to freedom?

Making Connections

Between the readings: The first reading affirms that God's commands are trustworthy and true; obeying them is a source of life and goodness. The Law is not an obligation to be lived in begrudging obedience; it is a gift from God, an assurance that goodness and righteousness are within our reach. The second reading acknowledges that God's wisdom is distinct from human wisdom; it often seems to us to be mysterious and hidden. Even so, it is worthy of trust.

To experience: Many of us at some time or another struggle with the moral teachings of the church, especially when leaders teach them without integrity. It is demoralizing to receive challenging teachings from people who themselves are not able to live by them. But what Jesus really wants for us is healing and freedom from the things that hold us back from the fullness of life with him. As you read this gospel, can you hear Jesus reissuing these teachings not as a way to control but as a loving invitation?

Homily Points

• Jesus holds his disciples to a high standard. What does God desire for creation and how are we to live out the divine will? Today's gospel could read as another list of religious dos and don'ts. The law Jesus came to fulfil manifests in a myriad of ways. Whatever your relationship to the issues named—anger, adultery, divorce, and staying faithful to vows—Jesus offers these teachings as a means of drawing us closer to God.

• These teachings reveal something about the divine will—and thus, God's very self. Our God is a God of truth and justice, who values reconciliation and desires right relationship for all of creation. In light of today's gospel, consider: Is there a relationship in your life that needs mending? How might you take a step toward reconciliation this week?

• Today's gospel may be difficult to digest for those of us who have personal experience with the issues named by Jesus. Perhaps there is anger festering right now between you and a loved one. Maybe you have been the victim or perpetrator of adultery. Who among us has never looked upon another with lust? Who among us does not care about someone who is divorced? Let us be gentle with ourselves and with each other as we take in Jesus's message. In coming to fulfil the law, Jesus did not come to shame or berate. He came to help us grow more faithful each day—and to help us strengthen our muscles of repentance and reconciliation.

Model Penitential Act

Presider: In today's first reading, the prophet Sirach reminds us of the "[i]mmense . . . wisdom of the Lord," who is "mighty in power, and all-seeing." For the times we have not trusted in God, let us ask for pardon and forgiveness . . . *[pause]*

Lord Jesus, you give life to those who trust in you: Lord, have mercy.

Christ Jesus, you call us to reconcile with our brothers and sisters: Christ, have mercy.

Lord Jesus, you came to fulfil the law for the good of your people: Lord, have mercy.

Model Universal Prayer (Prayer of the Faithful)

Presider: In today's second reading, St. Paul speaks of the "mysterious" and "hidden" wisdom of God. With hearts full of awe, let us bring our needs before the Lord.

Response: Lord, hear our prayer.

Bring a swift end to the clerical abuse and cover-up crisis plaguing the church . . .

Foster a spirit of reconciliation between nations at war . . .

Draw out hope for new life in those people experiencing divorce and their families . . .

Inspire all of us gathered here to work toward healing of hurting relationships . . .

Presider: God whose love stretches beyond all telling, you sent your son to show us the way to eternal life. Hear our prayers that we might follow his way in both word and deed. We ask this through Christ our Lord. **Amen.**

Liturgy and Music

Ministerial Presence: We belong to each other. This is a fundamental truth of collaborative music ministry. This Sunday, the law is one of love and of life with each other. Set some time during rehearsal this week to speak of ministerial presence. In other words, think about what it means to be present in ministry to others not only in our own parish community but to the greater community of the diocese or archdiocese. Are we aware of the number of parishes in your own deanery? Do you know the pastors and music directors of neighboring parishes? How can we be more present to each other?

Set up an expectation that each choir member's ministerial presence is vital to the prayer and spiritual life of the choir and parish community. We thrive on singing and praying with each other. Our presence and absence matters. When relational ministry becomes a part of our own ministry, we begin to think beyond the confines of our own space and to lean toward helping the other, being part of the greater community of believers. A ministerial presence comes with deeper spiritual reflection. This Sunday, take time to discuss how the law leads us to love one another and how the law breathes new life into our work in ministry.

COLLECT

Let us pray.

Pause for silent prayer

O God, who teach us that you abide
in hearts that are just and true,
grant that we may be so fashioned by
        your grace
as to become a dwelling pleasing to you.
Through our Lord Jesus Christ, your Son,
who lives and reigns with you in the unity
        of the Holy Spirit,
God, for ever and ever. **Amen.**

FIRST READING

Sir 15:15-20

If you choose you can keep the
        commandments, they will save you;
    if you trust in God, you too shall live;
he has set before you fire and water;
    to whichever you choose, stretch forth
        your hand.
Before man are life and death, good and
        evil,
    whichever he chooses shall be given
        him.
Immense is the wisdom of the Lord;
    he is mighty in power, and all-seeing.
The eyes of God are on those who fear
        him;
    he understands man's every deed.
No one does he command to act unjustly,
    to none does he give license to sin.

RESPONSORIAL PSALM

Ps 119:1-2, 4-5, 17-18, 33-34

R̸. (1b) Blessed are they who follow the
law of the Lord!

Blessed are they whose way is blameless,
    who walk in the law of the Lord.
Blessed are they who observe his decrees,
    who seek him with all their heart.

R̸. Blessed are they who follow the law of
the Lord!

You have commanded that your precepts
    be diligently kept.
Oh, that I might be firm in the ways
    of keeping your statutes!

R̸. Blessed are they who follow the law of
the Lord!

Be good to your servant, that I may live
    and keep your words.
Open my eyes, that I may consider
    the wonders of your law.

R̸. Blessed are they who follow the law of
the Lord!

Instruct me, O Lᴏʀᴅ, in the way of your statutes,
    that I may exactly observe them.
Give me discernment, that I may observe your law
    and keep it with all my heart.

R℣. Blessed are they who follow the law of the Lord!

SECOND READING
1 Cor 2:6-10

Brothers and sisters:
We speak a wisdom to those who are mature,
    not a wisdom of this age,
    nor of the rulers of this age who are passing away.
Rather, we speak God's wisdom,
    mysterious, hidden,
    which God predetermined before the ages for our glory,
    and which none of the rulers of this age knew;
    for, if they had known it,
    they would not have crucified the Lord of glory.
But as it is written:
    What eye has not seen, and ear has not heard,
        and what has not entered the human heart,
        what God has prepared for those who love him,
        this God has revealed to us through the Spirit.

For the Spirit scrutinizes everything, even the depths of God.

Living Liturgy

Love and Life: Jesus challenges us in the gospel reading today to go beyond the minimum requirements of the law to respond to others in love. In another way, Sr. Irene Nowell states in her book *Sing a New Song*: "We sometimes see the law as the limitation of our freedom or the inhibition of our desires. But the reason for our freedom, the goal of our desires, is life."

These two perspectives of the Law give us a wider compass for understanding why and how we do liturgy. On one hand we hear that the law promotes love, and on the other we learn that the law fosters life. How might we use these two markers of love and life when we consider adhering to liturgical rubrics? Those who approach liturgical preparations with an air of certitude ultimately deny room for God's work.

Be open to God's work when considering pastoral choices outside of the liturgical norms that might sometimes be made to minister to the needs of the assembly, or perhaps because the immediate situation at hand necessitates an alternate pastoral option. Liturgy is living and dynamic. It is a moving relationship between God and God's people. The embodiment of each liturgy only happens when rubrics and texts are joined together to tradition and need. God's spirit breathes life and love onto those who are faithful to the spirit of the law that engages us to look beyond the mere act of following rules. We pray with the psalmist: "Open my eyes, that I may consider / the wonders of your law."

PROMPTS FOR FAITH-SHARING

• Which of Jesus's commands in this gospel is most challenging to you here and now?

• How could letting go of internal sins such as anger and lust enable you to live more wholeheartedly as a disciple of Jesus?

• What moral teachings of the church do you struggle with? Is there anything that could help you see them as a loving invitation to a life of wholeness?

✝ SPIRITUALITY

GOSPEL ACCLAMATION
1 John 2:5

℟. Alleluia, alleluia.
Whoever keeps the word of Christ,
the love of God is truly perfected in him.
℟. Alleluia, alleluia.

Gospel   Matt 5:38-48; L79A

Jesus said to his disciples:
   "You have heard that it was said,
   An eye for an eye and a tooth for a
      tooth.
But I say to you, offer no resistance to
      one who is evil.
When someone strikes you on your
      right cheek,
   turn the other one as well.
If anyone wants to go to law with you
      over your tunic,
   hand over your cloak as well.
Should anyone press you into service
      for one mile,
   go for two miles.
Give to the one who asks of you,
   and do not turn your back on one
      who wants to borrow.

   "You have heard that it was said,
   You shall love your neighbor and
      hate your enemy.
But I say to you, love your enemies
   and pray for those who persecute
      you,
   that you may be children of your
      heavenly Father,
   for he makes his sun rise on the bad
      and the good,
   and causes rain to fall on the just and
      the unjust.
For if you love those who love you,
   what recompense will you have?
Do not the tax collectors do the same?
And if you greet your brothers only,
   what is unusual about that?
Do not the pagans do the same?
So be perfect, just as your heavenly
      Father is perfect."

Reflecting on the Gospel

We live in a world where retaliation seems almost an automatic response—from the playground to the floors of government. When speaking about the Old Testament response of "an eye for an eye and a tooth for a tooth" (Exod 21:24; Deut 19:21; Lev 24:20), Jesus is not trying to distinguish between Old Testament harshness and the New Testament love ethic—a false dichotomy. The

lex talionis, or "law of retaliation," was formulated in both the pagan and Jewish world as a principle of proportionate retribution, and therefore a moral advance over unbridled and excessive revenge or "payback" in tribal societies. What Jesus proclaims is again a radical reinterpretation of the Law, and with the dramatic skill of a great teacher he presents his audience with some "case studies" to make his point.

If someone strikes a disciple's cheek, instead of retaliating, the disciple should offer the other cheek as well. If a debtor is taken to court and ordered to surrender his tunic as collateral for the loan, the disciple should also give his cloak. Palestinian eyebrows would be raised at the memorable mental picture of the debtor disciple standing publicly naked in the court, bereft of both his under and outer garments, the latter often used also as a blanket at night! The third example is that of a disciple's response to what could be legally demanded by a Roman soldier: that a Palestinian carry the soldier's heavy pack for a mile (1,000 paces). As one trudged past the milestone, not to dump the pack but to offer to go another mile with the occupying enemy would seem absolute foolishness. Likewise, to give to anyone who wants to borrow seems extreme.

But God is so generous, and a disciple should be so secure in this love that there is no need to insist on one's rights. Writing his gospel through the prism of the death and resurrection of Jesus, Matthew sees the light of Jesus's response to love broken into the colors of the generous, practical, and radical. For the sake of others, even enemies, Jesus went the "extra mile" to his death, did not retaliate against the blows during his passion, and was stripped naked, not only of clothes but of life itself.

But how to understand the words "[B]e perfect, just as your heavenly Father is perfect" in a way that does not seem impossibly unattainable? The meaning of *perfect* here, based on the words in Hebrew and Greek, is "wholeness," or "maturity." God will still be God and we will still be human, but a disciple is called to act wholeheartedly, maturely, focused on God's universal, generous, and impartial love for all that God has created. This response is much the same as the earlier mention of "clean of heart" in the Beatitudes (Matt 5:8). Our love is to be a countercultural, kingdom response to the love of God. Perhaps at times we can only struggle and thank God for what he loves in those we find it hard to love—as we go on struggling to do just that.

Preparing to Proclaim

Key words and phrases: "[L]ove your enemies."

To the point: Like last week, Jesus explains to his disciples that being his followers will ask more of them than a literal reading of the law they have always been taught. They are called not to an approach of compliance with minimum requirements, but to a life of radical generosity that imitates the love of God, whose love spills forth and gives us life. They are called to offer forgiveness and love that is not deserved by the recipients. "Be perfect" is an intimidating instruction, but it may help to think of "perfect" in the sense of whole or complete. The life to which Jesus calls us is one of integrity, one where our hearts and minds and actions are all in alignment with each other. Living as Jesus asks is healing. It brings us to wholeness. It enables us to follow him with our whole hearts.

Psalmist Preparation

This psalm offers an important counterbalance to the demands of the gospel. We will often fail in our mission to imitate God's perfection and holiness, but God is infinitely patient with our slow progress, faithfully awaiting us with boundless mercy. As you prepare this psalm, think of a time you have made a misstep in your own journey of holiness. If you have brought this misstep to the sacrament of confession, thank God for the mercy you encountered there. If you have not, make a plan to respond to God's endless invitation to experience that mercy. Either way, say a prayer of thanks to God for the mercy he promises, and bring your gratitude to your proclamation of this psalm.

Making Connections

Between the readings: Jesus's gospel teachings are not the first time God has given commandments to love profoundly: "[L]ove your neighbor as yourself" is already pretty radical. As in the gospel, this love is commanded in imitation of God; we are to strive for the holiness and perfection that characterizes God's very self. The second reading also reminds us of our dignity and our call to holiness; here, the image of the temple is used to illustrate how God dwells within us. The psalm offers an important counterbalance to the commands of the other readings: even when we fail in our quest for holiness, God is ready to greet us with mercy.

To experience: This gospel can be very much misused in cases of abuse; victims are not morally required to continuously turn the other cheek to one who has hurt them. An important mark of maturity in Christian life is the ability to discern between suffering we are called to accept and suffering we are called to resist. Remember that God wants justice for the oppressed and is always on the side of those who are downtrodden.

Homily Points

• Jesus demands a radical kind of love in today's gospel. It is not enough to love those who love you, the Son of God says. We must also love the enemy, the stranger, the one who gnaws at our last nerve. How? Jesus asks us to do what seems impossible—and the call may very well be impossible if we try to take it up alone. Jesus knows the shortcomings of the human condition. He knows we get annoyed, jealous, judgmental, and prone to a whole host of other emotions that make it hard to love others. That is why Jesus makes this summons in the context of community. The work of loving as God loves is the work of all of us, together.

• Guided by Christ's example and ongoing presence in our lives, we can take up a seemingly impossible task. For we are temples of God, as St. Paul reminds us. The Spirit of God dwells in us. Even with our human frailties, we can love bigger and bolder than we ever thought possible. We will soon enter the season of Lent, a time for doing the hard work of discipleship. The way of the cross is demanding, no doubt, yet Jesus promises we will make it through.

• Keep today's gospel in mind as you prepare for Lent. Who are the people you find difficult to love? With Christ's help, how can you open your heart more fully to these people in the days ahead?

Model Penitential Act

Presider: Jesus puts forth difficult commands in today's gospel. To give so generously of one's love and very being is the ongoing work of discipleship. For the many times we have fallen short in loving others, let us ask for God's mercy . . . *[pause]*

    Lord Jesus, you guide us to grow in holiness: Lord, have mercy.
    Christ Jesus, you call us into divine love: Christ, have mercy.
    Lord Jesus, you show us the way to eternal life: Lord, have mercy.

Model Universal Prayer (Prayer of the Faithful)

Presider: Today's psalm reminds us that our Lord is kind and merciful. With trust, let us place before God our prayers and petitions.

Response: Lord, hear our prayer.

Let your love be known to catechumens preparing for initiation into the church . . .

Let your love be known to medical workers, chaplains, and all who provide end-of-life care . . .

Let your love be known to those who struggle with eating disorders and other body image issues . . .

Let your love be known to the young people of our community . . .

Presider: Loving God, you call us to love as you love—fully and without distinction. Hear our prayers that by following your example we might help to let your love be known throughout the world. We ask this through Christ our Lord. **Amen.**

Liturgy and Music

Entering Lent: As we head into the season of Lent this coming Ash Wednesday, let us be mindful of the upcoming season's songs. We fast from the singing of the Alleluia as we await the resurrection day. In its place we sing instead a Lenten gospel acclamation, just as the singing of the Glory to God is paused. Our music making becomes less festive and robust in tone and texture. Simpler arrangements and orchestrations are recommended during this time and perhaps a more solemn Mass setting or a simpler arrangement of an existing one. Think of incorporating plainchant or singing some pieces unaccompanied.

    Take advantage of the season's simpler music to schedule a lighter selection for Sunday music and instead look ahead to the ritual music of the Sacred Triduum and the festivities of Easter Sunday. Contract extra musicians who will play at the Triduum and Easter liturgies now, if you have not already done so. Fill rehearsals each week with a sensible amount of Triduum or Easter music without over-rehearsing. Take your time to explain the significance of each piece in relation to the ritual action. You may have to balance your rehearsal time accordingly between Sunday and Triduum music to efficiently rehearse everything. Peace to you as you enter this holy season.

COLLECT

Let us pray.

Pause for silent prayer

Grant, we pray, almighty God,
that, always pondering spiritual things,
we may carry out in both word and deed
that which is pleasing to you.
Through our Lord Jesus Christ, your Son,
who lives and reigns with you in the unity
    of the Holy Spirit,
God, for ever and ever. **Amen.**

FIRST READING

Lev 19:1-2, 17-18

The LORD said to Moses,
    "Speak to the whole Israelite
        community and tell them:
    Be holy, for I, the LORD, your God, am
        holy.

"You shall not bear hatred for your brother
    or sister in your heart.
Though you may have to reprove your
    fellow citizen,
    do not incur sin because of him.
Take no revenge and cherish no grudge
    against any of your people.
You shall love your neighbor as yourself.
I am the LORD."

RESPONSORIAL PSALM

Ps 103:1-2, 3-4, 8, 10, 12-13

℟. (8a) The Lord is kind and merciful.

Bless the LORD, O my soul;
    and all my being, bless his holy name.
Bless the LORD, O my soul,
    and forget not all his benefits.

℟. The Lord is kind and merciful.

He pardons all your iniquities,
    heals all your ills.
He redeems your life from destruction,
    crowns you with kindness and
        compassion.

℟. The Lord is kind and merciful.

Merciful and gracious is the LORD,
    slow to anger and abounding in
        kindness.
Not according to our sins does he deal
    with us,
    nor does he requite us according to our
        crimes.

℟. The Lord is kind and merciful.

As far as the east is from the west,
   so far has he put our transgressions
      from us.
As a father has compassion on his
   children,
   so the LORD has compassion on those
      who fear him.

R⁊. The Lord is kind and merciful.

SECOND READING
1 Cor 3:16-23

Brothers and sisters:
Do you not know that you are the temple
   of God,
   and that the Spirit of God dwells in
      you?
If anyone destroys God's temple, God will
      destroy that person;
   for the temple of God, which you are,
      is holy.

Let no one deceive himself.
If any one among you considers himself
      wise in this age,
   let him become a fool, so as to become
      wise.
For the wisdom of this world is
      foolishness in the eyes of God,
   for it is written:
      God catches the wise in their own
         ruses,
and again:
      The Lord knows the thoughts of the
         wise,
         that they are vain.
So let no one boast about human beings,
   for everything belongs to you,
   Paul or Apollos or Cephas,
   or the world or life or death,
   or the present or the future:
   all belong to you, and you to Christ, and
      Christ to God.

Living Liturgy

Embrace the Enemy: Jesus asks his followers to take a different approach by re-sisting retaliation altogether. We are asked to go beyond the ways of our world to serve God's kingdom on earth. In addition to this, the other difficult demand of true disciple-ship lies in embracing the enemy. The psalmist cries out: "Merciful and gracious is the LORD." And so we are summoned to love as God loves. And God's love is unconditional.

In Los Angeles, there is a program that provides a blueprint for living out this mes-sage of God's love. Homeboy Industries, founded by Jesuit priest Fr. Greg Boyle, is the largest gang intervention, rehabilitation, and re-entry program in the world. Homeboy Industries provides hope, training, and support to formerly gang-involved and previ-ously incarcerated people, allowing them to redirect their lives and become contribut-ing members of the City of Los Angeles community. By creating an ever widening "circle of compassion," the program practices radical kinship in creating a space of second, third and fourth chances and in the unconditional embrace of the broken.

A "culture of relational tenderness" embraces Homeboy's ethos where healing hap-pens. Program members are given a safe haven to discover and inhabit their authentic selves and become whole as they begin to believe in themselves again—"So be perfect, just as your heavenly Father is perfect." Discerning this last phrase of Sunday's gospel passage through the lens of Homeboy Industries teaches us that this perfection that we strive for is not to be perfect in the sense of doing everything correctly or following strict moral laws. Instead, the goal of being perfect is in aiming for completeness, for wholeness in God. Through striving for this completeness, we share radical kinship with each other and we are able to glimpse the kingdom of heaven.

PROMPTS FOR FAITH-SHARING

• Where in your life could you extend forgiveness? Knowing that forgiveness doesn't al-ways mean offering a blank slate to one with a pattern of hurting you, what would forgive-ness look like in your situation?

• The first reading instructs us to love others as ourselves, but sometimes we struggle to love ourselves! In prayer, ask God to reveal to you how you appear through God's eyes, and reflect on the experience here.

• How have you experienced God's mercy? Where do you still need it?

SEASON
OF LENT

GOSPEL ACCLAMATION
See Ps 95:8

If today you hear his voice,
harden not your hearts.

Gospel   Matt 6:1-6, 16-18; L219

Jesus said to his disciples:
  "Take care not to perform righteous
      deeds
  in order that people may see them;
  otherwise, you will have no recompense
      from your heavenly Father.
When you give alms,
  do not blow a trumpet before you,
  as the hypocrites do in the synagogues
      and in the streets
  to win the praise of others.
Amen, I say to you,
  they have received their reward.
But when you give alms,
  do not let your left hand know what
      your right is doing,
  so that your almsgiving may be secret.
And your Father who sees in secret will
      repay you.

"When you pray,
  do not be like the hypocrites,
  who love to stand and pray in the
      synagogues and on street corners
  so that others may see them.
Amen, I say to you,
  they have received their reward.
But when you pray, go to your inner room,
  close the door, and pray to your Father in
      secret.
And your Father who sees in secret will
      repay you.

"When you fast,
  do not look gloomy like the hypocrites.
They neglect their appearance,
  so that they may appear to others to be
      fasting.
Amen, I say to you, they have received their
      reward.
But when you fast,
  anoint your head and wash your face,
  so that you may not appear to be fasting,
  except to your Father who is hidden.
And your Father who sees what is hidden
      will repay you."

See Appendix A, p. 268, for the other readings.

Reflecting on the Gospel

Anyone who has had the experience of purchasing a new home understands the importance of looking beyond what can be seen. One must assess the foundation, investigate the structure, go down into the basement and check for level ground. The difference between a shelter and a mere structure is that while both may appear to be standing, a shelter has the integrity and reinforcements to protect us from the fiercest elements and guard the things that matter most to us.

What awaits us at the end of the Lenten season is the story of Christ's passion and death—a series of harrowing and horrific events that tested the faith of all who witnessed it. Even now, knowing the full story, it is not for the faint of heart. What glory could come from the gore of scourgings and beatings, from the tears and public trauma, from the intense, agonizing pain that ends in a humiliating death? Sometimes it is hard to remember and embrace the idea that the work of entering into glory requires us to go beyond the feel-good truisms and sink down into the dark and less visible places.

In today's gospel, Jesus instructs his listeners on how not to pray, how not to present themselves to God. In contrast to public deeds and words that may serve to glorify the doer and speaker, Jesus tells listeners to "go to your inner room, close the door, and pray to your Father in secret." This method of prayer is not simply satisfying to God because it is more private and less boastful. This method of prayer enables us to journey to the center of our spirits, the temple in which God dwells in us, and assess whether the structure is sturdy enough to endure the storms of our broken world. It creates a strong and secure channel by which we can more clearly hear the voice of God. It allows us to realize the truth about ourselves and how we are called to move throughout our lives.

When we go into our inner rooms and pray to God in secret, the needs and hopes of our hearts may not yet be clear to us. Going down into the inner room, away from the eyes of potential critics or commenders, creates the conditions for us to come before God without ego and without agenda. When we surrender our pride, our plans, and our desire for praise, we can more easily receive that which God intends for us.

The cross made of ashes that we receive on this day serves as a reminder that the path to renewal is gritty and unglamorous. The practices of fasting and almsgiving are reminders that paring down and abstaining from certain luxuries can clear the path by which we will return to God. The way in which we pray can prepare us to return to God with hearts ready to receive the strength and hope that will sustain us through trials and tests of faith. May we learn to reinforce our spiritual shelters by following Christ's advice. Let us go into our inner rooms in humility and with the trust that God will give us what we need to lay a sturdy foundation.

Preparing to Proclaim

Key words and phrases: "[Y]our Father who sees what is hidden will repay you."

To the point: These readings taken together remind us that Lent has both individual and communal dimensions. The gospel reminds us that we do not engage in the Lenten practices of prayer, fasting, and almsgiving in order to be perceived by others as holy. There is a privacy to these practices; we are engaging in individual repentance for our personal sins. But just as the Israelites do in the first reading, we also gather with our community to experience God's bountiful mercy together.

Model Penitential Act

Presider: As we begin this Lenten season, Jesus invites us into a space of repentance so that we might grow ever closer to our Creator. Let us pause for a moment and embrace the mercy God longs to offer us . . . *[pause]*

  Confiteor: I confess . . .

Model Universal Prayer (Prayer of the Faithful)

Presider: In today's first reading, the Lord calls to us: "[R]eturn to me with your whole heart." Let us voice aloud the petitions resting on our hearts.

Response: Lord, hear our prayer.

Strengthen the spiritual practices of prayer, fasting, and almsgiving within all members of the Body of Christ . . .

Animate a spirit of humility among world leaders of wealthy nations whose power impacts the lives of many . . .

Bring relief to all victims of violence and persecution who are burdened under the weight of the crosses they carry . . .

Form all of us gathered here into ambassadors for Christ, particularly as we honor the death and resurrection of Jesus . . .

Presider: God of all blessings, you gifted creation with your only Son who gave his own life so that we might dwell with you forever. Draw us closer to Christ and the whole Christian community during these solemn Lenten days. We ask this through Christ our Lord. **Amen.**

Living Liturgy

Sacred Space: Now is the acceptable time to be reconciled to God. It is also the time to take the psalmist's prayer of prophetic hope into the center of our beings, into our hearts and into our homes—that God's abundant compassion will blot out our offences. Learning from my grandmother, I have created a simple prayer space at my home. In this space I place a cross I acquired on a pilgrimage, a candle given to me by a close friend, and a prayer book that my beloved mother prayed with. During these days of reflection, find sacred space for fasting, prayer, and almsgiving.

FOR REFLECTION

• Which of the three Lenten practices (prayer, fasting, and almsgiving) comes most easily to you? Which is hardest?

• Do you perceive Lent as a sad, somber time of obligatory repentance or a joyful time of loving invitation from God?

• In this Lenten season, how might God be inviting you to grow closer to who God calls you to be?

Homily Points

• Fast from understanding. Feast on mystery. A spiritual director offered this Ash Wednesday advice years ago and it stuck. What a gift it is to get lost in the messiness of mystery, to revel in the ways God reveals God's love to us in new and unexpected ways during the Lenten season.

• Then, on Ash Wednesday 2018, a gunman killed seventeen people at Marjorie Stoneman Douglas High School in a horrific school shooting. The messy mystery of Ash Wednesday took on new meaning as the world grieved young people who were returned to dust too soon.

• In this season of journeying with Jesus toward the cross, let us hold close the countless people dying on their own crosses every day because of violence plaguing our world.

✠ SPIRITUALITY

GOSPEL ACCLAMATION
Matt 4:4b

One does not live on bread alone,
but on every word that comes forth
from the mouth of God.

Gospel

Matt 4:1-11; L22A

At that time Jesus was led by
the Spirit into the desert
to be tempted by the devil.
He fasted for forty days and
forty nights,
and afterwards he was
hungry.
The tempter approached and
said to him,
"If you are the Son of God,
command that these stones
become loaves of bread."
He said in reply,
"It is written:
One does not live on bread alone,
but on every word that comes
forth
from the mouth of God."

Then the devil took him to the holy city,
and made him stand on the parapet
of the temple,
and said to him, "If you are the Son
of God, throw yourself down.
For it is written:
He will command his angels
concerning you
and with their hands they will
support you,
lest you dash your foot against a
stone."
Jesus answered him,
"Again it is written,
You shall not put the Lord, your
God, to the test."

Continued in Appendix A, p. 269.

Reflecting on the Gospel

In today's gospel, Jesus is led by the Spirit, immediately after his baptism, into the wilderness. At his baptism, he was named as God's Son, the Beloved, and in the wilderness, he will be tested in his fidelity to this identity and obedience to 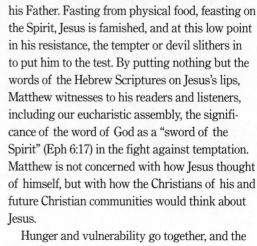 his Father. Fasting from physical food, feasting on the Spirit, Jesus is famished, and at this low point in his resistance, the tempter or devil slithers in to put him to the test. By putting nothing but the words of the Hebrew Scriptures on Jesus's lips, Matthew witnesses to his readers and listeners, including our eucharistic assembly, the significance of the word of God as a "sword of the Spirit" (Eph 6:17) in the fight against temptation. Matthew is not concerned with how Jesus thought of himself, but with how the Christians of his and future Christian communities would think about Jesus.

Hunger and vulnerability go together, and the first temptation is for Jesus to work a miracle and command the stones to become bread. The Hebrews in the desert grumbled and tried to manipulate God's will, demanding food from heaven and then becoming dissatisfied with the manna, so Jesus's response to this first temptation is the reminder that "one does not live on bread alone, but on every word that comes forth from the mouth of God" (quoting Deut 8:3). Is this word our sustaining nourishment, or are we more addicted to overeating, to junk food, to keeping a full kitchen pantry while millions of our sisters and brothers go hungry?

The devil then takes Jesus up to a high part of the Jerusalem temple and tempts him to another miracle. Let Jesus toss himself off this pinnacle and force God's hand so that angels will catch him. But Jesus has other "wings" that will save him—his trust in God's loving protection (Ps 91:4)—and again he refuses to put God to the test (see Deut 6:16). We may wish for, pray for the miraculous intervention of God in our lives, but often this has much to do with our self-centeredness and little to do with faith in God's care for us.

Finally, the devil takes Jesus up a high mountain and there presents himself as the one with dominion over the powers of the world. But Jesus will have nothing to do with the seductions of political power and wealth. He will be the powerless servant, but the one who has the authority to command, "Get away, Satan!" because homage is due to God alone (Deut 6:13). At the end of Matthew's gospel, after Jesus has passed through the wilderness of suffering and death and has been exalted in his resurrection, he will stand on another mountain with his disciples, and there they will worship him with a very human mixture of faith and doubt. Jesus, the Son of God, then gives them a share in his authority so that they may go to make disciples of all nations, baptizing them, and teaching them to obey all that Jesus has taught them (Matt 28:16-20).

Preparing to Proclaim

Key words and phrases: "Get away, Satan!"

To the point: Jesus demonstrates his sinlessness in this gospel as he responds to the devil's temptations with strength and confidence, rebuffing his advances without missing a beat. These temptations are perhaps relatable; all of them encourage Jesus to put something—food, safety, power—ahead of his relationship with God. The middle temptation is particularly chilling, as we hear the devil himself quote Scripture to support a twisted agenda that is not of God. This one can be confusing; it seems that the devil is asking Jesus to trust in God, which is surely a good thing. But trusting God does not mean treating God like a vending machine that will dispense favors at our command; in fact, telling God what he ought to do for us stands in direct opposition to true trust in his providence. Fortunately, Jesus knows better than the devil's most clever tricks; his relationship with God is built on a loving trust that will carry him all the way to the cross.

Psalmist Preparation

Our sin is a sure thing; thankfully, so is God's mercy. The joy of Lent is often hidden beneath its solemn tone of repentance, but this psalm reveals its secret. We have sinned, yes, and this is cause for sorrow; but the psalm ends with us returning to praise. Lenten work is not about taking on sacrifice for its own sake, but about enabling God to continue the work of creation and renewal that God loves to do. We ask God to return us to "the joy of salvation," and we can rest assured that God wants to do so. Can you infuse your Lenten practices with joy? Does this change your attitude toward the season?

Making Connections

Between the readings: Jesus's response to the devil stands in contrast to Adam and Eve's; he outsmarts temptation at every turn where their naivete caused them to cave immediately. Unfortunately, this is not enough to undo the consequences of sin; this work will be continued all the way to Calvary. The second reading affirms Jesus as the mirror image of Adam. Through Adam we inherit sin and death; from Jesus we inherit freedom and life.

To experience: The temptations the devil throws at Jesus are versions of those we encounter all the time. Food and power and security are constantly present in our lives; they are not bad in and of themselves, but when we allow them to take the place in our hearts that ought to belong only to God, they keep us from living the fullness of life that comes only from union with God.

Homily Points

• Matthew moves from the story of Jesus's baptism right to his journey into the desert. Other translations use the term "wilderness." The desert can quite literally be a wild space. Birds of prey fly freely. The hot sun scorches. Water and food are likely scarce, if available at all. The scene Jesus now finds himself in stands in stark contrast to the day of his baptism when his beloved John the Baptist stood with him in the flowing waters of the Jordan River.

• The sequence of events reminds us how quickly life can change. We can move from a spiritual high to a devastating low without much warning. No matter where we find ourselves, the Spirit of God never leaves our side. Notice what is not said in this passage. Nowhere does it say the Spirit leaves Jesus alone with the devil. Just like in the waters of baptism, God's Spirit remains with Jesus—and each of us—during our times in the wilderness.

• The devil puts Jesus, in all his humanity, to the test in today's gospel. Imagine how Jesus must have felt after forty days and forty nights of fasting. The gospel writer's description that "afterwards he was hungry" is surely the understatement of the year! Think about how you felt on Ash Wednesday if you observed a day of fasting. Perhaps you moved slower or found yourself getting irritated more quickly than usual. Our bodies need fuel to function. Times of fasting force us to pay attention to our bodies—and the God who created them. Jesus placed all his trust in God during those forty days of fasting. May we do the same as we observe the Lenten practices.

Model Penitential Act

Presider: The devil tempts Jesus in today's gospel—and Jesus remains rooted in his faith. We are made in the image of the Son of God who withstands the enticements of the evil one, and yet at times we succumb to temptations. For those times, let us ask for mercy . . . *[pause]*

 Confiteor: I confess . . .

Model Universal Prayer (Prayer of the Faithful)

Presider: In today's second reading, St. Paul writes of how the grace of God overflows for many. Emboldened by this grace, let us bring our needs before the Lord.

Response: Lord, hear our prayer.

Rouse Christians around the world to resist temptations that draw us away from gospel living . . .

Give integrity and a strong sense of justice to judges and others who work in legal affairs . . .

Nourish those who lack adequate food, water, or other basic necessities . . .

Advance efforts to recognize and utilize the gifts of women in our communities . . .

Presider: Creator God, by your breath we come to have life. You are the source of all that is good and holy. Guide us in our prayer, fasting, and almsgiving this Lent that we might be cleansed and healed. We offer this prayer through Christ our Lord. **Amen.**

Liturgy and Music

Intentional Silence: This Lenten time of retreat to a reflective desert space requires a conscious shift in our attitude and tone of music making. As part of the simplicity, our music and worship ought to welcome periods of sacred silence. Within the discomfort that silence sometimes brings, we seek to live and breathe graced quiet moments that allow God's spirit to speak.

 In all there are six opportunities for silence that we are encouraged to observe at every Eucharistic liturgy—before Mass begins; during the penitential act; after the presider says "Let us pray" at each collect; after each Scripture reading; after the homily; and after Communion.

 Take care to shape the amount of time spent in silence at liturgy. As I've mentioned, place intentionality at the heart of our music making and prayer. Be intentional with the silences at Mass. Encourage stillness to accompany silence. While we are collectively praying, reflecting, or simply sitting in silence, encourage all music ministers (singers and instrumentalists) to embody silence. Try not to prepare for what is coming next by turning pages or moving microphones. Be still and present to God's movement in the silence.

COLLECT

Let us pray.

Pause for silent prayer

Grant, almighty God,
through the yearly observances of holy Lent,
that we may grow in understanding
of the riches hidden in Christ
and by worthy conduct pursue their effects.
Through our Lord Jesus Christ, your Son,
who lives and reigns with you in the unity of the Holy Spirit,
God, for ever and ever. **Amen.**

FIRST READING

Gen 2:7-9; 3:1-7

The LORD God formed man out of the clay of the ground
 and blew into his nostrils the breath of life,
 and so man became a living being.

Then the LORD God planted a garden in Eden, in the east,
 and placed there the man whom he had formed.
Out of the ground the LORD God made various trees grow
 that were delightful to look at and good for food,
 with the tree of life in the middle of the garden
 and the tree of the knowledge of good and evil.

Now the serpent was the most cunning of all the animals
 that the LORD God had made.
The serpent asked the woman,
 "Did God really tell you not to eat from any of the trees in the garden?"
The woman answered the serpent:
 "We may eat of the fruit of the trees in the garden;
 it is only about the fruit of the tree in the middle of the garden that God said,
 'You shall not eat it or even touch it, lest you die.'"
But the serpent said to the woman:
 "You certainly will not die!
No, God knows well that the moment you eat of it
 your eyes will be opened and you will be like gods
 who know what is good and what is evil."
The woman saw that the tree was good for food,
 pleasing to the eyes, and desirable for gaining wisdom.

So she took some of its fruit and ate it;
  and she also gave some to her husband,
    who was with her,
  and he ate it.
Then the eyes of both of them were
    opened,
  and they realized that they were naked;
  so they sewed fig leaves together
  and made loincloths for themselves.

RESPONSORIAL PSALM

Ps 51:3-4, 5-6, 12-13, 17

R̞. (cf. 3a) Be merciful, O Lord, for we have sinned.

Have mercy on me, O God, in your
    goodness;
  in the greatness of your compassion
    wipe out my offense.
Thoroughly wash me from my guilt
  and of my sin cleanse me.

R̞. Be merciful, O Lord, for we have sinned.

For I acknowledge my offense,
  and my sin is before me always:
"Against you only have I sinned,
  and done what is evil in your sight."

R̞. Be merciful, O Lord, for we have sinned.

A clean heart create for me, O God,
  and a steadfast spirit renew within me.
Cast me not out from your presence,
  and your Holy Spirit take not from me.

R̞. Be merciful, O Lord, for we have sinned.

Give me back the joy of your salvation,
  and a willing spirit sustain in me.
O Lord, open my lips,
  and my mouth shall proclaim your praise.

R̞. Be merciful, O Lord, for we have sinned.

SECOND READING

Rom 5:12-19

Brothers and sisters:
Through one man sin entered the world,
  and through sin, death,
  and thus death came to all men,
    inasmuch as all sinned—
  for up to the time of the law, sin was in
    the world,
  though sin is not accounted when there
    is no law.
But death reigned from Adam to Moses,
  even over those who did not sin
  after the pattern of the trespass of
    Adam,
  who is the type of the one who was to
    come.

*Continued in Appendix A, p. 269, or
Rom 5:12, 17-19 in Appendix A, p. 269.*

Living Liturgy

The Temptation to Be Relevant: Over these first three weeks of Lent, I draw from the reflections of theologian and author Henri Nouwen, from his book on spiritual life, *The Selfless Way of Christ,* about the spirituality of servant leadership as framework to discern the gospel story of temptations that faced Jesus on his desert journey. Nouwen urges us to take a path of downward mobility in stark contrast to the ways of the world that lure us toward upward mobility. Nouwen proposes a countercultural journey downward toward the cross and urges us into deeper reflection about our own sense of ministry to help us see God present in the midst of our struggles.

Nouwen states that the first temptation of turning stones to loaves of bread is a temptation to be relevant, something that most of us struggle with in our own work in pastoral ministry—to do something that is "needed" and "appreciated." In his response to the tempter, Jesus did not deny the importance of bread but rather relativized it in comparison with the nurturing power of the word of God. This is not to say that relevant behavior needs to be despised, but that it should not be the basis of our identity as Christians and as leaders of worship. The challenge for us is to allow God and God's word to shape and reshape us as human beings, that we can continue to witness to God's presence in the world with few or no visible results.

What has been our ministerial identity thus far and what should it look like moving into this season of Lent? Is it one preoccupied with visible results, product output, tangible goods, and progress? Resist the temptation to be relevant by doing irrelevant things. Instead, find relevancy in God's word.

PROMPTS FOR FAITH-SHARING

• Which of Jesus's temptations do you relate to most? How could you find inspiration for dealing with this struggle in Jesus's response?

• What does trust in God look like in your life? Where do you struggle to trust?

• The psalm reveals that Lent is a joyful season even amidst the sorrow we bear for our sins. How can you live the joy of this season, celebrating God's ever-constant mercy?

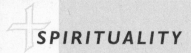

SPIRITUALITY

GOSPEL ACCLAMATION

cf. Matt 17:5

From the shining cloud the Father's voice is
    heard:
This is my beloved Son, hear him.

Gospel   Matt 17:1-9; L25A

Jesus took Peter, James, and John his
    brother,
  and led them up a high mountain by
    themselves.
And he was transfigured before them;
  his face shone like the sun
  and his clothes became white as
    light.
And behold, Moses and Elijah appeared
    to them,
  conversing with him.
Then Peter said to Jesus in reply,
  "Lord, it is good that we are here.
If you wish, I will make three tents
    here,
  one for you, one for Moses, and one
    for Elijah."
While he was still speaking, behold,
  a bright cloud cast a shadow over
    them,
  then from the cloud came a voice that
    said,
  "This is my beloved Son, with whom
    I am well pleased;
  listen to him."
When the disciples heard this, they fell
    prostrate
  and were very much afraid.
But Jesus came and touched them,
    saying,
  "Rise, and do not be afraid."
And when the disciples raised their
    eyes,
  they saw no one else but Jesus alone.

As they were coming down from the
    mountain,
  Jesus charged them,
  "Do not tell the vision to anyone
  until the Son of Man has been raised
    from the dead."

Reflecting on the Gospel

This week we hear the story of the "transfiguration" of Jesus, although a
better description might be "transformation." His face and garments become
transformed; the glory of God shines on his face and the dazzling white of his
clothes radiates his holy identity. Two of his ancestors, Moses and Elijah, appear in conversation with him. They talk with Jesus who is both in continuity
with and the fulfillment *of* the law and the prophets.

Then Peter makes what he thinks is
a brilliant suggestion: that Jesus, Moses,
and Elijah be settled down here in three
tents (or booths), which Peter will build
in order to celebrate a kind of extended
feast of Booths/Tabernacles. Since child-
hood, Jesus and the disciples had celebrated this feast, so Peter grasps at an
action that will restore some familiarity
to this unfamiliar event. But the Transfiguration is not about slipping back
into the security of the past, not about
settling down, and what seems to Peter
to be his dazzling contribution to the
scenario is immediately overshadowed
as the Father takes the initiative and
tents over the mountain with a bright
cloud.

Peter's words are silenced by the voice
from the cloud: "This is my beloved Son,
with whom I am well pleased; listen
to him." The identity of the Son was
proclaimed at his baptism, but now the command to "listen to him" is added.
To understand Jesus, the disciples must listen and listen and listen to what
Jesus says about suffering and death and resurrection; they must hear his good
news that is announced in his transfiguration of crippled bodies and minds into
whole and healed humanity, in the transfiguration of sinners through forgiveness, in the transfiguration of bread and wine into his body and blood. And
after they have seen Jesus on another hill, raised up and broken on a cross, they
will learn to believe in the transfiguration that brings him from the tomb to the
mountain of their great commissioning by Jesus, the risen and glorified One.

As a sign of this transfiguration that is to come, Jesus touches and raises
the disciples from their fear—fear of what might be the implications of this
mountain revelation for themselves. Then they see "no one else but Jesus" on
the mountain. For all disciples in every age, he is the one whom we must trust
to grasp us, raise us up from our fears, and lead us into the new. As Jesus tells
Peter, James, and John, they are to say nothing about him until they have understood that suffering and glory both belong in his mystery.

Immediately after the mountain transfiguration, down on the plain, Jesus will
heal and transfigure the lives of an epileptic boy and his father. This is where
transfiguration belongs: not only in the privileged peak experiences of our
lives, but also in the trudge across the flat plains of the everyday. In Lent, our
prayer, fasting, and almsgiving are the practices that will help transform us into
the likeness of Jesus as we journey toward the celebration of his Easter glory.

Preparing to Proclaim

Key words and phrases: "This is my beloved Son . . . listen to him."

To the point: The transfiguration is a mysterious thing; it reveals something about who Jesus is but leaves the disciples (and us) with as many questions as answers. There is both light and shadow in this moment of revelation. We may wish that God would communicate more directly with us; we ask for signs and signals to indicate God's will. Here, though, the disciples who do actually hear God's voice fall to the ground in fear. God does not say anything terribly challenging; the voice in fact affirms that they are doing well in entrusting their lives to Jesus. But there is something about it that overwhelms them. Encountering God in all God's mystery and wildness is not always a reassuring prospect; we are never ready for the ways in which God might call us to change.

Psalmist Preparation

Like last week's psalm, this one pairs God's mercy and our trust. The two go together. God deserves our trust because God is trustworthy; his unfailing offer of unconditional love enables us to draw ever closer to him despite our ongoing failings. At the same time, the last stanza of this psalm reminds us that God does not often work on the timeline we choose. We often find ourselves waiting for God's voice and God's healing. As you prepare this psalm, think of an area of your life where you find yourself waiting for God. Strive to wait with trust rather than impatience.

Making Connections

Between the readings: Like the disciples in the gospel, Abram receives explicit directions from God. He does not respond in fear but in trust, immediately fulfilling the instructions he receives. His life of love and obedience prepares him to respond when God asks something big of him. The second reading affirms the role of the transfiguration. Along with the entire life of Jesus, the transfiguration makes manifest the grace of God, which has been with us all along.

To experience: We do not often hear the voice of God as explicitly as the disciples do in the gospel. For most of us, God tends to speak in whispers and hints. This does not mean that God is any less present, but it does make God's presence less obvious. Following God's will for our lives is not always as easy as it is for Abram, who receives clear and direct instructions. For us, it is a matter of learning the tools of discernment so that we can hear God's voice—and remain assured of God's loving presence—as we piece together our paths in life.

Homily Points

• Today's first reading from Genesis showcases one of God's greatest characteristics: faithfulness. God's talk with Abram comes after generations of human failure. The early chapters of Genesis are riddled with instances of humans falling short: Adam and Eve disobey God in the garden; Cain murders his brother Abel; the wickedness of humankind rises to the point that God wipes out nearly all of creation in a flood. Time and again, God's beloved people disappoint. Time and again, God forgives. God chooses to remain faithful to the ones whom God carefully knit together. God promises the divine blessing will be with Abram and, through him, with all communities of the earth. Across time, God never gives up on us. May we not give up on each other either. Made in the image of God, may we strive to grow more faithful each day.

• Peter, James, and John experienced an incredibly intense spiritual moment as they witnessed Jesus's transfiguration atop the mountain. They saw a great light. They heard the voice of their Creator. They felt the movement of the Spirit washing over them. Then, in a matter of moments, the intensity ended. The three friends needed to make their way down the mountain, back to everyday life. Except, their lives could never be the same. Such a powerful experience of the divine must have awakened something within these men, right?

• In our own ways, we each navigate between moments of spiritual intensity and spiritual ordinary. Perhaps you had a "mountaintop moment" during a focused morning of prayer or on a weekend retreat. These moments may feel few and far between—yet we can carry their energy when we head back down the mountain and into daily life.

Model Penitential Act

Presider: In the first reading, God promises to bless Abram and all the communities on earth. God's faithfulness endures forever. For the times our words and actions have betrayed God's faithfulness, let us ask for pardon and mercy . . . *[pause]*

Confiteor: I confess . . .

Model Universal Prayer (Prayer of the Faithful)

Presider: Christ Jesus, the light of the world, shines brightly for all to see. Basking in his glow, let us bring our needs before the Lord.

Response: Lord, hear our prayer.

Strengthen the baptized and those preparing for baptism this Easter season to follow the way of Christ . . .

Further the conservation efforts working to protect the earth's mountains, forests, and bodies of water from the climate crisis . . .

Give relief to those bearing their share of hardships for the gospel, including LGBTQ+ members of the church . . .

Grace each of us gathered here with growing awareness of the blessings you gift us . . .

Presider: Faithful God, you sent your beloved Son to show us the way to eternal life. Hear our prayers that we might dwell in the light of Christ all the days of our lives and reflect that light in all we say and do. We ask this through Christ our Lord. **Amen.**

Liturgy and Music

The Assembly's Voice: The General Instruction of the Roman Missal states that during Lent the playing of the organ and musical instruments is allowed only in order to support the singing. Exceptions, however, are Laetare Sunday (Fourth Sunday of Lent) and solemnities and feasts (313). The guideline encourages unaccompanied singing during the Lenten season. Perhaps this is something new for your choir and congregation to explore and implement at this time.

Unaccompanied congregational singing requires the participation of the entire assembly in listening for and singing with each other. It is a communal activity that in many ways lays bare vulnerabilities as each member of the assembly relies on the neighbor for pitch and support. Use either handbells, the organ, piano or a keyboard to help the group stay on pitch. Once assembly members are able to hear each other and sing together, confidence will grow and the volume of the assembly's voice will eventually increase.

COLLECT

Let us pray.

Pause for silent prayer

O God, who have commanded us
to listen to your beloved Son,
be pleased, we pray,
to nourish us inwardly by your word,
that, with spiritual sight made pure,
we may rejoice to behold your glory.
Through our Lord Jesus Christ, your Son,
who lives and reigns with you in the unity
    of the Holy Spirit,
God, for ever and ever. **Amen.**

FIRST READING

Gen 12:1-4a

The LORD said to Abram:
  "Go forth from the land of your kinsfolk
    and from your father's house to a land
      that I will show you.

  "I will make of you a great nation,
    and I will bless you;
  I will make your name great,
    so that you will be a blessing.
  I will bless those who bless you
    and curse those who curse you.
  All the communities of the earth
    shall find blessing in you."

Abram went as the LORD directed him.

RESPONSORIAL PSALM
Ps 33:4-5, 18-19, 20, 22

R̄. (22) Lord, let your mercy be on us, as
we place our trust in you.

Upright is the word of the Lord,
    and all his works are trustworthy.
He loves justice and right;
    of the kindness of the Lord the earth
        is full.

R̄. Lord, let your mercy be on us, as we
place our trust in you.

See, the eyes of the Lord are upon those
    who fear him,
    upon those who hope for his kindness,
to deliver them from death
    and preserve them in spite of famine.

R̄. Lord, let your mercy be on us, as we
place our trust in you.

Our soul waits for the Lord,
    who is our help and our shield.
May your kindness, O Lord, be upon us
    who have put our hope in you.

R̄. Lord, let your mercy be on us, as we
place our trust in you.

SECOND READING
2 Tim 1:8b-10

Beloved:
Bear your share of hardship for the gospel
    with the strength that comes from God.

He saved us and called us to a holy life,
    not according to our works
    but according to his own design
    and the grace bestowed on us in Christ
        Jesus before time began,
    but now made manifest
    through the appearance of our savior
        Christ Jesus,
    who destroyed death and brought life
        and immortality
    to light through the gospel.

Living Liturgy
The Temptation to Be Spectacular: This week we continue to reflect with Henri Nouwen on our own ministerial identity by discerning the second temptation of Jesus, of making a spectacular gesture to prove that he is indeed the Son of God. Nouwen links the desire for relevance (from last week's reflection) with a hunger for the spectacular and states that it has to do with a search for selfhood. He comments that our insecurities, doubtfulness, and loneliness within our ministerial settings spark a greater need for popularity and praise. Our world valorizes visibility and notoriety. Statistics measuring success—the best, the fastest, the biggest—show signs that we are dealing with something significant in our society. And this hunger is never satisfied.

Jesus's response to the tempter ought to inspire us: "You shall not put the Lord, your God, to the test." It gives us an option to retreat from the world and realize that "the search for spectacular glitter is an expression of doubt in God's complete and unconditional acceptance of us" (Nouwen, *Selfless Way of Christ*). We return to the center of our ministry, to the heart of our vocational identity, to hear God's voice assuring and affirming us, freeing us from our compulsion to be seen, praised, and admired. The work of our hands ought to point to God and not to ourselves. This discipline can only be practiced through contemplative prayer and now is the time to begin.

The gospel story of the transfiguration describes a vision showing Jesus in his heavenly glory. But before that point is reached, Jesus must first be raised from the dead, emphasizing the paschal mystery and that there can be no eternal life with God without death. Dying to our desires for relevance and for the spectacular is part of our journey to manifest the fullness of ministerial identity. The experience of God's acceptance frees us from our needy self. Through continual prayer and communion with God, God can reveal to us our true selfhood, a life set free to act according to God's truth and not according to our need for the spectacular.

PROMPTS FOR FAITH-SHARING

• What helps to reassure you of God's presence when it is not obvious?

• What helps you listen to the voice of God, especially when—as is most common for most of us—God is speaking in whispers and hints?

• Where in your life of faith do you need patience with God? What would help you to faithfully wait for God, who does not often work on the timelines we would have chosen for ourselves?

✝ SPIRITUALITY

GOSPEL ACCLAMATION
cf. John 4:42, 15

Lord, you are truly the Savior of the world;
give me living water, that I may never thirst
   again.

Gospel John 4:5-42; L28A

Jesus came to a town of Samaria
      called Sychar,
   near the plot of land that Jacob had
         given to his son Joseph.
Jacob's well was there.
Jesus, tired from his journey, sat
      down there at the well.
It was about noon.

A woman of Samaria came to draw
      water.
Jesus said to her,
   "Give me a drink."
His disciples had gone into the town
      to buy food.
The Samaritan woman said to him,
   "How can you, a Jew, ask me,
         a Samaritan woman, for a
         drink?"
—For Jews use nothing in common with
      Samaritans.—
Jesus answered and said to her,
   "If you knew the gift of God
   and who is saying to you, 'Give me a
         drink,'
   you would have asked him
   and he would have given you living
      water."
The woman said to him,
   "Sir, you do not even have a bucket
         and the cistern is deep;
   where then can you get this living
      water?
Are you greater than our father Jacob,
   who gave us this cistern and drank
         from it himself
   with his children and his flocks?"

Continued in Appendix A, p. 270, or
John 4:5-15, 19b-26, 39a, 40-42 *in Appendix A,*
p. 271.

Reflecting on the Gospel

When John wrote his gospel, he was well aware that Samaria had been the first region beyond Jerusalem to receive the good news (see Acts 8:2-9; 9:31). John is writing after the fact of the historical acceptance of the Gospel, but he sees it as what it truly is: an encounter with Jesus through the preaching of the early church. An intelligent, daring *woman* is at the center of the shocking inclusiveness for which our contemporary church is still striving.

Then as now, Jesus makes those who respond to him sharers in his freedom. The despised woman—who comes to the well in the heat of high noon in order to avoid the judgmental eyes and tongues of the other women at the usual drawing time of morning and evening—hurries back to her own town. She is no longer ashamed of the story of her life, because she has a more urgent story to tell about the man who lowered a bucket into the well of her soul and drew up the deep living water within her. She has been helped to see what she was looking for, what her own inner reality and truth are, and that she must worship the God in this spirit and truth. John presents us with a "litany" of names for Jesus. First the woman speaks to him as "Jew," then "prophet." As she hesitates to call him "Messiah," or "the Christ," Jesus reveals himself as the one anointed with the Holy Name, the "I AM," "YHWH," in his human presence; and after Jesus has stayed in the woman's Samaritan city, its inhabitants name him as "savior of the world."

When the disciples return with food, they are shocked, not so much because Jesus has been talking with a Samaritan, but because he has been relating to a woman! What Jesus tells them is that he has food that they know nothing about: the woman's questions, her insights, her energy and acceptance have nourished Jesus, for in such an encounter he is doing the will of the One who sent him and sowing in Samaria the grain that will be harvested for eternal life.

The woman announces to her Samaritan village what she experienced with Jesus, but until they have experienced him personally, they cannot truly believe. Only then can he be named "savior of the world." This is the faith that calls us, with the elect of our parish communities, to a scrutiny of what quenches our deepest "thirsts," of what nourishes our spirits as well as our bodies. Do pleasure, power, exclusiveness satisfy us? With what "enemy" are we unwilling to sit and talk, to eat and drink? How tolerant are we of those who belong to other religious or cultural traditions? Do we believe in the value of creative conversation, even when exhausted, even with our own young people who may have questions—sometimes abrasive, often welling up from deep longings within them? Can we move out of our comfort zones, leave our old "water jars" behind, and welcome the gifts of God that are being offered to us, especially in this privileged season of Lent?

Preparing to Proclaim

Key words and phrases: "[W]hoever drinks the water I shall give will never thirst."

To the point: In her encounter with Jesus, we see a healing narrative arc for the woman at the well. She begins from a place of defensiveness; she knows what Jews usually think of Samaritans. She continues in a guarded manner, giving only a partial answer when asked about her husband. Deciding that this must be a prophet, she moves to challenge Jesus, asking intelligent questions to probe his wisdom. When he reveals to her his identity as Messiah, she finally arrives in a place of trust—such trust that she leaves her water jar behind and becomes a powerful evangelist, her testimony the cause of many neighbors' belief. Such is the power of encounter with Christ; one who is known to be sinful, who slinks to the well in the heat of the day to avoid the crowds of cooler times, is transformed into one whose testimony is so powerfully true that the same townspeople who would have judged her are transformed, too.

Psalmist Preparation

Most of us assume that when we hear God's voice, we'll be ready to listen. Surely it's God's uncommunicativeness that's the issue, not our ability to hear him! But this psalm reminds us that our hearts need to stay open in order to keep hearing God. God is always reaching out to us, but often in ways we miss because we're not expecting them. As part of your preparation to proclaim this psalm, spend some time in silence. Ask God to reveal to you one place you've been overlooking God's presence in your life. Pray for a softer heart so that you might more readily notice God in all the gentle ways God comes to us.

Making Connections

Between the readings: The first reading shares the strong water imagery of the gospel; God provides for us in all ways, including our very human need for water. Our physical thirst reveals the neediness of our human condition; it is never satisfied for long, and we must stay close enough to a source of water to constantly fulfill a need that was satisfied not long ago. The second reading is more oblique, but does speak of the love of God being "poured out" into our hearts—an indication that physical thirst is neither our primary need nor the primary way that God provides.

To experience: Our physical thirst is only an echo of the way in which our hearts are meant to ache for God. Our need for God is infinite, for it takes an infinite God to satisfy the need. That means that our capacity is infinite. We are made for so much more than we realize.

Homily Points

• Water emerges as a major player in today's readings. The Israelites thirst for water. Jesus encounters the Samaritan woman drawing water from a well. In both cases, water serves to meet a basic biological need—and more. Jesus speaks of living water, the kind that satisfies thirst forever. Those who drink of it shall enjoy eternal life.

• This focus on water midway through Lent draws our attention and prayers to those in our community and around the world who are preparing for baptism. In a few short weeks, they will be submerged in lifegiving water and emerge forever changed as members of the Body of Christ. The Lord provides all the water we need to never thirst again. Let us follow him ever more closely.

• The conversation between the Samaritan woman and Jesus at the well causes a scandal in the minds of the disciples. Jewish men in charge did not converse with women in public. The gender difference creates scandal. The difference in cultures further divides the two. Jesus, who is Jewish, and the woman, who is Samaritan, should be on opposing sides. Their people were long-time enemies, divided over beliefs of the proper place for worship. The woman should have turned around when she saw Jesus sitting by the well. She should not have engaged. She should have avoided scandal. Instead, the Samaritan woman stays at the well, and her life is forever changed. She goes on to testify to the power of the one called Christ. Her persistence demonstrates how breaking the rules is not always a bad thing. Risking it all to encounter Christ is, in fact, exactly what we are called to do.

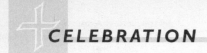
Model Penitential Act

Presider: In today's second reading, St. Paul writes of God's great love for us, proclaiming that "while we were still sinners Christ died for us." Trusting that God loves us through our faults, let us ask for mercy . . . *[pause]*

    Confiteor: I confess . . .

Model Universal Prayer (Prayer of the Faithful)

Presider: Confident in the Lord who provides for our every need, let us offer our prayers and petitions.

Response: Lord, hear our prayer.

Fortify the faith of those preparing to enter the waters of baptism this Easter . . .

Further the work of environmentalists and those working to protect the earth's resources . . .

Provide access to safe drinking water to every community in the world . . .

Help us to steward water well in our homes, schools, workplaces, and community centers . . .

Presider: Sustaining God, you call your creation to eternal life with you out of great love. Receive our prayers spoken aloud and those held in the silence of our hearts, that we might grow ever closer to you. We ask this through Christ our Lord. **Amen.**

Liturgy and Music

Singing the Scrutinies: The scrutinies are celebrated today and over the following two Sundays if there are members of the elect present in the assembly. Note that all three scrutinies are required. Additional music accompanies the simple rite.

Prepare familiar music ahead of time to be included at two places during the rite. First, prepare music for the intercessions for the elect (a chant similar to the Prayers of the Faithful), and secondly, include music after the prayer of exorcism (a brief song as an acclamation of thanksgiving would work here). Choose a familiar hymn, a single refrain of a song or perhaps a simple phrase to sing during the rite. Sing different verses (ones that relate more closely to the gospel story) of the same hymn over the three weeks of scrutinies.

Note that there should not be any music during the laying of hands that takes place during the prayer of exorcism. Silence adds to the solemnity during the ritual laying of hands. Also note that the presentations of the Creed and the Lord's Prayer are not part of the scrutinies and should not be combined. Each of these rituals has a set of prescribed readings and therefore cannot be celebrated within the same liturgy.

COLLECT

Let us pray.

Pause for silent prayer

O God, author of every mercy and of all
    goodness,
who in fasting, prayer and almsgiving
have shown us a remedy for sin,
look graciously on this confession of our
    lowliness,
that we, who are bowed down by our
    conscience,
may always be lifted up by your mercy.
Through our Lord Jesus Christ, your Son,
who lives and reigns with you in the unity
    of the Holy Spirit,
God, for ever and ever. **Amen.**

FIRST READING

Exod 17:3-7

In those days, in their thirst for water,
    the people grumbled against Moses,
    saying, "Why did you ever make us
        leave Egypt?
Was it just to have us die here of thirst
    with our children and our livestock?"
So Moses cried out to the LORD,
    "What shall I do with this people?
A little more and they will stone me!"
The LORD answered Moses,
    "Go over there in front of the people,
    along with some of the elders of Israel,
    holding in your hand, as you go,
    the staff with which you struck the
        river.
I will be standing there in front of you on
    the rock in Horeb.
Strike the rock, and the water will flow
    from it
    for the people to drink."
This Moses did, in the presence of the
    elders of Israel.
The place was called Massah and
    Meribah,
    because the Israelites quarreled there
    and tested the LORD, saying,
    "Is the LORD in our midst or not?"

RESPONSORIAL PSALM
Ps 95:1-2, 6-7, 8-9

R̲. (8) If today you hear his voice, harden not your hearts.

Come, let us sing joyfully to the LORD;
  let us acclaim the Rock of our salvation.
Let us come into his presence with
    thanksgiving;
  let us joyfully sing psalms to him.

R̲. If today you hear his voice, harden not your hearts.

Come, let us bow down in worship;
  let us kneel before the LORD who made
    us.
For he is our God,
  and we are the people he shepherds, the
    flock he guides.

R̲. If today you hear his voice, harden not your hearts.

Oh, that today you would hear his voice:
  "Harden not your hearts as at Meribah,
  as in the day of Massah in the desert,
where your fathers tempted me;
  they tested me though they had seen
    my works."

R̲. If today you hear his voice, harden not your hearts.

SECOND READING
Rom 5:1-2, 5-8

Brothers and sisters:
Since we have been justified by faith,
  we have peace with God through our
      Lord Jesus Christ,
    through whom we have gained access
        by faith
    to this grace in which we stand,
    and we boast in hope of the glory of
        God.

And hope does not disappoint,
  because the love of God has been
        poured out into our hearts
    through the Holy Spirit who has been
        given to us.
For Christ, while we were still helpless,
  died at the appointed time for the
        ungodly.
Indeed, only with difficulty does one die
      for a just person,
  though perhaps for a good person one
        might even find courage to die.
But God proves his love for us
  in that while we were still sinners Christ
      died for us.

Living Liturgy

The Temptation to Be Powerful: The third temptation of Jesus centers around the desire for power. I continue to share the thoughts and writings of Henri Nouwen in the third section of this three-part reflection on ministerial identity. Nouwen posits that our society idolizes feelings of power and that from power comes more power. A sense of security and control can come from power, as well as the illusion that life is ours to dispose of. Power takes many forms: money, connections, fame, intellectual ability, and skills. The challenge of authentic ministerial identity is to overcome this desire. Power does not give us the sense of security we desire, but instead reveals our own weaknesses and limitations. Even so, we continue to convince ourselves that our needs will be met through greater power.

"The Lord, your God, shall you worship / and him alone shall you serve" (Matt 4:10). Jesus's response to the tempter guides our way through the mystery of ministry, that we are called to serve not with power but with our powerlessness. Through this we enter into solidarity with the weak. We recognize God's mercy and healing from being in community with the oppressed. We might also then encounter the woman of Samaria who gradually recognizes the Messiah. Her sense of who Jesus is becomes strengthened as she spends more time in conversation with him. Like the woman from Samaria, we too will gradually be revealed to and deepened in Christ as we follow his own example of servant leadership. Powerless ministry can only happen when we take the time to serve our neighbors for their sake and not for our own.

PROMPTS FOR FAITH-SHARING

• How do you experience desire for God?

• How does the Samaritan woman's encounter with Jesus compare to your own moments of encounter with him?

• How does God speak to you? Where might you need to open your ears to hear him more clearly?

• After her encounter with Christ, the Samaritan woman became a powerful witness whose testimony brought others to believe. To whom in your life could you be a witness of the love of God?

SPIRITUALITY

GOSPEL ACCLAMATION
John 8:12

I am the light of the world, says the Lord;
whoever follows me will have the light of life.

Gospel

John 9:1-41; L31A

As Jesus passed by he saw a man
    blind from birth.
His disciples asked him,
  "Rabbi, who sinned, this man or his
      parents,
   that he was born blind?"
Jesus answered,
  "Neither he nor his parents sinned;
   it is so that the works of God might
      be made visible through him.
We have to do the works of the one
      who sent me while it is day.
Night is coming when no one can
      work.
While I am in the world, I am the light
   of the world."
When he had said this, he spat on the
      ground
   and made clay with the saliva,
   and smeared the clay on his eyes,
      and said to him,
  "Go wash in the Pool of Siloam"—
      which means Sent—.
So he went and washed, and came back
      able to see.

His neighbors and those who had seen
      him earlier as a beggar said,
  "Isn't this the one who used to sit
      and beg?"
Some said, "It is,"
   but others said, "No, he just looks
      like him."
He said, "I am."

Continued in Appendix A, p. 272, or
John 9:1, 6-9, 13-17, 34-38 *in Appendix A, p. 273.*

Reflecting on the Gospel

The Gospel of John's dramatic ninth chapter describes the healing of the blind man and the range of responses to it. The stuff of the miracle is spittle, mud, and the fingers of Jesus—the first two the images of messiness and the stuff of folkloric healing, but both transformed by the humanity of Jesus and the power of his outstretched hand that reveals the creative work of God (e.g., Deut 26:8) as incarnate and continuing in him. The blind man, however, must also do his part, must obey Jesus, the Sent One (see John 7:28-29; 10:36; 12:44-45) and go to the Pool of Siloam (which means "sent") to wash his eyes. Then the blind man will see and himself become a *sent* one, a witness to what has happened to him not merely physically, but also because the eyes of his spirit have been opened to the truth of Jesus.

The healed man immediately becomes the center of attention and controversy, yet he remains steadfast in his witness to Jesus as the one who healed him, and se-cure in his identity as the one "born-blind" but now re-created and seeing. A cast of players appears on stage: neighbors, Pharisees, parents. The man's witness to Jesus is the cause of division among the religious leaders, those supposed to be insightful but blind to the truth about Jesus. Like the Pharisees with their Sabbath myopia, we can misjudge others because of our ingrained religious prejudices; like the man's parents, we can be too frightened to get involved in any controversy, especially with a powerful yet unjust authority. There is so much finger-pointing in this gospel, so much accu-sation of sinfulness. The man born blind, his parents, and Jesus himself are all accused by Jesus's opponents. Abandoned by his neighbors, rejected by his par-ents, driven away by the Pharisees, the once-blind man is found again by Jesus in the last few verses. In the absence of Jesus, he has clung to the strange new experience of light. Just as the Samaritan woman in last week's gospel read-ing progressively named Jesus with greater insight as her faith in him grew, so with this man. From simply knowing him as Jesus (v. 11), he calls him a prophet (v. 17) and then proclaims that he comes from God (v. 33). As always, Jesus seeks out the abandoned one and finds him in the temple. When Jesus reveals his identity, the man makes his profession of faith: "I do believe, Lord." And he worships this Son of Man.

This gospel challenges us, as individuals and communities, to examine how we see with the eyes of faith and whether we are willfully blind to the Sent One, turning away from the Light of the World. What are our contemporary blind-nesses? Sin gets clicks. Are we more interested in sin than in grace? Are we brave enough to accept being sometimes ostracized by others when we choose to walk in the light of Christ rather than stumble away from him along our complacent, selfish, and socially pressurized paths of darkness?

Preparing to Proclaim

Key words and phrases: "I am the light of the world."

To the point: Like many of our Lenten readings, this gospel plays with themes of light and darkness, seeing and blindness. Here, Jesus makes clear that it is easier for God to heal physical blindness than willful refusal to see God at work. Most of us struggle with some level of spiritual blindness; after all, most of us do not get to witness these clear, decisive miracles of Jesus's time on earth. God does not always operate in ways that are easy for us to perceive. The Pharisees, though, are choosing blindness. Having their eyes opened will challenge a system that keeps them comfortably in power. What God reveals is not always comfortable or easy. We are sometimes called to sacrifice and to use our positions of privilege to advocate for others in unpopular ways. But if we *want* to see, God can heal our spiritual blindness, too.

Psalmist Preparation

Shepherds were not people of prominence in the ancient world; shepherding was dirty, smelly, humble work. It would not have been immediately obvious that identifying God as a shepherd was a form of praise. Like our other readings, this psalm is about defying expectations; the shepherd here provides such tender care that gratitude spills forth as praise. This psalm can sometimes feel mind-numbingly familiar. When was the last time you really tried to pray with it? Spend some time with it this week as you prepare to proclaim it and ask God to make it new for you.

Making Connections

Between the readings: The first reading contains a much more mundane form of blindness. Jesse merely *overlooks* David, assuming his youngest son cannot be the one chosen by God. But God is clear that his perception is not the same as ours; what God values is not the same as what we value. The second reading continues the themes of light and darkness, exhorting us to choose light over darkness—which is to say, sight over blindness.

To experience: The Pharisees are comfortable with their blindness, unable to recognize how much they don't see. We, too, are often content to remain in ignorance, especially when God's light reveals truth that is uncomfortable. We know God sides with the oppressed, and so we'd rather not know when we've benefited from oppression. This is the work of Lent, though: all the prayer and fasting and almsgiving are meant to illumine places where our lives are keeping us from God, and to aid us in turning away from them, uncomfortable though it may be.

Homily Points

• In today's first reading, God choses Samuel's youngest son, David, to be the anointed king. From the time of his anointing, it is said that "the spirit of the Lord rushed upon David." This powerful image connects well with the ways the spirit of the Lord is at work among those preparing for Christian initiation at the Easter Vigil. We rejoice with candidates and catechumens around the world and in our own parish community who will deepen their relationships with Christ and the church through the sacraments of initiation. The spirit of the Lord will no doubt rush upon them, just as the spirit rushes upon us, in the waters of baptism, in the anointing at confirmation, and each time we gather for Eucharist.

• Jesus uses the gifts of the earth and the gifts of his body to heal the man born blind. The Son of God does not summon a chorus of angels or some other-worldly tools. He simply spits on the ground, rubs the saliva and dirt together, and touches the man's eyes. Instantly, the man can see.

• We are made in the image of Christ the healer. In our own ways, we too can use the gifts of the earth and the gifts of our bodies to help others on the path of healing. Maybe you bring flowers to a friend who just received hard news. Maybe you hold the hand of a loved one going through chemotherapy, reminding her that she is not alone. We may not be able to restore someone's sight, but we can be agents of healing for our hurting world.

Model Penitential Act

Presider: In today's second reading, St. Paul warns the Ephesians to "[t]ake no part in the fruitless works of darkness." Indeed, darkness is too often its own garden. For the times we have chosen darkness over light, let us ask for mercy . . . *[pause]*

    Confiteor: I confess . . .

Model Universal Prayer (Prayer of the Faithful)

Presider: Grateful for God's steady presence among us, let us humbly offer our needs before the Lord.

Response: Lord, hear our prayer.

Deepen the faith of those preparing for Christian initiation at the Easter Vigil . . .

Inspire confidence in young people called into civil and religious leadership . . .

Animate greater recognition of and respect for the gifts of people with disabilities . . .

Attune our senses to those in need of healing in our local communities . . .

Presider: Almighty God, in you we find the source of all hope and healing. Hear our prayers that we might freely share this hope and healing with the world in need. We ask this through Christ our Lord. **Amen.**

Liturgy and Music

Laetare Sunday: We have reached the midway point of our Lenten journey and the church allows both musical instruments and joyful flourishes of flowers at the altar. While we are given this little respite from the abstinence of Lent, continue to practice moderation and save the larger, festive arrangements for the Triduum and Easter season.

    This might be a good time to take stock of how far we've come or how much we've done in our Lenten journey. How have we brought the Lenten practices of prayer, fasting, and almsgiving to bear over these past weeks? A music ministry day of recollection or reflection might be an appropriate activity in these middle days of Lent to allow choir members to share their Lenten experiences and prepare for the upcoming liturgies of the Triduum and Easter Sunday.

    Both the second reading and gospel today emphasize light and vision. In the Ephesians reading Christians are charged to live as children of light because Christ has given them light. We take on our Christian identity through baptism and as music ministers, we sing and pray for wisdom and enlightenment with those who celebrate the second scrutiny today on their own journey toward the waters of baptism.

COLLECT

Let us pray.

Pause for silent prayer

O God, who through your Word
reconcile the human race to yourself in a
    wonderful way,
grant, we pray,
that with prompt devotion and eager faith
the Christian people may hasten
toward the solemn celebrations to come.
Through our Lord Jesus Christ, your Son,
who lives and reigns with you in the unity
    of the Holy Spirit,
God, for ever and ever. **Amen.**

FIRST READING

1 Sam 16:1b, 6-7, 10-13a

The LORD said to Samuel:
    "Fill your horn with oil, and be on your
        way.
I am sending you to Jesse of Bethlehem,
    for I have chosen my king from among
        his sons."

As Jesse and his sons came to the sacrifice,
    Samuel looked at Eliab and thought,
    "Surely the LORD's anointed is here
        before him."
But the LORD said to Samuel:
    "Do not judge from his appearance or
        from his lofty stature,
    because I have rejected him.
Not as man sees does God see,
    because man sees the appearance
    but the LORD looks into the heart."
In the same way Jesse presented seven
        sons before Samuel,
    but Samuel said to Jesse,
    "The LORD has not chosen any one of
        these."
Then Samuel asked Jesse,
    "Are these all the sons you have?"
Jesse replied,
    "There is still the youngest, who is
        tending the sheep."
Samuel said to Jesse,
    "Send for him;
    we will not begin the sacrificial banquet
        until he arrives here."
Jesse sent and had the young man brought
        to them.
He was ruddy, a youth handsome to behold
    and making a splendid appearance.
The LORD said,
    "There—anoint him, for this is the one!"
Then Samuel, with the horn of oil in hand,
    anointed David in the presence of his
        brothers;
    and from that day on, the spirit of the
        LORD rushed upon David.

RESPONSORIAL PSALM
Ps 23:1-3a, 3b-4, 5, 6

R℣. (1) The Lord is my shepherd; there is
nothing I shall want.

The LORD is my shepherd; I shall not want.
   In verdant pastures he gives me repose;
beside restful waters he leads me;
   he refreshes my soul.

R℣. The Lord is my shepherd; there is
nothing I shall want.

He guides me in right paths
   for his name's sake.
Even though I walk in the dark valley
   I fear no evil; for you are at my side
with your rod and your staff
   that give me courage.

R℣. The Lord is my shepherd; there is
nothing I shall want.

You spread the table before me
   in the sight of my foes;
you anoint my head with oil;
   my cup overflows.

R℣. The Lord is my shepherd; there is
nothing I shall want.

Only goodness and kindness follow me
   all the days of my life;
and I shall dwell in the house of the LORD
   for years to come.

R℣. The Lord is my shepherd; there is
nothing I shall want.

SECOND READING
Eph 5:8-14

Brothers and sisters:
You were once darkness,
   but now you are light in the Lord.
Live as children of light,
   for light produces every kind of
      goodness
   and righteousness and truth.
Try to learn what is pleasing to the Lord.
Take no part in the fruitless works of
      darkness;
   rather expose them, for it is shameful
      even to mention
   the things done by them in secret;
   but everything exposed by the light
      becomes visible,
   for everything that becomes visible is
      light.
Therefore, it says:
   "Awake, O sleeper,
   and arise from the dead,
   and Christ will give you light."

Living Liturgy

The Word of God: Rich imagery and beautiful story fill the gospel readings of the third, fourth, and fifth Sundays of Lent. Lengthy Cycle A readings allow us all to immerse ourselves into each scriptural scene more fully, to imagine, as St. Ignatius of Loyola believes, that we are placed within the particular gospel scene. For some communities, this imagining manifests in more than a liturgical or gospel proclamation. It might take the form of an enactment of the gospel story, sometimes with elaborate staging, costumes, and props. The gifts of the community are rightly celebrated during the preparation of such reenactments. As much as these are wonderful ways to engage in community-building experiences and exercise communal contemplation, how much of God's word is retained in the production and telling of the story?

Within such dramatic gospel story reenactments, we sometimes lose sight of our initial, more intimate connection to the story. With all the staging and production, it becomes less the narrative that we first imagined and takes on someone else's interpretation. More importantly with such theatrical productions, we have lost the chance to receive the full meaning of God's word.

A more vibrant way of celebrating these sacred stories would be to prepare the script well and the readers with narrations that come from a place of deeper faith. Stay close to the meaning of the texts and proclaim them in a sensitive way. Authenticity in prayerful narration comes with thoughtful, spiritual preparation weeks before the actual Sunday. Give time and space for God's word to work in our hearts.

PROMPTS FOR FAITH-SHARING

• Where might there be a pocket of blindness in your own life? How could you invite God in to heal it?

• What are your real values in life—where do you *really* spend your time, attention, energy, and money? Do any of these conflict with who you profess to be?

• Does anything about God's work in these readings make you uncomfortable? How might that be a call to action?

Blessed are those who dwell in your house,
O Lord;
they never cease to praise you.

Gospel

Matt 1:16, 18-21, 24a; L543

Jacob was the father of Joseph,
the husband of Mary.
Of her was born Jesus who is
called the Christ.

Now this is how the birth of Jesus
Christ came about.
When his mother Mary was betrothed to Joseph,
but before they lived together,
she was found with child through
the Holy Spirit.
Joseph her husband, since he was
a righteous man,
yet unwilling to expose her to
shame,
decided to divorce her quietly.
Such was his intention when,
behold,
the angel of the Lord appeared to
him in a dream and said,
"Joseph, son of David,
do not be afraid to take Mary your
wife into your home.
For it is through the Holy Spirit
that this child has been conceived in
her.
She will bear a son and you are to
name him Jesus,
because he will save his people from
their sins."
When Joseph awoke,
he did as the angel of the Lord had
commanded him
and took his wife into his home.

or Luke 2:41-51a in Appendix A, p. 274.

See Appendix A., p. 274, for the other readings.

Reflecting on the Gospel

Anne-Marie Bonneau is an activist in the environmental justice movement and the creator of a blog called *Zero-Waste Chef.* To be living a "zero-waste lifestyle" means that one strives to make purchasing, diet, and living decisions that will bring the amount of waste produced by their household as close to zero as possible. It means avoiding unnecessary packaging and non-recyclable materials, as well as food and products that one knows are produced through wasteful processes. To one who is not currently living the zero-waste lifestyle, it can seem extremely challenging and perhaps impossible. Bonneau has written about the guilt that can emerge in the quest to live a zero-waste lifestyle. She came to an important realization in a blog post from February 2019 where she wrote, "We don't need a handful of people doing zero waste perfectly. We need millions of people doing zero waste imperfectly." We don't need to wait until we are perfectly knowledgeable and equipped to improve a difficult situation.

Little is known about the details of St. Joseph's life, but one theme from his life is that he trusted God's directives even when he could not see the whole picture. Scripture and tradition tell us that he was a descendant of King David and that his trade was carpentry. St. Joseph is the patron saint of the universal church, craftsmen, families, and a happy death among other things. Images of him frequently include a lily (a symbol of purity) and a carpenter's square (a symbol of truth). None of his own words are recorded in Scripture, but believers come to know him through his actions.

When Joseph was betrothed to Mary and learned that she was pregnant, the Gospel of Matthew tells us that he considered divorcing her quietly. However, he was visited by an angel of the Lord and reassured that Mary's pregnancy was caused not by scandal, but rather by the will and power of God. Later in the gospel, Matthew recounts the dangerous threat that King Herod posed to the infant Jesus and listeners hear again how, through a dream, Joseph was instructed to protect his family by seeking refuge in Egypt.

How many of us today would, when faced with a heavy conundrum, be moved to a decision by what we heard in a dream? It may feel incredible, but one lesson that we draw from these moments of salvation history is that God will speak to us in ways God knows we'll understand. What are the channels through which you are most attuned to God's voice? Is it through the worship and ritual of church life? Is it through Scripture study? Is it through acts of service and seeking solidarity with those on the margins?

The few stories we have about St. Joseph show us that even though he was asked to embrace a life that included mystery and, at times, danger, he fulfilled God's will by listening to God's instruction and doing the next right thing. On this feast day of St. Joseph, may we strive to emulate his example and remember that God will speak to us in times of desperation and confusion and that we can trust in the message that we hear.

Preparing to Proclaim

Key words and phrases: "[H]e did as the angel of the Lord had commanded him."

To the point: Joseph acts not out of obligation but out of extraordinarily generous love. He technically has no obligation to Mary or Jesus, but he takes on the huge task of raising her son with her. He participates in the mundane realities of parenthood—feeding, providing, teaching. Like all parents, he is at times baffled by this person God has entrusted to him; we see this especially when Joseph and Mary find Jesus teaching in Jerusalem. Like all parents, though, he is fulfilling a sacred duty, one for which he is uniquely appointed.

Model Penitential Act

Presider: St. Joseph trusted in God's desires for his family. He remained faithful to Mary when she conceived a child through the Holy Spirit and loved Jesus as his own. With this holy man as our guide, let us ask God for mercy . . . *[pause]*

Lord Jesus, you are the Son of God and Son of Mary: Lord, have mercy.

Christ Jesus, you grew up under the care of your earthly father, Joseph: Christ, have mercy.

Lord Jesus, you will come again to save your people from sin: Lord, have mercy.

Model Universal Prayer (Prayer of the Faithful)

Presider: Guided by the intercession of St. Joseph, let us bring our prayers and petitions before the Lord.

Response: Lord, hear our prayer.

Renew the spirits of all fathers, godfathers, and father-figures working to raise good and faithful children . . .

Kindle a spirit of openness and generosity in families who could create loving foster homes for children in need . . .

Bring a swift end to domestic abuse and healing to those who have suffered through it . . .

Inspire each of us gathered here to listen closely for God's callings in our lives . . .

Presider: God of surprises, you called Joseph and Mary to parenthood in the most unlikely of ways. Your power knows no bounds. Receive our prayers that, through the witness of St. Joseph, we might grow in faithfulness and trust. We ask this through Christ our Lord. **Amen.**

Living Liturgy

Patron of the Universal Church: In his 2020 apostolic letter celebrating the 150th anniversary of the proclamation of St. Joseph as patron of the universal church, *Patris Corde*, Pope Francis describes the important attributes of a father and fatherhood through the faithfulness of St. Joseph. A father is beloved, tender, loving, obedient, accepting, creatively courageous, an honest worker, and a "father in the shadows" in terms of finding happiness in self-gift. Pope Francis through this letter reminds us that the lives of the saints are concrete proof that it is possible to put the gospel into practice.

FOR REFLECTION

• If you are a parent, what might you learn from the model of Joseph's extravagant generosity toward his own family?

• Famously, Joseph does not speak throughout the gospels; we have no record of his words. What is one thing you imagine he would have said repeatedly to Jesus?

• Joseph takes on a protective role for Jesus and Mary. Where could you use his protective intercession in your life?

Homily Points

• Scripture is relatively quiet about the details of St. Joseph's life. We come to know the most about the father of the holy family through his dreams. Joseph trusted the movements of the Holy Spirit even when he was asleep. It can be easy to write off dreams as silly or insignificant. However, the stories of Joseph and other figures in Scripture like Samuel and Jacob show that dreams can be one space through which God calls us.

• Scripture does tell us that Joseph was a carpenter. He worked with his hands to create, fix, and build. Joseph reminds us of the great value of manual labor. It is not only practical, providing tables on which to eat and the like, but such labor is also a forum for self-expression. May we take a moment today to notice the items in our homes crafted by the hands of carpenters.

GOSPEL ACCLAMATION
John 1:14ab

The Word of God became flesh and made his
dwelling among us;
and we saw his glory.

Gospel

Luke 1:26-38; L545

The angel Gabriel was sent
from God
to a town of Galilee called
Nazareth,
to a virgin betrothed to a
man named Joseph,
of the house of David,
and the virgin's name was
Mary.
And coming to her, he said,
"Hail, full of grace! The
Lord is with you."
But she was greatly troubled
at what was said
and pondered what sort of
greeting this might be.
Then the angel said to her,
"Do not be afraid, Mary,
for you have found favor
with God.
Behold, you will conceive in your womb
and bear a son,
and you shall name him Jesus.
He will be great and will be called Son
of the Most High,
and the Lord God will give him the
throne of David his father,
and he will rule over the house of
Jacob forever,
and of his Kingdom there will be no
end."
But Mary said to the angel,
"How can this be,
since I have no relations with a
man?"
And the angel said to her in reply,
"The Holy Spirit will come upon you,
and the power of the Most High will
overshadow you.

Continued in Appendix A, p. 275.

See Appendix A, p. 275, for the other readings.

Reflecting on the Gospel

Many people know the name Rosa Parks and remember her as the mother of the Montgomery Bus Boycott. Fewer people know about Claudette Colvin, who in March 1955, nine months before Rosa Parks, was forcibly removed from a city bus and arrested for refusing to give up her seat for a young White woman.

At fifteen years old, Colvin was the first person to be arrested for defying Montgomery's policy of segregation on public transportation. She was taken to an adult jail rather than a juvenile detention center and waited three hours for her mother and pastor to post her bail. For many nights thereafter, her neighbors and family kept watch over the Colvins' home fearing violent retaliation from the Ku Klux Klan. Claudette Colvin is part of a long legacy of Black women willing to put their bodies on the line in the name of justice and dignity.

As we listen to the gospel story of Mary's visit from the angel Gabriel, we can see parallels between what was asked of Mary in ancient Israel and what was asked of Claudette Colvin in 1955 in Alabama. After being called "full of grace" and being told that she had found favor with God, Mary is told that God has a plan to bring "the Son of the Most High" into the world to rule over the house of Jacob forever. Mary, in her youth and through the power of her womanhood, is invited to help bring forth a new era of possibility for humankind. In a similar way, Colvin responded when the opportunity to take a stand presented itself.

There are several reasons why Claudette Colvin was a lesser-known figure in the history of the civil rights movement. Some of it had to do with the fact that she did not meet certain respectability standards of the time. She was young and not as established in the community. With her darker complexion and natural hair, she did not meet Eurocentric standards of beauty. Perhaps most significantly, soon after her encounter on the bus, she became pregnant. The local NAACP chapter feared that the teenage mother would cause controversy and distract from the cause of desegregation. Even though she would not become an icon in this chapter of the civil rights movement, Colvin's action was an initial spark that ignited many others. After Rosa Parks took similar actions in December 1955, the Montgomery Bus Boycott began in earnest and 40,000 African Americans boycotted the system for over a year before the laws upholding segregation were struck down by the US Supreme Court.

Today, we celebrate Mary's *fiat* and the idea of God inviting lowly figures to be collaborators in the divine plan. This solemnity also challenges us to acknowledge the women and men proclaiming the good news in our present world and disrupt the patterns of thinking that cause us to overlook their prophetic messages. Collaborating with God is a spiritual labor as well as a physical one. Let us give thanks for all the figures who came before us and gave of themselves—body and spirit—to help bring about God's kingdom. May we show the bravery of Mary and of Claudette the next time we are invited to participate in God's great work.

Preparing to Proclaim

Key words and phrases: "Do not be afraid, Mary."

To the point: This feast day, exactly nine months before our celebration of Jesus's birth, is when we celebrate Mary's great "fiat" that enabled salvation history as we know it to unfold. She was being asked not just for nine months of her life but for the rest of her life. Becoming a mother turns a woman's entire life and identify completely inside out, permanently. We know she was afraid; the angel had to tell her not to be. And yet she says "yes," offering up everything she has and everything she is to the God she knows will not leave her.

Model Penitential Act

Presider: Mary said a brave "yes" to God's great ask of her: to bear God's son. For the times we have not done what God asks of us, let us ask for forgiveness . . . *[pause]*

Lord Jesus, you are the Son of God: Lord, have mercy.

Christ Jesus, you are the Son of Mary: Christ, have mercy.

Lord Jesus, your kingdom will rule forever: Lord, have mercy.

Model Universal Prayer (Prayer of the Faithful)

Presider: The angel assured Mary that the Lord was with her. The Lord is with us, too. Through the intercession of Mary, we bring our prayers and petitions before God.

Response: Lord, hear our prayer.

Call forth the gifts of lay and religious women within the church . . .

Incline the ears of elected officials to listen to the call of God and the needs of the marginalized . . .

Give hope to couples who are struggling with infertility and all people longing to be parents . . .

Inspire each of us gathered here to trust that in God, all things are possible . . .

Presider: Gracious God, you sent your beloved Son into the world to dwell with creation. Receive our prayers that in communion with the Blessed Virgin Mary we might listen ever more closely to God's callings in our lives and use our gifts for the betterment of the world. We ask this through Christ our Lord. **Amen.**

Living Liturgy

Celebrating Vocation: God begins conversation with Mary through the angel Gabriel. God speaks to us—as with Mary—in often unexpected ways. How surprised are we when we receive an unexpected greeting card, find a text message from an old friend, or catch a glimpse of a rainbow? We experience something outside of ourselves that is God's presence. We come into relationship with God when we answer God, when we respond. This Annunciation, we celebrate the richness of that conversation with God and our vocation as liturgical ministers. How and when did and do you answer God's call into ministry?

FOR REFLECTION

• How do you hear God's call in your life? Where have you learned to hear it?

• How have you said "yes" to God? Where do you still struggle to do so?

• How might Mary be a model of courage for you?

Homily Points

• Through the angel Gabriel, God asks Mary for her consent to conceive and bear God's son. Mary actively says "yes" before anything is done to her body. The story of the Annunciation highlights the importance of consent in such deeply intimate encounters. May it be a model for all of us.

• As we rejoice with Mary at the conception of her son, let us be mindful today of the many couples in our community who are struggling to conceive. Infertility issues are painfully common, yet often remain hidden. May all couples know of God's great love.

✝ SPIRITUALITY

GOSPEL ACCLAMATION
John 11:25a, 26

I am the resurrection and the life, says the Lord;
whoever believes in me, even if he dies, will
never die.

Gospel
John 11:1-45; L34A

Now a man was ill, Lazarus from
    Bethany,
    the village of Mary and her sister
        Martha.
Mary was the one who had anointed
        the Lord with perfumed oil
    and dried his feet with her hair;
    it was her brother Lazarus who
        was ill.
So the sisters sent word to Jesus
        saying,
    "Master, the one you love is ill."
When Jesus heard this he said,
    "This illness is not to end in
        death,
    but is for the glory of God,
    that the Son of God may be
        glorified through it."
Now Jesus loved Martha and her sister
        and Lazarus.
So when he heard that he was ill,
    he remained for two days in the place
        where he was.
Then after this he said to his disciples,
    "Let us go back to Judea."
The disciples said to him,
    "Rabbi, the Jews were just trying to
        stone you,
    and you want to go back there?"
Jesus answered,
    "Are there not twelve hours in a day?
If one walks during the day, he does
        not stumble,
    because he sees the light of this
        world.

Continued in Appendix A, p. 276, or
John 11:3-7, 17, 20-27, 33b-45 *in Appendix A,*
p. 277.

Reflecting on the Gospel

Today's remarkable gospel story proclaims that no one is so far gone into death that Jesus cannot call him or her back to life, for he *is* the resurrection and the life, which is more than just physical life, in the present as well as on the other side of death. Martha and Mary are models for our journey—never a direct, straight-line event—to profound faith. Martha takes the initiative in welcoming Jesus and professes a typical Jewish faith (held by the Pharisee party) in the resurrection "on the last day," the day of judgment and resurrection at the end of time. But in John's Gospel, it is important that faith is not just focused on a distant event but is a death-defying affirmation of the "now" reality of God's presence and power in Jesus. That reality calls us to come forth trustingly into life from the narrow confines of our daily anxieties, from the fears of our mortality, and from what seems to wither and die in us from day to day. So to Martha, Jesus proclaims, "I am the resurrection and the life," and Martha professes her faith in him as the Messiah, the Son of God. Mary and the other mourners arrive at the scene and Mary, like her sister, makes straight for Jesus. Then, together, they move toward the tomb of Lazarus. There Jesus weeps—not only tears of friendship for his friend, but also tears of anger at the last enemy, death, which he has been sent to destroy.

We can surely feel sympathy for Martha who, having just professed her faith in Jesus, now protests at his command to take away the stone because of her expectation of the stench of four-day death. As it does for Peter (see Matt 16:16), and for ourselves, faith can waver when what seems to be "reality" intrudes with its apparent unpleasant consequences for our lives. Jesus's prayer to his Father and his loud cry—"Lazarus, come out!"—tear open both heaven and earth to witness to the truth that, for the glory of God, Jesus will bring us out of death. Lazarus emerges, his face and body still wrapped in his burial cloths, and Jesus commands the watchers, "Untie him and let him go." Soon Jesus himself will be a tomb-dweller for three days, but he will leave his burial cloths in the tomb, will come forth unaided and unveiled by human help as the risen and sent One who goes into the presence of his Father.

Although called forth to life by Jesus in our baptism, we, like Lazarus, need others to help us go free, and during Lent this command to untie, or unbind, one another has a special urgency. The last scrutiny is celebrated today, and with the elect, the parish community prays for both their unbinding from sin as they are called to the new life of baptism in two weeks' time, and for ourselves, the already baptized, who are still bound in our sinfulness. For all of us, Jesus is our hope of coming forth into the new life of his Easter mysteries.

Preparing to Proclaim

Key words and phrases: "Yes, Lord. I have come to believe that you are the Christ, the Son of God."

To the point: Mary and Martha reverse roles here. Where Mary once sat at the feet of Jesus, she now sits at home in her grief. Martha, however, the one who was too busy to listen, comes to him as interlocutor, intelligently and faithfully interacting with him. She does not see the whole picture, though, for Jesus is still in the process of revealing all that his life means for the world. Lazarus here becomes a sort of firstfruits, one restored to life before the full restoration occurs. Wonderful as this miracle is, it is a jarring one; this simply does not happen. People who have been dead for four days do not come back to life. And we know nothing of Lazarus's experience here. Whatever his experience was of death, it must have been unsettling to be jolted back to life. Jesus is here to bring life, yes, but he brings it in ways that disrupt the order of things to which we have grown accustomed.

Psalmist Preparation

We begin to see in this gospel the "fullness of redemption" promised in the psalm. Jesus's work of healing the sick and blind has all been a prelude to this, the restoration of life even to those who are dead. And so, as the psalm affirms, we trust in the Lord, waiting to experience the fullness of life he promises. As you prepare this psalm, think about ways you are still waiting for God to work in your life. Bring something specific to your proclamation of the psalm and make it an earnest prayer of trust.

Making Connections

Between the readings: In the first reading, God reveals through Ezekiel that death does not have the final say. Despite death's appearance of permanence, God's power is greater still, and what God wants for us is life. The second reading affirms that while our bodies still die, this is no longer the end it once was. Christ's Spirit living in us allows us to share in his triumph over death.

To experience: When Jesus calls us to fuller life in him, it is not always comfortable or easy. There are often demands and sacrifices we would not have expected and certainly would not have chosen for ourselves. But while Lazarus stood alone as the first called forth from the tomb, we are never left alone with our challenges; it is Christ's own life that we share, and he accompanies us always.

Homily Points

• The raising of Lazarus surfaces difficult questions about life and death. In their grief, Martha and Mary speak bluntly to Jesus: "Lord, if you had been here, my brother would not have died." They know Jesus to be the Son of God. They know his track record of healing the sick. Martha and Mary are dear friends of Jesus. How could he not save their beloved Lazarus? The sisters cry out, and Jesus weeps with them. Moved with compassion, Jesus commands the dead man Lazarus to come out of the cave—and behold, he does.

• Some of us may hear this story and rejoice. Lazarus receives a second chance at life! Others of us may feel jealous of Mary and Martha for the extra time they got with their brother. Such a miraculous event begs big questions: Why does Jesus not raise all our loved ones to new life on this earth immediately after their deaths? Why does suffering exist if our Lord is all-powerful? What might our resurrections look like? These questions have no easy answers, yet they point us to some of the most profound truths of the Christian faith.

• Our God is utterly mysterious. God's timing is beyond all human comprehension. There is so much about God and God's ways that we cannot know yet. But we can choose to believe Christ's proclamation: "I am the resurrection and the life . . . everyone who lives and believes in me will never die." We can grieve the earthly death of loved ones and be confident that they are now enjoying new life with Christ. We can choose to live each day with trust in Christ's abiding love for all of creation.

Model Penitential Act

Presider: Today we hear the psalmist cry out: "With the Lord there is mercy and fullness of redemption." Trusting in the Lord's eagerness to forgive, let us call to mind our sins . . . *[pause]*

   Confiteor: I confess . . .

Model Universal Prayer (Prayer of the Faithful)

Presider: As the season of Lent nears its conclusion and we look ahead to Holy Week, let us place our prayers and petitions before our Lord who suffered, died, and rose to new life.

Response: Lord, hear our prayer.

Open the hearts of the baptized to be agents of healing for our world . . .

Advance the healing work of doctors, nurses, therapists, and all medical personnel . . .

Make your loving presence known to all those who face serious illness . . .

Comfort those among us who grieve the death of a loved one . . .

Presider: God of life, your Son raised Lazarus from the dead so that all might come to know your saving power. Hear our prayers that we, along with all peoples of the world, might enjoy the fullness of redemption. We ask this through Christ our Lord. **Amen.**

Liturgy and Music

Sung Responses: Many parishes have adopted the practice of singing a short refrain or musical phrase interspersed throughout the lengthy Cycle A readings of the third, fourth, and fifth Sundays of Lent, and during the passion readings of Palm Sunday and Good Friday. While the liturgical documents do not necessarily mention this inclusion to the proclamation of the gospel, does it mean that it is not permitted? The answer is both yes and no.

   The lack of explicit permission or the mention of this practice in the liturgical rubrics and laws does not necessarily mean that it is prohibited. On the other hand, if the rubrics don't forbid the practice, it doesn't mean that it is allowed. We have learned that liturgical law, rubrics, and ritual books are living documents. These liturgical decisions about occasional sung responses during the gospel reading ought to be discussed openly at liturgy team meetings. The members of this worship should thoughtfully discern this matter and make a decision that will continue to bring the people of God together.

COLLECT

Let us pray.

Pause for silent prayer

By your help, we beseech you, Lord our God,
may we walk eagerly in that same charity
with which, out of love for the world,
your Son handed himself over to death.
Through our Lord Jesus Christ, your Son,
who lives and reigns with you in the unity
   of the Holy Spirit,
God, for ever and ever. **Amen.**

FIRST READING

Ezek 37:12-14

Thus says the Lord GOD:
   O my people, I will open your graves
   and have you rise from them,
   and bring you back to the land of Israel.
Then you shall know that I am the LORD,
   when I open your graves and have you
      rise from them,
   O my people!
I will put my spirit in you that you may
   live,
   and I will settle you upon your land;
   thus you shall know that I am the LORD.
I have promised, and I will do it, says the
   LORD.

RESPONSORIAL PSALM
Ps 130:1-2, 3-4, 5-6, 7-8

R̗. (7) With the Lord there is mercy and
fullness of redemption.

Out of the depths I cry to you, O LORD;
   LORD, hear my voice!
Let your ears be attentive
   to my voice in supplication.

R̗. With the Lord there is mercy and
fullness of redemption.

If you, O LORD, mark iniquities,
   LORD, who can stand?
But with you is forgiveness,
   that you may be revered.

R̗. With the Lord there is mercy and
fullness of redemption.

I trust in the LORD;
   my soul trusts in his word.
More than sentinels wait for the dawn,
   let Israel wait for the LORD.

R̗. With the Lord there is mercy and
fullness of redemption.

For with the LORD is kindness
   and with him is plenteous redemption;
and he will redeem Israel
   from all their iniquities.

R̗. With the Lord there is mercy and
fullness of redemption.

SECOND READING
Rom 8:8-11

Brothers and sisters:
Those who are in the flesh cannot please
   God.
But you are not in the flesh;
   on the contrary, you are in the spirit,
   if only the Spirit of God dwells in you.
Whoever does not have the Spirit of Christ
   does not belong to him.
But if Christ is in you,
   although the body is dead because of
      sin,
   the spirit is alive because of
      righteousness.
If the Spirit of the One who raised Jesus
   from the dead dwells in you,
   the One who raised Christ from the dead
   will give life to your mortal bodies also,
   through his Spirit dwelling in you.

Living Liturgy

Postures of Prayer: At some parishes that I've ministered at the presider would usually invite the whole assembly to be seated during the lengthy Cycle A readings that we hear today and over the past two weeks. In the guide *Praying with Body, Mind, and Voice*, the USCCB says that our common postures and gestures are both symbol of unity of the gathered faithful as well as a means of fostering unity. When we stand, kneel, sit, bow, and sign ourselves in common action, we give unambiguous witness that we are indeed the Body of Christ, united in body, mind, and voice.

At liturgy, standing is seen as a sign of respect and honor, an acknowledgment of the wonderful gift of baptism in which we have been given a share in the life of God, and a stance of those who have risen with Christ taken not in pride but with humble gratitude. Sitting is the posture of listening and meditation. All who are in this seated position during Mass should attempt to assume a posture that is attentive rather than merely taking a position of rest. Should we then sit or stand during the proclamation of these lengthy Cycle A readings?

At play are two competing concerns: (1) the care for those who are unable to stand for a very long time and (2) giving honor and reverence to the presence of Christ in the gospel. The pastoral concern for the ones who are unable to stand for long periods ought to be directed specifically to the group rather than to the entire assembly. This encourages the posture of standing for the gospel reading in prayer and praise practiced by the more able-bodied ones. However, if the decision is for a communal seated position, then perhaps a call for active listening be made during the invitation to be seated. Whatever the posture, we engage our bodies in prayer and we pray with our entire person.

PROMPTS FOR FAITH-SHARING

• How have you experienced Jesus's life-giving power? Is it easy or challenging to live out the demands of life with him?

• How has inviting God into your life upended your expectations?

• Does your life of faith lead to rest or to further restlessness? Knowing that God can work through either, how do you choose to respond?

✝ SPIRITUALITY

GOSPEL ACCLAMATION
Phil 2:8-9

Christ became obedient to the point of death,
even death on a cross.
Because of this, God greatly exalted him
and bestowed on him the name which is above
every name.

Gospel at the procession with palms

Matt 21:1-11; L37A

When Jesus and the disciples drew
near Jerusalem
and came to Bethphage on the Mount
of Olives,
Jesus sent two disciples, saying to
them,
"Go into the village opposite you,
and immediately you will find an ass
tethered,
and a colt with her.
Untie them and bring them here to me.
And if anyone should say anything to
you, reply,
'The master has need of them.'
Then he will send them at once."
This happened so that what had been
spoken through the prophet
might be fulfilled:
Say to daughter Zion,
"Behold, your king comes to you,
meek and riding on an ass,
and on a colt, the foal of a beast
of burden."
The disciples went and did as Jesus
had ordered them.
They brought the ass and the colt and
laid their cloaks over them,
and he sat upon them.
The very large crowd spread their
cloaks on the road,
while others cut branches from the
trees
and strewed them on the road.

Continued in Appendix A, p. 278.

Gospel at Mass   Matt 26:14–27:66; L38A
or Matt 27:11-54 *in Appendix A, pp. 278–280.*

Reflecting on the Gospel

The passion narrative that we proclaim today is a story of many people who, as Paul wrote to the Romans, do not do what they want, but do the very thing they hate and find it hard to believe that they could act this way (see Rom 7:15). Sinfulness is doing what, in our personal depths, we know is evil, because of fear, greed, social pressure, lust for power, or disregard for human life. In the Garden

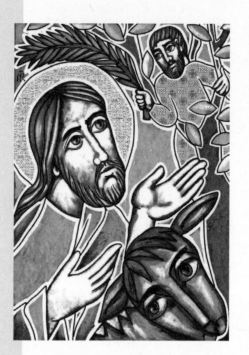

of Gethsemane, Peter the rock crumbles into a soft sand-drift of sleep, and the dozing Zebedee brothers (see Matt 20:20-23) no longer seem to care whether they are at the right-hand or the left-hand places of the man who lies in agony among the olive trees. The traitor's kiss smacks them from their sleep, and the violence spawns a feeble swordplay until the words of Jesus, even in the context of such violence, command peace. Then those who had once left everything to follow Jesus (see Matt 4:22) now leave everything to run away from him.

Peter crawls away to crouch like a spider in the dark corner of the high priest Caiaphas's courtyard. While Jesus is on trial inside, he is spinning his web of lies outside. Impetuous speech has often been Peter's downfall; tragically, tonight it is more deliberate, trapping him three times in what he does not want to do but does, choosing self-protection over faithfulness to his Master. And the terrible anomaly of this is symbolized by the cockcrow that does not herald dawn but deepest night in Peter's soul. But Matthew tells us that Peter will be saved, as we will be, by the remembrance of Jesus's words and by our tears over our betrayals of Jesus.

Jesus is handed over to Pilate, the Roman governor, who is unnerved by Jesus's silence. Pilate would much prefer this Jew to be as slippery as the blood that he suspects he will cause to be shed; he wishes that Jesus would wriggle out of his conscience and this trial. Instead, it is Barabbas that the weak Pilate allows to slip out free. Pilate might not want to hand Jesus over, but again here is someone who compromises himself because of social pressure from the crowd and the fear of losing favor with Caesar. Only Pilate's wife honestly intervenes to try to save Jesus. Just as Matthew's infancy narrative had dreamers like Joseph and the magi, so here is another dreamer. But a woman's dreams and witness are unacceptable. Pilate washes his hands of the whole dirty matter. Compromise, dismissal of the "dreams" of others, peer pressure, and fear of losing upward social mobility: these can also send our truth as followers of Jesus gurgling down the drain.

In this story, there is so much here to reflect on and ask ourselves about: friendship, betrayal, forgiveness, our own small and large violences, our too easy and too frequent excuses for our failures in Christian discipleship. And so we, too, wait and watch through this Holy Week.

Preparing to Proclaim

Key words and phrases: "Truly, this was the Son of God!"

To the point: The paired gospels of this Sunday give us the whole narrative arc of Holy Week. The triumph of Jesus's entrance into Jerusalem contrasts painfully with the crowds that turn on him in the passion narrative. One moment, though, brings us back to the truth; the centurion, a most unexpected source, affirms that this man truly was the Son of God. This is not the only time the passion story subverts expectations. The women epitomize bravery, staying near the grisly scene of the cross while the disciples who most staunchly averred their bravery are the first to run away. Religious leaders insist on Jesus's death while the occupying government tries to find ways to release him. Jesus's death does not happen quietly but affects the earth. We do not hear the end of the story here, the resurrection to which we so look forward, but we see very clearly that God is doing something new.

Psalmist Preparation

This psalm is heart wrenching but relatable. All of us, at some moment in our lives of faith, will feel that we have been abandoned by God. The demands of faith do not always reward us with warm feelings that reassure us of God's presence and approval. But at the end of this psalm the writer issues a reminder: even without those pleasant feelings, we can still praise the God who deserves our trust even when all seems lost. This is the God who brings life out of death itself. As you prepare this psalm, think of a time you have felt abandoned by God. Ask God to show you how God was present in that time.

Making Connections

Between the readings: The first reading provides the first moment of stark contrast between the procession's triumphant tones and the gravity of the passion. The glory of Jesus's entrance into Jerusalem was not for its own sake. The beautiful hymn of the second reading captures this paradox in all its fullness: Jesus shares God's being by rights, but by choice humbles himself to death. It is this humility that allows his even greater exaltation and the worship we now bring to the one who gives us life.

To experience: Crucifixes are a common sight for us as Catholics, so common that we can fail to let them call to mind this story in its entirety. On the surface this looks like a gory, tragic story, but we know that it is, more truly, the story of the greatest love the world has ever known. The crucifix also points beyond itself; it is not the end of the story. We know that the resurrection is coming, and we trust in God's ability to make life ever new even as we share in the sorrow of the passion.

Homily Points

• Jesus's divinity is always a reality—and, the readings of Holy Week draw our attention to Jesus's humanity in particular ways. Over the coming days, the church invites us to accompany our brother Jesus on his journey to Jerusalem. The liturgies of Holy Week offer chances to feel with Jesus and his disciples—the palm branches waving in the streets, the water that washes over our feet, the bread and wine shared in memory of Christ, the wood of the cross. We can also feel the difficult emotions that may have welled within Jesus during his final days—sadness over saying goodbye to his beloved disciples, loneliness from a friend's betrayal, anguish over his impending death. These core elements of Holy Week, both the tangible objects and the emotions, are central to human life. Our God knows them intimately.

• As St. Paul writes, Jesus came in human likeness. He emptied himself and took on the form of a slave. The Son of God knows what it is like to feel sad and hurt, to say hard goodbyes, and to suffer injustices. Our Savior lived the hard realities of humanity just like us. He gifts his very self to humankind. On the night he was betrayed, Jesus took the bread and said, "Take and eat; this is my body." Then he took the cup of wine, the blood of the covenant, poured out for the forgiveness of sins.

• As we celebrate the Eucharist today, let us give thanks for Jesus and his great gift of self. Let us each consider how we might journey with Jesus during this holiest of weeks.

Model Penitential Act

Presider: To mark our entrance into the most sacred week of the liturgical year, let us pause to ask God for mercy and healing from our sins . . . *[pause]*

Confiteor: I confess . . .

Model Universal Prayer (Prayer of the Faithful)

Presider: Jesus cries out to God in his time of need. With trust that God listens to our prayers, let us bring our needs before the Lord.

Response: Lord, hear our prayer.

Strengthen the wills of the baptized to accompany those in times of suffering . . .

Thwart the plans of those who seek to harm others this day . . .

Grant peace to people who are in their final days of life . . .

Unite all of us gathered here in a spirit of prayer, fasting, and almsgiving as we approach the Easter Triduum . . .

Presider: God of the suffering, Jesus Christ willingly gave himself up to death on the cross so that our sins might be forgiven. Receive our prayers that during this Holy Week we might draw ever closer to the faith of the cross and the hope of resurrection. We ask this through Christ our Lord. **Amen.**

Liturgy and Music

Praying the Stations of the Cross: Many of us are familiar with the traditional fourteen Stations of the Cross displayed in every modern Catholic church. During these weeks of Lent, some have found grace and deep meaning in praying this devotion. This devotional practice of following Jesus's steps on the way to the cross has been promoted by the Franciscans since the fourteenth century. Some place its roots in an ancient tradition that the Blessed Virgin Mary visited daily the sites of Jesus's suffering death and resurrection. Regardless of how this devotion developed, there are many different ways to pray the Stations.

We must remain open to various ways of praying the Stations of the Cross. As you prepare this prayer, consider creative ways to incorporate music with the devotion. Perhaps a slideshow presentation of images of current events in the nation or around world that correspond to each Station of the Cross could be another way of deepening reflection and prayer along the Way.

COLLECT

Let us pray.

Pause for silent prayer

Almighty ever-living God,
who as an example of humility for the
    human race to follow
caused our Savior to take flesh and submit
    to the Cross,
graciously grant that we may heed his
    lesson of patient suffering
and so merit a share in his Resurrection.
Who lives and reigns with you in the unity
    of the Holy Spirit,
God, for ever and ever. **Amen.**

FIRST READING

Isa 50:4-7

The Lord God has given me
    a well-trained tongue,
that I might know how to speak to the
    weary
    a word that will rouse them.
Morning after morning
    he opens my ear that I may hear;
and I have not rebelled,
    have not turned back.
I gave my back to those who beat me,
    my cheeks to those who plucked my
      beard;
my face I did not shield
    from buffets and spitting.

The Lord God is my help,
    therefore I am not disgraced;
I have set my face like flint,
    knowing that I shall not be put to
      shame.

RESPONSORIAL PSALM

Ps 22:8-9, 17-18, 19-20, 23-24

R̸. (2a) My God, my God, why have you
    abandoned me?

All who see me scoff at me;
    they mock me with parted lips, they
      wag their heads:
"He relied on the Lord; let him deliver him,
    let him rescue him, if he loves him."

R̸. My God, my God, why have you
    abandoned me?

Indeed, many dogs surround me,
a pack of evildoers closes in upon me;
they have pierced my hands and my feet;
I can count all my bones.

R℣. My God, my God, why have you
abandoned me?

They divide my garments among them,
and for my vesture they cast lots.
But you, O Lᴏʀᴅ, be not far from me;
O my help, hasten to aid me.

R℣. My God, my God, why have you
abandoned me?

I will proclaim your name to my brethren;
in the midst of the assembly I will
praise you:
"You who fear the Lᴏʀᴅ, praise him;
all you descendants of Jacob, give glory
to him;
revere him, all you descendants of
Israel!"

R℣. My God, my God, why have you
abandoned me?

SECOND READING
Phil 2:6-11

Christ Jesus, though he was in the form
of God,
did not regard equality with God
something to be grasped.
Rather, he emptied himself,
taking the form of a slave,
coming in human likeness;
and found human in appearance,
he humbled himself,
becoming obedient to the point of
death,
even death on a cross.
Because of this, God greatly exalted him
and bestowed on him the name
which is above every name,
that at the name of Jesus
every knee should bend,
of those in heaven and on earth and
under the earth,
and every tongue confess that
Jesus Christ is Lord,
to the glory of God the Father.

Living Liturgy

Highs and Lows: There is no Sunday in the liturgical year quite like Palm Sunday in terms of its dramatic quality. The liturgy today captures contrasts of highs and lows. It begins in triumph as Jesus enters Jerusalem and quickly shifts into the commemoration of the Lord's passion. The entrance into the holy city also marks the entrance into the paschal mystery of his suffering, death, and resurrection. The challenge for our liturgy today and throughout Holy Week is to find a balance between triumph and passion, always honoring the community's diverse character.

We remember that Jesus was an innocent victim of capital punishment. According to the Death Penalty Information Center, as of July 2021, the death penalty is authorized by twenty-seven states and the federal government and prohibited in twenty-three states and the District of Columbia. Similarly, a July 2021 Pew Research Center Survey reports that the views of the death penalty differ by religious affiliation. Around two-thirds of Protestants in the United States favor capital punishment, though support is much higher among White evangelical Protestants and White non-evangelical Protestants than it is among Black Protestants. Around six-in-ten Catholics also support capital punishment, a figure that includes 61% of Latinx Catholics and 56% of White Catholics. Opposition to the death penalty also varies among the religiously unaffiliated. Around two-thirds of atheists oppose it, as do more than half of agnostics. Among those who say their religion is "nothing in particular," 63% support capital punishment. Atheists oppose the death penalty about as strongly as Protestants favor it. As of September 1, 2021, 1,534 prisoners have been executed in the US since 1976.

On October 3, 2020, Pope Francis issued an encyclical titled *Fratelli Tutti*, which ratified the position of the Catholic Church against the death penalty and called upon all Catholics to advocate for the abolition of the death penalty worldwide, respecting the dignity of every human.

PROMPTS FOR FAITH-SHARING

• With which character of the passion story do you most identify? Why?

• How can you imitate the humility of Jesus, who chose to empty himself out of love?

• How have you seen God transform sorrow into joy? Where would you like God to do so?

EASTER TRIDUUM

GOSPEL ACCLAMATION
John 13:34

I give you a new commandment, says the Lord:
love one another as I have loved you.

Gospel   John 13:1-15; L39ABC

Before the feast of Passover, Jesus knew
    that his hour had come
    to pass from this world to the
        Father.
He loved his own in the world and
    he loved them to the end.
The devil had already induced
    Judas, son of Simon the
    Iscariot, to hand him over.
So, during supper,
    fully aware that the Father had
        put everything into his
        power
    and that he had come from God
        and was returning to God,
    he rose from supper and took off
        his outer garments.
He took a towel and tied it around
    his waist.
Then he poured water into a basin
    and began to wash the disciples'
        feet
    and dry them with the towel
        around his waist.
He came to Simon Peter, who said to him,
    "Master, are you going to wash my
        feet?"
Jesus answered and said to him,
    "What I am doing, you do not
        understand now,
    but you will understand later."
Peter said to him, "You will never wash
    my feet."
Jesus answered him,
    "Unless I wash you, you will have no
        inheritance with me."
Simon Peter said to him,
    "Master, then not only my feet, but my
        hands and head as well."
Jesus said to him,
    "Whoever has bathed has no need
        except to have his feet washed,
    for he is clean all over;
    so you are clean, but not all."

Continued in Appendix A, p. 281.
See Appendix A, p. 281, for the other readings.

Reflecting on the Gospel

Tonight we do not hear any of the Synoptic Gospels recounting the institution of the Eucharist. The institution tradition is left to Paul in the second reading from his First Letter to the Corinthians. By proclaiming John's Last Supper narrative, the Lectionary links this celebration with the Johannine passion that is read on Good Friday and with the Sunday gospels of the Easter season, most of which are from John.

Jesus celebrates this last meal with his friends, and with a friend-become-enemy. Tonight he clothes himself with a towel; tomorrow he will be clothed as a fool and then stripped naked. The "hour" has come: the hour of Jesus's love for his own to the very end, the hour when the Father has given all things into his hands. John tells us what these "things" are tonight: a towel, a bowl of water, and the feet of his disciples—such ordinary, humble, human realities with which Jesus will show the depths of his love. Tomorrow, the salvation of the world will be put into his hands that are nailed to the wood. And on the third day, Jesus will be clothed in the glory of his risen life.

Tonight Jesus kneels on the floor to wash the feet of his disciples, and we might wonder why this gospel reading is chosen on the night when we remember the institution of the Eucharist. Perhaps, like John's community at the end of the first century, we are used to celebrating Eucharist, but familiarity may have eroded its meaning for us. John reminds us by the washing of the feet, this "parable in action," that Jesus is Servant, one who is ready to do the dirty jobs, to be at the bottom of the social heap, to take the last place along with all those whom we shove down: the abused, the marginalized, the refugees, the unemployed, those with physical and psychological disabilities. Bearing down on them are those at the top of the pyramid: the powerful, the rich, the successful.

Peter finds Jesus as Servant hard to accept. He surely suspects that if Jesus is like this, so must his disciples be—and he panics; he objects.

Jesus returns to the table as Lord and Teacher to help his disciples to understand that "as I have done for you, you should also do." Some commentators have called these words the Johannine words of institution, for the Eucharist is about sharing the love and life of Jesus who humbled himself, even to death on a cross. In the vulnerability of bread eaten and wine drunk, Jesus asks us to follow his example: to get down, metaphorically, and serve one another, despite the dust and smell and misunderstandings; to be hospitable to our sisters and brothers and in communion with them; to be vulnerable in a society of loving service offered and received when so often we have been encouraged to value self-reliance autonomy, getting to the top. Then we, too, will have a share in the hospitality of the kingdom.

Preparing to Proclaim

Key words and phrases: "I have given you a model to follow, / so that as I have done for you, you should also do."

To the point: On this day when we so wholeheartedly celebrate the institution of the Eucharist, the gospel does not tell that story (although we do hear it in the second reading). It serves as a reminder that our eucharistic lives do not end in the celebration of the Mass; they rather begin there. We are sent out, dismissed to do the work that Jesus models here. Our communion is consummated by acts of service and love.

Model Penitential Act

Presider: In today's gospel, Jesus calls his disciples to follow his model of servant leadership and love. As we prepare to celebrate the Eucharist, let us ask for forgiveness for the times we have failed to love as Christ . . . *[pause]*

Lord Jesus, you give us your body, the bread of life: Lord, have mercy.

Christ Jesus, you give us your blood, the cup of salvation: Christ, have mercy.

Lord Jesus, you will come again in glory: Lord, have mercy.

Model Universal Prayer (Prayer of the Faithful)

Presider: Trusting in Christ's great love for us, let us lay at the feet of Jesus the prayers and petitions of our community.

Response: Lord, hear our prayer.

Draw the church ever closer to the heart of Christ during these sacred Triduum days . . .

Grow the spirit of love within all those who serve their families or communities . . .

Transform the hearts of those who seek to betray or harm another person this night . . .

Sustain the energy of liturgists, musicians, lay ministers, ordained ministers, and all others who lead worship . . .

Presider: Loving God, you came into this world to save us and model for us the way of everlasting life. Receive our prayers this night. Strengthen us so that we might act ever more graciously in remembrance of you. We ask this through Christ our Lord. **Amen.**

Living Liturgy

Entering the Three Days: The Universal Norms on the Liturgical Year and the Calendar tells us that "[t]he Paschal Triduum of the Passion and Resurrection of the Lord begins with the evening Mass of the Lord's Supper, has its center in the Easter Vigil, and closes with Vespers (Evening Prayer) of the Sunday of the Resurrection" (19). Tonight's liturgy is entrance into these three days. As we commemorate these sacred days we remember the essential element of Christian identity—service. We imitate Jesus in service to others. The *Mandatum* holds many different meanings. What does it mean in your community and your ministry?

FOR REFLECTION

• How and from whom have you received the humble service that Jesus models in this gospel?

• Where might you be called to become a servant leader?

• How does your participation in liturgy shape you for acts of service, hospitality, and justice?

Homily Points

• The Triduum call can be summed up in one word: love. To live in remembrance of Jesus is to love with our whole bodies. The Son of God models the messy movements of love during the Last Supper when he stoops to scrub the feet of his disciples.

• As we journey through the Triduum, we will see the stakes of Christ's love rise higher and higher. To love in the face of death, to love in the hope of new life—indeed, the love of Christ knows no bounds. Neither should our love. Jesus shows us the way during these most sacred days. Nourished at his table, may we embody Christ's love to the ends of the earth.

GOSPEL ACCLAMATION
Phil 2:8-9

Christ became obedient to the point of death,
even death on a cross.
Because of this, God greatly exalted him
and bestowed on him the name which is above
    every other name.

Gospel   John 18:1–19:42; L40ABC

Jesus went out with his disciples across
    the Kidron valley
  to where there was a garden,
  into which he and his disciples
      entered.
Judas his betrayer also knew the place,
  because Jesus had often met there
      with his disciples.
So Judas got a band of soldiers and
    guards
  from the chief priests and the
      Pharisees
  and went there with lanterns, torches,
      and weapons.
Jesus, knowing everything that was
    going to happen to him,
  went out and said to them, "Whom
      are you looking for?"
They answered him, "Jesus the
    Nazorean."
He said to them, "I AM."
Judas his betrayer was also with them.
When he said to them, "I AM,"
  they turned away and fell to the ground.
So he again asked them,
  "Whom are you looking for?"
They said, "Jesus the Nazorean."
Jesus answered,
  "I told you that I AM.
So if you are looking for me, let these
    men go."
This was to fulfill what he had said,
  "I have not lost any of those you gave me."
Then Simon Peter, who had a sword,
    drew it,
  struck the high priest's slave, and cut
      off his right ear.
The slave's name was Malchus.
Jesus said to Peter,
  "Put your sword into its scabbard.
Shall I not drink the cup that the Father
    gave me?"

Continued in Appendix A, pp. 282–283.
See Appendix A, p. 284, for the other readings.

Reflecting on the Gospel

In the Gospel of John's account of Jesus's death, the drama of dispossession is acted out in three scenes. First, Jesus is dispossessed of his clothing by the soldiers. Then he dispossesses himself of his mother and the beloved disciple, the woman and man who are his ideal disciples. Here we see women and men

as equal disciples, given into each other's care, accepting one another as Jesus's gifts, and all this under the shadow of the cross that is the glory tree. In this silent space we lay down our defenses and try to identify with such discipleship.

In this gospel there is no agonized dying cry, only the silent triumph of one who has accomplished what he came into the world to do. As his final dispossession, Jesus hands over his last breath to his Father, the breath that animates the new creation. No bones of this Paschal Lamb are broken, no cosmic darkness falls upon the earth, but from the pierced side of Jesus flow blood and water, John's signs of Eucharist and baptism through which all peoples and nations can enter into the new temple of the body of the crucified and risen One. He who thirsted becomes in death the source of the living water of the Spirit (see John 7:37b-39).

With deliberate irony, John proclaims that it is with the dead body of Jesus in their arms that hesitant Israel comes to faith: Joseph of Arimathea, a secret disciple because of his fear of Jesus's enemies and his own associates, and Nicodemus, the nighttime seeker, take the body of Jesus and bind it in the swaddling bands of death. They surround him with an extravagant amount of costly spices and oil, for this is a royal cortege and burial. The seed of Christ's body is buried in the earth, hidden there until it bears fruit on Easter morning.

Silence was God's answer on Golgotha; silence is our answer today when we come forward to touch or kiss the cross. Young people welcoming some activity, children interested in this novelty, old people doing what they have done for years, parents carrying their babies, the poor and the disabled heading with determination for what they are so familiar with: together we are the people who hope that this tree will drip its salvation upon us. "Were you there when they crucified my Lord?" we may sing, but there is another question to be answered: "Where are we now in relation to the cross and the crucified?" When we encounter it with hope and love, we speak its mystery to the world for which Jesus died.

On this day of dispossession, we are dispossessed even of the celebration of Mass and receive the hosts that were consecrated on Holy Thursday night. In deep silence we leave the church to move into our own preparation day for the Passover of Jesus, the preparation that will allow Jesus to burst forth from the tombs of our hearts on the night of nights.

Preparing to Proclaim

Key words and phrases: "It is finished."

To the point: John's version of the passion is replete with promises fulfilled; he likes to remind us that Jesus's death is a realization of Scripture. He also portrays Jesus as more divine than human; here, Jesus is calm and in control, responding with enviable tranquility to the chaos around him. While the story is not yet over—we have yet to see the resurrection and ascension—he is already acting as the king Pilate will name him as, sovereign over the world even as evil rages in very close proximity to him.

Living Liturgy

Adoring the Cross: The adoration of the holy cross allows us to behold the cross not only as sign of crucifixion and death but also as sign of glory and victory over death. Today the sacred paschal fast is observed and, if appropriate, also on Holy Saturday until the Easter Vigil. In fasting we also remove ourselves from the distractions of the world. Through our contemplation of the cross, our praying and fasting, we remember Jesus's passion. By recognizing Christ's suffering, how do we address our own struggles in life and suffering in the world?

FOR REFLECTION

• The second reading affirms that Jesus has experienced our weaknesses and has come through them without sin. Where do you need Jesus's help to conquer a weakness or a sinful tendency?

• How do you react to Jesus's sense of calm and control in the gospel? Is it reassuring to you or does it feel distancing?

• From the cross, Jesus entrusts his mother to the beloved disciple, and by extension to all of us. How would you care for Mary at the foot of the cross? How can you bring this to those you know who are grieving?

COLLECT

Let us pray.

Pause for silent prayer

Remember your mercies, O Lord,
and with your eternal protection sanctify your
    servants,
for whom Christ your Son,
by the shedding of his Blood,
established the Paschal Mystery.
Who lives and reigns for ever and ever. **Amen.**

or:

O God, who by the Passion of Christ your
    Son, our Lord,
abolished the death inherited from ancient sin
by every succeeding generation,
grant that just as, being conformed to him,
we have borne by the law of nature
the image of the man of earth,
so by the sanctification of grace
we may bear the image of the Man of heaven.
Through Christ our Lord. **Amen.**

Homily Points

• The Son of God suffers. On this Good Friday, the church slows down to be present to the incredible gift Jesus gives the world: his very self. Today the Word made flesh, the all-powerful one born of the Father before all ages, gets whipped. He gets spat at and mocked. He gets nailed to the cross. Today we listen as our Savior cries out in agony. We kneel in reverence as he breathes his last breath.

• Soon, our Savior will rise again. But for today, we carry the grief of death. We lament the sin and evil that brought Christ to this place. We mourn the countless people who face similar fates in our world today.

Gospel   Matt 28:1-10; L41ABC

After the sabbath, as the first day of
    the week was dawning,
    Mary Magdalene and the other Mary
        came to see the tomb.
And behold, there was a great
        earthquake;
    for an angel of the Lord
        descended from heaven,
    approached, rolled back the
        stone, and sat upon it.
His appearance was like
    lightning
    and his clothing was white as
        snow.
The guards were shaken with
    fear of him
    and became like dead men.
Then the angel said to the
    women in reply,
"Do not be afraid!
I know that you are seeking
    Jesus the crucified.
He is not here, for he has been
    raised just as he said.
Come and see the place where
    he lay.
Then go quickly and tell his
    disciples,
    'He has been raised from the dead,
    and he is going before you to Galilee;
    there you will see him.'
    Behold, I have told you."
Then they went away quickly from the
    tomb,
    fearful yet overjoyed,
    and ran to announce this to his
        disciples.
And behold, Jesus met them on their
    way and greeted them.
They approached, embraced his feet,
    and did him homage.
Then Jesus said to them, "Do not be
    afraid.
Go tell my brothers to go to Galilee,
    and there they will see me."

*See Appendix A, pp. 285–290, for the other
readings.*

Reflecting on the Gospel

In his resurrection account, Matthew tells us that a small group of women had seen the crucifixion of Jesus, had watched his burial, had sat contemplating his tomb. After the Sabbath, they return again to see the tomb—nothing more, no greater expectation—and to continue their vigil at the grave. We understand; we know how hard it is to leave the place where we have just buried a loved one.

There is no thought of rolling away the stone; the Roman guards are still there. But then there is the earthquake. An angel descends from heaven, the stone is rolled away, and the messenger of God sits triumphantly on it in front of the women. The angel proclaims to the women the emptiness of the tomb, the futility of human attempts to seal in the grave "Jesus the crucified."

There is more seeing for the women to do. As we are tonight, they are called to look at the empty tomb and believe that Jesus is risen and goes before us into new life. At the beginning of his gospel, Matthew places a woman, Mary of Nazareth, whose empty, virginal womb would give birth to Jesus the Savior, conceived by the Holy Spirit. At the end of his gospel, Matthew places Mary Magdalene and the other Mary at the empty tomb, where they are told that risen life has been conceived and brought forth. They believe, and they are enlivened. In contrast, the guards are shaken with uncomprehending fear and become "like dead men."

But there is more: the women are to tell Jesus's disciples this good news of his resurrection and of his going ahead of them to Galilee, where the disciples will also see him. As the women hurry away with this mission, Jesus himself approaches. It is the risen One's personal affirmation of the angel's message. Jesus announces one change from the angel's message: "his disciples" become "my brothers," forgiven brothers. Jesus is going before them into Galilee—Galilee of the Gentiles, Galilee of the springtime of their call, where the winter of their infidelity will thaw in the presence of the warmth of the forgiving, trustful love of their risen Master, and they will be commissioned by him to make disciples of all nations.

Our faith in the resurrection is built on the word of God and on the presence and witness of the risen Christ in human experience, in women and men who have received the gift of faith and have had it nourished in the community of believers. This is what the newly baptized tell us tonight; this is the responsibility we have for one another. We will fail; we will be called back to "Galilee" again and again, called to leave the place of the dead and follow Jesus who offers us his new life that will continue to transform us into the image of the crucified and risen One. For all this, we will loudly and constantly sing "Alleluia!" for the next fifty days.

Preparing to Proclaim

Key words and phrases: "[He] has been raised from the dead."

To the point: This empty tomb narrative has more drama than any of the others. Rather than quietly finding the stone already rolled away, the women feel an earthquake and actually witness an angel descend to move it aside. They also get to see Jesus as they leave the tomb, another departure from the other Synoptics that leave Jesus's appearance for later. The women leave the tomb feeling both fear and joy; there is room for both of these in a response to the resurrection. This drama is appropriate in this great narrative that changes the whole world.

Model Universal Prayer (Prayer of the Faithful)

Presider: Called to walk as children of the light, let us joyfully voice to God our prayers and petitions.

Response: Lord, hear our prayer.

Animate God's holy church to "make the buildings shake with joy" on this most sacred of nights . . .

Bless with faith, hope, and love all those who are being baptized, confirmed, and welcomed to the eucharistic table tonight . . .

Shine the paschal flame upon those who dwell in darkness . . .

Strengthen the baptismal call of all gathered here in celebration of Christ's resurrection . . .

Presider: God of hope, you sent your son Jesus into this world to live among creation. Through his resurrection, we are forever freed from the power of sin and death. Hear our prayers, that our lives may reflect your great love. We ask this through Christ our Lord. **Amen.**

Living Liturgy

Dispelling the Darkness: The church awaits the resurrection of Christ and celebrates it in the sacraments. The entire celebration must take place in darkness, beginning after nightfall and ending before the dawn on Sunday. Symbols at this liturgy must communicate clearly what they mean. Let the flames of the new fire genuinely dispel the darkness and light up the night. A small fire from a barbecue grill will neither be enough to illuminate the night nor symbolize the "light of Christ rising in glory" that will "dispel the darkness of our hearts and minds" (Roman Missal, The Easter Vigil, 14). What does that mean for your parish? Prepare these celebrations in community with intentionality.

COLLECT

Let us pray.

Pause for silent prayer

O God, who make this most sacred night radiant with the glory of the Lord's Resurrection, stir up in your Church a spirit of adoption, so that, renewed in body and mind, we may render you undivided service. Through our Lord Jesus Christ, your Son, who lives and reigns with you in the unity of the Holy Spirit, God, for ever and ever. **Amen.**

FOR REFLECTION

• The epistle affirms that we who are baptized have participated in Christ's death and thus are able to share in his life. How do you live out the call of your baptism to leave sin behind and live with Christ in freedom?

• Where and how do you encounter the risen Christ? What emotions does it evoke in you? How does he send you forth to witness to his presence?

Homily Points

• This is the night! In Matthew's resurrection account, Jesus meets Mary Magdalene and the other Mary on the road. The two women are on their way to share news of Jesus's resurrection to the disciples. Women—who have been marginalized and discounted since the beginning—are the first people entrusted with preaching the good news.

• Generations of women and others followed Mary Magdalene and the other Mary's lead. As we rejoice in tonight's great feast of victory, let us be thankful for the witnesses of these first evangelizers. Let us also be emboldened to share the good news in our own communities.

GOSPEL ACCLAMATION
cf. 1 Cor 5:7b-8a

R̸. Alleluia, alleluia.
Christ, our paschal lamb, has been sacrificed;
let us then feast with joy in the Lord.
R̸. Alleluia, alleluia.

Gospel

John 20:1-9; L42ABC

On the first day of the week,
Mary of Magdala came to the
tomb early in the morning,
while it was still dark,
and saw the stone removed
from the tomb.
So she ran and went to Simon
Peter
and to the other disciple whom
Jesus loved, and told
them,
"They have taken the Lord
from the tomb,
and we don't know where they
put him."
So Peter and the other disciple
went out and came to the
tomb.
They both ran, but the other
disciple ran faster than Peter
and arrived at the tomb first;
he bent down and saw the burial cloths
there, but did not go in.
When Simon Peter arrived after him,
he went into the tomb and saw the
burial cloths there,
and the cloth that had covered his head,
not with the burial cloths but rolled up
in a separate place.
Then the other disciple also went in,
the one who had arrived at the tomb
first,
and he saw and believed.
For they did not yet understand the
Scripture
that he had to rise from the dead.

or

Matt 28:1-10; L41A *in Appendix A, p. 291,
or, at an afternoon or evening Mass*
Luke 24:13-35; L46 *in Appendix A, p. 291.*

See Appendix A, p. 292, for the other readings.

Reflecting on the Gospel

The beginning of this gospel reading shows Mary of Magdala coming to the tomb early in the morning while it is still dark. The narrative quickly shifts to what is unusual about the scene—Mary noticing that the stone had been removed from the tomb. Without a doubt, that is a tremendous and paradigm-shifting occurrence. When Simon Peter and the other disciple arrive at the tomb and realize that Jesus is no longer dead and no longer housed in the dark tomb, one layer of this incredible event is unveiled. Christ's physical resurrection demonstrates the mighty power of God. We bear witness to God's abiding love for humankind, a love that declares "I love you so much that I will journey with you unto death and bring you out on the other side."

In a smaller, quieter way it is also quite moving to imagine Mary and the other women visiting the tomb and tending to Jesus's body in the days between the crucifixion and the resurrection. These women may have overcome fear of judgment or even violence from the community to go and care for Jesus's body. They may have had to overcome shame or embarrassment after watching their spiritual leader endure such an undignified execution. Then, of course, there is the soul-rocking grief of mourning a beloved friend.

The Easter story is overflowing with miracles, and perhaps one such miracle is that Mary and the disciples exhibit a love and devotion that was not extinguished by fear or by a gruesome and humiliating death. What love, what tenacity of spirit compels one to return and willingly encounter profound trauma again and again? Even without fully understanding what Jesus meant when he said that he would rise again, Mary of Magdala and the disciples returned to the tomb believing that their love held significance regardless of whether it could change the circumstances.

It evokes images of first responders working tirelessly at a scene of a disaster. Or medical care professionals who provide palliative care to terminally ill patients. Or counselors and psychiatrists who provide treatment for people living with debilitating mental illness for which there may never be a cure. It is a beautiful aspect of our human nature that we are so often driven to return, to strive, to persist, and to care even against all odds. That kernel of hope that reveals itself during our worst moments is perhaps a glimpse of the divine likeness breathed into each of us by God at the moment of our creation.

Although this Easter narrative shows us a mournful vigil that culminates in an astonishing and miraculous revelation, let us consider how the spirit of resurrection is also present in the perpetual vigil—in the ways we keep showing up day after day to break chains, nurture relationships, and show mercy and compassion. Although we live in hope, it is true that we may not see the fruit of our labors. Or, as this Easter story also demonstrates, the miracle we receive may be grander than our imaginings. Let us nurture the hope that lives within our hearts while also placing our trust and our joy in the resurrection God has in store for us—whatever its form.

Preparing to Proclaim
Key words and phrases: "They have taken the Lord from the tomb."

To the point: John's empty tomb narrative is mysterious. We do not see Jesus here, and not even the angel of the Synoptics reassures these witnesses about what is happening. There are only oblique signs: a moved stone, burial cloths, and no body. The gospel ends without understanding and there is still a journey ahead of coming to understand what God has done here. Our Easter joy is not always immediate; we cannot start it on demand. But God remains with us in the journey of coming to share in this joy more fully.

Model Penitential Act
Presider: Christ has risen, he has risen indeed! As we celebrate the Easter victory, let us be grateful for the merciful love of our Savior . . . *[pause]*
　　Lord Jesus, you rose from the grave and conquered death: Lord, have mercy.
　　Christ Jesus, you shine brightly for all to see: Christ, have mercy.
　　Lord Jesus, you will live forever in glory: Lord, have mercy.

Model Universal Prayer (Prayer of the Faithful)
Presider: Christ our Savior rose from the dead and is now seated at the right hand of God. With praise and thanksgiving, let us offer our Easter prayers and petitions.

Response: Lord, hear our prayer.

Shower Easter joy upon the newly baptized, confirmed, and communed members of the Body of Christ . . .

Imbue those who work in healthcare and chaplaincy with the gifts of the Spirit . . .

Envelop in divine hope those who grieve the death of a loved one . . .

Transform the lives of each of us gathered here to reflect ever more deeply the good news of Christ . . .

Presider: Redeeming God, you promise your people life in glory alongside your son Jesus. Hear our prayers, that through the paschal mystery we may grow in faith, hope, and love. We ask this through Christ our risen Lord. **Amen.**

Living Liturgy
Welcoming Wholeheartedly: Creating inclusive space for welcome is essential today with so many visitors attending Easter Sunday Mass, perhaps for the first time. Be present to these new guests and greet them as they enter the worship space. Prepare a worship aid that details the order of service, possibly with some directions on liturgical posture. Brief all liturgical ministers to carry a welcoming spirit through this joyful day and throughout the Easter season. Hospitality requires gratitude, generosity, joy, and humility to leave judgments behind and welcome the guest wholeheartedly.

COLLECT
Let us pray.

Pause for silent prayer

O God, who on this day,
through your Only Begotten Son,
have conquered death
and unlocked for us the path to eternity,
grant, we pray, that we who keep
the solemnity of the Lord's Resurrection
may, through the renewal brought by your Spirit,
rise up in the light of life.
Through our Lord Jesus Christ, your Son,
who lives and reigns with you in the unity of
　　the Holy Spirit,
God, for ever and ever. **Amen.**

FOR REFLECTION
• We know so well how this story ends, but try to put yourself in the place of Mary Magdalene or one of the disciples as they put the pieces together for the first time. What would you be thinking and feeling as this absolutely unthinkable thing unfolds?

• Like the characters of this gospel, we also often encounter the risen Christ in oblique signs and symbols, things that are easy to overlook in all our busyness. What in your life might be an overlooked symbol of resurrection?

Homily Points
• In company with the psalmist, let us pray once more: "This is the day the Lord has made; let us rejoice and be glad!" Our call for the next fifty days of Easter is to spread Christ's joy to all we meet. This does not mean we need to be happy every second of every day. It does not mean we ignore the real suffering plaguing our world.

• Easter joy is strong enough to carry the wounds of the world together with the deep conviction that hope always wins. Death does not have the final say. Through Christ, the Easter victory is ours for eternity.

SEASON OF EASTER

✠ SPIRITUALITY

GOSPEL ACCLAMATION
John 20:29

℟. Alleluia, alleluia.
You believe in me, Thomas, because you have
    seen me, says the Lord;
blessed are those who have not seen me, but still
    believe!
℟. Alleluia, alleluia.

Gospel   John 20:19-31; L43A

On the evening of that first day of the
    week,
    when the doors were locked, where the
        disciples were,
    for fear of the Jews,
    Jesus came and stood in their midst
    and said to them, "Peace be with you."
When he had said this, he showed them
    his hands and his side.
The disciples rejoiced when they saw the
    Lord.
Jesus said to them again, "Peace be with
    you.
As the Father has sent me, so I send you."
And when he had said this, he breathed
    on them and said to them,
    "Receive the Holy Spirit.
Whose sins you forgive are forgiven them,
    and whose sins you retain are retained."

Thomas, called Didymus, one of the
    Twelve,
    was not with them when Jesus came.
So the other disciples said to him, "We
    have seen the Lord."
But he said to them,
    "Unless I see the mark of the nails in
        his hands
    and put my finger into the nailmarks
    and put my hand into his side, I will
        not believe."

Now a week later his disciples were again
    inside
    and Thomas was with them.
Jesus came, although the doors were locked,
    and stood in their midst and said,
        "Peace be with you."

Continued in Appendix A, p. 292.

Reflecting on the Gospel

Today's gospel is the same in each of the three yearly cycles, a fact that underlines its significance. It proclaims that the risen Christ is often in our midst in ways that we do not expect and that even though Jesus is risen, we still have to confront the mystery and the glory of the wounds.

Terrified by the death of Jesus, dispirited and disillusioned over their own failures and their desertion of their Master, the disciples huddle behind closed doors. Mary Magdalene has announced to them that she had seen the Lord

and delivered to them his message, but she is just a woman and, according to the socioreligious views of the time, a woman's evidence did not count! So these Jewish disciples (probably a more inclusive group than the Twelve become Eleven through Judas's treachery) lock their doors against "the Jews" (the Johannine term for the opponents of Jesus) and barricade their hearts against hope. But for the One who can break the bonds of death, locks are no obstacles. Suddenly the Tomb Breaker is in their midst, and his first gift to them is his peace.

Biblical peace is much more than the absence of war; it is a wholeness and holiness of spirit, soul, and body. Its opposite is chaos, and this community is a community in chaos. To re-create the lives of these vulnerable disciples and bring them out of their chaos and hurt, Jesus then shows them his wounded hands and side. He stands before them in the glorified reality of his humanity, of all that he has become by his life, death, and resurrection—and this includes his wounds. A risen Lord without his wounds would have little to say to the wounded ones in that Jerusalem room, just as he would have little to say to us. We can be rather cynical about the devotions of some cultures that seem to delight in processions, images, wayside shrines of a bloodied Christ, judging that they have not learned to go forward to his resurrection. And yet these people are usually the ones who know what it is to suffer with the crucified Christ who by his resurrection is now present with them.

Charles Pegúy recounts a story about a man who died and arrived at heaven's gates. The recording angel said to him, "Show me your wounds." "Wounds?" replied the man, "I haven't got any." And the angel asked, "Did you never think that anything was worth fighting for?" The crucified Christ knew that all his sisters and brothers were worth fighting for.

Our wounds tell us something about who we are. The death camp numbers branded on a Jew's arm, the distinctive and advertised scars of the missing person, the scars of lifesaving surgery, the hated or denied wounds to our own hearts: much of our identity lies in our wounds. Some of us allow our life to drain from our wounds; others grow to new life at these broken places, and this is resurrection—this is a call to go and be wounded healers of others.

Preparing to Proclaim

Key words and phrases: "We have seen the Lord."

To the point: Poor Thomas here gets such a bad reputation, known mockingly as "Doubting Thomas" when in reality he demonstrates great faith. His need for proof is only human; the other disciples were shown Jesus's hands and side before they came to believe, too! In fact, Thomas's questioning demonstrates an intelligent and responsible engagement with his faith. He ponders the truth of what he hears and brings his questions to the table, not shutting down when something does not immediately make sense to him. At the same time, he does not blindly accept what he has been told, even though it is something he deeply hopes is true. And when he does encounter Jesus, his response is immediate: "My Lord and my God!" He gives over his heart and life to the one who has risen from the dead.

Psalmist Preparation

This psalm connects Easter back to Lent, thrice repeating that "His mercy endures forever." The sheer, wholehearted rejoicing of this psalm still reminds us that God is working in unexpected ways, for it is the stone rejected by the builders that God chooses as the cornerstone. God's ways continue not to be our ways, but in the light of Easter we see more clearly that God's ways are better. As you prepare this psalm, make a list of five wonderful things in your life. Bring your gratitude for these things to your proclamation, letting your joy for them spill out into an invitation to share that joy.

Making Connections

Between the readings: The gospel tells the story of one of the first encounters with the risen Christ; the first reading tells us about a community living in the wake of such an encounter. They respond to the gospel with awe and generosity, with prayer and communal living. The second reading is written to a community slightly more removed from immediately witnessing the resurrection; while they (and we) need to rely on the testimony of others, it affirms that joy and hope are at the heart of their response.

To experience: Most of us do not get to experience the risen Christ as tangibly and viscerally as Thomas does. Our encounters will more likely be encounters of the heart, more subtle and less subject to the proof that he asks for. Our firsthand encounters usually need to be contextualized by the tradition we have inherited; we are dependent on the testimony of those who came before us.

Homily Points

• Tradition can be quick to judge Thomas for his reaction to the risen Christ. He does not take the disciples' claim lightly: "We have seen the Lord." Thomas asks for more. He asks to see and touch Jesus so that he too might come to believe. Thomas's doubt can be interpreted as a desire to dive deeper into the mystery of the resurrection. By all human logic, Jesus should still be dead. His heart stopped beating. His lungs stopped breathing. Jesus died, full stop. His resurrection three days later defies everything we thought to be true about the workings of the world.

• The other disciples did not rejoice in belief until the resurrected Jesus showed them his wounds. They too needed to see. Who among us would not jump at the chance for a physical encounter with our Lord who lived and died and now lives again?

• Jesus does not scold Thomas for his request. When he appears to the disciples a week later, Jesus gives Thomas exactly what he needs to believe. Jesus's invitation to touch, see, and believe in his resurrection is enough for Thomas to cry out: "My Lord and my God!" Did Thomas actually put his hands in Jesus's side? The gospel account does not say. But the invitation was enough for the doubter to make a profound declaration of faith. Jesus wants Thomas to believe. Jesus meets Thomas in his uncertainty and desire for more. Jesus gives Thomas what he needs to persevere on the path of faith.

Model Rite for the Blessing and Sprinkling of Water

In the healing waters of baptism, we are freed from the powers of sin and death. May these waters draw us ever closer to Christ and his resurrection . . . *[pause]*

> *[continue with* The Roman Missal, *Appendix II]*

Model Universal Prayer (Prayer of the Faithful)

Presider: Sustained by God's divine mercy, let us bring forward our prayers and petitions for the church and the world.

Response: Lord, hear our prayer.

Foster thoughtful questions and a sense of curiosity among the faithful . . .

Bless the work of activists striving to bring about peace in our neighborhoods . . .

Grace with community people who are lonely, anxious, or depressed . . .

Increase our sense of awe of and respect for the gifts of the created world . . .

Presider: Merciful Creator, you sent your son into the world to bring about peace. Receive our prayers that we too may be agents of peace in communities everywhere. We ask this through Christ our resurrected Lord. **Amen.**

Liturgy and Music

Full Community: This Sunday will mark the first Sunday that neophytes of the parish will be in full community with the rest of the gathered assembly as they attend Mass without being dismissed before the Liturgy of the Eucharist. What joy to witness through song and prayer the newly baptized as they experience the eucharistic liturgy as a whole for the first time! As music ministers, we play an important role in continuing to journey with these new members of our faith, to help them and ourselves recognize and live fully the paschal mystery. Choir members should be reminded of the important work of what Austin Fleming calls "a ministry that reaches the deepest recesses of the human heart" (*Preparing for Liturgy*). Our work is soul-stirring.

Most parish communities already include the Rite for the Blessing and Sprinkling of Water throughout the Easter season which aids the community and the community of newly baptized to contemplate and participate in the Easter mysteries. *Vidi aquam* is the text that accompanies this ritual action and is found in Appendix II of The Roman Missal. This beautiful text may be set to a psalm tone and chanted simply by choir and assembly. This rite is a reminder of baptism and it should precede the Glory to God.

COLLECT

Let us pray.

Pause for silent prayer

God of everlasting mercy,
who in the very recurrence of the paschal feast
kindle the faith of the people you have made your own,
increase, we pray, the grace you have bestowed,
that all may grasp and rightly understand
in what font they have been washed,
by whose Spirit they have been reborn,
by whose Blood they have been redeemed.
Through our Lord Jesus Christ, your Son,
who lives and reigns with you in the unity of the Holy Spirit,
God, for ever and ever. **Amen.**

FIRST READING

Acts 2:42-47

They devoted themselves
 to the teaching of the apostles and to the communal life,
 to the breaking of bread and to the prayers.
Awe came upon everyone,
 and many wonders and signs were done through the apostles.
All who believed were together and had all things in common;
 they would sell their property and possessions
 and divide them among all according to each one's need.
Every day they devoted themselves
 to meeting together in the temple area
 and to breaking bread in their homes.
They ate their meals with exultation and sincerity of heart,
 praising God and enjoying favor with all the people.
And every day the Lord added to their number those who were being saved.

RESPONSORIAL PSALM

Ps 118:2-4, 13-15, 22-24

℟. (1) Give thanks to the Lord for he is good, his love is everlasting.
 or: ℟. Alleluia.

Let the house of Israel say,
 "His mercy endures forever."
Let the house of Aaron say,
 "His mercy endures forever."
Let those who fear the Lord say,
 "His mercy endures forever."

℟. Give thanks to the Lord for he is good, his love is everlasting.
 or: ℟. Alleluia.

I was hard pressed and was falling,
    but the LORD helped me.
My strength and my courage is the LORD,
    and he has been my savior.
The joyful shout of victory
    in the tents of the just.

R⸱. Give thanks to the Lord for he is good,
his love is everlasting.
    or: R⸱. Alleluia.

The stone which the builders rejected
    has become the cornerstone.
By the LORD has this been done;
    it is wonderful in our eyes.
This is the day the LORD has made;
    let us be glad and rejoice in it.

R⸱. Give thanks to the Lord for he is good,
his love is everlasting.
    or: R⸱. Alleluia.

SECOND READING
1 Pet 1:3-9

Blessed be the God and Father of our Lord
    Jesus Christ,
    who in his great mercy gave us a new
        birth to a living hope
    through the resurrection of Jesus Christ
        from the dead,
    to an inheritance that is imperishable,
        undefiled, and unfading,
    kept in heaven for you
    who by the power of God are
        safeguarded through faith,
    to a salvation that is ready to be
        revealed in the final time.
In this you rejoice, although now for a
        little while
    you may have to suffer through various
        trials,
    so that the genuineness of your faith,
    more precious than gold that is
        perishable even though tested by
        fire,
    may prove to be for praise, glory, and
        honor
    at the revelation of Jesus Christ.
Although you have not seen him you love
        him;
    even though you do not see him now yet
        believe in him,
    you rejoice with an indescribable and
        glorious joy,
    as you attain the goal of your faith, the
        salvation of your souls.

CATECHESIS

Living Liturgy

Experience Mystery: The story of Thomas shows us that the experience of the risen Christ is necessary for faith. We relate to Thomas's human nature and in our doubt, we often demand proof. Yet our ministry invites us to always contemplate the paschal mystery. During this Easter season, we continue to journey in community with the parish's neophytes (new plants) as the newly baptized enter into a period of mystagogy. The *Catechism of the Catholic Church* describes mystagogy as a "liturgical catechesis that aims to initiate people into the mystery of Christ and discernment of the paschal mystery" (1075).

The reading from the Acts of the Apostles today charts out in concrete examples the ways in which early Christians made the paschal mystery a part of their lives. This final period of the Rite of Christian Initiation of Adults (RCIA) journey is described as a "time for the community and the neophytes together to grow in deepening their grasp of the paschal mystery and making it part of their lives" (244). From the reading, we learn that this method of Christian discipleship is threefold—meditating on the gospel, sharing in the Eucharist, and doing works of charity. We accompany the newly initiated over these Easter weeks and continue to unpack and explore the spiritual treasures contained in the sacraments by reflecting on their meaning and significance in our personal lives.

Our work in ministry ought to lead us and others into more faith-filled ways to reverence the word, celebrate the sacraments, and witness Christ to the world. Our faith calls us through our baptism to live outside what Pope Francis calls a "throwaway culture" and turn toward a culture that shares concern for the other. Through mystagogy, we rediscover how the external signs of ritual and liturgical prayer might allow us to deeply ponder and experience the inner, spiritual meaning of the divine life which they signify. We are among the "blessed" because we believe without having seen.

PROMPTS FOR FAITH-SHARING

• We often struggle to celebrate Easter as a full season in the way we do with Lent. As we complete the Easter octave, how do you plan to continue to celebrate the resurrection?

• The first reading describes a community living in the aftermath of their immediate encounter with the risen Christ. How does your community compare?

• What moments of encounter in your life have made the risen Jesus present to you? How can you share the gift of Jesus's abundant life with others?

APRIL 16, 2023
SECOND SUNDAY OF EASTER
(or of DIVINE MERCY)

✝ SPIRITUALITY

GOSPEL ACCLAMATION

cf. Luke 24:32

℟. Alleluia, alleluia.
Lord Jesus, open the Scriptures to us;
make our hearts burn while you speak to us.
℟. Alleluia, alleluia.

Gospel   Luke 24:13-35; L46A

That very day, the first day of the week,
    two of Jesus' disciples were going
    to a village seven miles from Jerusalem
        called Emmaus,
    and they were conversing about all the
        things that had occurred.
And it happened that while they were
        conversing and debating,
    Jesus himself drew near and walked
        with them,
    but their eyes were prevented from
        recognizing him.
He asked them,
    "What are you discussing as you walk
        along?"
They stopped, looking downcast.
One of them, named Cleopas, said to him
        in reply,
    "Are you the only visitor to Jerusalem
    who does not know of the things
    that have taken place there in these
        days?"
And he replied to them, "What sort of
        things?"
They said to him,
    "The things that happened to Jesus the
        Nazarene,
    who was a prophet mighty in deed and
        word
    before God and all the people,
    how our chief priests and rulers both
        handed him over
    to a sentence of death and crucified
        him.

Continued in Appendix A, p. 293.

Continued in Appendix A, p. 293.

Reflecting on the Gospel

For Luke, Easter day is filled with action. The spice-bearing women go to the tomb and announce the resurrection to the Eleven, who consider this "idle tales." Peter goes to the tomb but comes away not sure what he has seen. Two disciples leave Jerusalem and head for Emmaus. It is a day of journeying, a day that illustrates that with Jesus we are a journeying, pilgrim people. The Emmaus event is about being "on the road," about the new things we are called to do by the risen Christ after we have heard the story and shared the broken bread.

As the two disciples approach the village with the Stranger, the day is drawing to a close, but faith is about to dawn. Jesus acts as if to go farther. He will not impose himself on disciples, then or now; he waits for an invitation to stay with them, and when this is offered as a first response of the travelers to his story, he accepts it readily. Jesus enters the house as guest and becomes the Host. At table he takes, blesses, breaks, and gives the bread. On the road he had already broken the Scriptures for them, and these ritual actions at table complete the revelation. Then he vanishes from their sight. The bread has been eaten, the story has been told, the hospitality has been offered and accepted. Word and bread and hospitality—these will continue to make Jesus present to and understood in his post-resurrection church.

Emmaus is the place of conversion, of broken people healed by the broken word and the broken bread. Wounded hearts have become burning hearts, disfigured dreams are transfigured, and death is recognized as the way to invincible life. But Emmaus is not the place to stay. The two disciples turn and return to the Jerusalem community, driven on their mission of proclaiming the risen One to the wounded community of the Eleven. There they hear that the forgiving and compassionate Jesus has already appeared to Simon (Peter), the disciple most wounded by his denial of his Master.

Week after week in the Liturgy of the Word, as we gather at the eucharistic table, we share in the new story and new hospitality that Jesus offered to the Emmaus disciples. The temptation is to prefer the old story, the old bread of power and violence and exclusion; to prefer the option of escape from suffering rather than seeing it as inevitable in our traveling with Jesus; to rationalize about what is too difficult and too unjust to forgive. But Emmaus challenges us to walk through our daily lives in the company of the Christ who reveals himself in Scripture and Eucharist, and also in the other unexpected "strangers" whom we may meet and who share with us the bread of their lives that proclaim hope in the face of suffering and apparent hopelessness. The climax of the Emmaus narrative does not happen in the house but in the mission that takes the disciples, with burning hearts, back onto the road.

Preparing to Proclaim

Key words and phrases: "Were not our hearts burning within us / while he spoke to us on the way . . . ?"

To the point: This Easter encounter is a beloved story, and with good reason. It transitions us from the disciples' encounters with the risen Christ to our ongoing encounters with Christ in the Mass. Their hearts burn within them as he speaks to them about Scripture, a forerunner to our Liturgy of the Word, when we hear Scripture opened for us and meet Jesus alive and speaking to us there. Then they recognized him in the breaking of the bread, which is how he will remain with them—and us—long beyond his ascension into heaven. For us, too, Mass serves as a point of encounter in the midst of our lifelong journey. Jesus chooses to be with us and walk with us, and while we might not always recognize him, we are never left alone.

Psalmist Preparation

This psalm's path imagery pairs perfectly with today's gospel, where the disciples encounter Jesus while walking. Journeys and pathways are common imagery for life with God; "walking with God" is a favorite image of the Old Testament for those who lived faithfully. This psalm has a pondering quality, affirming the deep, true ways that God remains with us even if it is not always evident. If you are able, consider praying with this text while walking sometime this week. Reflect on your own journey of faith and the times that God has shown you the path. Remember that some choices God leaves to us, and even when God does not give clear or obvious signposts, God promises to be with us on whatever path we choose.

Making Connections

Between the readings: The first reading shows Peter in his redemption arc—after his cowardly denial of Jesus in the passion narrative, he here stands up and proclaims the truth of Jesus's life, death, and resurrection. He is ready to take a risk because his encounter with the risen Jesus has transformed him; this courage comes from God. The second reading continues his preaching and reminds us of the source of his courage, a courage that would enable him to follow Jesus to a death by crucifixion: this is not human courage, but courage that only comes when our "faith and hope are in God."

To experience: We may be tempted to think of the disciples as extremely privileged to have encountered the Risen Christ so immediately. They certainly are, but so are we, who continue to encounter Jesus at every Mass as he humbly comes to be with us, fully and completely, in the Scriptures and Eucharist we receive at every Mass.

Homily Points

• Cleopas and his companion pose a profound question after their encounter with the risen Christ: "Were not our hearts burning within us?" The two disciples feel the flames of faith within their very beings as they walk and talk with Jesus along the road to Emmaus. Their experience reminds us that discipleship is meant to be a full body experience. Following Christ attunes our various senses to the holy in everyday life.

• When is the last time you felt your heart burn within you? Find those spaces where your heart burns and dwell there. As theologian Howard Thurman says, "Don't ask what the world needs. Ask what makes you come alive, and go do it. Because what the world needs is more people who have come alive." The Easter season gifts us with fifty days to reflect on our calling to be disciples of the risen Christ. Use this time to discern the people, places, work, and social causes that make you come alive.

• Discipleship is best lived out in community. Jesus sends us out to share the good news together. Cleopas and his companion debate and discuss all that has taken place over the last few days. They bounce ideas off each other. Perhaps they scheme their next steps. Who are your discipleship companions? In what ways can our church community support our newest companions—those who were received into the church at the Easter Vigil? Together the Body of Christ can spread Easter hope to the ends of the earth.

Model Rite for the Blessing and Sprinkling of Water

Presider: In baptism, we begin a special relationship with Jesus who journeys alongside us forever. By the sprinkling of this water, may we be reminded of Christ's great love for us . . . *[pause]*

    [continue with The Roman Missal, *Appendix II]*

Model Universal Prayer (Prayer of the Faithful)

Presider: Accompanied by Jesus our eternal companion, let us entrust our needs to the Lord.

Response: Lord, hear our prayer.

Steer the church toward greater awareness of the divine presence in our midst . . .

Grace the work of soup kitchens, food pantries, and other organizations feeding the hungry . . .

Safeguard migrants and refugees forced to make dangerous journeys in the hopes of finding safety . . .

Set aflame with the fire of your love the hearts of each person gathered here . . .

Presider: God of hope, through the breaking of the bread we come to know the love of your son Jesus. Hear our prayers that strengthened by his constant presence we might live with the flames of faith alive in our hearts. We ask this through Christ our resurrected Lord. **Amen.**

Liturgy and Music

First Communion and the Communion Song: The celebration of First Communion often takes place during the Easter season. When celebrating this during regular Sunday Mass, take care to prepare liturgical music that will incorporate eucharistic hymns and Easter songs that reflect the Scripture readings. Find a balance in the repertoire sung that Sunday. When making decisions on ministerial roles at these liturgies, there seems to be a tendency to focus entirely on the children that will be receiving the sacrament. Allow others in the community to participate and ensure a balance of participation.

    In preparing for these liturgies, it would be good for us to think about when the communion song begins. The General Instruction of the Roman Missal (GIRM) clearly states that: "While the Priest is receiving the Sacrament, the Communion Chant is begun" (86). However, most music ministers leave a time of silence for the priest to consume the body and blood of Christ and wait to begin the communion song. Know that the purpose of this piece is "to express the spiritual union of the communicants by means of the unity of their voices, to show gladness of heart, and to bring out more clearly the 'communitarian' character of the procession to receive the Eucharist" (86). The priest receiving Communion is part of the expression of spiritual union that all communicants share. We are all united, and therefore, begin the communion song when the priest receives.

Let us pray.

Pause for silent prayer

May your people exult for ever, O God,
in renewed youthfulness of spirit,
so that, rejoicing now in the restored glory
    of our adoption,
we may look forward in confident hope
to the rejoicing of the day of resurrection.
Through our Lord Jesus Christ, your Son,
who lives and reigns with you in the unity
    of the Holy Spirit,
God, for ever and ever. **Amen.**

FIRST READING
Acts 2:14, 22-33

Then Peter stood up with the Eleven,
    raised his voice, and proclaimed:
    "You who are Jews, indeed all of you
        staying in Jerusalem.
Let this be known to you, and listen to my
    words.
You who are Israelites, hear these words.
Jesus the Nazorean was a man
    commended to you by God
    with mighty deeds, wonders, and signs,
    which God worked through him in your
        midst, as you yourselves know.
This man, delivered up by the set plan and
    foreknowledge of God,
    you killed, using lawless men to crucify
        him.
But God raised him up, releasing him from
    the throes of death,
    because it was impossible for him to be
        held by it.
For David says of him:
    I saw the Lord ever before me,
        with him at my right hand I shall not
        be disturbed.
    Therefore my heart has been glad and
        my tongue has exulted;
    my flesh, too, will dwell in hope,
    because you will not abandon my soul to
        the netherworld,
    nor will you suffer your holy one to
        see corruption.
    You have made known to me the paths
        of life;
    you will fill me with joy in your
        presence.

"My brothers, one can confidently say to
    you
    about the patriarch David that he died
        and was buried,
    and his tomb is in our midst to this day.

But since he was a prophet and knew that
   God had sworn an oath to him
that he would set one of his
      descendants upon his throne,
he foresaw and spoke of the
      resurrection of the Christ,
that neither was he abandoned to the
      netherworld
nor did his flesh see corruption.
God raised this Jesus;
   of this we are all witnesses.
Exalted at the right hand of God,
   he received the promise of the Holy
      Spirit from the Father
   and poured him forth, as you see and
      hear."

RESPONSORIAL PSALM
Ps 16:1-2, 5, 7-8, 9-10, 11

R℣. (11a) Lord, you will show us the path
of life. or: R℣. Alleluia.

Keep me, O God, for in you I take refuge;
   I say to the LORD, "My Lord are you."
O LORD, my allotted portion and my cup,
   you it is who hold fast my lot.

R℣. Lord, you will show us the path of life.
   or:
R℣. Alleluia.

I bless the LORD who counsels me;
   even in the night my heart exhorts me.
I set the LORD ever before me;
   with him at my right hand I shall not be
      disturbed.

R℣. Lord, you will show us the path of life.
   or:
R℣. Alleluia.

Therefore my heart is glad and my soul
      rejoices,
   my body, too, abides in confidence;
because you will not abandon my soul to
      the netherworld,
   nor will you suffer your faithful one to
      undergo corruption.

R℣. Lord, you will show us the path of life.
   or:
R℣. Alleluia.

You will show me the path to life,
   abounding joy in your presence,
   the delights at your right hand forever.

R℣. Lord, you will show us the path of life.
   or:
R℣. Alleluia.

SECOND READING
1 Pet 1:17-21

See Appendix A, p. 293.

Living Liturgy
Regaining Hope: This week and last, we learn how the first community of disciples came to believe that Jesus had risen from the dead. We hear the beloved journey to Emmaus story today. Through these gospel stories we gain insight about the formation of the early church community and discover that the first community met and recognized Jesus in the breaking of the bread. The two on the road were perhaps afraid but chose not to hide in the locked upper room.

Pope Francis offers these words about journey and mission. He tells us that "[i]t is a swift encounter, that of Jesus with the two disciples of Emmaus. But in it there is all the destiny of the Church. It tells us that the Christian community is not closed up in a fortified citadel, but walks in its most vital space, namely the road. And there it encounters people, with their hopes and disappointments, at times heavy. The Church listens to all our stories, as they emerge from the casket of our personal conscience; to then offer the Word of life, the witness of love, love that is faithful unto the end. And then people's hearts once more burn with hope" (Catechesis of the Holy Father, General Audience, May 24, 2017).

Regaining hope becomes our ministerial call to move out of our fear to recognize Jesus in the invisible ones, the strangers on the journey, the unknown guests at the feast. Regaining hope through the breaking of bread, we are sent to discern a culture of encounter and accompaniment through the highs and lows of life, which ought to lead to a transformation of ourselves and the unknown ones inside and outside our faith community. Our own hearts burn with transformational hope, joy, and love through the encounter of Jesus in Scripture and in sacraments. Do we witness this joy and hope with others to form inclusive community and set the world ablaze?

PROMPTS FOR FAITH-SHARING

• What is your experience of encountering Jesus in the Eucharist? What might help you renew your eucharistic practice as an encounter with the risen Christ?

• The first reading shows a courageous Peter preaching the truth of Christ's life and making up for his cowardly denial at the passion. How might you be called to greater courage in witnessing to what you know to be true about Jesus?

• The image of journeying or pathways is a common one for the life of faith. Reflect on your own journey so far; how have you encountered Christ along the way?

✠ SPIRITUALITY

GOSPEL ACCLAMATION
John 10:14

℟. Alleluia, alleluia.
I am the good shepherd, says the Lord;
I know my sheep, and mine know me.
℟. Alleluia, alleluia.

Gospel John 10:1-10; L49A

Jesus said:
"Amen, amen, I say to you,
    whoever does not enter a sheepfold
        through the gate
    but climbs over elsewhere is a thief
        and a robber.
But whoever enters through the gate is
    the shepherd of the sheep.
The gatekeeper opens it for him, and the
    sheep hear his voice,
    as the shepherd calls his own sheep by
        name and leads them out.
When he has driven out all his own,
    he walks ahead of them, and the sheep
        follow him,
    because they recognize his voice.
But they will not follow a stranger;
    they will run away from him,
    because they do not recognize the voice
        of strangers."
Although Jesus used this figure of
    speech,
    the Pharisees did not realize what he
        was trying to tell them.

So Jesus said again, "Amen, amen, I say
    to you,
    I am the gate for the sheep.
All who came before me are thieves and
    robbers,
    but the sheep did not listen to them.
I am the gate.
Whoever enters through me will be
    saved,
    and will come in and go out and find
        pasture.
A thief comes only to steal and slaughter
    and destroy;
    I came so that they might have life and
        have it more abundantly."

Reflecting on the Gospel

On Easter morning, Mary Magdalene had heard the one most personal word—her own name, "Mary!"—called by the risen Shepherd, and she responded to the One who called her by naming him: "Master!" We need to familiarize ourselves with the voice of Jesus our Shepherd in order to hear him calling our own name. That call comes in our daily prayer, in our study of Scripture, often in our small parish and home groups, in our attentive and mindful listening to the Liturgy of the Word at Mass, and, hopefully, in the homilies that break it open for us.

There are many voices of "thieves and robbers" shouting at us today, and the pastoral image of leaders of the church has been damaged in recent years, especially by the sexual abuse committed by some who are supposed to be trusted shepherds. There are voices of the drug dealers stealing life from so many of our young people and the economic rationalists who are enticing us into selfish materialism and consumerism. Some of the harshest voices are those of the ultra-conservative critics in the sheepfold itself who are busily robbing the flock of their Vatican II inheritance and doing subtle violence to anyone whose view differs from their self-righteous positions.

In front of the Jerusalem crowds, Peter burns hotly with Pentecost fire as he proclaims that salvation comes through the Shepherd whose body was ravaged on the cross and who rose again as Lord and Christ of God. Peter's words cut into the hearts of his listeners, and their response to his words is a question from the heart: "What are we to do?" From his own wounded experience of betraying Jesus, cauterized now by the Spirit's fire, Peter knows only too well what is needed: repentance and its ritual expression in baptism. This echoes the challenge of John the Baptist (see Luke 3:10), but now Easter and Pentecost have happened, and the baptism is not only one of water for repentance, but baptism in the Spirit and fire kindled by the resurrection of Jesus and so "in his name." The repentance is not just "being sorry," but is an act of *metánoia*, of radical conversion of heart and mind that turns one's life to Christ.

Beyond those to whom Peter spoke, the promise of the gift of the Holy Spirit is also for those who are as "far off" as us, who have responded to the voice of the Lord who calls us. Numbers are a symbolic rather than a real concern of the Scriptures; whatever was the exact number of those baptized in response to Peter's sermon, Luke's aim is to show us that the large number is a wonderful and foundational restoration of the people of God within historic Judaism, and at its heart in Jerusalem. The joy and enthusiasm will be contagious. Is it still contagious so that people ask us: "What are we to do?" Perhaps the response to the Rite of Christian Initiation (RCIA) in our parishes is an indicator.

Preparing to Proclaim

Key words and phrases: "I came so that they might have life and have it more abundantly."

To the point: In this gospel for Good Shepherd Sunday, Jesus mixes his metaphors a bit. We usually think of him as the Good Shepherd, and he is that; he is the one who contrasts with the thief sneaking in to steal and slaughter. He is the one who calls us by name and whose voice we know. He is the one who provides our sustenance and protection. But in this parable, he also identifies himself as the gate into the sheepfold. This is an even humbler image than that of shepherd, for in this metaphor, he is not even human. He is our way, our path to all that is good and real. It is through him that we enter safety and rest. And it is he who serves as our protection, because he has conquered those evil forces in the world that would wish us harm.

Psalmist Preparation

This psalm can sometimes feel blunted by familiarity; it comes up frequently in the liturgical year, plus it is ubiquitous on wall plaques and throw pillows, sometimes to the point of watering down its beautiful and powerful imagery of God as our shepherd. If you find your eyes glazing over at this psalm, try to spend some time with it in imaginative prayer. Really bring to life the scenes it paints, including what each of your five senses would experience if you were in the loving care of God as described here. When you proclaim the psalm, strive to do so with tender gratitude, knowing that God cares for each member of the congregation this dearly.

Making Connections

Between the readings: The second reading explicitly repeats the sheep and shepherd image of the gospel; sheep sometimes go astray, but returning to their shepherd keeps them safe. Peter's preaching of baptism in the first reading is an important connection to the sheepfold gate of the gospel. Baptism is how we share in Christ's death and thus his life. It is our entry point to the safety of Christ's flock.

To experience: For many of us, baptism was long ago. We take for granted that we are part of God's flock of sheep and do not remember what it was like to ever be outside it. This is an important season to listen to the witness of those more newly initiated into the church; their stories of coming in from the outside are often very powerful and can remind us of what we're about. If you are a newer convert, consider ways you might share your story with those around you.

Homily Points

• Too often, unjust distinctions between who is "in" and who is "out" plague our communities. People are welcomed or cast aside based on who they voted for, the amount of money in their bank account, the color of their skin, and countless other human-made categories. In today's gospel, Christ the Good Shepard does establish a boundary for his sheep, but he does so for the sake of drawing all people toward fullness of life. The Good Shepherd's fence is ever-expanding. Our Lord longs to welcome all of creation into his pastures—and indeed, calls each of us into the sheepfold by name.

• In today's gospel, we are told Jesus came so that we "might have life and have it more abundantly." Now is a good time to take stock of our realities and consider: Am I living my life to the fullest? If not, what is preventing me? How can I live more deeply into Christ's gift of life?

• Today's psalm is one of the more popular ones in Scripture. The familiar phrase is often prayed in times of trial: "The Lord is my shepherd; there is nothing I shall want." The psalmist does not claim that the Lord will take away all suffering. Instead, the psalmist assures us of God's constant presence as we wade through the darkness. God will not leave us to face our fears alone. No matter what happens in this life, we can be assured that goodness and kindness will follow us always. Dwelling in the house of the Lord is our destiny.

Model Rite for the Blessing and Sprinkling of Water

Presider: Through the waters of baptism, the Good Shepherd welcomes us into the divine flock. By the sprinkling of this water, let us recall the beloved community to which we belong, now and forever . . . *[pause]*

> [continue with The Roman Missal, Appendix II]

Model Universal Prayer (Prayer of the Faithful)

Presider: Christ the Good Shepherd provides for his sheep, leading and guiding us along the right path. With trust, we bring our prayers and petitions before him.

Response: Lord, hear our prayer.

Arouse the church to advocate for racial justice and the dismantling of white supremacy . . .

Instill work supervisors with compassion, generosity, and empathy . . .

Guide young people discerning their next steps in life . . .

Receive into the house of the Lord our neighbors and loved ones who have died . . .

Presider: God of everlasting goodness, by the care of your son we have come to know the fullness of life. Receive our prayers that we might draw others into your sheepfold. We ask this through Christ our resurrected Lord. **Amen.**

Liturgy and Music

Music and Metaphor: There are so many beautiful songs and texts that sing of the Good Shepherd. Our reading today challenges us to consider the juxtaposition of titles for Jesus—as shepherd who tends the flock, as gate keeper who provides a safe refuge and as lamb slain for the life of the world. A much richer musical landscape will form when we discern texts closely.

Music and metaphor go hand in hand, for metaphors enliven the imagination. Take time to go through the Sunday readings again even though we have heard them or read them before. For this Sunday and future ones, list topics gleaned from the readings and note the many titles of Jesus.

From his book *Themes and Variations* (GIA Publications), Don Saliers shares a beautiful reflection on music and metaphor. I include this excerpt for our work in music ministry: "Good music orders sound to the themes, rhythms, harmonics, and pulse to patterns in human life. This, of course, leads us to the truth that music-making is itself a metaphor for coming fully alive. The deeper matters of life—especially of the religious and spiritual dimensions of life—are awakened and sustained when music brings a new imagination and new way of receiving hope, faith and love." Consider Saliers's reflection when reaching for a "favorite" song to schedule on Good Shepherd Sunday and imagine a new way of receiving God's grace through music.

COLLECT

Let us pray.

Pause for silent prayer

Almighty ever-living God,
lead us to a share in the joys of heaven,
so that the humble flock may reach
where the brave Shepherd has gone before.
Who lives and reigns with you in the unity
    of the Holy Spirit,
God, for ever and ever. **Amen.**

FIRST READING
Acts 2:14a, 36-41

Then Peter stood up with the Eleven,
    raised his voice, and proclaimed:
"Let the whole house of Israel know for
    certain
    that God has made both Lord and Christ,
    this Jesus whom you crucified."

Now when they heard this, they were cut
    to the heart,
    and they asked Peter and the other
    apostles,
    "What are we to do, my brothers?"
Peter said to them,
    "Repent and be baptized, every one of
    you,
    in the name of Jesus Christ for the
    forgiveness of your sins;
    and you will receive the gift of the Holy
    Spirit.
For the promise is made to you and to your
    children
    and to all those far off,
    whomever the Lord our God will call."
He testified with many other arguments,
    and was exhorting them,
    "Save yourselves from this corrupt
    generation."
Those who accepted his message were
    baptized,
    and about three thousand persons were
    added that day.

RESPONSORIAL PSALM
Ps 23:1-3a, 3b-4, 5, 6

℟. (1) The Lord is my shepherd; there is
nothing I shall want.
    or: ℟. Alleluia.

The LORD is my shepherd; I shall not want.
    In verdant pastures he gives me repose;
beside restful waters he leads me;
    he refreshes my soul.

℟. The Lord is my shepherd; there is
nothing I shall want.
    or: ℟. Alleluia.

He guides me in right paths
　for his name's sake.
Even though I walk in the dark valley
　I fear no evil; for you are at my side
with your rod and your staff
　that give me courage.

℞. The Lord is my shepherd; there is
nothing I shall want.
　or: ℞. Alleluia.

You spread the table before me
　in the sight of my foes;
you anoint my head with oil;
　my cup overflows.

℞. The Lord is my shepherd; there is
nothing I shall want.
　or: ℞. Alleluia.

Only goodness and kindness follow me
　all the days of my life;
and I shall dwell in the house of the Lord
　for years to come.

℞. The Lord is my shepherd; there is
nothing I shall want.
　or: ℞. Alleluia.

SECOND READING

1 Pet 2:20b-25

Beloved:
If you are patient when you suffer for
　doing what is good,
　this is a grace before God.
For to this you have been called,
　because Christ also suffered for you,
　leaving you an example that you should
　　follow in his footsteps.
He committed no sin, and no deceit was
　found in his mouth.

When he was insulted, he returned no
　insult;
　when he suffered, he did not threaten;
　instead, he handed himself over to the
　　one who judges justly.
He himself bore our sins in his body upon
　the cross,
　so that, free from sin, we might live for
　　righteousness.
By his wounds you have been healed.
For you had gone astray like sheep,
　but you have now returned to the
　　shepherd and guardian of your
　　souls.

Living Liturgy

Listening Patterns: Sometimes it is difficult to hear the voice of Jesus amid the noisy distractions of everyday living. Jesus's voice gets lost not only in the false wisdom of this world but from our own assertion that simply because we have said something, we understand what it means—a condition which comes from a curious conceit of our culture. At these moments we must listen more closely to what our lives are really saying, take notes and be guided by the voice of the Shepherd. Our vocation comes from listening, quite literally, to the call and voice.

Together with the church's neophytes, the new lambs, we constantly listen to the voice of Jesus that calls us into the safety and security of a belonging community. We hear the call to find Christian identity within a flock that listens to each other and embraces love for all. Through the distractions of this world, are we able to identify various voice patterns for diversity, equity, and inclusion? Each pattern locates a particular need and each cry for help provides an entry point to compassionate listening. Like the two on the road to Emmaus, we sometimes miss recognizing the voice and presence of Jesus in our midst.

St. Oscar Romero was able to identify the voice of Jesus in the voice of the downtrodden and prepared a place of refuge in the cathedral for the persecuted ones of El Salvador, saying in a Sunday homily: "In the name of God, then, and in the name of this suffering people whose cries rise daily more loudly to heaven, I plead with you . . . : put an end to this repression!" (*Saint Oscar Romero: Voice of the Voiceless*, trans. Michael E. Lee). How might we break through a culture of conceitful rhetoric to truly listen for the voice of Jesus present especially in the oppressed? How can we maintain a special bond with the shepherd and through the connection listen for truths and values that bring us into fellowship with each other?

PROMPTS FOR FAITH-SHARING

• There are at least two related images for Christ in today's readings: he is both the shepherd who guides and protects us and the gate into the sheepfold, our point of entry into safety and rest. Which of these images do you prefer? Why?

• The first reading emphasizes that repentance and baptism are the appropriate responses to the good news of Christ. How do you live out the call of your baptism in a continuous way, even if it occurred long ago?

• It can feel like the members of a flock of sheep have no individuality, but Christ's images of shepherding often stress the individual love he carries for each of us. How could you care for a member of your community in an individualized way this Easter season?

✠ SPIRITUALITY

GOSPEL ACCLAMATION
John 14:6

℟. Alleluia, alleluia.
I am the way, the truth and the life, says the Lord;
no one comes to the Father, except through me.
℟. Alleluia, alleluia.

Gospel   John 14:1-12; L52A

Jesus said to his disciples:
   "Do not let your hearts be troubled.
You have faith in God; have faith also in me.
In my Father's house there are many dwelling places.
If there were not,
   would I have told you that I am going to prepare a place for you?
And if I go and prepare a place for you,
   I will come back again and take you to myself,
   so that where I am you also may be.
Where I am going you know the way."
Thomas said to him,
   "Master, we do not know where you are going;
   how can we know the way?"
Jesus said to him, "I am the way and the truth and the life.
No one comes to the Father except through me.
If you know me, then you will also know my Father.
From now on you do know him and have seen him."
Philip said to him,
   "Master, show us the Father, and that will be enough for us."
Jesus said to him, "Have I been with you for so long a time
   and you still do not know me, Philip?
Whoever has seen me has seen the Father.
How can you say, 'Show us the Father'?
Do you not believe that I am in the Father and the Father is in me?

Continued in Appendix A, p. 293.

Reflecting on the Gospel

There is a gentle urgency about the first words of this gospel: "Do not let your hearts be troubled. You have faith in God; have faith also in me." This is a rallying cry to faithfulness as Jesus draws near to his passion and death through which he will return to his Father's house. It is a rallying cry to all his disciples who will also go into death—but with the confidence that is born out of Jesus's resurrection from the dead. The "Father's house" is not spatial but relational, and so there is room for everyone who abides in Jesus as he abides "at the Father's side" (John 1:18). Jesus does not deny that anxiety is looming and absence is threatening as he speaks, but his departure will only be that of a good host who excuses himself for "a little while" (John 14:19) in order to make rooms ready for the guests who have been invited to his Father's house.

And yet Thomas's question haunts us. "Master, we do not know where you are going; how can we know the way?" In even the most faithful life, there may come a time when we seem either to stumble suddenly into darkness or gradually wander away from old certainties. We would all like a simple, clearly marked road to direct us to the Father's house through what is often the dark wood of our lives. What we are offered is not a map but a *person*, Jesus Christ, who replies to Thomas's question with another solemn "I am the way and the truth and the life." When we journey along a well-traveled road, we trust the road because we know it has been made and used by others who have been there before us, putting in bridges, median strips, detours where necessary. Others have traveled this way safely. When both the way and the Traveler who has gone before us is Jesus, we should journey with the greatest confidence.

On display in Auschwitz is a large map clearly marked with the rail systems that carried over two million people, especially Jews, from all over Europe to this place of death. At the Yad Vashem Holocaust Museum in Jerusalem, a memorial to those transported, is a rail wagon hanging on a piece of broken track over a gap into the valley below. Jesus is the map that we follow to life, the way across the gap to those who fear that his leaving them will mean abandonment, and the truth that will carry us to life not death.

For the Jewish people, the prohibition against making images of God flows from the Genesis tradition that humanity, male and female together, reflects the image of God (see Gen 1:26). So the answer that Jesus gives to Philip's question is, in one sense, the traditional Jewish answer: Jesus shows his disciples the face of God in his own humanity (see 2 Cor 4:6). In another sense, it is radically different because, in words and works, Jesus is the unique and saving revelation of God, one with God.

Preparing to Proclaim

Key words and phrases: "I am the way and the truth and the life."

To the point: We are past the midpoint of the Easter season, and the readings start to turn from the immediate aftermath of the resurrection and toward the ongoing work the church will face after Jesus's bodily presence departs earth. We see that while the work of Easter is complete in one sense—Jesus has conquered death once and for all—it will be an ongoing project to bring it to its fullness. Jesus has gone ahead of us in death and has conquered it for us so that we might participate in his life. In this gospel, Jesus tells us that he will go ahead of us to heaven, as well, but it is not to leave us alone. He goes ahead to open the way for us and to prepare our place there. Jesus also affirms his unity with his Father here; he already dwells in the Father and the Father in him, and we are called to follow him into such intimacy with God, which is truly heaven.

Psalmist Preparation

The psalm reflects the shift of the other readings this week, moving from early Easter's wholehearted outpouring of praise to late Easter's reassurances that our trust in God remains well-founded even as we wait for the work of Easter to be seen in all its fullness. As in Lent, we have a psalm that pairs mercy and trust. We know that God will not abandon us, and we rejoice in that truth. As you prepare this psalm, think about times you have found God to be trustworthy. What is a time when God's promises were fulfilled for you? Bring your gratitude for that moment to your proclamation of this psalm.

Making Connections

Between the readings: Like the gospel, the second reading calls us to follow in Christ's footsteps. Here, we are to follow him in becoming "living stones" that might be built into a "spiritual house." This house is akin to the temple, a place for offering sacrifice. But it can also serve as shelter for others. The first reading reminds us that part of the work of the church is to distribute goods in a just way. This is so important that a new group is established: deacons are initiated to oversee the social work of the church.

To experience: Some of the metaphors in these readings can seem obscure and unreachable. We are to wait for Jesus to prepare a place for us in his Father's house; we are in the meantime to become living stones built into another house. Reflecting on themes of home and hospitality might help these readings take on a more robust meaning.

Homily Points

• "Do not let your hearts be troubled." Jesus's decree comes on the heels of what any observer would call a troubling time for the disciples. Jesus just told the Twelve that he is to die—and that his death will be brought about in part by the betrayal of one of them. Life is about to change drastically for the disciples. Grief looms on the horizon. Jesus knows the challenges to come—and still he declares, "Do not let your hearts be troubled." Jesus assures the disciples—and in turn, each of us—that the divine dwells with us always. We need not fear. We need not hold all the answers. We need only to believe in God's great love and power to bring light into the darkest places.

• Does such a belief mean our hearts will never feel troubled again? Most likely not. Our world is hurting. People on the planet are suffering under the weights of individual and structural sin and misfortune.

• It is natural to feel pain ourselves and to feel with the pains of our neighbors. This is empathy. Jesus is not suggesting that we disavow ourselves of the world's troubles. Rather, he is encouraging us to bring the stirrings of our hearts to God. He is inviting us to trust that he is indeed "the way, the truth, and the life." He is inviting us to trust that all will be made well once more when the kingdom finally comes. Until then, we are to claim our royal priesthood and announce the praises of our God.

Model Rite for the Blessing and Sprinkling of Water

Presider: Through the waters of baptism we die and rise with Christ anew. May these waters purify our hearts and draw us ever closer to the dwelling place of God . . . *[pause]*

    [*continue with* The Roman Missal, *Appendix II]*

Model Universal Prayer (Prayer of the Faithful)

Presider: Trusting in Christ Jesus, "the way, the truth, and the life," let us place our needs and petitions before the Lord.

Response: Lord, hear our prayer.

Deepen the priestly call of all believers, that the word of God may continue to spread to the ends of the earth . . .

Support the work of therapists, counselors, chaplains, and others who serve in times of crisis, that more people may be brought out of darkness and into light . . .

Soothe the hurting hearts of people in tense or broken relationships, that they may experience healing . . .

Keep our family and friends safe from harm, that we may enter this new week with health and hope . . .

Presider: God of peace, you promise to create an everlasting home for us so that we may dwell with you forever. Hear our prayers·that our hearts might rejoice at your saving help. We ask this through Christ our resurrected Lord. **Amen.**

Liturgy and Music

Marian Songs during Eastertime: While the month of May is dedicated to the Blessed Virgin Mary, remember to keep the Easter season in mind when preparing liturgical music. There are several Easter hymns that reference Mary's witness to the resurrection—*Regina Caeli* (O Queen of Heaven) and "Be Joyful, Mary" are just two examples. Try to weave these songs into the community's repertoire throughout this month's Sunday liturgies.

    In addition, some of the rich facets of today's readings—church, discipleship, Jesus as the way, truth, and life, the word of God—give music ministers plenty to focus on in terms of choosing appropriate music as the Easter season continues. This week, music ministers might connect the discipleship of the early Christians with that of Mary's willingness to do God's will.

    During this month, some parishes might include devotional practices of the rosary and the novena for the community. Consider recycling one or two of these devotional songs at Sunday Mass as a way of connecting the rosary and novena group with the parish community.

    If your parish is one that has implemented a year-round process for the catechumenate, catechumens will continue to be dismissed before the Creed. Choose an Easter-themed, more festive dismissal song to accompany the procession from the pews.

COLLECT

Let us pray.

Pause for silent prayer

Almighty ever-living God,
constantly accomplish the Paschal
    Mystery within us,
that those you were pleased to make new
    in Holy Baptism
may, under your protective care, bear
    much fruit
and come to the joys of life eternal.
Through our Lord Jesus Christ, your Son,
who lives and reigns with you in the unity
    of the Holy Spirit,
God, for ever and ever. **Amen.**

FIRST READING

Acts 6:1-7

As the number of disciples continued to
    grow,
    the Hellenists complained against the
      Hebrews
    because their widows
    were being neglected in the daily
      distribution.
So the Twelve called together the
    community of the disciples and said,
    "It is not right for us to neglect the word
      of God to serve at table.
Brothers, select from among you seven
    reputable men,
    filled with the Spirit and wisdom,
    whom we shall appoint to this task,
    whereas we shall devote ourselves to
      prayer
    and to the ministry of the word."
The proposal was acceptable to the whole
    community,
    so they chose Stephen, a man filled with
      faith and the Holy Spirit,
    also Philip, Prochorus, Nicanor, Timon,
      Parmenas,
    and Nicholas of Antioch, a convert to
      Judaism.
They presented these men to the apostles
    who prayed and laid hands on them.
The word of God continued to spread,
    and the number of the disciples in
      Jerusalem increased greatly;
    even a large group of priests were
      becoming obedient to the faith.

RESPONSORIAL PSALM

Ps 33:1-2, 4-5, 18-19

℟. (22) Lord, let your mercy be on us, as
we place our trust in you.
    or: ℟. Alleluia.

Exult, you just, in the LORD;
  praise from the upright is fitting.
Give thanks to the LORD on the harp;
  with the ten-stringed lyre chant his
    praises.

R̶. Lord, let your mercy be on us, as we
place our trust in you.
  or: R̶. Alleluia.

Upright is the word of the LORD,
  and all his works are trustworthy.
He loves justice and right;
  of the kindness of the LORD the earth
    is full.

R̶. Lord, let your mercy be on us, as we place
our trust in you.
  or: R̶. Alleluia.

See, the eyes of the LORD are upon those
    who fear him,
  upon those who hope for his kindness,
to deliver them from death
  and preserve them in spite of famine.

R̶. Lord, let your mercy be on us, as we place
our trust in you.
  or: R̶. Alleluia.

SECOND READING
1 Pet 2:4-9

Beloved:
Come to him, a living stone, rejected by
    human beings
  but chosen and precious in the sight of
    God,
  and, like living stones,
  let yourselves be built into a spiritual
    house
  to be a holy priesthood to offer spiritual
    sacrifices
  acceptable to God through Jesus Christ.
For it says in Scripture:
Behold, I am laying a stone in Zion,
a cornerstone, chosen and precious,
and whoever believes in it shall not be
* put to shame.*
Therefore, its value is for you who have
    faith, but for those without faith:
The stone that the builders rejected
has become the cornerstone,
and
A stone that will make people stumble,
and a rock that will make them fall.
They stumble by disobeying the word, as
    is their destiny.

You are "a chosen race, a royal priesthood,
  a holy nation, a people of his own,
  so that you may announce the praises"
    of him
  who called you out of darkness into his
    wonderful light.

Living Liturgy

Living Stones: Over these two weeks we listen to the Last Supper discourse. Jesus tells us that if we believe in him, we will do the works that he does, and the news we hear is even more amazing because in doing Jesus's work, we are doing the Father's. Jesus continues to reveal himself in answer to Thomas's question, as the way, the truth, and the life. Yet the disciples through Philip's questioning still cannot recognize Jesus's intimate connection with the Father. Through this story we learn that the kingdom of heaven is more than a place. It is an abiding relationship with God and all that has gone before and all that will follow. Doing the work of Jesus means to be in close relationship with each other, to accompany the other.

The image of accompaniment that Peter's letter gives us is one of church as a building made of living stones with Christ as the foundation for all the ways that we turn our faith into action. Catholic Relief Services (CRS) gives us one avenue to activate a living faith through helping the suffering and vulnerable communities of the world. The CRS website (www.crs.org) offers ways to give and to get involved. CRS works with a vast network of partners worldwide to carry out the commitment of the USCCB to assist the poor, partnering with local churches around the globe. A web browse through the guiding principles of the organization gives greater context for the kind of relational ministry that we continue to foster in our own faith communities in the practice of accompaniment. CRS's guiding principles are shared across religious and cultural boundaries and articulate values that are common among people who seek to promote and work toward true justice and lasting peace.

From this example of turning faith into action we can draw a template for living like we belong to each other. And for our ministerial contexts we recognize that we are a "chosen race, a royal priesthood, a holy nation" announcing God's praises and living our baptismal call out of darkness into wonderful light.

PROMPTS FOR FAITH-SHARING

• Reflect on what the word "home" means to you and the places that have been your home. How do these places impact how you envision the place Jesus is preparing for you?

• What role does hospitality play in your life? How might you, called to be a "living stone," help to create a home for others?

• Do you find it easy or hard to trust God in the long wait for God's promises to be fully realized?

✝ SPIRITUALITY

GOSPEL ACCLAMATION
John 14:23

℟. Alleluia, alleluia.
Whoever loves me will keep my word, says the
    Lord,
and my Father will love him and we will come
    to him.
℟. Alleluia, alleluia.

Gospel

John 14:15-21; L55A

Jesus said to his disciples:
  "If you love me, you will keep my
      commandments.
And I will ask the Father,
  and he will give you another
      Advocate to be with you always,
  the Spirit of truth, whom the world
      cannot accept,
  because it neither sees nor knows
      him.
But you know him, because he remains
      with you,
  and will be in you.
I will not leave you orphans; I will come
      to you.
In a little while the world will no longer
      see me,
  but you will see me, because I live
      and you will live.
On that day you will realize that I am
      in my Father
  and you are in me and I in you.
Whoever has my commandments and
      observes them
  is the one who loves me.
And whoever loves me will be loved by
      my Father,
  and I will love him and reveal myself
      to him."

Reflecting on the Gospel

"We must be still and still moving / Into another intensity / For a further union, a deeper communion." T. S. Eliot wrote these words in his *Four Quartets*. The communion that we hear proclaimed in today's gospel is the deepest, most intense, and most personal of unions, expressed in Jesus's repeated use of the word *in*. The union is the indwelling of the Paraclete "in you" (meaning Jesus's disciples); of Jesus "in my Father"; of the disciples who are gathered, "you are in me and I in you." This indwelling happens through mutual love, which frames the reading in its first and last verses.

Our TV screens are tragically filled with images of contemporary orphans of war, of HIV/AIDS, of natural disasters. We see how the untimely death of their parents has left some children in deep sorrow and with feelings of abandonment. Jesus's leaving his disciples is not "untimely"; it is part of his "hour" that reveals the fullness of his mystery. To help them understand this, to enable them to move from fear to faith, Jesus promises his disciples "another" Advocate. *Advocate* is only one translation of *parákletos*, a word rich in its various meanings of comforter, encourager, counselor. We admire those generous, if too rare, men and women who advocate in our courts of law (often without charging legal fees) for the downtrodden, the dispossessed. We can become enthralled in courtroom dramas on television or in a gripping novel. The Advocate whom Jesus will send will care for the disciples who are "dispossessed" of the human presence of Jesus and will be the real drama of their lives, as Luke will show in the Acts of the Apostles.

This Advocate will do what Jesus did, but in "another" way, through the Spirit of Jesus abiding in his disciples. If they want to cling to the Jesus they knew on this side of death, they will never know him as the risen Lord who shares new life with them.

It is all a work of love, and not love that is a private, mystical relationship with Jesus, but love that is as communal as that between the Father and Son and the Spirit of them both; love that reflects the communion between disciples and is expressed in works of love, which reflect the life, death, and resurrection of Jesus; love that is the empowering reason for the obedience of disciples to Jesus's words and works.

For each one of us there will come a time of "farewell discourse" as we face the prospect of our own biological death. Pierre Teilhard de Chardin wrote powerfully of the ultimate indwelling of God in us that can come only through death, as it did for Jesus: "O God, grant that I may understand (provided only my faith is strong enough) that it is you who are painfully parting the fibers of my being in order to penetrate to the very marrow of my substance and bear me away within yourself."

Preparing to Proclaim

Key words and phrases: "I will not leave you orphans."

To the point: This gospel echoes the themes of last week as Jesus is preparing his disciples to live without him for a time, or at least without the bodily presence they have come to know and which will depart earth at the ascension. This week adds a foreshadowing of the upcoming Pentecost feast; Jesus's presence will remain in the Holy Spirit, who will accompany the disciples and the church beyond their lifetime in their remaining work on earth. For us, too, the Holy Spirit is a promised companion, providing continuity with these earliest of Jesus's followers. Like the disciples, we are not left alone in the struggle.

Psalmist Preparation

Last week's psalm was a throwback to Lenten themes of God's mercy and our need for patient trust; this one returns to the fullness of Easter rejoicing. The Holy Spirit's ongoing presence, promised in the gospel and demonstrated in the first reading, is reason for a renewed outpouring of gratitude and thanksgiving. As you prepare this psalm, spend some time reflecting on the role of the Holy Spirit in your life; think especially about the gifts of the Spirit (wisdom, understanding, counsel, fortitude, knowledge, piety, and fear of the Lord) and how they play a role in seeing you through the challenges of the life of faith.

Making Connections

Between the readings: In the first reading, we see an affirmation of the gospel's idea of the Holy Spirit as an ongoing presence with us beyond Christ's bodily presence on earth. This is depicted in a forerunner of what we now know as the sacrament of confirmation. Those who have been baptized in Samaria have their baptisms completed in a sense when the apostles lay hands on them and the Holy Spirit descends.

To experience: There have always been and will always be struggles that accompany a life of faith, and we might wonder why Jesus does not make his presence more visible and obvious to us and to those who would criticize us. But God is not about "winning" in the way we would sometimes choose; the "win" here is not that we will never struggle or suffer but that we will never be left alone in our struggles.

Homily Points

• Great joy came upon the crowds of Samaria who paid attention to the speech and signs pointing to Christ. Their witness reminds us that joy—profound Easter joy—can spark from simply paying attention. The world teems with resurrection moments: a brother's depression slowly lifts, warring countries call for a cease-fire, fresh buds bloom at the start of spring. Pay attention for resurrection moments in your life this week. When one happens, sink into the joy it evokes and give praise to God for the Easter victory that is ours.

• Why do you hope? St. Peter puts forth a challenging summons in today's second reading: "Always be ready to give an explanation to anyone who asks you for a reason for your hope." In a world pained by suffering, violence, and oppression, it can be easy to lose hope. It could be easy to feel let down by political systems, broken promises, and other entities not of God. For we have been promised that in Christ—and only in Christ—rests all our hope. How do we communicate this hope in compelling ways? What does it look like to share a reality as mysterious as Christ's resurrection? This is the call of the Easter season and beyond.

• In today's gospel, Jesus assures us that God's Spirit "remains with you and will be in you." How have you seen the Spirit alive in yourself? In your family and friends? In this congregation? As we approach the celebration of Pentecost, let us be ever more mindful of the Spirit's lasting presence in our lives.

Model Rite for the Blessing and Sprinkling of Water

Presider: God's Spirit came upon us in the waters of baptism and dwells with us always. May the Spirit of truth continue to transform our hearts and inspire our lives . . . *[pause]*

   [continue with The Roman Missal, *Appendix II]*

Model Universal Prayer (Prayer of the Faithful)

Presider: Holding fast to the hope of Christ, let us offer to the Lord our prayers and petitions.

Response: Lord, hear our prayer.

Increase love and respect for LGBTQ+ people in the church and broader world . . .

Fix oppressive political and economic systems in our world that cause suffering . . .

Inspire the work of artists, writers, musicians, and other creatives who bring hope to the world . . .

Open our senses to the wonders of your creation and the joy of Christ alive in our world . . .

Presider: Generous God, you draw us closer to you through the gifts of your son and the Holy Spirit. Receive our prayers that with joy and gratitude we might live into your hopes for the world. We ask this through Christ our Lord. **Amen.**

Liturgy and Music

Singing the Communion Song: The communion song should generally be a piece that is familiar to the congregation or one that can be memorized easily and sung without the aid of a hymnal or handout. By this time, if you've introduced new music at the start of the Easter season, especially communion songs, the assembly will already be familiar with these songs. If the refrain is short and repetitive, encourage the choir to sing these pieces by heart to enter more deeply into prayer with the community. Another way to encourage the assembly's participation would be to select songs that require the assembly's response in a simple phrase that would come after a cantor's verse.

   Today we celebrate Mother's Day and a blessing is usually prayed over all the mothers, mothers-to-be and mother figures of the parish. A short acclamation or phrase of a song might be woven into this blessing prayer and the full piece or refrain might be sung in conclusion of the short rite.

   As the assembly progresses through the middle weeks of Easter, may our Alleluia songs remain fresh and exciting. Vary the arrangements, add more instruments (or take away some) and think of creative ways to refresh and enliven these remaining festive Easter liturgies.

COLLECT

Let us pray.

Pause for silent prayer

Grant, almighty God,
that we may celebrate with heartfelt
   devotion these days of joy,
which we keep in honor of the risen Lord,
and that what we relive in remembrance
we may always hold to in what we do.
Through our Lord Jesus Christ, your Son,
who lives and reigns with you in the unity
   of the Holy Spirit,
God, for ever and ever. **Amen.**

FIRST READING
Acts 8:5-8, 14-17

Philip went down to the city of Samaria
   and proclaimed the Christ to them.
With one accord, the crowds paid attention
   to what was said by Philip
   when they heard it and saw the signs he
      was doing.
For unclean spirits, crying out in a loud
   voice,
   came out of many possessed people,
   and many paralyzed or crippled people
      were cured.
There was great joy in that city.

Now when the apostles in Jerusalem
   heard that Samaria had accepted the
      word of God,
   they sent them Peter and John,
   who went down and prayed for them,
   that they might receive the Holy Spirit,
   for it had not yet fallen upon any of
      them;
   they had only been baptized in the
      name of the Lord Jesus.
Then they laid hands on them
   and they received the Holy Spirit.

RESPONSORIAL PSALM
Ps 66:1-3, 4-5, 6-7, 16, 20

R̷. (1) Let all the earth cry out to God with
joy.
   or:
R̷. Alleluia.

Shout joyfully to God, all the earth,
   sing praise to the glory of his name;
   proclaim his glorious praise.
Say to God, "How tremendous are your
   deeds!"

R̷. Let all the earth cry out to God with joy.
   or:
R̷. Alleluia.

"Let all on earth worship and sing praise
　　to you,
　　sing praise to your name!"
Come and see the works of God,
　his tremendous deeds among the
　　children of Adam.

R̷. Let all the earth cry out to God with joy.
　or:
R̷. Alleluia.

He has changed the sea into dry land;
　through the river they passed on foot.
Therefore let us rejoice in him.
　He rules by his might forever.

R̷. Let all the earth cry out to God with joy.
　or:
R̷. Alleluia.

Hear now, all you who fear God, while I
　　declare
　what he has done for me.
Blessed be God who refused me not
　my prayer or his kindness!

R̷. Let all the earth cry out to God with joy.
　or:
R̷. Alleluia.

SECOND READING
1 Pet 3:15-18

Beloved:
Sanctify Christ as Lord in your hearts.
Always be ready to give an explanation
　to anyone who asks you for a reason for
　　your hope,
　but do it with gentleness and reverence,
　keeping your conscience clear,
　so that, when you are maligned,
　those who defame your good conduct
　　in Christ
　may themselves be put to shame.
For it is better to suffer for doing good,
　if that be the will of God, than for
　　doing evil.
For Christ also suffered for sins once,
　the righteous for the sake of the
　　unrighteous,
　that he might lead you to God.
Put to death in the flesh,
　he was brought to life in the Spirit.

Living Liturgy

Love Beyond Boundary: Love is at the center of the gospel reading today. Christian love extends beyond thinking only about a list of rules to practicing a living relationship with Christ and through Christ, the triune God. The reading continues with Jesus's Last Supper discourse which we read from last Sunday. The Advocate promised is available for all, not just for the first disciples. Through this we recognize that the Spirit is non-discriminatory and unencumbered by borders and boundaries. However, we ourselves often limit the work of the Spirit.

In the encyclical *Fratelli Tutti*, Pope Francis uses the parable of the Good Samaritan to reflect on an unhealthy society that turns its back on suffering. Both the passers-by in the story, the priest and the Levite, ignore the injured one. This shows that belief in and the worship of God while following all the commandments are not enough to ensure just ministry. By only focusing on rules, we deny the full outpouring of the Holy Spirit in us and a deepening relationship with God and each other. By offering this story, Pope Francis answers this question: "Who is my neighbor?"

The psalm today celebrates this understanding of boundless ministry to the neighbor with joy and praise, a joy given to all the nations. We learn that even in suffering we can bless God who has kept us alive. In suffering we still proclaim to our neighbors to come and see the tremendous deeds of God. God's word transcends the boundaries of human experience. Within our liturgical remembering we dissolve the boundaries of time and bring God's glorious deeds into the present. As a belonging community, we celebrate the unlimited flow and the unencumbered movement of the Holy Spirit present in our hearts that transforms suffering into hope and love.

PROMPTS FOR FAITH-SHARING

• Reflect on your confirmation; what do you remember of that day?

• How do you experience the Holy Spirit's promised presence in your life?

• The gifts of the Spirit are wisdom, understanding, counsel, fortitude, knowledge, piety, and fear of the Lord. Which of these do you need to increase in order to meet your current challenges in life?

✝ SPIRITUALITY

GOSPEL ACCLAMATION
Matt 28:19a, 20b

℟. Alleluia, alleluia.
Go and teach all nations, says the Lord;
I am with you always, until the end of the world.
℟. Alleluia, alleluia.

Gospel

Matt 28:16-20; L58A

The eleven disciples went to
    Galilee,
  to the mountain to which
      Jesus had ordered them.
When they saw him, they
      worshiped, but they
      doubted.
Then Jesus approached and
      said to them,
  "All power in heaven and on
      earth has been given to
      me.
Go, therefore, and make
      disciples of all nations,
  baptizing them in the name of
      the Father,
  and of the Son, and of the
      Holy Spirit,
  teaching them to observe all that I
      have commanded you.
And behold, I am with you always, until
      the end of the age."

Reflecting on the Gospel

The gospel reading chosen for this feast of the Ascension is the conclusion to Matthew's Gospel. It does not recount Jesus's ascension (we get that in the first reading), but it confirms Jesus's promise to be always with his disciples. At the beginning of his gospel, while telling the story of Jesus's birth, Matthew has named him as "Emmanuel," "God is with us" (Matt 1:23), and at the end he repeats the promise to be "with you always, until the end of the age" (Matt 28:20). It is only in the context of this promise that there can be any hope of fragile disciples fulfilling the imperatives of their great commissioning to "Go! . . . baptize! . . . make disciples! . . . teach!" All this is spoken to the Eleven, whom we last saw forsaking Jesus when he was arrested (Matt 26:31-56). They had struggled through to enough belief in what the women had told them—that Jesus was going before them into Galilee and would meet them there—to get themselves to Galilee.

Why Galilee? Matthew's concern is not with geographical exactitude, which never brought anyone to faith. Rather, he makes geography serve his theology. The Eleven have passed through the harsh winter of their disillusionment with themselves and the pain of Jesus's passion and death. What more appropriate setting for a second spring of discipleship than Galilee, the place of their first call, first enthusiasms, first mission? In the eyes of Jewish orthodoxy, Galilee was also a marginalized region, less sophisticated and more populated by Gentiles than was Jerusalem. What Matthew is announcing to his own and future communities like our own is that we, too, are being called again and again, with new responsibilities, to our "Galilees": the world of the less privileged, the place and time of new beginnings of our discipleship, and that here is the starting point for the proclamation of the gospel. The Galilee setting is also Matthew's subtle way of emphasizing the identity between the earthly and risen Jesus. For Matthew, mountains are important as places of temptation (see Matt 4:8), teaching (Matt 5–7), and transfiguration (Matt 17:1-8). Here, in this last scene of his gospel, the final teaching is given, healing forgiveness is offered, and the Eleven are transfigured into teachers, evangelizers, and baptizers in the name of the Father, Son, and Holy Spirit.

When the disciples see Jesus, "they worshiped, but they doubted." The mixture of postresurrection faith and doubt is not so much skepticism or disbelief as fearful doubt, a struggle to accept the call and its responsibility, knowing only too well their own weakness. The only other time that Matthew describes the disciples as worshipping Jesus is after the calming of the storm on the Sea of Galilee and Jesus's rescue of Peter from the waves when his faith in Jesus falters. We can easily see ourselves, individually and communally, in the same mix of worshipping faith and doubt. True discipleship does not exclude doubt but takes it before God and into the mystery of Christ in whose absent presence we fall down and worship.

Preparing to Proclaim

Key words and phrases: "And behold, I am with you always, until the end of the age."

To the point: Finally comes the moment for which the last weeks have prepared us. Jesus is going away, at least in one sense: the disciples will not have his bodily presence to which they have become accustomed. He gives them their mission for while he is away: to make disciples, to baptize, to teach all that Jesus has taught. This will be the ongoing work of the church, work that continues even today. And Jesus does not leave the disciples—or us—alone in this work. Many of our Easter season readings have prepared us for this moment. He remains present in the breaking of the bread; he has promised the Holy Spirit as guide and companion. He is with us always, never leaving us alone, even when the life of faith is a struggle.

Psalmist Preparation

This psalm, written centuries before the life of Christ, directly connects with the narrative of Jesus ascending into heaven. In Jesus's ascension, God takes his rightful place as ruler over heaven and earth. We respond with rejoicing, even as we await this to be achieved in its fullness. For it remains true that Jesus's kingship is not always clear: sin still happens, suffering still exists, the poor and oppressed become more so. As you prepare this psalm, think of a few ways you wish Jesus's reign were more apparent. Pray for their actualization as you proclaim this psalm; let it be an earnest prayer for the fulfillment of God's promises.

Making Connections

Between the readings: The second reading affirms the power of Christ and that the church, his body, continues his work on earth beyond the ascension. While the gospel has another moment of Jesus's preparing the disciples for his departure, the first reading contains the actual ascension narrative. Here, too, he leaves them with a mission—they are to be his witnesses all through the world. And here, too, there is a promise to return. This is still not the end of the story.

To experience: Each of us is called to share in the evangelizing work that Christ entrusts to the disciples here. For laypersons, it is not always apparent how we are making disciples or teaching the faith or leading others to baptism. But opportunities abound and every relationship is a chance to make Christ more present to someone, baptized or not, who might not know him well.

Homily Points

• The ascension of the Lord ushers us into a week of waiting. Jesus has ascended into heaven and the Holy Spirit has not yet come down. Pentecost is still days away. Times of waiting can often be uncomfortable, yet this unique time in the liturgical year affords us the space to step back with the original eleven disciples and ponder: What does Christ's resurrection mean for our lives? How can I carry the hope of Easter into the next season?

• Relationships change. People constantly grow and evolve. Think back to a time when you reconnected with a longtime friend. This person cared for you at precious times in life and now has the chance to experience you in a new stage, perhaps as you wrestle with big questions or live more deeply into your callings. The disciples know what it is like to see a friend change. They accompanied Jesus throughout his earthly ministry. They witnessed his great care for the poor and compassion for the suffering. Then, Jesus died. The relationship necessarily changed. Perhaps some disciples even wondered if the relationship ended.

• Then Jesus appeared to them days later in the upper room. The disciples reconnected with their beloved friend and Lord who just made a sacrifice that changed the world forever. How did their relationships with Christ change after the resurrection and at the time of his ascension? What about our relationships with Christ—in what ways will the Easter victory impact your connection to Christ?

Model Rite for the Blessing and Sprinkling of Water

Presider: In the waters of baptism, we die and rise with Christ. By the sprinkling of this water, may we be empowered to "make disciples of all nations" and spread the hope of baptism to the ends of the earth . . . *[pause]*

> [continue with The Roman Missal, *Appendix II]*

Model Universal Prayer (Prayer of the Faithful)

Presider: Fortified by our Lord who ascended into heaven and now sits at the right hand of God, let us offer our prayers and petitions.

Response: Lord, hear our prayer.

Enlighten the hearts of those who preach the gospel in word and deed . . .

Grant success to farmers and all who grow, produce, and distribute our food . . .

Ease the anxieties and fears of people waiting for medical test results . . .

Shape each of us gathered here into faithful witnesses of the love of Christ . . .

Presider: God of all ages, your son Jesus promised to be with us always until the end of the age. Hear our prayers that we might embrace his presence in our lives and encourage others to do the same. We ask this through Christ our resurrected Lord. **Amen.**

Liturgy and Music

From Ascension to Pentecost: Whether Ascension is celebrated on a Thursday or a Sunday in your diocese, today would be the day to incorporate songs of the Spirit as we journey as community through this Easter time toward the solemnity of Pentecost. One way to musically connect Ascension to Pentecost would be to play a scaled-down version (perhaps refrain without verses with a simpler accompaniment) of a setting of *Veni Sancte Spiritus* or a piece to the Holy Spirit. This piece might be selected as a prelude song or song for the preparation of the gifts. The full setting of this piece would then be sung at the Pentecost liturgy.

The psalm today is a festive one. The imagery is vivid and its triumph echoes in the words of the great commission in Matthew's Gospel. With Psalm 47, as music ministers, we enter into the joy of the disciples who have been entrusted with the good news of authority and kingdom building, and accept the awesome responsibility of continuing to bear witness through our ministry. What steps will we take to carry out this responsibility? The summer months are quickly approaching. Will we consider continuing education in our various fields of liturgical and music ministry?

Let us pray.

Pause for silent prayer

Gladden us with holy joys, almighty God,
and make us rejoice with devout
    thanksgiving,
for the Ascension of Christ your Son
is our exaltation,
and, where the Head has gone before in
    glory,
the Body is called to follow in hope.
Through our Lord Jesus Christ, your Son,
who lives and reigns with you in the unity
    of the Holy Spirit,
God, for ever and ever. **Amen.**

FIRST READING
Acts 1:1-11

In the first book, Theophilus,
    I dealt with all that Jesus did and taught
    until the day he was taken up,
    after giving instructions through the
        Holy Spirit
    to the apostles whom he had chosen.
He presented himself alive to them
    by many proofs after he had suffered,
    appearing to them during forty days
    and speaking about the kingdom of
        God.
While meeting with them,
    he enjoined them not to depart from
        Jerusalem,
    but to wait for "the promise of the
        Father
    about which you have heard me speak;
    for John baptized with water,
    but in a few days you will be baptized
        with the Holy Spirit."

When they had gathered together they
        asked him,
    "Lord, are you at this time going to
        restore the kingdom to Israel?"
He answered them, "It is not for you to
        know the times or seasons
    that the Father has established by his
        own authority.
But you will receive power when the Holy
        Spirit comes upon you,
    and you will be my witnesses in
        Jerusalem,
    throughout Judea and Samaria,
    and to the ends of the earth."
When he had said this, as they were
        looking on,
    he was lifted up, and a cloud took him
        from their sight.

While they were looking intently at the
    sky as he was going,
      suddenly two men dressed in white
        garments stood beside them.
They said, "Men of Galilee,
    why are you standing there looking at
      the sky?
This Jesus who has been taken up from
    you into heaven
    will return in the same way as you have
      seen him going into heaven."

RESPONSORIAL PSALM
Ps 47:2-3, 6-7, 8-9

R℣. (6) God mounts his throne to shouts of
joy: a blare of trumpets for the Lord.
    or:
R℣. Alleluia.

All you peoples, clap your hands,
    shout to God with cries of gladness,
for the Lᴏʀᴅ, the Most High, the awesome,
    is the great king over all the earth.

R℣. God mounts his throne to shouts of joy:
a blare of trumpets for the Lord.
    or:
R℣. Alleluia.

God mounts his throne amid shouts of joy;
    the Lᴏʀᴅ, amid trumpet blasts.
Sing praise to God, sing praise;
    sing praise to our king, sing praise.

R℣. God mounts his throne to shouts of joy:
a blare of trumpets for the Lord.
    or:
R℣. Alleluia.

For king of all the earth is God;
    sing hymns of praise.
God reigns over the nations,
    God sits upon his holy throne.

R℣. God mounts his throne to shouts of joy:
a blare of trumpets for the Lord.
    or:
R℣. Alleluia.

SECOND READING
Eph 1:17-23

See Appendix A, p. 293.

Living Liturgy

Witnessing Absence: The disappearance of the risen Christ today echoes the gospel reading from the Third Sunday of Easter. The disciples on the way to Emmaus only recognize Jesus at the breaking of bread where he vanished from their sight. Christ is no longer present in body but instead remains embodied by an entire community of believers, sent out to be his presence in the world. In a sermon on the ascension, St. Leo the Great said this: "What was visible in our Savior has passed over into his mysteries" (*Catechism of the Catholic Church* 1115), which means that Christ becomes present in the sacraments that we celebrate.

Through each sacrament then we are summoned to witness to the world. John August Swanson depicts through his serigraph *The Last Supper* an example of radical table fellowship that witnesses to the world our compassion and care. In his notes about the artwork, Swanson tells us that the theme of his serigraph is "community, and what it means to share a meal together. . . . It is the table where we come to know and love each other in the breaking of bread, and are not alone anymore."

The focal point of the serigraph is Swanson's round Last Supper table, showing his mind and heart's "vision of a feast of companionship and sharing" where there is "no hierarchy of seating and no one can be excluded from the conversation." But a more intriguing feature of the artwork is the illuminated narrative border of seventy-eight miniature scenes that emphasize the labor of those who grow and prepare the food. Often forgotten and invisible are those who make the meal possible, the work of so many other hands. We have the choice at every eucharistic gathering to remember and witness the presence of Christ in his absence. Swanson witnesses the absence by expressing the sacred. He shares this: "As in many of my other works, the sacred is expressed in the ordinary acts we do, in the care that we put into each of the daily activities that sustain us, our loved ones and our community."

PROMPTS FOR FAITH-SHARING

• Do you feel Christ's presence with you? In what ways is it easy or hard to trust?

• How do you feel when you imagine Christ's return to earth? What do you still need to do to be ready for it?

• In the gospel, Jesus gives his disciples three tasks for while he is away: They are to make disciples, to baptize, and to teach all that Jesus has taught. This is now the ongoing mission of the church. In what ways do you participate in these tasks?

✝ SPIRITUALITY

GOSPEL ACCLAMATION
cf. John 14:18

℟. Alleluia, alleluia.
I will not leave you orphans, says the Lord.
I will come back to you, and your hearts will
    rejoice.
℟. Alleluia, alleluia.

Gospel   John 17:1-11a; L59A

Jesus raised his eyes to heaven and said,
    "Father, the hour has come.
Give glory to your son, so that your
      son may glorify you,
      just as you gave him authority over all
        people,
      so that your son may give eternal
        life to all you gave him.
Now this is eternal life,
      that they should know you, the
        only true God,
    and the one whom you sent,
      Jesus Christ.
I glorified you on earth
    by accomplishing the work that
      you gave me to do.
Now glorify me, Father, with you,
    with the glory that I had with
      you before the world
      began.

"I revealed your name to those whom you
      gave me out of the world.
They belonged to you, and you gave them
      to me,
    and they have kept your word.
Now they know that everything you gave me
      is from you,
    because the words you gave to me I have
      given to them,
    and they accepted them and truly
      understood that I came from you,
    and they have believed that you sent me.
I pray for them.
I do not pray for the world but for the ones
      you have given me,
    because they are yours, and everything of
      mine is yours
    and everything of yours is mine,
    and I have been glorified in them.
And now I will no longer be in the world,
    but they are in the world, while I am
      coming to you."

Reflecting on the Gospel

The gospel we hear today is the prayer that Jesus offers for his disciples before he is arrested in the Garden of Gethsemane. Jesus clearly and concisely summarizes the mission that was his to fulfill on earth: that all people would have eternal life, hear and accept God's word, and remember that they belong to God. Perhaps it was that clarity of vision that gave him the strength to see the mission through to its divine conclusion—from arduous passion to painful death to glorious resurrection. This gospel can serve as a reminder that fruitful work is done with intention and integrity. As believers who are called to continue God's mission, we will find direction when we are lost and strength when we are weary by keeping our eyes fixed on the ultimate goal. But what can we do to stay focused and attuned to God's will?

We hear throughout Scripture how Jesus remained connected to the Creator and to his earthly mission through prayer, retreat, and ritual. There are many examples of Jesus praying, including in John 11:41-42 where Jesus prays before raising Lazarus from the dead. In that instance, Jesus thanks God for listening to his words and acknowledges that God is always listening. Do we trust that God is always with us throughout our life journey? Do we testify to that belief through our words and actions?

Jesus also took time to retreat, to withdraw to private places for renewal and rest. In these moments, Jesus had experiences that clarified his vision. Consider the forty days Jesus spent fasting in the desert. During that time, Satan tempted Jesus with offers of wealth and power and tried to persuade Jesus to test God. The temptations Jesus faced are also placed before us in our day-to-day lives. How often are we tempted to sacrifice our integrity, our principles, or our welfare in exchange for some financial reward? How often do we see political parties compromise on deeply held principles out of fear that they will lose votes at the ballot box and seats at the tables where decisions are made? When we follow Jesus's example of undertaking spiritual retreats, we give ourselves the opportunity to reorient our hearts and realign our will so that both are more closely linked with God.

Jesus also demonstrated for us the power of shared ritual. An observant Jewish man, Jesus participated in the celebrations and high holy days of his ancestors. At the Last Supper, Jesus celebrated the Passover meal with his disciples. Through the washing of their feet and the breaking of the bread, Jesus taught the disciples how ritual can express not just devotion and submission to God, but also abiding care for the sisters and brothers who walk through life with us every day.

How do we uniquely celebrate, remember, or show honor? In what ways does a retreat into our inner selves provide relief from the world and rest in God? Let us use this season to pause, seek opportunity for retreat, and grow closer to God through the example of Jesus. In our mission to bring about the kingdom of God, let us focus our vision on the Divine and grow in trust each step of the way.

Preparing to Proclaim

Key words and phrases: "Give glory to your son . . . so that your son may give eternal life to all you gave him."

To the point: John's Gospel tends to give us the most sophisticated trinitarian theology of the four, and this gospel with its dizzying array of prepositions shows how the early church was coming to understand the relationship between Jesus and his Father. There is shared glory here—glory that Jesus had "before the world began" but to which he now needs to be returned after he has humbled himself to share in the human condition even up to death. There is a reciprocity; what glorifies the son also glorifies the father. And there is unity—all who belong to the son belong also to the father, and they will remain on earth to continue Jesus's work while he returns to the fullness of his glory in heaven.

Psalmist Preparation

This psalm affirms Jesus's statement in the gospel that we are all called to share in eternal life. The "land of the living" is not where we are now, where death still has far too great a hold. We are intended for something much greater, something that is beyond the limited imaginings of our small human minds. As you prepare this psalm, spend some time reflecting on your working image of eternal life. How does it compare to this life? What does it look like, sound like, smell like? Who is there with you? Invite God into your imaginings, and bring your image to your proclamation of this week's psalm.

Making Connections

Between the readings: The first reading shows the disciples in the state Jesus describes in the gospel—remaining faithfully in the world after he has returned to heaven. The Holy Spirit has not yet descended, and they have not yet taken up their missions of preaching and service to the poor. Before these things, they devote themselves to prayer, maintaining a relationship with God that will become the basis of their mission in a very short time.

To experience: The promise of eternal life can sometimes sound too big for us, and as with Jesus's words in the gospel it can be hard to even wrap our minds around it. This is an astonishingly huge thing that we've been promised, and it can seem sometimes that we don't have the capacity for it. But the truth of the matter is that we do. God made us with an infinite capacity for God, with a space in our hearts that can only be filled by the infinitude of God.

Homily Points

• The apostles gathered in the upper room to pray together. So much had taken place in the previous days: from Jesus's entry into Jerusalem to his suffering and death on the cross to his resurrection and ascension into heaven. These are many of the most significant, mysterious moments of the Christian faith. Imagine being one of the apostles trying to take it all in! The men and women who followed Christ needed space to come together and reflect on everything they experienced. The upper room provided a safe haven.

• Imagine all they could have talked about and all the questions they could have pondered with one another. What is a favorite memory of our time with Jesus? How did you feel watching him hang on the cross? What went through your mind when he showed up alive after death? Do you think he'll be back again? Or perhaps it was all too much to take in at the moment. Maybe the apostles stayed quiet, holding space for one another to grieve, rejoice, or feel whatever else they needed to feel.

• However the scene played out, it mattered that the apostles came together. It mattered that they devoted themselves to prayer. Their witness models for us a way to live as church as the Easter season draws to a close. Soon Ordinary Time will be upon us. How can we as a community devote ourselves to prayer in this new season? What will it take for us to keep the Easter spirit alive in our pews in the weeks and months to come?

Model Rite for the Blessing and Sprinkling of Water

Presider: Through the sacrament of baptism we come to share in the glory of God through Jesus Christ. By the sprinkling of this water may our hearts be united in the joy of Christ . . . *[pause]*

  [continue with The Roman Missal, *Appendix II]*

Model Universal Prayer (Prayer of the Faithful)

Presider: Drawn into the light and life of Christ, let us proclaim our prayers and petitions before the Lord.

Response: Lord, hear our prayer.

Bless the spaces in our church and wider community that facilitate prayer and connection like the upper room . . .

Inspire government officials to enact policies that safeguard the most vulnerable among us . . .

Give safety and peace of mind to people fleeing abusive relationships . . .

Welcome into the peace of eternal life those in our community who have died . . .

Presider: Good and gracious God, you give glory to your son who in turn gives the promise of everlasting life in heaven to all people. Hear our prayers that we might reflect your glory to the ends of the earth. We ask this through Christ our resurrected Lord. **Amen.**

Liturgy and Music

Accomplishing the Work: From today's gospel we learn that Jesus glorified God by "accomplishing the work he was given to do" (John 17:4). In an earlier post, I mentioned that our work in ministry is never complete. It is always ongoing. Sometimes our work in liturgical and music ministry requires us to wear multiple hats and the work becomes overwhelmingly busy. But take heart and always remember that we do this work to help all believers pray and indeed, pray better. Sometimes doubt takes over in our ministry and we become discouraged. Take comfort that you are not alone and that your work never goes unrecognized. You will never know how much your ministry will touch the hearts and lives of other people. When I am doubtful in my ministry, I turn to this prayer by Thomas Merton from his *Thoughts in Solitude*: "My Lord God, I have no idea where I am going. I do not see the road ahead of me. I cannot know for certain where it will end. . . . But I believe that the desire to please you does in fact please you. And I hope I have that desire in all that I am doing. . . . I will not fear, for you are ever with me, and you will never leave me to face my perils alone."

COLLECT
Let us pray.

Pause for silent prayer

Graciously hear our supplications, O Lord,
so that we, who believe that the Savior of
    the human race
is with you in your glory,
may experience, as he promised,
until the end of the world,
his abiding presence among us.
Who lives and reigns with you in the unity
    of the Holy Spirit,
God, for ever and ever. **Amen.**

FIRST READING
Acts 1:12-14

After Jesus had been taken up to heaven
    the apostles
    returned to Jerusalem
    from the mount called Olivet, which is
        near Jerusalem,
    a sabbath day's journey away.

When they entered the city
    they went to the upper room where they
        were staying,
    Peter and John and James and Andrew,
    Philip and Thomas, Bartholomew and
        Matthew,
    James son of Alphaeus, Simon the
        Zealot,
    and Judas son of James.
All these devoted themselves with one
    accord to prayer,
    together with some women,
    and Mary the mother of Jesus, and his
        brothers.

RESPONSORIAL PSALM
Ps 27:1, 4, 7-8

R⃰. (13) I believe that I shall see the good
things of the Lord in the land of the
living.
  or:
R⃰. Alleluia.

The LORD is my light and my salvation;
  whom should I fear?
The LORD is my life's refuge;
  of whom should I be afraid?

R⃰. I believe that I shall see the good things
of the Lord in the land of the living.
  or:
R⃰. Alleluia.

One thing I ask of the LORD;
  this I seek:
To dwell in the house of the LORD
  all the days of my life,
that I may gaze on the loveliness of the
  LORD
  and contemplate his temple.

R⃰. I believe that I shall see the good things
of the Lord in the land of the living.
  or:
R⃰. Alleluia.

Hear, O LORD, the sound of my call;
  have pity on me, and answer me.
Of you my heart speaks; you my glance
  seeks.

R⃰. I believe that I shall see the good things
of the Lord in the land of the living.
  or:
R⃰. Alleluia.

SECOND READING
1 Pet 4:13-16

Beloved:
Rejoice to the extent that you share in the
  sufferings of Christ,
  so that when his glory is revealed
  you may also rejoice exultantly.
If you are insulted for the name of Christ,
  blessed are you,
  for the Spirit of glory and of God rests
    upon you.
But let no one among you be made to
  suffer
  as a murderer, a thief, an evildoer, or as
    an intriguer.
But whoever is made to suffer as a
  Christian should not be ashamed
  but glorify God because of the name.

Living Liturgy

Entering Prayer: Most dioceses in the United States celebrate Ascension Sunday today instead of the Seventh Sunday of Easter. If your diocese celebrates the Seventh Sunday of Easter, the readings focus on prayer—the prayer of the earliest Christians and the final prayer of Jesus before being betrayed on the night before his death.

When I reflected on this set of readings, I kept thinking of my mother's love of family and care for others. Because of her serious heart condition, she would frequently be in and out of hospital. During her hospital stays, she would always ask how my brother and I were doing. I would always respond not to worry about me but to take care of her own recovery. The thirteenth hospital visit was a slightly longer one which worried me. In classic form, she responded, "Don't worry about me. I'll be ok. It's all in God's hands." A few days later, she passed into the embrace of God. My mother loved her faith and her family. She would pray fervently and volunteer in ministry generously. She would assure the family and others of her love, care and prayer.

Jesus prays not only for his disciples but also for us and whatever we encounter in this world. This brings hope to all followers then and now. Within the story of the earliest followers of Christ, we are given a roadmap for our own journeys of faith. We have been summoned to proclaim Christ in word and in action to all those that we meet. Jesus is concerned about those whom he loves, those who will be left to carry on the work of evangelization and mission of love. Both my mother's and Jesus's love remain alive in our midst. Jesus's disciples, as we see in the Acts of the Apostles, carry on with their lives to complete Jesus's mission and vision. Likewise, my family and I continue to realize the heritage entrusted to us by the ones who first loved us.

PROMPTS FOR FAITH-SHARING

• When Jesus speaks of those who belong to him, do you include yourself in that number? Why or why not?

• The first reading shows that prayer is the baseline work of the disciples; it is established as their daily task before the Holy Spirit arrives to send them out with their other missions of preaching and baptizing and caring for the poor. How does prayer fit into your other callings in life? How might you make more room for it?

• How do you imagine eternal life? Does it feel like something you're ready for?

✝ SPIRITUALITY

Gospel

John 20:19-23; L63A

On the evening of that first
    day of the week,
  when the doors were
      locked, where the
      disciples were,
  for fear of the Jews,
  Jesus came and stood in
    their midst
  and said to them, "Peace
    be with you."
When he had said this, he
    showed them his hands
    and his side.
The disciples rejoiced when
    they saw the Lord.
Jesus said to them again,
    "Peace be with you.
As the Father has sent me,
    so I send you."
And when he had said this, he breathed
    on them and said to them,
  "Receive the Holy Spirit.
Whose sins you forgive are forgiven
    them,
  and whose sins you retain are
    retained."

Reflecting on the Gospel

Location, location, location. Anyone who has attended a large concert, a play, or a sporting event knows that your location as an audience member plays a big role in how you experience an event. Can you see and hear what's going on or are there obstacles blocking your way? What are the people around you doing and saying? How far away are you from the stage? Are you close enough to feel connected to the performers or players? All of these factors help determine whether an experience will be enjoyable or miserable.

The story of Pentecost is inspiring not only because of the transformation the apostles experience, but also because God demonstrates, yet again, that God is willing to bridge whatever distance exists between believers and Godself. At a moment when the apostles are at their most frightened, going so far as to hide in a secret location, God bursts into the space "like a strong driving wind." God assures the apostles that even in the depths of their despair, they are not beyond the reach of God's protective, empowering, loving care. And just like that moment at a concert where the performers invite the audience to sing along with them, God impels the apostles to go out into the streets and proclaim the "mighty acts of God" before the large crowds gathered "from every nation under heaven."

Another remarkable part of the Pentecost story is how the large crowd comprised of people "from every nation under heaven" heard the apostles speaking in each of their individual languages. This is sometimes interpreted as a reversal of the tower of Babel story in which the Babylonians' attempt to build a tower that would reach the heavens (a prideful act) is thwarted by God, who makes the workers unable to communicate with each other, thus creating the diverse languages of the world. The Pentecost story as told in Scripture suggests the crowds heard the apostles speaking with familiar words, but perhaps in those moments, what the crowds understood was the feeling of liberation from fear, of renewed hope. Maybe the crowds could see the lines of anxiety melting from the apostles' faces as they boldly proclaimed the things God had done for them. Maybe the crowds saw the apostles reach their hands toward the sky the way people do when seeing the sun for the first time after a long, frightful storm and felt their own limbs extending upward. Perhaps this miraculous connection was not literal understanding, but a figurative and emotional one in which the assembled realized that all people experience dark nights of the soul, but that we are not alone during those trials and that they will not last forever.

Where we choose to position ourselves matters. Although fear or hopelessness can make us feel disconnected or isolated from others, they need not separate us from each other or God. May our senses be heightened so that we can better feel God's spirit moving in us—even in difficult times. May our hearts be opened so that we can better receive the joyful testimony of God's majesty that is being proclaimed by all of creation. And in doing so, may we be brought out of hiding and into the fray where we can more fully encounter God and our neighbor.

Preparing to Proclaim
Key words and phrases: "Receive the Holy Spirit."

To the point: It can come as a surprise, even for those of us who are attentive to the cycle of readings, that the Pentecost narrative is not today's gospel. Instead, we have a preliminary passing on of the Holy Spirit at another Easter encounter story. In this one, Jesus's breath is the means of transmission, a gentler image than the driving wind and tongues of fire we associate with this day. The Pentecost story we might expect here occurs only in Acts, and thus remains in the position of first reading. This reminds us that Pentecost is removed enough from the life of Jesus that it does not appear in the gospels. This story is about what the church will do now that Jesus's bodily presence has left earth. And what it does is run out and preach, unable to contain the good news of Jesus.

Psalmist Preparation
We have just heard, in the first reading, about God sending out his Spirit, and now in the psalm we ask him to do so again. The Spirit's coming is not a one-and-done deal. Rather, it is an ongoing transmission that brings life. The work of renewing and recreating the earth is never done in our lifetimes. We still wait for Jesus to return and bring it to fullness. As you prepare this psalm, spend some time recognizing ways the Holy Spirit is active in your life. Also acknowledge where you might need the Spirit, and ask God to pour it forth into your individual life as well as the life of the church.

Making Connections
Between the readings: The gospel narrates a small, contained passing of the Holy Spirit. Jesus appears behind locked doors only to those who knew him. He offers them something of a commission, but the story ends the way it started: in a small room in a contained community, behind locked doors. The first reading begins in a similar way but ends with a massively inclusive image: the disciples are preaching not only to those who share their language and culture but to those outside these bounds.

To experience: All of us are part of some culture or another. "Culture" does not just mean racial or ethnic background but includes things like our age, our social location, and even the micro-cultures of each of our families. The Holy Spirit can and does work through all of these, but the Pentecost story makes clear that we are also called to a unity that transcends them.

Homily Points
• As we come to the end of the Easter season, let us reflect on the incredible journey undertaken by Jesus out of love for us. Eight weeks ago, we entered the church waving palm branches to mark Jesus's entry into Jerusalem. During that holiest of weeks, we remember how Jesus, on the night he was betrayed, shared bread and wine with his disciples. Then, after an agonizing evening in the garden, Jesus takes up his cross. Nails pierce his skin as he hangs and cries out and soon, breathes his last. The story should have ended here with death—but we know that is not what happened.

• Throughout the last fifty days of Easter, we soaked in stories of the resurrected Lord who still had some teaching and revealing to do. Jesus was not ready to leave quite yet. Now, on this solemnity of Pentecost, Jesus turns the work over to his disciples. Jesus's journey continues, though now we are the ones to take on the preaching and praying, the forgiving and healing. Guided by the Holy Spirit, we—the disciples of today—are called to carry on Christ's saving work.

• How do we take on such a major mission? We do so by coming together like our ancestors did for that first Pentecost celebration—a diverse group of people bonded by their amazement at the mighty acts of God. We do so by remembering that we are part of one body with many parts, each part called to use its gifts for the betterment of the whole.

Model Rite for the Blessing and Sprinkling of Water

Presider: The Holy Spirit embraced us in the waters of baptism. Through the sprinkling of this water, may the Spirit animate us to live as sisters and brothers in Christ . . . *[pause]*

[*continue with* The Roman Missal, *Appendix II*]

Model Universal Prayer (Prayer of the Faithful)

Presider: Gathered as one body in Christ, let us bring our prayers and petitions before the Lord.

Response: Lord, hear our prayer.

Unite Christians of all traditions in our common baptismal call . . .

Bring peace to communities caught in the cycles of war and violence . . .

Forgive the sins of all people with repentant hearts who are struggling to forgive themselves . . .

Deepen our amazement and reverence for the diverse gifts present in the human family . . .

Presider: Gracious God, you sent your Spirit to dwell with disciples past and present. On this Solemnity of Pentecost, we give thanks and praise for your Spirit's attention to our prayers and abiding presence in our lives. We offer this prayer through Christ our Lord. **Amen.**

Liturgy and Music

Citizens of Heaven: On this Pentecost Sunday, we commemorate Memorial Day weekend in the United States. Catholics should pray for their nation and remember those who have died in service of this country, yet when we gather as people of God to celebrate the rituals of our faith at the eucharistic celebration, God and God's love through the Holy Spirit should be the center of our song and prayer. Christian liturgy is not tied to any one country since we are all counted as citizens of heaven baptized by the Holy Spirit, "speaking in our own tongues of the mighty acts of God."

Songs for the nation, while included in some hymnals, should be reserved for celebrations and events of the nation when we gather as a nation (see Thirteenth Sunday in Ordinary Time—"Liturgy and Music: Music Connects with Liturgical Action"). We sing songs to the Holy Spirit today in joy and hope praising our God who renews the face of the earth. It is our responsibility to pray for the dead as a spiritual act of mercy and we also seek to bear in mind our mission of working toward the peace of God's kingdom. Include both an intercession remembering the brave souls who have died in service to this country as well as an intercession for the end of war.

Let us pray.

Pause for silent prayer

O God, who by the mystery of today's
    great feast
sanctify your whole Church in every
    people and nation,
pour out, we pray, the gifts of the Holy Spirit
across the face of the earth
and, with the divine grace that was at work
when the Gospel was first proclaimed,
fill now once more the hearts of believers.
Through our Lord Jesus Christ, your Son,
who lives and reigns with you in the unity
    of the Holy Spirit,
God, for ever and ever. **Amen.**

FIRST READING
Acts 2:1-11

When the time for Pentecost was fulfilled,
    they were all in one place together.
And suddenly there came from the sky
    a noise like a strong driving wind,
    and it filled the entire house in which
        they were.
Then there appeared to them tongues as
    of fire,
    which parted and came to rest on each
        one of them.
And they were all filled with the Holy
    Spirit
    and began to speak in different tongues,
    as the Spirit enabled them to proclaim.

Now there were devout Jews from every
    nation under heaven
    staying in Jerusalem.
At this sound, they gathered in a large
    crowd,
    but they were confused
    because each one heard them speaking
        in his own language.
They were astounded, and in amazement
    they asked,
    "Are not all these people who are
        speaking Galileans?
Then how does each of us hear them in
    his native language?
We are Parthians, Medes, and Elamites,
    inhabitants of Mesopotamia, Judea and
        Cappadocia,
    Pontus and Asia, Phrygia and
        Pamphylia,
    Egypt and the districts of Libya near
        Cyrene,
    as well as travelers from Rome,
    both Jews and converts to Judaism,
        Cretans and Arabs,
    yet we hear them speaking in our own
        tongues
    of the mighty acts of God."

RESPONSORIAL PSALM
Ps 104:1, 24, 29-30, 31, 34

R̸. (cf. 30) Lord, send out your Spirit, and renew the face of the earth.
    or: R̸. Alleluia.

Bless the LORD, O my soul!
    O LORD, my God, you are great indeed!
How manifold are your works, O LORD!
    The earth is full of your creatures.

R̸. Lord, send out your Spirit, and renew the face of the earth.
    or: R̸. Alleluia.

If you take away their breath, they perish and return to their dust.
When you send forth your spirit, they are created,
    and you renew the face of the earth.

R̸. Lord, send out your Spirit, and renew the face of the earth.
    or: R̸. Alleluia.

May the glory of the LORD endure forever;
    may the LORD be glad in his works!
Pleasing to him be my theme;
    I will be glad in the LORD.

R̸. Lord, send out your Spirit, and renew the face of the earth.
    or: R̸. Alleluia.

SECOND READING
1 Cor 12:3b-7, 12-13

Brothers and sisters:
No one can say, "Jesus is Lord," except by the Holy Spirit.

There are different kinds of spiritual gifts but the same Spirit;
    there are different forms of service but the same Lord;
    there are different workings but the same God
    who produces all of them in everyone.
To each individual the manifestation of the Spirit
    is given for some benefit.

As a body is one though it has many parts,
    and all the parts of the body, though many, are one body,
    so also Christ.
For in one Spirit we were all baptized into one body,
    whether Jews or Greeks, slaves or free persons,
    and we were all given to drink of one Spirit.

SEQUENCE

See Appendix A, p. 294.

Living Liturgy

Understanding Gift: The second reading of today reminds us of the importance of recognizing our diverse gifts while celebrating our unity in God. St. Paul tells us that the Holy Spirit is the one who brings together the many—while we are all different, we are united by the same Holy Spirit. In a Pentecost homily, Pope Francis comments that the secret of unity in the church, the secret of the Spirit, is gift. He continues to say: "It is important to believe that God is gift, that he acts not by taking away, but by giving. Why is this important? Because our way of being believers depends on how we understand God. If we have in mind a God who takes away and who imposes himself, we too will want to take away and impose ourselves: occupying spaces, demanding recognition, seeking power. But if we have in our hearts a God who is gift, everything changes. If we realize that what we are is his gift, free and unmerited, then we too will want to make our lives a gift. By loving humbly, serving freely and joyfully, we will offer to the world the true image of God. The Spirit, *the living memory of the Church*, reminds us that we are born from a gift and that we grow by giving: not by holding on but by giving of ourselves" (May 31, 2020). So, in our ministerial contexts, what is our understanding of God?

The gospel reading reminds us that we are also called to be a reconciling presence in the world. This is one way of sharing our gifts with the world, as agents of reconciliation. If our ministry setting is a multicultural one, what steps do we take to celebrate unity in diversity? How might we highlight cultural differences to create a welcome and inclusive space for the Spirit to work in?

PROMPTS FOR FAITH-SHARING

• Jesus promises peace in the gospel. Where in your life do you need the peace of Christ?

• Name the cultures of which you are a part, remembering that "culture" here can be as small as family culture and can include things like age, profession, and social location. What aspects of your culture do you find limiting when it comes to preaching the gospel? How might the Holy Spirit be inviting you to overcome these divisions?

• The second reading reminds us that the Spirit unites us as one body. What role do you play in the Body of Christ? How do you need others to support you?

ORDINARY TIME II

SPIRITUALITY

GOSPEL ACCLAMATION
cf. Rev 1:8

R҃. Alleluia, alleluia.
Glory to the Father, the Son, and the Holy Spirit;
to God who is, who was, and who is to come.
R҃. Alleluia, alleluia.

Gospel

John 3:16-18; L164A

God so loved the world that he gave his
    only Son,
  so that everyone who believes in him
    might not perish
  but might have eternal life.
For God did not send his Son into the
    world to condemn the world,
  but that the world might be saved
    through him.
Whoever believes in him will not be
    condemned,
  but whoever does not believe has
    already been condemned,
  because he has not believed in the
    name of the only Son of God.

Reflecting on the Gospel

In Alice Walker's novel *The Color Purple*, Celie, a battered and exploited woman, meets the exotic and freespirited Shug. She tells Celie that mutual love should be the reality behind all our relationships; that love transfigures and brutality disfigures; that it's not only pleasing God that matters, because God is always trying to please us back with surprises—just as Shug, the mistress of Celie's cold, distant husband, is a surprise for Celie.

The biggest "surprise" that God has sprung on the world is the love that takes flesh and comes among us in the Son. The gospel of today's feast again proclaims that God is not intent on judging and condemning the world, but judgment will happen—not as a future event but as a present reality for which we ourselves are responsible when we accept or reject the Son. Like Nicodemus—whose encounter with Jesus begins in the verses immediately preceding today's gospel (which most regard as continuing the dialogue between him and Jesus)—we are often "night visitors" to the mystery of God, afraid to come into the light, wanting to keep our acceptance and understanding of God within the confines of our own manageable and limited experiences. Today's feast invites us to remember God's most gracious hospitality, most free and generous love for all created reality. Through Christ and the Spirit, in whom our humanity is born again when the womb waters of baptism break over us, we are a precious and privileged part of this creation.

It will often be a struggle to live what we are, and we need the encouragement that Paul gives to the Corinthians in his Second Letter. This is a letter in which Paul has to deal with the pain of attacks on his apostolic credentials, has admitted his weakness, and has needed to write strong criticism to this often-cantankerous church that he still loves dearly. In his closing, Paul bids the Corinthians farewell with words that encourage them to live in joy, peace, and love for one another, because this is the life that reflects their God. Liturgically, this is shown by the "holy kiss" (the sign of peace). Paul ends with the blessing that we would now describe as trinitarian: the grace that is received through the gift of Jesus Christ, the all-embracing love of God, and the communion of the Holy Spirit. This is the dynamism that binds together every Christian community. It is also the challenge to love, to comfort, to live in peace with one another.

As Augustine wrote, "If you see love, you see the Trinity." Over and above all theological speculation, the best way of meditating on and understanding something of the extraordinary mystery of the Trinity is to reflect on the love that we ordinary Christians show in our daily lives. Beautiful though this may be, it is only the faintest image of the love of Father, Son, and Spirit, whose communion is the source not only of our responsibility to one another but also to the whole interdependent cosmos.

Preparing to Proclaim

Key words and phrases: "God so loved the world that he gave his only Son."

To the point: At first glance, this gospel may seem an odd choice for the Sunday we celebrate the tripartite personhood of God. The Father and Son are mentioned, but the Holy Spirit is nowhere to be seen. But despite the lack of explicit mention, this gospel is rich in the Spirit. It is through the Spirit overshadowing Mary that Jesus comes to be in the world, and the Spirit accompanies Jesus throughout his ministry and mission on earth. The silence here is often part of how the Spirit works, in subtleties and whispers rather than in obvious or understandable ways. We might prefer the Spirit's work—like all of God's work—to be more evident to us, but the wisdom of God differs from ours and so our work is training our eyes to see the quiet hints of God's hand in the world.

Psalmist Preparation

Sometimes psalms of praise are repetitive in nature, and it can be tempting to think of them as boring. But this form of Hebrew poetry has an elegance to it; the repeated phrase "praiseworthy and exalted above all forever" cycles back after lines that draw us deeper and deeper into something that cannot actually be expressed in words. This is a lovely, poetic depiction of the mystery of the Trinity that we celebrate today. We cannot fully comprehend it, but we can be drawn more fully into it. As our understanding grows deeper and realer, so too can our praise.

Making Connections

Between the readings: The second reading finally names all three members of the Trinity explicitly on this Trinity Sunday. St. Paul uses their names as a greeting, one we still use at Mass today. This is a powerful greeting. We begin everything we do in the names of these three persons in one God. The familiarity of this triad—Father, Son, and Spirit—can make us forget that there is a beautiful mystery at play here. God's very essence is relationship, is love, to the point that God needs to be three persons so that the love has someplace to go.

To experience: We live out the mystery of the Trinity in the ongoing dance of all our human relationships. As the ancient hymn "Ubi Caritas" reminds us, wherever love is, God is present. God is the source and sustenance of all the different ways we experience love in our human relationships.

Homily Points

• We can never know the fullness of our almighty, mysterious God. But today's readings point to a crucial aspect of the divine human relationship: our triune God—Father, Son, and Holy Spirit—dwells with us, always. Our God is not one to stay up in the clouds. Just the opposite—in today's first reading, Moses encounters the Lord coming down from the clouds. The Lord stands close enough to have a conversation with Moses. Many of us may wish the Lord would speak as clearly and directly to us. Frustration can arise in prayer when we do not receive the clarity desired from God. Yet while our divine dialogue may look different than Moses's, God assures us that God will be with us always until the end of the ages.

• In today's gospel, we receive further assurance of God's presence. Out of great love for us, God sent God's only son to save the world. We spent the last few months of Lent and Easter hearing stories of Jesus's time on earth, both before and after his death on the cross. Even death cannot separate us from God!

• Then last week we celebrated the outpouring of the Holy Spirit, breathed upon the earliest disciples by Christ himself, who continues to be our advocate and guide. Our triune God dwells with us. St. Paul sums this blessing up well in today's second reading: "The grace of the Lord Jesus Christ and the love of God and the fellowship of the Holy Spirit be with all of you."

143

Model Penitential Act

Presider: In his letter to the Corinthians, St. Paul calls on us to mend our ways. For all that needs mending in our lives, let us ask God for mercy and forgiveness . . . *[pause]*

Lord Jesus, you are the Son of God: Lord, have mercy.

Christ Jesus, you came into the world so that we might have eternal life: Christ, have mercy.

Lord Jesus, you sent the Holy Spirit to animate the world: Lord, have mercy.

Model Universal Prayer (Prayer of the Faithful)

Presider: Believing that God dwells with us always, let us give voice to our needs and the needs of our world.

Response: Lord, hear our prayer.

Inspire bishops, that they may use their power to rid the church of clerical abuse and systems of cover-up . . .

Protect the land growing our food, that it may be safe from floods, fires, and other disasters . . .

Free victims of human trafficking, that they may know peace and healing . . .

Send your Spirit upon each of us gathered here, that we may know the divine presence ever more deeply in the days ahead . . .

Presider: Triune God, in your great love, you create, redeem, and sanctify the world. Receive our prayers that guided by the Spirit we might be beacons of your love throughout the world. We ask this through Christ our Lord. **Amen.**

Liturgy and Music

Singing the Love of the Trinity: We enter Ordinary Time with these two important solemnities of our Christian faith—the Holy Trinity today and the Body and Blood of Christ next week. Make sure there is enough music to accompany the liturgical action if you use incense during the entrance procession at these celebrations. Be sure to sing all the verses of a trinitarian hymn, for it allows the text of the hymn to describe the whole mystery surrounding the Trinity, a love that should be revealed in our ministry.

June is also a month often filled with wedding liturgies, another opportunity to enter the love of the Trinity. The revision of the Order of Celebrating Matrimony has brought some new rituals. One in particular is the entrance procession which involves the bride and groom processing in together following the ministers and the wedding party, accompanied by a gathering song or entrance processional sung by everyone present, just as at Sunday Mass. How beautiful is this expression of trinitarian love—where the rite of marriage is not simply between husband and wife, but one that binds together the couple and the community through the love of Christ encountered in the sacrament.

COLLECT

Let us pray.

Pause for silent prayer

God our Father, who by sending into the world
the Word of truth and the Spirit of sanctification
made known to the human race your wondrous mystery,
grant us, we pray, that in professing the true faith,
we may acknowledge the Trinity of eternal glory
and adore your Unity, powerful in majesty.
Through our Lord Jesus Christ, your Son,
who lives and reigns with you in the unity of the Holy Spirit,
God, for ever and ever. **Amen.**

FIRST READING
Exod 34:4b-6, 8-9

Early in the morning Moses went up Mount Sinai
as the LORD had commanded him,
taking along the two stone tablets.

Having come down in a cloud, the LORD stood with Moses there
and proclaimed his name, "LORD."
Thus the LORD passed before him and cried out,
"The LORD, the LORD, a merciful and gracious God,
slow to anger and rich in kindness and fidelity."
Moses at once bowed down to the ground in worship.
Then he said, "If I find favor with you, O LORD,
do come along in our company.
This is indeed a stiff-necked people; yet pardon our wickedness and sins,
and receive us as your own."

RESPONSORIAL PSALM
Dan 3:52, 53, 54, 55

℟. (52b) Glory and praise forever!

Blessed are you, O Lord, the God of our
   fathers,
   praiseworthy and exalted above all
      forever;
and blessed is your holy and glorious
      name,
   praiseworthy and exalted above all for
      all ages.

℟. Glory and praise forever!

Blessed are you in the temple of your holy
      glory,
   praiseworthy and glorious above all
      forever.

℟. Glory and praise forever!

Blessed are you on the throne of your
      kingdom,
   praiseworthy and exalted above all
      forever.

℟. Glory and praise forever!

Blessed are you who look into the depths
   from your throne upon the cherubim,
   praiseworthy and exalted above all
      forever.

℟. Glory and praise forever!

SECOND READING
2 Cor 13:11-13

Brothers and sisters, rejoice. Mend your
      ways, encourage one another,
   agree with one another, live in peace,
   and the God of love and peace will be
      with you.
Greet one another with a holy kiss.
All the holy ones greet you.

The grace of the Lord Jesus Christ
   and the love of God
   and the fellowship of the Holy Spirit be
      with all of you.

Living Liturgy

Creating Space: Today's reading challenges us to deeply contemplate the profound mystery of the Holy Trinity. During these next two solemnities in Ordinary Time, I invite us to think about the Christian act of creating space.

Sometimes the theological richness of the mystery of the Holy Trinity gets lost when explanations become watered down and oversimplified. Take time to consider the vast space in which the sacred three persons work in relationship with each other and how this impacts our ministry so not to risk overlooking a fundamental doctrine of our faith. If we leave this work only to theologians, then the action of God in this space, which is always in love of our world, goes unrecognized at best and underutilized at worst.

Think about the space where God is at work. This space and how we create it through our ministry ought to reflect the Trinity's complex yet simple relationship dance. This space might be thought of in terms of radical hospitality.

God loves the world and sends the Son to save it. Through death and resurrection we have been given the gift of the Holy Spirit. We understand this space to be one that allows each believer to fully be in relationship with God and each other, to have trust to reveal their true selves. This space is a liminal one, like a doorway, where God alone alters time and space, hearts and minds, where believers are transformed. This space is also a physical one where hands are outstretched in blessing, tears are shed, joys are expressed, strangers are included, and differences accepted. It is a space where we work with God's grace and mercy, and, as liturgical ministers, we faithfully prepare this sacred place that embraces the trinitarian mystery. The more we embrace the mystery, the more faithful we become. Our mission is finding meaning in the mystery.

PROMPTS FOR FAITH-SHARING

• Is there a person of the Trinity you think of most often when you pray? While the unity of the Trinity means that of course God in God's fullness hears your prayers, what might it be like to try praying to one of the other persons more explicitly?

• Where might God be inviting you to keep an eye out for the Spirit's subtle movements?

• Which relationships in your life reveal God's love to you? In which relationships is it challenging to see God at work?

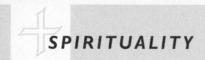

SPIRITUALITY

GOSPEL ACCLAMATION

John 6:51

℞. Alleluia, alleluia.
I am the living bread that came down from heaven,
    says the Lord;
whoever eats this bread will live forever.
℞. Alleluia, alleluia.

Gospel

John 6:51-58; L167A

Jesus said to the Jewish crowds:
  "I am the living bread that came
    down from heaven;
  whoever eats this bread will live
    forever;
  and the bread that I will give
  is my flesh for the life of the world."

The Jews quarreled among themselves,
    saying,
  "How can this man give us his flesh
    to eat?"
Jesus said to them,
  "Amen, amen, I say to you,
  unless you eat the flesh of the Son
    of Man and drink his blood,
  you do not have life within you.
Whoever eats my flesh and drinks my
    blood
  has eternal life,
  and I will raise him on the last day.
For my flesh is true food,
  and my blood is true drink.
Whoever eats my flesh and drinks my
    blood
  remains in me and I in him.
Just as the living Father sent me
  and I have life because of the Father,
  so also the one who feeds on me
  will have life because of me.
This is the bread that came down from
    heaven.
Unlike your ancestors who ate and still
    died,
  whoever eats this bread will live
    forever."

Reflecting on the Gospel

This is the day when we acknowledge that we have Christ in our blood; that we are the people for whom the Word takes flesh, the people who are hungry and thirsty for God.

Jesus's proclamation, in today's gospel reading, that his flesh is to be eaten and his blood drunk shocks his Jewish audience. His words are meant to shock us, too, into hearing with new ears and understanding with new and open hearts. In the prologue to his gospel (John 1:14), as in this reading, John uses the word *sarx* ("flesh") instead of *soma* ("body"). The latter meant a body tangible to our human senses, while *sarx* implies human nature in its completeness. In English, the phrase "flesh and blood" is a common way of referring to or characterizing a human being. In positioning this solemnity so soon after the close of the Easter season, we are reminded that the resurrection spills over into the Eucharist and is central to its reality. What we receive is the risen Christ who is now present to his church, and so to eat and drink, to *accept*, his whole risen, sacramental presence of flesh and blood and to abide in its mystery, is a pledge of sharing in Christ's resurrection.

In the wilderness, Jesus's ancestors experienced the new and unexpected gift of the manna. God gave them this when they were hungering after the bread of Pharaoh, even though that tasted of injustice. Better, they cried to Moses, our stomachs full of slavery than the empty hunger of desert freedom. In that dangerous, vulnerable moment, God tested the people to see if they would commit themselves to doing things God's way. Jesus reminds the people around him of this past complaint (see John 6:49), because to accept Jesus as broken bread to be eaten and wine to be poured out is to take the "manna risk" of the new covenant. Today when we hold out our hands and accept the broken bread, we are daring to take hold of a body that was broken in death and rose for freedom and justice. When we drink the cup, we pledge ourselves to solidarity—especially with the losers, the powerless, the have-nots, the "dregs" of society, the sinners—for whom Jesus drained the cup of suffering.

This solemnity, therefore, should focus our attention on what we can so easily forget: that every Eucharist should create in us a great sense of unease about any disunity, discrimination, and hypocrisy in the Body of Christ. No matter how liturgically correct or ritually beautiful our celebration, much is missing from the "full, conscious and active participation" of the assembly (Constitution on the Sacred Liturgy 14) if we do not do this in memory of the just Servant. Liturgical memory is not a nostalgic or romantic recall of the past, but a present reality that demands that, in Jesus's name, we do justice now and in the future. The Eucharist is a gathering place and a stopping place for us nomads on our own exodus way toward the kingdom of justice and peace.

Preparing to Proclaim

Key words and phrases: "Whoever eats my flesh and drinks my blood remains in me and I in him."

To the point: The latter part of the Easter season is all about the Holy Spirit; Jesus promises to send an advocate who will not leave us orphaned. Now, two Sundays after Pentecost, we celebrate another astonishing way that Jesus remains with us after the ascension. Through the power of that Spirit, he becomes fully present at every Mass; his body and blood are really there. While we might envy the disciples who got to walk alongside Jesus in his lifetime, we are given the extraordinary gift of being united with him—deeply and really—at every eucharistic celebration. Eating is one of the few acts that bypasses the barriers of the human body; the closeness is such that even on a molecular level, Jesus becomes part of us. The humility of God joining us in our human condition was an inconceivable gift; the humility of giving his flesh and blood as food and drink continues the mind-bending generosity of our God.

Psalmist Preparation

Here we offer praise for the special gift with which God has entrusted God's people. As you prepare this psalm, reflect on eucharistic experiences from your own lifetime. Do any jump out as particularly powerful experiences of God's presence? How has the reception of Communion and the regular discipline of liturgical participation shaped your faith? When you proclaim this psalm, let its praise be for all that the Eucharist has been to you—and all that will still unfold in your ongoing relationship with Jesus there.

Making Connections

Between the readings: The first reading shows that God has a long history of providing food and drink for God's people. The Eucharist carries on this long tradition, but in an entirely new way that gives life previously unimaginable. The second reading reminds us that the Eucharist is a way of participating in the life of Jesus himself. We become his Body by participating. We are also bound together, becoming united in a reality that transcends all the human divisions we continue to enforce.

To experience: The Second Vatican Council calls the Eucharist the "source and summit" of our faith, but its repeatability can make it feel less special or exciting than some of the other sacraments. But Jesus reminds us of the reason for this repeatability; this sacrament is food, and like the food we eat to nourish our physical selves, this meal needs to be repeated for spiritual health and vigor.

Homily Points

• On the night of the Last Supper, Jesus broke bread and proclaimed it his body. He took the cup filled with wine and declared it his blood. Jesus entrusted the promise of eternal life to two of the most essential—and enjoyable!—human actions: eating and drinking. Jesus does not require special skills to attain eternal life. Rather he reveals the hope of everlasting joy in heaven from the ordinary fruits of the earth. Jesus's gifts of the bread and wine, his very body and blood, make the heavenly kingdom accessible to all who believe.

• Our regular partaking of the body and blood in the Eucharist strengthens us for the journey to heaven and draws us around a common table with others who believe in the power of Christ. The body and blood of Christ is entirely gift—a grace-filled meal. We cannot earn our place at the eucharistic table, nor can we lose our seat. Jesus sat among saints and sinners at the Last Supper and throughout his earthly ministry. He welcomed all to join in the feast—and he continues that welcome to us today. We are invited to receive the bread of life and the cup of salvation each week.

• Christ's body and blood serve as fuel so that we might go out and live into our God-given callings with energy and spirit. The grace broken and poured at the altar extends out into the world. Strengthened by Christ's body and blood, we will enjoy the fullness of everlasting life with Christ.

Model Penitential Act

Presider: In today's first reading, Moses reminds the Israelites: "Do not forget the Lord, your God." For the times we have neglected our relationship with God, let us ask for mercy and pardon . . . *[pause]*

Lord Jesus, you are the living bread that came down from heaven: Lord, have mercy.

Christ Jesus, you intercede for us as the right hand of God: Christ, have mercy.

Lord Jesus, you promise eternal life to all who partake in your body: Lord, have mercy.

Model Universal Prayer (Prayer of the Faithful)

Presider: Beloved by Christ who gave of his very flesh and blood for us, let us offer our prayers and petitions.

Response: Lord, hear our prayer.

Unite Christians around a common table and a common mission to bring Christ's love to all corners of the world . . .

Bless blood donors, organ donors, and all who give of their bodies to help others . . .

Nurture the growing bodies of children and ensure all children have access to nutritious foods and drinks . . .

Bring hope to all gathered here so that, nourished by the body and blood of Christ, we may be beacons of light to our communities . . .

Presider: God of everlasting goodness, you sent your son, Jesus, to nourish your people. Receive our prayers that we too may work to feed others in word, sacrament, and service. We ask this through Christ our Lord. **Amen.**

Liturgy and Music

Proper Timing of the Fraction Rite: The Fraction Rite is the part of the Mass that follows the sign of peace. During this rite, the *Agnus Dei* or Lamb of God is sung. Make every effort to time properly the singing of the *Agnus Dei* to coincide with the ritual action of the breaking of the bread. The General Instruction of the Roman Missal tells us, "This invocation accompanies the fraction of the bread and, for this reason, may be repeated as many times as necessary until the rite has been completed" (83). This means that the *Agnus Dei* is sung as a litany and should be repeated as many times as needed until the presider is ready to say, "Behold the Lamb of God." In this way, music and ritual action are connected. Time the first invocation with the moment the presider breaks the host. Anticipate how much of the introduction to the *Agnus Dei* you will need to play. In some cases, a single note cue works better than a lengthy intro. Bear in mind that the text for each invocation is "Lamb of God"; other titles, for example, "Jesus, Bread of Life" or "Jesus, Wine of Hope," may not be used.

COLLECT

Let us pray.

Pause for silent prayer

O God, who in this wonderful Sacrament
have left us a memorial of your Passion,
grant us, we pray,
so to revere the sacred mysteries of your
    Body and Blood
that we may always experience in
    ourselves
the fruits of your redemption.
Who live and reign with God the Father
in the unity of the Holy Spirit,
God, for ever and ever. **Amen.**

FIRST READING

Deut 8:2-3, 14b-16a

Moses said to the people:
    "Remember how for forty years now the
        LORD, your God,
    has directed all your journeying in the
        desert,
    so as to test you by affliction
    and find out whether or not it was your
        intention
    to keep his commandments.
He therefore let you be afflicted with
        hunger,
    and then fed you with manna,
    a food unknown to you and your
        fathers,
    in order to show you that not by bread
        alone does one live,
    but by every word that comes forth
        from the mouth of the LORD.

"Do not forget the LORD, your God,
    who brought you out of the land of
        Egypt,
    that place of slavery;
    who guided you through the vast and
        terrible desert
    with its saraph serpents and scorpions,
    its parched and waterless ground;
    who brought forth water for you from
        the flinty rock
    and fed you in the desert with manna,
    a food unknown to your fathers."

RESPONSORIAL PSALM
Ps 147:12-13, 14-15, 19-20

R⎖. (12) Praise the Lord, Jerusalem.
   or:
R⎖. Alleluia.

Glorify the Lord, O Jerusalem;
   praise your God, O Zion.
For he has strengthened the bars of your
      gates;
   he has blessed your children within you.

R⎖. Praise the Lord, Jerusalem.
   or:
R⎖. Alleluia.

He has granted peace in your borders;
   with the best of wheat he fills you.
He sends forth his command to the earth;
   swiftly runs his word!

R⎖. Praise the Lord, Jerusalem.
   or:
R⎖. Alleluia.

He has proclaimed his word to Jacob,
   his statutes and his ordinances to Israel.
He has not done thus for any other nation;
   his ordinances he has not made known
      to them.
Alleluia.

R⎖. Praise the Lord, Jerusalem.
   or:
R⎖. Alleluia.

SECOND READING
1 Cor 10:16-17

Brothers and sisters:
The cup of blessing that we bless,
   is it not a participation in the blood of
      Christ?
The bread that we break,
   is it not a participation in the body of
      Christ?
Because the loaf of bread is one,
   we, though many, are one body,
   for we all partake of the one loaf.

OPTIONAL SEQUENCE

See Appendix A, p. 294.

Living Liturgy

Rehearsing Inclusivity: In preparation for today's solemnity, as we contemplate the meaning of this phrase from the Dogmatic Constitution on the Church (*Lumen Gentium*), "[The Eucharist is] the source and summit of the Christian life" (11), I also hope we will spend some time in meditation on Pope Francis's invitation to everyone to share in the life of the church: "The Eucharist, although it is the fullness of sacramental life, is not a prize for the perfect but a powerful medicine and nourishment for the weak" (*Evangelii Gaudium* 47).

Eucharist in community gives foundation for rehearsing inclusive space for the Body of Christ. Eucharistic remembering transforms lives. Our hearts should be healed, reconciled, given new life to live in union with God and the saints. However, as Francis adds, "[f]requently, we act as arbiters of grace rather than its facilitators."

Take some time to consider how we might be better at recognizing God's grace in our ministerial spaces and to see how our complete participation in eucharistic celebration strengthens us to be the body and blood of Christ in the world. In our brokenness we share the transformative power of eucharistic healing with the world. We become broken for the broken. When we do this, we continue to cultivate spaces of belonging community through acknowledging and accepting vulnerabilities, we open wide our church doors so that whole community might exist. Having been fed, we go forth to offer everyone the life of Christ. It is what St. Oscar Romero meant when he said: "The church does not ignore the earth, but in the eucharist it says to all who work on the earth: look beyond" (*The Violence of Love*, trans. James R. Brockman, SJ). Looking beyond with eucharistic and eschatological vision acknowledges the Body of Christ living in the liminal space of the "already and the not yet." We participate as Body of Christ in God's presence and activity with eyes and ears fully open to the possibility and promise of transformative love in rehearsal for what is to come.

PROMPTS FOR FAITH-SHARING

• What is your participation in Eucharist like these days? Do you come to Communion wholeheartedly or out of habit?

• Mothers live out Jesus's model of giving up his body as food and drink in a special way; pregnancy and breastfeeding are some of the most literal ways one can give up one's body for another. What might your experience of mothering or being mothered teach you about what Jesus is doing in the Eucharist?

• Who in the church do you find it difficult to understand yourself as being in communion with? How might the Eucharist serve as an invitation to transcend the boundaries between you?

THE MOST HOLY BODY AND BLOOD OF CHRIST (CORPUS CHRISTI)

℟. Alleluia, alleluia.
Take my yoke upon you, says the Lord;
and learn from me, for I am meek and humble
of heart.
℟. Alleluia, alleluia.

Gospel   Matt 11:25-30; L170A

At that time Jesus exclaimed:
"I give praise to you,
   Father, Lord of
      heaven and earth,
   for although you have
      hidden these things
      from the wise and the
      learned
   you have revealed them
      to little ones.
Yes, Father, such has been
   your gracious will.
All things have been
   handed over to me
   by my Father.
No one knows the Son
   except the Father,
   and no one knows
      the Father
      except the Son
   and anyone to whom the Son wishes
      to reveal him.

"Come to me, all you who labor and are
   burdened,
   and I will give you rest.
Take my yoke upon you and learn from
   me,
   for I am meek and humble of heart;
   and you will find rest for yourselves.
For my yoke is easy, and my burden
   light."

See Appendix A, p. 295, for the other readings.

Reflecting on the Gospel

The Solemnity of the Sacred Heart of Jesus reminds us of the deep and abiding love God has for humanity. The Sacred Heart of Jesus illustrates the nuanced and complicated nature of love. Images of the Sacred Heart of Jesus often depict a flaming heart shining with divine light, pierced by a lance, and encircled by a crown of thorns. This dynamic and evocative image speaks to a love that is charged and vigorous, as well as harrowing and demanding. This image of love is vivid and at work in large and small, public and private ways in today's world.

As a young woman, Greta Thunberg became an outspoken advocate for government and economic policies that would mitigate the effects of climate change. In 2019, activated by her concern for the welfare of the earth, Thunberg embarked on a voyage across the Atlantic Ocean from Plymouth in the United Kingdom to New York City in the United States to attend the United Nations Climate Action Summit. She made the trip in fifteen days, riding aboard a solar-powered sailing yacht that ensured she could make the journey with zero carbon emissions. When our hearts are inflamed, an image mirroring the Sacred Heart of Jesus, we are empowered to act in radically countercultural ways out of integrity and for the sake of the beloved. Consider the flaming heart and reflect on the elements and issues in your life that embolden and enkindle you.

Another image found within the Sacred Heart is one that is wounded and surrounded by a crown of thorns. Parenthood may serve as an example for this image. To care for and raise up another life is to be perpetually vulnerable, frequently misunderstood, and sometimes attacked, making this a vocation that often requires both physical and emotional sacrifice. Many parents come to know their children in the way bittersweetly described by Kahlil Gibran in *The Prophet:* "souls that dwell in the house of tomorrow, which you cannot visit, not even in your dreams." The experience of parenthood can be as gratifying as it is gritty, as miraculous as it is miry. Through parents and guardians, we can witness another casting of the Sacred Heart of Jesus out into our world.

The readings that accompany this feast speak to the generosity of the Sacred Heart of Jesus, forever shining on humankind even when we fail to appreciate its dignifying effect on our lives. In the first reading from Deuteronomy, we hear Moses tell the Israelites of God's enduring love for them, not because of their size or might, but simply because of their identity and because of the promise God made to their ancestors. In the gospel, we hear Jesus promise his followers rest when they are weary and help with their burdens. These images of the Sacred Heart of Jesus invite us to accept the love that God holds out to us. May we respond to that invitation with earnest and grateful hearts. May we come to know intimately the love of God through the Sacred Heart of Jesus.

Preparing to Proclaim

Key words and phrases: "I am meek and humble of heart."

To the point: In one sense, the heart is an anatomical organ, one that is central to our lives and beings and to which every part of us needs to connect in order to stay, well, part of us. In another sense, the word "heart" is used to refer to something much deeper, to one's inmost being and deepest desires and point of connection with the divine. Today, we celebrate the heart of Jesus, which in one sense was a very real anatomical organ that traversed this earth with him.

In another sense, though, this feast invites us to reflect on the core of who Jesus is. And this gospel reveals deep wisdom about the heart of Jesus that we celebrate today. Jesus's heart is one that is meek and humble, rich in patience and kindness and gentleness. It is a heart that rejoices in God's privileged treatment of the "little ones," truly celebrating that God is always on the side of those who are small and lowly and oppressed and ignored. And it is a heart that loves us, that calls us to rest and ease in life with God.

Model Penitential Act

Presider: The Lord longs to give us rest and to relieve us from our burdens. With trust in God's everlasting mercy, let us call to mind our sins and ask for forgiveness . . . *[pause]*

Lord Jesus, you are the son of God and son of Mary: Lord, have mercy.

Christ Jesus, you draw us into your sacred heart: Christ, have mercy.

Lord Jesus, you gave your life out of love for us: Lord, have mercy.

Model Universal Prayer (Prayer of the Faithful)

Presider: As God's beloved children, let us bring our needs and the needs of the world before the Lord.

Response: Lord, hear our prayer.

Open the hearts of your faithful to the needs of people in pain or distress . . .

Grant wisdom to religious communities discerning their futures . . .

Give strength and peace to people preparing for surgery and their caregivers and medical teams . . .

Tend to the broken hearts of people in our community who are grieving . . .

Presider: God of every good gift, in your great love you opened wide the heart of your son, Jesus, so that all of us might enjoy life with you. Hear these our prayers that in the days ahead we might serve you with grateful hearts and willing spirits. We ask this through Christ our Lord. **Amen.**

Living Liturgy

Binding Love: In the middle of the Loyola Marymount University campus sits the Chapel of the Sacred Heart, the spiritual center of the university. In the chapel choir loft is a beautiful rose window image of the Sacred Heart of Jesus. These icons of stained glass and sacred space transmit messages of mercy, charity, love, and light that echo the readings of the day. Through the Sacred Heart we imagine a binding love which connects us to God and all God's people, especially the forgotten and disinherited ones. These images of love send us forth to be humble disciples who minister with generous hearts.

COLLECT

Let us pray.

Pause for silent prayer

Grant, we pray, almighty God,
that we, who glory in the Heart of your
      beloved Son
and recall the wonders of his love for us,
may be made worthy to receive
an overflowing measure of grace
from that fount of heavenly gifts.
Through our Lord Jesus Christ, your Son,
who lives and reigns with you in the unity of
      the Holy Spirit,
God, for ever and ever. **Amen.**

or:

O God, who in the Heart of your Son,
wounded by our sins,
bestow on us in mercy
the boundless treasures of your love,
grant, we pray,
that, in paying him the homage of our devotion,
we may also offer worthy reparation.
Through our Lord Jesus Christ, your Son,
who lives and reigns with you in the unity of
      the Holy Spirit,
God, for ever and ever. **Amen.**

FOR REFLECTION

• Reflect on the many things the word "heart" can mean and how you use it most often. What does it mean to you to hear the claim that God has a heart?

• What burdens might Jesus be asking you to leave with him in this gospel? How could you put them down—or at least put them aside for a time—in order to free up room in your heart for Jesus?

• How do you fulfill the second reading's call to "love one another"? How could you do better?

Homily Points

• In the sacred heart of Jesus, we will find the rest longed for by our weary souls. What does it look like to dwell in Jesus's sacred heart? How can we take Christ's yoke upon us in the busyness of our daily lives? Rest is not a given in today's fast-paced culture. Like any relationship, drawing close to the heart of Jesus requires time and attention.

• Knowledge of God is not something to be grasped or gained through intensive study. Rather, anything we come to know about the divine is a total gift from God. Today's gospel notes that God reveals Godself to those people who are positioned to receive such a gift with humility and gratitude.

SPIRITUALITY

GOSPEL ACCLAMATION
Mark 1:15

R̸. Alleluia, alleluia.
The kingdom of God is at hand.
Repent and believe in the Gospel.
R̸. Alleluia, alleluia.

Gospel   Matt 9:36–10:8; L91A

At the sight of the crowds, Jesus' heart
   was moved with pity for them
   because they were troubled and
      abandoned,
   like sheep without a shepherd.
Then he said to his disciples,
   "The harvest is abundant but the
      laborers are few;
   so ask the master of the harvest
   to send out laborers for his harvest."

Then he summoned his twelve disciples
   and gave them authority over unclean
      spirits
   to drive them out and to cure every
      disease and every illness.
The names of the twelve apostles are
   these:
   first, Simon called Peter, and his
      brother Andrew;
   James, the son of Zebedee, and his
      brother John;
   Philip and Bartholomew, Thomas and
      Matthew the tax collector;
   James, the son of Alphaeus, and
      Thaddeus;
   Simon from Cana, and Judas Iscariot
      who betrayed him.

Jesus sent out these twelve after
   instructing them thus,
   "Do not go into pagan territory or enter
      a Samaritan town.
Go rather to the lost sheep of the house
   of Israel.
As you go, make this proclamation: 'The
   kingdom of heaven is at hand.'
Cure the sick, raise the dead, cleanse
   lepers, drive out demons.
Without cost you have received; without
   cost you are to give."

Reflecting on the Gospel

In today's gospel passage from Matthew, we find the only occasion that Matthew uses the word *apostle*, meaning "sent one," to describe the follower of Jesus. While the meaning of *disciple* is "learner," today's gospel emphasizes the *sending out* of those whom Jesus has chosen. They are individuals; about some of them we know their background and the circumstances of their calling,

while others are named here and then simply become part of "the Twelve." That is enough to encourage us about the possibility of becoming a community around Jesus. If fishermen (two sets of brothers, with the family dynamics that might involve), a tax collector, a hot-headed revolutionary Zealot, a traitor, and the rest could be chosen and harvested by Jesus as the first laborers in the field, then surely there is hope for the disparate humanity that is our local or universal church today.

Jesus had to work hard, and not always successfully, with these apprentices. The fact that they are twelve is an important symbolic statement. Just as there were the twelve tribes of God's people in the Old Testament, so in the New Testament we again have the Twelve. And there's a wonderful description of heaven in the book of Revelation—again highly symbolic—as the new Jerusalem whose twelve gates are inscribed with "[the names] of the twelve tribes of the Israelites," and the twelve foundations of the city are inscribed with "the twelve names of the twelve apostles of the Lamb" (Rev 21:10-14).

Like all apprenticeships, it was "on the job" training, and the Twelve are immediately sent out on a mission. That Jesus sends his apostles only to "the lost sheep of the house of Israel," with instruction to avoid the Gentiles and Samaritans, may disconcert us. Jesus himself has already ministered with compassion to the Gentiles: the Roman centurion's servant (Matt 8:5-13) and the Gadarene demoniacs (Matt 8:28-34). Soon he will meet the Canaanite woman (Matt 15:21-28) and praise her faith in front of the objecting disciples, but it is not until after the resurrection that Jesus will commission the disciples themselves to go to all nations (Matt 28:19). After the resurrection they will have been sufficiently, painfully, and joyfully taught by Jesus for their larger mission. The mission of the Twelve at this stage is urgent and limited to the region and culture with which they were most familiar. Here they are to do what they have seen Jesus doing. Matthew's community of mainly Jewish Christians can identify with this priority, but it must also learn the often-difficult acceptance of the Gentiles who were joining the early church.

Here, in our own life situations, we are to try and do the same: minister with the gift of faith and Christ's compassion to the sick in mind and body, raise people from deathdealing despair, cast out the addictions that so destructively take hold of our sisters and brothers. Baptized into Christ, God has loved us at no charge; now we have to love the unlovable, without recompense.

Preparing to Proclaim

Key words and phrases: "[H]e summoned his twelve disciples and gave them authority over unclean spirits . . . and to cure every disease and every illness."

To the point: This gospel reveals Jesus's human nature in a number of ways. First, he is moved with pity; he has an emotional response to seeing people in need. Next, he seems to realize that he cannot do this work alone; there are too many needs to meet. Even Jesus, the second person of the Trinity, needs to ask for help. This is not a weakness of the human condition, not an effect of sin, but rather a normal part of our healthy functioning. And finally, he gives instructions that we know will be incomplete: at this point he sends his disciples only "to the lost sheep of the house of Israel." Jesus allows himself to be limited by the human constraints of time and resources and personnel. The fullness of his mission, where all nations are joined in praise of the one God, will develop over time.

Psalmist Preparation

This psalm expands the first reading's notion of Israel as God's chosen people; we, too, have been adopted by God in baptism and now belong to this beloved assembly. This psalm is appropriate for the image of a flock. It has a simple joy to it that suggests the childlike faith with which we are called to follow our shepherd. As you prepare this psalm, think of moments when your faith was simple and easy, when God's presence was clear and your response of love came naturally. Give thanks to God for these moments, which often help sustain us when faith feels more complicated and God's presence is harder to discern. Know that God remains with you; that promise is clear.

Making Connections

Between the readings: The first reading affirms Jesus's understanding of Israel as God's particularly beloved people. They are to be "a kingdom of priests," tasked with acting as something of a liaison between God and the rest of the world. In the gospel, the disciples take part in this priesthood in a new way, sent out to bring God back to Israel and Israel back to God. Ultimately, they will be further commissioned to go to all nations; the Holy Spirit at Pentecost will enable them to speak beyond the boundaries of their own language and culture.

To experience: This gospel shows Jesus getting organized. While his personal touch is irreplaceable, his ministry will be more effective with delegation and teamwork. There is a model of servant leadership here; good leaders are both willing to do the work themselves and willing to step aside when the situation calls for it.

Homily Points

• God wants the Israelites to stay close. "Hearken to my voice and keep my covenant," God tells the Israelites through Moses. At the time, the Israelites had pitched camp right at the foot of the mountain where God dwells. They believed they were in close proximity to God in a special way, perhaps similar to how we feel when we gather in church for Eucharist. The Israelites journeyed toward God—and God journeyed toward the Israelites. The relationship between God and God's beloved people goes two ways. Just as we desire closeness with God, God also desires closeness with us. God delights when we carve out time for prayer, serve our neighbors in need, advocate for justice, and take part in the myriad of other ways we keep the divine covenant.

• God delights in us. Savor that truth for a moment. God lifts us toward God's very self. God embraces us just as God embraced our ancestors in Israel. God draws us close—and then remains with us as we go into the world to labor the divine love into being.

• Today's gospel tells of Jesus calling disciples to help enact the gospel work of curing the sick, raising the dead, cleansing the lepers, driving out demons, and proclaiming to the lost: "The kingdom of heaven is at hand." Jesus calls disciples to labor for the harvest of the Lord. The Son of God is all-powerful and could take care of everything on his own. But like God the Creator, Jesus wants his people to be part of the mission too.

Model Penitential Act

Presider: In today's second reading, St. Paul reminds us that "while we were still sinners Christ died for us." Eager to grow in holiness, let us ask for mercy and forgiveness . . . *[pause]*

Lord Jesus, your heart was moved with pity for people in need: Lord, have mercy.

Christ Jesus, you call on disciples to cure the sick and drive out demons: Christ, have mercy.

Lord Jesus, you seek laborers for the harvest of justice: Lord, have mercy.

Model Universal Prayer (Prayer of the Faithful)

Presider: Believing in God's constant presence in our lives, let us confidently voice our prayers and petitions.

Response: Lord, hear our prayer.

Incline the ear of the church to listen ever closer to God's voice . . .

Grant success and good weather to all farmers whose labor feeds and sustains us . . .

Drive out the evils of racism, sexism, homophobia, and all other systems of oppression . . .

Empower each of us gathered here today to claim our call to discipleship . . .

Presider: Good and gracious God, you dwell within and among your chosen people, encouraging us and challenging us to grow in faith. Hear our prayers that with courage we might answer the call to discipleship each day. We ask this through Christ our Lord. **Amen.**

Liturgy and Music

A Generous Heart: Among the prayers attributed to St. Ignatius of Loyola, one stands out to me in terms of establishing a ministry that reaches out to the world—a prayer that helps to form a ministerial heart filled with generosity in service. A line from the gospel reading today guides our ministry to the world: "Without cost you have received; without cost you are to give." Ministry to the world calls us to form generous hearts within ourselves and in those that we serve with.

In our prayer and music making this week, place generosity at the center. At rehearsal, schedule some time to invite each person to reflect on their contributions to music ministry. What have we done to ensure a smooth and generous flow of ministry? Also take the time to thank one another for the generous contributions that each one brings to the group. Generosity and gratitude go hand in hand. When we are grateful for what we have and acknowledge the gifts and blessings that we have received, we are more open to sharing our gifts and blessings with the world. Music ministers, keep making the job look easy. Know that it does not go unnoticed.

COLLECT

Let us pray.

Pause for silent prayer

O God, strength of those who hope in you,
graciously hear our pleas,
and, since without you mortal frailty can
	do nothing,
grant us always the help of your grace,
that in following your commands
we may please you by our resolve and our
	deeds.
Through our Lord Jesus Christ, your Son,
who lives and reigns with you in the unity
	of the Holy Spirit,
God, for ever and ever. **Amen.**

FIRST READING

Exod 19:2-6a

In those days, the Israelites came to the
	desert of Sinai and pitched camp.
While Israel was encamped here in front
	of the mountain,
	Moses went up the mountain to God.
Then the LORD called to him and said,
	"Thus shall you say to the house of
		Jacob;
	tell the Israelites:
	You have seen for yourselves how I
		treated the Egyptians
	and how I bore you up on eagle wings
	and brought you here to myself.
Therefore, if you hearken to my voice and
	keep my covenant,
	you shall be my special possession,
	dearer to me than all other people,
	though all the earth is mine.
You shall be to me a kingdom of priests, a
	holy nation."

RESPONSORIAL PSALM
Ps 100:1-2, 3, 5

R℣. (3c) We are his people: the sheep of his flock.

Sing joyfully to the LORD, all you lands;
    serve the LORD with gladness;
    come before him with joyful song.

R℣. We are his people: the sheep of his flock.

Know that the LORD is God;
    he made us, his we are;
    his people, the flock he tends.

R℣. We are his people: the sheep of his flock.

The LORD is good:
    his kindness endures forever,
    and his faithfulness to all generations.

R℣. We are his people: the sheep of his flock.

SECOND READING
Rom 5:6-11

Brothers and sisters:
Christ, while we were still helpless,
    yet died at the appointed time for the
        ungodly.
Indeed, only with difficulty does one die
    for a just person,
    though perhaps for a good person
    one might even find courage to die.
But God proves his love for us
    in that while we were still sinners Christ
        died for us.
How much more then, since we are now
    justified by his blood,
    will we be saved through him from the
        wrath.
Indeed, if, while we were enemies,
    we were reconciled to God through the
        death of his Son,
    how much more, once reconciled,
    will we be saved by his life.
Not only that,
    but we also boast of God through our
        Lord Jesus Christ,
    through whom we have now received
        reconciliation.

Living Liturgy

Mission Statements: Parishes and worship communities articulate mission statements characteristic of the nature of their service to the world. Sometimes this is posted on the community's web page, and in other situations it might be framed and placed in an important place in the administrative office visible for all to see. Are you familiar with yours?

In Matthew's Gospel today we come to a transitionary moment. The focus has shifted from the ministry of Jesus to the work of the community that he has summoned. Especially in the Gospel of Matthew, the work of the church after the death and resurrection of Jesus is central and rightly emphasized. Our work and mission in ministry continue into the church's period of Ordinary Time.

When I joined the campus ministry team at Loyola Marymount University in Los Angeles, I learned that our campus ministry mission statement was a simple three-word phrase or mantra—belong, believe, become. These three words along with the charisms of the Jesuits and the Marymount sisters have shaped the ways in which I have ministered to students on campus. It has given me the graced opportunities to question belonging, believing and becoming. What does it mean or take to belong to or believe in or become a group of Christian disciples that proclaim the kingdom of heaven, a community of believers that "[c]ure the sick, raise the dead, cleanse lepers, drive out demons"?

When we learn to work together with others to achieve a common goal, we have learned something of what it means to do the work of Christ, to proclaim the kingdom of heaven. A parish, school, or campus ministry community or family provides a welcome place for working together, sharing a common task and a common goal of promoting all the good that comes from the gospel and from our mission statements.

PROMPTS FOR FAITH-SHARING

• We are all called to be both members of Jesus's flock and, in ways appropriate to our state in life, shepherds of that flock. Which of these calls feels more natural to you? How could the other be an invitation to grow?

• Do you feel that you share in the disciples' mission as described in the gospel? How do you (or how could you) help in healing and comforting those who are sick?

• When you are moved with pity for another, how do you respond? How could your response be more like Jesus's response—immediate and loving?

GOSPEL ACCLAMATION
cf. Luke 1:76

℞. Alleluia, alleluia.
You, child, will be called prophet of the Most
    High,
for you will go before the Lord to prepare his
    way.
℞. Alleluia, alleluia.

Gospel   Luke 1:57-66, 80; L587

**When the time arrived for Elizabeth to
    have her child
    she gave birth to a son.
Her neighbors and relatives heard
    that the Lord had shown his great
        mercy toward her,
    and they rejoiced with her.
When they came on the eighth day to
        circumcise the child,
    they were going to call him Zechariah
        after his father,
    but his mother said in reply,
    "No. He will be called John."
But they answered her,
    "There is no one among your
        relatives who has this name."
So they made signs, asking his father
    what he wished him to be called.**

Continued in Appendix A, p. 296.

See Appendix A, p. 296, for the other readings.

Reflecting on the Gospel

I have a handful of questions I like to ask students at the start of a new school year to help us get to know each other. My favorite question by far is, "What is your full name and where does it come from?" At first, students jokingly demand to know why I want to know their middle names and swear me to secrecy. Eventually, though, they begin to share stories about eager parents who had settled on a name as soon as they realized they were expecting or nervous parents who only realized the perfect name in the delivery room after meeting their child face-to-face. I learn about grandparents, great-grandparents, and other namesakes. I learn about names that are a combination of their parents' names, or names that begin with the same letter as all of their siblings' names. There may be some common patterns or habits in naming, but the students' names tell unique stories about who they are. Hearing about the origins of their names gives me insight into who they are and what they mean to their families and communities.

The significance of naming is a prominent theme in today's readings. In the book of Isaiah, the prophet recounts how God gifted him with his name, and in turn, bestowed upon him power and protection. ("He made me a polished arrow, / in his quiver he hid me.") The psalmist sings of how we are intimately known, seen, and loved by God. The reading from the Acts of the Apostles recalls King David, reminding us that each named figure in salvation history had a specific role to play in God's plans. In the gospel reading, we hear the story of Elizabeth defying expectations by choosing to give her son the name John. An unusual choice, the neighbors and relatives remark, because no one in their family has that name. Zechariah affirms Elizabeth's announcement and is immediately freed from the silence that settled upon him months prior.

"John is his name." In Hebrew, the name John means "graced by God." Today, the name continues to be popular across cultures. The curious relatives and neighbors did not know this would be the case. They simply wondered, "What, then, will this child be?"

The readings for this day emphasize the idea that God sees and graces each person individually. Although every creature is part of an intricate web of interdependence and interconnectedness, we also exist as singularly unique beings with a specific purpose and vocation. John the Baptist's vocation was to testify to the coming of Christ and to prepare the people of Israel to encounter God enfleshed. When new parents gaze at the face of their child for the first time and call them by name, they too may wonder, "What, then, will this child be?" Every member of the Body of Christ has a role to play in God's story of salvation. Whether that role is epic and public or quiet and private will vary, but one thing that remains consistently true is that no person, no name is small. Each of us is the product of generations of hopes and dreams, and our names are expressions of future aspirations and thanksgiving for former blessings. What can we learn about our purpose and our vocation by investigating and embracing our lovingly given names? What will be unlocked in us once we recognize ourselves as God's chosen and beloved ones?

Preparing to Proclaim

Key words and phrases: "He will be called John."

To the point: This gospel passage completes the wondrous events surrounding the conception of both John the Baptist and Jesus. We have seen multiple angels, conceptions by two women who should not have been able to conceive, the visitation and *Magnificat.* Here, finally, John is born, and more wonderful things ensue: the miraculous unanimity of his parents on an unexpected name and the resulting loosening of Zechariah's tied tongue. All this makes clear even from his birth that this is a child for whom God has great things in mind. His role as Jesus's forerunner is so unique that he stands with Mary and Jesus as being someone whose birthday we celebrate in the church year.

Model Penitential Act

Presider: In today's first reading, the prophet Isaiah cries out, "The Lord called me from birth, from my mother's womb God gave me my name." God names and claims each of us from birth. For the times we have not taken God's call seriously enough, let us ask for mercy . . . *[pause]*

Lord Jesus, you sought wisdom from John the Baptist: Lord, have mercy.
Christ Jesus, you bring peace to the world: Christ, have mercy.
Lord Jesus, in you we find everlasting life: Lord, have mercy.

Model Universal Prayer (Prayer of the Faithful)

Presider: Through the intercession of St. John the Baptist, let us offer our prayers and petitions to the Lord.

Response: Lord, hear our prayer.

Energize ministers of your church to follow the radical calls of Christ . . .

Protect people experiencing homelessness and all who will sleep on the streets this night . . .

Comfort and renew hope in couples struggling with infertility . . .

Equip this congregation to share the prophetic message of Jesus to the ends of the earth . . .

Presider: Everlasting God, in your kindness and mercy you make all things possible. Raise up in your church prophets like John the Baptist who prepare the way of the Lord and empower others to serve you in our sisters and brothers. We ask this through Christ our Lord. **Amen.**

Living Liturgy

Pointing the Way to Christ: We remember the great saint today and recall the significance of our own birth and baptism. How wonderfully made we are in the eyes of God and how we long to follow St. John the Baptist's way of heralding the way, words, and attitude of Christ. John the Baptist points us toward the direction we will take to lead others to Christ. May we realize that we are fragile and imperfect vessels that facilitate the work of God's Spirit within our communities. Like the Baptist, we show through our compassionate ministry the path to bridge building and bridge crossing, illuminating the world with the light of Christ.

COLLECT

Let us pray.

Pause for silent prayer

O God, who raised up Saint John the Baptist
to make ready a nation fit for Christ the Lord,
give your people, we pray,
the grace of spiritual joys
and direct the hearts of all the faithful
into the way of salvation and peace.
Through our Lord Jesus Christ, your Son,
who lives and reigns with you in the unity
of the Holy Spirit,
God, for ever and ever. **Amen.**

FOR REFLECTION

• John the Baptist's birth is surrounded by wonderful events that make God's presence and action clear. While your life might not have such clear evidence of God's hand, where have you seen God at work in your own life?

• Elizabeth was of what doctors like to call "advanced maternal age," making this pregnancy, wonderful though it was, a dangerous thing. God often works in liminal spaces where life and death intersect, such as childbirth. Can you think of other similar spaces that you or others you know have experienced?

Homily Points

• Neighbors gather to rejoice with Elizabeth and Zechariah over the most improbable birth of their son. The words of the angel came true: Nothing shall be impossible with God. Our prayers are not always answered exactly as we want. God is not a magician, after all! But there are precious moments in life where our hopes become reality. We ought to take time to come together as a community to celebrate and give thanks to God for such marvelous gifts.

• Earlier in Luke's Gospel, Zechariah questioned God at the announcement of his wife's miraculous pregnancy. Immediately, the angel Gabriel struck Zechariah silent. As the baby grew in Elizabeth's belly, Zechariah undoubtably reflects on his relationship with God and trust in God's almighty power. God strengthens Zechariah's faith through months of silence.

SPIRITUALITY

GOSPEL ACCLAMATION
cf. John 15:26b, 27a

R℣. Alleluia, alleluia.
The Spirit of truth will testify to
    me, says the Lord;
and you also will testify.
R℣. Alleluia, alleluia.

Gospel

Matt 10:26-33; L94A

Jesus said to the Twelve:
    "Fear no one.
Nothing is concealed that
    will not be revealed,
    nor secret that will not be
    known.
What I say to you in the
    darkness, speak in the
    light;
what you hear whispered,
    proclaim on the
    housetops.
And do not be afraid of
    those who kill the body
    but cannot kill the soul;
    rather, be afraid of the one who can
    destroy
    both soul and body in Gehenna.
Are not two sparrows sold for a small
    coin?
Yet not one of them falls to the ground
    without your Father's knowledge.
Even all the hairs of your head are
    counted.
So do not be afraid; you are worth
    more than many sparrows.
Everyone who acknowledges me before
    others
    I will acknowledge before my
        heavenly Father.
But whoever denies me before others,
    I will deny before my heavenly
        Father."

Reflecting on the Gospel

In today's gospel reading, before the disciples are sent out to share the mission of Jesus, they must dare to listen to him explain the tough demands of that mission. Three times Jesus tells them not to be afraid: not to fear those who (in the previous verse) malign them, or disregard them as worthless, or can injure and even kill them. Jesus has gathered them as a community of disciples and sown his word in the soil of their hearts so that it may push through this darkness and bear fruit by their proclamation of the gospel.

Just as Jesus trusts his Father, so it is to be with his disciples. Their one Father is so aware of his beloved creation that he is even aware of the death of the insignificant and dispensable little sparrows that are the cheapest food of the poor. Jesus says that if God has this concern for sparrows, how much more will he be concerned with the life and death of human beings. This greater concern is imaged as that of a caring parent who knows so much about his children—even the number of the hairs on their head—and will take care of them.

"Everyone" who hears these words of Jesus—each one of us in the Sunday assembly—is called to fearlessly proclaim the gospel, to acknowledge Jesus openly and without embarrassment in our families, communities, workplaces, and wider social situations. If we do this, Jesus assures us of an acknowledgment by his Father when we come to our final judgment. It is a pastoral challenge for every baptized Christian to find the right words that are more than "church speak" that says nothing to the doubts and anxieties, the truth of who people are.

What are the difficulties in climbing to the contemporary "housetops" where the right words can be spoken and heard? Married people struggling with fidelity, young people at war with their hormones, those with disabilities longing to be recognized first of all as people, men and women searching for their sexual identity, the poor and disadvantaged who are ashamed or angry: all of these need Christians to first of all listen to and then respond to their stories.

To be able to find new words, the experience and wisdom of the whole people of God is needed, and situations need to be created where this can be heard and shared without fear. For example, this is what happens in a parish that has a weekly session welcoming anyone to help in the preparation of the homily for the coming Sunday. The priest or a lay leader who has studied the readings says a few words, usually about the gospel. Then those gathered are asked what the word of God meant to them, what they would like to hear explained, how they are challenged, bored, or angered by what they have heard. Everyone's response is respected; there is no argument, no judgment. What the priest has dared to listen to from his parishioners then can help him to shape his homily for the following Sunday.

Preparing to Proclaim

Key words and phrases: "Even all the hairs of your head are counted."

To the point: In this gospel, Jesus is reassuring the disciples, for he has just revealed that their mission of preaching and healing will also lead them into the path of persecutions and hatred. In this passage, he reminds them at least three times not to be afraid. Their mission is true and trustworthy and worth the pain it will bring. More importantly, they do not go alone; they are accompanied always by a God who knows all and sees all and loves them intimately. The image of God seeing and noting the deaths of even sparrows is a charming one; sparrows are referred to by birders as "little brown jobs," interesting in their own way but nondescript, good at camouflage, and hard to tell apart. We know now of their ecological importance, but on the surface they are not the most interesting bird there is to see. But God sees and notices each of them individually, and God's care for us is many orders of magnitude more.

Psalmist Preparation

The psalm echoes the sentiments of both the gospel and the first reading: a life of faith is not always easy. Sometimes, in the context of a sinful world, it even causes suffering. There is reason for fear. But there is also reason for courage, for we do not face our suffering alone. God, who is all-powerful, promises to accompany us always in love. As you prepare this psalm, reflect on any fears you have about living your faith. Where do you need an increase in courage? Know that God hears and answers the plea you make in this psalm.

Making Connections

Between the readings: Jeremiah here acknowledges the same fear the disciples experience in the gospel. Being a messenger for God can make us unpopular; encountering God often calls people to change in ways for which they are not ready, and their resulting scorn is sometimes directed at those who bring the message. But again, strength is found in God's companionship and protection. Courage is called for, and it is justified, because the one who goes with us can do all things.

To experience: In the contemporary Western world, Christians often do not face the sort of persecutions encountered by the disciples. For us, courageous faith is still needed but occurs in much more subtle ways: in standing up for truth in a conversation with a loved one, in treating those with love whose choices might make us uncomfortable. Wherever and whenever we need courage, God goes with us, seeing our fears and accompanying us through them.

Homily Points

• The prophet Jeremiah was never one to hold back his feelings from God. His book of Scripture is filled with wailing and lamentations. Jeremiah suffered betrayal and frustrations throughout his life—and he let God know it. Jeremiah bared his soul to God—the good, the bad, and everything in between. Through this honesty, trust grew between the great prophet and God almighty. Jeremiah did not lash out for show. He came to believe God could handle anything stirring in his heart. Jeremiah saw God as a partner, one who "is with me, like a mighty champion."

• We too can call upon God in every moment of our lives, even—and perhaps especially—the moments that are not so neat and tidy. God does not need to be protected from our trials. Rather, God longs to draw ever closer to us just as God drew closer to Jeremiah and the great prophets throughout time. God can handle us. God wants to handle us.

• Jesus makes God's close presence known to the disciples in today's gospel. He assures them that "even all the hairs of your head are counted" by God. Our God is a God of abundance who creates and reveals all the time. We need only to pay attention. We need only to be honest. We need only to trust God's great love for us.

Model Penitential Act

Presider: In today's second reading, St. Paul reminds us that all people sin—and still the gracious gift of Jesus Christ overflows. For the times we have sinned this week, let us pause to ask for mercy . . . *[pause]*

Lord Jesus, you are our help and salvation: Lord, have mercy.

Christ Jesus, you intercede for us before God the Father: Christ, have mercy.

Lord Jesus, you will come again to break the bonds of death: Lord, have mercy.

Model Universal Prayer (Prayer of the Faithful)

Presider: Trusting that God listens to our prayers, let us offer our prayers and petitions with confidence.

Response: Lord, hear our prayer.

Safeguard all children in our churches, schools, and communities . . .

Increase respect for indigenous communities and the lands under their care . . .

Grant protection and peace to migrants, refugees and all people forced to flee their homes . . .

Incline the hearts of each of us gathered here to greater partnership and honesty with God . . .

Presider: Ever-present God, through the gift of your son Jesus Christ you promise to bring all things into the light. Hear our prayers that with boldness we might proclaim your good news. We ask this through Christ our Lord. **Amen.**

Liturgy and Music

To Sing Blessing: Our church teaches that "Sacramentals derive from the baptismal priesthood: every baptized person is called to be a 'blessing,' and to bless. Hence lay people may preside at certain blessings; the more a blessing concerns ecclesial and sacramental life, the more is its administration reserved to the ordained ministry" (*Catechism of the Catholic Church* 1669). At certain times of the year or on various occasions at Sunday Mass, the community might bless a certain person or group of people. Although not required, music to accompany such blessings adds to the beauty and reverence of the ritual action.

While there are a variety of short pieces composed specifically to accompany a blessing, you could also consider singing a refrain or a phrase from a refrain of a song familiar to the parish community. Weave the simple acclamation within the blessing prayer. This allows the entire assembly to participate in the blessing through song.

Entering the summer months, it would be appropriate to invite the pastor to offer a blessing of thanksgiving to all the liturgical ministers (including music ministers) as parish ministries take some time off for rest and recreation. In acknowledging these generous volunteers, the whole parish community encounters Christ through the blessing and service of these faithful people.

COLLECT

Let us pray.

Pause for silent prayer

Grant, O Lord,
that we may always revere and love your
holy name,
for you never deprive of your guidance
those you set firm on the foundation of
your love.
Through our Lord Jesus Christ, your Son,
who lives and reigns with you in the unity
of the Holy Spirit,
God, for ever and ever. **Amen.**

FIRST READING

Jer 20:10-13

Jeremiah said:
"I hear the whisperings of many:
'Terror on every side!
Denounce! Let us denounce him!'
All those who were my friends
are on the watch for any misstep of
mine.
'Perhaps he will be trapped; then we can
prevail,
and take our vengeance on him.'
But the LORD is with me, like a mighty
champion:
my persecutors will stumble, they
will not triumph.
In their failure they will be put to utter
shame,
to lasting, unforgettable confusion.
O LORD of hosts, you who test the just,
who probe mind and heart,
let me witness the vengeance you take
on them,
for to you I have entrusted my cause.
Sing to the LORD,
praise the LORD,
for he has rescued the life of the poor
from the power of the wicked!"

RESPONSORIAL PSALM
Ps 69:8-10, 14, 17, 33-35

R̶/. (14c) Lord, in your great love, answer me.

For your sake I bear insult,
    and shame covers my face.
I have become an outcast to my brothers,
    a stranger to my children,
because zeal for your house consumes me,
    and the insults of those who blaspheme
        you fall upon me.

R̶/. Lord, in your great love, answer me.

I pray to you, O Lᴏʀᴅ,
    for the time of your favor, O God!
In your great kindness answer me
    with your constant help.
Answer me, O Lᴏʀᴅ, for bounteous is your
        kindness;
    in your great mercy turn toward me.

R̶/. Lord, in your great love, answer me.

"See, you lowly ones, and be glad;
    you who seek God, may your hearts
        revive!
For the Lᴏʀᴅ hears the poor,
    and his own who are in bonds he spurns
        not.
Let the heavens and the earth praise him,
    the seas and whatever moves in them!"

R̶/. Lord, in your great love, answer me.

SECOND READING
Rom 5:12-15

Brothers and sisters:
Through one man sin entered the world,
    and through sin, death,
    and thus death came to all men,
        inasmuch as all sinned—
for up to the time of the law, sin was in
        the world,
    though sin is not accounted when there
        is no law.
But death reigned from Adam to Moses,
    even over those who did not sin
    after the pattern of the trespass of
        Adam,
    who is the type of the one who was to
        come.

But the gift is not like the transgression.
For if by the transgression of the one the
        many died,
    how much more did the grace of God
    and the gracious gift of the one man
        Jesus Christ
    overflow for the many.

Living Liturgy

Love Wins Fear: Throughout the gospels Jesus makes it clear to his disciples, "Fear no one." And so it is with a certain amount of fearlessness that we continue in the work of Christian discipleship within liturgical and pastoral ministries. The psalmist's plea is to God to remove the evil that causes the psalmist's own suffering, and echoed in the gospel reading, we hear that only God is to be feared, for God in God's great love will answer us when we cry out. Authentic discipleship challenges us to continually overcome our own prejudices and implicit biases when ministering to the broken.

Throughout the month of June, we recognize and stand in love and solidarity with persons of the LGBTQ+ community, a people who have endured suffering, shame, and hate, who have lived in the shadows of abuse and discrimination. The church teaches that members of the LGBTQ+ community "must be accepted with respect, compassion and sensitivity. Every sign of unjust discrimination in their regard should be avoided" (*Catechism of the Catholic Church* 2358).

Pride Month invites all Christians, including queer Christians, to live out fully God's summons to ease the suffering of the persecuted. It challenges all God's children to fear no one and to speak up fearlessly for human dignity. We are greatly loved by our Creator who has counted all the hairs on our head. As the disciples are emboldened, so are we to speak in the light what we have heard in the dark and to proclaim from the rooftops what we have heard in whispers —love always wins.

PROMPTS FOR FAITH-SHARING

• Have you experienced suffering because of your faith in Jesus? What was it like?

• How does your suffering compare to that of the early church?

• Where in your life do you need an increase in courage?

GOSPEL ACCLAMATION
Matt 16:18

℟. Alleluia, alleluia.
You are Peter and upon this rock I will build my Church,
and the gates of the netherworld shall not prevail against it.
℟. Alleluia, alleluia.

Gospel Matt 16:13-19; L591

When Jesus went into the region of Caesarea Philippi
he asked his disciples,
"Who do people say that the Son of Man is?"
They replied, "Some say John the Baptist, others Elijah,
still others Jeremiah or one of the prophets."
He said to them, "But who do you say that I am?"
Simon Peter said in reply,
"You are the Christ, the Son of the living God."
Jesus said to him in reply, "Blessed are you, Simon son of Jonah.
For flesh and blood has not revealed this to you, but my heavenly Father.

Continued in Appendix A, p. 297.

See Appendix A, p. 297, for the other readings.

Reflecting on the Gospel

St. Peter and St. Paul are figures who loom large in the history of the faith. Because of their courage and their ardent dedication to the will of God, the good news of Jesus Christ was spread throughout the world. As they carried God's message of hope to new lands, they supported newly forming communities of Christians with their teaching and correspondence. Sts. Peter and Paul illustrate what it means to make one's life a living testimony to the love and power of God. Peter and Paul's stories also remind us that God does not depend on perfect humans to bring about God's divine plans; rather, the plans are accomplished when imperfect people continue to show up faithfully and do their best.

Throughout the gospels, Peter plays a prominent role. He is an eyewitness to the ministry of Jesus, but we see that many times he is slow to comprehend all of Jesus's intentions. At the Last Supper, Peter initially rebuffs Jesus's offer to wash his feet. When Jesus insists, Peter overcorrects saying, "Master, then not only my feet, but my hands and head as well" (John 13:9). However, in today's gospel from Matthew, we see that Peter understands the most essential tenet of the faith: that Jesus Christ is the Son of God and Savior. St. Peter represents believers whose hearts are fiercely focused on Christ but are still growing as they follow in Christ's footsteps.

We also draw wisdom from the story in which Peter followed Jesus Christ out of the boat and momentarily walked on water. When his faith began to waver, Peter began to sink in the water but Jesus reached out and saved Peter. If we come face-to-face with our weakness and start to experience doubt, we too can call out to Christ and be rescued. Like Peter, we can journey out to the place where Christ leads us.

St. Paul figures more prominently after Jesus's earthly ministry comes to an end and is an example of how God's collaborators are sometimes pulled from unlikely places. Paul's conversion experience on the way to Damascus compelled him to dedicate the rest of his life to God's service. Here we see our past does not have to dictate or limit the potential of our future. It is never too late for us to change course and reorient ourselves so that we are better aligned with God's will. Where are the blind spots in our vision? Where are the opportunities for us to grow in our understanding of what God wants from us?

When we consider God's conversion of Paul on the road to Damascus, the way the scales were removed from Paul's eyes, we can be assured that we, too, will be given new eyes with which to see and understand God's plans. On this solemnity celebrating Sts. Peter and Paul, let us rejoice in the way that God saw the potential of those two flawed men, entered into their lives, and invited them to participate in this great work. We are asked to remember that even when our flaws are on display, God graciously invites us to be collaborators and constructors of God's kingdom.

Preparing to Proclaim

Key words and phrases: "You are the Christ, the Son of the living God."

To the point: The gospel depicts Jesus giving Peter his utterly unique role in the church. Peter is the first to correctly identify Jesus as Messiah and Son of God. He becomes the rock upon which the church is built and is given the keys to the kingdom of heaven. We know him as the first leader of the church, the predecessor to the pope. But this is not Peter's whole story. We have been through the Easter season and know that he will prove to be one of Jesus's most inconsistent and imperfect followers. This reminds us that Peter was not left alone to carry on

Jesus's work. Even in his uniqueness he sits among the other apostles and will later be both supported and challenged by Paul, who forever shares his feast day.

Model Penitential Act

Presider: In today's gospel, Jesus asks his disciples, "Who do you say that I am?" Peter replies, "You are the Christ, the Son of the living God." Trusting in God's living presence among us, let us ask for pardon and mercy . . . *[pause]*

Lord Jesus, you rescue us from every evil: Lord, have mercy.

Christ Jesus, you promise safety in the heavenly kingdom: Christ, have mercy.

Lord Jesus, to you be glory forever and ever: Lord, have mercy.

Model Universal Prayer (Prayer of the Faithful)

Presider: With hearts open to God's call, let us offer our prayers and petitions.

Response: Lord, hear our prayer.

Raise up leaders within the church, particularly those who help guide our liturgical ministries, outreach ministries, and faith formation . . .

Guide leaders of nations to uphold the common good and take special care of the most vulnerable . . .

Eradicate the sin of racism from all social systems and human hearts . . .

Grace the lives of all gathered here with strength and resolve to live the Christian life . . .

Presider: God of power and might, you call leaders like Sts. Peter and Paul to guide your church. Receive our prayers that we too might contribute to the building up of your kingdom on earth. We ask this through Christ our Lord. **Amen.**

Living Liturgy

Christ Remains with Us: Saints Peter and Paul give us hope. The movements of our own life in ministry and our faith journey mirror the lives of these two saints in their countless ups and downs. Through our doubt, misunderstandings, denials, weaknesses, and sheer stupidity, Christ remains with us in our human struggle and keeps calling us to be witnesses of our faith. Our triumphs and failures are all matters of the grace of God. With Peter and Paul, we recognize our call into a faith community not our own, a community centered in Christ.

COLLECT

Let us pray.

Pause for silent prayer

O God, who on the Solemnity of the Apostles Peter and Paul
give us the noble and holy joy of this day,
grant, we pray, that your Church
may in all things follow the teaching
of those through whom she received
the beginnings of right religion.
Through our Lord Jesus Christ, your Son,
who lives and reigns with you in the unity of the Holy Spirit,
God, for ever and ever. **Amen.**

FOR REFLECTION

• Reflect on your experience of leaders within the church. Which leaders have you known who make God's presence clear? Which have been more challenging to work with?

• Knowing Peter's whole story, how do you feel about him being chosen as the "rock" upon which Jesus builds the church? Is there reassurance there that God can work with you in all your imperfection?

• In the second reading, Paul uses athletic metaphors to describe the challenges of Christian life: "I have competed well; I have finished the race." What might we learn from athletes' disciplined training about what the life of faith calls for from us?

Homily Points

• Every saint faced their share of hardships. Living a life committed to Christ takes risks. It can be easy to imagine saints sitting dutifully in church, hands clasped together in quiet prayer. Or one might imagine saints arriving into town with great fanfare, hurling miracles left and right. Yet take up most books about the saints and you will quickly notice that the Christian life is no walk in the park.

• Today's Scripture readings tell of St. Peter chained up in a prison cell after the execution of James, his fellow apostle. Paul writes of being rescued from every evil threat. Following Christ does not ensure security. Rather, such a life ensures stability through the ongoing presence of Christ in good times and bad, on earth and in heaven. Saints like Peter and Paul serve as witnesses to the strength that comes from aligning with Christ.

• "But who do you say that I am?" Jesus poses this intimate question to Peter—and to each of us. Throughout history, Jesus has accumulated many titles: Word made flesh, Redeemer, Light of the World, and Prince of Peace just to name a few. These titles point to particular characteristics or realities of Jesus. They help us come to know Jesus. They help us to name our relationships with him. Who is Jesus to you? Who is Jesus for our church community? For our neighborhood and world? Inspired by Peter, may we share what we know to be true about Jesus.

SPIRITUALITY

GOSPEL ACCLAMATION
1 Peter 2:9

R⁊. Alleluia, alleluia.
You are a chosen race, a royal
    priesthood, a holy nation;
announce the praises of him who
    called you out of darkness into
    his wonderful light.
R⁊. Alleluia, alleluia.

Gospel

Matt 10:37-42; L97A

Jesus said to his apostles:
    "Whoever loves father or
        mother more than me is
        not worthy of me,
    and whoever loves son or
        daughter more than me
        is not worthy of me;
    and whoever does not take
        up his cross
    and follow after me is not
        worthy of me.

"Whoever finds his life will
        lose it,
    and whoever loses his life for my
        sake will find it.
Whoever receives you receives me,
    and whoever receives me receives
        the one who sent me.
Whoever receives a prophet because he
        is a prophet
    will receive a prophet's reward,
    and whoever receives a righteous
        man
    because he is a righteous man
    will receive a righteous man's
        reward.
And whoever gives only a cup of cold
        water
    to one of these little ones to drink
    because the little one is a disciple—
    amen, I say to you, he will surely not
        lose his reward."

Reflecting on the Gospel

A precious gem of early Christian literature is the *Passion of Perpetua and Felicity*, an account of the martyrdom (around CE 203) in North Africa of Perpetua, a twenty-two-year-old married woman of noble Roman birth, and her slavegirl, Felicity. It is written as a diary account by Perpetua, in first-person style—which, if true, would make it an incredibly important witness from one of the earliest Christian female writers—but some scholars suggest someone else was the principal author, perhaps the early Christian author Tertullian.

Both Perpetua and Felicity are condemned to the arena at Carthage. One part of the account describes Perpetua's pain because of her father's attitude. Weary and exhausted with grief, he tries to make his daughter change her mind, to remember the love of her family, and especially her baby son, whom she was still nursing. Faced with such distress, Hilarion, the administrator, begs her to offer sacrifice for the emperors. Perpetua steadfastly refuses, and Hilarion puts to her the deciding question: "Are you a Christian?" When she simply answers, "I am a Christian," her father makes a last attempt to try to get his daughter to deny her faith. Instead, Hilarion orders that her father be thrown down and beaten with a rod. This pain, says Perpetua, hurt her as if she herself had been struck. Then the judgment is passed: "To the wild beasts."

Today, the simple answer "Yes, I am a Christian" may not have the dramatic result of martyrdom in many places. In other countries, however, it is still the very real experience of Christians whose faith has to withstand persecution and tyranny or refuse to be conformed to personal, social, or even ecclesial comfort zones. No committed Christian can escape the demanding priorities of the cross in our daily lives. We do not pray for the cross, but we accept its often surprising arrival, trying to recognize it for what it is: a challenge to trust in God and God's future, and to discover that selfgiving is selffulfillment.

If in our lives we do prioritize the love of Jesus and his gospel, and if in doing this we have to painfully bid farewell to people who are precious to us, Jesus offers us a great welcome into a new "family" and community. A chain of hospitality (the lifegiving Middle Eastern virtue) binds the disciple to Jesus and Jesus to the Father. To welcome one is to welcome the others. We are not all Perpetuas or Felicitys, but if disciples no longer have family structures to support them because of rifts that come with allegiance to Jesus, the Christian community has the obligation of offering hospitality to them. It may be a gesture as small and ordinary as a neighborly "cuppa," or the affirmation (using modern means of communication as well as personal contact) of those prophets and seekers of justice in our midst who may be persecuted not only by those outside the church but also by those "in [their] native place and in [their] own house" (Matt 13:57).

Preparing to Proclaim
Key words and phrases: "Whoever finds his life will lose it, and whoever loses his life for my sake will find it."

To the point: This gospel calls us to hospitality; it is about receiving others and thereby receiving Christ. But this hospitality goes beyond what we usually mean by the word. It is not about throwing parties or offering a bed when it will make us look good or give us fodder for our social media feeds. It's not a hospitality of convenience. This is rather a hospitality of the heart; it is about being willing to move around our very selves in order to make space for others. That's why Jesus's words about receiving others and offering cups of cold water are paired with those about taking up our crosses and losing our lives. This hospitality is about giving of ourselves, which is sometimes uncomfortable. But Jesus is calling us to something deeper here. We do not give up our lives for no reason, but because in doing so we imitate the self-giving love of God. By making this space for others, we find our truest selves.

Psalmist Preparation
This is a lovely psalm to proclaim; you get to sing about singing and to pledge through your very song the church's intention to always offer praise for God's goodness. The vow we make here is a big one: "forever" is a lot to promise! But we can make it precisely because of the goodness of the Lord. It is God's faithfulness that comes first, and because God fulfills his promises, we can fulfill ours. As you prepare this psalm, seek out evidence of God's goodness in your own life. Sing this psalm in thanksgiving for what you find and let it be an earnest prayer of praise.

Making Connections
Between the readings: The first reading shows a practice of radical hospitality, the same kind to which we are called by the gospel. The Shunammite woman and her husband do not just provide for Elisha's needs as is convenient for them. They rearrange their very lives and home to make space for him. In the end, this is what hospitality is all about—making space for others, in our homes, in our lives, and in our hearts.

To experience: Many of us are adept at surface-level hospitality; we know how to greet someone new, to make conversation, to be friendly. Many of us know how to open our homes to others, to create a pleasant experience and tend to the immediate needs of those who eat or sleep under our roofs. But Jesus asks us for something more; hospitality of the heart requires deeper vulnerability, radical generosity, and profound trust in God.

Homily Points
• In his rule for monastic living, St. Benedict calls on his brothers to "receive all as Christ." Hospitality is a hallmark of Benedictine spirituality—and the broader Christian life. We need not be monks or nuns to practice the radical hospitality called for in St. Benedict's Rule and today's gospel. Jesus puts himself in the place of a guest when he tells his apostles: "Whoever receives you receives me." He ups the ante even further by adding: "and whoever receives me receives the one who sent me."

• To welcome another person is to welcome God, the source of all life, and Christ's very self. For all people are made in the image of God. God dwells within and among each one of us. The friend and the foe, the loved one and the stranger, the joyful, the hurting, the weary and the lost—everyone reflects the image of God in a unique way and deserves to be treated as such.

• What does it look like to receive or welcome another as Christ? How can we answer Jesus's call to take up our cross and follow him? Discipleship demands a radical embrace of the divine in our daily lives. Maybe that looks like seeking forgiveness from a colleague. Maybe it looks like welcoming the pain of unhoused neighbors into your heart and allowing it to move you to action. Maybe the radical welcome to which Jesus calls us looks as simple as offering a "hi, how are you?" to the person sitting by themselves a few pews over. As we move into a new week, consider how you can take up the Christian call to receive others as if you are receiving Christ's very self.

Model Penitential Act

Presider: In today's second reading, St. Paul reminds us that we must think of ourselves as dead to sin and living for God in Christ Jesus. As we work to root out sin from our lives, let us ask God for mercy and forgiveness . . . *[pause]*

Lord Jesus, you took up the cross for our sake: Lord, have mercy.

Christ Jesus, you draw us ever closer to God, the source of life: Christ, have mercy.

Lord Jesus, you will come again to shower us with compassion: Lord, have mercy

Model Universal Prayer (Prayer of the Faithful)

Presider: Having received the word of God, let us offer our petitions to the one who welcomes us with great love.

Response: Lord, hear our prayer.

Transform our church into a place and a people who welcome all as Christ . . .

Bless people who work in hospitality and service industries . . .

Stop the harmful effects of the climate crisis and help all people to deepen their care for the natural world . . .

Further the work of our local communities to provide adequate housing and healthcare to people in need . . .

Presider: Almighty God, through your son Jesus you beckon us to draw ever closer to you. Receive our prayers that we may be beacons of welcome to all those searching for divine assistance. We ask this through Christ our Lord. **Amen.**

Liturgy and Music

Music Connects with Liturgical Action: Our music making at Mass supports liturgical action, for liturgical music ought to be in complete service of the ritual. When preparing music for this weekend, be mindful of what the Constitution on the Sacred Liturgy states: "[S]acred music is to be considered the more holy, the more closely connected it is with the liturgical action, whether making prayer more pleasing, promoting unity of minds, or conferring greater solemnity on the sacred rites" (112).

While liturgy is closely connected to life, Christ and the paschal mystery is the focus at Mass. Pay attention to this when considering music for this Independence Day weekend. Instead of singing nationalistic songs, decorating in red, white, and blue, and displaying flags in the sanctuary (which the USCCB has discouraged), focus on Christ. Sing instead songs that proclaim God's justice and peace for all peoples. Note that in the Roman Missal for the USA, there is a Mass that may be used for the Fourth of July, but non-liturgical texts in the form of national documents or speeches have no place in the liturgy. It would be most appropriate and necessary to include a prayer for our nation during the universal prayer or intercessions.

COLLECT

Let us pray.

Pause for silent prayer

O God, who through the grace of adoption
chose us to be children of light,
grant, we pray,
that we may not be wrapped in the
    darkness of error
but always be seen to stand in the bright
    light of truth.
Through our Lord Jesus Christ, your Son,
who lives and reigns with you in the unity
    of the Holy Spirit,
God, for ever and ever. **Amen.**

FIRST READING

2 Kgs 4:8-11, 14-16a

One day Elisha came to Shunem,
    where there was a woman of influence,
        who urged him to dine with her.
Afterward, whenever he passed by, he
    used to stop there to dine.
So she said to her husband, "I know that
    Elisha is a holy man of God.
Since he visits us often, let us arrange a
    little room on the roof
    and furnish it for him with a bed, table,
        chair, and lamp,
    so that when he comes to us he can stay
        there."
Sometime later Elisha arrived and stayed
    in the room overnight.

Later Elisha asked, "Can something be
    done for her?"
His servant Gehazi answered, "Yes!
    She has no son, and her husband is
        getting on in years."
Elisha said, "Call her."
When the woman had been called and
    stood at the door,
    Elisha promised, "This time next year
    you will be fondling a baby son."

RESPONSORIAL PSALM
Ps 89:2-3, 16-17, 18-19

℟. (2a) Forever I will sing the goodness of the Lord.

The promises of the LORD I will sing
forever,
through all generations my mouth shall
proclaim your faithfulness.
For you have said, "My kindness is
established forever";
in heaven you have confirmed your
faithfulness.

℟. Forever I will sing the goodness of the
Lord.

Blessed the people who know the joyful
shout;
in the light of your countenance, O
LORD, they walk.
At your name they rejoice all the day,
and through your justice they are
exalted.

℟. Forever I will sing the goodness of the
Lord.

You are the splendor of their strength,
and by your favor our horn is exalted.
For to the LORD belongs our shield,
and to the Holy One of Israel, our king.

℟. Forever I will sing the goodness of the
Lord.

SECOND READING
Rom 6:3-4, 8-11

Brothers and sisters:
Are you unaware that we who were
baptized into Christ Jesus
were baptized into his death?
We were indeed buried with him through
baptism into death,
so that, just as Christ was raised from
the dead
by the glory of the Father,
we too might live in newness of life.

If, then, we have died with Christ,
we believe that we shall also live with
him.
We know that Christ, raised from the dead,
dies no more;
death no longer has power over him.
As to his death, he died to sin once and
for all;
as to his life, he lives for God.
Consequently, you too must think of
yourselves as dead to sin
and living for God in Christ Jesus.

Living Liturgy

Extending Hospitality: In the gospel reading today Jesus explains the difficulties of discipleship. The demand of discipleship in Matthew's Gospel may appear harsh. Yet the truth is, when we choose to do anything wholeheartedly, especially in our liturgical ministries, we must be prepared for the consequences. The ultimate paradox of discipleship is that to gain life, we must give it away. Choosing to take up the cross and follow Christ, to have a life with Christ, means that everything we do, every interaction we have, must be understood from a new perspective. Sometimes this means switching points of view from the one who offers welcome to the one who is being welcomed.

When we offer Christian hospitality, it must extend further than simply welcoming a guest or a stranger. Rather, it involves walking together in community with the new person or the seeker. The gospel reveals that Christ walks with and welcomes all and that those who welcome the disciples have also welcomed Christ. Authentic Christian hospitality requires going one step further in our encounter of the other as we engage in an act of accompaniment. A phrase that I've learned in campus ministry is "to meet students where they are at," which might be one way to describe this sense of accompaniment.

How hospitable is your parish community at meeting new parishioners where they are at? Does the worship community reflect a warm welcoming presence as a sign of God's love? Does the parish's hospitality style follow a prescribed and formalized pattern or is it a free joyful response to God's grace?

In many ways, when we think of extending Christian hospitality we must also reflect on our own journey of faith and discipleship. In order to welcome someone fully into community we need to first feel that we also completely belong to the community, the community that connects us to God's love.

PROMPTS FOR FAITH-SHARING

• What do you usually mean by hospitality, and how do you practice it in your life? How might these readings challenge you to expand its practice?

• We are sometimes hesitant to think of the rewards God promises—we want to do the right thing simply because it is right—but these readings make clear that there is a reward for those who receive Christ in others. What reward do you hope for? What hopes are you hesitant to bring even to God?

• How could your parish's liturgy become an experience of the radical hospitality to which Jesus calls us in this gospel?

✚ SPIRITUALITY

GOSPEL ACCLAMATION
cf. Matt 11:25

℟. Alleluia, alleluia.
Blessed are you, Father, Lord of heaven and
earth;
you have revealed to little ones the mysteries
of the kingdom.
℟. Alleluia, alleluia.

Gospel

Matt 11:25-30; L100A

At that time Jesus exclaimed:
"I give praise to you, Father, Lord
of heaven and earth,
for although you have hidden
these things
from the wise and the learned
you have revealed them to little
ones.
Yes, Father, such has been your
gracious will.
All things have been handed over to
me by my Father.
No one knows the Son except the
Father,
and no one knows the Father except
the Son
and anyone to whom the Son wishes
to reveal him.

"Come to me, all you who labor and are
burdened,
and I will give you rest.
Take my yoke upon you and learn from
me,
for I am meek and humble of heart;
and you will find rest for yourselves.
For my yoke is easy, and my burden
light."

Reflecting on the Gospel

In the verses from Matthew's Gospel that come immediately before the passage we hear today, Jesus has reproached the cities that rejected him. But then out of this lamentation there erupts his hymn of praise and thanks to his Father for the "little ones," those who have no status but can recognize in Jesus the One who is "gracious and merciful, / slow to anger and of great kindness," who lifts up the fallen and those who are burdened, as the responsorial Psalm 145 prays. This recognition is God's revelation, a gift of God's grace, for such people have no other way of coming to this response.

As Jesus has just told John the Baptist's disciples, a sign of the messianic times would be the preaching to and welcoming of the good news by the poor and disadvantaged. These words are not only for Jesus's immediate audience or for Matthew's community of powerless "little ones" struggling with the religious authorities fifty years or more after Jesus's death and resurrection. They are also a present and future challenge to those whose theological and religious pretensions or spiritual elitism ignore or downgrade the wisdom and experience of those who have come to know God through simple but often hard-won and faithful commitment.

Matthew then gives us one of our very few glimpses into the prayer of Jesus. As when he had earlier taught his disciples to pray, Jesus addresses God as "Father," not to idolize a name or gender or metaphor, but to focus on *a relationship*: the reign of his Abba over his life and the lives of all those who become daughters and sons of this same God by accepting Jesus as the Word and Wisdom of God. There are echoes here of the hymn that closes the book of Sirach (see Sir 51:22-30). Like Lady Wisdom, Jesus offers an invitation to those who are overburdened and weary: "Come to me . . ."

It is Jesus, not the rigorous law enforcers of his day, who will offer rest. Jesus uses the image of his easy "yoke" to encourage the people to accept his invitation. To the Palestinian peasant, the yoke was a familiar farming object. It was a wooden frame, designed to be fitted over the necks of two oxen or horses to evenly distribute the weight of the load that they had to pull. When yoked, plowing animals were more effectively kept in step with one another. It was usually the local carpenter who would make and fit a yoke, with great concern for the individual animal's neck muscles and the maximum direction of its energy. (One wonders how many yokes Jesus and Joseph had built in Joseph's workshop.)

"*My* yoke," says Jesus, will be well-fitted to each disciple. It will distribute the weight of our heavy burdens between each one of us and Jesus, and it will keep us in step with the One who is the Way as we plow through life.

Preparing to Proclaim

Key words and phrases: "[M]y yoke is easy, and my burden light."

To the point: After several weeks of affirming the challenges of following him, Jesus offers here a word of consolation. "My yoke is easy, and my burden light" does not sound like it aligns well with all we have been hearing about persecution and suffering. But Jesus is reminding us that even though suffering might be part of the life of his followers, it is not of God and is not God's will for us—it is a side effect of living in a world where sin still has a hold. Following Jesus is in fact a joyful thing; this is the God who loves us desperately and wants nothing but our good. Jesus wants peace for us; he *promises* peace for us. This peace comes at many different levels: between nations, between individuals, and within our own hearts.

Psalmist Preparation

This is an iconic psalm of praise, pouring out thanksgiving for all God has done and continues to do for us. Our response is one of gratitude and of speaking. When we experience the fullness of God's love we are compelled to share what we have seen with others. This psalm is also a familiar one—one of the frequent flyers of Ordinary Time. As you prepare to proclaim it this week, consider ways you have witnessed God at work in your own life. If time permits, write your own psalm of praise and use your own words to express your gratitude for all God has done. Bring the energy and love of your new psalm into your proclamation of these old words.

Making Connections

Between the readings: The first reading also speaks a word of consolation: God comes to save us, and our response is to rejoice. God is not a God of war who will deal harsh justice to our enemies. Rather, he comes meekly, in a way we would not expect. He banishes not Israel's enemies but the very tools of war. Once again, God subverts our expectations. He does not engage in the futile means humans have for fighting each other but rather bypasses the fight altogether.

To experience: There is an invitation in these readings to rest, an invitation our productivity-driven culture doesn't often let us hear clearly. The life of faith often calls us to hard work—to self-gift, to mission, to tireless preaching of the gospel. But God does not expect us to do this all the time. Our creator made us to need rhythms that include times of repose. He even *commands* us to rest in the Old Testament, carving out one of every seven days as a time to set aside our work.

Homily Points

• Today's first reading from Zechariah and the gospel from Matthew showcase the call we answer each time we gather for Eucharist: the call to rejoice and give praise to God. These sacred acts unite us with our ancestors in faith across time, people who also marveled at the power and graciousness of God. Rejoicing and praising God draws us closer to the Lord of heaven and earth. It heightens our awareness of the spirit of God dwelling in us. As we prepare to receive the Eucharist, let us carry a spirit of thanksgiving in our hearts for God's abiding love for us.

• Let us also rejoice and give praise for the gift of children present in our pews! Thank you, parents and guardians, for making your young ones a part of this faith community. Jesus exclaims in today's gospel that God reveals Godself to the little ones. Today we give thanks for the children whose very presence is a revelation of God. May each of us approach the Lord with childlike awe and wonder this week.

• Jesus longs to give rest to the weary— those laboring under unjust conditions, those burdened by medical debt, care giving, the loss of a reliable paycheck. The list of those who labor and are burdened is long. To those of us facing hardships right now, please know that Jesus sees you. Jesus loves you. Jesus is yoked to you and will never leave you to face your trials alone.

Model Penitential Act

Presider: In today's gospel Jesus offers rest to those who labor and are burdened. At the beginning of this Eucharist, let us lay our burdens of sin before Jesus and ask for mercy . . . *[pause]*

Lord Jesus, you are meek and humble of heart: Lord, have mercy.

Christ Jesus, you reveal the Father's love to the world: Christ, have mercy.

Lord Jesus, you will lighten the burden of all who believe in you: Lord, have mercy.

Model Universal Prayer (Prayer of the Faithful)

Presider: Sanctified by God's great love for us, let us place our needs and petitions before the Lord.

Response: Lord, hear our prayer.

Animate the work of Christian social services and outreach ministries . . .

Give rest to single parents, new parents, caretakers, and all who tend to the needs of others . . .

Envelop in love those who struggle with body image issues that they may feel God's Spirit dwelling within them . . .

Nurture the hearts and minds of the children in our community . . .

Presider: Merciful God, you recognize the good in all your creation and celebrate the gifts of the littlest among us. Receive our prayers that with childlike faith we may grow in works of service and justice. We ask this through Christ our Lord. **Amen.**

Liturgy and Music

Cura Personalis: Over these summer months we allow ourselves and the members of our liturgical and music ministry teams to take time to rest and rejuvenate. I offer this reflection on the Ignatian-Jesuit characteristic of *cura personalis*, which is Latin for "care for the whole person." When we are active in ministry, we tend to lose track of this. The body, mind, and soul are equally worthy of care and attention.

Our Christian faith insists that we nourish ourselves fully, for glorifying God requires our healthy head, heart, and soul. Nourishment comes both through action and contemplation. Care for yourself with whichever option brings you most life. Restful prayer, meditation, spiritual exercises, and communal interaction with physical activity are all ways of recreating help to deepen our understanding and love of God and of our own work in ministry. Both allow us to connect to a greater community and to come alive in body, mind, and soul. Theologian Howard Thurman said it best: "Don't ask yourself what the world needs. Ask yourself what makes you come alive, and go do that, because what the world needs is people who have come alive" (Gil Bailie, *Violence Unveiled*). *Cura personalis* invites us to reconnect with our deepest self and in the process reconnect in God and in the world.

COLLECT

Let us pray.

Pause for silent prayer

O God, who in the abasement of your Son
have raised up a fallen world,
fill your faithful with holy joy,
for on those you have rescued from slavery
    to sin
you bestow eternal gladness.
Through our Lord Jesus Christ, your Son,
who lives and reigns with you in the unity
    of the Holy Spirit,
God, for ever and ever. **Amen.**

FIRST READING

Zech 9:9-10

Thus says the LORD:
Rejoice heartily, O daughter Zion,
    shout for joy, O daughter Jerusalem!
See, your king shall come to you;
    a just savior is he,
meek, and riding on an ass,
    on a colt, the foal of an ass.
He shall banish the chariot from Ephraim,
    and the horse from Jerusalem;
the warrior's bow shall be banished,
    and he shall proclaim peace to the
        nations.
His dominion shall be from sea to sea,
    and from the River to the ends of the
        earth.

RESPONSORIAL PSALM

Ps 145:1-2, 8-9, 10-11, 13-14

℟. (cf. 1) I will praise your name forever,
my king and my God.
    or:
℟. Alleluia.

I will extol you, O my God and King,
    and I will bless your name forever and
        ever.
Every day will I bless you,
    and I will praise your name forever and
        ever.

℟. I will praise your name forever, my
king and my God.
    or:
℟. Alleluia.

The LORD is gracious and merciful,
  slow to anger and of great kindness.
The LORD is good to all
  and compassionate toward all his
    works.

R̸. I will praise your name forever, my
king and my God.
    or:
R̸. Alleluia.

Let all your works give you thanks, O
  LORD,
  and let your faithful ones bless you.
Let them discourse of the glory of your
    kingdom
  and speak of your might.

R̸. I will praise your name forever, my
king and my God.
    or:
R̸. Alleluia.

The LORD is faithful in all his words
  and holy in all his works.
The LORD lifts up all who are falling
  and raises up all who are bowed down.

R̸. I will praise your name forever, my
king and my God.
    or:
R̸. Alleluia.

SECOND READING
Rom 8:9, 11-13

Brothers and sisters:
You are not in the flesh;
  on the contrary, you are in the spirit,
  if only the Spirit of God dwells in you.
Whoever does not have the Spirit of Christ
    does not belong to him.
If the Spirit of the one who raised Jesus
    from the dead dwells in you,
  the one who raised Christ from the dead
  will give life to your mortal bodies also,
  through his Spirit that dwells in you.
Consequently, brothers and sisters,
  we are not debtors to the flesh,
  to live according to the flesh.
For if you live according to the flesh, you
    will die,
  but if by the Spirit you put to death the
    deeds of the body,
  you will live.

Living Liturgy

A Learning Community: In contrast to the gospel message we heard last week about the difficulties of discipleship in taking up the cross, this week we learn that Jesus offers us his yoke, which is easy and light. When Jesus says, "Take my yoke," he means work closely with him in our pastoral ministry to bring God's love into the world. Jesus tells his disciples that he is meek and humble of heart and that taking on his yoke would include becoming like Jesus in attitude, disposition, and way of being in the world. In Jesus's teaching we learn that God has revealed the hidden things to the "little ones," not "the wise and the learned." Who might the "little ones" among us be? Would they be the ones who are younger in age, less developed in faith, shorter in social stature? I imagine that "the wise and the learned" ones are being challenged today to ask the question: How can we learn from each other in community about taking on the Christlike attitude and disposition of lifting burdens and helping each other?

As a community of active believers, we ought to be open to mentoring each other: carrying the heavy burdens in the world today, supporting those in need, relieving especially the pressures and stresses of those who live in underprivileged communities. As more Americans disaffiliate from religion and religious groups, are we able to offer a place for honest conversations about Christian life? Are we ready to consider true partnerships within our parish communities between youth and adults in the real work of Christian discipleship?

Think of investing in young people as liturgical leaders through mentoring and training programs, that is, accompany each other through our liturgical ministries into a community of learning, bringing God's love into the world with the attitude and disposition of Christ serving the ones with the heaviest burdens.

PROMPTS FOR FAITH-SHARING

• What consolations does Jesus offer you in your Christian journey? What consolations do you wish he would offer?

• Do you find Jesus's yoke easy and light? What makes it hard to carry sometimes?

• How do you honor God's invitations—and even commands!—to rest?

JULY 9, 2023
FOURTEENTH SUNDAY
IN ORDINARY TIME

✝ SPIRITUALITY

GOSPEL ACCLAMATION

R⁊. Alleluia, alleluia.
The seed is the word of God, Christ is the sower.
All who come to him will have life forever.
R⁊. Alleluia, alleluia.

Gospel Matt 13:1-23; L103A

On that day, Jesus went out of the
    house and sat down by the
    sea.
Such large crowds gathered around
    him
    that he got into a boat and sat
        down,
    and the whole crowd stood along
        the shore.
And he spoke to them at length in
    parables, saying:
    "A sower went out to sow.
And as he sowed, some seed fell
    on the path,
    and birds came and ate it up.
Some fell on rocky ground, where
    it had little soil.
It sprang up at once because the
    soil was not deep,
    and when the sun rose it was
        scorched,
    and it withered for lack of roots.
Some seed fell among thorns, and
    the thorns grew up and choked it.
But some seed fell on rich soil, and
    produced fruit,
    a hundred or sixty or thirtyfold.
Whoever has ears ought to hear."

The disciples approached him and said,
    "Why do you speak to them in parables?"
He said to them in reply,
    "Because knowledge of the mysteries of
        the kingdom of heaven
    has been granted to you, but to them it
        has not been granted.
To anyone who has, more will be given and
    he will grow rich;
    from anyone who has not, even what he
        has will be taken away.

Continued in Appendix A, p. 298, or
Matt 13:1-9 *in Appendix A, p. 298.*

Reflecting on the Gospel

Palestinian sowing was not the precise, tidy process of modern farming. The farmer scattered generous handfuls of seed onto the unplowed field and then after—not before—this sowing, plowed or raked them into the soil. There was no way that a sower could take credit for extraordinary harvests that yielded "a hundred or sixty or thirtyfold," when a *fivefold* yield was considered a good crop. The idea of the returns Jesus spoke of here would boggle the imagination with the prospect of well-fed families, paid taxes, and some profit stored away! Such a yield was God's work and blessing. And so Jesus "hooks" or "teases" his

listeners into a new understanding: it is God who gives the increase when the seed of the word of God is planted among people.

For Matthew's community there was internal tension and division between Christians grounded in their Jewish heritage and Gentile Christians who knew nothing of this, and external tension between Christians and Jews, and especially with those of the Pharisee party after the destruction of the Jerusalem temple in CE 70. The latter were suspicious of anything or anyone whom they suspected of undermining the already devastated Jewish community. Matthew's community needed to be encouraged by hearing that God was the Lord of the harvest, despite the poor soil, the rocks and thorns that was their church and world. We are in no less need of such encouragement today.

The seed is a wonderful symbol of the kingdom—small, hard, unattractive to the senses. Yet within it lies the promise of life, of growth, of harvest. But for all its promise, it remains only a seed, unless it surrenders itself to an environment that can realize its potential. When that happens, the seed grows gently, quietly; there is no instant produce. This is a good parable for Ordinary Time when the festal seasons are behind and before us, and we are in the weeks of patient planting and slow germination, of cultivating and fertilizing the word of God in the soil of our daily lives, persevering in the hope of the coming kingdom.

This parable can help us review how well we live our discipleship. At different times, even in the same day, and individually or communally, we can be the different "soils" about which Jesus speaks. We can be people who receive the Word on the edge of the path, those who skirt the real issues, disciples of surface commitment and no depth. Or our lives can be rocky soil, enthusiasts of the moment who soon lose interest. Again, we may offer a patchy, thorn-infested welcome to the seed of the Word, and the potential for its growth is endangered by our entanglement with selfseeking concerns or apathy, and so the seed does not come to maturity and bear fruit. Then there are the times when we are "good soil" for the seed, when we welcome, obey, and witness to the Word, and God enables us to bear a fruitful harvest for the kingdom.

Preparing to Proclaim

Key words and phrases: "[S]ome seed fell on rich soil, and produced fruit."

To the point: Midsummer is a powerful time to hear this parable for the earth has warmed and is starting to produce. If you visit a local farmer's market you will start to see a rich and wide variety of produce from now until the fall. And the work of growing plants—whether in pots on an apartment balcony or on large-scale agricultural operations—is rich with imagery that can be meaningful for the life of faith. Plants start as seeds, which are not living things on their own. But they carry potential for far more than seems possible at first glance. Given the right conditions, they grow to many times their size, eventually bearing fruit (whose botanical job, by the way, is to produce and spread more seeds!). We, too, need the right conditions and care to grow and bear good fruit; God offers us all this so that we might bear life abundantly.

Psalmist Preparation

This is a gorgeous, underused psalm. It praises God for the beauty of the earth and the wisdom with which God designed its seasons to feed and nourish us. If you can, sit outside as you rehearse this psalm. Use all your senses to notice the lush growth and vibrant life of summertime: see greenery, hear birdsong, and so on. Notice how your singing voice sounds outside; open air often carries sound differently from closed spaces. Notice all that God has created and give thanks for it; bring your gratitude for your little corner of the natural world into your proclamation of this psalm.

Making Connections

Between the readings: The first reading and psalm echo the farming imagery of the gospel. God's word is likened to the rain that comes forth from heaven to nourish the earth and to feed us. The second reading pairs our seed and fruit imagery with another of nature's great wonders—that of childbirth. Labor pains are another reflection of God's cyclical work, for great pain and groaning bring new life and abundant joy. The pain of labor, like the suffering of Christ, is lifegiving. It is not pain without purpose.

To experience: If you hear the longer version of this gospel, Jesus makes clear what each seed is a metaphor for. Lack of understanding, lack of rootedness, and worldly anxiety can all prevent us from bearing fruit for Christ. If we are not deeply rooted, challenges can easily topple us. It takes constant weeding away of distractions and unimportant things to maintain space in our lives and hearts for God's word.

Homily Points

• Today's readings teach us about the word of God. Three characteristics stand out. First, the word of God is expansive. The prophet Isaiah offers a beautiful image of the word of God coming down from heaven like rain and snow, with enough strength to nourish the whole world. God sends out God's word to the ends of the earth. Like rain and snow, God's word gets to work sparking growth and new life in all who encounter it. God's reach knows no bounds. Where do you experience the expansiveness of God's word?

• The word of God is also contextual. In the gospel parable of the sower and the seed, Jesus lays out a variety of options for where the seeds can land—and image for how people can receive God's word. Some people are not prepared to absorb the word of God, like seeds on the path. Others find great joy in God's word at first but cannot sustain it. They are like seeds sown on rocky ground. Still others deal with anxieties and temptations that make it nearly impossible to truly take in the word of God, like seeds sown among thorns. The word of God does not change, but the context of the hearer makes a big difference in how well it will be received. How might you cultivate rich soil to truly hear the word of God this week?

• Finally, today's readings show the connection between the word of God and the natural world. Both Isaiah and Jesus use nature imagery to teach about God's word—for it is not stuck somewhere in the heavens out of reach. Rather, the word of God is all around us, ready to be discovered and engaged. Spend some prayerful time in nature this week and listen for God's revelation.

Model Penitential Act

Presider: In today's second reading, St. Paul assures us that humankind will be "set free from slavery to corruption and share in the glorious freedom of the children of God." Let us ask for mercy for the times we have fallen victim to corruption . . . *[pause]*

Lord Jesus, you teach us the way to salvation: Lord, have mercy.

Christ Jesus, you sow seeds of hope across the world: Christ, have mercy.

Lord Jesus, you cultivate rich soil in the kingdom of God: Lord, have mercy.

Model Universal Prayer (Prayer of the Faithful)

Presider: In God's great goodness, God longs to satisfy our every need and nourish us with all that is right and just. With confidence let us bring our needs before the Lord.

Response: Lord, hear our prayer.

Gladden the hearts of catechists, youth ministers, and all who share the word of God with children . . .

Grant success and good weather to gardeners, farmers, day laborers, and all who feed us by the work of their hands . . .

Support and prosper efforts to ensure affordable and safe housing for all people . . .

Enlighten writers and artists in our community to find creative ways to spread the word of God . . .

Presider: Creator God, you sow seeds of faith generously across time and space. Receive our prayers that in the days ahead we may find ourselves in rich soil, ready to do your work. We offer this prayer through Christ our Lord. **Amen.**

Liturgy and Music

Sowing New Seeds: When considering introducing new music to the assembly, I often think of Austin Fleming's reflection from *Preparing for Liturgy*: "Open your hearts and voices to new songs worthy of God's people at prayer. Let your repertoire change as all living things must, but not so much that the song of God's people is lost." This statement helps shape a music program that not only honors tradition but also looks ahead and allows room for focused, intentional change.

When thinking about adding or taking away from a community's music repertoire, discern if this change will continue to allow the voice of the assembly to remain heard. By this I mean choose new songs that allow the gathered faithful to continually sing in unison which forms and keeps an identity of congregational song. Create a communal identity for song and prayer, one that is collectively faithful to God's command and anticipates heaven. Ensure that the songs we sing are "worthy of God's people at prayer." From the Scriptures, know well what calls forth praise. Fleming adds: "Let the lyrics of your songs be strong and true and rooted in the scriptures; those who sing the Lord's word sing the Lord's song. Make no room for the maudlin, the sentimental." Trends come and go. Be mindful of the melodies and texts that will remain in the hearts and minds of the faithful community.

COLLECT

Let us pray.

Pause for silent prayer

O God, who show the light of your truth
to those who go astray,
so that they may return to the right path,
give all who for the faith they profess
are accounted Christians
the grace to reject whatever is contrary to
    the name of Christ
and to strive after all that does it honor.
Through our Lord Jesus Christ, your Son,
who lives and reigns with you in the unity
    of the Holy Spirit,
God, for ever and ever. **Amen.**

FIRST READING
Isa 55:10-11

Thus says the LORD:
Just as from the heavens
    the rain and snow come down
and do not return there
    till they have watered the earth,
    making it fertile and fruitful,
giving seed to the one who sows
    and bread to the one who eats,
so shall my word be
    that goes forth from my mouth;
my word shall not return to me void,
    but shall do my will,
    achieving the end for which I sent it.

RESPONSORIAL PSALM

Ps 65:10, 11, 12-13, 14

R̦. (Luke 8:8) The seed that falls on good ground will yield a fruitful harvest.

You have visited the land and watered it;
    greatly have you enriched it.
God's watercourses are filled;
    you have prepared the grain.

R̦. The seed that falls on good ground will yield a fruitful harvest.

Thus have you prepared the land:
    drenching its furrows,
    breaking up its clods,
softening it with showers,
    blessing its yield.

R̦. The seed that falls on good ground will yield a fruitful harvest.

You have crowned the year with your
        bounty,
    and your paths overflow with a rich
        harvest;
the untilled meadows overflow with it,
    and rejoicing clothes the hills.

R̦. The seed that falls on good ground will yield a fruitful harvest.

The fields are garmented with flocks
    and the valleys blanketed with grain.
    They shout and sing for joy.

R̦. The seed that falls on good ground will yield a fruitful harvest.

SECOND READING

Rom 8:18-23

Brothers and sisters:
I consider that the sufferings of this
        present time are as nothing
    compared with the glory to be revealed
        for us.
For creation awaits with eager expectation
    the revelation of the children of God;
    for creation was made subject to futility,
    not of its own accord but because of the
        one who subjected it,
    in hope that creation itself
    would be set free from slavery to
        corruption
    and share in the glorious freedom of the
        children of God.
We know that all creation is groaning in
        labor pains even until now;
    and not only that, but we ourselves,
    who have the firstfruits of the Spirit,
    we also groan within ourselves
    as we wait for adoption, the redemption
        of our bodies.

Living Liturgy

Revolution of the Heart: Over these next three Sundays we encounter the parables of Matthew 13. One would think that since parables are drawn from everyday life, it would be easier for listeners to understand Jesus's message. However, the meanings of parables are not self-evident. As listeners and worship leaders, we must engage in some degree of reflection on the story told to comprehend its message. In some way this medium of storytelling, the parable, models the actual point of the parable of the sower itself. Those who are willing to engage themselves with the effort to understand will reap the reward of discovering its message and will bear fruit.

What are our obstacles to listening and understanding Jesus's teachings and the meaning of these parables? What do we hear in Jesus's teaching about the kingdom of heaven? As a community of welcome and belonging, we ought to till the soil for God's word to take root in our heart to produce abundant fruit.

Dorothy Day, founder of the Catholic Worker Movement, tells us: "The biggest challenge of the day is: how to bring about a revolution of the heart, a revolution that has to start with each one of us" (catholicworker.org). I think about the significance of Dorothy Day's statement as I reflect on the agrarian imagery of the parable today. Her social justice movement planted seeds to bring about a revolution. In her transformative work, she connected farming communities with houses of hospitality in the cities where members would organize soup kitchens to feed the hungry. Whether the seed falls on the path, on rocky ground, among thorns or on fertile soil, we respond as community of beloved belonging that we will help each other to transform and recognize the kingdom of heaven. We till the soil of our heart and our pastoral ministry to accept God's word which will lead us to spreading more seed in works of mercy, peace and justice.

PROMPTS FOR FAITH-SHARING

• Jesus names three dangers in this gospel: lack of understanding, lack of rootedness, and worldly anxiety can all prevent us from bearing fruit for Christ. Which of these feels like it carries the most risk for you?

• When your faith is challenging, what keeps you rooted in the word of God? How do you maintain trust in Jesus in times of trial?

• What anxieties do you have that threaten to smother your faith? How can you set them aside to make space for God's word to take root in your heart?

JULY 16, 2023
FIFTEENTH SUNDAY IN ORDINARY TIME

✚ SPIRITUALITY

GOSPEL ACCLAMATION
cf. Matt 11:25

℟. Alleluia, alleluia.
Blessed are you, Father, Lord of heaven
    and earth;
you have revealed to little ones the
    mysteries of the kingdom.
℟. Alleluia, alleluia.

Gospel   Matt 13:24-43; L106A

Jesus proposed another parable to
    the crowds, saying:
"The kingdom of heaven may be
    likened
  to a man who sowed good seed in
    his field.
While everyone was asleep his
    enemy came
  and sowed weeds all through the
    wheat, and then went off.
When the crop grew and bore fruit,
    the weeds appeared as well.
The slaves of the householder
    came to him and said,
  'Master, did you not sow good
    seed in your field?
Where have the weeds come from?'
He answered, 'An enemy has done this.'
His slaves said to him,
  'Do you want us to go and pull them up?'
He replied, 'No, if you pull up the weeds
  you might uproot the wheat along with
    them.
Let them grow together until harvest;
  then at harvest time I will say to the
    harvesters,
  "First collect the weeds and tie them in
    bundles for burning;
  but gather the wheat into my barn."'"

He proposed another parable to them.
"The kingdom of heaven is like a
    mustard seed
  that a person took and sowed in a field.
It is the smallest of all the seeds,
  yet when full-grown it is the largest of
    plants.

*Continued in Appendix A, p. 299, or
Matt 13:24-30 in Appendix A, p. 299.*

Reflecting on the Gospel

In this Sunday's gospel, Jesus is again the storyteller who uses vivid images as a vehicle to carry the truth of his words to the crowd.

In the first of the three parables, the weed with which the enemy overseeded the wheat was probably darnel. In its early appearance, this is almost indistinguishable from wheat, and it is only when the heads of the plants begin to fruit that the weeds are recognized. If it is harvested and milled with the wheat, the flour will be spoiled, so the immediate response of the landowner's slave is to uproot the weeds. But their master has a shrewd confidence in the ability of his wheat crop to survive competition with the entangled weeds for nutrition and irrigation. He tells his slaves to wait until the harvest time when the reapers will more easily distinguish the weeds from the wheat, and so not only will he have rescued a good harvest, but he will also have a useful supply of fuel from the dried weeds.

The central meaning of the parable is that the kingdom of God takes root in imperfect communities of "wheat and weeds," and in both an imperfect church and world. Even in the Twelve there was good and bad, loyalty and disloyalty, understanding and obtuseness—and we surely recognize this in ourselves as individuals and communities. Unbridled zeal that wants to create a pure and perfect community becomes intolerant fanaticism, which is not how the kingdom is established. The leaders of a Christian community need the discernment of the Spirit of Jesus to know when and how to emphasize patience and restraint, or warning and judgment.

The short parable of the mustard seed provides encouragement for the Christian community struggling with its small beginnings or, like today's church, faced in some places with the diminution of what once was "big," such as priestly and religious vocations or wellattended Masses. For the reign of the kingdom, says Jesus, small seeds are enough to grow into welcoming bushes where people can rest and nest.

Finally, Jesus suggests that God is also like a woman with hands in the flour, mixing in "three measures of wheat flour," enough for an extravagant loaf that would feed about 150 people! This is Matthew's only parable with a female image of God, and the only positive reference to leaven that causes fermentation and so usually symbolizes corruption. And here is the challenge: as Jesus taught, the realm of God is permeated by those whom many "purists" might consider "corrupt"—the poor, the outcast, the marginalized—who will be the active ingredient for the growth of the kingdom. They are welcomed by Jesus who was crucified and rose again to leaven and transform the world, and who still mixes with us in all our weaknesses and sinfulness. This parable not only challenges us to consider the feminine aspects of God's nature, but also to reflect on the ministry of women in the growth of the kingdom, and to hope for more and more leavening as women and men mix together in leadership roles.

Preparing to Proclaim

Key words and phrases: "[G]ather the wheat into my barn."

To the point: The farming and harvest imagery of last week continues with this gospel's parables. The perils of farming are still at play; abundant life is a potential outcome, but so too are weeds that threaten to choke out the long-anticipated good harvest. God has taken a risk on us, on creating humanity and bestowing us with free will. When young people learn about the Fall, they often ask why God gave us free will at all or why God didn't create the world in such a way that evil would not really be an option. We might not fully understand this mystery, but apparently, God thought it was worth the risk. Like farmers who every year take on unpredictable weather and swarming pests and a myriad of fungal diseases, God hopes in us and believes that the fruit we can bear is worth all that can go wrong.

Psalmist Preparation

This psalm praises God for the endless forgiveness that characterizes God's dealings with us. None of us really deserves the grace God pours forth abundantly, but God gives it anyway. If you can, participate in the sacrament of reconciliation this week as part of your preparation of this psalm. This is a private sacrament, but it has a communal dimension as well; it is as an assembly that we receive God's mercy. Let your experience of God's mercy illuminate these words as you lead the assembly in praise for God's mercy for all of us.

Making Connections

Between the readings: The gospel shows God as a farmer who rather harshly separates the intended harvest from the weeds that are not meant to be there. The first reading balances this image by reminding us that this is a God of forgiveness, known for leniency and repeated mercies. The psalm echoes this theme, praising God for the abounding kindness and never-ending patience that none of us deserves but which we receive anyway.

To experience: We who are adults know that the moral life is not as cut-and-dry as it is in this parable. None of us is fully good or fully evil; judging our hearts is much more complicated than separating us into "children of the kingdom" and "children of the evil one." This is where God's mercy comes in. God knows our hearts deeply and intimately. God knows all of our motivations and our struggles. Still, God is prepared to offer us the utmost generosity in judgment.

Homily Points

• Jesus lays out a feast of parables in today's gospel. Last week, we took in the parable of the sower and the seed. You may recall issues that some seeds faced just getting into the ground like rough soil and thorns. It seemed at least somewhat left up to chance which seeds prospered and which did not. The first of this week's parables introduces new problems for the crops: weeds and intentionality. Any farmer or gardener knows the pain that comes with weeds, which take significant time to uproot and can spread quickly. One wrong move and the good crops surrounding the weeds can be ruined. The weeds in today's parable did not appear by a stroke of bad luck, either. When asked where the weeds came from, the master of the house offers an ominous reply: "An enemy has done this."

• This parable points to the reality of evil in the world. Jesus is acknowledging that there are forces at work that want to see good falter—and often, these forces persist. Like pesky weeds that will not stop spreading, forces of evil continue to wreak havoc on our world. We need only consider the realities of racism, sexism, violence, and the many other forms of hate to realize how widespread the weeds have grown.

• Still, in the end, let us hold out hope that God the master gardener can and will separate the good plants from the evil weeds. God who made heaven and earth will surely make all things right in the end.

Model Penitential Act

Presider: In today's second reading, St. Paul assures us that "the Spirit comes to the aid of our weakness . . ." For those areas of our lives in which we need the Spirit's aid, let us ask God for mercy . . . *[pause]*

Lord Jesus, you weed out evil from our world: Lord, have mercy.

Christ Jesus, you sow seeds of faith among us: Christ, have mercy.

Lord Jesus, you will come again to unite us in everlasting life: Lord, have mercy.

Model Universal Prayer (Prayer of the Faithful)

Presider: With confidence in the power of Christ to bring about healing and wholeness, let us place our needs before the Lord.

Response: Lord, hear our prayer.

Grace parish staffs and other ministry teams with hearts eager to listen and respond to the needs of the community . . .

Guide local and national leaders to prioritize legislation that will help people experiencing poverty . . .

Root out all forms of violence in our streets, countrysides, and homes . . .

Bless the lands on which we live with suitable rain and fruitful soil . . .

Presider: Almighty God, you sent your son into the world to free creation from the bonds of sin and death so that we might flourish. Hear our prayers that we might listen to Christ's teachings and allow our hearts to be transformed by his saving love. We ask this through Christ our Lord. **Amen.**

Liturgy and Music

Singing **Magis:** Another word to contemplate for our life of music ministry comes from an Ignatian-Jesuit spirituality: *magis.* The word comes from the *Spiritual Exercises* in which St. Ignatius Loyola reminds us (and especially those in ministry) to make pathways that are "conducive to the greater service of God and the universal good." It is a complex word that in one way means to do the more, the better, the greater for God and in another way moderates the ministerial drive for doing too much. The word gives space for us to know that sometimes *more* does not always mean *better.*

Striving for the best, the most, the greatest all the time often hinders our ability to do our most authentic and loving work in ministry. In our desire for doing the more, we overlook the real purpose of our work—the glorification of God and not ourselves. Quantity and quality become things that we must cautiously balance. Of course, this all ought to be considered within our diverse and unique contexts of ministry. For me, living the *magis* in campus music ministry means to know honestly what I can and cannot achieve daily, to make decisions that bring out the best in those that I serve, and to strive to do more at my own pace. Always for God.

COLLECT

Let us pray.

Pause for silent prayer

Show favor, O Lord, to your servants
and mercifully increase the gifts of your
    grace,
that, made fervent in hope, faith, and
    charity,
they may be ever watchful in keeping your
    commands.
Through our Lord Jesus Christ, your Son,
who lives and reigns with you in the unity
    of the Holy Spirit,
God, for ever and ever. **Amen.**

FIRST READING

Wis 12:13, 16-19

There is no god besides you who have the
    care of all,
    that you need show you have not
        unjustly condemned.
For your might is the source of justice;
    your mastery over all things makes you
        lenient to all.
For you show your might when the
    perfection of your power is
    disbelieved;
    and in those who know you, you rebuke
        temerity.
But though you are master of might, you
    judge with clemency,
    and with much lenience you govern us;
    for power, whenever you will, attends
        you.
And you taught your people, by these
    deeds,
    that those who are just must be kind;
and you gave your children good ground
    for hope
    that you would permit repentance for
        their sins.

RESPONSORIAL PSALM
Ps 86:5-6, 9-10, 15-16

R̸. (5a) Lord, you are good and forgiving.

You, O LORD, are good and forgiving,
   abounding in kindness to all who call
      upon you.
Hearken, O LORD, to my prayer
   and attend to the sound of my pleading.

R̸. Lord, you are good and forgiving.

All the nations you have made shall come
   and worship you, O LORD,
   and glorify your name.
For you are great, and you do wondrous
      deeds;
   you alone are God.

R̸. Lord, you are good and forgiving.

You, O LORD, are a God merciful and
      gracious,
   slow to anger, abounding in kindness
      and fidelity.
Turn toward me, and have pity on me;
   give your strength to your servant.

R̸. Lord, you are good and forgiving.

SECOND READING
Rom 8:26-27

Brothers and sisters:
The Spirit comes to the aid of our
      weakness;
   for we do not know how to pray as we
      ought,
   but the Spirit himself intercedes with
      inexpressible groanings.
And the one who searches hearts
   knows what is the intention of the
      Spirit,
   because he intercedes for the holy ones
   according to God's will.

Living Liturgy

Community in Collaboration with God: We continue to hear the parable discourse of Matthew. Three parables are given to us to contemplate today—the parables of the sower, the mustard seed, and the yeast. The first parable describes the twofold reality of the kingdom of heaven that has its beginnings in this world and its fruition at the final judgment. Jesus cautions that any effort to judge is premature. To uproot weeds in our ministerial settings would prematurely harm the wheat.

The first parable invites us to think beyond living within finite binary systems which we are so often instinctually drawn to. Instead of living in the binary of good and bad, of big and small, of you or me, it is perhaps more about living in Christian community recognizing all our diversity and difference, celebrating intersectional bodies, and acknowledging our own gifts and limitations. Rather than uproot the weeds or "darnel" from the wheat, the sower waits for the harvest. Perfect, imperfect, and everything in between grow side by side in this field. Different seeds grow together in this kinship of the community of believers awaiting the harvest day.

What does it mean to be intertwined in a community of difference, intersectionality, and diversity? Community in collaboration with God and each other appears when we begin to recognize differences that confront our interconnectedness. Without seeing or celebrating each other's differences, a community remains broken, wounded. It is in confronting our own capacity to wound and acknowledging our own brokenness that our truth telling begins to happen, to take shape, to gain voice, and to become articulated in words and ways of healing. As Christian disciples, we must speak up and act up in ways that shine light on the very least among us, on whom some might consider the "darnel"—the homeless, the immigrant, the addict, the queer person.

PROMPTS FOR FAITH-SHARING

• God cares for us as a farmer cares for the crop. How do you experience God's care in your life? In what ways do you long for God's care?

• What is the fruit that your life is bearing? What do you have to offer to God at the harvest?

• How have you experienced God's mercy? Where do you still need it?

✚ SPIRITUALITY

R̸. Alleluia, alleluia.
Blessed are you, Father, Lord of heaven
    and earth;
you have revealed to little ones the
    mysteries of the kingdom.
R̸. Alleluia, alleluia.

Gospel Matt 13:44-52; L109A

Jesus said to his disciples:
  "The kingdom of heaven is like a
      treasure buried in a field,
  which a person finds and hides
      again,
  and out of joy goes and sells all
      that he has and buys that
      field.
Again, the kingdom of heaven is
      like a merchant
  searching for fine pearls.
When he finds a pearl of great
      price,
  he goes and sells all that he has
      and buys it.
Again, the kingdom of heaven is
      like a net thrown into the sea,
  which collects fish of every kind.
When it is full they haul it ashore
  and sit down to put what is good into
      buckets.
What is bad they throw away.
Thus it will be at the end of the age.
The angels will go out and separate the
      wicked from the righteous
  and throw them into the fiery furnace,
  where there will be wailing and
      grinding of teeth.

"Do you understand all these things?"
They answered, "Yes."
And he replied,
  "Then every scribe who has been
      instructed in the kingdom of
      heaven
  is like the head of a household
  who brings from his storeroom both the
      new and the old."

or Matt 13:44-46 in Appendix A, p. 299.

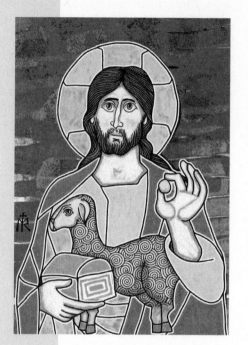

Reflecting on the Gospel

In the ancient world without access to bank or strongbox storage, burying valuables was a common practice (see, for example, Matt 25:18), especially under threat of invasion. If the original owner died or was unable to return to his land, if no one had been told the whereabouts of the treasure, or if the land was confiscated, the treasure might lie hidden for many years, unknown to the descendants of the original owner or those who subsequently acquired that land. Then someone finds the treasure. "Finders keepers" does not apply in Palestinian society unless the field is one's own property, so the one who finds the treasure determines to sell all that he has and buy the field. It is—Jesus suggests in this first of three parables of today's gospel—this joy of discovery, the attitude of readiness to give up everything in order to obtain the treasure, that should characterize his disciples to whom God discloses the treasure of the kingdom. Perhaps through a friendship, an event at work, a book read, or in the everyday but humanly significant events of birth, sickness, or death, we may stumble on the Unexpected One who transforms our lives and makes everything else relative forever. Then we know the joy of the kingdom.

Twinned with the parable of the buried treasure is the parable of the pearl of great price. The surprise of this parable is not the discovery of the pearl because, unlike the one who found the buried treasure, the traveling merchant was deliberately seeking the precious pearl; the surprise is its great value. Consequently, the merchant sells everything he owns to purchase the pearl, considered in the ancient world as among the most valuable of goods. The kingdom of God is beyond all price, and even though a person may be seeking it, when God reveals it to the seeker it is beyond all expectations.

The third of this Sunday's parables, about the dragnet, is not concerned with the "now," but the "not yet." A dragnet was a large net supported by floats and held in place by sinkers, used for surface fishing. Its catch was indiscriminate: edible and inedible, ritually clean and unclean, marketable or worthless, the fish would be sorted out by the fishermen when brought ashore. As with the parable of the weeds and wheat, the dragnet catch is an image of the Christian community of committed disciples and sinners, of good and evil—the mix that we can recognize in ourselves. There will, however, come a moment of endtime judgment when disciples will be finally accountable for their obedience or disobedience to what Jesus has revealed and their readiness or resistance to allow this to rule over them.

The disciples give a perhaps too ready "yes" when Jesus asks them if they have understood, and certainly the power of the storytelling helps us, like them, to understand something of the joy and value of the kingdom of God. But it is our living as kingdom people that is our true assent to Jesus.

Preparing to Proclaim

Key words and phrases: "[H]e goes and sells all that he has and buys it."

To the point: This week's series of parables tells us something about how we are to receive the kingdom of God. Finding it and participating in it is like finding a treasure. It probably brings a bit of wonder; how did we get so lucky as to be included in this? But above all it brings joy, the kind of breathtaking joy that leads us to wholehearted pursuit of the thing that brings it. This is the joy of a child who has found an interest that overrides their brain's developmental limits on attention span. This is the joy of someone who has fallen in love. All of these people will find that the object of their interest does not always bring this easy joy. Lovers will find some of their beloveds' flaws hard to live with; children may move on when a new interest fizzles in a challenge they can't overcome; and even God's kingdom makes demands of us and sometimes the sacrifice may seem too much. But the initial joy and wonder tells us something important: this movement of our hearts is how God gets to us.

Psalmist Preparation

This psalm praises God's commands, God's law, as a great gift or treasure. The psalmist's response to it is not one of begrudging compliance but of grateful joy. The law is seen as a gift that God has given in order that we might participate in God's kingdom and share in God's eternal life. As you prepare this psalm, think about how you respond to the idea of God as a king who rules and leads. As you understand God right now, is this someone you want to follow? Does the idea of obedience to God bring you joy or does it feel like a burden?

Making Connections

Between the readings: Solomon asks for something that pleases God: an understanding heart. He pursues wisdom with the wholeheartedness with which we are to pursue the kingdom, which tells us something else about what pursuing the kingdom entails. It is deeply related to this wisdom. The psalm continues this theme, for encountering God's leadership—even his commands—inspires a response of love from us.

To experience: Many of us have some experience of encountering God and responding with the kind of wonder and joy and love that causes the person of the parable to sell all he has in pursuit of it. But the long slog of Christian life in a sinful world often causes these feelings to wear off. Love is not measured by our emotional response to the beloved but by our commitment to living out its demands, with consistency and integrity.

Homily Points

• How does God appear to you? In today's first reading, God comes to Solomon in a dream. Several biblical figures receive a calling or message from God while they sleep—prophets like Daniel and Samuel as well as Joseph, the father of Jesus. These appearances are certainly valid. Perhaps even some of you have encountered God in a dream.

• But this is not the only way in which God makes Godself known to us. Some people meet God in the daily praying of Scripture. Others encounter God while outside in nature or gathered around a table of dear friends. If you struggle to know how or where to encounter God, do not worry. You are in the right place. God is fully present each time we gather for Eucharist. In the bread, wine, and gathered assembly, God is here imparting wisdom and nourishment for our journeys.

• "The kingdom of heaven is like . . ." For the last few weeks, we have heard Jesus compare the kingdom of heaven to many things—a merchant searching for pearls, a net thrown into the sea, a person who sows seeds in good soil, and more. Jesus uses metaphors as a tool for teaching about God's ways that are beyond human understanding. God's kingdom cannot be distilled into one statement. God's kingdom is too vast, too mysterious to be fully known and explained. Jesus points us to familiar images with the hopes that we might come to know just a small sliver about the glory that awaits us.

Model Penitential Act

Presider: In today's second reading, St. Paul assures the people that "all things work for good for those who love God." For the times we have forgotten or failed to love God with our whole hearts, let us ask for mercy . . . *[pause]*

    Lord Jesus, you give hope to the weary: Lord, have mercy.

    Christ Jesus, you call us to serve those in need: Christ, have mercy.

    Lord Jesus, you will open the doors to the kingdom of heaven: Lord, have mercy.

Model Universal Prayer (Prayer of the Faithful)

Presider: Believing in God's desire to make known to us the riches of the kingdom of heaven, let us offer our prayers and petitions.

Response: Lord, hear our prayer.

Inspire the work of Christian writers, editors, publishers, and all who share about the kingdom of God through the written word . . .

Strengthen the work of local food pantries, meal programs, and other agencies that feed the hungry . . .

Thwart the plots of terrorists and those who wish harm upon others . . .

Bless the elders, teachers, and other storytellers of our community and all who receive their wisdom . . .

Presider: God of all wisdom, by your grace we will one day come to see good triumph over evil. Hear our prayers that as we move toward such a time, our hearts might expand in love of you and neighbor. We ask this through Christ our Lord. **Amen.**

Liturgy and Music

Bringing Forth the Old and the New: Today's gospel speaks directly to our ministry within liturgical music of keeping the old and finding the new to shape the church of today and tomorrow. We are summoned by Jesus to be like the scribe and become the head of a household "who brings from his storeroom both the new and the old." First, we must identify songs in our community's sacred treasury of music that have held us together through time. Then we can consider possibilities of new music that might bring the community renewed hope. The Constitution on the Sacred Liturgy tells us, "The treasury of sacred music is to be preserved and cultivated with great care. Choirs must be diligently developed, especially in cathedral churches. Bishops and other pastors of souls must do their best to ensure that whenever a liturgical service is to be accompanied by chant, the whole body of the faithful may be able to take that active part which is rightly theirs" (114).

Reflect on this statement as you consider this next one: "Composers, animated by the christian spirit, should accept that it is part of their vocation to cultivate sacred music and increase its store of treasures. Let them produce compositions which have the qualities proper to genuine sacred music, and which can be sung not only by large choirs but also by smaller choirs, and which make possible the active participation of the whole congregation" (121).

COLLECT

Let us pray.

Pause for silent prayer

O God, protector of those who hope in you,
without whom nothing has firm foundation, nothing is holy,
bestow in abundance your mercy upon us
and grant that, with you as our ruler and guide,
we may use the good things that pass
in such a way as to hold fast even now
to those that ever endure.
Through our Lord Jesus Christ, your Son,
who lives and reigns with you in the unity of the Holy Spirit,
God, for ever and ever. **Amen.**

FIRST READING

1 Kgs 3:5, 7-12

The Lord appeared to Solomon in a dream at night.
God said, "Ask something of me and I will give it to you."
Solomon answered:
    "O Lord, my God, you have made me, your servant, king
    to succeed my father David;
    but I am a mere youth, not knowing at all how to act.
I serve you in the midst of the people whom you have chosen,
    a people so vast that it cannot be numbered or counted.
Give your servant, therefore, an understanding heart
    to judge your people and to distinguish right from wrong.
    For who is able to govern this vast people of yours?"

The Lord was pleased that Solomon made this request.
So God said to him:
    "Because you have asked for this—
    not for a long life for yourself,
    nor for riches,
    nor for the life of your enemies,
    but for understanding so that you may know what is right—
    I do as you requested.
I give you a heart so wise and understanding
    that there has never been anyone like you up to now,
    and after you there will come no one to equal you."

RESPONSORIAL PSALM

Ps 119:57, 72, 76-77, 127-128, 129-130

℟. (97a) Lord, I love your commands.

I have said, O LORD, that my part
    is to keep your words.
The law of your mouth is to me more
    precious
    than thousands of gold and silver
    pieces.

℟. Lord, I love your commands.

Let your kindness comfort me
    according to your promise to your
    servants.
Let your compassion come to me that I
    may live,
    for your law is my delight.

℟. Lord, I love your commands.

For I love your commands
    more than gold, however fine.
For in all your precepts I go forward;
    every false way I hate.

℟. Lord, I love your commands.

Wonderful are your decrees;
    therefore I observe them.
The revelation of your words sheds light,
    giving understanding to the simple.

℟. Lord, I love your commands.

SECOND READING

Rom 8:28-30

Brothers and sisters:
We know that all things work for good for
    those who love God,
    who are called according to his purpose.
For those he foreknew he also predestined
    to be conformed to the image of his Son,
    so that he might be the firstborn
    among many brothers and sisters.
And those he predestined he also called;
    and those he called he also justified;
    and those he justified he also glorified.

Living Liturgy

The Valuable Community: This Sunday's gospel reading concludes the parable discourse of Matthew with a set of three parables. Jesus continues to offer ways for his listeners to catch a glimpse of the kingdom of heaven. The first two parables describe the immense value of the kingdom of heaven—like buried treasure and a valuable pearl—things that we would give up everything to possess. As those who work in liturgical ministry, we continue to bring about God's kingdom in our actions and in our words. We also discern what we find most valuable in our ministry.

Time is often thought of as valuable currency. Anti-apartheid hero and Nobel laureate Nelson Mandela comments on wasting time: "We must use time wisely and forever realize that the time is always ripe to do right." To invest in the kingdom of heaven, we ought to spend quality time with those we are most in community with. First, spend time with God. This would mean in addition to preparing for Sunday Mass, taking time for personal prayer and devotions. Then spend quality time with the ones whom we are in significant relationships with—our spouse, children, siblings, parents, loved ones. All of this requires taking some time away from other activities, which is a sacrifice on our part. When this happens, we live the point of the parable by giving up something to buy something greater. We trade earthly treasures for heavenly ones.

In the midst of a materialistic world, we must teach each other how to love according to God's will as we struggle to recognize what is of true value. In *Fratelli Tutti* Pope Francis comments on the unique value of love in community: "Love, then, is more than just a series of benevolent actions. Those actions have their source in a union increasingly directed towards others, considering them of value, worthy, pleasing and beautiful. . . . Only by cultivating this way of relating to one another will we make possible a social friendship that excludes no one" (94).

PROMPTS FOR FAITH-SHARING

• What do you truly value? Consider where you spend your money, your time, and your attention. Do they align with what you claim is important to you?

• Where and when have you encountered God in such a way that it brought you great joy and wonder?

• What have you been called to sacrifice for your commitment to the Christian life? How does that make you feel?

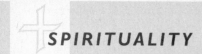 SPIRITUALITY

℟. Alleluia, alleluia.
This is my beloved Son with whom I am
    well pleased;
listen to him.
℟. Alleluia, alleluia.

Gospel   Matt 17:1-9; L614

Jesus took Peter, James, and his
    brother, John,
  and led them up a high mountain
    by themselves.
And he was transfigured before them;
  his face shone like the sun
  and his clothes became white as
    light.
And behold, Moses and Elijah
    appeared to them,
  conversing with him.
Then Peter said to Jesus in reply,
  "Lord, it is good that we are here.
If you wish, I will make three tents
    here,
  one for you, one for Moses, and one
    for Elijah."
While he was still speaking, behold,
  a bright cloud cast a shadow over them,
  then from the cloud came a voice that
    said,
  "This is my beloved Son, with whom I
    am well pleased;
  listen to him."
When the disciples heard this, they fell
    prostrate
  and were very much afraid.
But Jesus came and touched them,
    saying,
  "Rise, and do not be afraid."
And when the disciples raised their eyes,
  they saw no one else but Jesus alone.

As they were coming down from the
    mountain,
  Jesus charged them,
  "Do not tell the vision to anyone
  until the Son of Man has been raised
    from the dead."

Reflecting on the Gospel

In today's gospel from Matthew, Jesus takes Peter, James, and John high up on a mountain where they are given a glimpse of the Son of God glorified. Jesus's face shines like the sun, his clothes transform and appear to be white as snow, and a voice from the sky proclaims that he indeed is the Son of God. Prophets from the Old Testament—Moses and Elijah—attend this spectacular event, lending credence to the idea that Jesus Christ was the one foretold in the prophecies. Jesus Christ was the one who had been sent by the Creator to reconcile the world and bring it back into oneness with God in heaven. Jesus Christ was in fact the Messiah that the people of God had been waiting for.

Yet, this was still the same Jesus that the disciples ate, drank, and traveled with each day. This was the same Jesus who they would accompany down the mountain and with whom they would resume their normal lives. No wonder they fell prostrate and were in shock! How could anyone hold such dramatically different realities together at once? How can anyone expect to simply go back to normal after an event like that? At one point, Peter tells Jesus that it is good that they are here and offers to set up three tents for Jesus and the two prophets. This, however, is not the plan; they are not meant to stay on the mountain. They must return.

When we have powerful experiences of God through worship or community, it can transform the way we see everything. Physical spaces take on a heightened, new aura. The objects we use and interact with feel newly sacred. People whom we encounter seem more precious to us. Thank God for those moments and the way they buoy our spirits! They remind us of the power of God and the goodness that comes from union with the Creator.

We must find ways to bring those feelings with us as we descend from the mountaintop. The truth is that all of creation is imbued with the glory of God. All matter and all creatures are pulsing and are powered by God's spirit dwelling within them. Our sensitivity to that reality can weaken as we go about the ordinary business of being alive, but our lack of awareness doesn't make it any less true. In the book *Conjectures by a Guilty Bystander,* Trappist monk Thomas Merton writes, "There is no way to tell people that they are all walking around shining like the sun." This revelation came to him while he was walking down an ordinary street in Louisville, Kentucky. Of course, we cannot all walk around with this euphoric knowledge at the forefront of our minds at all times, but perhaps it is more accessible to us than we realize. Perhaps we can bring that knowledge into the moments of our lives that feel tiresome, monotonous, or purposeless and experience renewal.

When Jesus was transfigured before his disciples on the mountaintop, he was revealing to them a highly concentrated truth about who he was. When we experience moments of transfiguration, may we carry those moments in our hearts to remind us of the inherent goodness of life, of creation, and of God.

Preparing to Proclaim

Key words and phrases: "Rise, and do not be afraid."

To the point: On retreats, the story of the transfiguration is often used to charge participants with living out the retreat as they return to the more mundane rhythms of daily life. They may have experienced God in a powerful way, but like the disciples in this story, they must come down from the "mountaintop" of that experience to walk in the valleys below. Talking about their experience might be met with doubt or suspicion, and it is unlikely that the demands of real life will allow them the space and time to have the emotionally powerful experience of God that often occurs in a retreat setting. But, like the disciples, they do not go forth alone. Jesus remains with them—and with us. And our more powerful experiences of intimacy with him can go a long way in enlightening and empowering the more normal parts of our journeys of faith.

Psalmist Preparation

This psalm proclaims God as ruler over all the earth, but in our everyday lives it is not always evident that God is in charge. The psalm claims that "mountains melt like wax before the Lord," but to us mountains seem really rather permanent—as do tragedy and loss and suffering. God is a humble king and rather than make all well from a detached throne on high, he uses his power to accompany us, to walk amongst us in all our suffering. As you prepare this psalm, think of a part of your life where it is not evident that God is in control. Try to imagine God—the king of the universe—walking with you in your suffering.

Making Connections

Between the readings: Like the gospel, the first reading shows a vision of God as a bright and fiery king in all his glory. It also hints at a trinitarian God; there is at least a Father (the "Ancient One") and a Son here. The second reading, too, speaks of the relationship between the Father and the Son. We see the early church working out its understanding of the three persons of God and how they relate to each other.

To experience: Many of us are blessed at some point with "mountaintop experiences," where God's presence is clear and obvious and stimulates an emotional response commensurate with God's vast goodness. But our lives are not usually lived under conditions that permit constant emotional stimulus. Emotions are part of our human condition—changeable, unpredictable, tied closely to the last time we ate and whether we got enough sleep last night. Walking in the everyday "valleys" of our life calls for staying committed to God when the emotional payoff is low. This is where love becomes a virtue rather than an emotion.

Homily Points

• The gospels tend to highlight "mountaintop moments," times that display Jesus's power as the Son of God. Stories like Jesus multiplying loaves and fishes, healing the sick, or transfiguring before his disciples illuminate the uniqueness of Jesus's vocation. He is a member of the holy Trinity, born into this world to bring about salvation for all.

• Yet most of the time, Jesus probably seemed pretty ordinary to Peter, James, and John. The gospel writers could not record everything. For every mountaintop moment like we hear in today's gospel, Jesus no doubt experienced many other mundane moments that received no fanfare—times hanging out with friends, cooking dinner, relaxing, or doing the countless other actions that fill every human's day.

• Both kinds of moments—the mountaintop ones and the mundane ones—hold value for the Christian life. We receive life from a God who does marvelous deeds in the created world. Our almighty God interacts with humankind, lifting up the lowly in situations that seem impossible and gracing us with blessings beyond belief. It is right to approach God—Creator, Son, and Holy Spirit—with awe in these mountaintop moments. It is also right to approach God with awe during the mundane times, giving thanks and praise for simply existing. On this feast of Transfiguration, let us rejoice for the many ways God encounters us each day.

Model Penitential Act

Presider: In today's gospel, the voice of God proclaims: "This is my beloved Son, with whom I am well pleased." Confident that God is pleased with each of us—and that we can always be more faithful witnesses to God's love in the world—let us ask for mercy . . . *[pause]*

Lord Jesus, you shine brightly for all to see: Lord, have mercy.

Christ Jesus, the great prophets stand by your side: Christ, have mercy.

Lord Jesus, you call your disciples to rise—and not be afraid: Lord, have mercy.

Model Universal Prayer (Prayer of the Faithful)

Presider: With faith in Christ's constant presence in our lives, let us offer our prayers and petitions to the Lord.

Response: Lord, hear our prayer.

Advance the work of Christian retreat centers and other places of refuge in our church . . .

Inspire elected officials to put forth policies that eliminate systemic racism from our communities . . .

Shine the light of hope on all people struggling with anxiety, depression, and other mental health issues . . .

Grace each of us with the gifts of awe and wonder in our daily lives . . .

Presider: Creator God, you instruct the disciples to listen to Jesus your beloved son. Hear our prayers that we too might listen to Jesus and allow our hearts to be transformed by his saving power. We ask this through Christ our Lord. **Amen.**

Liturgy and Music

Proclaiming the Psalm: It takes a lot of preparation to sing the responsorial psalm well at each Sunday liturgy, and today's psalm, Psalm 97, requires even more focus and skill. Psalmody is an integral part in the Liturgy of the Word. It would benefit cantors and psalmists to review paragraphs 34–36 of the USCCB handbook for music ministers, *Sing to the Lord: Music in Divine Worship*. Pay attention to this statement when preparing to proclaim the psalm today: "As one who proclaims the Word, the psalmist should be able to proclaim the text of the psalm with clarity, conviction, and sensitivity to the text. the musical setting, and those who are listening" (35).

The psalms give us words to express the full range of human emotion. While the psalm today is a psalm of enthronement (also sung at Christmas Dawn Mass and at the Seventh Sunday of Easter [Cycle C]), on other Sundays, the psalm might be a wisdom psalm, a psalm of confidence, a song of thanksgiving, or a lament. Take seriously the nature of each psalm and how it reflects the readings of the day. Research its context and how it accompanies the first and the gospel readings. The psalm functions to lead worshippers to both understand and to appropriate the readings, to allow listeners to say that we, too, are part of this story. Prepare well.

COLLECT

Let us pray

Pause for silent prayer

O God, who in the glorious
        Transfiguration
of your Only Begotten Son
confirmed the mysteries of faith by the
        witness of the Fathers
and wonderfully prefigured our full
        adoption to sonship,
grant, we pray, to your servants,
that, listening to the voice of your beloved
        Son,
we may merit to become co-heirs with him.
Who lives and reigns with you in the unity
        of the Holy Spirit,
God, for ever and ever. **Amen.**

FIRST READING
Dan 7:9-10, 13-14

As I watched:
    Thrones were set up
        and the Ancient One took his throne.
    His clothing was snow bright,
        and the hair on his head as white as
            wool;
    his throne was flames of fire,
        with wheels of burning fire.
    A surging stream of fire
        flowed out from where he sat;
    Thousands upon thousands were
            ministering to him,
        and myriads upon myriads attended
            him.
The court was convened and the books
        were opened.

As the visions during the night continued,
        I saw
    One like a Son of man coming,
        on the clouds of heaven;
    When he reached the Ancient One
        and was presented before him,
    The one like a Son of man received
            dominion, glory, and
            kingship;
        all peoples, nations, and languages
            serve him.
    His dominion is an everlasting dominion
        that shall not be taken away,
        his kingship shall not be destroyed.

RESPONSORIAL PSALM
Ps 97:1-2, 5-6, 9

R̶. (1a, 9a) The Lord is king, the Most High over all the earth.

The LORD is king; let the earth rejoice;
  let the many islands be glad.
Clouds and darkness are round about him;
  justice and judgment are the foundation
    of his throne.

R̶. The Lord is king, the Most High over all the earth.

The mountains melt like wax before the
  LORD,
  before the LORD of all the earth.
The heavens proclaim his justice;
  all peoples see his glory.

R̶. The Lord is king, the Most High over all the earth.

Because you, O LORD, are the Most High
  over all the earth,
  exalted far above all gods.

R̶. The Lord is king, the Most High over all the earth.

SECOND READING
2 Pet 1:16-19

Beloved:
We did not follow cleverly devised myths
  when we made known to you
    the power and coming of our Lord Jesus
      Christ,
  but we had been eyewitnesses of his
    majesty.
For he received honor and glory from God
    the Father
  when that unique declaration came to
    him from the majestic glory,
  "This is my Son, my beloved, with
    whom I am well pleased."
We ourselves heard this voice come from
  heaven
  while we were with him on the holy
    mountain.
Moreover, we possess the prophetic
  message that is altogether reliable.
You will do well to be attentive to it,
  as to a lamp shining in a dark place,
  until day dawns and the morning star
    rises in your hearts.

Living Liturgy

Leaving the Mountaintop: At the beginning of each academic year, the campus ministry team at Loyola Marymount University (LMU), where I minister, takes first-year students up to a campground retreat center by Lake Arrowhead in the San Bernardino Mountains for the First Year Retreat. Most students have a mountaintop experience and almost always no one wants to leave the mountaintop.

Today we go from learning about the demands of discipleship and finding the kingdom of heaven through the ordinariness of the parables to something quite spectacular—God breaks into our world and our lives. The transfiguration gives us a brief and fleeting glimpse of Jesus in all his glory. With the benefit of hindsight, we see an anticipation of Jesus's resurrection, a foreshadowing of his glory in heaven and we are filled with hope for the promise of our own resurrection.

Leaving the mountaintop proves to be a challenge. How do we reacclimate to daily life? Perhaps remembering special moments of grace, of meaningful and important times, will bring some perspective to our work in the field. Jesus's warning to not tell anyone about the events on the mountain privileges a leadership of action over one driven by words.

In the transfiguration experience, light and glory emanate and through this we live our baptismal call to take light down the mountain to the world. Today would be an appropriate time to celebrate the rite for receiving other baptized Christians into full communion with the Catholic Church, although this could happen at any time throughout the year. This moment of complete welcome would be another way to recognize God's light and glory as we walk toward a community of kinship. As God breaks into our world and our daily life, we become aware of the transfiguration moments of peace, joy, reconciliation, and forgiveness. Placing our faith into action in identifying these graced moments deepen our care and concern for each other, reflecting God's own reach to us.

PROMPTS FOR FAITH-SHARING

• What "mountaintop experiences" have you had where Jesus felt very real and present? What did they reveal to you about him?

• What in your daily life makes it hard to experience God's presence and power?

• What tools do you use when Jesus's presence is not so obvious or emotional? Are there prayer techniques you rely on?

✠ SPIRITUALITY

GOSPEL ACCLAMATION
cf. Ps 130:5

R̷. Alleluia, alleluia.
I wait for the Lord;
my soul waits for his word.
R̷. Alleluia, alleluia.

Gospel   Matt 14:22-33; L115A

After he had fed the people, Jesus
    made the disciples get into a boat
    and precede him to the other side,
    while he dismissed the crowds.
After doing so, he went up on the
    mountain by himself to pray.
When it was evening he was there
    alone.
Meanwhile the boat, already a few
    miles offshore,
    was being tossed about by the
        waves, for the wind was
        against it.
During the fourth watch of the night,
    he came toward them walking on
    the sea.
When the disciples saw him walking
    on the sea they were terrified.
"It is a ghost," they said, and they cried
    out in fear.
At once Jesus spoke to them, "Take
    courage, it is I; do not be afraid."
Peter said to him in reply,
    "Lord, if it is you, command me to
        come to you on the water."
He said, "Come."
Peter got out of the boat and began to
    walk on the water toward Jesus.
But when he saw how strong the wind
    was he became frightened;
    and, beginning to sink, he cried out,
        "Lord, save me!"
Immediately Jesus stretched out his hand
    and caught Peter,
    and said to him, "O you of little faith,
        why did you doubt?"
After they got into the boat, the wind
    died down.
Those who were in the boat did him
    homage, saying,
    "Truly, you are the Son of God."

Reflecting on the Gospel

In today's gospel reading, as Jesus walks upon the surface of the lake in the midst of a storm, the terrified disciples mistake him for a ghostly apparition. "Take courage," Jesus says, "it is I; do not be afraid." It is Peter who responds: "Lord, if it is you, command me to come to you on the water."

What are we to make of this response? Is this Peter the confident risk-taker, disregarding all that he knows about the dangers of the deep in the lake where he once earned a living? Or is this a painful postresurrection memory of an overconfident Peter who blusters that his faith would never be overwhelmed by the waves of passion and death, only to sink a few hours later in the storm of his betrayal of Jesus (Matt 26:33-35; 69-75)? Or is this Peter a mixture of both possibilities, the best and the worst, that we so often experience in ourselves? Jesus speaks the simple, single, and commanding word "Come." And Peter gets out of the boat to approach Jesus. But then the reality of the storm around him overwhelms his faith and his daring confidence in Jesus, and immediately he begins to sink.

To his credit, Peter knows the right response to his failure, and he again acknowledges Jesus as "Lord," as he had done before he left the boat, but now he adds the cry for salvation. And Jesus immediately responds, reaching out to him not as a man of no faith, but as one of "little faith." Again Matthew reminds us of the God who so often in the Old Testament is described as reaching out to save his people with "great power" and an "outstretched arm" (see Deut 9:29; 26:8). Here, in Jesus the Lord is that saving hand that holds Peter above the threatening waters, the arm that supports Peter as, together, they walk back to the boat. They get into the boat, and the disciples bow down before Jesus and acknowledge him as the Son of God. Out of their traumatic experience new insight about Jesus has emerged, but its significance for them is still to be tested.

It is to the church, to individuals and communities of disciples of "little faith," that the hand of Jesus is always outstretched to save. We, too, are "water walkers" today when we are enabled to tread the threatening waves or blustering winds that can sweep over us because of our confidence in the presence and power of the stormstriding and compassionate Jesus. Sunday after Sunday we come together to praise and adore God, despite—or perhaps because of—the storms of the past week. We, too, are an assembly of people who have a "little faith" in Jesus mixed with some doubt that he is in the midst of our ordinary and often chaotic lives, people who struggle to keep faithful, people who sometimes risk a great deal for Jesus in terms of relationships and vocations, in the broad sense of our many and different callings. Yet we come to worship him.

Preparing to Proclaim

Key words and phrases: "Take courage, it is I; do not be afraid."

To the point: Peter's emotional trajectory is relatable here; it shows us that having faith is never a one-and-done proposition. His bravado seems to be rewarded when he steps out of the boat and finds himself able to walk on water, but when he encounters new fears, it is as if he never had courage at all. For us, too, the journey of faith is circuitous; it brings moments of courage and confidence as well as moments of doubt and distress. We sometimes find that our most confident moments precede a new experience that throws off everything we thought we knew. All the while, though, Jesus is with us. He goes before us, walking on the water and making it safe; and he stands prepared to catch us when our resolve falters.

Psalmist Preparation

Like the other readings, the psalm proclaims God as one whose rulership is found in gentle ways. He proclaims not powerfully demonstrative revenge on enemies but a peace that transcends the need for vengeance. His presence is found in a good harvest, in the natural rhythms of the earth yielding abundance to provide for our needs. As you prepare to proclaim this psalm, think about the gentle ways God is present in your life. Strive to pay closer attention to at least one of these whispered hints of God's presence.

Making Connections

Between the readings: In both the first reading and the gospel, God's power is found in calmness and stillness. Elijah expects God's power to be made manifest in wind and earthquake and fire, but God is in fact found in the tiny whispering sound, one that could be missed if Elijah weren't paying attention. The gospel takes this one step further. Not only does Jesus bring stillness, he shows power over the forces of water and wind that so frighten the disciples. God is all-powerful, yes, but God chooses to exercise this power in gentleness.

To experience: There is a group of seabirds called petrels and they earned St. Peter as their eponym because they move their feet in such a way that they appear to walk on water as they feed. Many of our plants and animals were named by people who saw God powerfully present in the natural world. This gospel with its mighty weather imagery and the first reading with its tiny whisper can serve as reminders to pay attention to God's presence in all we encounter—nature, relationships, and even our own gifts.

Homily Points

• Today's gospel brims with drama—at least at first glance. A vicious storm tosses the disciples around in their boat. Suddenly Jesus appears from the water—or is it a ghost? Peter tests Jesus and starts to drown, only to have the Son of God triumphantly pull him to safety. It is a made-for-TV scene!

• All of the action tends to overshadow the beginning of this passage—verses that are less flashy but just as telling about Jesus. After a full day of feeding people, Jesus withdraws to the mountains to pray by himself. Even the Son of God needs time to center and recharge. Even Jesus—the one to whom we so often direct our prayers—makes prayer a priority. His pause in the midst of all the other needs that clamor for his attention models the way for us. We too are called to retreat and pray in the midst of our daily lives.

• We might not be able to escape to the mountainside, but can we wake up ten minutes earlier and read the daily Mass readings? Can we leave our phones at home when we go out for a walk and spend that time conversing with God? Can we turn off the radio and drive in contemplative quiet on the way to work? Consider when and where you can stow away for even a moment of prayer. God will reveal Godself to us whenever we make the time and space to listen for the tiny, whispering sound of the divine.

Model Penitential Act

Presider: In today's first reading, Elijah encounters God not in the heavy winds or earthquake, but in a tiny whispering sound. For those times when we have not paid close enough attention to God in our midst, let us ask for mercy . . . *[pause]*

Lord Jesus, you instruct your disciples to take courage: Lord, have mercy.

Christ Jesus, you save all those who are falling: Christ, have mercy.

Lord Jesus, you truly are the Son of God: Lord, have mercy.

Model Universal Prayer (Prayer of the Faithful)

Presider: God reveals Godself to all of creation, across time and space. With confidence, we offer our prayers and petitions before the Lord.

Response: Lord, hear our prayer.

Prosper and uphold the work of religious sisters and brothers across the world . . .

Bolster the work of conservationists, environmental activists, and all those striving to combat the climate crisis . . .

Pour out your grace and peace upon people experiencing food or housing insecurity . . .

Inspire everyone in our congregation to share their gifts and talents to make our community stronger . . .

Presider: Almighty God, by your generous spirit you let us see your kindness and grant us your salvation. Receive our prayers and the prayers of all the world that together we might find peace. We ask this through Christ our Lord. **Amen.**

Liturgy and Music

Don't Cause a Distraction: In the first parish where I directed music, the choir was situated in the choir loft until the new pastor redesigned a music ministry space beside the altar area. It was interesting to observe that some choir members seemed not to realize that they were in full view of the assembly and continued to conduct themselves as if they were hidden up in the loft. I refer to this note from *Sing to the Lord:* "When not engaged in the direct exercise of their particular role, music ministers, like all ministers of the Liturgy, remain attentive members of the gathered assembly and should never constitute a distraction" (96).

We eventually become comfortable in our role as music leaders and with the space that we minister in. After all, it is almost a second home. Be mindful of the times during the liturgy when we are not making music and give reverence to the space by participating in prayer. Be discreet in preparing for the next song or part of the liturgy. All these directions should have been finalized at the week's rehearsal or during the pick-up practice before Mass. All cues to the cantors and choir should not distract from prayer and the liturgical action before us. Plan ahead to minimize distractions.

COLLECT

Let us pray.

Pause for silent prayer

Almighty ever-living God,
whom, taught by the Holy Spirit,
we dare to call our Father,
bring, we pray, to perfection in our hearts
the spirit of adoption as your sons and
    daughters,
that we may merit to enter into the
    inheritance
which you have promised.
Through our Lord Jesus Christ, your Son,
who lives and reigns with you in the unity
    of the Holy Spirit,
God, for ever and ever. **Amen.**

FIRST READING

1 Kgs 19:9a, 11-13a

At the mountain of God, Horeb,
    Elijah came to a cave where he took
      shelter.
Then the LORD said to him,
    "Go outside and stand on the mountain
      before the LORD;
    the LORD will be passing by."
A strong and heavy wind was rending the
    mountains
    and crushing rocks before the LORD—
    but the LORD was not in the wind.
After the wind there was an earthquake—
    but the LORD was not in the earthquake.
After the earthquake there was fire—
    but the LORD was not in the fire.
After the fire there was a tiny whispering
    sound.
When he heard this,
    Elijah hid his face in his cloak
    and went and stood at the entrance of
      the cave.

RESPONSORIAL PSALM
Ps 85:9, 10, 11-12, 13-14

R℣. (8) Lord, let us see your kindness, and
grant us your salvation.

I will hear what God proclaims;
    the LORD—for he proclaims peace.
Near indeed is his salvation to those who
        fear him,
    glory dwelling in our land.

R℣. Lord, let us see your kindness, and
grant us your salvation.

Kindness and truth shall meet;
    justice and peace shall kiss.
Truth shall spring out of the earth,
    and justice shall look down from
        heaven.

R℣. Lord, let us see your kindness, and
grant us your salvation.

The LORD himself will give his benefits;
    our land shall yield its increase.
Justice shall walk before him,
    and prepare the way of his steps.

R℣. Lord, let us see your kindness, and
grant us your salvation.

SECOND READING
Rom 9:1-5

Brothers and sisters:
I speak the truth in Christ, I do not lie;
    my conscience joins with the Holy Spirit
        in bearing me witness
    that I have great sorrow and constant
        anguish in my heart.
For I could wish that I myself were
        accursed and cut off from Christ
    for the sake of my own people,
    my kindred according to the flesh.
They are Israelites;
    theirs the adoption, the glory, the
        covenants,
    the giving of the law, the worship, and
        the promises;
    theirs the patriarchs, and from them,
    according to the flesh, is the Christ,
    who is over all, God blessed forever.
        Amen.

Living Liturgy

Authentic Prayer Builds Faith: Peter's imperfect faith reminds us of the work we have left to do. The more we pray, the less we fear.

On March 27, 2020, Pope Francis presided over an Extraordinary Moment of Prayer during the early COVID-19 pandemic where he reminded the faithful that trust in God during challenging times calls for a removal of things that keep us from belonging authentically to each other: "The storm exposes our vulnerability and uncovers those false and superfluous certainties around which we have constructed our daily schedules, our projects, our habits and priorities." For our work in liturgical ministry, Francis offers a challenge to put aside the distractions of busy habits and schedules to spend time in what "nourishes our people's souls." Resetting our priorities during times of crisis requires prayer and trust in God. Francis adds: "In this storm, the façade of those stereotypes with which we camouflaged our egos, always worrying about our image, has fallen away, uncovering once more that (blessed) common belonging, of which we cannot be deprived: our belonging as brothers and sisters."

Who is in the boat and who is outside of it? Who is included and who is excluded? In a society more and more polarized by race, religion, and politics, how does the gospel speak to us about how to navigate these waters so that all may feel welcome into the security of a blessed, common belonging in the safety of a supportive and empowering faith community? May we have the humility to risk removing façades to honestly pray and cry out to God for God's kindness and salvation already present within the community of belonging we serve.

PROMPTS FOR FAITH-SHARING

• Elijah finds God present not in the loud powers of the natural world but in a tiny whispering sound, one that would be easy to overlook were he not paying attention. What small, gentle ways might God be present in your life? Where could God be calling you to pay closer attention?

• Jesus issues a one-word invitation to Peter: "Come." It echoes many of Jesus's other commands and invitations throughout the gospels. How do you hear this invitation in your own life? How is Jesus calling you to come closer to him?

• While Peter's faith falters in this story, he also shows another level of faith: when he starts to sink, he does not turn back to the boat. His immediate reaction is to call out to Jesus for help. When you find your faith faltering, how do you respond? Do you trust Jesus to bolster your efforts when they are not enough?

GOSPEL ACCLAMATION
R7. Alleluia, alleluia.
Mary is taken up to heaven;
a chorus of angels exults.
R7. Alleluia, alleluia.

Gospel   Luke 1:39-56; L622

Mary set out
  and traveled to the hill coun-
      try in haste
  to a town of Judah,
  where she entered the house
      of Zechariah
  and greeted Elizabeth.
When Elizabeth heard Mary's
      greeting,
  the infant leaped in her
      womb,
  and Elizabeth, filled with the
      Holy Spirit,
  cried out in a loud voice and
      said,
  "Blessed are you among
      women,
  and blessed is the fruit of
      your womb.
And how does this happen to
      me,
  that the mother of my Lord
      should come to me?
For at the moment the sound of
      your greeting reached my ears,
  the infant in my womb leaped for joy.
Blessed are you who believed
  that what was spoken to you by the Lord
  would be fulfilled."

And Mary said:

  "My soul proclaims the greatness of
      the Lord;
    my spirit rejoices in God my Savior
    for he has looked with favor on his
      lowly servant.

Continued in Appendix A, p. 300.

See Appendix A, p. 300, for the other readings.

Reflecting on the Gospel

What can Mary teach us about what it means to be a woman of God? When we celebrate Marian feasts, we have a unique opportunity to consider this question. The events of Mary's life are both incredibly challenging and incredibly inspiring. Although God directly touched Mary's life in extraordinary ways, all people—and especially women—can look to the person of Mary and trust that the lessons of her life are timeless, resonating in hearts across nations and across cultures.

We should take care not to only lift up particular aspects of Mary's life, aspects that are overly simplistic or generalized and that have been used to subjugate women for centuries. For example, when we consider Mary's *fiat* at the annunciation, we can celebrate Mary's faith-filled "yes" to God without perpetuating the idea that women are uniquely positioned and called to exercise submission within their families or the institutions in which they are members. Mary's response to God was active. Her willingness to carry the Son of God in her own body demonstrated radical hospitality. Are all of us, regardless of gender, being similarly responsive to God's requests to be welcomed lovingly into our bodies and lives? When we celebrate the immaculate conception, the teaching that Mary, imbued with special grace, was born without original sin, we need not hold Mary up and measure our purity against hers. Rather, we can reflect on how God imbues all people with grace and talents. We can discern in our own hearts what special gifts we have been born with and how God wishes for us to use them to grow our world's capacity for compassion and mercy.

What does it mean to be a woman of God? In addition to being a miraculous virgin who humbled herself before God, Mary was a pregnant teenager at risk of being punished by her community. She was a refugee fleeing the violent wrath of a dangerous political figure. She was a mother who witnessed the unjust execution of her son by corrupt civil authorities. We look upon the face of Mary every day when we look out at our world and see women still experiencing similar hardships. These women embody Mary's example of godly womanhood by continuing to survive, protect their families, and remain faithful in a world that is still yearning for justice.

In the *Magnificat*, which we hear in today's gospel, Mary passionately extols the virtues of God, lifting God up as a fount of justice and mercy. The God that Mary proclaims in these verses is swift, active, and shows preference to the oppressed and lowly. Mary shows us that godly womanhood can also sound radical and prophetic. When greeting Mary, Elizabeth affirms Mary's trust in God, proclaiming, "Blessed are you who believed that what was spoken to you by the Lord would be fulfilled."

On this solemnity celebrating the Assumption of Mary, may all of us take time to reflect on the unique calling God has for our lives. May we faithfully follow the path that God lays out for us, as Mary did, and may we believe that what God says to us will be fulfilled in due course.

Preparing to Proclaim

Key words and phrases: "The Almighty has done great things for me, / and holy is his Name."

To the point: The visitation narrative gives us the great canticle of the *Magnificat*, in which Mary proclaims God's preference for the poor and lowly and downtrodden. Her prediction that all generations will call her blessed is appropriate today as we do that very thing, recalling her courage in participating in God's redemptive work. It is also appropriate that she names God's work as "lifting up the lowly," on this day when we celebrate her final reward of being raised, body and soul, into the ultimate joy and rest that Jesus has prepared for her and for us.

Model Penitential Act

Presider: Today's first reading points out great signs that appeared in the sky from God. For the times we have not been attentive to the signs of God's presence and love in our lives, let us ask the Lord for mercy and forgiveness . . . *[pause]*

Lord Jesus, you are the Son of God and son of Mary: Lord, have mercy.
Christ Jesus, you fill the hungry with good things: Christ, have mercy.
Lord Jesus, you send the rich away empty: Lord, have mercy.

Model Universal Prayer (Prayer of the Faithful)

Presider: Through the intercession of the Blessed Virgin Mary, let us offer to God our prayers and petitions.

Response: Lord, hear our prayer.

Further the ministries of women in the church to proclaim the greatness of the Lord . . .

Bless the Elizabeths in our lives who support and celebrate us . . .

Grant comfort and healing to couples who are struggling to conceive or who have experienced miscarriage . . .

Inspire our community to stand by the poor and the oppressed with the vigor of Mary . . .

Presider: God, source of joy and anticipation, you gifted Mary with the courage to carry your son and embrace his call to justice. Receive our prayers that through Mary's intercession we might give praise to God by our lives. We ask this through Christ our Lord. **Amen.**

Living Liturgy

Prophetic Voice: Mary's song is a political and prophetic one. The words of the *Magnificat* forever link the incarnation with social justice in every age. Whenever we sing the canticle at evening prayer and during Marian feast days, remember that it is linked to all song that comes out of struggle, suffering, and courage in the face of oppression. Singing it would indeed be a political act, yet how might Mary's song offer a healing counterpoint to political divide? A society afflicted by such divide needs Mary's prophetic voice accompanied by healing music.

COLLECT
Let us pray.

Pause for silent prayer

Almighty ever-living God,
who assumed the Immaculate Virgin Mary,
  the Mother of your Son,
body and soul into heavenly glory,
grant, we pray,
that, always attentive to the things that are above,
we may merit to be sharers of her glory.
Through our Lord Jesus Christ, your Son,
who lives and reigns with you in the unity of
  the Holy Spirit,
God, for ever and ever. **Amen.**

FOR REFLECTION

• It is with wonder that Elizabeth gives us the second sentence of the Hail Mary: "Blessed are you among women, and blessed is the fruit of your womb." How could you encounter the amazing realities of Mary's life with renewed appreciation?

• In the *Magnificat*, do you see yourself as one of the lowly and hungry ones that God sides with? Or as one of the proud, mighty, and rich whose fate is less promising? Most of us are on both sides in this life. How could you stand more firmly with those who are poor and oppressed?

Homily Points

• The Solemnity of the Assumption of the Blessed Virgin Mary invites us to give thanks and praise for our bodies. We are not just brains sitting across from each other at dinner or souls floating past each other at the grocery store. We are embodied people, called to glorify God with our full selves.

• God resurrected Mary into heaven, body and all. We await the day when, like Mary, we will encounter our Creator in the halls of heaven. Until then, let us consider the people and places in which we meet God in our daily lives. What makes your heart leap for joy? When are you prompted to proclaim the greatness of the Lord?

✚ SPIRITUALITY

GOSPEL ACCLAMATION
cf. Matt 4:23

℟. Alleluia, alleluia.
Jesus proclaimed the Gospel of the
    kingdom
and cured every disease among the
    people.
℟. Alleluia, alleluia.

Gospel

Matt 15:21-28; L118A

At that time, Jesus withdrew
    to the region of Tyre and
    Sidon.
And behold, a Canaanite
    woman of that district
    came and called out,
"Have pity on me, Lord, Son
    of David!
My daughter is tormented by a
    demon."
But Jesus did not say a word in
    answer to her.
Jesus' disciples came and
    asked him,
"Send her away, for she keeps calling
    out after us."
He said in reply,
"I was sent only to the lost sheep of
    the house of Israel."
But the woman came and did Jesus
    homage, saying, "Lord, help me."
He said in reply,
"It is not right to take the food of the
    children
and throw it to the dogs."
She said, "Please, Lord, for even the
    dogs eat the scraps
that fall from the table of their
    masters."
Then Jesus said to her in reply,
"O woman, great is your faith!
Let it be done for you as you wish."
And the woman's daughter was healed
    from that hour.

Reflecting on the Gospel

Today's strange gospel reading is about crossing boundaries into new territory that is not only geographical but also a venture into differences of culture, gender, and religion. In "pagan" territory, Jesus is confronted by a Canaanite woman, a descendant of one of the ancient enemies of Israel. She is the mother of a daughter in dire need of help. No husband or father is mentioned. The

woman is devoting her life to the one she loves, but she is nearly at the end of her tether. So, despite the fact that she is a Gentile, she shouts her faithfilled words at Jesus, hailing him as "Lord, Son of David."

Jesus's response to her cry may surprise us. He is silent, struggling with his identity, his mission, his prejudices. If we deny Jesus such struggles, we minimize the reality of the incarnation—the mystery of the Word made flesh, fully sharing our humanity in a certain time and place, with a particular ancestry, ethnicity, and culture—and we deny his relevance for our own struggles.

As though he is thinking aloud, he says not to her but to his disciples, "I was sent only to the lost sheep of the house of Israel." Tenacious and bold, yet humble, the woman gets down into the dust in front of Jesus, kneels where dogs play and crumbs fall, and asks a second time for his help. This Gentile is challenging him in a way that is painful for both of them. Jesus asks her if it is fair to take Israelite "food," the sustaining gift of God's salvation, and offer it to the Gentile "dogs." At least he is now addressing the woman, and she seizes the opportunity for some serious wordplay.

Like a dog, she says, she will be content with any scraps of help that Jesus can offer her from the table of the children of Israel. And Jesus, who had to learn to read the signs of the times in the Hebrew Scriptures, in prayer, in events, and in people, reads this woman. And now he says to this stranger and Gentile "great is your faith" as she desperately seeks healing for her daughter.

Impelled by this faith, Jesus crosses into new territory of understanding himself and his mission to the nations. After his resurrection, the salvation first offered to the Jews through Jesus will be the gift that the community of disciples must offer to all the nations (Matt 28:19-20). As Matthew's predominantly Jewish Christian community struggled with the increasing number of Gentile Christians who were joining then, it was significant that the evangelist could point to this incident and say, see how *Jesus himself* had to struggle with a Gentile—and see how he recognized her great faith. Not only Matthew's first-century community needs to look carefully. It is also our own racism, sexism, and cultural superiority that we see reflected in this gospel. As long as there are "dogs [under] the table"—people in misery, people on the margins of or excluded from the church—we are challenged to cross boundaries and offer them the crumbs of our compassion.

Preparing to Proclaim

Key words and phrases: "O woman, great is your faith!"

To the point: This is one of the places where the gospels show us Jesus's full humanity; it would seem that his understanding of his own mission is expanded by his encounter with the Canaanite woman. He is the Son of God, and yet he is *moved* here from unresponsiveness to resistance to, finally, realization that perhaps his work is bigger than even he had realized. He begins his life and work within the context of God's pre-established relationship to Israel. In this moment, it is made clear to him and to us that Jesus is for all people. Faith in him is available to all and his healing ministry is not meant to be limited to some pre-approved group. It is very human to draw boundaries and establish groups; we seek to understand what we need to do to be "in." But God's generosity and hospitality are more radical and inclusive than we can ever understand.

Psalmist Preparation

The psalm very clearly echoes the message of the other readings: God is for all, for all nations and all peoples. The ultimate hope is for all to be united in praise of the one God; this end will fulfill the shared mission of Israel and of the church. As part of your preparation to proclaim this psalm, think of a story you've heard of someone who doesn't feel fully included in the church. If you don't know one, find one; the internet abounds with such stories. Pray for this person as you proclaim the psalm, that they may experience the radical hospitality of God by experiencing welcome in the church.

Making Connections

Between the readings: The first reading gives a foretaste of what we learn in the gospel: while Israel plays a special role in God's saving work, salvation is for all peoples, regardless of race or origin. The second reading, too, shows Paul striving to resolve the differences between Jews and Gentiles in his community. Both groups have a history of disobedience, but God's greater mercy is also for all.

To experience: Unfortunately, even the church is not exempt from the human tendency to draw exclusive boundaries that name who is in and who is out. Many in the church are excluded because of their gender or income or sexual orientation. On a smaller level, parish activities often unintentionally exclude families whose children don't attend the parochial school and parents who need to work. But God calls us to a more radical inclusiveness, to hospitality that truly loves and receives all.

Homily Points

• The prophet Isaiah paints a picture of radical inclusivity in today's first reading. Throughout the Old Testament, we hear of God's special relationship with the Israelites, the people God called and claimed as God's own. Yet God's loving care is not bound to the Israelites or any one group of people. God welcomes all. God loves all. God creates a house of prayer for all people who join themselves to the Lord. God's embrace of the foreigner models how we are to approach people from different backgrounds today.

• Every line of Scripture offers a wellspring of insights and opportunities for reflection. St. Paul is a particularly gifted writer who draws audiences in with his powerful observations. One such line from today's second letter to the Romans reads: "For the gifts and the call of God are irrevocable." Let us take a moment to soak in this reality. God gives us gifts that can never be taken away, gifts like love, mercy, and complete acceptance. God also calls each of us to lives of discipleship—and within that, to a myriad of relationships, works, and service opportunities. The specific contexts may change as we move through life, but the presence of God's call will remain with each of us forever.

• The Canaanite woman in today's gospel models an authentic, vulnerable way of interacting with Jesus. She recognizes Jesus as Lord and asks directly for help. She persists when Jesus rebukes and insults her. By the end, Jesus changes heart and praises the woman's faith. In what ways could this woman's witness inspire your own faith life?

Model Penitential Act

Presider: Today's first reading from the prophet Isaiah reminds us to "observe what is right, do what is just." For the times we have fallen short of doing what is right and just, let us ask God for mercy and forgiveness . . . *[pause]*

Lord Jesus, you answer those who cry for help: Lord, have mercy.

Christ Jesus, you exult the Canaanite woman's faith: Christ, have mercy.

Lord Jesus, you will come again to heal every one of our ills: Lord, have mercy.

Model Universal Prayer (Prayer of the Faithful)

Presider: Today's second reading assures us that God has mercy upon all. Trusting in God's infinite mercy, let us turn to the Lord with our prayers and petitions.

Response: Lord, hear our prayer.

Advance deepening respect and dialogue among Christians, Jews, and Muslims . . .

Grant success to politicians and advocates working toward peace in the Middle East . . .

Give aid to people facing unemployment or underemployment . . .

Fill with hope those in our community who are near death . . .

Presider: God of abundant blessings, you grace figures like the Canaanite woman with great faith. Hear our prayers that we too might receive the gift of faith that grows and stretches to be shared with all who we encounter. We ask this through Christ our Lord. **Amen.**

Liturgy and Music

Broadening Our Network: The summer months give many involved in liturgy, especially those in music ministry, some time off to relax and attend Mass with friends and family members. During this time, neighboring liturgical ministers might also be enjoying some down time. Apart from attending annual conferences to enhance our ministerial skills and broaden our network of pastoral musician friends, this would be a good time to also get to know the neighboring parish's music director and the music program there. Host a simple lunch or dinner. It would also be fruitful to include music ministers from neighboring Christian churches and communities. Exchanging ideas and sharing stories of ministry and life allow us to witness the beauty of God and gain greater understanding of the internal life and activity of the church. This connection with our local colleagues in ministry enables us to deepen our identity as Body of Christ. We draw from one another through personal experiences and ministerial encounters some ways in which to plan for the new choir year ahead. As Christian disciples and coworkers in the vineyard of the Lord, we rely on each other for help as we continue this transformative work of communion and community.

COLLECT

Let us pray.

Pause for silent prayer

O God, who have prepared for those who
    love you
good things which no eye can see,
fill our hearts, we pray, with the warmth
    of your love,
so that, loving you in all things and above
    all things,
we may attain your promises,
which surpass every human desire.
Through our Lord Jesus Christ, your Son,
who lives and reigns with you in the unity
    of the Holy Spirit,
God, for ever and ever. **Amen.**

FIRST READING

Isa 56:1, 6-7

Thus says the LORD:
Observe what is right, do what is just;
    for my salvation is about to come,
      my justice, about to be revealed.

The foreigners who join themselves to the
    LORD,
    ministering to him,
loving the name of the LORD,
    and becoming his servants—
all who keep the sabbath free from
    profanation
    and hold to my covenant,
them I will bring to my holy mountain
    and make joyful in my house of prayer;
their burnt offerings and sacrifices
    will be acceptable on my altar,
for my house shall be called
    a house of prayer for all peoples.

RESPONSORIAL PSALM

Ps 67:2-3, 5, 6, 8

R̶. (4) O God, let all the nations praise you!

May God have pity on us and bless us;
    may he let his face shine upon us.
So may your way be known upon earth;
    among all nations, your salvation.

R̶. O God, let all the nations praise you!

May the nations be glad and exult
    because you rule the peoples in equity;
    the nations on the earth you guide.

R̶. O God, let all the nations praise you!

May the peoples praise you, O God;
    may all the peoples praise you!
May God bless us,
    and may all the ends of the earth fear
      him!

R̶. O God, let all the nations praise you!

SECOND READING

Rom 11:13-15, 29-32

Brothers and sisters:
I am speaking to you Gentiles.
Inasmuch as I am the apostle to the
    Gentiles,
    I glory in my ministry in order to make
      my race jealous
    and thus save some of them.
For if their rejection is the reconciliation
    of the world,
    what will their acceptance be but life
      from the dead?

For the gifts and the call of God are
    irrevocable.
Just as you once disobeyed God
    but have now received mercy because
      of their disobedience,
    so they have now disobeyed in order
      that,
    by virtue of the mercy shown to you,
    they too may now receive mercy.
For God delivered all to disobedience,
    that he might have mercy upon all.

Living Liturgy

Breaking Barriers for Unity: The gospel reading today gives us an opportunity to connect our ministry with Jesus's ministry of breaking down barriers. A large part of the ministry of Jesus involves the dismantling of cultural barriers and the creation of borders that are porous enough to extend sincere welcome and belonging for those especially cast down by societal norms—the foreigner, the tax collector, the sinner, the leper. As we think of various ways in which we welcome the seeker or the newcomer to the parish community, here are a few probing questions to reflect on: What boundary lines have we unintentionally drawn in our process of offering welcome? Have we been open to building bridges within our ministerial efforts? Have we approached ministry through a transformative experience of welcome for both ourselves and those that receive our welcome?

Through ecumenical efforts, the church hopes for and strives toward the unity of all Christians. Ecumenism emphasizes what is viewed as the universality of the Christian faith and unity among churches. It comes from the Greek word *oikoumene,* which means "the inhabited earth." According to the USCCB, "The ecumenical movement finds its roots in holiness, so individual prayerfulness always comes first. A grasp of the faith from study of it lets one present the faith clearly. If you are uncertain about what the Church teaches about a particular issue or why, say so and offer to find the explanation. Humility is essential, for when you meet with other Christians for dialogue you must meet them on equal footing" (Sara Perla, "Decree on Ecumenism: At a Glance").

At the center of ecumenical dialogue is the grace of humility, to quiet the self into a place where one might be open to listening and participating in conversations without the distraction of personal preoccupations of pride and power. It is the grace of the Canaanite woman, her faith, her persistence, and confidence in Jesus to allow learning and eventually healing to happen.

PROMPTS FOR FAITH-SHARING

• What do you make of Jesus in this scene, who seems to change his mind about his own mission?

• What groups are excluded by the culture of the church? In your own parish setting, who might be excluded without you realizing it?

• How might your parish better live out the radical hospitality of God?

• How might you, personally, more fully live out the fundamental inclusiveness that is a trademark of how God works in the world?

AUGUST 20, 2023

TWENTIETH SUNDAY
IN ORDINARY TIME

SPIRITUALITY

GOSPEL ACCLAMATION
Matt 16:18

℞. Alleluia, alleluia.
You are Peter and upon this rock I will
    build my Church
and the gates of the netherworld shall
    not prevail against it.
℞. Alleluia, alleluia.

Gospel

Matt 16:13-20; L121A

Jesus went into the region of
    Caesarea Philippi and
    he asked his disciples,
    "Who do people say that the
        Son of Man is?"
They replied, "Some say John
    the Baptist, others Elijah,
    still others Jeremiah or one
    of the prophets."
He said to them, "But who do
    you say that I am?"
Simon Peter said in reply,
    "You are the Christ, the Son
    of the living God."
Jesus said to him in reply,
    "Blessed are you, Simon son of
        Jonah.
For flesh and blood has not revealed
    this to you, but my heavenly
    Father.
And so I say to you, you are Peter,
    and upon this rock I will build my
        church,
    and the gates of the netherworld
        shall not prevail against it.
I will give you the keys to the kingdom
    of heaven.
Whatever you bind on earth shall be
    bound in heaven;
    and whatever you loose on earth
        shall be loosed in heaven."
Then he strictly ordered his disciples
    to tell no one that he was the Christ.

Reflecting on the Gospel

In northern Galilee, a few miles from the present border between Lebanon and Syria, is a place of majestic beauty called, in Jesus's day, Caesarea Philippi. It's here, dwarfed by a huge rock cavern and temples, that Jesus asks his disciples, "Who do people say that the Son of Man is?" This is a safe question requiring no personal involvement. They answer quickly, evoking the haunting memory of John the Baptist, the passionate preaching of Jeremiah, the legendary expectation of Elijah. Then comes Jesus's direct question: "But who do *you* say that I am?"

In the boat after the storm, the disciples had paid homage to him and confessed him as the Son of God. Here all the confessional attention is fixed on Peter. He confesses more than he himself understands about the identity of Jesus. But now Jesus is going to tell him how the identity and mission of both of them are linked together. Jesus pronounces a blessing over Peter because of God's revelation to him, gives him a new name and a new mission. The renaming of Simon Peter as the "rock" on which Jesus's church would be built is a wordplay between the Greek name *Petros* (Peter) and *petra* (rock). It is almost a biblical and ambivalent "nickname" for this "rocky" man who was to be both the foundation stone of the community of disciples and ironically, some time later, the unstable one who on the night of Jesus's passion would crumble into shifting sand. But as a leader for his church, Jesus surely wants someone with whom we can identify in our own weaknesses. In Matthew's Gospel, it is only Peter who receives a personal beatitude, a blessing of God pronounced over him by Jesus. The assurance is given that no matter what destructive powers are hurled at the church, and not withstanding Peter's role in it, the church will stand firm because, as Jesus says, it is "*my* church."

It will be Peter's privilege, and the privilege of his successors in the Petrine ministry, to be given the "keys," the authority that will enable him to unlock the riches of the revelation of Jesus Christ that has been entrusted to the church. In contrast, the scribes and Pharisees who oppose Jesus will later be accused by him of locking people out of the kingdom by their teaching and example (Matt 23:13). "To bind" and "to loose" were rabbinic terms for "to permit" and "to forgive," and Peter is assured that Jesus will always be present in the authority that Jesus delegates to him to interpret the law, to make exceptions, to forgive, or to demand obedience. Peter is to be a good steward of the church's treasure house of grace. However, until Peter and the other disciples have learned fully what it means for Jesus to be the Messiah, until he has suffered, died, and risen, and until they have been drawn into this mystery, they are not to tell people about what has been revealed here at Caesarea Philippi, for it would be only the partial truth.

Preparing to Proclaim

Key words and phrases: "You are the Christ, the Son of the living God."

To the point: Peter is an imperfect, problematic, very human person. Here he shows great faith and insight into the reality of who Jesus is, yet at the passion he will be the first to run away from the frightful scene and will repeatedly deny his connection to Christ. In this scene, he appears to earn his status as first among the disciples by giving the right answer to a tricky question. But in reality, his power and leadership are unearned gifts from God; Jesus even says that it is God who revealed this answer to Peter. Leadership in the church is not earned or deserved. All too often its leaders fail to live out the holiness to which we are all called. But because it is given by God, it still has some level of trust-worthiness; the church is never left alone with the imperfection of solely human leadership.

Psalmist Preparation

The refrain of this psalm both affirms God's eternal love and then asks God not to forsake us; it operates as if God needs from us a reminder of God's own characteristics. Of course, God does not really need this reminder, but this is a common formula for prayer. We praise something about God, then we make a request that that good thing could bring about. God is generous, so we ask for God's generosity; God is powerful, so we ask that God will exert that power on our behalf. As you prepare this psalm, think about what else you regularly find yourself asking God for. Practice prefacing your requests in prayer with a word of praise or gratitude.

Making Connections

Between the readings: The first reading shows another instance of God delegating power to a human. It is not earned or deserved, but because God gives it, it is real. The key imagery is consistent between these readings, too; key holders have power because they are able to open and shut doors that others cannot. We don't always get to know why certain people have more power than others, and when it comes to church leadership, we are asked to trust that God holds the ultimate power and is really in control.

To experience: When church leadership fails us, it can often cause a crisis of faith. This is absolutely understandable, especially given the ways that we are often miscatechized about the relationship between power and holiness. But the leadership never really belonged to the imperfect humans who failed us. It is, in the end, God who gave the power and who promises to side with the lowly ones.

Homily Points

• Jesus gives the keys of the kingdom of heaven to . . . Peter? It may seem like an odd choice at first glance to anyone familiar with Peter's track record. This is the same man who Jesus calls "Satan" just a few verses later when Peter takes issue with Jesus's suffering. This is the same man who denies Jesus three times on the night when Jesus could have used support the most. Time and again, we see Peter misspeak or misstep. Yet Jesus decides that Peter is the rock upon whom he will build the church. Why?

• Jesus recognizes in Peter a deep, abiding faith. Peter believes Jesus is "the Christ, the Son of the living God," and he is not afraid to say it. Peter is not a perfect person. Jesus does not expect him to be perfect. Rather, Jesus's hope for Peter—and for all of us—is that we will faithfully witness to the truth of the living God, the Almighty One, who sent God's only son into the world out of profound love for all of creation. This is the witness upon which our church is built.

• Imagine Christ asking you the central question from today's gospel: "Who do you say that I am?" How would you respond? We cannot know the fullness of Jesus right now—the mystery of his life, death, and resurrection continues to be revealed. But like Peter, we can say with confidence that Christ is brother, friend, confidant, Redeemer, Savior, Son of the living God, and so much more.

Model Penitential Act

Presider: In today's responsorial psalm, we give praise to the Lord whose love is eternal. For the times we have not witnessed God's love in the world, let us ask for mercy and forgiveness . . . *[pause]*

Lord Jesus, you are the Christ, the Son of the living God: Lord, have mercy.

Christ Jesus, you are seated at the right hand of God: Christ, have mercy.

Lord Jesus, you will open the gates to the kingdom of heaven: Lord, have mercy.

Model Universal Prayer (Prayer of the Faithful)

Presider: Trusting in the depth of the riches and wisdom and knowledge of God, let us offer our needs and petitions.

Response: Lord, hear our prayer.

Animate Christian congregations everywhere with the joy of the Gospel . . .

Invigorate the work of teachers, administrators, ministers, and all who are getting ready for the new school year . . .

Keep safe all those who are in the path of severe weather and experiencing the effects of the climate crisis . . .

Prosper the hospitality and outreach efforts of our congregation . . .

Presider: Shepherding God, through your son, Jesus, you assure us of a home in the kingdom of heaven. Receive our prayers that by following his example we might spread love and hope to all we meet. We ask this through Christ our Lord. **Amen.**

Liturgy and Music

An Identity-Shaping Activity: A familiar question: Is this piece of music appropriate for use in this particular liturgy? Some already know the three criteria used to evaluate the quality of music for the liturgy. The USCCB guidelines are categorized as liturgical, pastoral, and musical. Read through paragraphs 126–36 of *Sing to the Lord: Music in Divine Worship,* which offers valuable information. Be mindful that these deliberations should be made with "cooperation, consultation, collaboration, and mutual respect" of those involved in preparing music for liturgy. Maintain a generous spirit in the music planning committee for imagining a diverse music program that incorporates different musical styles and genres. If liturgy is an identity marker of our Christian faith and living, then what we choose to sing and give voice to at worship shapes our collective Catholic identity.

John Bell, when interviewed about the importance of congregational singing, said, "That sense of being a corporate body comes out in the song of the church more than anything else. We are doing something together for God." Music making is a fully embodied practice. He goes on: "Congregational singing is an identity-shaping activity. . . . I think we now are in an era in which communities can be reshaped by what we sing. . . . The song of the church will tell us that. . . . Part of the job of the church is both to be faithful to God's command and to anticipate heaven" ("Sing a New Song," *The Christian Century,* July 25, 2006). Shaping identity might be added to the list of criteria when the time comes again to contemplate appropriate music for liturgy.

COLLECT

Let us pray.

Pause for silent prayer

O God, who cause the minds of the
    faithful
to unite in a single purpose,
grant your people to love what you
    command
and to desire what you promise,
that, amid the uncertainties of this world,
our hearts may be fixed on that place
where true gladness is found.
Through our Lord Jesus Christ, your Son,
who lives and reigns with you in the unity
    of the Holy Spirit,
God, for ever and ever. **Amen.**

FIRST READING
Isa 22:19-23

Thus says the LORD to Shebna, master of
    the palace:
"I will thrust you from your office
    and pull you down from your station.
On that day I will summon my servant
    Eliakim, son of Hilkiah;
I will clothe him with your robe,
    and gird him with your sash,
    and give over to him your authority.
He shall be a father to the inhabitants of
    Jerusalem,
    and to the house of Judah.
I will place the key of the House of David
    on Eliakim's shoulder;
    when he opens, no one shall shut;
    when he shuts, no one shall open.
I will fix him like a peg in a sure spot,
    to be a place of honor for his family."

RESPONSORIAL PSALM
Ps 138:1-2, 2-3, 6, 8

R̸. (8bc) Lord, your love is eternal; do not forsake the work of your hands.

I will give thanks to you, O LORD, with all my heart,
for you have heard the words of my mouth;
in the presence of the angels I will sing your praise;
I will worship at your holy temple.

R̸. Lord, your love is eternal; do not forsake the work of your hands.

I will give thanks to your name,
because of your kindness and your truth:
when I called, you answered me;
you built up strength within me.

R̸. Lord, your love is eternal; do not forsake the work of your hands.

The LORD is exalted, yet the lowly he sees,
and the proud he knows from afar.
Your kindness, O LORD, endures forever;
forsake not the work of your hands.

R̸. Lord, your love is eternal; do not forsake the work of your hands.

SECOND READING
Rom 11:33-36

Oh, the depth of the riches and wisdom and knowledge of God!
How inscrutable are his judgments and how unsearchable his ways!
For who has known the mind of the Lord
or who has been his counselor?
Or who has given the Lord anything that he may be repaid?
For from him and through him and for him are all things.
To him be glory forever. Amen.

Living Liturgy

What Kind of Identity? The act of questioning becomes part of our faith experience. It is part of our journey as liturgical and music ministers to live into the uncertainties of our vocation knowing that we neither have all the answers nor the right answer. Over these next weeks in the gospel readings, we take some time to reflect on the questions and responses of Jesus, Peter, and the disciples. It is important to discern as a whole this gospel story spread over these two weeks. The certainty and uncertainty in the answers that we hear from Peter and the disciples over these two weeks mark a path for our own ministerial responses to Jesus's questioning. This week we hear a response from Peter that is God-inspired, while next week Peter responds more from thinking not as God does but as humans do. This week Peter is exalted by Jesus and the next, he is rebuked.

Theologian and mystic Howard Thurman suggests a spirituality that embraces the mystery of life, a spirituality that does not deny the unsettling power of uncertainty. The certainty we cling to, which engages challenges and overcomes risks, is the certainty of God. Our questioning is vital to our journey of faith as we witness in this story and in our individual stories of ministerial identity. The way Peter answers and behaves should bring us hope in that we too are challenged by life's uncertainties and that our responses, while well-intentioned, might not yield the best answers.

Who do people say you are as a leader of liturgy and music? How would you describe your parish's ministerial identity? What markers are important to you as you continue to establish an inclusive identity for ministry? What kind of identity would you speak of when asked about your own personal vocation story?

PROMPTS FOR FAITH-SHARING

• Who do you say that Jesus is? Reflect on your working image of him. Which titles or characteristics stand out as prominent to you? Where might your understanding of Jesus be lacking?

• Jesus tells his disciples not to share the truth that he is the Christ; there is a time and place to proclaim, and this is not it. We, too, need to exercise prudence in deciding when and where and how to talk about our faith. We are charged with spreading the good news, but there are times when our delivery would do more harm than good. How do you discern the right times and places to talk about Jesus?

• The second reading talks about God's ways being inscrutable and unsearchable. What do you currently find most confusing about God and how God works in the world?

✦ SPIRITUALITY

Gospel

Matt 16:21-27; L124A

Jesus began to show his
    disciples
  that he must go to Jerusalem
      and suffer greatly
  from the elders, the chief
      priests, and the scribes,
  and be killed and on the
      third day be raised.
Then Peter took Jesus aside
    and began to rebuke him,
  "God forbid, Lord! No such
      thing shall ever happen
      to you."
He turned and said to Peter,
  "Get behind me, Satan! You are an
      obstacle to me.
You are thinking not as God does, but
    as human beings do."

Then Jesus said to his disciples,
  "Whoever wishes to come after me
      must deny himself,
  take up his cross, and follow me.
For whoever wishes to save his life will
    lose it,
  but whoever loses his life for my
      sake will find it.
What profit would there be for one to
    gain the whole world
  and forfeit his life?
Or what can one give in exchange for
    his life?
For the Son of Man will come with his
    angels in his Father's glory,
  and then he will repay all according
      to his conduct."

Reflecting on the Gospel

Last Sunday we heard Jesus pronounce a personal blessing over Peter when he acclaimed his master as God's Messiah. Jesus responds by naming Peter as the "rock" on which Jesus will found his church. It all sounds positive for Peter—until the next, immediate exchange in today's gospel. Flush with the new name and new responsibility, Peter today starts to exercise this role—on Jesus! He not only takes Jesus aside, but he *rebukes* him for talking of his impending death. "No such thing shall ever happen to you!"

In strong language that does not exclude love, Jesus puts Peter in his place: behind him, following him, which is the right place for every disciple. He addresses Peter as "Satan." When the rock puts himself in front of Jesus, he becomes "an obstacle" or a scandal (Greek *skándalon*). Peter's good-hearted but false interpretation of Jesus's mission is a temptation like that of Satan in the wilderness, a temptation for Jesus to follow an easier path, to have life on his own terms rather those of his Father. Peter has a long journey to make with Jesus, with much blundering along the way, before he realizes how costly the discipleship of a crucified and risen messiah will be. So Jesus explains not only to Peter, but to all disciples, that those who follow him will have to share his cross. This is not a call to self-destruction, but a challenge to find life by living with all our energies centered on God rather than on the false idol of the autonomous self which can be so dear to us, especially in circumstances of affluence and upward mobility. Jesus promises that there will be a reward for those who have done what the unselfish orientation of their lives to him and their sisters and brothers demands. This reward will be revealed at the end time when Jesus, as the Son of Man, comes for the final judgment (see Matt 25:31-46).

There is a wonderful and ecumenical tribute in stone to suffering discipleship in the very familiar West Front of Westminster Abbey. When the twenty-five-year-long restoration program of the abbey's exterior was completed in 1995, there remained a row of ten niches above the front door that had been empty for five hundred years. It was decided not to fill these with saintly or worthy figures of the past, but to proclaim the message of the costly Christian witness of those who had been willing to take up their cross and die for Christ in the twentieth century. These ten statues are of individual martyrs, some well known, others not, but the intention was to represent those who have died, and continue to die, in circumstances of oppression and persecution throughout the world. They include victims of the struggle for human rights in North and South America, those who confessed Christ and died in the Nazi and Soviet persecutions in Europe, martyrs of religious prejudice and dictatorial rule in Africa, of fanaticism on the Indian subcontinent, of brutalities during the Second World War in Asia and the Cultural Revolution in China. The statues were unveiled in 1998.

Preparing to Proclaim

Key words and phrases: "You are thinking not as God does, but as human beings do."

To the point: Last week Peter answered Jesus's question correctly and was affirmed as a conduit of divine knowledge and received the delegation of divine power. But later in the very same conversation, he messes up. He hears of God's unthinkable plan for Jesus—one that involves a horrific and humiliating death—and he responds as any of us would if a friend started talking like that. He responds with loving protectiveness; but in this case, that is not the right response. God's logic is not our own, and here Jesus introduces the contradictory idea that saving our life causes us to lose it while giving up our life enables us to find it. Mystics reconcile this contradiction by pointing out that much of what we cling to is a superficial self that gives a false sense of what life is. By letting go of all that is not real or permanent, we find our true selves, which are at home with God.

Psalmist Preparation

This psalm speaks of the sort of ardent desire for God that can aid us in following the gospel's call to deny ourselves and follow Christ. This intensity, though, is not always a predictable part of being a person of faith. Emotionally charged experiences are a gift, but emotions are a very fickle thing. A life of faith is rather built on disciplines, on sustainable practices that maintain our commitment even when the emotional payoff is low. As you prepare this psalm, think about times when you have shared the psalmist's passionate love for God. Think about how you live out that love when you do not feel it emotionally. Renew your commitment to some part of your practice of the faith, and know that doing so is an act of great love.

Making Connections

Between the readings: The first reading echoes the idea that human logic is not the same as divine logic; we can feel "duped" by God when our faith brings us humiliation in the eyes of the world. But as Jeremiah finds, God has a way of drawing us back. As St. Augustine famously wrote, our hearts remain restless until they rest in God. The second reading also affirms that the life of faith involves sacrifice. We are not to conform to this world, which means it will often not feel much like home.

To experience: The crosses we are called to take up often seem small in comparison to Christ's. But Christ walks with us even in our smallest sufferings. Even mundane moments of irritation and struggle can become moments in which we practice virtue. We can follow Christ by responding to these frustrations with patience, fortitude, and empathy for others who are involved.

Homily Points

• The sacred Triduum celebrations are likely far from our thoughts as we glory in the joys of summer. The Easter baskets are tucked away in the attic. The palms lay discreetly on our mantels. Our shift of focus makes sense. It is Ordinary Time after all—the church declares it so. And yet, the suffering, death, and resurrection of Jesus Christ anchors the Christian story year-round. We are always an Easter people, called each day to take up our crosses and follow Jesus. Today's gospel begins with the Triduum reminder—or at the time, the Triduum foreshadowing. Jesus knew the suffering, death, and resurrection that awaited him. He kept these moments always before his eyes. Formed in Christ's image, we are called to do the same.

• In today's gospel, Peter displays the misdirected confidence that can be all too prevalent in faith circles. Jesus gives Peter the keys to the kingdom of heaven and declares Peter the rock upon which he will build the church. In the very next passage, Peter takes matters into his own hands and rebukes Jesus. Peter thinks he has the authority to decide what Jesus should or should not do, who Jesus should or should not be.

• How often do we claim that same authority, declaring with mistaken confidence Jesus's intentions and actions that fit our image of the Lord? In reality, Jesus is far more radical than we may care to admit. He is far more loving, generous, and merciful that we may dare to imagine. Rather than rebuking Jesus, we are called to follow in his footsteps, to take up our crosses and find life in Christ.

Model Penitential Act

Presider: In today's second reading, St. Paul tells the people to "not conform yourselves to this age." For the times we have given into the temptations of today, let us ask for pardon and mercy . . . *[pause]*

Lord Jesus, you suffered out of great love for us: Lord, have mercy.

Christ Jesus, you died out of great love for us: Christ, have mercy.

Lord Jesus, you rose again out of great love for us: Lord, have mercy.

Model Universal Prayer (Prayer of the Faithful)

Presider: Let us place our prayers and petitions at the foot of Christ's cross with confidence.

Response: Lord, hear our prayer.

Grace the work of sanctuary churches and social services who provide aid to undocumented immigrants . . .

Foster the efforts of scientists, medical researchers, and all who are working to combat the spread of infectious diseases . . .

Bless the lives and lands of indigenous people . . .

Strengthen the will of each of us to take up our crosses and follow Jesus . . .

Presider: Liberating God, you sent your son Jesus to be our Savior and guide. Hear our prayers that by his example we live lives of service and justice. We ask this through Christ our Lord. **Amen.**

Liturgy and Music

Recruiting for Ministry: The academic year has begun for most parish communities. Parish ministries might organize a Fall Ministry Recruitment Fair around this time with informational flyers including QR codes about registering to serve in different areas of church ministry—liturgical ministries, social outreach, sacramental preparation, etc. One thing I have learned through time, however, is that the most important invitation is a personal one. Consider personally inviting young singers and instrumentalists to sing and play at liturgy. Everyone has a busy schedule so be flexible with reassigning meeting or rehearsal times.

As more young people volunteer time in ministry, ensure that all proper diocesan safety regulations have been sought and fulfilled. After doing so, set up a music ministry mentorship system where the more experienced musicians, cantors and psalmists would actively care for the musical and pastoral development of the newcomers. Sharing information and experience of ministry in a positive setting will help young musicians gain confidence in their singing, playing and ministry. Encourage mutual partnerships in these ministry friendships where one learns from the other. This kind of ministry building engages faith in a relational way and offers a collaborative ministerial experience.

COLLECT

Let us pray.

Pause for silent prayer

God of might, giver of every good gift,
put into our hearts the love of your name,
so that, by deepening our sense of
   reverence,
you may nurture in us what is good
and, by your watchful care,
keep safe what you have nurtured.
Through our Lord Jesus Christ, your Son,
who lives and reigns with you in the unity
   of the Holy Spirit,
God, for ever and ever. **Amen.**

FIRST READING
Jer 20:7-9

You duped me, O LORD, and I let myself
   be duped;
   you were too strong for me, and you
      triumphed.
All the day I am an object of laughter;
   everyone mocks me.

Whenever I speak, I must cry out,
   violence and outrage is my message;
the word of the LORD has brought me
   derision and reproach all the day.

I say to myself, I will not mention him,
   I will speak in his name no more.
But then it becomes like fire burning in
   my heart,
   imprisoned in my bones;
I grow weary holding it in, I cannot
   endure it.

RESPONSORIAL PSALM

Ps 63:2, 3-4, 5-6, 8-9

R̸. (2b) My soul is thirsting for you, O Lord my God.

O God, you are my God whom I seek;
   for you my flesh pines and my soul
      thirsts
   like the earth, parched, lifeless and
      without water.

R̸. My soul is thirsting for you, O Lord my God.

Thus have I gazed toward you in the
      sanctuary
   to see your power and your glory,
for your kindness is a greater good than
      life;
   my lips shall glorify you.

R̸. My soul is thirsting for you, O Lord my God.

Thus will I bless you while I live;
   lifting up my hands, I will call upon
      your name.
As with the riches of a banquet shall my
      soul be satisfied,
   and with exultant lips my mouth shall
      praise you.

R̸. My soul is thirsting for you, O Lord my God.

You are my help,
   and in the shadow of your wings I
      shout for joy.
My soul clings fast to you;
   your right hand upholds me.

R̸. My soul is thirsting for you, O Lord my God.

SECOND READING

Rom 12:1-2

I urge you, brothers and sisters, by the
      mercies of God,
   to offer your bodies as a living sacrifice,
   holy and pleasing to God, your spiritual
      worship.
Do not conform yourselves to this age
   but be transformed by the renewal of
      your mind,
   that you may discern what is the will
      of God,
   what is good and pleasing and perfect.

Living Liturgy

Identity in a Different Way: The gospel story today continues last week's gospel reading. Jesus calls Peter the "rock," yet Jesus also rebukes Peter as he shows the limitations of his understanding of Jesus's identity. The common view was that the Messiah would be a political figure, a king that would free Israel from Roman rule. However, Jesus reveals the identity of a true Messiah whose life and death would offer a different understanding of what it means to be the Messiah, an identity akin more to the suffering servant described by the prophet Isaiah than to a political liberator. Peter's expectation of Jesus is limited by thinking about God in human ways.

Today we also continue to think about the identity of Jesus and our own ministerial identity as liturgical and music ministers. We deliberate the difference between thinking "as God does" and "as human beings do." What expectations have we set up for God in our ministry and in our life? What expectations will you have for building community after the restful summer months?

The cost of following Jesus is not in pride and power but in holiness that is found in the love of the neighbor. When we build community, what might we imagine as markers of our Christian identity? Given Peter's responses over the past two weeks, how might we live ministry with one foot in the certainty of Christ, Son of the living God, and the other in the uncertainty of Peter's response in relation to Messianic expectation?

PROMPTS FOR FAITH-SHARING

• How does Jesus's rebuke of Peter make you feel? Do you sympathize with Peter's stance?

• What crosses are you carrying? How could your community better support you in your struggle with them?

• Have you ever had an experience where self-sacrifice returned you to yourself? Has a hard choice ever brought you to deeper authenticity and self-knowledge?

• What about God's logic is hard for you to accept?

SEPTEMBER 3, 2023
TWENTY-SECOND SUNDAY
IN ORDINARY TIME

✠ SPIRITUALITY

GOSPEL ACCLAMATION
2 Cor 5:19

R︎. Alleluia, alleluia.
God was reconciling the world to
      himself in Christ
and entrusting to us the message of
      reconciliation.
R︎. Alleluia, alleluia.

Gospel

Matt 18:15-20; L127A

Jesus said to his disciples:
  "If your brother sins against
      you,
  go and tell him his fault
      between you and him
      alone.
If he listens to you, you have
      won over your brother.
If he does not listen,
  take one or two others along
      with you,
  so that 'every fact may be
      established
on the testimony of two or
      three witnesses.'
If he refuses to listen to them, tell the
      church.
If he refuses to listen even to the
      church,
  then treat him as you would a Gentile
      or a tax collector.
Amen, I say to you,
  whatever you bind on earth shall be
      bound in heaven,
  and whatever you loose on earth
      shall be loosed in heaven.
Again, amen, I say to you,
  if two of you agree on earth
  about anything for which they are to
      pray,
  it shall be granted to them by my
      heavenly Father.
For where two or three are gathered
      together in my name,
  there am I in the midst of them."

Reflecting on the Gospel

The offering of forgiveness to a sister or brother is one of the sometimes-painful ways that we take up our cross and follow Jesus, whether in the first-century Matthean community or in today's church. In today's gospel reading, Jesus tells his disciples how this painful but healing process of forgiveness is to be conducted.

The model that Jesus presents to the disciples is one of "gospel subsidiarity," not a "pyramid" model. Subsidiarity means that we do not do something at a higher level when it can be done at a lower, in contrast to starting at the top of the pyramid with the highest authority. So the first approach in reconciliation is to be the one-to-one conversation between the offended and the offender. It is the former who is to seek out the latter, in courage and loving humility, and with no intention of a judgmental confrontation, hard as this may be.

If the person who has done wrong is deaf to the words of this initial and personal encounter, the next step to be taken is not an exasperated resignation to the misconduct: "Too bad! Now it's up to you." Rather, pastoral zeal requires that one or two other members of the community accompany the wronged one to witness the effort being made and confirm that there is a just attempt to win back the sinner without misconceptions, arbitrariness, or personal prejudice on either side. If this fails, then the matter is to be brought before the "church."

If the community cannot bring the offending member to repentance, that person is to be treated "as you would a Gentile or a tax collector." This is not, however, the harsh and permanent severance of relationships that it might at first sound to be. In the gospel context, it is a reminder that it was Gentiles and tax collectors, people on the religious and social margins, whom Jesus befriended, never giving up on his efforts with the "hundredth lost sheep." (This parable in Matt 18:12-14 comes immediately before today's reading.)

The mention of the "two or three gathered" in Jesus's name would have reminded Jewish Christians of what was said of the study of Torah, traditionally and still done together by two companions (*chaverim*): "If two or three sit together and the words of the Torah pass between them, the Divine Presence (*shekhinah*) abides between them" (tractate *'Abot* 3:2 in the Jewish Mishnah). Now, in the Spirit, the words of Jesus, his gospel teaching, must be continuously studied and prayed by the church, especially at such times of serious decision-making about the exclusion of the unrepentant sinner and the church's continuing responsibility to care for the excluded one. The risen Christ will intercede for both his community and the sinner. In the context of the faith community, such prayer makes reconciliation much more than conflict management or legal mediation. For both their own sake and that of the Christian community, troublesome people cannot just be ignored, yet this is sometimes a very real temptation for those in authority.

Preparing to Proclaim

Key words and phrases: "For where two or three are gathered together in my name, there am I in the midst of them."

To the point: In this gospel, Jesus gives us some clear directions for the on-going life in community we are still living out. Sin and offense will never be absent, even within the Christian community; our human tendency to err is too strong. But our unity is too important to let that reality stand alone. Instead, we are to strive to lovingly win back over those who have hurt us; first by ourselves, then with the support of the community. But Jesus does not tell us to withstand endless abuse; he introduces the idea here that setting boundaries can be an acceptable form of loving others. This ought to be discerned within the context of unity as an important value; gathering together in Jesus's name is one way to secure his presence.

Psalmist Preparation

The gospel addresses its instructions to those who need to correct another, but the psalm reminds us that we might also find ourselves on the other side of that exchange. All of us are sometimes the ones who need correction and forgiveness, and the psalm tells us to receive such correction with an open heart rather than defensiveness. As you prepare to proclaim this psalm, think of a time your behavior has been corrected, whether or not the correction was graciously delivered and whether or not you feel you deserved it. Strive to let go of any embarrassment or defensiveness surrounding this memory, and open your heart to the love that was hopefully behind it.

Making Connections

Between the readings: In the first reading, there is an even stronger sense of shared responsibility for sins within the community; we owe it to each other to call each other back to the Christian life. But again, our responsibility for others is limited; if they choose not to hear us, we are not called to continuously harp on what we see as their failings. And the second reading rounds out these commands; love is the context for all of this and our ultimate responsibility to each other.

To experience: This gospel implies the need not only for fraternal correction but also for forgiveness; when we inform another of the ways they have hurt us, we are meant to be truly reconciled with them rather than holding it over them or imagining ourselves morally superior. Jesus's instructions here are a recipe for letting go of grudges and moving on to fuller reconciliation.

Homily Points

• The actions we take today have ramifications for eternity. Today's gospel sets the stakes high. Jesus tells the disciples, "whatever you bind on earth shall be bound in heaven, and whatever you loose on earth shall be loosed in heaven." This line, likely a later addition to the Matthean text, describes what is allowed and not allowed in church life. It also reminds us that church life—life lived alongside fellow believers in praise and glory of Christ—does not end when we take our final breaths. We are members of the Body of Christ for eternity. Our participation in the life of the church today matters.

• Questions of church authority can be difficult to wrestle with, particularly for women and other people who rarely if ever see themselves represented in church leadership. Earlier in Matthew, Jesus grants Peter the authority to bind and loose the things of earth. Peter is the rock upon whom Jesus builds the church—and Catholics believe Peter's authority lives on through bishops.

• It is certainly true that the men who assume the chair of Peter hold significant authority. And, in today's gospel, Jesus grants the authority to bind and loose to the church at large. He promises to be present with us always. Guided by Christ's presence, every member of the church is called to claim the authority bestowed by Christ at baptism and work to make the church ever more caring, forgiving, and loving.

Model Penitential Act

Presider: In today's second reading, St. Paul proclaims that we are to "owe nothing to anyone, except to love one another." For the times we have chosen hate or indifference over love, let us ask God for mercy and pardon . . . *[pause]*

Lord Jesus, you are love incarnate: Lord, have mercy.

Christ Jesus, you came to show us the way to salvation: Christ, have mercy.

Lord Jesus, you are present when we gather in your name: Lord, have mercy.

Model Universal Prayer (Prayer of the Faithful)

Presider: Jesus calls us to be a church that listens to and prays for the needs of the world. Let us place our petitions before him.

Response: Lord, hear our prayer.

Grant all Christians the awareness and courage to claim their baptismal authority for the strengthening of the church . . .

Deliver us from political and religious authority figures who abuse their power . . .

Shine the light of your love on people who are incarcerated and their families . . .

Draw more people into the life of this gathered assembly, graced by Christ's presence . . .

Presider: Loving God, you empower each of us to proclaim the good news of your son, Jesus Christ. Receive our prayers that with faith and courage we might follow in the way of Jesus to everlasting life. We ask this through Christ our Lord. **Amen.**

Liturgy and Music

Receiving Negative Feedback: Austin Fleming's prayer for music ministers ends this way: "When your brothers and sisters / thank and praise you for your work, / take delight in the song their prayer has become, / and rejoice in the work / the Lord has accomplished through you. / Be faithful in the work you do, / for through it the Lord saves his people" ("The Ministry of Music," in *Preparing for Liturgy*).

But what happens when we receive less than positive comments on our music making? How do we react when we receive negative feedback about some aspect of our music ministry? If the comment is made anonymously, it would be best to overlook it. However, if the person offers a name, then connect with the person and listen. Listening is an important trait for ministry. You may agree or disagree with the opinion rendered and either way it will be a learning moment. Open and honest dialogue is essential in gaining trust and understanding. Our vocation in ministry calls us to greater service, to greater love of God and God's church. Approach each negative comment with gratitude and grace, take it to prayer and perhaps to a time of discernment with a close colleague. And as Fleming reminds us, the faithful work we do makes room for God to save God's people.

COLLECT

Let us pray.

Pause for silent prayer

O God, by whom we are redeemed and
    receive adoption,
look graciously upon your beloved sons
    and daughters,
that those who believe in Christ
may receive true freedom
and an everlasting inheritance.
Through our Lord Jesus Christ, your Son,
who lives and reigns with you in the unity
    of the Holy Spirit,
God, for ever and ever. **Amen.**

FIRST READING
Ezek 33:7-9

Thus says the LORD:
    You, son of man, I have appointed
        watchman for the house of Israel;
    when you hear me say anything, you
        shall warn them for me.
If I tell the wicked, "O wicked one, you
      shall surely die,"
    and you do not speak out to dissuade
        the wicked from his way,
    the wicked shall die for his guilt,
    but I will hold you responsible for his
        death.
But if you warn the wicked,
    trying to turn him from his way,
    and he refuses to turn from his way,
    he shall die for his guilt,
    but you shall save yourself.

RESPONSORIAL PSALM
Ps 95:1-2, 6-7, 8-9

R̸. (8) If today you hear his voice, harden not your hearts.

Come, let us sing joyfully to the LORD;
    let us acclaim the rock of our salvation.
Let us come into his presence with
    thanksgiving;
    let us joyfully sing psalms to him.

R̸. If today you hear his voice, harden not your hearts.

Come, let us bow down in worship;
    let us kneel before the LORD who made
    us.
For he is our God,
    and we are the people he shepherds, the
    flock he guides.

R̸. If today you hear his voice, harden not your hearts.

Oh, that today you would hear his voice:
    "Harden not your hearts as at Meribah,
    as in the day of Massah in the desert,
where your fathers tempted me;
    they tested me though they had seen
    my works."

R̸. If today you hear his voice, harden not your hearts.

SECOND READING
Rom 13:8-10

Brothers and sisters:
Owe nothing to anyone, except to love one
    another;
    for the one who loves another has
      fulfilled the law.
The commandments, "You shall not
    commit adultery;
    you shall not kill; you shall not steal;
      you shall not covet,"
    and whatever other commandment
      there may be,
    are summed up in this saying, namely,
    "You shall love your neighbor as
      yourself."
Love does no evil to the neighbor;
    hence, love is the fulfillment of the law.

Living Liturgy

Temperaments and Dispositions: Conflicts and disagreements are a natural part of community life, especially within a community of Christian believers. This Sunday's gospel reading reflects just that. Jesus does not discourage disagreement within the community of the church; he acknowledges conflict and error with all its realities and offers ways to address and resolve them. One of the many causes of breakdowns and collapses in communication in ministerial settings is burnout. While many are beginning the academic year and various ministerial programs in community with much enthusiasm and energy, the gospel today prepares us for the ongoing journey of discipleship, and how to anticipate these times of communication breakdown from ministry burnout and to think of ways to resolve conflict.

Religion professor Bobbi Patterson's study of *Building Resilience Through Contemplative Practices* gives an outline for identifying what our temperaments and dispositions in service offer to ministerial work. For example, through contemplation, dispositions of kindness and non-judgment help shape a better temperament for reaching a goal that is mindful and generous of another person's opinion. From this perspective, dispositions are malleable like soil while temperaments are mostly rock solid. Patterson tells us that "[k]nowledge of our own and others' dispositions and temperaments in service and burnout encourages us to get to know our co-volunteers and co-professionals better."

Contemplative traditions value both dispositions and temperaments. Dispositional shifts help us work through the realities we face without demanding our point of view or demeaning someone else's. Thinking about others' dispositions encourages us to team train, to learn specific skills from each other. Furthermore, considering the temperament of a co-worker or co-leader in ministry fosters diversity and encourages humility and empathy. Embrace your own temperament and disposition to find opportunities that overcome burnout.

PROMPTS FOR FAITH-SHARING

• Have you ever needed to deliver a correction to another member of the Christian community? How do you feel it went? Could you have delivered it more lovingly?

• Have you ever received correction from a peer? How did it make you feel? Did it help you improve in virtue?

• Unity is presented here as a strong value for the Christian community. What do you see as some of the primary challenges to Christian unity? How could you play a part in overcoming them?

✝ SPIRITUALITY

℟. Alleluia, alleluia.
I give you a new commandment, says
    the Lord;
love one another as I have loved you.
℟. Alleluia, alleluia.

Gospel

Matt 18:21-35; L130A

Peter approached Jesus and
    asked him,
    "Lord, if my brother sins
        against me,
    how often must I forgive?
As many as seven times?"
Jesus answered, "I say to
    you, not seven times but
    seventy-seven times.
That is why the kingdom of
    heaven may be likened to
    a king
who decided to settle
    accounts with his
    servants.
When he began the accounting,
    a debtor was brought before him who
        owed him a huge amount.
Since he had no way of paying it back,
    his master ordered him to be sold,
    along with his wife, his children, and
        all his property,
    in payment of the debt.
At that, the servant fell down, did him
    homage, and said,
    'Be patient with me, and I will pay
        you back in full.'
Moved with compassion the master of
    that servant
    let him go and forgave him the loan.
When that servant had left, he found
    one of his fellow servants
    who owed him a much smaller
        amount.

Continued in Appendix A, p. 300.

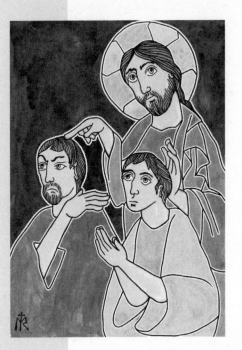

Reflecting on the Gospel

In today's gospel, Peter indulges in what he thinks is a very generous calculation in response to Jesus's call to forgiveness of a sister or brother, and he answers his own question about how many times he should do this with "seven times?" But Jesus replies with a disconcerting, "I say to you, not seven times but seventy-seven times." Such a multiple of seven, the Hebrew number symbolic of perfection or fullness, implies that forgiveness is to be "infinite" because it is to reflect God's unconditional and enduring forgiveness of us.

To help a no-doubt-deflated Peter understand more about the quality rather than the quantity of forgiveness, Jesus tells a "shocking" parable which, by its conclusion, is intended for all his followers and not only Peter. It is a drama in three acts: the dealing of the king with his high-ranking, bureaucratic slave; the dealing of that slave with his fellow slave; and the second encounter of the king and the slave in the light of what happened between the two slaves. Jesus likens membership in the kingdom of heaven to the expectation that is at the heart of the parable—namely, that forgiveness received from a loving and compassionate God, as God is named in the responsorial Psalm 103, is the basis for forgiveness offered in return to others. There can be dire consequences when such an expectation is not met.

To "forgive and forget" is usually a psychological contortion that is not humanly possible. The real challenge is to remember and forgive. Forgiveness is a personal demand of discipleship of Jesus, but in a world where we have experienced so much destructive bitterness between peoples, often bred from generation to generation, there is also a need for forgiveness among nations. Do we believe that the forgiveness the disciples offer to one another can help create a healing milieu for our world whose time we share?

In Eastern Europe, Africa, Ireland, the Middle East—and where tomorrow?—memory has so often caused hatred, not forgiveness. In his book *The Dignity of Difference*, Rabbi Jonathan Sacks writes about the pain of generations of exile, persecution, and pogroms, culminating with the Holocaust, that is written into the Jewish soul and so into their identity. It cannot be forgotten, and so he struggles: "How can I let go of that pain, when it is written into my very soul? And yet I must. For the sake of my children and theirs (the enemy's), not yet born. I cannot build their future on the hatred of the past, nor can I teach them to love God more by loving people less. Asking God to forgive me, I hear, in the very process of making that request, His demand of me that I love others. I forgive because I have a duty to my children as well as my ancestors. . . . I honor the past not by repeating it but by learning from it—by refusing to add pain to pain, grief to grief. That is why we must answer hatred with love, violence with peace, resentment with generosity of spirit and conflict with reconciliation."

Preparing to Proclaim

Key words and phrases: "I say to you, not seven times but seventy-seven times."

To the point: In this gospel, Jesus calls us to radically generous forgiveness, a magnitude of forgiveness far above Peter's guess at what generous forgiveness should be. Again, God's logic is not ours; this is not a transaction that makes sense on human terms. This is one more way that we are called to imitate God, whose mercy is boundless and to whom we owe much more than we are owed. Imitating God in forgiveness is about making us bigger; it expands our hearts so that we may participate more fully in God's life and triumph and joy. But as we saw last week, this call to generous forgiveness doesn't mean we can't have boundaries. While most of us can stand to be more forgiving, God does not will for us to put up with true abuse. Forgiveness in such cases does not mean returning to an abuser with a blank slate and allowing the abuse to happen all over again; it might instead mean coming to a place of understanding even if the relationship cannot be restored.

Psalmist Preparation

This psalm describes the bountiful mercy of God that the gospel calls us to emulate. God always gives us more than we deserve or earn, and we are called to treat others with that same generosity. Note too that God is "slow to anger" in the first place; when we do wrong, God is not moved or changed but simply keeps responding to us in love. As you prepare the psalm this week, think of a relationship in your life that could use fuller forgiveness. Ask God for strength in moving toward deeper healing and reconciliation. Know that God promises the same for you.

Making Connections

Between the readings: The first reading makes clear what the gospel hints at: forgiveness is a gift to the one forgiven, but it has an even more powerful impact on the one who forgives. When we refuse to forgive, it is our own hearts that become dry and hardened. Granting others the grace of forgiveness expands our own capacity to live out God's love and thus to become more truly ourselves.

To experience: Even Peter's question is flawed; forgiveness is rarely a discreet, countable act. Granting forgiveness is not always as simple as checking a box to accomplish time number thirteen of the seventy-seven allotted. It can be hard to know when we've "achieved" full forgiveness; old hurts sometimes come back unexpectedly, revealing that they were not as healed as we once thought. More often, it is an ongoing process, one of changing our hearts, embracing humility and compassion, and being willing to be generous with others as God is with us.

Homily Points

• Jesus practiced forgiveness that knew no bounds. Time and time again, he forgave people who hurt him or his disciples. Jesus even forgave those who sentenced him to death, crying out from the cross, "Forgive them, Father, for they know not what they do." Today's gospel challenges us to practice this same spirit of forgiveness, a spirit that is generous and ongoing.

• Jesus poses a tall task. Forgiveness is rarely easy. The need for it only comes about because of harm inflicted on another (or many others). Forgiveness reminds us that we are far from perfect. Pain is part of our realities. Given the sensitivities surrounding forgiveness, let us consider a few key points about the type of forgiveness advocated for by Jesus.

• Jesus calls his disciples to forgive their sisters and brothers "from your heart"—a practice of transformation. Forgiveness is not about forgetting, despite what the popular adage says. A real harm has been perpetrated. Jesus would never want a person to put themselves back in an abusive or dangerous situation. Rather, the act of forgiving frees a person to begin healing. Forgiveness does not always happen overnight. Sometimes the response is immediate, like when the king in today's gospel forgave the servant on the spot. But oftentimes, forgiveness is a longer process of acknowledging the harm, working through the feelings and thoughts that were provoked, and praying for God's help.

Model Penitential Act

Presider: In today's second reading, St. Paul tells us that "None of us lives for oneself, and no one dies for oneself." For the times our pride and selfishness have shielded us from embracing the gifts of others, let us ask for mercy . . . *[pause]*

Lord Jesus, you show us the way to forgiveness: Lord, have mercy.

Christ Jesus, you lift up the lowly and forgotten: Christ, have mercy.

Lord Jesus, you will come again to bring us into life everlasting: Lord, have mercy.

Model Universal Prayer (Prayer of the Faithful)

Presider: With gratitude for God's presence among us, let us place before the Lord our prayers and petitions.

Response: Lord, hear our prayer.

Bless priests who hear confessions and all those who work for healing in the church with graciousness and empathy . . .

Kindle the fires of justice in our communities, particularly in communities of color . . .

Strengthen conservation efforts and provoke people to combat the climate crisis . . .

Open our hearts to Christ's generous spirit of forgiveness . . .

Presider: Gracious God, you inspire disciples across generations to be people of mercy and hope. Receive our prayers that we may be strengthened to proclaim your word to all those we meet, today and always. We ask this through Jesus our brother. **Amen.**

Liturgy and Music

Finding God in All Things: At the beginning of each academic year on the campus where I work, the liturgy team prepares a welcome liturgy for incoming and continuing students. Much work goes into finalizing every detail. One year, just before Mass began, the main chapel lighting and sound system failed to work. Mass went on as scheduled. We sang unamplified with limited lighting streaming through the stained glass. It was beautiful.

It was beautiful because we could hear each other sing and the assembly singing (surprisingly louder and more enthusiastically) along with us, and there was something about struggling to read music in the fading light that also brought us physically and spiritually closer together. Of course, the first-year students thought this prayer experience happened at every 8 p.m. liturgy. I wish it did because it gave us a chance to pray in an unknown, unfamiliar setting where all our senses were tuned into the moment and to each other. The absence of accompaniment and additional instrumentation helped us listen to each other and for the assembly's voice, the primary music minister of the Mass. While we had done everything as liturgy team to prepare well for this liturgy, this was something we could not prepare for, and it was just this that allowed us to experience God in a fresh way, to find God in all things.

COLLECT

Let us pray.

Pause for silent prayer

Look upon us, O God,
Creator and ruler of all things,
and, that we may feel the working of your mercy,
grant that we may serve you with all our heart.
Through our Lord Jesus Christ, your Son,
who lives and reigns with you in the unity of the Holy Spirit,
God, for ever and ever. **Amen.**

FIRST READING

Sir 27:30—28:7

Wrath and anger are hateful things,
    yet the sinner hugs them tight.
The vengeful will suffer the Lord's vengeance,
    for he remembers their sins in detail.
Forgive your neighbor's injustice;
    then when you pray, your own sins will be forgiven.
Could anyone nourish anger against another
    and expect healing from the Lord?
Could anyone refuse mercy to another like himself,
    can he seek pardon for his own sins?
If one who is but flesh cherishes wrath,
    who will forgive his sins?
Remember your last days, set enmity aside;
    remember death and decay, and cease from sin!
Think of the commandments, hate not your neighbor;
    remember the Most High's covenant, and overlook faults.

RESPONSORIAL PSALM

Ps 103:1-2, 3-4, 9-10, 11-12

R℟. (8) The Lord is kind and merciful, slow to anger, and rich in compassion.

Bless the LORD, O my soul;
and all my being, bless his holy name.
Bless the LORD, O my soul,
and forget not all his benefits.

R℟. The Lord is kind and merciful, slow to anger, and rich in compassion.

He pardons all your iniquities,
heals all your ills.
He redeems your life from destruction,
he crowns you with kindness and
compassion.

R℟. The Lord is kind and merciful, slow to anger, and rich in compassion.

He will not always chide,
nor does he keep his wrath forever.
Not according to our sins does he deal
with us,
nor does he requite us according to our
crimes.

R℟. The Lord is kind and merciful, slow to anger, and rich in compassion.

For as the heavens are high above the
earth,
so surpassing is his kindness toward
those who fear him.
As far as the east is from the west,
so far has he put our transgressions
from us.

R℟. The Lord is kind and merciful, slow to anger, and rich in compassion.

SECOND READING

Rom 14:7-9

Brothers and sisters:
None of us lives for oneself, and no one
dies for oneself.
For if we live, we live for the Lord,
and if we die, we die for the Lord;
so then, whether we live or die, we are
the Lord's.
For this is why Christ died and came to
life,
that he might be Lord of both the dead
and the living.

Living Liturgy

Restoring Stability: The gospel today follows last week's gospel where Jesus teaches the disciples how to negotiate disputes and conflict with the community of Christian believers. There is a temptation to quantify forgiveness as Peter tries to do, but Jesus tells us that forgiveness is not about quantity, it is more about the depth of forgiveness. When we forgive, we must forgive one another from the heart, sincerely and abundantly. More importantly, we learn today that our own forgiveness depends on our openness to forgive others.

To forgive fully also means to restore justice and in so many ways to restore stability into our lives and to the world. The idea of restorative justice emphasizes repairing the harm of unjust behavior. It is a broader look at how punitive policy neglects the hurt experienced by victims, fails to call offenders to account and overlooks the needs of the greater community. Restorative justice attempts to describe a justice system that is rooted in human dignity, healing, and interconnectedness.

Last week we reflected on how our different temperaments and dispositions might search for hidden ways to overcome burnout in ministry, to transform hearts for resolving conflict. This week, we contemplate how forgiveness affects the broader community by activating peace over punishment through *shalom*, a universal flourishing of wholeness and delight that saves and redeems relationships. Consider some recent times when someone you are closely connected to at home or work sought your forgiveness. Were any statements made that placed conditions on forgiveness?

At the center of the gospel message today comes the desire of the community to act alongside God in showing compassion to the world. This outward radiating pattern of acting with compassion anchors all relationships within Christian community. This way of complete forgiveness, to forgive sincerely just as God has forgiven us, transforms us in our ministry to return healing stability to our lives and into our world.

PROMPTS FOR FAITH-SHARING

• Are there faults and hurts that you find easy to forgive? Are there any that you struggle to forgive fully?

• Sometimes forgiveness fully restores relationships and sometimes it moves them to a new phase with new boundaries. What does forgiveness look like in your life?

• Which relationships in your life still need forgiveness's healing power?

✝ SPIRITUALITY

GOSPEL ACCLAMATION
cf. Acts 16:14b

℟. Alleluia, alleluia.
Open our hearts, O Lord,
to listen to the words of your Son.
℟. Alleluia, alleluia.

Gospel   Matt 20:1-16a; L133A

Jesus told his disciples this parable:
   "The kingdom of heaven is like a
     landowner
  who went out at dawn to hire
     laborers for his vineyard.
After agreeing with them for the
     usual daily wage,
  he sent them into his vineyard.
Going out about nine o'clock,
  the landowner saw others standing
     idle in the marketplace,
  and he said to them, 'You too go
     into my vineyard,
  and I will give you what is just.'
So they went off.
And he went out again around noon,
  and around three o'clock, and did
     likewise.
Going out about five o'clock,
  the landowner found others standing
     around, and said to them,
  'Why do you stand here idle all day?'
They answered, 'Because no one has
     hired us.'
He said to them, 'You too go into my
     vineyard.'
When it was evening the owner of the
     vineyard said to his foreman,
  'Summon the laborers and give them
     their pay,
  beginning with the last and ending with
     the first.'
When those who had started about five
     o'clock came,
  each received the usual daily wage.
So when the first came, they thought that
     they would receive more,
  but each of them also got the usual
     wage.

Continued in Appendix A, p. 301.

Reflecting on the Gospel

Perhaps many of us can we remember what it was like to be "picked last." As children, perhaps, it was for the playground teams; as adults, it may have been an issue of promotion or missing out being on the short list after a job application. This parable is about the landowner's generosity toward the last-picked people. The scenario would be familiar to first-century Palestinian society: the

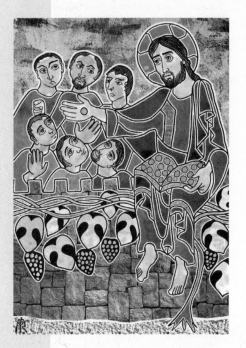

hopeful gathering of the unemployed in the marketplace, anxious for the subsistent but average daily wage of one denarius, and then the process of hiring. Everything is done justly; the wage is offered, which is neither overgenerous nor miserly, and is accepted by the laborers. As the demands of the day's work unroll, more laborers are hired in the morning and early afternoon. At the "eleventh hour" (about 5 p.m.), the landowner comes out for the last time and finds some men still hanging around hopefully. With the patient hope of the poor, the "not chosen" have stood there all day, worried that they would have to go home emptyhanded to their families.

Now comes the time for payment of the wages. The last to be hired are the first paid, because the parable requires an audience for what is coming next. There are probably some raised eyebrows and delighted nudging among those hired earlier when they do their comparative mathematical calculations. After more hours in the vineyard there will surely be more of a payoff for them. Then comes the painful grumbling from the other workers, who, it turns out, are paid the same as the "eleventh hour" workers, for more work and for working in more grueling conditions in the heat of the day. The landowner reminds one of the workers that he has been given the just wage agreed on when they were hired; the denarius is the laborer's right; generosity is the landowner's right, "because I am generous." But what earns an even stronger rebuke is the complaint that "you have made them equal to us."

The parable ends with a reversal of expectations: "The last will be first and the first will be last." We are in the territory of God's kingdom where we realize that the generosity of the landowner God reaches out to the last called as equally as to the first; that, in Jesus, God is present to the people who are poor, sick, disabled; that the tax collectors and the prostitutes all have equal access if they answer the call into the "vineyard," a symbol of God's holy people (see Ezek 17:6, 8; Hos 10:1; 14:7).

As we listen to this parable as a eucharistic community, we are powerfully reminded of the equality and solidarity of all God's laboring disciples who receive the same food at the same table. Yet are there people about whose presence we are judgmental? And outside of Mass, is our vision of our brothers and sisters darkened by envy, and even by an unexpressed suspicion of or open grumbling about God who seems to be unfair with his generosity—especially to me? Does making comparisons override being in communion?

Preparing to Proclaim

Key words and phrases: "Thus, the last will be first, and the first will be last."

To the point: A common reaction to this gospel is to feel affronted: it really does seem unfair that all the laborers receive the same wage for unequal amounts of work. But Jesus is once again telling us that God's logic does not follow ours. Our sense of justice is too small. God's generosity is always bigger than what we had envisioned, and then is bigger again still. Part of the problem is that most of us identify with the early laborers in the story. We believe we have put in the work and really deserve the good things God gives us and will give us. But none of us really deserves the gifts of God; they are not something that *can* be earned but are by their nature free and gracious gifts. And God promises us the free and undeserved generosity that the latecomers receive in this parable.

Psalmist Preparation

This psalm refrain shows the stunning generosity of God; to be near to God, all we need to do is call. God is already there awaiting our appeal. It's not as mind-bending an image as the gospel, but it's the same breathtaking truth: God's generosity far exceeds anything we could expect or imagine. As you prepare this psalm, reflect on what it means to you for God to be near. How do you know God's closeness? Are there times it is it hard to perceive? Try to find a moment or two this week that can serve as evidence of God's personal love for you, and proclaim this psalm as a prayer of thanksgiving for those moments.

Making Connections

Between the readings: The first reading reminds us in no uncertain terms that God's ways are not our ways. God operates on a different kind of logic, one which surpasses everything we would call logical but rather operates out of a love that overflows with lifegiving power. As St. Paul voices in the second reading, we are called to imitate God's ongoing self-gift. We can be united to Christ in both life and death when we strive to follow his example.

To experience: In many ways, it is fair and just that the world does not operate on the divine logic demonstrated in the gospel. Employers should *not* work like the landowner in this parable. A job that paid the same amount for an evening of labor as for a backbreaking dawn-to-dusk day would be what we call a toxic workplace. But the kingdom of heaven does not work like earth; the generosity that awaits us there is beyond our wildest imaginings.

Homily Points

• Grapes grow riper and sweeter in the autumn days leading up to harvest. Many factors impact grape growth: air temperature, sun exposure, the health of other grapes in the cluster. Even the best laborers cannot plan the perfect picking day. Vineyards need workers who are nimble, attentive, and eager to embrace the unexpected—both when it comes to picking grapes and, as we see in today's gospel, in matters of money.

• The first group of laborers in today's parable get stuck in binary thinking at payment time: Either you work a full day and get paid the usual wage, or you work part of the day and get paid part of the usual wage. But then they see the later hires get paid the full wage, and the first group makes an assumption: If those who work part of the day get the full wage, then those of us who work the full day will get the full wage plus a bonus. This thinking seems fair.

• But the landowner rebukes this reasoning—and through his actions, Jesus shows us once again: God is far too creative for binaries. God is far too mysterious for assumptions. Our God is a God of infinite possibilities, whose ways are high above the human ways to which we've grown accustomed. Our God cannot be tamed within the made-up constructs of in or out, worthy or unworthy, last or first. Our God is near to *all* who call upon the divine name in truth, no matter if we got to work at the crack of dawn or right before quitting time. Through the landowner, Jesus shows us a God eager to break down the binaries and assumptions through which we so often operate, and to build up the dignity of every person.

Model Penitential Act

Presider: Jesus calls us to be generous and merciful in all things. For the times we have not lived into this call, let us ask the Lord for forgiveness . . . *[pause]*

Lord Jesus, you are near to all who call upon you: Lord, have mercy.

Christ Jesus, you defend people who are poor and oppressed: Christ, have mercy.

Lord Jesus, you will bring all creation into the peace of everlasting life: Lord, have mercy.

Model Universal Prayer (Prayer of the Faithful)

Presider: Confident that we can turn to God for mercy and healing, let us entrust our prayers and petitions to the Lord.

Response: Lord, hear our prayer.

Inspire congregations to use their buildings, grounds, and materials in ways that show respect for the earth . . .

Sustain the work of laborers, farmers, gardeners, and all who work to draw nourishment from the gifts of the earth . . .

Give hope and success to people who are unemployed or underemployed . . .

Open our hearts to an ever-growing spirit of generosity, particularly to the people entrusted to our care . . .

Presider: Creator God, your ways are high above our ways, and still you make yourself known to us in word, sacrament, and the created world. Hear our prayers that we might grow more aware of your presence each day. We ask this through Christ our Lord. **Amen.**

Liturgy and Music

Fair Compensation: According to a 2020 report from the US Bureau of Labor Statistics, musicians earned an average of $31.40 per hour. Church music directors, however, earned a lower median pay of $25.12 per hour. How fairly are church musicians compensated? Most church musician positions are either volunteer or part-time. While the liturgy remains the most important thing that we do as a parish community, there are few full-time paid music directors working in parishes these days. Sometimes the funds just aren't available. In other cases, some parishes do not prioritize an excellent liturgical music program and settle for whomever is available to lead music, relying on part-time musicians to lead music at some Sunday liturgies and volunteers to sing at the others. Unfortunately, these methods of music ministry often result in a disconnected community, and without proper leadership and a common collection of songs and hymns to bring worshippers together, the quality of liturgy suffers.

On the flip side, as volunteer, full-time, or part-time music ministers, we must equally take seriously the call of liturgical music ministry as vocation. Yes, it is important that we are justly compensated for our time. It is also important that we take every measure to do our best work in ministry by actively deepening our faith, caring for the community we serve, preparing well for rehearsals, ongoing study, practicing our instrument, and by making the liturgy the most important thing we do each week.

COLLECT

Let us pray.

Pause for silent prayer

O God, who founded all the commands of
   your sacred Law
upon love of you and of our neighbor,
grant that, by keeping your precepts,
we may merit to attain eternal life.
Through our Lord Jesus Christ, your Son,
who lives and reigns with you in the unity
   of the Holy Spirit,
God, for ever and ever. **Amen.**

FIRST READING

Isa 55:6-9

Seek the LORD while he may be found,
   call him while he is near.
Let the scoundrel forsake his way,
   and the wicked his thoughts;
let him turn to the LORD for mercy;
   to our God, who is generous in
      forgiving.
For my thoughts are not your thoughts,
   nor are your ways my ways, says the
      LORD.
As high as the heavens are above the
   earth,
   so high are my ways above your ways
   and my thoughts above your thoughts.

RESPONSORIAL PSALM

Ps 145:2-3, 8-9, 17-18

R℣. (18a) The Lord is near to all who call upon him.

Every day will I bless you,
　and I will praise your name forever and
　　ever.
Great is the LORD and highly to be praised;
　his greatness is unsearchable.

R℣. The Lord is near to all who call upon him.

The LORD is gracious and merciful,
　slow to anger and of great kindness.
The LORD is good to all
　and compassionate toward all his
　　works.

R℣. The Lord is near to all who call upon him.

The LORD is just in all his ways
　and holy in all his works.
The LORD is near to all who call upon him,
　to all who call upon him in truth.

R℣. The Lord is near to all who call upon him.

SECOND READING

Phil 1:20c-24, 27a

Brothers and sisters:
Christ will be magnified in my body,
　whether by life or by death.
For to me life is Christ, and death is gain.
If I go on living in the flesh,
　that means fruitful labor for me.
And I do not know which I shall choose.
I am caught between the two.
I long to depart this life and be with
　Christ,
　for that is far better.
Yet that I remain in the flesh
　is more necessary for your benefit.

Only, conduct yourselves in a way worthy
　of the gospel of Christ.

Living Liturgy

Abundant Generosity: This Sunday we hear of the generosity of God. When we witness generosity given to others, we expect to receive some of that generosity as well. We bank on getting paid a just day's wage for our labor and sometimes we complain, become jealous and envious even when we receive what we have from God. Occasionally, we even think that our own efforts deserve more reward than the work of others. But God's generosity cannot be quantified and, as we discerned last week, neither can God's forgiveness. In quantifying God's generosity, we contain God within our own human terms rather than experience God within God's infinitely different ways.

The gospel invites us to think instead of justice for all. We are called to turn our attention to the poor and to care for their well-being, just as we are called to review our priorities and to educate ourselves on the root causes of poverty. Take some time this week to identify the structural barriers that perpetuate poverty in the United States. In 1964, President Lyndon B. Johnson identified some of these barriers in his *War on Poverty* speech—access to good education, good housing, nurturing family life, good healthcare and an end to racial inequality and injustice. How much have our priorities changed since tearing down this wall? What new perspectives might we envision as church community that consider the abundant generosity of God?

The landowner in the parable is exceptionally just, making sure that all are compensated fairly, just as we receive from God more than what is justifiable. Human nature foolishly compares, complains, and holds on to preconceived notions of fairness and equality. Rather than cultivating a spirit of gratitude, this way of thinking devolves into a spirit of entitlement. May we find ourselves always open to accept God's abundant love freely and generously and share that same love with others.

PROMPTS FOR FAITH-SHARING

• Do you identify more with the early risers or the latecomers in the gospel parable? How does that make you feel about the landowner's unthinkable generosity?

• Our human interactions would not be healthy if we always followed the example of this parable, but how can you bring God's generosity more fully to life?

• In the second reading, Paul writes of the fruitful labor he has left in this life. What fruitful labor do you feel God has given you? What makes you feel that you are participating in God's lifegiving work?

• The psalm promises that God's closeness is dependent only on our calling out to God; we do not need to earn God's love. When and how do you most fully know that God is close to you?

✠ SPIRITUALITY

GOSPEL ACCLAMATION
John 10:27

℟. Alleluia, alleluia.
My sheep hear my voice, says the
Lord;
I know them, and they follow me.
℟. Alleluia, alleluia.

Gospel

Matt 21:28-32; L136A

Jesus said to the chief priests
and elders of the people:
"What is your opinion?
A man had two sons.
He came to the first and said,
'Son, go out and work in the
vineyard today.'
He said in reply, 'I will not,'
but afterwards changed his
mind and went.
The man came to the other son
and gave the same order.
He said in reply, 'Yes, sir,' but
did not go.
Which of the two did his
father's will?"
They answered, "The first."
Jesus said to them, "Amen, I say to you,
tax collectors and prostitutes
are entering the kingdom of God
before you.
When John came to you in the way of
righteousness,
you did not believe him;
but tax collectors and prostitutes did.
Yet even when you saw that,
you did not later change your minds
and believe him."

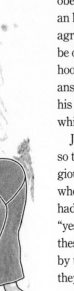

Reflecting on the Gospel

First-century Palestinian life was essentially communal. Honor was a highly prized virtue, just as shame was considered a despicable vice, and the significance of both the virtue and vice was that they were obvious to the community, as in today's parable. The first son offers an honest "no," a shameful insult to a father to whom he should be obedient. Later he regrets his response and goes obediently into the vineyard. The second son gets an honorable approval rating when he readily agrees to his father's request, but this turns out to be only lip service. Then Jesus puts in the parable hooks and drags the chief priests and elders into answering his question as to which of the sons did his father's will. They cannot escape the reply in which Jesus has netted them: "The first."

Jesus then makes an application of the parable so that it reflects the shameful action of the religious leaders and the honorable response of those whom they despised and ostracized. The leaders had seen tax collectors and prostitutes say their "yes" to the Baptist's call to repentance. Both of these groups were considered shameful, especially by the Jewish religious and civil leaders, because they collaborated with the Romans, one through employment in the imperial tax system, the other by providing sexual services to their clients, many of whom were Roman soldiers. The tax collectors and prostitutes who repented would go into the kingdom before the chief priests and elders, says Jesus. It is important to note that the marginalized people whose hearts were changed will *precede* the chief priests and elders; Jesus does not exclude them definitively. The door will always be left open for anyone who repents. The kingdom is to be inclusive, and the early history of the church shows that many of the priests became "obedient to the faith" and entered the Christian community (Acts 6:7).

So often it is easy to say an initial "yes" when fervor is high, failure seems impossible, and the future looks golden. But time passes, the enthusiasms cool, the relationships that have to endure through the long haul of married love, the promises of friendship or vocation have to be truthfully discerned and embraced every day, and the original "yes" is repeated—not with an initial blaze but with the burning embers that are daily fanned by our fidelity, in good times and bad.

We may have been disillusioned in recent years by those in the church who have failed in integrity, respect for their flock, or management of abuse accusations, but no matter how tragic these revelations have been for both the victims and the church, we need to remember what today's parable tells us: that the kingdom door is never closed; that we are all an imperfect "yes and no" community of disciples no matter what our role in the church, and that we are people for whom not only one but many changes of heart and conversion to the Father's will are possible and necessary.

Preparing to Proclaim

Key words and phrases: "He said in reply, 'I will not,' but afterwards changed his mind and went."

To the point: This week's gospel finds us in another parable and another vineyard. We're still talking about the exceeding generosity of God and how it surpasses all our hopes and imaginings. Here, it is about second chances, and it is good news for all of us. Life brings countless opportunities to fail to do right, and all of us fail sometimes. But it is never too late to change course, and we are never too far gone to come back. God's love reaches far beyond what we expect; in fact, our limited imaginations often cause us to exclude daughters and sons with whom God is well pleased. God's love is not limited to those who appear to be living moral and religious lives; it most fully embraces those on the margins of what we and our too-small imaginations have deemed acceptable.

Psalmist Preparation

Note who God teaches in the last verse of this psalm: it is the humble whom God guides to justice and to whom God teaches his way. Those who are proud are not able to receive guidance, for they believe they know what they need to know and so their hearts are hardened to learning more. Those who are humble are able to receive God's guidance and teaching; their hearts are oriented to learn. As you prepare this psalm, reflect on what humility means to you. How can you cultivate this virtue so that you might be more receptive to what God wants to teach you?

Making Connections

Between the readings: The first reading stresses again that God does not think like us; divine logic is based on love. Our human notions of "fairness" are only marginally related to the true justice that God is bringing about. The second reading takes up a similar theme; we are not only to love others as ourselves but to see them as *more* important than we are. This is illogical and does not fit into the human way of being in the world, but it imitates the lavish love that God offers to all of us.

To experience: In the gospel, neither brother acts with complete honesty or integrity; it would be nice if there were a son who obeyed his father in both word and deed. Perhaps this is pointing to the fact that none of us is perfect, that all of us are in need of God's generous mercy. We don't always think of ourselves as being needy before God; we would like to believe we have merited the good things God gives us. But this gospel challenges us to remember to receive them all as gifts given freely.

Homily Points

• How open are we to changing our minds? We are often told to stay in our camps in today's deeply divided political and social climate. Shouting matches replace civil debate in many pockets of the community. To some, changing one's mind is a sign of weakness or disloyalty. Jesus takes a different stance in today's gospel.

• Changing one's mind is a point of growth for the first son. After an initial decline, he does as his father says and goes to work in the vineyard. The first son ultimately makes a good decision, even if he started off on a rocky foot. The second son, meanwhile, appears to be in alignment with his father's wishes. He gives a suitable answer, presumably because he knew what should be done. But in the end, his actions do not live up to his words. Talk is cheap when it is not followed up by actions. Today's gospel invites us to consider who is worthy to enter the kingdom of God—and to beware that the answer might not be apparent at first glance.

• Jesus celebrates when we change our minds. The one who God greatly exalted, who emptied himself and took the form of a slave out of love for us, longs for us to draw closer to him. Are there areas of your life that could use a change or a different answer? What will it take for such a conversion to happen? Let us ask the Lord for help and healing.

Model Penitential Act

Presider: In today's second reading, St. Paul calls the people to "[d]o nothing out of selfishness or out of vainglory." For the times we have put ourselves before others, let us ask for healing and mercy . . . *[pause]*

Lord Jesus, you emptied yourself and took on the form of a slave: Lord, have mercy.

Christ Jesus, you became obedient to the point of death on a cross: Christ, have mercy.

Lord Jesus, you are exalted to the glory of God: Lord, have mercy.

Model Universal Prayer (Prayer of the Faithful)

Presider: Strengthened by the word of God, let us place before the Lord our prayers and the prayers of the world.

Response: Lord, hear our prayer.

Guide the work of the World Council of Churches and all ecclesial bodies striving for greater unity among Christians . . .

Enlighten local and national politicians to develop stronger responses to the needs of the most vulnerable . . .

Comfort people who are hospitalized or in long-term care . . .

Open our minds and hearts to the word of God and the divine presence in our world . . .

Presider: Gracious God, you open the way to eternal life to your beloved creation. In you rests all our hope. Receive our prayers that we might grow in openness and fidelity each day. We ask this through Christ our Lord. **Amen.**

Liturgy and Music

Prayer of St. Francis: The importance of placing words into action is what we learn from the gospel today. When we apply this to our music ministry, we bring a closer awareness to the hymn texts of song lyrics that we sing and think about how we might practice these words we sing more intentionally in everyday living. Think about what it means to authentically live the words of the Prayer of St. Francis, which in many ways lay bare our human imperfection and search for wholeness.

Take for example the phrase "to be understood as to understand." Have we taken a position on an issue or made a decision in our ministry where we expect others to agree? In reverse, have we taken time to fully understand the person whose thoughts and convictions are different from ours on a particular topic? How do we activate in our lives these Franciscan words of understanding and being understood?

Notice in the prayer text of Francis that the word "pardon" is repeated. Why? Have we thought about the ways in which we might bridge differences through taking the humble stand of asking for forgiveness? Or are we struggling to forgive? Take time, as we do with Scripture, to allow God's Spirit to bring clarity to our reflection on the song texts that we sing and not to take for granted the faithful work that comes from engaging in these words.

COLLECT

Let us pray.

Pause for silent prayer

O God, who manifest your almighty power
above all by pardoning and showing
    mercy,
bestow, we pray, your grace abundantly
    upon us
and make those hastening to attain your
    promises
heirs to the treasures of heaven.
Through our Lord Jesus Christ, your Son,
who lives and reigns with you in the unity
    of the Holy Spirit,
God, for ever and ever. **Amen.**

FIRST READING
Ezek 18:25-28

Thus says the LORD:
You say, "The LORD's way is not fair!"
Hear now, house of Israel:
    Is it my way that is unfair, or rather, are
        not your ways unfair?
When someone virtuous turns away from
        virtue to commit iniquity, and dies,
    it is because of the iniquity he
        committed that he must die.
But if he turns from the wickedness he
      has committed,
    and does what is right and just,
    he shall preserve his life;
    since he has turned away from all the
        sins that he has committed,
    he shall surely live, he shall not die.

RESPONSORIAL PSALM
Ps 25:4-5, 6-7, 8-9

R̸. (6a) Remember your mercies, O Lord.

Your ways, O LORD, make known to me;
    teach me your paths,
guide me in your truth and teach me,
    for you are God my savior.

R̸. Remember your mercies, O Lord.

Remember that your compassion, O LORD,
    and your love are from of old.
The sins of my youth and my frailties
    remember not;
    in your kindness remember me,
    because of your goodness, O LORD.

R̸. Remember your mercies, O Lord.

Good and upright is the LORD;
 thus he shows sinners the way.
He guides the humble to justice,
 and teaches the humble his way.

R̂. Remember your mercies, O Lord.

SECOND READING
Phil 2:1-11

Brothers and sisters:
If there is any encouragement in Christ,
 any solace in love,
 any participation in the Spirit,
 any compassion and mercy,
 complete my joy by being of the same
   mind, with the same love,
 united in heart, thinking one thing.
Do nothing out of selfishness or out of
   vainglory;
 rather, humbly regard others as more
   important than yourselves,
 each looking out not for his own
   interests,
 but also for those of others.

Have in you the same attitude
 that is also in Christ Jesus,
   Who, though he was in the form of
     God,
    did not regard equality with God
     something to be grasped.
   Rather, he emptied himself,
    taking the form of a slave,
    coming in human likeness;
    and found human in appearance,
    he humbled himself,
    becoming obedient to the point of
      death,
    even death on a cross.
   Because of this, God greatly exalted him
    and bestowed on him the name
    which is above every name,
    that at the name of Jesus
    every knee should bend,
    of those in heaven and on earth
      and under the earth,
    and every tongue confess that
    Jesus Christ is Lord,
    to the glory of God the Father.

or Phil 2:1-5

See Appendix A, p. 301.

Living Liturgy

To Preach and to Practice: You may remember a quote attributed to St. Francis of Assisi, "Preach the gospel at all times. When necessary, use words." Whether the saint said this or not, this quote has taken hold of our imagination and allowed us to reflect on the quality of our ministerial efforts. While we embrace the wisdom of these words or reject it as compromise, it is hard to deny the deep commitment to preaching and practice, or to proclamation and embodiment of the gospel message.

Today we hear "actions speak louder than words," which reminds us of the inconsistencies present in some way within our lives and Christian ministries. The reminder comes in being consistent about both worshipping God and following Christ, and the journey to that meeting point which must include a conversion of the heart offered by John the Baptist. What we say ought to inform and manifest in what we do. When these two are in conflict (saying and doing), our witness of faith is compromised and those who seek to belong to our community (especially younger seekers) receive, at best, an incoherent message and, at worst, an insincere one. A change of mind should be accompanied by a change of heart. How might we send a clear message of faith and action through the work of worship and liturgical ministry?

In truth, a change of heart resists the temptation to sustain places of power and privilege, which compromises authority and credibility. In the example of St. Francis of Assisi, imagine the radical life of peace, grace, and love characterized by Christ, bringing community together, a gathering of believers that practice humility and love over self-righteousness and bigotry. Our words and actions in ministry hope to carry God's love through these more nuanced words attributed to the saint, "It is no use walking anywhere to preach unless our walking is our preaching."

PROMPTS FOR FAITH-SHARING

• Do you identify more with the first or second son in Jesus's parable? Do you feel frustration or relief at this gospel passage?

• Do you identify more with the chief priests and elders that Jesus addresses or the tax collectors and prostitutes whose place in the kingdom he affirms? Why do you think that is?

• In what ways do you feel you succeed in answering the second reading's call to look out for the interests of others? In what ways could you improve?

OCTOBER 1, 2023
TWENTY-SIXTH SUNDAY IN ORDINARY TIME

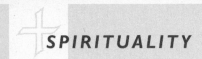

SPIRITUALITY

R̸. Alleluia, alleluia.
I have chosen you from the world, says
the Lord,
to go and bear fruit that will remain.
R̸. Alleluia, alleluia.

Gospel   Matt 21:33-43; L139A

Jesus said to the chief priests
and the elders of the people:
"Hear another parable.
There was a landowner who
planted a vineyard,
put a hedge around it, dug a
wine press in it, and built
a tower.
Then he leased it to tenants and
went on a journey.
When vintage time drew near,
he sent his servants to the
tenants to obtain his
produce.
But the tenants seized the
servants and one they beat,
another they killed, and a
third they stoned.
Again he sent other servants, more
numerous than the first ones,
but they treated them in the same way.
Finally, he sent his son to them, thinking,
'They will respect my son.'
But when the tenants saw the son, they
said to one another,
'This is the heir.
Come, let us kill him and acquire his
inheritance.'
They seized him, threw him out of the
vineyard, and killed him.
What will the owner of the vineyard do to
those tenants when he comes?"
They answered him,
"He will put those wretched men to a
wretched death
and lease his vineyard to other tenants
who will give him the produce at the
proper times."

Reflecting on the Gospel

Absentee landowners were well known to Galilean peasants. Sometimes they would rent out their land to tenant farmers who worked the land and then received a certain meager percentage of the crop's return. At harvest time, the owner's agents would be sent to collect his dues. The vineyard in the parable we hear today—the third of a trilogy of vineyard parables; we heard the first two over the past two Sundays—has been created by the landowner God who planted it, protected it, built a winepress in it for the crushing of the grapes and a watchtower from which to guard it. With our biblical antennae well-tuned after three weeks, we recognize the vineyard as Israel and the landowner's servants who are sent to collect the fruit of the harvest as the prophets who were mistreated and abused (see 2 Chr 24:21-22).

Finally, after the repeated sending of servants, the landowner's son is sent with the full authority of his Father, only to be killed by the tenant farmers. Jesus is the last and greatest of the line of servant prophets who are resisted by the chief priests and elders who attempt to usurp control over the people of God. But the vineyard is not destroyed; only those who failed in their stewardship of God's precious possession are punished.

The parable stresses the need to bear fruit, which in Matthew is a metaphor for productive, life-giving conduct that results from repentance and the conversion to kingdom living. This conversion was preached by John the Baptist (Matt 3:8, 10) and Jesus (Matt 7:16, 20). Jesus asks the chief priests and elders two boomerang type of questions: one that comes back to hit them with their role as failing tenants of God's vineyard; the other, a quotation from Psalm 118:22-23 and a returning challenge to accept Jesus as the authoritative interpreter of the Hebrew Scriptures. Heard in Matthew's and our postresurrection communities, these words affirm that Jesus, the rejected stone, has become the cornerstone that holds together the walls of the building of living stones (Acts 4:11; 1 Pet 2:7).

This parable offers a warning to those who are unproductive and bear no fruit, especially at vintage time when the Son of Man will come to claim the harvest of our lives in the gospel. Do we believe that suffering and rejection in our own lives can be a way of following the Servant Son who is the beloved of the Vineyard God and whose rising to new life is the Lord's own doing, which we will share if we share his sufferings? Are we possessive rebels who want people and possessions to serve our own ambitions, with no thought of offering service or dispossessing ourselves for the sake of others? Can we honestly recognize that by our hypocrisy or integrity, our deafness to the prophets in our own times, we run the risk of becoming self-condemned tenants of God's vineyard? And in a post-Holocaust age when interfaith dialogue is so important, are we making any attempts to be involved in, or at least supportive of, such rapprochement?

Continued in Appendix A, p. 301.

Preparing to Proclaim

Key words and phrases: "[B]y the Lord has this been done, / and it is wonderful in our eyes"

To the point: The image of God as a vineyard keeper continues this week, and the harvest imagery grows stronger as the Northern Hemisphere enters more firmly into fall. To Jesus's audience, this parable would have been head-scratchingly mysterious, but for those of us who know the rest of Jesus's story, it foreshadows the passion rather chillingly. But good news still prevails. God's life-giving and saving work does not end when human wickedness tries to stand in its way. Amidst all the pain and brokenness and suffering of this sin-burdened world, God finds ways to continue to give life and bear fruit. God is persistent, not only in carrying out God's plans but also in loving us. God wins and will have final victory, even when it is not apparent. And because God is always on our side, this is very good news.

Psalmist Preparation

This psalm reminds us of the ever-enduring faithfulness of God. Composed during a time of exile, this psalm expresses confidence in God's desire to love us and make us fruitful, even when we have failed to do so in the past. Even when all seems lost, God is on our side, never willing to fully abandon those he created out of love. This psalm calls on God to offer another chance, to enact the abundant generosity we have seen in so many of the readings of these last weeks. As you prepare this psalm, think about where you need God's generosity to become more apparent in your life. Bring your needs and desires fully before God in prayer; God can handle even the pain with which you might bring them. Sing these verses with the yearning of Israel far from home, longing to be reunited with God's special presence in the temple.

Making Connections

Between the readings: The first reading echoes the vineyard imagery that has been so strong in the gospels of the past several weeks. Israel is the vineyard that God refuses to give up on; life and love will win out over human failure to participate in them. The second reading balances the anxiety that might be produced by the harsh judgments of the other readings. Paul reassures us that God is a God of peace, who remains with us whenever we choose what is true and good and beautiful.

To experience: This is a parable where it can be hard to identify strongly with any characters. Were it not for Jesus's direct second-person "the kingdom of God will be taken away from you," we might not know what we are supposed to take from it. But yes, even we are prone to rejection of God's messengers and even God's Son. But God never stops trying to reach us, determined to make us partners in bringing forth life.

Homily Points

• We continue the series of gospel parables this week, with a landowner and his tenants taking center stage. Today's story reads harsh: tenants who are supposed to be caring for the land decide to seize and kill the people whom the landowner sent to obtain his produce, first the servants and then the landowner's very son. The tenants are ruthless in their rejection—and Jesus insists that they will pay for their stance.

• As with all parables, the meaning extends beyond the story itself. A first clue of what Jesus may have meant by this parable comes at the very beginning. Jesus addresses the parable to the chief priests and elders of the people. He wants these religious leaders to hear the consequences that come with rejecting the work of the gospel—and even more, the person who embodies the gospel. Note that the tenants do not attack the produce. They attack the people who come to collect it, even the landowner's own son.

• We can draw parallels between the landowner's son and Jesus, the Son of God. In telling this parable, Jesus reminds the religious leaders that the kingdom of God comes as a person—Jesus. Their ministries must always draw people to the truth of Jesus. Those who try to turn Jesus into something he is not will face dire consequences. This is true for all of us. We are called to embrace the fullness of Christ, for it is only through him that we might one day enter the kingdom of God.

Model Penitential Act

Presider: In today's second reading, St. Paul tells the people to "make your requests known to God" in everything. For the times we have turned away from God, let us ask for mercy and forgiveness . . . *[pause]*

Lord Jesus, you are the way of truth: Lord, have mercy.

Christ Jesus, you are worthy of all praise: Christ, have mercy.

Lord Jesus, you promise us a share of everlasting life: Lord, have mercy.

Model Universal Prayer (Prayer of the Faithful)

Presider: Trusting in God's endless compassion for the world and its many needs, let us bring our prayers and petitions to the Lord.

Response: Lord, hear our prayer.

Embolden the church to combat the clerical abuse crisis and aid in the care of survivors of abuse . . .

Raise up young people into leadership roles within the church and society at large . . .

Fill people struggling with mental illness with the peace of God that surpasses all understanding . . .

Awaken in this community of faith the gifts of stewardship and respect . . .

Presider: Gracious God, you sent your son to lead us and teach us the ways to your kingdom. Hear our prayers that we might listen to his voice and allow our hearts to be transformed by the joy of the gospel. We ask this through Christ our Lord. **Amen.**

Liturgy and Music

Contemplative Prayer with Mary: October is the month of the rosary. We are aware that Mary's song, the perennial *Magnificat*, sings of breaking barriers of cultural stereotypes, of overcoming adversity and oppression through prayer, praise, and willing action. During this month, think of incorporating Marian songs in the liturgy as choral prelude or as song for the preparation of the gifts as a meditation piece.

If we aren't familiar with praying the rosary and devotion to Mary, study and spend some time in catechesis with the group. We learn from the gospel the importance of producing good fruit for building the kingdom of God and we reflect on this phrase of the *Hail Mary*: "And blessed is the fruit of your womb, Jesus."

We connect in contemplative prayer our actions in ministerial discipleship with the Blessed Virgin Mary's openness to God's will. This time of prayer allows us to engage in mystery. Reflect on the Luminous Mysteries or the Mysteries of Light instituted by St. John Paul II in 2002 in his apostolic letter *Rosarium Virginis Mariae*, and walk through key aspects of Jesus's ministry and life on earth meditating on the significance of each story in our own ministry of liturgical music. John Paul II says: "With the Rosary, the Christian people *sits at the school of Mary* and is led to contemplate the beauty on the face of Christ and to experience the depths of his love."

COLLECT

Let us pray.

Pause for silent prayer

Almighty ever-living God,
who in the abundance of your kindness
surpass the merits and the desires of
    those who entreat you,
pour out your mercy upon us
to pardon what conscience dreads
and to give what prayer does not dare to
    ask.
Through our Lord Jesus Christ, your Son,
who lives and reigns with you in the unity
    of the Holy Spirit,
God, for ever and ever. **Amen.**

FIRST READING

Isa 5:1-7

Let me now sing of my friend,
    my friend's song concerning his vineyard.
My friend had a vineyard
    on a fertile hillside;
he spaded it, cleared it of stones,
    and planted the choicest vines;
within it he built a watchtower,
    and hewed out a wine press.
Then he looked for the crop of grapes,
    but what it yielded was wild grapes.

Now, inhabitants of Jerusalem and people
    of Judah,
    judge between me and my vineyard:
What more was there to do for my vineyard
    that I had not done?
Why, when I looked for the crop of grapes,
    did it bring forth wild grapes?
Now, I will let you know
    what I mean to do with my vineyard:
take away its hedge, give it to grazing,
    break through its wall, let it be trampled!
Yes, I will make it a ruin:
    it shall not be pruned or hoed,
    but overgrown with thorns and briers;
I will command the clouds
    not to send rain upon it.
The vineyard of the LORD of hosts is the
    house of Israel,
    and the people of Judah are his
        cherished plant;
he looked for judgment, but see,
    bloodshed!
    for justice, but hark, the outcry!

RESPONSORIAL PSALM

Ps 80:9, 12, 13-14, 15-16, 19-20

℟. (Isaiah 5:7a) The vineyard of the Lord is the house of Israel.

A vine from Egypt you transplanted;
   you drove away the nations and planted
     it.
It put forth its foliage to the Sea,
   its shoots as far as the River.

℟. The vineyard of the Lord is the house
of Israel.

Why have you broken down its walls,
   so that every passer-by plucks its fruit,
the boar from the forest lays it waste,
   and the beasts of the field feed upon it?

℟. The vineyard of the Lord is the house of
Israel.

Once again, O LORD of hosts,
   look down from heaven, and see;
take care of this vine,
   and protect what your right hand has
     planted,
   the son of man whom you yourself
     made strong.

℟. The vineyard of the Lord is the house of
Israel.

Then we will no more withdraw from you;
   give us new life, and we will call upon
     your name.
O LORD, God of hosts, restore us;
   if your face shine upon us, then we
     shall be saved.

℟. The vineyard of the Lord is the house of
Israel.

SECOND READING
Phil 4:6-9

Brothers and sisters:
Have no anxiety at all, but in everything,
   by prayer and petition, with
     thanksgiving,
   make your requests known to God.
Then the peace of God that surpasses all
    understanding
   will guard your hearts and minds in
    Christ Jesus.

Finally, brothers and sisters,
   whatever is true, whatever is honorable,
   whatever is just, whatever is pure,
   whatever is lovely, whatever is gracious,
   if there is any excellence
   and if there is anything worthy of
     praise,
   think about these things.
Keep on doing what you have learned and
    received
   and heard and seen in me.
Then the God of peace will be with you.

Living Liturgy

To Bear Fruit: We hear another parable today. This story and the writings of the prophets shake us from complacency to take account of our duties in ministry. In connection with last week's challenge, we are urged into action again; this time, to produce good fruit for kingdom building. The gospel invites us to think of the importance of listening to God's word in relation to bearing fruit as God speaks through Scripture, through the church's tradition and teaching, and through modern-day prophets. The Letter to the Philippians gives us some description of good fruit—whatever is true, honorable, just, pure, lovely and gracious. Jesus exposes the religious leaders for their failure to heed God's messengers. How do we respond through our ministry work to those who are God's messenger's today?

Let us now consider a modern-day prophet. Breaking down racial and cultural barriers, Sr. Thea Bowman, an educator and prophet of our time, vowed to "live until I die" as a steward of God's gifts of joy and love. In 1984, reluctant to let the pain of cancer further deteriorate her body and spirit, she spoke to the USCCB and enlightened church leaders to what it meant to live as Black and Catholic, and of the history and spirituality of the Black Catholic community. She explained the importance of continuing to evangelize the African American community, promoting inclusivity and full participation of African Americans within church leadership and understanding the necessity and value of Catholic schools in the Black community. Sister Thea's profound spiritual impact and example of holiness continue to bear good fruit through schools, an education foundation to assist students in need, housing units for the poor and elderly, and a health clinic named in her honor for people who are marginalized. How might we seize the opportunity from today's gospel to consider how we respond to God's messengers today? Would we also consider being witnesses and messengers for kingdom building?

PROMPTS FOR FAITH-SHARING

• What fruit is God calling you to bear in your life? What keeps you from fully producing this fruit?

• Are there "stones" in your life you might inadvertently be rejecting? In other words, are there things in your life that God might be building with in unexpected ways? People you overlook? Qualities you dislike about yourself?

• The second reading reminds us that God is a God of peace; peace is what God wants for us. Where do you need God's peace in your life?

✠ SPIRITUALITY

GOSPEL ACCLAMATION
cf. Eph 1:17-18

℟. Alleluia, alleluia.
May the Father of our Lord Jesus Christ
enlighten the eyes of our hearts,
so that we may know what is the hope
that belongs to our call.
℟. Alleluia, alleluia.

Gospel   Matt 22:1-14; L142A

Jesus again in reply spoke to the chief
    priests and elders of the people
  in parables, saying,
  "The kingdom of heaven may be
      likened to a king
  who gave a wedding feast for his son.
He dispatched his servants
  to summon the invited guests to the
      feast,
  but they refused to come.
A second time he sent other servants,
    saying,
  'Tell those invited: "Behold, I have
      prepared my banquet,
  my calves and fattened cattle are
      killed,
  and everything is ready; come to the
      feast."'
Some ignored the invitation and went away,
  one to his farm, another to his business.
The rest laid hold of his servants,
  mistreated them, and killed them.
The king was enraged and sent his troops,
  destroyed those murderers, and burned
      their city.
Then he said to his servants, 'The feast is
    ready,
  but those who were invited were not
      worthy to come.
Go out, therefore, into the main roads
  and invite to the feast whomever you find.'
The servants went out into the streets
  and gathered all they found, bad and good
      alike,
  and the hall was filled with guests.

Continued in Appendix A, p. 302, or
Matt 22:1-10 *in Appendix A, p. 302.*

Reflecting on the Gospel

In this Sunday's gospel, we are still in the temple precincts in the same company as the last two Sundays: with the chief priests and elders of the people. In this context, Jesus tells a parable about a wedding and the crises that result from the refusal of the invited guests to attend. It is obviously an allegory, a story that speaks of one thing yet signifies something else.

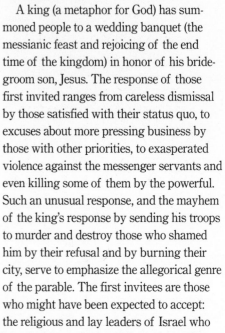

A king (a metaphor for God) has summoned people to a wedding banquet (the messianic feast and rejoicing of the end time of the kingdom) in honor of his bridegroom son, Jesus. The response of those first invited ranges from careless dismissal by those satisfied with their status quo, to excuses about more pressing business by those with other priorities, to exasperated violence against the messenger servants and even killing some of them by the powerful. Such an unusual response, and the mayhem of the king's response by sending his troops to murder and destroy those who shamed him by their refusal and by burning their city, serve to emphasize the allegorical genre of the parable. The first invitees are those who might have been expected to accept: the religious and lay leaders of Israel who should have heard the call of God through the prophets and through the Hebrew Scriptures. But they reject God's invitation. The invitation is now offered to the street people: the beggars, the prostitutes, the socially outcast and vulnerable. Allegorically, the invitation passes to the Gentiles.

There will be a judgment about the worthiness of the guests because participation in the wedding feast of the Son means more than just showing up. Such judgment, however, belongs to the king, who comes into the assembly of guests and finds there someone "not dressed in a wedding garment." Again, the allegorical nature of the parable is obvious. "Clothing" is often a metaphor for good works and faithful discipleship. Those who wish to share the Son's wedding feast must always be clothed and ready in this way of love.

Like Matthew's community, as a church we are also servants sent out to invite others to the wedding feast, to proclaim that God's door is always open and welcoming. Our mission is not to judge, but to carry the message to our streets and workplaces, and suffer unconcern, ridicule, and sometimes even persecution for the sake of the King and his Son. But we are also the invited guests. Do we reject the invitation because of priorities that disregard the Gospel: addiction to personal success, selfishness, materialism, fear of judgment of others rather than mercy for them? At the feast of the Eucharist, do we just show up, not caring much about the guests around us, not caring if we are clothed in love for God and our sisters and brothers, just partaking of the bread and wine but not offering ourselves to others, both present and absent, as broken bread and drained wine for their nourishment? And does all this make our baptismal clothing tattered and grubby, unfit for a holy feast?

Preparing to Proclaim

Key words and phrases: "Behold, I have prepared my banquet . . . come to the feast."

To the point: This Sunday, we also begin to see the eschatological themes that will be with us through the end of the church year. They begin on a hopeful note, one in which it is clear that God wants to provide for our needs and have us partake in all that God can offer. In this parable, we see the end game of the lavish generosity the last few weeks' parables have been hinting at. This is more than absurdly recurrent forgiveness and illogical wages. This is a feast, a party. For celebration is the appropriate response when we realize who God is, one whose entire way of being is extravagant, lavish with generosity, and whose whole all-powerful self is constantly spilling forth in self-gift. No one is excluded from this invitation unless they exclude themselves. God's loving abundance is for all.

Psalmist Preparation

We've heard this psalm several times throughout the liturgical year; it echoes this week's other readings as another beautiful image of the abundant care God has for us. God promises us fullness and rest and vibrant, plentiful life. Our final goal is life with God, a life in which all our needs will be cared for and tended to. As part of your preparation to proclaim this psalm, be sure to spend some time with the other readings for the week to round out your image of the abundant feast that God prepares and wills for all of us. Spend some prayer time envisioning yourself in these scenes.

Making Connections

Between the readings: The first reading gives us a foretaste of the gospel's feast: God provides and God provides abundantly. We are not provided just the bread and water we need to live; this is a tasty, lavish feast. It tends to not just our bare physical needs but to our emotional ones, too: God removes our guilt and wipes away our tears. The second reading also assures us of God's providence; God has all we need (and all we could ever want) and God's "glorious riches" are there to provide for our needs.

To experience: Many of us hesitate to ask God for too much; we strive to pray for the "right" things so that we will not be too disappointed if our desires aren't met. But God already knows all our needs and all our desires and all our thoughts; bringing them to prayer is a way of growing our knowledge of God, not God's knowledge of us. Our neediness before God is an unchangeable and indisputable fact; our acknowledgment of it is simply a way to grow in humility.

Homily Points

• Today's readings highlight the covenant relationship between God and the chosen people. The reading from the prophet Isaiah showcases the joy that can come from a life dedicated to the Lord. God will provide for God's chosen people. Every tear will be wiped away. Death will no longer have the final say. The people look to the Lord in awe and wonder: "This is the LORD for whom we looked; / let us rejoice and be glad that he has saved us!"

• Today's gospel highlights a different side of the covenant relationship. God desires to have a people and to provide a rich banquet for them. God expects the chosen people to show up. Covenant relationships must go both ways. God provides for the people—and the people must obey God. Obedience has never been the easiest practice. People then and now get busy, make other plans, and rebel against powers that appear to tread on their freedom. The chosen people in the parable reject the king's invitation—so the king calls others to the feast and warns the chosen ones of their impending doom. Obeying God matters. Showing up for significant relationships matters.

• Today's readings may challenge us to reflect on the ways we show up for God—and the ways we fall short. We are members of God's chosen people today, baptized into the life of Christ and his church. May our minds and hearts be open to God's gracious invitation.

Model Penitential Act

Presider: Jesus calls us to answer his invitation to be people of peace and goodwill. Knowing that we can always grow in holiness, let us bring our sins before the Lord and ask for healing . . . *[pause]*

Lord Jesus, you come in word and sacrament to strengthen your people: Lord, have mercy.

Christ Jesus, you sustain the marginalized and oppressed: Christ, have mercy.

Lord Jesus, you invite all to the banquet of heaven: Lord, have mercy.

Model Universal Prayer (Prayer of the Faithful)

Presider: We believe in God's almighty love for the world and its needs. With trust, let us bring our prayers and petitions before the Lord.

Response: Lord, hear our prayer.

Grant discernment and grace to lay and ordained leaders of the church . . .

Guide the work of social service agencies who work to uphold the human rights of all people . . .

Comfort those who mourn the death of a beloved family member or friend . . .

Give strength and resources to those in our community facing economic hardship . . .

Presider: God of everlasting goodness, in you rests all our hope. Receive our prayers that through your gracious invitation, we might serve the world with justice and bring peace to those most in need. We ask this through Christ our Lord. **Amen.**

Liturgy and Music

Appropriate Attire: What is the appropriate attire for music ministers at Sunday Mass? The General Instruction of the Roman Missal says that lay ministers "may wear the alb or other appropriate and dignified clothing" (339). The United States bishops offer similar advice, in *Sing to the Lord*, that "[c]hoir and ensemble members may dress in albs or choir robes, but always in clean, presentable and modest clothing. Cassock and surplice, being clerical attire, are not recommended as choir vesture" (33). Similar guidance is given for cantors and psalmists. The choice to vest lay ministers in albs depends on each parish and should be practiced consistently at all the Masses, although this might vary throughout the year depending on the season and according to the degree of solemnity of a particular celebration. Vesting in more uniform attire for parish celebrations that involve multiple parish music groups signifies unity.

Recall the garments worn by the catechumens at the Easter Vigil and how the placing of the white garment is symbol and remembrance of baptism. Think also of how we dress when we attend Mass to lead in music and sung prayer and how this will signify our baptismal duty of serving God's people as light of Christ.

COLLECT
Let us pray.

Pause for silent prayer

May your grace, O Lord, we pray,
at all times go before us and follow after
and make us always determined
to carry out good works.
Through our Lord Jesus Christ, your Son,
who lives and reigns with you in the unity
    of the Holy Spirit,
God, for ever and ever. **Amen.**

FIRST READING
Isa 25:6-10a

On this mountain the LORD of hosts
    will provide for all peoples
a feast of rich food and choice wines,
    juicy, rich food and pure, choice wines.
On this mountain he will destroy
    the veil that veils all peoples,
the web that is woven over all nations;
    he will destroy death forever.
The Lord GOD will wipe away
    the tears from every face;
the reproach of his people he will remove
    from the whole earth; for the LORD has
        spoken.
    On that day it will be said:
"Behold our God, to whom we looked to
        save us!
    This is the LORD for whom we looked;
    let us rejoice and be glad that he has
        saved us!"
For the hand of the LORD will rest on this
    mountain.

RESPONSORIAL PSALM

Ps 23:1-3a, 3b-4, 5, 6

R̸. (6cd) I shall live in the house of the Lord all the days of my life.

The LORD is my shepherd; I shall not want.
In verdant pastures he gives me repose;
beside restful waters he leads me;
he refreshes my soul.

R̸. I shall live in the house of the Lord all the days of my life.

He guides me in right paths
for his name's sake.
Even though I walk in the dark valley
I fear no evil; for you are at my side
with your rod and your staff
that give me courage.

R̸. I shall live in the house of the Lord all the days of my life.

You spread the table before me
in the sight of my foes;
you anoint my head with oil;
my cup overflows.

R̸. I shall live in the house of the Lord all the days of my life.

Only goodness and kindness follow me
all the days of my life;
and I shall dwell in the house of the LORD
for years to come.

R̸. I shall live in the house of the Lord all the days of my life.

SECOND READING

Phil 4:12-14, 19-20

Brothers and sisters:
I know how to live in humble
circumstances;
I know also how to live with abundance.
In every circumstance and in all things
I have learned the secret of being well
fed and of going hungry,
of living in abundance and of being in
need.
I can do all things in him who strengthens
me.
Still, it was kind of you to share in my
distress.

My God will fully supply whatever you
need,
in accord with his glorious riches in
Christ Jesus.
To our God and Father, glory forever and
ever. Amen.

Living Liturgy

Peaceable Kingdom: The refrain of today's responsorial psalm comes from the last half of Psalm 23 and emphasizes the image of hospitality—I will live in the house of the Lord all the days of my life. The readings today portray God as host. In this last parable in a series of three parables, God invites us all into God's kingdom. Within familiar banquet imagery, Jesus offers a glimpse of the kingdom of heaven. The psalm provides a similar image of unity and welcome, highlighting the shepherd-king who not only provides protection but spreads a table and anoints the head of the guest. Yet, the images of violence that fills the story today draw our imagination away from a merciful and welcoming God.

Unfortunately, violence has accompanied human history to this very day. The early church drew wisdom from the experience of Jesus's death and resurrection. Through time we have witnessed those who bring harm and hurt into church community, the unholy ones who "live in the house of the Lord." The weeds that live alongside the wheat, as we have heard in an earlier parable, left only to God's judgment on the final day.

John August Swanson offers another perspective of Psalm 23 through his serigraph based on an earlier sketch titled *Peaceable Kingdom*, which incorporates elements of the mighty laying down with the meek, and the innocent and peaceful overcoming deceit and hypocrisy. Swanson comments on violence through his depiction of two sojourners: "Moving forward barefoot and without fear, two figures travel through a valley transformed by their own beliefs; a world where lions and lambs can lie together in peaceful harmony. The language of Psalm 23 has a message of strength. This story connects with our own lives, as we listen to those who encourage and empower others to speak out and stand against death, violence and hate." How will we respond to God's invitation knowing that there are duties expected of the guest?

PROMPTS FOR FAITH-SHARING

• How does God invite you to the feast? Where do you hear the call to share in the abundant life and joy that God promises?

• What needs do you have that often go unseen? How do you wish God would provide for these?

• In this parable, "bad and good alike" rub shoulders at the same celebration. Who in the church is a struggle for you to be in communion with? How might God be inviting you to greater love for them?

✠ SPIRITUALITY

GOSPEL ACCLAMATION
Phil 2:15d, 16a

℟. Alleluia, alleluia.
Shine like lights in the world
as you hold on to the word of life.
℟. Alleluia, alleluia.

Gospel

Matt 22:15-21; L145A

**The Pharisees went off
and plotted how they might entrap
Jesus in speech.
They sent their disciples to him,
with the Herodians, saying,
"Teacher, we know that you are a
truthful man
and that you teach the way of God
in accordance with the truth.
And you are not concerned with
anyone's opinion,
for you do not regard a person's
status.
Tell us, then, what is your opinion:
Is it lawful to pay the census tax
to Caesar or not?"
Knowing their malice, Jesus said,
"Why are you testing me, you
hypocrites?
Show me the coin that pays the census
tax."
Then they handed him the Roman coin.
He said to them, "Whose image is this
and whose inscription?"
They replied, "Caesar's."
At that he said to them,
"Then repay to Caesar what belongs
to Caesar
and to God what belongs to God."**

Reflecting on the Gospel

Determined to destroy Jesus, the Pharisees and the Herodians seize on the issue of the collection of the "census tax" as their common cause. This was a one-denarius (the day's wage of a laborer) tax imposed by the Roman Empire on every person of Judea. It was bitterly resented, especially by the poor. When Jesus is tackled about the tax issue, if he speaks out against it, he can be charged with sedition and arrested; if he supports the tax, he will discredit himself as a prophet in the eyes of the oppressed.

Jesus reads the malice of their hearts, lets them know that he is not deceived by their collusion, and calls them hypocrites. Then he springs his own trap. He asks them to show him the coin used for the census tax. He does not have one himself, but before his opponents have time to think, someone in the group readily produces a coin. It is something that most Jews considered blasphemous. Not only did it bear the image of the emperor, but it was also inscribed on one side with the words: *Tiberius Caesar Divi Augusti Filius Augustus* (Tiberius Caesar, august son of the divine Augustus), and on the other, *Pontifex Maximus* (High Priest). This granted political honor and divine status to the emperor, and it should have been abhorrent to any Jew of the time. In fact, the Pharisees had even devised ways to avoid handling the coins by using foreign moneychangers to exchange Roman for Judean coins. In one swift move, Jesus has changed the whole issue from that of paying the tax to one of accepting images, a highly sensitive issue in Judaism (see Exod 20:4). In Jesus's hand, the coin becomes a kind of parable. Like the Pharisees, Jesus probably is not opposed to paying taxes if this is necessary for peaceful coexistence, but such an obligation is worthless when compared to the ultimate loyalty that is owed to God.

Jesus's response of "[R]epay to Caesar what belongs to Caesar and to God what belongs to God" is not to be read as an explanation for the contemporary separation of church and state. Jesus doesn't "compartmentalize" life, and such a dualistic interpretation would have been completely contrary to his worldview. Real wisdom recognizes the legitimate function of human authority in relation to God's authority. What is demanded is that we discern how to live in history and society while holding onto our commitment to the reign of God. Jesus does not elaborate on the "how" of this. His followers must discern how, within the overall claim of God, to discharge civic obligations in their own times and places.

Such an ethical task demands the action that Jesus exemplified: truthfulness rather than hypocrisy, honesty rather than flattery, justice rather than opportunism. This is still a challenge to leadership—both political and ecclesial—as well as to every Christian disciple. We might ask, where is God's impression in the "coinage" of our daily life? The answer is: on everything that God has made, and especially on other women and men.

Preparing to Proclaim

Key words and phrases: "Then repay to Caesar what belongs to Caesar and to God what belongs to God."

To the point: This gospel makes a distinction between the political and the spiritual realms and implies that we have duties to both of them. The church's tradition does not call lay persons to withdraw from secular life; involvement in the political can be part of our partnership with God, how we make the kingdom of heaven present here on earth. It can be an expression of faith, part of how we participate in God's work of love and justice, making this world more holy. But this world, in its current sin-marred state, is not our final home. Political action can be an expression of our faith, but its fruits are only temporary. Political campaigns or candidates or parties can run the risk of becoming idols when we place our hopes in them. In the end, politics leaves us homeless; they will ultimately fail us because our true home is with God. While we are meant to strive for justice, only God can bring about the final justice we seek.

Psalmist Preparation

"Give the Lord glory and honor." Implied in this psalm's outpouring of praise is that it is *only* God who deserves this glory and honor. God's power is ultimate, above all others, and God deserves our whole hearts and our utmost in love and loyalty. As you prepare this psalm, reflect on those things in your life that threaten to become idols—that is, those things that run the risk of taking the place in your heart that ought to belong only to God. Make a resolution to distance yourself from one of these things in some small way this week so that there is more room in your heart to sincerely proclaim the praises of this psalm.

Making Connections

Between the readings: Like the gospel, the first reading makes an important distinction between earthly and divine power. Human leaders may do good work that is willed by God, but God affirms that "I am the Lord and there is no other, there is no God besides me." No other power, no matter how good, can fulfill what is God's to fulfill.

To experience: Political leaders are not the only thing in our lives that run the risk of becoming an idol. Money is a common one; on its own it is a morally neutral tool that can be used for good, but when we pursue it for its own sake it can start to take a place in our hearts that ought to belong to God alone. Security is another; the way we live sometimes betrays that we value our own safety and comfort far above the solidarity to which the gospel calls us.

Homily Points

• The Second Vatican Council made many bold claims when it convened more than fifty years ago. It put forth practical reforms, like the ability to celebrate Mass in native languages, and set forth guidance for Catholics interacting with their diversifying communities. Guided by the Holy Spirit, the council set a vision for the "church in the modern world." It recognized that while the ultimate authority rests in God, we also live in a world with varying systems of governance.

• How do we discern what authority to listen to? What happens if the will of the government clashes with the will of God? These are questions people of faith have asked throughout time, from church councils to the days of Christ. Today's gospel could have inspired the types of discussions happening at Vatican II. The religious leaders of the day ask Jesus a legitimate question—even if their intent was to trick him: "Is it lawful to pay the census tax to Caesar or not?" They are in essence asking where their allegiances should lie. Jesus's answer may have surprised them: "Repay to Caesar what belongs to Caesar and to God what belongs to God."

• Jesus recognizes that his followers are responsible to both heaven and earthly matters. The ultimate question is not whether to avoid taxes. The issue is how should Christians hold the government accountable for practicing values like peace and justice? We have a responsibility to engage in the political lives of our communities, to advocate for the marginalized as Jesus did. Being a church in the modern world is not easy. With the Spirit's help, we can discern a right and just way forward.

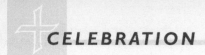

Model Penitential Act

Presider: In today's second reading, St. Paul calls to mind the faith, hope, and love that God showers upon God's people. For the times our hardness of heart has caused us to turn away from God's goodness, let us ask for mercy . . . *[pause]*

Lord Jesus, you are the wisdom of God: Lord, have mercy.

Christ Jesus, you shine God's glory across creation: Christ, have mercy.

Lord Jesus, you will come again to draw us into the peace of everlasting life: Lord, have mercy.

Model Universal Prayer (Prayer of the Faithful)

Presider: With concern for the needs of the world and trust in God's almighty power to heal, let us offer our prayers and petitions before the Lord.

Response: Lord, hear our prayer.

Advance dialogue and collaboration between church and civic leaders . . .

Inspire people in positions of authority to use their power for the common good . . .

Rid the sins of systemic racism from our communities . . .

Strengthen each of us gathered here to care for neighbors who are isolated and lonely . . .

Presider: Merciful God, you are the Lord, there is no other. All that is right and just comes from you. Receive our prayers that we might be stewards of your good work in the world. We ask this through Christ our Lord. **Amen.**

Liturgy and Music

Belonging to God: Today we are reminded that whatever we possess is from God. St. Ignatius of Loyola's *Suscipe* prayer comes to mind as I think about surrendering everything back to God in return for only God's love and grace. So, whenever we sing or play music in church, we engage more than just our musicality and skill, we engage in our faith in returning our gifts back in belonging to God.

As music ministers, our vocation is not just creating beautiful music, we are participating in both external and internal spirituality. Through our public worship, we awaken our personal faith. We should never be discouraged when the assembly does not respond in a way that we expect them to, in some cases God's song may be quieter than we imagine. Sometimes we may be too sad to sing a song of praise and at other times we may feel too joyful to lament. Let God's music invite us into the meaning of a particular text and allow the assembly's voice to guide our spirit. At times we may be asked to sing or play a song that is often used or one that we don't care to sing or play at all. When this happens, try to remain open to encountering God in new ways.

COLLECT

Let us pray.

Pause for silent prayer

Almighty ever-living God,
grant that we may always conform our
will to yours
and serve your majesty in sincerity of
heart.
Through our Lord Jesus Christ, your Son,
who lives and reigns with you in the unity
of the Holy Spirit,
God, for ever and ever. **Amen.**

FIRST READING

Isa 45:1, 4-6

Thus says the LORD to his anointed, Cyrus,
    whose right hand I grasp,
subduing nations before him,
    and making kings run in his service,
opening doors before him
    and leaving the gates unbarred:
For the sake of Jacob, my servant,
    of Israel, my chosen one,
I have called you by your name,
    giving you a title, though you knew me
    not.
I am the LORD and there is no other,
    there is no God besides me.
It is I who arm you, though you know me
    not,
    so that toward the rising and the setting
    of the sun
    people may know that there is none
    besides me.
I am the LORD, there is no other.

RESPONSORIAL PSALM

Ps 96:1, 3, 4-5, 7-8, 9-10

R̸. (7b) Give the Lord glory and honor.

Sing to the LORD a new song;
 sing to the LORD, all you lands.
Tell his glory among the nations;
 among all peoples, his wondrous deeds.

R̸. Give the Lord glory and honor.

For great is the LORD and highly to be
 praised;
 awesome is he, beyond all gods.
For all the gods of the nations are things
 of nought,
 but the LORD made the heavens.

R̸. Give the Lord glory and honor.

Give to the LORD, you families of nations,
 give to the LORD glory and praise;
 give to the LORD the glory due his name!
Bring gifts, and enter his courts.

R̸. Give the Lord glory and honor.

Worship the LORD, in holy attire;
 tremble before him, all the earth;
say among the nations: The LORD is king,
 he governs the peoples with equity.

R̸. Give the Lord glory and honor.

SECOND READING

1 Thess 1:1-5b

Paul, Silvanus, and Timothy to the church
 of the Thessalonians
 in God the Father and the Lord Jesus
 Christ:
 grace to you and peace.
We give thanks to God always for all of
 you,
 remembering you in our prayers,
 unceasingly calling to mind your work
 of faith and labor of love
 and endurance in hope of our Lord
 Jesus Christ,
 before our God and Father,
 knowing, brothers and sisters loved by
 God,
 how you were chosen.
For our gospel did not come to you in
 word alone,
 but also in power and in the Holy Spirit
 and with much conviction.

Living Liturgy

Whose We Are: In Jesus's response to the Pharisees and Herodians, we have a new way of thinking about a lifestyle for discipleship, one that shares our possessions with the least among us. So far, we have done some reflection on creating an identity of inclusive community belonging. Today we reflect on belongings—who we are in relation to whose we are. The gospel reading today asks us to question what goods we have acquired and recognize that all we have belongs to God. In our individualistic society, we tend to become possessive of what we own and what we have earned. How willing are we to adjust our mindset to keep things in proper perspective, the perspective not of obtaining worldly things but of concern for the things of God? Today we are asked to reflect on our own sincerity as we seek a Christian response to the problems in our world today.

Perhaps this might be the time to declutter our spiritual life. In other words, to rid our hearts of possessions and distractions that keep us from effective ministry and turn our attention to seeking the things attached to God. Would this mean less time on social media, more time in prayer, more surrendering to God's will, less time for negative thoughts, more time for rest, less time for bad habits? St. Teresa of Calcutta expresses her simple life of prayer, detachment from worldly possessions, and attachment to Godly things, all of this to understand and be in solidarity with the lives of the poor: "There is but one love of Jesus, as there is but one person in the poor—Jesus. We take vows of chastity to love Christ with undivided love; to be able to love him with undivided love we take a vow of poverty which frees us from all material possessions, and with that freedom we can love him with undivided love, and from this vow of undivided love we surrender ourselves totally to him in the person who takes his place" (*A Gift for God*). May we surrender to God what belongs to God.

PROMPTS FOR FAITH-SHARING

• How do you participate in politics? Have you ever thought of this practice as an extension of your faith?

• What in your life runs the risk of becoming an idol? Where do you spend your time, talent, and treasure? Does this spending align with what you claim to value?

• What relationships do you have where you are in a position of power? How could you exercise that power in a way that is consistent with God's vision of justice for the world?

✝ SPIRITUALITY

GOSPEL ACCLAMATION
John 14:23

R7. Alleluia, alleluia.
Whoever loves me will keep my word, says the Lord,
and my Father will love him and we will come to him.
R7. Alleluia, alleluia.

Gospel

Matt 22:34-40; L148A

When the Pharisees heard that Jesus had silenced the Sadducees, they gathered together, and one of them, a scholar of the law, tested him by asking, "Teacher, which commandment in the law is the greatest?" He said to him, "You shall love the Lord, your God, with all your heart, with all your soul, and with all your mind. This is the greatest and the first commandment. The second is like it: You shall love your neighbor as yourself. The whole law and the prophets depend on these two commandments."

Reflecting on the Gospel

Those antagonistic to Jesus—we encountered them in last Sunday's gospel too—do not give up. In the gospel reading we hear today, the Sadducees have just been silenced by Jesus's interpretation of Scripture (see Matt 22:23-33), but now the Pharisees return to confront him. A lawyer, someone whose role we might recognize as a "professional theologian," poses a question about the greatest commandment among the 613 precepts of the Mosaic Torah (Law/Teaching). This is another bedeviling attempt to involve Jesus in a hairsplitting debate, not a typical discussion as was held in rabbinic circles for the sake of clarification.

As an observant Jew, Jesus responds to his tempter by saying that the first and greatest commandment is the fifth verse of the great Jewish profession of faith, the *Shema*: "[Hear, O Israel!] You shall love the Lord, your God, with all your heart, with all your soul, and with all your mind" (see Deut 6:4-9). Jews have recited this ancient love song every day down through the generations, even when attempts have been made to smother it on the funeral pyres of history. These holy words have drifted over the world in the tragic smoke of Auschwitz and other death camps; they have also risen as the incense of joyful prayer. Love is to bind together our interiority ("heart"), our life force ("soul"), and our rationality ("mind") into a dynamic and total engagement that integrates and directs the whole person toward God.

Although asked for one commandment, Jesus responds with two, quoting a verse from the Jewish Code of Holiness—a practical summary of the Jewish way of life—because, he says, the "second is *like*" the first (see Lev 19:18). It is equal in importance and inseparable from the first. Everything, Jesus says, hangs on these. A door hangs on two hinges, but if one is out of alignment, it will not swing properly or open easily. If love of God and neighbor are out of balance, our lives will be badly aligned. Jesus is not discounting the other commandments, not talking about "heavier" or "lighter" commandments, but emphasizing that their weight, and the tradition of the prophets, is borne by these two commandments that balance one another. Jesus defines for us in his own person what this love of God and neighbor is.

Perhaps our greatest temptation is to separate our love of God and love of people. We may leave today's Mass and go into our lives only to show how little we really are "in communion" with our brothers and sisters by failing to love them in the small but demanding ways of everyday neighborliness, or by hurting them. In the Old Testament, "neighbor" was another Israelite, or resident alien without rights of citizenship; but in Matthew's Gospel we have seen how Jesus has already extended this to love of enemies (Matt 5:43-44). And a month from now, on the last Sunday of the liturgical year, the solemnity of Our Lord Jesus Christ the King, in the parable of the Last Judgment, the challenge to practical love will reach out to disciples of all nations.

Preparing to Proclaim

Key words and phrases: "This is the greatest and the first commandment."

To the point: The Pharisees attempt to entrap Jesus with a trick question: Naming one commandment as the greatest would devalue the others by comparison, making it sound as if he does not value God's word in its fullness. Instead, Jesus shows that he understands God's word far more deeply than those who are tied to reading the law literally. He names not one of the ten commandments but one that comes after them in Deuteronomy. He reveals that fulfilling the law is not about servile deference to what is written, but about love. If our hearts are formed in love, the other commandments will follow, flowing forth from our inner being instead of needing to be forced as outer actions. The second commandment, too, can be named as secondary because it also flows from love of God. If we truly love God, so will we love our neighbor.

Psalmist Preparation

In this psalm we sing of the love for God to which the gospel calls us. We also affirm that we are not called to give ourselves to God one-sidedly; we name here many of the things that God is for us. In this psalm, God is named as our "strength," "rock," "fortress," "deliverer," "shield," "horn of . . . salvation," "stronghold"—and this is just a small selection of the names for God we find in the Bible and in the Christian tradition. As you prepare this psalm, choose one of these titles to sit with. How does it resonate with your image of God? How does it challenge it or help it to expand?

Making Connections

Between the readings: The first reading shows that the God of the Old Testament is not some being foreign from the Jesus of the New Testament. The love that Jesus preaches does not *replace* the law. There is continuity here. God's Old Testament commandments are more specific, and make punishment clearer, but they are about the very love for neighbor that Jesus has named as so important. To treat foreigners and widows and orphans with justice is to fulfill the love to which we are called.

To experience: In this life, the moral teachings of the church will always be at times burdensome and challenging. This is simply part of being human; until we are fully united to God in heaven we will not be acting from hearts perfectly formed in love. We can, though, try to reframe our understandings of these teachings; while they are often poorly taught and uncompassionately preached, they are *meant* to help us live in the love Jesus calls us to.

Homily Points

• How are people of faith to act in the world? Today's set of readings offers clear practices by which to live. The first reading from Exodus tells people what not to do: do not oppress foreigners, do not wrong widows or orphans, do not extort neighbors in need. Knowing what practices to avoid helps build healthy boundaries. It's like putting up a fence— the harmful practices stay on the outside. We are left with bountiful space inside the fence to do God's will. Today's gospel makes that crystal clear: first, love the Lord your God; second, love your neighbor as yourself.

• These are two of the most well-known commandments for people of faith, having first been part of Jewish law. By this point, we have a good idea of what it means to love our neighbors, even if we struggle to live it out at times. Concrete practices that show love for our neighbors include feeding those in need, visiting the sick and lonely, and advocating for just wages and good healthcare for all. The list goes on for ways we can love the people around us.

• But the first and greatest commandment to love God with the fullness of our beings may not be as obvious. What does it look like to love God, in God's great vastness and mystery? How do we love something that is always present and often hard to see? What would it feel like to give all our hearts, souls, and minds— the totality of our beings—over to the love of God?

Model Penitential Act

Presider: Today's readings set forth the ways people of faith are called to act—to care for the vulnerable, to embrace the exploited, and to love God and neighbor. For the times we have fallen short of these commands, let us ask God for mercy . . . *[pause]*

Lord Jesus, you strengthen us for the journey of faith: Lord, have mercy.

Christ Jesus, you intercede for us at the right hand of God: Christ, have mercy.

Lord Jesus, you are love incarnate now and forever: Lord, have mercy.

Model Universal Prayer (Prayer of the Faithful)

Presider: Knowing that God loves us and wants to answer our needs, let us place before the Lord our prayers and petitions.

Response: Lord, hear our prayer.

Animate Christian congregations to receive all people as Christ . . .

Foster greater respect and assistance for migrants, immigrants, and refugees . . .

Give aid to people struggling to meet their basic needs for food, water, shelter, clothing, and healthcare . . .

Deepen our love for God and neighbor through prayer, study, and community living . . .

Presider: God of infinite glory, throughout time you have called people into greater relationship with you and with our neighbors. Hear our prayers that we might embody your graciousness in our homes and communities. We ask this through Christ our Lord. **Amen.**

Liturgy and Music

Black Catholic History Month: From the Office of Black Catholics, Archdiocese of Washington: On July 24, 1990, the National Black Clergy Caucus of the United States designated November as Black Catholic History Month to celebrate the long history and proud heritage of Black Catholics. Two commemorative dates fall within this month, Saint Augustine's birthday (November 13) and Saint Martin de Porres's feast day (November 3). More importantly, November not only marks a time when we pray for all saints and souls in loving remembrance, but also a time to recall the saints and souls of Africa and the African diaspora. Some people forget that Christianity did not originate in Europe and even express surprise when they learn that Black Catholic History began in the Acts of the Apostles (8:26-40) with the conversion of the Ethiopian Eunuch by Philip the Deacon.

Black Catholics trace their faith history back to Christian antiquity long before other nations heard the "good news." Christian Africa was indeed a "leading light" in early Christendom. Black Catholics point to three popes who were born in Africa: Saints Victor I, Melchiades, and Gelasius I. All three shepherded the early church through tough and tumultuous times in history. Black Catholics claim many Black Saints—Saints Cyprian, Zeno, Anthony of Egypt, Moses the Black, Pachomius, Maurice, Athanasius, Pisentius, Mary of Egypt, Cyril of Alexandria, Monica of Hippo, Augustine of Hippo, Perpetua, Felicitas, and Thecla. Black Catholic History Month provides opportunities to learn and share the whole history and rich heritage of our Catholicism.

COLLECT

Let us pray.

Pause for silent prayer

Almighty ever-living God,
increase our faith, hope and charity,
and make us love what you command,
so that we may merit what you promise.
Through our Lord Jesus Christ, your Son,
who lives and reigns with you in the unity
    of the Holy Spirit,
God, for ever and ever. **Amen.**

FIRST READING
Exod 22:20-26

Thus says the LORD:
"You shall not molest or oppress an alien,
    for you were once aliens yourselves in
        the land of Egypt.
You shall not wrong any widow or orphan.
If ever you wrong them and they cry out
    to me,
    I will surely hear their cry.
My wrath will flare up, and I will kill you
    with the sword;
    then your own wives will be widows,
        and your children orphans.

"If you lend money to one of your poor
    neighbors among my people,
    you shall not act like an extortioner
        toward him
    by demanding interest from him.
If you take your neighbor's cloak as a
    pledge,
    you shall return it to him before sunset;
    for this cloak of his is the only covering
        he has for his body.
What else has he to sleep in?
If he cries out to me, I will hear him; for I
    am compassionate."

RESPONSORIAL PSALM

Ps 18:2-3, 3-4, 47, 51

R̶̸. (2) I love you, Lord, my strength.

I love you, O LORD, my strength,
  O LORD, my rock, my fortress, my
    deliverer.

R̶̸. I love you, Lord, my strength.

My God, my rock of refuge,
  my shield, the horn of my salvation, my
    stronghold!
Praised be the LORD, I exclaim,
  and I am safe from my enemies.

R̶̸. I love you, Lord, my strength.

The LORD lives and blessed be my rock!
  Extolled be God my savior.
You who gave great victories to your king
  and showed kindness to your anointed.

R̶̸. I love you, Lord, my strength.

SECOND READING

1 Thess 1:5c-10

Brothers and sisters:
You know what sort of people we were
    among you for your sake.
And you became imitators of us and of
    the Lord,
  receiving the word in great affliction,
    with joy from the Holy Spirit,
  so that you became a model for all the
    believers
  in Macedonia and in Achaia.
For from you the word of the Lord has
    sounded forth
  not only in Macedonia and in Achaia,
  but in every place your faith in God has
    gone forth,
  so that we have no need to say anything.
For they themselves openly declare about
    us
  what sort of reception we had among
    you,
  and how you turned to God from idols
  to serve the living and true God
  and to await his Son from heaven,
  whom he raised from the dead,
  Jesus, who delivers us from the coming
    wrath.

Living Liturgy

Richer Community: Our faith is more than a personal relationship between us and God. Jesus's response to the Pharisees, who have been attempting to find reason to arrest him through questions on Mosaic Law, offers a twofold invitation to connect two aspects of Jewish Law—love of God that finds expression in love of neighbor. Our faith and liturgical ministry should not be centered only in pious prayer or within the Sunday Mass context. Rather, our faithful ministry ought to be set on fire to make places we live in reflective of the gospel message of rich community. Christian disciples are called to make the world a richer place by our choices, our actions, and where we spend our time, money, and energy. Pope Francis said this before an Angelus prayer: "As long as there is a brother or sister to whom we close our hearts, we will still be far from being disciples as Jesus asks us" (October 25, 2020).

We create spaces where hearts will continue to open in generous compassion for the neighbor and in love of God. Ours is a lifelong vocation. Taking inspiration from those that have wrestled with prayer and practice during their lifetimes of ministry and learning about their faith journeys will guide us in ours. Many have witnessed a solidarity with the oppressed neighbor.

Cesar Chavez fought for the migrant farm worker, for just wages, for fair and healthy working conditions. The United Farm Workers movement, through nonviolent actions, brought change and equality. Chavez's work drew inspiration from St. Francis and Mahatma Gandhi and sought recognition of the importance and dignity of all workers. Long periods of fasting would mark this movement for justice. During a fast against the use of pesticides, Chavez made a comment that joins love of God with love of neighbor: "I pray to God that this fast will be a preparation for a multitude of simple deeds for justice. Carried out by men and women whose hearts are focused on the suffering of the poor and who yearn, with us, for a better world. Together, all things are possible" (ufw.org).

PROMPTS FOR FAITH-SHARING

• Jesus asks for our whole selves: heart, soul, and mind. What parts of yourself do you find challenging to give to God in love?

• Which of the church's moral teachings is most challenging for you right now? Is there a way to see it as an invitation to form your heart in the love God calls us to? If not, bring this to God, who sits with us in all our suffering.

• Choose one of the images for God from the psalm and sit with it for a while. How does it resonate with your usual working image of God? How does it challenge it or help it to expand?

R⁊. Alleluia, alleluia.
Come to me, all you who labor and are burdened,
and I will give you rest, says the Lord.
R⁊. Alleluia, alleluia.

Gospel

Matt 5:1-12a; L667

When Jesus saw the crowds,
    he went up the mountain,
and after he had sat down,
    his disciples came to
    him.
He began to teach them,
    saying:

"Blessed are the poor in
    spirit,
    for theirs is the Kingdom
    of heaven.
Blessed are they who mourn,
    for they will be comforted.
Blessed are the meek,
    for they will inherit the
    land.
Blessed are they who
    hunger and thirst for
    righteousness,
    for they will be satisfied.
Blessed are the merciful,
    for they will be shown mercy.
Blessed are the clean of heart,
    for they will see God.
Blessed are the peacemakers,
    for they will be called children of
    God.
Blessed are they who are persecuted
    for the sake of righteousness,
    for theirs is the Kingdom of
    heaven.
Blessed are you when they insult you
    and persecute you
    and utter every kind of evil against
    you falsely because of me.
Rejoice and be glad,
    for your reward will be great in
    heaven."

See Appendix A, p. 302, for the other readings.

Reflecting on the Gospel

There is a concept called "mastery-based learning" that has been prominent among educators for the last few years. The core tenet of mastery-based learning is that students should demonstrate deep understanding, or mastery, of a topic before moving on to the next one. In mastery-based classrooms, teachers also recognize that all students may not grasp the material at the exact same time and should strive to give students multiple chances to demonstrate mastery. This means that students have the opportunity to retake tests or revise papers in hopes of earning a higher grade. Although this pedagogical model may be different from what many of us remember from school, it is one that reflects the realities of life. After all, how many of us had the opportunity to retake the driver's license exam? Or the SATs? Or a presentation for work?

Mastery-based learning depends on students' ability to develop a growth mindset—the belief that with time, consistent practice, and constructive feedback from a trusted guide, they can improve their knowledge and skills. "I don't know" and "I give up" don't exist in mastery-based classrooms where the growth mindset is fostered. With a growth mindset, students harness the power of "yet." The solemnity of All Saints is one that invites believers to assume a growth mindset, to embrace the power of "yet" with regard to our spiritual lives.

Today's gospel reading from Matthew gives us a clear list of the traits and characteristics that saintly people ought to possess: poverty of spirit, meekness, mercy, and purity of heart among others. The Beatitudes are a helpful yet challenging yardstick by which we can measure our spiritual and moral growth. Some of the Beatitudes may feel attainable, but others are radically countercultural. Who wants to live in a way that leads to insults and persecution? It is so much easier to go with the flow, to assimilate to the ways of the world even when they prove to be inhumane, materialistic, and wasteful.

But we are not called to go with the flow. We are called to be saints. As our second reading from the First Book of John tells us, "we are God's children now" and we are called to be living witnesses to God's saving power. This calling is a mighty challenge. Some days, we will successfully rise and meet it. Other days—many days—we will fall short. This is where we can apply the power of "yet." We may not be perfectly peaceful *yet.* We may not feel a deep hunger and thirst for righteousness *yet.* We may not have a deep well and high capacity for mercy *yet,* but thankfully God affords us many chances to develop these habits of spirit.

In a homily titled "In the Footsteps of Christ," St. Josemaría Escríva preached, "Don't forget that the saint is not the person who never falls, but rather the one who never fails to get up again, humbly and with a holy stubbornness." Although we will come up short again and again, we must assume a spirit of "holy stubbornness." We must develop a spiritual growth mindset so that we can grow ever closer to the saintly destiny God has in mind for us.

Preparing to Proclaim

Key words and phrases: "Rejoice and be glad, for your reward will be great in heaven."

To the point: In this gospel, Jesus describes different characteristics of saints. Their holiness might not always be apparent from the outside; people who have these characteristics could very well come across as strange or off-putting. What Jesus describes here are not external actions but interior dispositions. But saints also live with integrity, meaning that their external actions come forth from who they really are and what they really value. These dispositions would cause someone to take action, leaving evidence of holiness in the fruits of a person's life.

Model Penitential Act

Presider: Today's second reading reminds us that we are God's children, beloved by the one who creates and calls us. Trusting in God's mercy, let us call to mind our sins . . . *[pause]*

Lord Jesus, you are the Son of God: Lord, have mercy.

Christ Jesus, you bless people in need of your love: Christ, have mercy.

Lord Jesus, you promise a great reward in heaven to those who follow you: Lord, have mercy.

Model Universal Prayer (Prayer of the Faithful)

Presider: Guided by our ancestors in faith, let us bring our needs and the needs of the world before the Lord.

Response: Lord, hear our prayer.

Raise up in the church young people dedicated to service and justice . . .

Grant strength and perseverance to the mentors and teachers who show us how to embody the Christian faith . . .

Fulfill the desires of people seeking safe, affordable housing . . .

Welcome into the halls of heaven all those who have died . . .

Presider: Gracious God, you inspire people across time to live lives of holiness and to sacrifice for the good of the gospel. Receive our prayers that we might grow in holiness and readiness to serve you in word and deed. We ask this through Christ our Lord. **Amen.**

Living Liturgy

Communion of Saints: We think today not only of the well-known holy ones whose stories inspire us, but also of the saints from our own lives, real people who walk this earth through trials, triumphs, faults, and failings, witnesses who point us to the cross of Christ through their joys and suffering. I also think of the images of everyday people reflected in the beautiful *Communion of Saints* tapestries by John Nava that adorn the walls of the Cathedral of Our Lady of the Angels in Los Angeles. All facing the large alabaster cross window, this diverse group of holy ones accompany the gathered assembly toward the eucharistic table.

COLLECT

Let us pray.

Pause for silent prayer

Almighty ever-living God,
by whose gift we venerate in one celebration
the merits of all the Saints,
bestow on us, we pray,
through the prayers of so many intercessors,
an abundance of the reconciliation with you
for which we earnestly long.
Through our Lord Jesus Christ, your Son,
who lives and reigns with you in the unity
    of the Holy Spirit,
God, for ever and ever. **Amen.**

FOR REFLECTION

• Make a list of the characteristics you would expect a saint to have. How closely does it match up with the beatitudes?

• Which of the beatitudes feels easiest to live out? Which is most challenging for you? How might it be an invitation?

• In this gospel, Jesus describes interior dispositions that are holy. What external actions would serve as evidence to you of these dispositions?

Homily Points

• Saints give flesh to Jesus's Sermon on the Mount. They give faces and stories to the big "Blessed" statements. They witness to God's way of ordering creation—in which the poor, meek, hungry come first. Their witness is not without consequences. The wood of the cross paves the path of holiness. Our saints have splinters to prove it. But death doesn't end the saints' stories.

• A great cloud of witnesses surrounds us, always. Saints spanning centuries from every nation, race, people, and tongue form a communion rooted in Christ. It's the same communion you and I joined in baptism: a communion that defies death in favor of resurrection; a communion that shrinks the space between heaven and earth; a communion that knows the path of holiness can only be paved by the wood of the cross—and has the splinters to prove it.

GOSPEL ACCLAMATION
See John 6:40

This is the will of my Father, says the Lord,
that everyone who sees the Son and believes in
    him
may have eternal life.

Gospel

John 6:37-40; L668

**Jesus said to the crowds:
"Everything that the Father
    gives me will come to me,
    and I will not reject anyone
        who comes to me,
    because I came down from
        heaven not to do my own
        will
    but the will of the one who
        sent me.
And this is the will of the one
    who sent me,
    that I should not lose anything
        of what he gave me,
    but that I should raise it on
        the last day.
For this is the will of my Father,
    that everyone who sees the
        Son and believes in him
    may have eternal life,
    and I shall raise him on the last day."**

See Appendix A., p. 303, for the other readings.

Additional reading choices are in the Lectionary
for Mass *(L668) or those given in the Masses for
the Dead (L1011–1016).*

Reflecting on the Gospel
"I'm just living in the hands of God."

That is how a friend of mine used to answer the question "How are you?" during particularly busy days in college. Her answer has stayed with me all this time, and I now use it when I find myself buffeted around by the demands of work and community.

How am I? Well, I add things to my to-do list faster than I cross them off. I feel a little bit like an imposter in my job, but I seem to be doing a good job of fooling everyone. I have grand aspirations of the hobbies I'll pursue someday when I have time—recipes I will learn to cook or gifts that I will make for the people I love. For now, I am getting by. I am simply living in the hands of God. God graciously provides my daily bread and I strive to be grateful and content with the bounty that I receive. I will likely continue in this way—slightly harried, feeling both most fortunate and most inadequate—until of course I do not. One day this flurry and frenzy will stop. My life will end, and then my soul will be in the hands of God.

The readings we hear today remind us that our entire existence occurs under the loving gaze of God. God walks with us through both the momentous and the mundane parts of our lives. We are never beyond God's reach. We are never forsaken. We are never so lost that we cannot be found by God. Through all we experience and undertake, God is there with us offering guidance and care. The gospel we hear from John finds Jesus telling the crowds that no one will be lost, that it is the will of God that all who believe will be raised to eternal life on the last day. This is our destiny—to reside in God's loving care for all eternity.

The imagery of God as the Good Shepherd offers special comfort to those of us who may feel confounded by the complexity of life or gutted by the starkness of death. Psalm 23 reminds us, "Though I walk in the valley of darkness, I fear no evil, for you are with me." In both our living and our dying, God is there to hold us and bring us to Godself. The loss of a loved one often feels like "an affliction" or like "utter destruction"—and indeed, it may be. We cannot ignore the fact that senseless, untimely deaths happen every day. However, we can find solace by looking to the incarnate God. Through Jesus Christ, we have a God who intimately knows the experiences of grief, of pain, and of death. God knows what we are going through because God remembers. God also remembers what awaits us on the other side of death: glorious resurrection.

On this All Souls' Day, may we take comfort in the fact that we profess a God who is no farther from us than our own heartbeat. We profess a God who offers comfort and companionship through all of life's stages from beginning to end. With this knowledge, let us rest confidently in the hands of God.

Preparing to Proclaim

Key words and phrases: "I shall raise him on the last day."

To the point: In all the gospel options for today, we hear our common theme of subverting expectations. God has a preferential love for those who are poor and powerless. This love extends to all of us in the face of death, which seems to have power over us all. But even death is no longer the end it once was. Jesus's ability to overturn systems of power bestows all of us with the ability to live beyond our deaths. This is what we profess as we pray for all who have passed before us.

Model Penitential Act

Presider: Jesus Christ, the resurrected Lord, intercedes for us at the right hand of God. With faith and hope in his mercy, let us call to mind our sins . . . *[pause]*

Lord Jesus, you suffered out of love for your people: Lord, have mercy.

Christ Jesus, you died a painful death on the cross: Christ, have mercy.

Lord Jesus, you rose to new life and make way for us to do the same: Lord, have mercy.

Model Universal Prayer (Prayer of the Faithful)

Presider: As we await the coming of God's kingdom, let us lift up the needs of our community and the needs of the world.

Response: Lord, hear our prayer.

Bless those who minister to the dying with a compassionate spirit and listening heart . . .

Strengthen medical personnel, hospice workers, and all who care for the dying . . .

Make your loving presence known to all those who are near death . . .

Bring peace and consolation to everyone in this community who is grieving the death of a loved one . . .

Presider: Merciful God, you sent your son to comfort those who mourn and bring all people into the peace of everlasting life. Hear our prayers that we might be attentive to your presence and live out our days to the fullest in praise of you. We ask this through Christ our Lord. **Amen.**

Living Liturgy

Eternal Tones: I share this excerpt from a poem by John O'Donohue, "On the Death of the Beloved," to accompany us and those that we minister to on this holy day of remembrance. What a great privilege we have been given to accompany through our music those who have lost loved ones.

Let us not look for you only in memory,
Where we would grow lonely without you.
You would want us to find you in presence,
Beside us when beauty brightens,
When kindness glows
And music echoes eternal tones.

COLLECT (from the first Mass)
Let us pray.

Pause for silent prayer

Listen kindly to our prayers, O Lord,
and, as our faith in your Son,
raised from the dead, is deepened,
so may our hope of resurrection for your
    departed servants
also find new strength.
Through our Lord Jesus Christ, your Son,
who lives and reigns with you in the unity of
    the Holy Spirit,
God, for ever and ever. **Amen.**

FOR REFLECTION

• Do you find it easy or challenging to believe that God wants to bring us to life beyond death?

• How do you envision life after death? What about it do you look forward to? What questions or hesitations do you have?

• How do you think Jesus interacts with those we have lost? Envision a conversation between him and one of your departed loved ones.

Homily Points

• We are forever an Easter people. As we remember those who have died, let us find solace in the Easter truth: death does not have the final say. It never will. Jesus ensured this fate when he suffered, died, and then rose to new life. The Son of God paved the way for people whose time on this earth ends to enter the glory of the kingdom of God.

• Today's feast celebrates the gift of everlasting life. It also offers space to lament the changes in proximity and relationship that happen when a loved one dies. We should not glaze over this grief. Rather, we are called to come together as a praying community, to rejoice and to weep, to remember and to wonder.

✝ SPIRITUALITY

GOSPEL ACCLAMATION
Matt 23:9b, 10b

℟. Alleluia, alleluia.
You have but one Father in heaven
and one master, the Christ.
℟. Alleluia, alleluia.

Gospel Matt 23:1-12; L151A

Jesus spoke to the crowds and
    to his disciples, saying,
"The scribes and the
    Pharisees
have taken their seat on the
    chair of Moses.
Therefore, do and observe all
    things whatsoever they tell
    you,
but do not follow their
    example.
For they preach but they do not
    practice.
They tie up heavy burdens hard
    to carry
    and lay them on people's
    shoulders,
but they will not lift a finger to move
    them.
All their works are performed to be
    seen.
They widen their phylacteries and
    lengthen their tassels.
They love places of honor at banquets,
    seats of honor in synagogues,
    greetings in marketplaces, and the
    salutation 'Rabbi.'
As for you, do not be called 'Rabbi.'
You have but one teacher, and you are
    all brothers.
Call no one on earth your father;
    you have but one Father in heaven.
Do not be called 'Master';
    you have but one master, the Christ.
The greatest among you must be your
    servant.
Whoever exalts himself will be
    humbled;
    but whoever humbles himself will be
    exalted."

Reflecting on the Gospel

In today's gospel reading, Jesus uses denunciation as a method of illustrating the qualities of authentic leadership among his disciples.

His first criticism is of those who "preach but . . . do not practice." They are like play actors (that's the original meaning of the Greek word *hupocrites*, from which we get *hypocrites*) who wore stylized masks to denote their roles. Their public, performing faces do not match their inner, personal truth. Some religious leaders, says Jesus, exercise control by teaching interpretations that are excessively legalistic and burdensome. After the destruction of the temple and the disappearance of the active Jewish priesthood, the priestly purity laws were transferred over time to the whole people in an attempt to fortify a vulnerable Judaism from external attack and internal laxity. For many Jews, such laws became a heavy burden. What Jesus offers is burden-lifting mercy and rest to those who come to him (see Matt 11:28).

Clinging to terms of importance and power, seizing the public limelight, and attachment to ostentatious religious regalia are signs of exaltation rather than humility, says Jesus. He criticizes the Jewish leaders who wear showy phylacteries, the small leather cubes containing biblical texts that a Jewish man straps to his forehead (symbolizing his mind) and left biceps (nearest to his heart) during morning prayer in order to dramatize the command in Deuteronomy (Deut 6:6-8). Jesus also criticizes the excessively long tassels on the Jewish man's (then) outer garment, which were fringed and knotted symbolically as a reminder of the 613 precepts of the Mosaic Law, and the honorific titles that are another flamboyant effort to impress others with one's holy status.

If we are inclined to dismiss these criticisms as rather quaint and irrelevant, we might think about the meaning of titles like *Eminence, Excellency,* or *Monsignor* (literally, "my Lord") or expensive dwellings and insignia for some clergy, all of which are common aspects of Catholic life. In contrast, we have prophetic bishops like the late Hélder Câmara, who died in 1999 in his simple house at Olinda in the parched, impoverished northeast region of Brazil. At Vatican II, wearing his wooden cross over a simple black cassock, Dom Hélder had urged his fellow bishops to sell their silver and gold pectoral crosses and give the money to the poor. Together with Cardinals Pierre Gerlier and Giacomo Lecaro, he created a small think tank of about forty bishops, the "church of the poor" group, which met regularly during the council. Just before its close, they made a public declaration of "Thirteen Commitments." Having recognized, they said, the deficiencies of their life of poverty in accordance with the Gospel, the members of the group proclaimed the thirteen commitments, each of which was based on and referenced by gospel texts. Included among them were commitments to "renounce the appearance and reality of riches, especially in clothing (fine cloth, striking colors), insignia in precious materials, for these signs should be evangelical" and to "refuse to be addressed orally or in writing by names indicating importance and power (Eminence, Excellency, Monsignor). We prefer to be addressed by the evangelical title Father."

Preparing to Proclaim

Key words and phrases: "Whoever exalts himself will be humbled; but whoever humbles himself will be exalted."

To the point: This gospel has one of Jesus's familiar reversals of our expectations for this world. He states that the visible religious leaders of his time are not, in fact, in favor with God. Their misguided love for recognition and honor outweighs their love for God. They seem to hold power—and by earthly standards, they do—but they are not enacting the true power that is available to all of us. This power is God's gift and enables us to enact God's will. It doesn't look much like power, though; it rather looks a lot like servanthood. Jesus tells his followers to humble themselves, because humility is the basis of true exaltation in God's ordering of things. This humility is found in unity, joined as brothers and sisters under one loving teacher and father and master.

Psalmist Preparation

You might see some wry smiles from mothers this week when you sing about the still, quiet child on its mother's lap—if the mothers in your congregation even have a chance to hear the words you're singing! As you prepare this psalm, say a prayer for all the parents who will hear it while wrangling small children through Mass. They are icons of the humility to which the gospel calls us, and they could likely use the peace the psalmist has found. Pray, too, for their children, who may still be learning how to behave in church but who are also the face of Christ to all of us present.

Making Connections

Between the readings: Both the psalm and the second reading use images of being cared for as a mother cares for her children; in the psalm it is an image for God's care for us, and in Thessalonians it is an image for how church leaders ought to care for the flock entrusted to them. This is again a reversal of our expectations: the self-giving work of mothers often goes unseen and unacknowledged, yet it is here a mark of leadership.

To experience: We don't always get to see the promise of this gospel played out; too often in this life, it seems that those with power only get more power and those without only fall further and further. Our sinful structures are cyclical by nature, and these cycles can seem insurmountably hard to break. But sometimes cycles are broken: parents can break intergenerational cycles of abuse and trauma, for instance, by sacrificing a power-based relationship for one based on love.

Homily Points

• The old saying spoke truth then and it speaks truth now: "Practice what you preach." The scribes and Pharisees devoted themselves to the law—yet they did not live it out. Throughout the gospels, we see Jesus grow increasingly frustrated with the religious leaders of the day who wield their authority in ways he deems hypocritical. These religious leaders know the law—and the law matters. Jesus came "not to abolish [the law,] but to fulfill [it]" (Matt 5:17). Religions need well-formed people who can carry the tradition and sacred texts into the present day. Yet, any teacher or parent will tell you that true learning rarely happens by simply being told what to do. Knowing the law intellectually is only the first step. Jesus calls his disciples to embody the law with their whole being—mind, body, and spirit.

• Before we point fingers too quickly—and likely fall into the same hypocrite camp Jesus tells us to avoid!—let us consider how Jesus approaches the scribes and Pharisees. Note that Jesus first recognizes the truth in their teachings: "[D]o and observe all things whatsoever they tell you." Then Jesus speaks honestly and directly to the issues he sees, naming specific examples of ways their actions fall short of the law's intent. Jesus once again models how we should approach others who we believe are in the wrong.

• Surely, we can all think of someone who acts a little too righteous while trying to show off their faith and presents a hypocritical message in the process. Rather than bad-mouthing them or writing them off completely, what if we were to follow Jesus's way of respectful, honest, and direct dialogue?

CELEBRATION

Model Penitential Act

Presider: In today's first reading, the prophet Malachi laments how the people broke faith with one another and violated the covenant with God. For the times we have not been faithful to our neighbors or to God, let us ask for mercy . . . *[pause]*

Lord Jesus, you teach us the way of humble service: Lord, have mercy.

Christ Jesus, you are moved with compassion for all of creation: Christ, have mercy.

Lord Jesus, you deserve our everlasting gratitude and praise: Lord, have mercy.

Model Universal Prayer (Prayer of the Faithful)

Presider: With hearts filled with compassion for the many needs of the world, let us lift up our prayers and petitions to God.

Response: Lord, hear our prayer.

Strengthen the integrity of the church and animate its members so that we may practice what we preach . . .

Guide our civil and religious discourse to greater respect, honesty, and openness . . .

Grant relief and healing to people suffering from addiction to drugs or alcohol . . .

Channel our energies toward the work of the gospel, particularly the care for people who are poor and marginalized . . .

Presider: Almighty and ever-living God, in your generosity you grace us with the gifts of the Holy Spirit. Receive our prayers that, emboldened by the Spirit, we might serve your people with humility and respect. We offer this prayer through Christ our Lord. **Amen.**

Liturgy and Music

Preparing for the New Liturgical Year: The end of the liturgical year is quickly approaching, and you might already be looking ahead and preparing music for Advent and Christmastime. As the year ends, encourage music ministers to reflect on the past year and try to identify times of grace and gratitude. Some questions for reflection: How have we experienced loving God and loving neighbor through our ministry? How have we turned our performance into prayer this past year? In what ways have we encountered God's presence in our music making and those with whom we make music?

Find some rehearsal time to share these reflections with the group and invite members to share their hopes for the new liturgical year as they prepare their hearts to continue in ministry.

When you prepare music for liturgy, how far in advance do you do so? Seasonally, monthly, weekly? Do you prepare music in committee or alone? Do you read through all the readings and use a music planning guide or a liturgy resource?

The benefit of preparing music through a season or over a few months allows the music director to identify common topics within the readings, which helps with shaping the music program and to know when to include new songs and anticipate repeating these songs, which develops congregational singing. This kind of planning builds confidence in music making and deepens prayer. While it is good practice to prepare music seasonally, always be flexible to making changes to the plan to respond to the topical and pastoral realities.

COLLECT

Let us pray.

Pause for silent prayer

Almighty and merciful God,
by whose gift your faithful offer you
right and praiseworthy service,
grant, we pray,
that we may hasten without stumbling
to receive the things you have promised.
Through our Lord Jesus Christ, your Son,
who lives and reigns with you in the unity
of the Holy Spirit,
one God, for ever and ever. **Amen.**

FIRST READING
Mal 1:14b–2:2b, 8-10

A great King am I, says the LORD of hosts,
and my name will be feared among the nations.
And now, O priests, this commandment is for you:
If you do not listen,
if you do not lay it to heart,
to give glory to my name, says the LORD of hosts,
I will send a curse upon you
and of your blessing I will make a curse.
You have turned aside from the way,
and have caused many to falter by your instruction;
you have made void the covenant of Levi,
says the LORD of hosts.
I, therefore, have made you contemptible
and base before all the people,
since you do not keep my ways,
but show partiality in your decisions.
Have we not all the one father?
Has not the one God created us?
Why then do we break faith with one another,
violating the covenant of our fathers?

RESPONSORIAL PSALM

Ps 131:1, 2, 3

R̶. In you, Lord, I have found my peace.

O LORD, my heart is not proud,
    nor are my eyes haughty;
I busy not myself with great things,
    nor with things too sublime for me.

R̶. In you, Lord, I have found my peace.

Nay rather, I have stilled and quieted
    my soul like a weaned child.
Like a weaned child on its mother's lap,
    so is my soul within me.

R̶. In you, Lord, I have found my peace.

O Israel, hope in the LORD,
    both now and forever.

R̶. In you, Lord, I have found my peace.

SECOND READING

1 Thess 2:7b-9, 13

Brothers and sisters:
We were gentle among you, as a nursing
    mother cares for her children.
With such affection for you, we were
    determined to share with you
    not only the gospel of God, but our very
        selves as well,
    so dearly beloved had you become to us.
You recall, brothers and sisters, our toil
    and drudgery.
Working night and day in order not to
    burden any of you,
    we proclaimed to you the gospel of God.

And for this reason we too give thanks to
    God unceasingly,
    that, in receiving the word of God from
        hearing us,
    you received not a human word but, as
        it truly is, the word of God,
    which is now at work in you who
        believe.

Living Liturgy

Surrender: Over the Lenten season, we reflected on a downward journey toward the cross, a passage toward humility. Today we are reminded as we approach the end of the liturgical year, to once again root our ministry in the glory of God. Those involved in or considering Christian leadership must be like Jesus, a servant for all. Rather than fall into the trappings of honor and personal gain over the people's good as the scribes and Pharisees have, we are asked to contemplate the example of the psalmist's gentle surrender to the gracious will of God and reflect on the great responsibilities of ministry that we have been given—In you, Lord, I have found my peace. Humility requires surrender. What does it mean to surrender everything to God?

The message of the *Suscipe* (Latin for "take") prayer of St. Ignatius of Loyola gives us a starting point to begin thinking about surrender in relation to ministry for God's glory when we compare it against modern society's message which is often an individualistic one. Our world thrives on competition. It values climbing over others to rise to the top, claiming what comes to the individual.

Instead, the *Suscipe* prayer urges us to relinquish the need for control and power to acknowledge that everything belongs to God, and that love and grace alone are enough for us to thrive in ministry. Everything is for God's greater glory. Be humble and grateful to God for everything entrusted to us. So, as we practice what we preach in ministry with self-reflection and in openness to God's love, we reclaim our ministerial identity of servant leadership in the example of Jesus. In this way, we surrender all things in acceptance of a lower status, a status and place that knows intimately the hope only found in God.

PROMPTS FOR FAITH-SHARING

• What does humility mean to you? How do you live it out in your life? How do you struggle with it?

• Have you known any great examples of servant leadership? What did you learn from them?

• Both the gospel and the first reading call for unity. Are there people in the church with whom you would rather not be in communion? How might God be calling you to reconciliation with them?

✝ SPIRITUALITY

GOSPEL ACCLAMATION
Matt 24:42a, 44

℟. Alleluia, alleluia.
Stay awake and be ready!
For you do not know on what day your
　　Lord will come.
℟. Alleluia, alleluia.

Gospel　Matt 25:1-13; L154A

Jesus told his disciples this parable:
　"The kingdom of heaven will be
　　　like ten virgins
　who took their lamps and went out
　　　to meet the bridegroom.
Five of them were foolish and five
　　　were wise.
The foolish ones, when taking their
　　　lamps,
　brought no oil with them,
　but the wise brought flasks of oil
　　　with their lamps.
Since the bridegroom was long
　　　delayed,
　they all became drowsy and fell
　　　asleep.
At midnight, there was a cry,
　'Behold, the bridegroom! Come out to
　　　meet him!'
Then all those virgins got up and trimmed
　　　their lamps.
The foolish ones said to the wise,
　'Give us some of your oil,
　for our lamps are going out.'
But the wise ones replied,
　'No, for there may not be enough for us
　　　and you.
Go instead to the merchants and buy
　　　some for yourselves.'
While they went off to buy it,
　the bridegroom came
　and those who were ready went into
　　　the wedding feast with him.
Then the door was locked.
Afterwards the other virgins came and said,
　'Lord, Lord, open the door for us!'
But he said in reply,
　'Amen, I say to you, I do not know you.'
Therefore, stay awake,
　for you know neither the day nor the
　　　hour."

Reflecting on the Gospel

At the end of the baptism liturgy, a candle is lit from the paschal candle and handed to the parents of the child with these words: "Parents and godparents, this light is entrusted to you to be kept burning brightly, so that your child, enlightened by Christ, may walk always as a child of the light and, persevering in the faith, may run to meet the Lord when he comes with all the Saints in the heavenly court." Behind this prayer stands the parable we hear in the gospel reading today, about the five wise and five foolish young women.

Unique to Matthew, this is the only parable of watching and waiting where discipleship is portrayed in feminine imagery. In the parable, the kingdom of heaven "will be like" a gathering of young women, unmarried but of marriageable age—in first-century Palestine, that begins at age twelve—who according to cultural norms are waiting at the bride's parental home so that they can meet the bridegroom as he approaches the house. Jesus has earlier referred to himself in Matthew's Gospel as the "bridegroom" (Matt 9:15), and God as "husband" is a recurring Old Testament metaphor (see Isa 54:5; Jer 31:32; Hos 2:16). The parable presents us with both a positive and negative model of how disciples are to wait for the return of Jesus the Bridegroom at the end of human history. The emphasis is on the oil and the burning lamps, not on the falling asleep, which all ten girls do when the arrival of the bridegroom is delayed. In baptism, we are chosen to illumine the passage of Christ the Bridegroom through our world by the lives we live. For Matthew, "oil" and "lamps" are symbolic of good works and Christian witness that gives glory to God.

In gospel terms, readiness to greet the Bridegroom and go with him to the eternal wedding banquet means a life lived in constant vigilance for and obedience to the reign of God that Jesus proclaims. The baptized neophyte, the newly married, the newly professed or ordained, the beginner in a longed-for job—all are excited and determined about the life to which they have committed themselves; all have their "lamps" burning brightly. Deeper into the night, into the demands of decades of oil refilling and wick tending, some flames may have flickered out while others continue to burn steadily and brightly, even though some may light up paths that differ from the original way the lamp carriers thought they would walk.

Although the parable is primarily concerned with what lies behind the, as yet, closed doors of the end of cosmic history and Christ's second coming, the Bridegroom will also come to us in our own death. One Eucharist will be the last from which we take the oil from the two tables of word and sacrament that help us to keep our lamps burning and light our way to open the doors of our hearts to the Bridegroom.

Preparing to Proclaim

Key words and phrases: "[S]tay awake, for you know neither the day nor the hour."

To the point: The end of the liturgical year always presents us with Scripture passages that speak of the end times. This theme will continue into Advent's repetitive admonition to stay awake and ready for the ultimate coming of Christ. The Bible's images of this time are sometimes troubling; here, we have a locked door and a Bridegroom who refuses to recognize those who came unprepared for the wedding feast—hardly a reassuring image of Christ's boundless mercy. But this is not a gospel about the mechanics of our preparation; when put into dialogue with the other readings for today, it becomes a gospel about our longing to be with Jesus. Those whose hearts desire him will find ways to prepare their hearts. The specifics of that preparation will look different for all of us, but love and longing are at their core.

Psalmist Preparation

This is one of the most heart-wrenchingly passionate psalms we sing as a church. The image of the parched earth is powerful; its readiness to receive and absorb rain is the posture we are asked to possess toward Christ both at his final coming and in all his everyday comings into our hearts and lives. This psalm is especially powerful at Mass as we move toward the Liturgy of the Eucharist; our flesh pines and our soul thirsts, and God responds with giving us his flesh and his blood for drink. Try to bring this psalm into your preparation for and reception of the Eucharist this week, receiving Christ with the ardent love of which the psalmist sings here.

Making Connections

Between the readings: The second reading reminds us that, even in the face of all that is dark and scary in the world, we are called to live with hope—hope granted to us through faith in the one who has conquered even death. The first reading tells us more about the wisdom attributed to half the gospel's virgins; this wisdom character is also read as an Old Testament image of Christ. Here, she is not a hardhearted host but is always waiting and preparing for those who seek her. Our love for wisdom—and for Jesus, the wisdom of God—is always met with preexisting love that seeks us first.

To experience: These eschatological November readings are fitting for the month Catholics dedicate to remembrance of the dead. Even as we grieve our losses, this week offers us a reminder to live in hope, not just for ourselves but for all our departed loved ones.

Homily Points

• How can we prepare to wait? This odd question strikes at the heart of today's gospel. Jesus offers the parable of ten virgins waiting for the bridegroom to help his followers imagine what it will be like to wait for the Son of Man to return. First, we see the virgins arrive together and stay together. If only one virgin had been there alone all night, it would have been much easier for her to give up. Who would have kept her motivated? Who would she have turned to when the waiting got hard? Like the virgins, Jesus wants us to live in joyful hope for the coming of the kingdom as a community. Church at its best encourages and strengthens the community of believers.

• The wise virgins came prepared with flasks of oil—but not infinite amounts. Similarly, Jesus calls us to be ready to wait for the coming of God's kingdom with humility and patience, recognizing that we do not yet have the fullness of faith, hope, and love in our lamps. But we do have something. Our lamps need not run empty if we steward our oil well. Like the wise virgins, we are called to wait with anticipation. Surely the bridegroom will come back!

• If the wise virgins had no faith in the bridegroom's return, why would they have continued to wait? Something—likely those spiritual gifts of faith, hope, and love—convinced them to keep vigil. We too receive spiritual gifts through the sacraments and the life of the church that empower us to keep waiting and to keep believing that what has been promised by God will one day be fulfilled.

Model Penitential Act

Presider: In today's first reading, we hear that wisdom is "readily perceived by those who love her and found by those who seek her." Strengthened by wisdom, let us turn to the Lord for healing . . . *[pause]*

> Lord Jesus, you are the Word made flesh: Lord, have mercy.
>
> Christ Jesus, you show us the way of patient endurance: Christ, have mercy.
>
> Lord Jesus, you offered your life for the salvation of all: Lord, have mercy.

Model Universal Prayer (Prayer of the Faithful)

Presider: Trusting in God's abiding love for the world, let us place our needs and the needs of our community before the Lord.

Response: Lord, hear our prayer.

Equip the pope with the wisdom, compassion, and patience needed to guide the church . . .

Inspire spiritual artists, writers, and teachers with creativity and energy . . .

Grant comfort and communal support to people who are waiting for medical test results and their loved ones . . .

Bring reconciliation and peace to people in our community who are hurting from broken relationships . . .

Presider: God of justice, you sent your son into the world to show us the way of mercy and love. Receive our prayers that each day we might grow ever more aware of Christ's presence among us until at last, we are joined together in heaven. We ask this through Christ our Lord. **Amen.**

Liturgy and Music

Feast of St. Cecilia: The feast of St. Cecilia, patron saint of musicians and poets, is coming up on November 22. Think of celebrating this day with a concert or a retreat for the music ministers. During this time, reflect on your calling into the vocation of music ministry. What inspires you to make music? The liturgies of November are filled with remembrance and giving thanks in Christian faith. Offer a blessing over the musicians of the parish and gather all music ministers for a meal of thanksgiving.

Our vocation of music ministry calls us to keep the light of Christ that we have received in baptism burning brightly until we meet the Lord. We remind ourselves that music is not something that is in the liturgy, it is of the liturgy. Through music, we express our thanksgiving and God's love is revealed. St. Cecilia's connection with church music comes from reports of her singing to God in her heart. While there is limited evidence that she ever played the organ, she is a perfect model of giving her life to God and her story inspires future witnesses of the church's worship.

Continue to prepare for the new liturgical year by gaining more insight on music and liturgy through these documents: Constitution on the Sacred Liturgy, General Instruction of the Roman Missal, *Musicam Sacram, Music in Catholic Worship, Liturgical Music Today,* and *Sing to the Lord.*

COLLECT

Let us pray.

Pause for silent prayer

Almighty and merciful God,
graciously keep from us all adversity,
so that, unhindered in mind and body alike,
we may pursue in freedom of heart
the things that are yours.
Through our Lord Jesus Christ, your Son,
who lives and reigns with you in the unity of the Holy Spirit,
God, for ever and ever. **Amen.**

FIRST READING

Wis 6:12-16

Resplendent and unfading is wisdom,
   and she is readily perceived by those who love her,
   and found by those who seek her.
She hastens to make herself known in anticipation of their desire;
   whoever watches for her at dawn shall not be disappointed,
   for he shall find her sitting by his gate.
For taking thought of wisdom is the perfection of prudence,
   and whoever for her sake keeps vigil shall quickly be free from care;
because she makes her own rounds, seeking those worthy of her,
   and graciously appears to them in the ways,
   and meets them with all solicitude.

RESPONSORIAL PSALM

Ps 63:2, 3-4, 5-6, 7-8

℟. (2b) My soul is thirsting for you, O Lord my God.

O God, you are my God whom I seek;
   for you my flesh pines and my soul thirsts
   like the earth, parched, lifeless and without water.

℟. My soul is thirsting for you, O Lord my God.

Thus have I gazed toward you in the sanctuary
   to see your power and your glory,
for your kindness is a greater good than life;
   my lips shall glorify you.

℟. My soul is thirsting for you, O Lord my God.

Thus will I bless you while I live;
  lifting up my hands, I will call upon
    your name.
As with the riches of a banquet shall my
    soul be satisfied,
  and with exultant lips my mouth shall
    praise you.

℞. My soul is thirsting for you, O Lord
my God.

I will remember you upon my couch,
  and through the night-watches I will
    meditate on you:
you are my help,
  and in the shadow of your wings I
    shout for joy.

℞. My soul is thirsting for you, O Lord
my God.

SECOND READING
1 Thess 4:13-18

We do not want you to be unaware,
    brothers and sisters,
  about those who have fallen asleep,
  so that you may not grieve like the rest,
    who have no hope.
For if we believe that Jesus died and rose,
  so too will God, through Jesus,
  bring with him those who have fallen
    asleep.
Indeed, we tell you this, on the word of
    the Lord,
  that we who are alive,
  who are left until the coming of the
    Lord,
  will surely not precede those who have
    fallen asleep.
For the Lord himself, with a word of
    command,
  with the voice of an archangel and with
    the trumpet of God,
  will come down from heaven,
  and the dead in Christ will rise first.
Then we who are alive, who are left,
  will be caught up together with them in
    the clouds
  to meet the Lord in the air.
Thus we shall always be with the Lord.
Therefore, console one another with these
    words.

or 1 Thess 4:13-14

See Appendix A, p. 303.

Living Liturgy

Preparing Three Words: How well do we prepare for life and all its experiences, here and on the other side of eternity? There are many life experiences that are beyond our control—family emergencies, natural disasters, unexpected health crises. Having lived in California for over three decades, it has become a way of life to be prepared for earthquakes. Along with preparing and refreshing an earthquake kit regularly, we constantly remember these words of survival: Drop. Cover. Hold On.

We hear in this week's readings what it means to be prepared to receive the kingdom of heaven. As we approach the end of the liturgical year we are reminded of the importance to "stay awake" and to be ready as we await the return of Christ, the groom, knowing that that day and time cannot be predicted. So, we reflect on the end times and death. How best will we be prepared when the time comes? Which three words will help point us towards the coming kingdom?

Thomas Merton through his life lived according to the gospel and the Rule of St. Benedict, which encourages us to keep death in our field of vision. And we come to realize that we were created for eternal life with God. Through a life of prayer and service—scriptural, liturgical, and personal—Merton urges a dedication to prayer, which helps us to "unclench our fists which cling to memories of the past and plants for the future so we might live fully and without fear in the present moment"(Gregory J. Ryan, "Thomas Merton on Death").

So, the three words that I hold on to for reflection during spiritual preparation of my passage into the eternal kingdom circle around prayer and ministry. The three words I hold in my heart are gratitude, joy, and imagination. Prepare your three words.

PROMPTS FOR FAITH-SHARING

• Do you identify more with the wise or foolish virgins in the gospel?

• How do you think you, particularly, are called to prepare your heart for Christ's coming?

• Re-read the first reading, remembering that "wisdom of God" is one of Christ's ancient titles. How does this reading work for you as an image of Christ? How does it compare with the gospel?

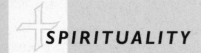

SPIRITUALITY

℟. Alleluia, alleluia.
Remain in me as I remain in you, says the
    Lord.
Whoever remains in me bears much fruit.
℟. Alleluia, alleluia.

Gospel   Matt 25:14-30; L157A

Jesus told his disciples this parable:
  "A man going on a journey
  called in his servants and entrusted
      his possessions to them.
To one he gave five talents; to another,
    two; to a third, one—
  to each according to his ability.
Then he went away.
Immediately the one who received five
    talents went and traded with them,
    and made another five.
Likewise, the one who received two
    made another two.
But the man who received one went off
    and dug a hole in the ground
    and buried his master's money.

"After a long time
  the master of those servants came back
    and settled accounts with them.
The one who had received five talents
    came forward
  bringing the additional five.
He said, 'Master, you gave me five talents.
See, I have made five more.'
His master said to him, 'Well done, my
    good and faithful servant.
Since you were faithful in small matters,
  I will give you great responsibilities.
Come, share your master's joy.'
Then the one who had received two
    talents also came forward and said,
  'Master, you gave me two talents.
See, I have made two more.'
His master said to him, 'Well done, my
    good and faithful servant.

Continued in Appendix A, p. 304, or
Matt 25:14-15, 19-21 *in Appendix A, p. 304.*

Reflecting on the Gospel

The parable we hear Jesus tell his disciples in the gospel today continues his teaching about the last days. The opening words cue us in to the fact that Jesus is again using allegory to teach about the kingdom of heaven. We are not really talking about high financial investment, but investment in gospel living. Shares will come to maturity when Jesus returns at the end of human history on the

cosmic Day of the Lord. The master's concluding harsh words and actions that we may find disturbing are dictated by the logic of the story and not by a theological imaging of God as revealed in Jesus.

Every disciple, like the master's slaves in the parable, has the responsibility of using the gifts we have been given by God for the sake of the kingdom. There is to be no "playing safe" in such an investment.

To each of the three slaves the master gives an enormous amount of money in the currency of "talents." At a conservative estimate, a talent was worth more than fifteen years of wages for a laborer, and this is the lowest amount given to the third slave! The amount for the five and two talent recipients soars correspondingly, and again the literary device of exaggeration comes into play for the sake of impressive and attention-catching storytelling. The slaves are given no instructions about what they are to do with the money; they are simply entrusted with it, each according to his own ability. Each must decide how to exercise his stewardship during the master's absence; there is no question of the slaves being in competition with one another. The master has taken a risk with both his money and his slaves, and the first two slaves respond by taking risks and trading with the money in order to make more, not for themselves, but for their master. The third slave "plays it safe." Cautious, unimaginative, and fearful, he buries the one talent. In the ancient world this was considered a safe way of hiding money, especially in a time of war (see Matt 13:44), but safety is not the issue here.

Discipleship is not just a comfortable holding on to the gifts that God has given us. It challenges us to action, to risk-taking, to increasing the yield of good works and sharing these with others, and to refraining from excuses for our failures. We cannot take refuge in our own preconceived and often sterile images of God, nor revel in what we regard as a "victim" relationship with God. The risks that earn us affirmation as "good and trustworthy" servants are the ordinary kingdom exchanges of daily life: forgiving rather than burying a grudge in our hearts; standing by another in times of sorrow, failure, or misunderstanding; giving someone the benefit of the doubt; associating with those whom many consider the "wrong kind" of people; laying down one's life for another—perhaps a misunderstood friend, a rebellious child, a terminally ill spouse, or an aged parent. All this "now" effort is preparing us for the "not yet" entry into the kingdom.

Preparing to Proclaim

Key words and phrases: "Come, share your master's joy."

To the point: This gospel introduces an important concept for our life of faith: faithfulness in small matters is how we practice our readiness to be faithful in greater ways. As athletes train through consistent training, we grow in virtue through the discipline of consistent practice whenever the opportunity arises. Small moral choices might seem not to matter, but they do; they are an opportunity to develop our holiness muscles. While the servants deal with their master's money for a limited time, we are responsible for our gifts for the entirety of our lives. This can be an overwhelming proposition, but there is reassurance here: practicing trustworthiness in small ways prepares us for the great joy that God promises. In all the ordinary ways we act with compassion and justice and integrity, we are practicing and preparing for nothing less than heaven.

Psalmist Preparation

The idea of "walking" in God's ways is a lovely one for our life of ongoing growth in faith. It is a journey we make one step at a time, and the steps are often small ones. But our faithfulness is rewarded with fruitfulness—not always as visible as it is in this psalm's image of blissful domestic life, but real nonetheless. Think of one discipline in your own faith life that might be bettered by increased consistency; it might be a greater commitment to daily prayer or the regular practice of a work of mercy. Consider making a resolution and be sure to invite God into your intention. This can help make this psalm's response an earnest prayer: to persevere in faithfulness, we need God's blessing and accompaniment, each and every day.

Making Connections

Between the readings: The first reading echoes the idea that faithfulness in daily labors is how one lives out a lifelong commitment, whether that commitment is to one's spouse or to a life of faith. The second reading has those late fall pre-Advent vibes, when we are reminded of the end times and of our need to stay prepared. In light of the gospel and first reading, we know how to do this: through commitments to our small, daily acts of faith and love.

To experience: Whatever our life circumstances, there are countless opportunities every day to make right or wrong choices. This can seem overwhelming and demanding: why would God ask so much of us? But it can also be seen as an opportunity, one provided by God's endless mercy. We have countless opportunities to do wrong, but we also have boundless chances to correct course, to try again, to participate anew in God's work of making us holy and whole.

Homily Points

• How are you using the gifts God gives you? Do you live life to the fullest, or do you tend to play it safe? Are you willing to take risks for who and what you believe in, or does fear drive your days? These are the sorts of challenging questions evoked in today's gospel. Jesus tells this parable to his followers toward the end of his life, when he too faces big questions about what was and what is to come. The Son of God chose to leave the safety of Galilee and journey to Jerusalem, where those in power wait to persecute him. Yet Jesus goes anyway. He knows his life means something beyond himself. Jesus loves the world so deeply that he is willing to risk his very life for our growth and prosperity.

• What would it look like for us, his disciples, to live the same way? God gifts us lives filled with meaning and purpose. Like the master in today's gospel, God gives us talents and expects us to grow them, especially for the sake of the poor, the marginalized, and the suffering.

• Two weeks from now, we begin a new liturgical year—and a new calendar year kicks off a few weeks after that. Let us take time to consider how we can live more fully into our discipleship this next year. Where is God calling us to take risks for our faith? How is God calling us to act with bravery and boldness for the sake of the gospel?

Model Penitential Act

Presider: As we prepare to encounter God in Scripture and in sacrament, let us call to mind our sins and ask for God's forgiveness . . . *[pause]*

Lord Jesus, you are the light of the world: Lord, have mercy.

Christ Jesus, you strengthen your people to do the hard gospel work: Christ, have mercy.

Lord Jesus, you will come again to draw us into the peace of everlasting life: Lord, have mercy.

Model Universal Prayer (Prayer of the Faithful)

Presider: Emboldened by God's never-ending mercy and trust, let us offer our prayers and petitions before the Lord.

Response: Lord, hear our prayer.

Advance respect and dialogue among Christians of different traditions . . .

Inspire civil and religious leaders to work together to abolish the death penalty . . .

Grant perseverance and healing to people going through cancer treatments . . .

Strengthen in all gathered here the gifts of discernment and risk-taking for the sake of the gospel . . .

Presider: God of all goodness, you called your son to risk his life for the salvation of your beloved people. Hear our prayers that each day we might grow in discipleship and seek to praise you with our words and actions. We ask this through Christ our Lord. **Amen.**

Liturgy and Music

Using Our Talents: Using our talents wisely means not only understanding our role as music ministers but embracing the power that liturgical music has in enriching community. Music has power to channel our emotions and beliefs. Music well-prepared and practiced has the ability to deepen prayer and move the inner heart to enter the heart of God. So, our role as music ministers is to assist the spiritual exchange between God and God's people at prayer. We also trust that the Lord will come with or without our help, but it is our task as music ministers to use our talents to ready the people for the Lord's holy advent.

To help focus our role as music ministers, try thinking less about what instrument accompanies the opening song and more about gathering the lost and disaffiliated ones into the community. Think less about whether the song for the preparation of the gifts is a motet or an Appalachian hymn and more about how we help the poor and give voice to the ones who are broken and struggling. Think less about how high the gospel book is carried in procession and more about how God's word calls us to heal the wounds of a community. We pray that we may use our gifts wisely to bring God's people together.

COLLECT

Let us pray.

Pause for silent prayer

Grant us, we pray, O Lord our God,
the constant gladness of being devoted
        to you,
for it is full and lasting happiness
to serve with constancy
the author of all that is good.
Through our Lord Jesus Christ, your Son,
who lives and reigns with you in the unity
        of the Holy Spirit,
God, for ever and ever. **Amen.**

FIRST READING

Prov 31:10-13, 19-20, 30-31

When one finds a worthy wife,
        her value is far beyond pearls.
Her husband, entrusting his heart to her,
        has an unfailing prize.
She brings him good, and not evil,
        all the days of her life.
She obtains wool and flax
        and works with loving hands.
She puts her hands to the distaff,
        and her fingers ply the spindle.
She reaches out her hands to the poor,
        and extends her arms to the needy.
Charm is deceptive and beauty fleeting;
        the woman who fears the LORD is to be
                praised.
Give her a reward for her labors,
        and let her works praise her at the city
                gates.

RESPONSORIAL PSALM

Ps 128:1-2, 3, 4-5

R℣. (cf. 1a) Blessed are those who fear the Lord.

Blessed are you who fear the LORD,
    who walk in his ways!
For you shall eat the fruit of your
      handiwork;
    blessed shall you be, and favored.

R℣. Blessed are those who fear the Lord.

Your wife shall be like a fruitful vine
    in the recesses of your home;
your children like olive plants
    around your table.

R℣. Blessed are those who fear the Lord.

Behold, thus is the man blessed
    who fears the LORD.
The LORD bless you from Zion:
    may you see the prosperity of
        Jerusalem
    all the days of your life.

R℣. Blessed are those who fear the Lord.

SECOND READING

1 Thess 5:1-6

Concerning times and seasons, brothers
      and sisters,
    you have no need for anything to be
        written to you.
For you yourselves know very well that
      the day of the Lord will come
    like a thief at night.
When people are saying, "Peace and
      security,"
    then sudden disaster comes upon them,
    like labor pains upon a pregnant
      woman,
    and they will not escape.

But you, brothers and sisters, are not in
      darkness,
    for that day to overtake you like a thief.
For all of you are children of the light
    and children of the day.
We are not of the night or of darkness.
Therefore, let us not sleep as the rest do,
    but let us stay alert and sober.

Living Liturgy

Active Discipleship: The parable Jesus offers today does not endorse a particular class of people. It instead echoes the fullness of the Matthean church, a community of some who contribute to the common purpose and others who make little or no effort at achieving a common goal. Every action in ministry is important. It is interesting to note that one who buries the talent, as a safer option, does so out of "fear" of losing it. Living out our gifts in service of others without counting the cost should motivate and rejuvenate our vocation in ministry. Living lives of discipleship means examining the excuses we make not to give generously, to hide gifts in fear and disengage in active kingdom building.

Paul's letter tells us that we tend to worry about the wrong things, sometimes looking for answers in the wrong places. We think we might be ready if we knew or could predict the time the master will return. While we cannot know the answer to that question, we are not left helpless, for we are children of light. Those of us who are afraid are not alone. Instead of repressing fear or allowing it to immobilize or conflict with our ministerial contribution, we might consider the lives of saints who turned to God in their fear and found hope for kingdom building, even if they felt seldom less afraid. St. Frances Xavier Cabrini lived through her fear of water, unwilling to let fear stand in the way of discipleship and her gift of saving souls, to make the transatlantic journey by ship to the United States at the request of the Holy Father. Take some time to think of which gifts of God we have "buried" out of worry, fear or laziness. Dig them up and use them to enter another liturgical year of active discipleship.

PROMPTS FOR FAITH-SHARING

• Are there areas in your life where you could practice greater faithfulness in seemingly small ways?

• Do you find it overwhelming or reassuring to think that there might be countless opportunities to grow in holiness in your everyday life?

• What do you think of the images of marriage presented in the first reading and the psalm? If you are married, do they resonate with your experience? If you are not, what might these readings be inviting you to consider about faithfulness and commitment in other areas of your life?

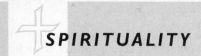

SPIRITUALITY

GOSPEL ACCLAMATION
Mark 11:9, 10

R7. Alleluia, alleluia.
Blessed is he who comes in the name of the Lord!
Blessed is the kingdom of our father David that
    is to come!
R7. Alleluia, alleluia.

Gospel   Matt 25:31-46; L160A

Jesus said to his disciples:
 "When the Son of Man comes in
    his glory,
 and all the angels with him,
 he will sit upon his glorious
    throne,
 and all the nations will be
    assembled before him.
And he will separate them one
    from another,
 as a shepherd separates the
    sheep from the goats.
He will place the sheep on his
    right and the goats on his left.
Then the king will say to those on
    his right,
 'Come, you who are blessed by
    my Father.
Inherit the kingdom prepared for
    you from the foundation of
    the world.
For I was hungry and you gave me food,
 I was thirsty and you gave me drink,
 a stranger and you welcomed me,
 naked and you clothed me,
 ill and you cared for me,
 in prison and you visited me.'
Then the righteous will answer him and say,
 'Lord, when did we see you hungry and
    feed you,
 or thirsty and give you drink?
When did we see you a stranger and
    welcome you,
 or naked and clothe you?
When did we see you ill or in prison, and
    visit you?'
And the king will say to them in reply,
 'Amen, I say to you, whatever you did
    for one of the least brothers of mine, you
    did for me.'

Continued in Appendix A, p. 304.

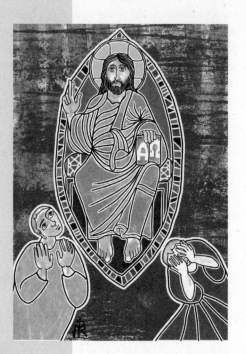

Reflecting on the Gospel

The solemnity of Our Lord Jesus Christ, King of the Universe, was instituted by Pope Pius XI in 1925 as a response to the social and political climate of the time. Pope Pius XI hoped to encourage believers to embrace Jesus Christ as not only the Sovereign of their hearts, but also the Sovereign of all nations and peoples.

It is clear throughout Scripture that Jesus Christ was indeed sent by God to exercise authority over heaven and earth and bring all of creation back into harmonious relationship with God. It is also clear that humanity's visions of "kingship" and God's visions have not always been in alignment. The Jewish people who came to know Jesus were expecting a messiah who would act as a political leader and overthrow the Roman Empire. This, of course, was not to be. In today's second reading from the first book of Corinthians, we hear specifically that Jesus's sovereignty would surpass all earthly powers and authorities. If Jesus did not come to exert himself as a secular, political leader, then how are we to understand Christ's sovereignty and power? And what, then, is the implication of this on our current understandings of power and authority?

First, we should look to the examples of leadership described in the other readings provided to us on this feast day. In the reading from the book of Ezekiel, we are presented with the image of the Good Shepherd. God promises to rescue his sheep, to seek the lost, to heal the sick, and give them rest. The Good Shepherd is a figure of authority, but a benevolent one whose main objective is to show care and compassion toward the sheep. Throughout the gospels, we see Christ manifest this vision when he dines with undesirables, heals the unclean, shows mercy to sinners. The leadership that Christ exercises is a servant-leadership, one that offers care rather than simply control. At a time in our society when trust in authority figures and institutions is discouragingly low, Christ the King offers up a vision of leadership that all people can put their faith in.

While we strive to put our faith in Christ who is our ultimate leader and guide, we can also determine the legitimacy of our earthly leaders by noting how closely they follow the example of the Good Shepherd. During his earthly ministry, Christ led by example. Do the leaders whom we look to today give us a powerful and Christlike example to follow—spiritually, politically, and otherwise? The leadership that Christ demonstrated and proclaimed while on earth was unconventional, subversive, and misunderstood by so many, from religious leaders to his own disciples. Are we receptive to leadership styles that may seem unconventional but whose essence is aligned with the radical call of the gospels? In his ministry, Christ showed a special concern for the overlooked and ostracized members of society, even when doing so threatened social norms. Do we hold our leaders to these standards of compassion and inclusion? Are we prepared to challenge the status quo by actively seeking out the lost, lonely, and injured?

As we honor Christ the King, let us also seek to raise up leaders among us who follow in his footsteps and will help usher in the kingdom of God.

Preparing to Proclaim

Key words and phrases: "[W]hatever you did for one of the least brothers of mine, you did for me."

To the point: When we envision royalty, we think of glamour and adventure, of triumph and power. Kings and queens are people set apart, people greater than others. In this gospel, Jesus offers us a radically different image. He comes in glory and power, yes, but underlying this is a radical solidarity with the least ones of his kingdom. Christ's power is used to encourage just and compassionate treatment of those we are all too quick to overlook: people who are poor, unfamiliar, and imprisoned. His power lies not primarily in shaming and banishing those who do not obey this command, but in his deep identification with those in need. We would probably claim that we would treat Jesus with the utmost respect, deserving of his unique place in the cosmic kingdom. Here he tells us, though, that we have opportunities to do so all the time. How we treat the least ones we encounter is how we treat Christ, our King.

Psalmist Preparation

This psalm's familiarity can sometimes blunt its impact, especially for those of us who lead congregations in song and thus hear the songs so many times over as we rehearse and prepare. But this one is replete with beautiful imagery for God's leadership; it is not about control but about care. God grants those in his charge rest and nourishment, safety and satisfaction. As you prepare this psalm, spend a little time trying to rest in God's presence. Can you place yourself into God's care as you proclaim this psalm? It might invite others to do the same.

Making Connections

Between the readings: The first reading also has an image of leadership being turned upside down; shepherds were not people who commanded much respect in the ancient world, but it is them with whom God identifies. In the second reading, Paul affirms that Christ's power does not exist for its own sake. Rather, it is part of God's greater plan to restore us to right relationship with each other, with our world, and with God.

To experience: Even when we know better, we often seek to exert power over those with whom we have been placed in relationship. This can be especially true of the children in our lives, who we often seek to control. But they, too, can bear Christ to us, and as "least ones" in our midst give us an opportunity to enact compassion and justice toward our very King.

Homily Points

• We have come to the end of another liturgical year. Before we jump too far into the freshness of Advent, let us pause and take stock of this past year of Christian living. Where did we encounter Christ? When did we act as Christ for another? In what ways did we succeed—and fall short—in answering the Christian call? Today's gospel reminds us of our core Christian practices: feeding the hungry, giving drink to the thirsty, welcoming the stranger, clothing the naked, caring for the sick, and visiting the imprisoned. Each of these actions makes the love of Christ known in the world. As we reflect back on the past year, may God draw our awareness to the people and places that benefited from our Christian practices and the areas in which we can grow in the year ahead.

• Today's gospel paints a vivid picture of the end times. Over the past few weeks, we have heard Jesus preach about the ways we are to live as we await the coming of God's kingdom. Matthew leaves little to the imagination in this final scene. When the Son of Man comes in glory, we will be judged by how we treated the poor and the marginalized—Christ in our midst.

• Caring for our neighbors in need is challenging work. How easy it is to walk by the person asking for grocery money or to keep at arm's length the immigrant family new to town. Yet easy is not the Christian way. Guided by the Holy Spirit, we can do the hard work of loving our neighbors.

Model Penitential Act

Presider: Jesus Christ, King of the universe, intercedes for us at the right hand of God. Grateful for his mercy, let us call to mind our sins and ask for forgiveness . . . *[pause]*

Lord Jesus, you are the Son of Man: Lord, have mercy.

Christ Jesus, you strengthen your people to spread the good news: Christ, have mercy.

Lord Jesus, you will come again in glory: Lord, have mercy.

Model Universal Prayer (Prayer of the Faithful)

Presider: As we celebrate the feast of Christ the King of the Universe, let us entrust the Lord with our prayers and petitions.

Response: Lord, hear our prayer.

Bless all catechists, ministers, priests, parish staff members, and volunteers who served the church over the past year . . .

Cultivate attention and care for the most vulnerable in elected and appointed government officials . . .

Reconcile friendships and family ties that are strained by hurt or misunderstanding . . .

Inspire all the baptized to live more deeply into our Christian calling to love God and neighbor in the new year ahead . . .

Presider: God of glory, in you we live and move and have our being. Hear our prayers that as we honor the kingship of Christ, we might contribute to the building up of your kingdom on earth. We ask this through Christ our Lord. **Amen.**

Liturgy and Music

Sing Then, but Keep Going: As we end this liturgical year with the joyful celebration of Christ the King, we continue to tend our faith as we tend our gifts for ongoing work in music ministry. There can be no greater purpose for our music making than to announce the coming of the Lord. St. Augustine makes this appeal on the last day of the liturgical year. At the Liturgy of the Hours, just before Advent begins, we meditate on Augustine's Sermon 256 where he summons us as music ministers to enter into a pilgrimage with hope and in song: "Let us sing now, not in order to enjoy a life of leisure, but in order to lighten our labors. You should sing as wayfarers do—sing, but continue your journey. Do not be lazy but sing to make your journey more enjoyable. Sing, but keep going. What do I mean by keep going? Keep on making progress. This progress, however, must be in virtue; for there are some the Apostle warns, whose only progress is in vice. If you make progress, you will be continuing your journey, but be sure that your progress is in virtue, true faith, and right living. Sing then, but keep going." Peace be with you.

COLLECT

Let us pray.

Pause for silent prayer

Almighty ever-living God,
whose will is to restore all things
in your beloved Son, the King of the
    universe,
grant, we pray,
that the whole creation, set free from
    slavery,
may render your majesty service
and ceaselessly proclaim your praise.
Through our Lord Jesus Christ, your Son,
who lives and reigns with you in the unity
    of the Holy Spirit,
God, for ever and ever. **Amen.**

FIRST READING

Ezek 34:11-12, 15-17

Thus says the Lord GOD:
    I myself will look after and tend my
        sheep.
As a shepherd tends his flock
    when he finds himself among his
        scattered sheep,
    so will I tend my sheep.
I will rescue them from every place where
        they were scattered
    when it was cloudy and dark.
I myself will pasture my sheep;
    I myself will give me rest, says the
        Lord GOD.
The lost I will seek out,
    the strayed I will bring back,
    the injured I will bind up,
    the sick I will heal,
    but the sleek and the strong I will
        destroy,
    shepherding them rightly.

As for you, my sheep, says the Lord GOD,
    I will judge between one sheep and
        another,
    between rams and goats.

RESPONSORIAL PSALM

Ps 23:1-2, 2-3, 5-6

℞. (1) The Lord is my shepherd; there is nothing I shall want.

The LORD is my shepherd; I shall not want.
    In verdant pastures he gives me repose.

℞. The Lord is my shepherd; there is nothing I shall want.

Beside restful waters he leads me;
    he refreshes my soul.
He guides me in right paths
    for his name's sake.

R︎. The Lord is my shepherd; there is
nothing I shall want.

You spread the table before me
    in the sight of my foes;
you anoint my head with oil;
    my cup overflows.

R︎. The Lord is my shepherd; there is
nothing I shall want.

Only goodness and kindness follow me
    all the days of my life;
and I shall dwell in the house of the LORD
    for years to come.

R︎. The Lord is my shepherd; there is
nothing I shall want.

SECOND READING
1 Cor 15:20-26, 28

Brothers and sisters:
Christ has been raised from the dead,
    the firstfruits of those who have fallen
        asleep.
For since death came through man,
    the resurrection of the dead came also
        through man.
For just as in Adam all die,
    so too in Christ shall all be brought to
        life,
    but each one in proper order:
    Christ the firstfruits;
    then, at his coming, those who belong
        to Christ;
    then comes the end,
    when he hands over the kingdom to his
        God and Father,
    when he has destroyed every
        sovereignty
    and every authority and power.
For he must reign until he has put all his
        enemies under his feet.
The last enemy to be destroyed is death.
When everything is subjected to him,
    then the Son himself will also be
        subjected
    to the one who subjected everything to
        him,
    so that God may be all in all.

Living Liturgy

Space, Time, Condition: Today we join the sacrifices of our life in ministry with Christ's self-giving and openness to receiving the love of God. We live in this way that our own openness to God and willingness to serve in ministry brings greater unity and peace to the entire world. I share this reflection by Gerald Darring on the kingdom of God as accompaniment for our ongoing ministry journey together.

The Kingdom of God is a space. It exists in every home where parents and children love each other. It exists in every region and country that cares for its weak and vulnerable. It exists in every parish that reaches out to the needy.

The Kingdom of God is a time. It happens whenever someone feeds a hungry person, or shelters a homeless person, or shows care to a neglected person. It happens whenever we overturn an unjust law, or correct an injustice, or avert a war. It happens whenever people join in the struggle to overcome poverty, to erase ignorance, to pass on the Faith.

The Kingdom of God is in the past (in the life and work of Jesus of Nazareth); it is in the present (in the work of the Church and in the efforts of many others to create a world of goodness and justice); it is in the future (reaching its completion in the age to come).

The Kingdom of God is a condition. Its symptoms are love, justice, and peace. Jesus Christ is king! We pray today that God may free all the world to rejoice in his peace, to glory in his justice, to live in his love (Gerald Darring, *The Perspective of Justice*, https://liturgy.slu.edu/ChristKingB112518/reflections_justice.html).

This imagination of the kingdom of God embraces all that this feast day hopes to inspire in our hearts and in our ministry. As we complete this liturgical year, I pray that we have taken time to journey into imagining or reimagining spaces in our various faith communities for rich belonging, courageous believing, and inclusive becoming.

PROMPTS FOR FAITH-SHARING

• The gospel reveals that Jesus calls us to compassionate care of the marginalized and vulnerable. What opportunities might you be overlooking in your life to pay homage to Christ the King?

• There is some harshness in the judgments passed by Christ in the gospel; how does this make you feel?

• In relationships where you hold power, how can you enact Christlike justice toward those who are less powerful?

NOVEMBER 26, 2023
OUR LORD JESUS CHRIST, KING OF THE UNIVERSE

Readings *(continued)*

Second Sunday of Advent, *December 4, 2022*

Gospel (cont.)
Matt 3:1-12; L4A

Even now the ax lies at the root of the trees.
Therefore every tree that does not bear good fruit
    will be cut down and thrown into the fire.
I am baptizing you with water, for repentance,
    but the one who is coming after me is mightier than I.
I am not worthy to carry his sandals.
He will baptize you with the Holy Spirit and fire.
His winnowing fan is in his hand.
He will clear his threshing floor
    and gather his wheat into his barn,
    but the chaff he will burn with unquenchable fire."

SECOND READING (cont.)
Rom 15:4-9

Welcome one another, then, as Christ welcomed you,
    for the glory of God.
For I say that Christ became a minister of the circumcised
    to show God's truthfulness,
    to confirm the promises to the patriarchs,
    but so that the Gentiles might glorify God for his mercy.
As it is written:
    Therefore, I will praise you among the Gentiles
    and sing praises to your name.

The Immaculate Conception of the Blessed Virgin Mary, *December 8, 2022*

Gospel (cont.)
Luke 1:26-38; L689

He will be great and will be called Son of the Most High,
    and the Lord God will give him the throne of David his father,
    and he will rule over the house of Jacob forever,
    and of his Kingdom there will be no end."
But Mary said to the angel,
    "How can this be,
    since I have no relations with a man?"
And the angel said to her in reply,
    "The Holy Spirit will come upon you,
    and the power of the Most High will overshadow you.
Therefore the child to be born
    will be called holy, the Son of God.
And behold, Elizabeth, your relative,
    has also conceived a son in her old age,
    and this is the sixth month for her who was called barren;
    for nothing will be impossible for God."
Mary said, "Behold, I am the handmaid of the Lord.
May it be done to me according to your word."
Then the angel departed from her.

FIRST READING
Gen 3:9-15, 20

After the man, Adam, had eaten of the tree,
    the Lord God called to the man and asked him, "Where are you?"
He answered, "I heard you in the garden;
    but I was afraid, because I was naked,
    so I hid myself."
Then he asked, "Who told you that you were naked?
You have eaten, then,
    from the tree of which I had forbidden you to eat!"
The man replied, "The woman whom you put here with me—
    she gave me fruit from the tree, and so I ate it."
The Lord God then asked the woman,
    "Why did you do such a thing?"
The woman answered, "The serpent tricked me into it, so I ate it."

Then the Lord God said to the serpent:
    "Because you have done this, you shall be banned
        from all the animals
        and from all the wild creatures;
    on your belly shall you crawl,
        and dirt shall you eat
        all the days of your life.
I will put enmity between you and the woman,
    and between your offspring and hers;
    he will strike at your head,
        while you strike at his heel."

The man called his wife Eve,
    because she became the mother of all the living.

RESPONSORIAL PSALM
Ps 98:1, 2-3ab, 3cd-4

℟. (1a) Sing to the Lord a new song, for he has done marvelous deeds.

Sing to the Lord a new song,
    for he has done wondrous deeds;
His right hand has won victory for him,
    his holy arm.

℟. Sing to the Lord a new song, for he has done marvelous deeds.

The Lord has made his salvation known:
    in the sight of the nations he has revealed
        his justice.
He has remembered his kindness and his
    faithfulness
    toward the house of Israel.

℟. Sing to the Lord a new song, for he has done marvelous deeds.

All the ends of the earth have seen
    the salvation by our God.
Sing joyfully to the Lord, all you lands;
    break into song; sing praise.

℟. Sing to the Lord a new song, for he has done marvelous deeds.

SECOND READING
Eph 1:3-6, 11-12

Brothers and sisters:
Blessed be the God and Father of our Lord
    Jesus Christ,
    who has blessed us in Christ
    with every spiritual blessing in the heavens,
    as he chose us in him, before the foundation
        of the world,
    to be holy and without blemish before him.
In love he destined us for adoption to himself
    through Jesus Christ,
    in accord with the favor of his will,
    for the praise of the glory of his grace
    that he granted us in the beloved.

In him we were also chosen,
    destined in accord with the purpose of the
    One
    who accomplishes all things according to
        the intention of his will,
    so that we might exist for the praise of his
    glory,
    we who first hoped in Christ.

Gospel (cont.)
Luke 1:26-38; L690A

He will be great and will be called Son of the Most High,
  and the Lord God will give him the throne of David his father,
  and he will rule over the house of Jacob forever,
  and of his Kingdom there will be no end."
But Mary said to the angel,
  "How can this be,
  since I have no relations with a man?"
And the angel said to her in reply,
  "The Holy Spirit will come upon you,
  and the power of the Most High will overshadow you.
Therefore the child to be born
  will be called holy, the Son of God.
And behold, Elizabeth, your relative,
  has also conceived a son in her old age,
  and this is the sixth month for her who was called barren;
  for nothing will be impossible for God."
Mary said, "Behold, I am the handmaid of the Lord.
May it be done to me according to your word."
Then the angel departed from her.

or Luke 1:39-47

Mary set out
  and traveled to the hill country in haste
  to a town of Judah,
  where she entered the house of Zechariah
  and greeted Elizabeth.
When Elizabeth heard Mary's greeting,
  the infant leaped in her womb,
  and Elizabeth, filled with the Holy Spirit,
  cried out in a loud voice and said,
  "Most blessed are you among women,
  and blessed is the fruit of your womb.
And how does this happen to me,
  that the mother of my Lord should come to me?
For at the moment the sound of your greeting reached my ears,
  the infant in my womb leaped for joy.
Blessed are you who believed
  that what was spoken to you by the Lord
  would be fulfilled."

And Mary said:

  "My soul proclaims the greatness of the Lord;
  my spirit rejoices in God my savior."

FIRST READING
Rev 11:19a; 12:1-6a, 10ab

God's temple in heaven was opened,
  and the ark of his covenant could be seen
    in the temple.

A great sign appeared in the sky, a woman
    clothed with the sun,
  with the moon under her feet,
  and on her head a crown of twelve stars.
She was with child and wailed aloud in pain
    as she labored to give birth.
Then another sign appeared in the sky;
  it was a huge red dragon, with seven heads
    and ten horns,
  and on its heads were seven diadems.
Its tail swept away a third of the stars in the
    sky
  and hurled them down to the earth.
Then the dragon stood before the woman
    about to give birth,
  to devour her child when she gave birth.
She gave birth to a son, a male child,
  destined to rule all the nations with an iron
    rod.
Her child was caught up to God and his
    throne.
The woman herself fled into the desert
  where she had a place prepared by God.

Then I heard a loud voice in heaven say:
  "Now have salvation and power come,
    and the Kingdom of our God
    and the authority of his Anointed."

or Zech 2:14-17

Sing and rejoice, O daughter Zion!
See, I am coming to dwell among you, says
    the Lord.
Many nations shall join themselves to the
    Lord on that day,
  and they shall be his people,
  and he will dwell among you,
  and you shall know that the Lord of hosts
    has sent me to you.
The Lord will possess Judah as his portion in
    the holy land,
  and he will again choose Jerusalem.
Silence, all mankind, in the presence of the
    Lord!
  For he stirs forth from his holy dwelling.

RESPONSORIAL PSALM
Judith 13:18bcde, 19

℟. (15:9d) You are the highest honor of our
    race.

Blessed are you, daughter, by the Most High
    God,
  above all the women on earth;
  and blessed be the Lord God,
  the creator of heaven and earth.

℟. You are the highest honor of our race.

Your deed of hope will never be forgotten
  by those who tell of the might of God.

℟. You are the highest honor of our race.

Gospel (cont.)

Matt 1:1-25; L13ABC

Asaph became the father of Jehoshaphat,
  Jehoshaphat the father of Joram,
  Joram the father of Uzziah.
Uzziah became the father of Jotham,
  Jotham the father of Ahaz,
  Ahaz the father of Hezekiah.
Hezekiah became the father of Manasseh,
  Manasseh the father of Amos,
  Amos the father of Josiah.
Josiah became the father of Jechoniah and his brothers
  at the time of the Babylonian exile.

After the Babylonian exile,
  Jechoniah became the father of Shealtiel,
  Shealtiel the father of Zerubbabel,
  Zerubbabel the father of Abiud.
Abiud became the father of Eliakim,
  Eliakim the father of Azor,
  Azor the father of Zadok.
Zadok became the father of Achim,
  Achim the father of Eliud,
  Eliud the father of Eleazar.
Eleazar became the father of Matthan,
  Matthan the father of Jacob,
  Jacob the father of Joseph, the husband of Mary.
Of her was born Jesus who is called the Christ.

Thus the total number of generations
  from Abraham to David
  is fourteen generations;
  from David to the Babylonian exile,
  fourteen generations;
  from the Babylonian exile to the Christ,
  fourteen generations.

Now this is how the birth of Jesus Christ came about.
When his mother Mary was betrothed to Joseph,
  but before they lived together,
  she was found with child through the Holy Spirit.
Joseph her husband, since he was a righteous man,
  yet unwilling to expose her to shame,
  decided to divorce her quietly.
Such was his intention when, behold,
  the angel of the Lord appeared to him in a dream and said,
  "Joseph, son of David,
  do not be afraid to take Mary your wife into your home.
For it is through the Holy Spirit
  that this child has been conceived in her.
She will bear a son and you are to name him Jesus,
  because he will save his people from their sins."
All this took place to fulfill
  what the Lord had said through the prophet:
    Behold, the virgin shall conceive and bear a son,
      and they shall name him Emmanuel,
    which means "God is with us."
When Joseph awoke,
  he did as the angel of the Lord had commanded him
  and took his wife into his home.
He had no relations with her until she bore a son,
  and he named him Jesus.

or Matt 1:18-25

This is how the birth of Jesus Christ came about.
When his mother Mary was betrothed to Joseph,
  but before they lived together,
  she was found with child through the Holy Spirit.
Joseph her husband, since he was a righteous man,
  yet unwilling to expose her to shame,
  decided to divorce her quietly.
Such was his intention when, behold,
  the angel of the Lord appeared to him in a dream and said,
  "Joseph, son of David,
  do not be afraid to take Mary your wife into your home.
For it is through the Holy Spirit
  that this child has been conceived in her.
She will bear a son and you are to name him Jesus,
  because he will save his people from their sins."
All this took place to fulfill
  what the Lord had said through the prophet:
    Behold, the virgin shall conceive and bear a son,
      and they shall name him Emmanuel,
    which means "God is with us."
When Joseph awoke,
  he did as the angel of the Lord had commanded him
  and took his wife into his home.
He had no relations with her until she bore a son,
  and he named him Jesus.

FIRST READING
Isa 62:1-5

For Zion's sake I will not be silent,
    for Jerusalem's sake I will not be quiet,
until her vindication shines forth like the
        dawn
    and her victory like a burning torch.

Nations shall behold your vindication,
    and all the kings your glory;
you shall be called by a new name
    pronounced by the mouth of the LORD.
You shall be a glorious crown in the hand of
        the LORD,
    a royal diadem held by your God.
No more shall people call you "Forsaken,"
    or your land "Desolate,"
but you shall be called "My Delight,"
    and your land "Espoused."
For the LORD delights in you
    and makes your land his spouse.
As a young man marries a virgin,
    your Builder shall marry you;
and as a bridegroom rejoices in his bride
    so shall your God rejoice in you.

RESPONSORIAL PSALM
Ps 89:4-5, 16-17, 27, 29

R℟. (2a) For ever I will sing the goodness of
the Lord.

I have made a covenant with my chosen one,
    I have sworn to David my servant:
forever will I confirm your posterity
    and establish your throne for all
        generations.

R℟. For ever I will sing the goodness of the
Lord.

Blessed the people who know the joyful shout;
    in the light of your countenance, O LORD,
        they walk.
At your name they rejoice all the day,
    and through your justice they are exalted.

R℟. For ever I will sing the goodness of the
Lord.

He shall say of me, "You are my father,
    my God, the rock, my savior."
Forever I will maintain my kindness toward
    him,
    and my covenant with him stands firm.

R℟. For ever I will sing the goodness of the
Lord.

SECOND READING
Acts 13:16-17, 22-25

When Paul reached Antioch in Pisidia and
        entered the synagogue,
    he stood up, motioned with his hand, and
        said,
    "Fellow Israelites and you others who are
        God-fearing, listen.
The God of this people Israel chose our
        ancestors
    and exalted the people during their sojourn
        in the land of Egypt.
With uplifted arm he led them out of it.
Then he removed Saul and raised up David
        as king;
    of him he testified,
    'I have found David, son of Jesse, a man
        after my own heart;
    he will carry out my every wish.'
From this man's descendants God, according
        to his promise,
    has brought to Israel a savior, Jesus.
John heralded his coming by proclaiming a
        baptism of repentance
    to all the people of Israel;
    and as John was completing his course, he
        would say,
    'What do you suppose that I am? I am not
        he.
Behold, one is coming after me;
    I am not worthy to unfasten the sandals of
        his feet.'"

Gospel (cont.)
Luke 2:1-14; L14ABC

She wrapped him in swaddling clothes and laid him in a manger,
  because there was no room for them in the inn.

Now there were shepherds in that region living in the fields
  and keeping the night watch over their flock.
The angel of the Lord appeared to them
  and the glory of the Lord shone around them,
  and they were struck with great fear.
The angel said to them,
  "Do not be afraid;
  for behold, I proclaim to you good news of great joy
  that will be for all the people.
For today in the city of David
  a savior has been born for you who is Christ and Lord.
And this will be a sign for you:
  you will find an infant wrapped in swaddling clothes
  and lying in a manger."
And suddenly there was a multitude of the heavenly host with the
    angel,
  praising God and saying:
    "Glory to God in the highest
      and on earth peace to those on whom his favor rests."

FIRST READING
Isa 9:1-6

The people who walked in darkness
  have seen a great light;
upon those who dwelt in the land of gloom
  a light has shone.
You have brought them abundant joy
  and great rejoicing,
as they rejoice before you as at the harvest,
  as people make merry when dividing spoils.
For the yoke that burdened them,
  the pole on their shoulder,
and the rod of their taskmaster
  you have smashed, as on the day of Midian.
For every boot that tramped in battle,
  every cloak rolled in blood,
  will be burned as fuel for flames.
For a child is born to us, a son is given us;
  upon his shoulder dominion rests.
They name him Wonder-Counselor, God-Hero,
  Father-Forever, Prince of Peace.
His dominion is vast
  and forever peaceful,
from David's throne, and over his kingdom,
  which he confirms and sustains
by judgment and justice,
  both now and forever.
The zeal of the Lᴏʀᴅ of hosts will do this!

RESPONSORIAL PSALM
Ps 96:1-2, 2-3, 11-12, 13

Rℐ. (Luke 2:11) Today is born our Savior,
    Christ the Lord.

Sing to the Lᴏʀᴅ a new song;
  sing to the Lᴏʀᴅ, all you lands.
Sing to the Lᴏʀᴅ; bless his name.

Rℐ. Today is born our Savior, Christ the Lord.

Announce his salvation, day after day.
  Tell his glory among the nations;
  among all peoples, his wondrous deeds.

Rℐ. Today is born our Savior, Christ the Lord.

Let the heavens be glad and the earth rejoice;
  let the sea and what fills it resound;
  let the plains be joyful and all that is in
    them!
Then shall all the trees of the forest exult.

Rℐ. Today is born our Savior, Christ the Lord.

They shall exult before the Lᴏʀᴅ, for he
    comes;
  for he comes to rule the earth.
He shall rule the world with justice
  and the peoples with his constancy.

Rℐ. Today is born our Savior, Christ the Lord.

SECOND READING
Titus 2:11-14

Beloved:
The grace of God has appeared, saving all
  and training us to reject godless ways and
    worldly desires
  and to live temperately, justly, and devoutly
    in this age,
  as we await the blessed hope,
  the appearance of the glory of our great
    God
  and savior Jesus Christ,
  who gave himself for us to deliver us from
    all lawlessness
  and to cleanse for himself a people as his
    own,
  eager to do what is good.

The Nativity of the Lord, *December 25, 2022 (Mass at Dawn)*

FIRST READING
Isa 62:11-12

See, the LORD proclaims
  to the ends of the earth:
say to daughter Zion,
  your savior comes!
Here is his reward with him,
  his recompense before him.
They shall be called the holy people,
  the redeemed of the LORD,
and you shall be called "Frequented,"
  a city that is not forsaken.

RESPONSORIAL PSALM
Ps 97:1, 6, 11-12

R̄. A light will shine on us this day: the Lord
  is born for us.

The LORD is king; let the earth rejoice;
  let the many isles be glad.
The heavens proclaim his justice,
  and all peoples see his glory.

R̄. A light will shine on us this day: the Lord
  is born for us.

Light dawns for the just;
  and gladness, for the upright of heart.
Be glad in the LORD, you just,
  and give thanks to his holy name.

R̄. A light will shine on us this day: the Lord
  is born for us.

SECOND READING
Titus 3:4-7

Beloved:
When the kindness and generous love
  of God our savior appeared,
not because of any righteous deeds we had
    done
  but because of his mercy,
he saved us through the bath of rebirth
  and renewal by the Holy Spirit,
whom he richly poured out on us
  through Jesus Christ our savior,
so that we might be justified by his grace
  and become heirs in hope of eternal life.

The Nativity of the Lord, *December 25, 2022 (Mass During the Day)*

Gospel (cont.)
John 1:1-18; L16ABC

And the Word became flesh
  and made his dwelling among us,
  and we saw his glory,
  the glory as of the Father's only Son,
  full of grace and truth.
John testified to him and cried out, saying,
  "This was he of whom I said,
  'The one who is coming after me ranks ahead of me
  because he existed before me.'"
From his fullness we have all received,
  grace in place of grace,
  because while the law was given through Moses,
  grace and truth came through Jesus Christ.
No one has ever seen God.
The only Son, God, who is at the Father's side,
  has revealed him.

or John 1:1-5, 9-14

In the beginning was the Word,
  and the Word was with God,
  and the Word was God.
He was in the beginning with God.

All things came to be through him,
  and without him nothing came to be.
What came to be through him was life,
  and this life was the light of the human race;
the light shines in the darkness,
  and the darkness has not overcome it.
The true light, which enlightens everyone,
  was coming into the world.
He was in the world,
  and the world came to be through him,
  but the world did not know him.
He came to what was his own,
  but his own people did not accept him.

But to those who did accept him
  he gave power to become children of God,
  to those who believe in his name,
  who were born not by natural generation
  nor by human choice nor by a man's decision
  but of God.
And the Word became flesh
  and made his dwelling among us,
  and we saw his glory,
  the glory as of the Father's only Son,
  full of grace and truth.

The Nativity of the Lord, December 25, 2022 (Mass During the Day)

FIRST READING
Isa 52:7-10

How beautiful upon the mountains
   are the feet of him who brings glad tidings,
announcing peace, bearing good news,
   announcing salvation, and saying to Zion,
   "Your God is King!"

Hark! Your sentinels raise a cry,
   together they shout for joy,
for they see directly, before their eyes,
   the LORD restoring Zion.
Break out together in song,
   O ruins of Jerusalem!
For the LORD comforts his people,
   he redeems Jerusalem.
The LORD has bared his holy arm
   in the sight of all the nations;
all the ends of the earth will behold
   the salvation of our God.

RESPONSORIAL PSALM
Ps 98:1, 2-3, 3-4, 5-6

R̸. (3c) All the ends of the earth have seen the
   saving power of God.

Sing to the LORD a new song,
   for he has done wondrous deeds;
his right hand has won victory for him,
   his holy arm.

R̸. All the ends of the earth have seen the
   saving power of God.

The LORD has made his salvation known:
   in the sight of the nations he has revealed
   his justice.
He has remembered his kindness and his
   faithfulness
   toward the house of Israel.

R̸. All the ends of the earth have seen the
   saving power of God.

All the ends of the earth have seen
   the salvation by our God.
Sing joyfully to the LORD, all you lands;
   break into song; sing praise.

R̸. All the ends of the earth have seen the
   saving power of God.

Sing praise to the LORD with the harp,
   with the harp and melodious song.
With trumpets and the sound of the horn
   sing joyfully before the King, the LORD.

R̸. All the ends of the earth have seen the
   saving power of God.

SECOND READING
Heb 1:1-6

Brothers and sisters:
In times past, God spoke in partial and
   various ways
   to our ancestors through the prophets;
in these last days, he has spoken to us
   through the Son,
   whom he made heir of all things
   and through whom he created the universe,
   who is the refulgence of his glory,
   the very imprint of his being,
   and who sustains all things by his mighty
   word.
   When he had accomplished purification
   from sins,
   he took his seat at the right hand of the
   Majesty on high,
   as far superior to the angels
   as the name he has inherited is more
   excellent than theirs.

For to which of the angels did God ever say:
   You are my son; this day I have begotten
    you?
Or again:
   I will be a father to him, and he shall be a
    son to me?
And again, when he leads the firstborn into
   the world, he says:
   Let all the angels of God worship him.

The Epiphany of the Lord, January 8, 2023

Gospel (cont.)
Matt 2:1-12; L20ABC

After their audience with the king they set out.
And behold, the star that they had seen at its rising preceded them,
   until it came and stopped over the place where the child was.
They were overjoyed at seeing the star,
   and on entering the house
   they saw the child with Mary his mother.
They prostrated themselves and did him homage.
Then they opened their treasures
   and offered him gifts of gold, frankincense, and myrrh.
And having been warned in a dream not to return to Herod,
   they departed for their country by another way.

Third Sunday in Ordinary Time, January 22, 2023

Gospel (cont.)
Matt 4:12-23; L67A

They were in a boat, with their father Zebedee, mending their nets.
He called them, and immediately they left their boat and their father
    and followed him.
He went around all of Galilee,
    teaching in their synagogues, proclaiming the gospel of the
        kingdom,
    and curing every disease and illness among the people.

or Matt 4:12-17

When Jesus heard that John had been arrested,
    he withdrew to Galilee.
He left Nazareth and went to live in Capernaum by the sea,
    in the region of Zebulun and Naphtali,
    that what had been said through Isaiah the prophet
    might be fulfilled:
        Land of Zebulun and land of Naphtali,
            the way to the sea, beyond the Jordan,
            Galilee of the Gentiles,
        the people who sit in darkness have seen a great light,
        on those dwelling in a land overshadowed by death
            light has arisen.
From that time on, Jesus began to preach and say,
    "Repent, for the kingdom of heaven is at hand."

Sixth Sunday in Ordinary Time, February 12, 2023

Gospel (cont.)
Matt 5:17-37; L76A

Therefore, if you bring your gift to the altar,
    and there recall that your brother
    has anything against you,
    leave your gift there at the altar,
    go first and be reconciled with your brother,
    and then come and offer your gift.
Settle with your opponent quickly while on the way to court.
Otherwise your opponent will hand you over to the judge,
    and the judge will hand you over to the guard,
    and you will be thrown into prison.
Amen, I say to you,
    you will not be released until you have paid the last penny.

"You have heard that it was said,
    You shall not commit adultery.
But I say to you,
    everyone who looks at a woman with lust
    has already committed adultery with her in his heart.
If your right eye causes you to sin,
    tear it out and throw it away.
It is better for you to lose one of your members
    than to have your whole body thrown into Gehenna.
And if your right hand causes you to sin,
    cut it off and throw it away.
It is better for you to lose one of your members
    than to have your whole body go into Gehenna.

"It was also said,
    Whoever divorces his wife must give her a bill of divorce.
But I say to you,
    whoever divorces his wife—unless the marriage is unlawful—
    causes her to commit adultery,
    and whoever marries a divorced woman commits adultery.

"Again you have heard that it was said to your ancestors,
    Do not take a false oath,
    but make good to the Lord all that you vow.

But I say to you, do not swear at all;
    not by heaven, for it is God's throne;
    nor by the earth, for it is his footstool;
    nor by Jerusalem, for it is the city of the great King.
Do not swear by your head,
    for you cannot make a single hair white or black.
Let your 'Yes' mean 'Yes,' and your 'No' mean 'No.'
Anything more is from the evil one."

or Matt 5:20-22a, 27-28, 33-34a, 37

Jesus said to his disciples:
    "I tell you, unless your righteousness surpasses
    that of the scribes and Pharisees,
    you will not enter the kingdom of heaven.

"You have heard that it was said to your ancestors,
    You shall not kill; and whoever kills will be liable to judgment.
But I say to you,
    whoever is angry with his brother
    will be liable to judgment.

"You have heard that it was said,
    You shall not commit adultery.
But I say to you,
    everyone who looks at a woman with lust
    has already committed adultery with her in his heart.

"Again you have heard that it was said to your ancestors,
    Do not take a false oath,
    but make good to the Lord all that you vow.
But I say to you, do not swear at all.
Let your 'Yes' mean 'Yes,' and your 'No' mean 'No.'
Anything more is from the evil one."

FIRST READING
Joel 2:12-18

Even now, says the LORD,
    return to me with your whole heart,
    with fasting, and weeping, and mourning;
Rend your hearts, not your garments,
    and return to the LORD, your God.
For gracious and merciful is he,
    slow to anger, rich in kindness,
    and relenting in punishment.
Perhaps he will again relent
    and leave behind him a blessing,
Offerings and libations
    for the LORD, your God.

Blow the trumpet in Zion!
    proclaim a fast,
    call an assembly;
Gather the people,
    notify the congregation;
Assemble the elders,
    gather the children
    and the infants at the breast;
Let the bridegroom quit his room
    and the bride her chamber.
Between the porch and the altar
    let the priests, the ministers of the LORD,
        weep,
And say, "Spare, O LORD, your people,
    and make not your heritage a reproach,
    with the nations ruling over them!
Why should they say among the peoples,
    'Where is their God?'"

Then the LORD was stirred to concern for his
        land
    and took pity on his people.

RESPONSORIAL PSALM
Ps 51:3-4, 5-6ab, 12-13, 14, and 17

R⁊. (see 3a) Be merciful, O Lord, for we have
    sinned.

Have mercy on me, O God, in your goodness;
    in the greatness of your compassion wipe
        out my offense.
Thoroughly wash me from my guilt
    and of my sin cleanse me.

R⁊. Be merciful, O Lord, for we have sinned.

For I acknowledge my offense,
    and my sin is before me always:
"Against you only have I sinned,
    and done what is evil in your sight."

R⁊. Be merciful, O Lord, for we have sinned.

A clean heart create for me, O God,
    and a steadfast spirit renew within me.
Cast me not out from your presence,
    and your Holy Spirit take not from me.

R⁊. Be merciful, O Lord, for we have sinned.

Give me back the joy of your salvation,
    and a willing spirit sustain in me.
O Lord, open my lips,
    and my mouth shall proclaim your praise.

R⁊. Be merciful, O Lord, for we have sinned.

SECOND READING
2 Cor 5:20–6:2

Brothers and sisters:
We are ambassadors for Christ,
    as if God were appealing through us.
We implore you on behalf of Christ,
    be reconciled to God.
For our sake he made him to be sin who did
        not know sin,
    so that we might become the righteousness
        of God in him.

Working together, then,
    we appeal to you not to receive the grace of
        God in vain.
For he says:

*In an acceptable time I heard you,
    and on the day of salvation I helped you.*

Behold, now is a very acceptable time;
    behold, now is the day of salvation.

Gospel (cont.)
Matt 4:1-11; L22A

Then the devil took him up to a very high mountain,
    and showed him all the kingdoms of the world in their magnificence,
    and he said to him, "All these I shall give to you,
    if you will prostrate yourself and worship me."
At this, Jesus said to him,
    "Get away, Satan!
It is written:
    The Lord, your God, shall you worship
      and him alone shall you serve."

Then the devil left him and, behold,
    angels came and ministered to him.

SECOND READING (cont.)
Rom 5:12-19

But the gift is not like the transgression.
For if by the transgression of the one, the
      many died,
    how much more did the grace of God
    and the gracious gift of the one man Jesus
      Christ
    overflow for the many.
And the gift is not like the result of the one
    who sinned.
For after one sin there was the judgment that
      brought condemnation;
    but the gift, after many transgressions,
      brought acquittal.
For if, by the transgression of the one,
    death came to reign through that one,
    how much more will those who receive the
      abundance of grace
    and of the gift of justification
    come to reign in life through the one Jesus
      Christ.
In conclusion, just as through one transgression
    condemnation came upon all,
    so, through one righteous act,
    acquittal and life came to all.
For just as through the disobedience of the
      one man
    the many were made sinners,
    so, through the obedience of the one,
    the many will be made righteous.

or Rom 5:12, 17-19

Brothers and sisters:
Through one man sin entered the world,
    and through sin, death,
    and thus death came to all men, inasmuch
      as all sinned.

For if, by the transgression of the one,
    death came to reign through that one,
    how much more will those who receive the
      abundance of grace
    and of the gift of justification
    come to reign in life through the one Jesus
      Christ.
In conclusion, just as through one
      transgression
    condemnation came upon all,
    so, through one righteous act,
    acquittal and life came to all.
For just as through the disobedience of the
      one man
    the many were made sinners,
    so, through the obedience of the one,
    the many will be made righteous.

Gospel (cont.)
John 4:5-42; L28A

Jesus answered and said to her,
 "Everyone who drinks this water will be thirsty again;
 but whoever drinks the water I shall give will never thirst;
 the water I shall give will become in him
 a spring of water welling up to eternal life."
The woman said to him,
 "Sir, give me this water, so that I may not be thirsty
 or have to keep coming here to draw water."

Jesus said to her,
 "Go call your husband and come back."
The woman answered and said to him,
 "I do not have a husband."
Jesus answered her,
 "You are right in saying, 'I do not have a husband.'
For you have had five husbands,
 and the one you have now is not your husband.
What you have said is true."
The woman said to him,
 "Sir, I can see that you are a prophet.
Our ancestors worshiped on this mountain;
 but you people say that the place to worship is in Jerusalem."
Jesus said to her,
 "Believe me, woman, the hour is coming
 when you will worship the Father
 neither on this mountain nor in Jerusalem.
You people worship what you do not understand;
 we worship what we understand,
 because salvation is from the Jews.
But the hour is coming, and is now here,
 when true worshipers will worship the Father in Spirit and truth;
 and indeed the Father seeks such people to worship him.
God is Spirit, and those who worship him
 must worship in Spirit and truth."
The woman said to him,
 "I know that the Messiah is coming, the one called the Christ;
 when he comes, he will tell us everything."
Jesus said to her,
 "I am he, the one speaking with you."

At that moment his disciples returned,
 and were amazed that he was talking with a woman,
 but still no one said, "What are you looking for?"
 or "Why are you talking with her?"
The woman left her water jar
 and went into the town and said to the people,
 "Come see a man who told me everything I have done.
Could he possibly be the Christ?"
They went out of the town and came to him.
Meanwhile, the disciples urged him, "Rabbi, eat."
But he said to them,
 "I have food to eat of which you do not know."
So the disciples said to one another,
 "Could someone have brought him something to eat?"
Jesus said to them,
 "My food is to do the will of the one who sent me
 and to finish his work.
Do you not say, 'In four months the harvest will be here'?
I tell you, look up and see the fields ripe for the harvest.
The reaper is already receiving payment
 and gathering crops for eternal life,
 so that the sower and reaper can rejoice together.
For here the saying is verified that 'One sows and another reaps.'
I sent you to reap what you have not worked for;
 others have done the work,
 and you are sharing the fruits of their work."

Many of the Samaritans of that town began to believe in him
 because of the word of the woman who testified,
 "He told me everything I have done."
When the Samaritans came to him,
 they invited him to stay with them;
 and he stayed there two days.
Many more began to believe in him because of his word,
 and they said to the woman,
 "We no longer believe because of your word;
 for we have heard for ourselves,
 and we know that this is truly the savior of the world."

Gospel (cont.)

or John 4:5-15, 19b-26, 39a, 40-42; L28A

Jesus came to a town of Samaria called Sychar,
  near the plot of land that Jacob had given to his son Joseph.
Jacob's well was there.
Jesus, tired from his journey, sat down there at the well.
It was about noon.

A woman of Samaria came to draw water.
Jesus said to her,
  "Give me a drink."
His disciples had gone into the town to buy food.
The Samaritan woman said to him,
  "How can you, a Jew, ask me, a Samaritan woman, for a drink?"
—For Jews use nothing in common with Samaritans.—
Jesus answered and said to her,
  "If you knew the gift of God
  and who is saying to you, 'Give me a drink,'
  you would have asked him
  and he would have given you living water."
The woman said to him,
  "Sir, you do not even have a bucket and the cistern is deep;
  where then can you get this living water?
Are you greater than our father Jacob,
  who gave us this cistern and drank from it himself
  with his children and his flocks?"
Jesus answered and said to her,
  "Everyone who drinks this water will be thirsty again;
  but whoever drinks the water I shall give will never thirst;
  the water I shall give will become in him
  a spring of water welling up to eternal life."
The woman said to him,
  "Sir, give me this water, so that I may not be thirsty
  or have to keep coming here to draw water."

"I can see that you are a prophet.
Our ancestors worshiped on this mountain;
  but you people say that the place to worship is in Jerusalem."
Jesus said to her,
  "Believe me, woman, the hour is coming
  when you will worship the Father
  neither on this mountain nor in Jerusalem.
You people worship what you do not understand;
  we worship what we understand,
  because salvation is from the Jews.
But the hour is coming, and is now here,
  when true worshipers will worship the Father in Spirit and truth;
  and indeed the Father seeks such people to worship him.
God is Spirit, and those who worship him
  must worship in Spirit and truth."
The woman said to him,
  "I know that the Messiah is coming, the one called the Christ;
  when he comes, he will tell us everything."
Jesus said to her,
  "I am he, the one speaking with you."

Many of the Samaritans of that town began to believe in him.
When the Samaritans came to him,
  they invited him to stay with them;
  and he stayed there two days.
Many more began to believe in him because of his word,
  and they said to the woman,
  "We no longer believe because of your word;
  for we have heard for ourselves,
  and we know that this is truly the savior of the world."

Gospel (long form cont.)
John 9:1-41; L31A

So they said to him, "How were your eyes opened?"
He replied,
  "The man called Jesus made clay and anointed my eyes
  and told me, 'Go to Siloam and wash.'
So I went there and washed and was able to see."
And they said to him, "Where is he?"
He said, "I don't know."

They brought the one who was once blind to the Pharisees.
Now Jesus had made clay and opened his eyes on a sabbath.
So then the Pharisees also asked him how he was able to see.
He said to them,
  "He put clay on my eyes, and I washed, and now I can see."
So some of the Pharisees said,
  "This man is not from God,
  because he does not keep the sabbath."
But others said,
  "How can a sinful man do such signs?"
And there was a division among them.
So they said to the blind man again,
  "What do you have to say about him,
  since he opened your eyes?"
He said, "He is a prophet."

Now the Jews did not believe
  that he had been blind and gained his sight
  until they summoned the parents of the one who had gained his sight.
They asked them,
  "Is this your son, who you say was born blind?
How does he now see?"
His parents answered and said,
  "We know that this is our son and that he was born blind.
We do not know how he sees now,
  nor do we know who opened his eyes.
Ask him, he is of age;
  he can speak for himself."
His parents said this because they were afraid of the Jews,
  for the Jews had already agreed
  that if anyone acknowledged him as the Christ,
  he would be expelled from the synagogue.
For this reason his parents said,
  "He is of age; question him."

So a second time they called the man who had been blind
  and said to him, "Give God the praise!
We know that this man is a sinner."
He replied,
  "If he is a sinner, I do not know.
One thing I do know is that I was blind and now I see."
So they said to him,
  "What did he do to you?
  How did he open your eyes?"
He answered them,
  "I told you already and you did not listen.
Why do you want to hear it again?
Do you want to become his disciples, too?"
They ridiculed him and said,
  "You are that man's disciple;
  we are disciples of Moses!

We know that God spoke to Moses,
  but we do not know where this one is from."
The man answered and said to them,
  "This is what is so amazing,
  that you do not know where he is from, yet he opened my eyes.
We know that God does not listen to sinners,
  but if one is devout and does his will, he listens to him.
It is unheard of that anyone ever opened the eyes of a person born
    blind.
If this man were not from God,
  he would not be able to do anything."
They answered and said to him,
  "You were born totally in sin,
  and are you trying to teach us?"
Then they threw him out.

When Jesus heard that they had thrown him out,
  he found him and said, "Do you believe in the Son of Man?"
He answered and said,
  "Who is he, sir, that I may believe in him?"
Jesus said to him,
  "You have seen him,
  and the one speaking with you is he."
He said,
  "I do believe, Lord," and he worshiped him.
Then Jesus said,
  "I came into this world for judgment,
  so that those who do not see might see,
  and those who do see might become blind."

Some of the Pharisees who were with him heard this
  and said to him, "Surely we are not also blind, are we?"
Jesus said to them,
  "If you were blind, you would have no sin;
  but now you are saying, 'We see,' so your sin remains."

Gospel (short form)

John 9:1, 6-9, 13-17, 34-38; L31A

As Jesus passed by he saw a man blind from birth.
He spat on the ground and made clay with the saliva,
   and smeared the clay on his eyes, and said to him,
   "Go wash in the Pool of Siloam"—which means Sent—.
So he went and washed, and came back able to see.

His neighbors and those who had seen him earlier as a beggar said,
   "Isn't this the one who used to sit and beg?"
Some said, "It is,"
   but others said, "No, he just looks like him."
He said, "I am."

They brought the one who was once blind to the Pharisees.
Now Jesus had made clay and opened his eyes on a sabbath.
So then the Pharisees also asked him how he was able to see.
He said to them,
   "He put clay on my eyes, and I washed, and now I can see."
So some of the Pharisees said,
   "This man is not from God,
   because he does not keep the sabbath."
But others said,

   "How can a sinful man do such signs?"
And there was a division among them.
So they said to the blind man again,
   "What do you have to say about him,
   since he opened your eyes?"
He said, "He is a prophet."

They answered and said to him,
   "You were born totally in sin,
   and are you trying to teach us?"
Then they threw him out.

When Jesus heard that they had thrown him out,
   he found him and said, "Do you believe in the Son of Man?"
He answered and said,
   "Who is he, sir, that I may believe in him?"
Jesus said to him,
   "You have seen him,
   and the one speaking with you is he."
He said,
   "I do believe, Lord," and he worshiped him.

Gospel
Luke 2:41-51a; L543

Each year Jesus' parents went to Jerusalem for the feast of Passover,
　and when he was twelve years old,
　they went up according to festival custom.
After they had completed its days, as they were returning,
　the boy Jesus remained behind in Jerusalem,
　but his parents did not know it.
Thinking that he was in the caravan,
　they journeyed for a day
　and looked for him among their relatives and acquaintances,
　but not finding him,
　they returned to Jerusalem to look for him.
After three days they found him in the temple,
　sitting in the midst of the teachers,
　listening to them and asking them questions,
　and all who heard him were astounded
　at his understanding and his answers.

When his parents saw him,
　they were astonished,
　and his mother said to him,
　"Son, why have you done this to us?
Your father and I have been looking for you with great anxiety."
And he said to them,
　"Why were you looking for me?
Did you not know that I must be in my Father's house?"
But they did not understand what he said to them.
He went down with them and came to Nazareth,
　and was obedient to them.

FIRST READING
2 Sam 7:4-5a, 12-14a, 16

The LORD spoke to Nathan and said:
"Go, tell my servant David,
　'When your time comes and you rest with
　　your ancestors,
　I will raise up your heir after you, sprung
　　from your loins,
　and I will make his kingdom firm.
It is he who shall build a house for my name.
And I will make his royal throne firm forever.
I will be a father to him,
　and he shall be a son to me.
Your house and your kingdom shall endure
　forever before me;
　your throne shall stand firm forever.'"

RESPONSORIAL PSALM
Ps 89:2-3, 4-5, 27 and 29

R̸. (37) The son of David will live for ever.

The promises of the LORD I will sing forever,
　through all generations my mouth will
　　proclaim your faithfulness,
For you have said, "My kindness is
　established forever";
　in heaven you have confirmed your
　faithfulness.

R̸. The son of David will live for ever.

"I have made a covenant with my chosen one;
　I have sworn to David my servant:
Forever will I confirm your posterity
　and establish your throne for all
　generations."

R̸. The son of David will live for ever.

"He shall say of me, 'You are my father,
　my God, the Rock, my savior.'
Forever I will maintain my kindness toward
　him,
　and my covenant with him stands firm."

R̸. The son of David will live for ever.

SECOND READING
Rom 4:13, 16-18, 22

Brothers and sisters:
It was not through the law
　that the promise was made to Abraham
　　and his descendants
　that he would inherit the world,
　but through the righteousness that comes
　　from faith.
For this reason, it depends on faith,
　so that it may be a gift,
　and the promise may be guaranteed to all
　　his descendants,
　not to those who only adhere to the law
　but to those who follow the faith of
　　Abraham,
　who is the father of all of us, as it is
　　written,
　I have made you father of many nations.
He is our father in the sight of God,
　in whom he believed, who gives life to the
　　dead
　and calls into being what does not exist.
He believed, hoping against hope,
　that he would become *the father of many
　　nations,*
　according to what was said, *Thus shall your
　　descendants be.*
That is why *it was credited to him as
　righteousness.*

Gospel (cont.)
Luke 1:26-38; L545

Therefore the child to be born
  will be called holy, the Son of God.
And behold, Elizabeth, your relative,
  has also conceived a son in her old age,
    and this is the sixth month for her who was
      called barren;
    for nothing will be impossible for God."
Mary said, "Behold, I am the handmaid of the
  Lord.
May it be done to me according to your word."
Then the angel departed from her.

FIRST READING
Isa 7:10-14; 8:10

The Lord spoke to Ahaz, saying:
Ask for a sign from the Lord, your God;
  let it be deep as the nether world, or high as
    the sky!
But Ahaz answered,
  "I will not ask! I will not tempt the Lord!"
Then Isaiah said:
  Listen, O house of David!
Is it not enough for you to weary people,
  must you also weary my God?
Therefore the Lord himself will give you this
    sign:
  the virgin shall be with child, and bear a son,
  and shall name him Emmanuel,
  which means "God is with us!"

RESPONSORIAL PSALM
Ps 40:7-8a, 8b-9, 10, 11

R̶⁊. (8a and 9a) Here I am, Lord; I come to do
  your will.

Sacrifice or offering you wished not,
  but ears open to obedience you gave me.
Holocausts and sin-offerings you sought not;
  then said I, "Behold, I come."

R̶⁊. Here I am, Lord; I come to do your will.

"In the written scroll it is prescribed for me,
To do your will, O God, is my delight,
  and your law is within my heart!"

R̶⁊. Here I am, Lord; I come to do your will.

I announced your justice in the vast assembly;
  I did not restrain my lips, as you, O Lord,
    know.

R̶⁊. Here I am, Lord; I come to do your will.

Your justice I kept not hid within my heart;
  your faithfulness and your salvation I have
    spoken of;
I have made no secret of your kindness and
  your truth
  in the vast assembly.

R̶⁊. Here I am, Lord; I come to do your will.

SECOND READING
Heb 10:4-10

Brothers and sisters:
It is impossible that the blood of bulls and
    goats
  takes away sins.
For this reason, when Christ came into the
    world, he said:

  "Sacrifice and offering you did not desire,
    but a body you prepared for me;
  in holocausts and sin offerings you took no
    delight.
  Then I said, 'As is written of me in the scroll,
  behold, I come to do your will, O God.'"

First Christ says, "Sacrifices and offerings,
  holocausts and sin offerings,
  you neither desired nor delighted in."
These are offered according to the law.
Then he says, "Behold, I come to do your will."
He takes away the first to establish the second.
By this "will," we have been consecrated
  through the offering of the Body of Jesus
    Christ once for all.

Gospel (cont.)
John 11:1-45; L34A

But if one walks at night, he stumbles,
    because the light is not in him."
He said this, and then told them,
    "Our friend Lazarus is asleep,
    but I am going to awaken him."
So the disciples said to him,
    "Master, if he is asleep, he will be saved."
But Jesus was talking about his death,
    while they thought that he meant ordinary sleep.
So then Jesus said to them clearly,
    "Lazarus has died.
And I am glad for you that I was not there,
    that you may believe.
Let us go to him."
So Thomas, called Didymus, said to his fellow disciples,
    "Let us also go to die with him."

When Jesus arrived, he found that Lazarus
    had already been in the tomb for four days.
Now Bethany was near Jerusalem, only about two miles away.
And many of the Jews had come to Martha and Mary
    to comfort them about their brother.
When Martha heard that Jesus was coming,
    she went to meet him;
    but Mary sat at home.
Martha said to Jesus,
    "Lord, if you had been here,
    my brother would not have died.
But even now I know that whatever you ask of God,
    God will give you."
Jesus said to her,
    "Your brother will rise."
Martha said to him,
    "I know he will rise,
    in the resurrection on the last day."
Jesus told her,
    "I am the resurrection and the life;
    whoever believes in me, even if he dies, will live,
    and everyone who lives and believes in me will never die.
Do you believe this?"
She said to him, "Yes, Lord.
I have come to believe that you are the Christ, the Son of God,
    the one who is coming into the world."

When she had said this,
    she went and called her sister Mary secretly, saying,
    "The teacher is here and is asking for you."
As soon as she heard this,
    she rose quickly and went to him.

For Jesus had not yet come into the village,
    but was still where Martha had met him.
So when the Jews who were with her in the house comforting her
    saw Mary get up quickly and go out,
    they followed her,
    presuming that she was going to the tomb to weep there.
When Mary came to where Jesus was and saw him,
    she fell at his feet and said to him,
    "Lord, if you had been here,
    my brother would not have died."
When Jesus saw her weeping and the Jews who had come with her
        weeping,
    he became perturbed and deeply troubled, and said,
    "Where have you laid him?"
They said to him, "Sir, come and see."
And Jesus wept.
So the Jews said, "See how he loved him."
But some of them said,
    "Could not the one who opened the eyes of the blind man
    have done something so that this man would not have died?"

So Jesus, perturbed again, came to the tomb.
It was a cave, and a stone lay across it.
Jesus said, "Take away the stone."
Martha, the dead man's sister, said to him,
    "Lord, by now there will be a stench;
    he has been dead for four days."
Jesus said to her,
    "Did I not tell you that if you believe
    you will see the glory of God?"
So they took away the stone.
And Jesus raised his eyes and said,
    "Father, I thank you for hearing me.
I know that you always hear me;
    but because of the crowd here I have said this,
    that they may believe that you sent me."
And when he had said this,
    he cried out in a loud voice,
    "Lazarus, come out!"
The dead man came out,
    tied hand and foot with burial bands,
    and his face was wrapped in a cloth.
So Jesus said to them,
    "Untie him and let him go."

Now many of the Jews who had come to Mary
    and seen what he had done began to believe in him.

Gospel (cont.)
or John 11:3-7, 17, 20-27, 33b-45; L34A

The sisters of Lazarus sent word to Jesus saying,
"Master, the one you love is ill."
When Jesus heard this he said,
"This illness is not to end in death,
but is for the glory of God,
that the Son of God may be glorified through it."
Now Jesus loved Martha and her sister and Lazarus.
So when he heard that he was ill,
he remained for two days in the place where he was.
Then after this he said to his disciples,
"Let us go back to Judea."

When Jesus arrived, he found that Lazarus
had already been in the tomb for four days.
When Martha heard that Jesus was coming,
she went to meet him;
but Mary sat at home.
Martha said to Jesus,
"Lord, if you had been here,
my brother would not have died.
But even now I know that whatever you ask of God,
God will give you."
Jesus said to her,
"Your brother will rise."
Martha said,
"I know he will rise,
in the resurrection on the last day."
Jesus told her,
"I am the resurrection and the life;
whoever believes in me, even if he dies, will live,
and everyone who lives and believes in me will never die.
Do you believe this?"
She said to him, "Yes, Lord.
I have come to believe that you are the Christ, the Son of God,
the one who is coming into the world."

He became perturbed and deeply troubled, and said,
"Where have you laid him?"
They said to him, "Sir, come and see."
And Jesus wept.
So the Jews said, "See how he loved him."
But some of them said,
"Could not the one who opened the eyes of the blind man
have done something so that this man would not have died?"

So Jesus, perturbed again, came to the tomb.
It was a cave, and a stone lay across it.
Jesus said, "Take away the stone."
Martha, the dead man's sister, said to him,
"Lord, by now there will be a stench;
he has been dead for four days."
Jesus said to her,
"Did I not tell you that if you believe
you will see the glory of God?"
So they took away the stone.
And Jesus raised his eyes and said,
"Father, I thank you for hearing me.
I know that you always hear me;
but because of the crowd here I have said this,
that they may believe that you sent me."
And when he had said this,
he cried out in a loud voice,
"Lazarus, come out!"
The dead man came out,
tied hand and foot with burial bands,
and his face was wrapped in a cloth.
So Jesus said to them,
"Untie him and let him go."

Now many of the Jews who had come to Mary
and seen what he had done began to believe in him.

Gospel at the Procession with Palms (cont.)
Matt 21:1-11; L37A

The crowds preceding him and those following
 kept crying out and saying:
  "Hosanna to the Son of David;
   blessed is he who comes in the name of the Lord;
  hosanna in the highest."
And when he entered Jerusalem
 the whole city was shaken and asked, "Who is this?"
And the crowds replied,
 "This is Jesus the prophet, from Nazareth in Galilee."

Gospel at Mass
Matt 26:14–27:66; L38A

One of the Twelve, who was called Judas Iscariot, went to the chief priests and said, "What are you willing to give me if I hand him over to you?" They paid him thirty pieces of silver, and from that time on he looked for an opportunity to hand him over.

On the first day of the Feast of Unleavened Bread, the disciples approached Jesus and said, "Where do you want us to prepare for you to eat the Passover?" He said, "Go into the city to a certain man and tell him, 'The teacher says, "My appointed time draws near; in your house I shall celebrate the Passover with my disciples."'" The disciples then did as Jesus had ordered, and prepared the Passover.

When it was evening, he reclined at table with the Twelve. And while they were eating, he said, "Amen, I say to you, one of you will betray me." Deeply distressed at this, they began to say to him one after another, "Surely it is not I, Lord?" He said in reply, "He who has dipped his hand into the dish with me is the one who will betray me. The Son of Man indeed goes, as it is written of him, but woe to that man by whom the Son of Man is betrayed. It would be better for that man if he had never been born." Then Judas, his betrayer, said in reply, "Surely it is not I, Rabbi?" He answered, "You have said so."

While they were eating, Jesus took bread, said the blessing, broke it, and giving it to his disciples said, "Take and eat; this is my body." Then he took a cup, gave thanks, and gave it to them, saying, "Drink from it, all of you, for this is my blood of the covenant, which will be shed on behalf of many for the forgiveness of sins. I tell you, from now on I shall not drink this fruit of the vine until the day when I drink it with you new in the kingdom of my Father." Then, after singing a hymn, they went out to the Mount of Olives.

Then Jesus said to them, "This night all of you will have your faith in me shaken, for it is written: / *I will strike the shepherd, / and the sheep of the flock will be dispersed; /* but after I have been raised up, I shall go before you to Galilee." Peter said to him in reply, "Though all may have their faith in you shaken, mine will never be." Jesus said to him, "Amen, I say to you, this very night before the cock crows, you will deny me three times." Peter said to him, "Even though I should have to die with you, I will not deny you." And all the disciples spoke likewise.

Then Jesus came with them to a place called Gethsemane, and he said to his disciples, "Sit here while I go over there and pray." He took along Peter and the two sons of Zebedee, and began to feel sorrow and distress. Then he said to them, "My soul is sorrowful even to death. Remain here and keep watch with me." He advanced a little and fell prostrate in prayer, saying, "My Father, if it is possible, let this cup pass from me; yet, not as I will, but as you will." When he returned to his disciples he found them asleep. He said to Peter, "So you could not keep watch with me for one hour? Watch and pray that you may not undergo the test. The spirit is willing, but the flesh is weak." Withdrawing a second time, he prayed again, "My Father, if it is not possible that this cup pass without my drinking it, your will be done!" Then he returned once more and found them asleep, for they could not keep their eyes open. He left them and withdrew again and prayed a third time, saying the same thing again. Then he returned to his disciples and said to them, "Are you still sleeping and taking your rest? Behold, the hour is at hand when the Son of Man is to be handed over to sinners. Get up, let us go. Look, my betrayer is at hand."

While he was still speaking, Judas, one of the Twelve, arrived, accompanied by a large crowd, with swords and clubs, who had come from the chief priests and the elders of the people. His betrayer had arranged a sign with them, saying, "The man I shall kiss is the one; arrest him." Immediately he went over to Jesus and said, "Hail, Rabbi!" and he kissed him. Jesus answered him, "Friend, do what you have come for." Then stepping forward they laid hands on Jesus and arrested him. And behold, one of those who accompanied Jesus put his hand to his sword, drew it, and struck the high priest's servant, cutting off his ear. Then Jesus said to him, "Put your sword back into its sheath, for all who take the sword will perish by the sword. Do you think that I cannot call upon my Father and he will not provide me at this moment with more than twelve legions of angels? But then how would the Scriptures be fulfilled which say that it must come to pass in this way?" At that hour Jesus said to the crowds, "Have you come out as against a robber, with swords and clubs to seize me? Day after day I sat teaching in the temple area, yet you did not arrest me. But all this has come to pass that the writings of the prophets may be fulfilled." Then all the disciples left him and fled.

Those who had arrested Jesus led him away to Caiaphas the high priest, where the scribes and the elders were assembled. Peter was following him at a distance as far as the high priest's courtyard, and going inside he sat down with the servants to see the outcome. The chief priests and the entire Sanhedrin kept trying to obtain false testimony against Jesus in order to put him to death, but they found none, though many false witnesses came forward. Finally two came forward who stated, "This man said, 'I can destroy the temple of God and within three days rebuild it.'" The high priest rose and addressed him, "Have you no answer? What are these men testifying against you?" But Jesus was silent. Then the high priest said to him, "I order you to tell us under oath before the living God whether you are the Christ, the Son of God." Jesus said to him in reply, "You have said so. But I tell you: / From now on you will see 'the Son of Man / seated at the right hand of the Power' / and 'coming on the clouds of heaven.'" / Then the high priest tore his robes and said, "He has blasphemed! What further need have we of witnesses? You have now heard the blasphemy; what is your opinion?" They said in reply, "He deserves to die!" Then they spat in his face and struck him, while some slapped him, saying, "Prophesy for us, Christ: who is it that struck you?"

Now Peter was sitting outside in the courtyard. One of the maids came over to him and said, "You too were with Jesus the Galilean." But he denied it in front of everyone, saying, "I do not know what you are talking about!" As he went out to the gate, another girl saw him and said to those who were there, "This man was with Jesus the Nazorean." Again he denied it with an oath, "I do not know the man!" A little later the bystanders came over and said to Peter, "Surely you too are one of them; even your speech gives you away." At that he began to curse and to swear, "I do not know the man." And immediately a cock crowed. Then Peter remembered the word that Jesus had spoken: "Before the cock crows you will deny me three times." He went out and began to weep bitterly.

When it was morning, all the chief priests and the elders of the people took counsel against Jesus to put him to death. They bound him, led him away, and handed him over to Pilate, the governor.

Then Judas, his betrayer, seeing that Jesus had been condemned, deeply regretted what he had done. He returned the thirty pieces of silver to the chief priests and elders, saying, "I have sinned in betraying innocent blood." They said, "What is that to us? Look to it yourself." Flinging the money into the temple, he departed and went off and hanged himself. The chief priests gathered up the money, but said, "It is not lawful to deposit this in the temple treasury, for it is the price of blood." After consultation, they used it to buy the potter's field as a burial place for foreigners. That is why that field even today is called the Field of Blood. Then was fulfilled what had been said through Jeremiah the prophet, *And they took the thirty pieces of silver, the value of a man with a price on his head, a price set by some of the Israelites, and they paid it out for the potter's field just as the Lord had commanded me.*

Now Jesus stood before the governor, and he questioned him, "Are you the king of the Jews?" Jesus said, "You say so." And when he was accused by the chief priests and elders, he made no answer. Then Pilate said to him, "Do you not hear how many things they are testifying against you?" But he did not answer him one word, so that the governor was greatly amazed.

Now on the occasion of the feast the governor was accustomed to release to the crowd one prisoner whom they wished. And at that time they had a notorious prisoner called Barabbas. So when they had assembled, Pilate said to them, "Which one do you want me to release to you, Barabbas, or Jesus called Christ?" For he knew that it was out of envy that they had handed him over. While he was still seated on the bench, his wife sent him a message, "Have nothing to do with that righteous man. I suffered much in a dream today because of him." The chief priests and the elders persuaded the crowds to ask for Barabbas but to destroy Jesus. The governor said to them in reply, "Which of the two do you want me to release to you?" They answered, "Barabbas!" Pilate said to them, "Then what shall I do with Jesus called Christ?" They all said, "Let him be crucified!" But he said, "Why? What evil has he done?" They only shouted the louder, "Let him be crucified!" When Pilate saw that he was not succeeding at all, but that a riot was breaking out instead, he took water and washed his hands in the sight of the crowd, saying, "I am innocent of this man's blood. Look to it yourselves." And the whole people said in reply, "His blood be upon us and upon our children." Then he released Barabbas to them, but after he had Jesus scourged, he handed him over to be crucified.

Then the soldiers of the governor took Jesus inside the praetorium and gathered the whole cohort around him. They stripped off his clothes and threw a scarlet military cloak about him. Weaving a crown out of thorns, they placed it on his head, and a reed in his right hand. And kneeling before him, they mocked him, saying, "Hail, King of the Jews!" They spat upon him and took the reed and kept striking him on the head. And when they had mocked him, they stripped him of the cloak, dressed him in his own clothes, and led him off to crucify him.

As they were going out, they met a Cyrenian named Simon; this man they pressed into service to carry his cross.

And when they came to a place called Golgotha—which means Place of the Skull—, they gave Jesus wine to drink mixed with gall. But when he had tasted it, he refused to drink. After they had crucified him, they divided his garments by casting lots; then they sat down and kept watch over him there. And they placed over his head the written charge against him: This is Jesus, the King of the Jews. Two revolutionaries were crucified with him, one on his right and the other on his left. Those passing by reviled him, shaking their heads and saying,

"You who would destroy the temple and rebuild it in three days, save yourself, if you are the Son of God, and come down from the cross!" Likewise the chief priests with the scribes and elders mocked him and said, "He saved others; he cannot save himself. So he is the king of Israel! Let him come down from the cross now, and we will believe in him. He trusted in God; let him deliver him now if he wants him. For he said, 'I am the Son of God.'" The revolutionaries who were crucified with him also kept abusing him in the same way.

From noon onward, darkness came over the whole land until three in the afternoon. And about three o'clock Jesus cried out in a loud voice, *"Eli, Eli, lema sabachthani?"* which means, "My God, my God, why have you forsaken me?" Some of the bystanders who heard it said, "This one is calling for Elijah." Immediately one of them ran to get a sponge; he soaked it in wine, and putting it on a reed, gave it to him to drink. But the rest said, "Wait, let us see if Elijah comes to save him." But Jesus cried out again in a loud voice, and gave up his spirit.

(Here all kneel and pause for a short time.)

And behold, the veil of the sanctuary was torn in two from top to bottom. The earth quaked, rocks were split, tombs were opened, and the bodies of many saints who had fallen asleep were raised. And coming forth from their tombs after his resurrection, they entered the holy city and appeared to many. The centurion and the men with him who were keeping watch over Jesus feared greatly when they saw the earthquake and all that was happening, and they said, "Truly, this was the Son of God!" There were many women there, looking on from a distance, who had followed Jesus from Galilee, ministering to him. Among them were Mary Magdalene and Mary the mother of James and Joseph, and the mother of the sons of Zebedee.

When it was evening, there came a rich man from Arimathea named Joseph, who was himself a disciple of Jesus. He went to Pilate and asked for the body of Jesus; then Pilate ordered it to be handed over. Taking the body, Joseph wrapped it in clean linen and laid it in his new tomb that he had hewn in the rock. Then he rolled a huge stone across the entrance to the tomb and departed. But Mary Magdalene and the other Mary remained sitting there, facing the tomb.

The next day, the one following the day of preparation, the chief priests and the Pharisees gathered before Pilate and said, "Sir, we remember that this impostor while still alive said, 'After three days I will be raised up.' Give orders, then, that the grave be secured until the third day, lest his disciples come and steal him and say to the people, 'He has been raised from the dead.' This last imposture would be worse than the first." Pilate said to them, "The guard is yours; go, secure it as best you can." So they went and secured the tomb by fixing a seal to the stone and setting the guard.

or Matt 27:11-54; L38A

Jesus stood before the governor, Pontius Pilate, who questioned him,
    "Are you the king of the Jews?"
Jesus said, "You say so."
And when he was accused by the chief priests and elders,
    he made no answer.
Then Pilate said to him,
    "Do you not hear how many things they are testifying against you?"
But he did not answer him one word,
    so that the governor was greatly amazed.

Now on the occasion of the feast
    the governor was accustomed to release to the crowd
    one prisoner whom they wished.

And at that time they had a notorious prisoner called Barabbas.
So when they had assembled, Pilate said to them,
    "Which one do you want me to release to you,
    Barabbas, or Jesus called Christ?"
For he knew that it was out of envy
    that they had handed him over.
While he was still seated on the bench,
    his wife sent him a message,
    "Have nothing to do with that righteous man.
I suffered much in a dream today because of him."
The chief priests and the elders persuaded the crowds
    to ask for Barabbas but to destroy Jesus.
The governor said to them in reply,
    "Which of the two do you want me to release to you?"
They answered, "Barabbas!"
Pilate said to them,
    "Then what shall I do with Jesus called Christ?"
They all said,
    "Let him be crucified!"
But he said,
    "Why? What evil has he done?"
They only shouted the louder,
    "Let him be crucified!"
When Pilate saw that he was not succeeding at all,
    but that a riot was breaking out instead,
    he took water and washed his hands in the sight of the crowd,
    saying, "I am innocent of this man's blood.
Look to it yourselves."
And the whole people said in reply,
    "His blood be upon us and upon our children."
Then he released Barabbas to them,
    but after he had Jesus scourged,
    he handed him over to be crucified.

Then the soldiers of the governor took Jesus inside the praetorium
    and gathered the whole cohort around him.
They stripped off his clothes
    and threw a scarlet military cloak about him.
Weaving a crown out of thorns, they placed it on his head,
    and a reed in his right hand.
And kneeling before him, they mocked him, saying,
    "Hail, King of the Jews!"
They spat upon him and took the reed
    and kept striking him on the head.
And when they had mocked him,
    they stripped him of the cloak,
    dressed him in his own clothes,
    and led him off to crucify him.

As they were going out, they met a Cyrenian named Simon;
    this man they pressed into service
    to carry his cross.

And when they came to a place called Golgotha
    —which means Place of the Skull—,
    they gave Jesus wine to drink mixed with gall.
But when he had tasted it, he refused to drink.
After they had crucified him,
    they divided his garments by casting lots;
    then they sat down and kept watch over him there.
And they placed over his head the written charge against him:
    This is Jesus, the King of the Jews.

Two revolutionaries were crucified with him,
    one on his right and the other on his left.
Those passing by reviled him, shaking their heads and saying,
    "You who would destroy the temple and rebuild it in three days,
    save yourself, if you are the Son of God,
    and come down from the cross!"
Likewise the chief priests with the scribes and elders mocked him and said,
    "He saved others; he cannot save himself.
So he is the king of Israel!
Let him come down from the cross now,
    and we will believe in him.
He trusted in God;
    let him deliver him now if he wants him.
For he said, 'I am the Son of God.'"
The revolutionaries who were crucified with him
    also kept abusing him in the same way.

From noon onward, darkness came over the whole land
    until three in the afternoon.
And about three o'clock Jesus cried out in a loud voice,
    "Eli, Eli, lema sabachthani?"
    which means, "My God, my God, why have you forsaken me?"
Some of the bystanders who heard it said,
    "This one is calling for Elijah."
Immediately one of them ran to get a sponge;
    he soaked it in wine, and putting it on a reed,
    gave it to him to drink.
But the rest said,
    "Wait, let us see if Elijah comes to save him."
But Jesus cried out again in a loud voice,
    and gave up his spirit.

(Here all kneel and pause for a short time.)

And behold, the veil of the sanctuary
    was torn in two from top to bottom.
The earth quaked, rocks were split, tombs were opened,
    and the bodies of many saints who had fallen asleep were raised.
And coming forth from their tombs after his resurrection,
    they entered the holy city and appeared to many.
The centurion and the men with him who were keeping watch over Jesus
    feared greatly when they saw the earthquake
    and all that was happening, and they said,
    "Truly, this was the Son of God!"

Gospel (cont.)
John 13:1-15; L39ABC

For he knew who would betray him;
    for this reason, he said, "Not all of you are clean."

So when he had washed their feet
    and put his garments back on and reclined at table again,
    he said to them, "Do you realize what I have done for you?
You call me 'teacher' and 'master,' and rightly so, for indeed I am.
If I, therefore, the master and teacher, have washed your feet,
    you ought to wash one another's feet.
I have given you a model to follow,
    so that as I have done for you, you should also do."

FIRST READING
Exod 12:1-8, 11-14

The LORD said to Moses and Aaron in the land
    of Egypt,
    "This month shall stand at the head of
        your calendar;
    you shall reckon it the first month of the
        year.
Tell the whole community of Israel:
    On the tenth of this month every one of
        your families
    must procure for itself a lamb, one apiece
        for each household.
If a family is too small for a whole lamb,
    it shall join the nearest household in
        procuring one
    and shall share in the lamb
    in proportion to the number of persons
        who partake of it.
The lamb must be a year-old male and
    without blemish.
You may take it from either the sheep or the
    goats.
You shall keep it until the fourteenth day of
    this month,
    and then, with the whole assembly of Israel
        present,
    it shall be slaughtered during the evening
        twilight.
They shall take some of its blood
    and apply it to the two doorposts and the
        lintel
    of every house in which they partake of
        the lamb.
That same night they shall eat its roasted
    flesh
    with unleavened bread and bitter herbs.

"This is how you are to eat it:
    with your loins girt, sandals on your feet
        and your staff in hand,
    you shall eat like those who are in flight.

It is the Passover of the LORD.
For on this same night I will go through
    Egypt,
    striking down every firstborn of the land,
        both man and beast,
    and executing judgment on all the gods of
        Egypt—I, the LORD!
But the blood will mark the houses where you
    are.
Seeing the blood, I will pass over you;
    thus, when I strike the land of Egypt,
    no destructive blow will come upon you.

"This day shall be a memorial feast for you,
    which all your generations shall celebrate
    with pilgrimage to the LORD, as a perpetual
        institution."

RESPONSORIAL PSALM
Ps 116:12-13, 15-16bc, 17-18

℟. (cf. 1 Cor 10:16) Our blessing-cup is a
    communion with the Blood of Christ.

How shall I make a return to the LORD
    for all the good he has done for me?
The cup of salvation I will take up,
    and I will call upon the name of the LORD.

℟. Our blessing-cup is a communion with the
    Blood of Christ.

Precious in the eyes of the LORD
    is the death of his faithful ones.
I am your servant, the son of your handmaid;
    you have loosed my bonds.

℟. Our blessing-cup is a communion with the
    Blood of Christ.

To you will I offer sacrifice of thanksgiving,
    and I will call upon the name of the LORD.
My vows to the LORD I will pay
    in the presence of all his people.

℟. Our blessing-cup is a communion with the
    Blood of Christ.

SECOND READING
1 Cor 11:23-26

Brothers and sisters:
I received from the Lord what I also handed
    on to you,
    that the Lord Jesus, on the night he was
        handed over,
    took bread, and, after he had given thanks,
    broke it and said, "This is my body that is
        for you.
Do this in remembrance of me."
In the same way also the cup, after supper,
    saying,
    "This cup is the new covenant in my blood.
Do this, as often as you drink it, in
    remembrance of me."
For as often as you eat this bread and drink
    the cup,
    you proclaim the death of the Lord until he
    comes.

Gospel (cont.)
John 18:1–19:42; L40ABC

So the band of soldiers, the tribune, and the Jewish guards seized Jesus,
    bound him, and brought him to Annas first.
He was the father-in-law of Caiaphas,
    who was high priest that year.
It was Caiaphas who had counseled the Jews
    that it was better that one man should die rather than the people.

Simon Peter and another disciple followed Jesus.
Now the other disciple was known to the high priest,
    and he entered the courtyard of the high priest with Jesus.
But Peter stood at the gate outside.
So the other disciple, the acquaintance of the high priest,
    went out and spoke to the gatekeeper and brought Peter in.
Then the maid who was the gatekeeper said to Peter,
    "You are not one of this man's disciples, are you?"
He said, "I am not."
Now the slaves and the guards were standing around a charcoal fire
    that they had made, because it was cold,
    and were warming themselves.
Peter was also standing there keeping warm.

The high priest questioned Jesus
    about his disciples and about his doctrine.
Jesus answered him,
    "I have spoken publicly to the world.
I have always taught in a synagogue
    or in the temple area where all the Jews gather,
    and in secret I have said nothing. Why ask me?
Ask those who heard me what I said to them.
They know what I said."
When he had said this,
    one of the temple guards standing there struck Jesus and said,
    "Is this the way you answer the high priest?"
Jesus answered him,
    "If I have spoken wrongly, testify to the wrong;
    but if I have spoken rightly, why do you strike me?"
Then Annas sent him bound to Caiaphas the high priest.

Now Simon Peter was standing there keeping warm.
And they said to him,
    "You are not one of his disciples, are you?"
He denied it and said,
    "I am not."
One of the slaves of the high priest,
    a relative of the one whose ear Peter had cut off, said,
    "Didn't I see you in the garden with him?"
Again Peter denied it.
And immediately the cock crowed.

Then they brought Jesus from Caiaphas to the praetorium.
It was morning.
And they themselves did not enter the praetorium,
    in order not to be defiled so that they could eat the Passover.
So Pilate came out to them and said,
    "What charge do you bring against this man?"
They answered and said to him,
    "If he were not a criminal,
    we would not have handed him over to you."
At this, Pilate said to them,
    "Take him yourselves, and judge him according to your law."

The Jews answered him,
    "We do not have the right to execute anyone,"
    in order that the word of Jesus might be fulfilled
    that he said indicating the kind of death he would die.
So Pilate went back into the praetorium
    and summoned Jesus and said to him,
    "Are you the King of the Jews?"
Jesus answered,
    "Do you say this on your own
    or have others told you about me?"
Pilate answered,
    "I am not a Jew, am I?
Your own nation and the chief priests handed you over to me.
What have you done?"
Jesus answered,
    "My kingdom does not belong to this world.
If my kingdom did belong to this world,
    my attendants would be fighting
    to keep me from being handed over to the Jews.
But as it is, my kingdom is not here."
So Pilate said to him,
    "Then you are a king?"
Jesus answered,
    "You say I am a king.
For this I was born and for this I came into the world,
    to testify to the truth.
Everyone who belongs to the truth listens to my voice."
Pilate said to him, "What is truth?"

When he had said this,
    he again went out to the Jews and said to them,
    "I find no guilt in him.
But you have a custom that I release one prisoner to you at Passover.
Do you want me to release to you the King of the Jews?"
They cried out again,
    "Not this one but Barabbas!"
Now Barabbas was a revolutionary.

Then Pilate took Jesus and had him scourged.
And the soldiers wove a crown out of thorns and placed it on his head,
    and clothed him in a purple cloak,
    and they came to him and said,
    "Hail, King of the Jews!"
And they struck him repeatedly.
Once more Pilate went out and said to them,
    "Look, I am bringing him out to you,
    so that you may know that I find no guilt in him."
So Jesus came out,
    wearing the crown of thorns and the purple cloak.
And he said to them, "Behold, the man!"
When the chief priests and the guards saw him they cried out,
    "Crucify him, crucify him!"
Pilate said to them,
    "Take him yourselves and crucify him.
I find no guilt in him."
The Jews answered,
    "We have a law, and according to that law he ought to die,
    because he made himself the Son of God."
Now when Pilate heard this statement,

he became even more afraid,
and went back into the praetorium and said to Jesus,
"Where are you from?"
Jesus did not answer him.
So Pilate said to him,
"Do you not speak to me?
Do you not know that I have power to release you
and I have power to crucify you?"
Jesus answered him,
"You would have no power over me
if it had not been given to you from above.
For this reason the one who handed me over to you
has the greater sin."
Consequently, Pilate tried to release him; but the Jews cried out,
"If you release him, you are not a Friend of Caesar.
Everyone who makes himself a king opposes Caesar."

When Pilate heard these words he brought Jesus out
and seated him on the judge's bench
in the place called Stone Pavement, in Hebrew, Gabbatha.
It was preparation day for Passover, and it was about noon.
And he said to the Jews,
"Behold, your king!"
They cried out,
"Take him away, take him away! Crucify him!"
Pilate said to them,
"Shall I crucify your king?"
The chief priests answered,
"We have no king but Caesar."
Then he handed him over to them to be crucified.

So they took Jesus, and, carrying the cross himself,
he went out to what is called the Place of the Skull,
in Hebrew, Golgotha.
There they crucified him, and with him two others,
one on either side, with Jesus in the middle.
Pilate also had an inscription written and put on the cross.
It read,
"Jesus the Nazorean, the King of the Jews."
Now many of the Jews read this inscription,
because the place where Jesus was crucified was near the city;
and it was written in Hebrew, Latin, and Greek.
So the chief priests of the Jews said to Pilate,
"Do not write 'The King of the Jews,'
but that he said, 'I am the King of the Jews.'"
Pilate answered,
"What I have written, I have written."

When the soldiers had crucified Jesus,
they took his clothes and divided them into four shares,
a share for each soldier.
They also took his tunic, but the tunic was seamless,
woven in one piece from the top down.
So they said to one another,
"Let's not tear it, but cast lots for it to see whose it will be,"
in order that the passage of Scripture might be fulfilled that says:
They divided my garments among them,
and for my vesture they cast lots.
This is what the soldiers did.

Standing by the cross of Jesus were his mother
and his mother's sister, Mary the wife of Clopas,
and Mary of Magdala.
When Jesus saw his mother and the disciple there whom he loved
he said to his mother, "Woman, behold, your son."
Then he said to the disciple,
"Behold, your mother."
And from that hour the disciple took her into his home.

After this, aware that everything was now finished,
in order that the Scripture might be fulfilled,
Jesus said, "I thirst."
There was a vessel filled with common wine.
So they put a sponge soaked in wine on a sprig of hyssop
and put it up to his mouth.
When Jesus had taken the wine, he said,
"It is finished."
And bowing his head, he handed over the spirit.

Here all kneel and pause for a short time.

Now since it was preparation day,
in order that the bodies might not remain
on the cross on the sabbath,
for the sabbath day of that week was a solemn one,
the Jews asked Pilate that their legs be broken
and that they be taken down.
So the soldiers came and broke the legs of the first
and then of the other one who was crucified with Jesus.
But when they came to Jesus and saw that he was already dead,
they did not break his legs,
but one soldier thrust his lance into his side,
and immediately blood and water flowed out.
An eyewitness has testified, and his testimony is true;
he knows that he is speaking the truth,
so that you also may come to believe.
For this happened so that the Scripture passage might be fulfilled:
Not a bone of it will be broken.
And again another passage says:
They will look upon him whom they have pierced.

After this, Joseph of Arimathea,
secretly a disciple of Jesus for fear of the Jews,
asked Pilate if he could remove the body of Jesus.
And Pilate permitted it.
So he came and took his body.
Nicodemus, the one who had first come to him at night,
also came bringing a mixture of myrrh and aloes
weighing about one hundred pounds.
They took the body of Jesus
and bound it with burial cloths along with the spices,
according to the Jewish burial custom.
Now in the place where he had been crucified there was a garden,
and in the garden a new tomb, in which no one had yet been buried.
So they laid Jesus there because of the Jewish preparation day;
for the tomb was close by.

FIRST READING

Isa 52:13–53:12

See, my servant shall prosper,
he shall be raised high and greatly exalted.
Even as many were amazed at him—
so marred was his look beyond human
semblance
and his appearance beyond that of the sons
of man—
so shall he startle many nations,
because of him kings shall stand
speechless;
for those who have not been told shall see,
those who have not heard shall ponder it.

Who would believe what we have heard?
To whom has the arm of the Lord been
revealed?
He grew up like a sapling before him,
like a shoot from the parched earth;
there was in him no stately bearing to make
us look at him,
nor appearance that would attract us to him.
He was spurned and avoided by people,
a man of suffering, accustomed to infirmity,
one of those from whom people hide their
faces,
spurned, and we held him in no esteem.

Yet it was our infirmities that he bore,
our sufferings that he endured,
while we thought of him as stricken,
as one smitten by God and afflicted.
But he was pierced for our offenses,
crushed for our sins;
upon him was the chastisement that makes
us whole,
by his stripes we were healed.
We had all gone astray like sheep,
each following his own way;
but the Lord laid upon him
the guilt of us all.

Though he was harshly treated, he submitted
and opened not his mouth;
like a lamb led to the slaughter
or a sheep before the shearers,
he was silent and opened not his mouth.
Oppressed and condemned, he was taken away,
and who would have thought any more of
his destiny?
When he was cut off from the land of the
living,
and smitten for the sin of his people,
a grave was assigned him among the wicked
and a burial place with evildoers,
though he had done no wrong
nor spoken any falsehood.
But the Lord was pleased
to crush him in infirmity.

If he gives his life as an offering for sin,
he shall see his descendants in a long life,
and the will of the Lord shall be
accomplished through him.

Because of his affliction
he shall see the light
in fullness of days;
through his suffering, my servant shall justify
many,
and their guilt he shall bear.
Therefore I will give him his portion among
the great,
and he shall divide the spoils with the
mighty,
because he surrendered himself to death
and was counted among the wicked;
and he shall take away the sins of many,
and win pardon for their offenses.

RESPONSORIAL PSALM

Ps 31:2, 6, 12-13, 15-16, 17, 25

R⁄. (Luke 23:46) Father, into your hands I
commend my spirit.

In you, O Lord, I take refuge;
let me never be put to shame.
In your justice rescue me.
Into your hands I commend my spirit;
you will redeem me, O Lord, O faithful God.

R⁄. Father, into your hands I commend my
spirit.

For all my foes I am an object of reproach,
a laughingstock to my neighbors, and a
dread to my friends;
they who see me abroad flee from me.
I am forgotten like the unremembered dead;
I am like a dish that is broken.

R⁄. Father, into your hands I commend my
spirit.

But my trust is in you, O Lord;
I say, "You are my God.
In your hands is my destiny; rescue me
from the clutches of my enemies and my
persecutors."

R⁄. Father, into your hands I commend my
spirit.

Let your face shine upon your servant;
save me in your kindness.
Take courage and be stouthearted,
all you who hope in the Lord.

R⁄. Father, into your hands I commend my
spirit.

SECOND READING

Heb 4:14-16; 5:7-9

Brothers and sisters:
Since we have a great high priest who has
passed through the heavens,
Jesus, the Son of God,
let us hold fast to our confession.
For we do not have a high priest
who is unable to sympathize with our
weaknesses,
but one who has similarly been tested in
every way,
yet without sin.
So let us confidently approach the throne of
grace
to receive mercy and to find grace for
timely help.

In the days when Christ was in the flesh,
he offered prayers and supplications with
loud cries and tears
to the one who was able to save him from
death,
and he was heard because of his reverence.
Son though he was, he learned obedience from
what he suffered;
and when he was made perfect,
he became the source of eternal salvation
for all who obey him.

At the Easter Vigil in the Holy Night of Easter, *April 8, 2023*

FIRST READING
Gen 1:1–2:2

In the beginning, when God created the
heavens and the earth,
the earth was a formless wasteland, and
darkness covered the abyss,
while a mighty wind swept over the waters.

Then God said,
"Let there be light," and there was light.
God saw how good the light was.
God then separated the light from the
darkness.
God called the light "day," and the darkness
he called "night."
Thus evening came, and morning followed—
the first day.

Then God said,
"Let there be a dome in the middle of the
waters,
to separate one body of water from the
other."
And so it happened:
God made the dome,
and it separated the water above the dome
from the water below it.
God called the dome "the sky."
Evening came, and morning followed—the
second day.

Then God said,
"Let the water under the sky be gathered
into a single basin,
so that the dry land may appear."
And so it happened:
the water under the sky was gathered into
its basin,
and the dry land appeared.
God called the dry land "the earth,"
and the basin of the water he called "the
sea."
God saw how good it was.
Then God said,
"Let the earth bring forth vegetation:
every kind of plant that bears seed
and every kind of fruit tree on earth
that bears fruit with its seed in it."
And so it happened:
the earth brought forth every kind of plant
that bears seed
and every kind of fruit tree on earth
that bears fruit with its seed in it.
God saw how good it was.
Evening came, and morning followed—the
third day.

Then God said:
"Let there be lights in the dome of the sky,
to separate day from night.
Let them mark the fixed times, the days and
the years,

and serve as luminaries in the dome of the
sky,
to shed light upon the earth."
And so it happened:
God made the two great lights,
the greater one to govern the day,
and the lesser one to govern the night;
and he made the stars.
God set them in the dome of the sky,
to shed light upon the earth,
to govern the day and the night,
and to separate the light from the darkness.
God saw how good it was.
Evening came, and morning followed—the
fourth day.

Then God said,
"Let the water teem with an abundance of
living creatures,
and on the earth let birds fly beneath the
dome of the sky."
And so it happened:
God created the great sea monsters
and all kinds of swimming creatures with
which the water teems,
and all kinds of winged birds.
God saw how good it was, and God blessed
them, saying,
"Be fertile, multiply, and fill the water of
the seas;
and let the birds multiply on the earth."
Evening came, and morning followed—the
fifth day.

Then God said,
"Let the earth bring forth all kinds of living
creatures:
cattle, creeping things, and wild animals of
all kinds."
And so it happened:
God made all kinds of wild animals, all
kinds of cattle,
and all kinds of creeping things of the
earth.
God saw how good it was.
Then God said:
"Let us make man in our image, after our
likeness.
Let them have dominion over the fish of the
sea,
the birds of the air, and the cattle,
and over all the wild animals
and all the creatures that crawl on the
ground."
God created man in his image;
in the image of God he created him;
male and female he created them.
God blessed them, saying:
"Be fertile and multiply;
fill the earth and subdue it.
Have dominion over the fish of the sea, the
birds of the air,

and all the living things that move on the
earth."
God also said:
"See, I give you every seed-bearing plant all
over the earth
and every tree that has seed-bearing fruit
on it to be your food;
and to all the animals of the land, all the
birds of the air,
and all the living creatures that crawl on
the ground,
I give all the green plants for food."
And so it happened.
God looked at everything he had made, and he
found it very good.
Evening came, and morning followed—the
sixth day.

Thus the heavens and the earth and all their
array were completed.
Since on the seventh day God was finished
with the work he had been doing,
he rested on the seventh day from all the
work he had undertaken.

or

Gen 1:1, 26-31a

In the beginning, when God created the
heavens and the earth,
God said: "Let us make man in our image,
after our likeness.
Let them have dominion over the fish of the
sea,
the birds of the air, and the cattle,
and over all the wild animals
and all the creatures that crawl on the
ground."
God created man in his image;
in the image of God he created him;
male and female he created them.
God blessed them, saying:
"Be fertile and multiply;
fill the earth and subdue it.
Have dominion over the fish of the sea, the
birds of the air,
and all the living things that move on the
earth."
God also said:
"See, I give you every seed-bearing plant all
over the earth
and every tree that has seed-bearing fruit
on it to be your food;
and to all the animals of the land, all the
birds of the air,
and all the living creatures that crawl on
the ground,
I give all the green plants for food."
And so it happened.
God looked at everything he had made, and
found it very good.

285

RESPONSORIAL PSALM

Ps 104:1-2, 5-6, 10, 12, 13-14, 24, 35

℟. (30) Lord, send out your Spirit, and renew
    the face of the earth.

Bless the Lord, O my soul!
    O Lord, my God, you are great indeed!
You are clothed with majesty and glory,
    robed in light as with a cloak.

℟. Lord, send out your Spirit, and renew the
    face of the earth.

You fixed the earth upon its foundation,
    not to be moved forever;
with the ocean, as with a garment, you
    covered it;
    above the mountains the waters stood.

℟. Lord, send out your Spirit, and renew the
    face of the earth.

You send forth springs into the watercourses
    that wind among the mountains.
Beside them the birds of heaven dwell;
    from among the branches they send forth
        their song.

℟. Lord, send out your Spirit, and renew the
    face of the earth.

You water the mountains from your palace;
    the earth is replete with the fruit of your
        works.
You raise grass for the cattle,
    and vegetation for man's use,
producing bread from the earth.

℟. Lord, send out your Spirit, and renew the
    face of the earth.

How manifold are your works, O Lord!
    In wisdom you have wrought them all—
the earth is full of your creatures.
    Bless the Lord, O my soul!

℟. Lord, send out your Spirit, and renew the
    face of the earth.

or

Ps 33:4-5, 6-7, 12-13, 20 and 22

℟. (5b) The earth is full of the goodness of
    the Lord.

Upright is the word of the Lord,
    and all his works are trustworthy.
He loves justice and right;
    of the kindness of the Lord the earth is full.

℟. The earth is full of the goodness of the Lord.

By the word of the Lord the heavens were
    made;
    by the breath of his mouth all their host.
He gathers the waters of the sea as in a flask;
    in cellars he confines the deep.

℟. The earth is full of the goodness of the Lord.

Blessed the nation whose God is the Lord,
    the people he has chosen for his own
        inheritance.
From heaven the Lord looks down;
    he sees all mankind.

℟. The earth is full of the goodness of the Lord.

Our soul waits for the Lord,
    who is our help and our shield.
May your kindness, O Lord, be upon us
    who have put our hope in you.

℟. The earth is full of the goodness of the Lord.

SECOND READING

Gen 22:1-18

God put Abraham to the test.
He called to him, "Abraham!"
"Here I am," he replied.
Then God said:
    "Take your son Isaac, your only one, whom
        you love,
    and go to the land of Moriah.
There you shall offer him up as a holocaust
    on a height that I will point out to you."
Early the next morning Abraham saddled his
    donkey,
    took with him his son Isaac and two of his
        servants as well,
    and with the wood that he had cut for the
        holocaust,
    set out for the place of which God had told
        him.

On the third day Abraham got sight of the
    place from afar.
Then he said to his servants:
    "Both of you stay here with the donkey,
    while the boy and I go on over yonder.
We will worship and then come back to you."
Thereupon Abraham took the wood for the
    holocaust
    and laid it on his son Isaac's shoulders,
    while he himself carried the fire and the
        knife.
As the two walked on together, Isaac spoke to
    his father Abraham:
    "Father!" Isaac said.
"Yes, son," he replied.
Isaac continued, "Here are the fire and the
    wood,
    but where is the sheep for the holocaust?"
"Son," Abraham answered,
    "God himself will provide the sheep for the
        holocaust."
Then the two continued going forward.

When they came to the place of which God
    had told him,
    Abraham built an altar there and arranged
        the wood on it.

Next he tied up his son Isaac,
    and put him on top of the wood on the
        altar.
Then he reached out and took the knife to
    slaughter his son.
But the Lord's messenger called to him from
    heaven,
    "Abraham, Abraham!"
"Here I am," he answered.
"Do not lay your hand on the boy," said the
    messenger.
"Do not do the least thing to him.
I know now how devoted you are to God,
    since you did not withhold from me your
        own beloved son."
As Abraham looked about,
    he spied a ram caught by its horns in the
        thicket.
So he went and took the ram
    and offered it up as a holocaust in place of
        his son.
Abraham named the site Yahweh-yireh;
    hence people now say, "On the mountain
        the Lord will see."

Again the Lord's messenger called to
    Abraham from heaven and said:
    "I swear by myself, declares the Lord,
    that because you acted as you did
    in not withholding from me your beloved
        son,
    I will bless you abundantly
    and make your descendants as countless
    as the stars of the sky and the sands of the
        seashore;
    your descendants shall take possession
    of the gates of their enemies,
    and in your descendants all the nations of
        the earth
    shall find blessing—
    all this because you obeyed my command."

or

Gen 22:1-2, 9a, 10-13, 15-18

God put Abraham to the test.
He called to him, "Abraham!"
"Here I am," he replied.
Then God said:
    "Take your son Isaac, your only one, whom
        you love,
    and go to the land of Moriah.
There you shall offer him up as a holocaust
    on a height that I will point out to you."

When they came to the place of which God
    had told him,
    Abraham built an altar there and arranged
        the wood on it.
Then he reached out and took the knife to
    slaughter his son.

But the LORD's messenger called to him from
heaven,
"Abraham, Abraham!"
"Here I am," he answered.
"Do not lay your hand on the boy," said the
messenger.
"Do not do the least thing to him.
I know now how devoted you are to God,
since you did not withhold from me your
own beloved son."
As Abraham looked about,
he spied a ram caught by its horns in the
thicket.
So he went and took the ram
and offered it up as a holocaust in place of
his son.

Again the LORD's messenger called to
Abraham from heaven and said:
"I swear by myself, declares the LORD,
that because you acted as you did
in not withholding from me your beloved
son,
I will bless you abundantly
and make your descendants as countless
as the stars of the sky and the sands of the
seashore;
your descendants shall take possession
of the gates of their enemies,
and in your descendants all the nations of
the earth
shall find blessing—
all this because you obeyed my command."

RESPONSORIAL PSALM
Ps 16:5, 8, 9-10, 11

R̸. (1) You are my inheritance, O Lord.

O LORD, my allotted portion and my cup,
you it is who hold fast my lot.
I set the LORD ever before me;
with him at my right hand I shall not be
disturbed.

R̸. You are my inheritance, O Lord.

Therefore my heart is glad and my soul
rejoices,
my body, too, abides in confidence;
because you will not abandon my soul to the
netherworld,
nor will you suffer your faithful one to
undergo corruption.

R̸. You are my inheritance, O Lord.

You will show me the path to life,
fullness of joys in your presence,
the delights at your right hand forever.

R̸. You are my inheritance, O Lord.

THIRD READING
Exod 14:15–15:1

The LORD said to Moses, "Why are you crying
out to me?
Tell the Israelites to go forward.
And you, lift up your staff and, with hand
outstretched over the sea,
split the sea in two,
that the Israelites may pass through it on
dry land.
But I will make the Egyptians so obstinate
that they will go in after them.
Then I will receive glory through Pharaoh and
all his army,
his chariots and charioteers.
The Egyptians shall know that I am the LORD,
when I receive glory through Pharaoh
and his chariots and charioteers."

The angel of God, who had been leading
Israel's camp,
now moved and went around behind them.
The column of cloud also, leaving the front,
took up its place behind them,
so that it came between the camp of the
Egyptians
and that of Israel.
But the cloud now became dark, and thus the
night passed
without the rival camps coming any closer
together all night long.
Then Moses stretched out his hand over the
sea,
and the LORD swept the sea
with a strong east wind throughout the
night
and so turned it into dry land.
When the water was thus divided,
the Israelites marched into the midst of the
sea on dry land,
with the water like a wall to their right and
to their left.

The Egyptians followed in pursuit;
all Pharaoh's horses and chariots and
charioteers went after them
right into the midst of the sea.
In the night watch just before dawn
the LORD cast through the column of the
fiery cloud
upon the Egyptian force a glance that
threw it into a panic;
and he so clogged their chariot wheels
that they could hardly drive.
With that the Egyptians sounded the retreat
before Israel,
because the LORD was fighting for them
against the Egyptians.

Then the LORD told Moses, "Stretch out your
hand over the sea,
that the water may flow back upon the
Egyptians,
upon their chariots and their charioteers."
So Moses stretched out his hand over the sea,
and at dawn the sea flowed back to its
normal depth.
The Egyptians were fleeing head on toward
the sea,
when the LORD hurled them into its midst.
As the water flowed back,
it covered the chariots and the charioteers
of Pharaoh's whole army
which had followed the Israelites into the sea.
Not a single one of them escaped.
But the Israelites had marched on dry land
through the midst of the sea,
with the water like a wall to their right and
to their left.
Thus the LORD saved Israel on that day
from the power of the Egyptians.
When Israel saw the Egyptians lying dead on
the seashore
and beheld the great power that the LORD
had shown against the Egyptians,
they feared the LORD and believed in him
and in his servant Moses.

Then Moses and the Israelites sang this song
to the LORD:
I will sing to the LORD, for he is gloriously
triumphant;
horse and chariot he has cast into the sea.

RESPONSORIAL PSALM
Exod 15:1-2, 3-4, 5-6, 17-18

R̸. (1b) Let us sing to the Lord; he has covered
himself in glory.

I will sing to the LORD, for he is gloriously
triumphant;
horse and chariot he has cast into the sea.
My strength and my courage is the LORD,
and he has been my savior.
He is my God, I praise him;
the God of my father, I extol him.

R̸. Let us sing to the Lord; he has covered
himself in glory.

The LORD is a warrior,
LORD is his name!
Pharaoh's chariots and army he hurled into
the sea;
the elite of his officers were submerged in
the Red Sea.

R̸. Let us sing to the Lord; he has covered
himself in glory.

The flood waters covered them,
  they sank into the depths like a stone.
Your right hand, O Lord, magnificent in
    power,
  your right hand, O Lord, has shattered the
    enemy.

R7. Let us sing to the Lord; he has covered
  himself in glory.

You brought in the people you redeemed
  and planted them on the mountain of your
    inheritance—
the place where you made your seat, O Lord,
  the sanctuary, Lord, which your hands
    established.
The Lord shall reign forever and ever.

R7. Let us sing to the Lord; he has covered
  himself in glory.

FOURTH READING
Isa 54:5-14

The One who has become your husband is
    your Maker;
  his name is the Lord of hosts;
your redeemer is the Holy One of Israel,
  called God of all the earth.
The Lord calls you back,
  like a wife forsaken and grieved in spirit,
  a wife married in youth and then cast off,
  says your God.
For a brief moment I abandoned you,
  but with great tenderness I will take you
    back.
In an outburst of wrath, for a moment
  I hid my face from you;
but with enduring love I take pity on you,
  says the Lord, your redeemer.
This is for me like the days of Noah,
  when I swore that the waters of Noah
  should never again deluge the earth;
so I have sworn not to be angry with you,
  or to rebuke you.
Though the mountains leave their place
  and the hills be shaken,
my love shall never leave you
  nor my covenant of peace be shaken,
  says the Lord, who has mercy on you.
O afflicted one, storm-battered and
    unconsoled,
  I lay your pavements in carnelians,
  and your foundations in sapphires;
I will make your battlements of rubies,
  your gates of carbuncles,
  and all your walls of precious stones.
All your children shall be taught by the Lord,
  and great shall be the peace of your children.

In justice shall you be established,
  far from the fear of oppression,
  where destruction cannot come near you.

RESPONSORIAL PSALM
Ps 30:2, 4, 5-6, 11-12, 13

R7. (2a) I will praise you, Lord, for you have
  rescued me.

I will extol you, O Lord, for you drew me clear
  and did not let my enemies rejoice over me.
O Lord, you brought me up from the
    netherworld;
  you preserved me from among those going
    down into the pit.

R7. I will praise you, Lord, for you have
  rescued me.

Sing praise to the Lord, you his faithful ones,
  and give thanks to his holy name.
For his anger lasts but a moment;
  a lifetime, his good will.
At nightfall, weeping enters in,
  but with the dawn, rejoicing.

R7. I will praise you, Lord, for you have
  rescued me.

Hear, O Lord, and have pity on me;
  O Lord, be my helper.
You changed my mourning into dancing;
  O Lord, my God, forever will I give you
    thanks.

R7. I will praise you, Lord, for you have
  rescued me.

FIFTH READING
Isa 55:1-11

Thus says the Lord:
All you who are thirsty,
  come to the water!
You who have no money,
  come, receive grain and eat;
come, without paying and without cost,
  drink wine and milk!
Why spend your money for what is not bread,
  your wages for what fails to satisfy?
Heed me, and you shall eat well,
  you shall delight in rich fare.
Come to me heedfully,
  listen, that you may have life.
I will renew with you the everlasting covenant,
  the benefits assured to David.
As I made him a witness to the peoples,
  a leader and commander of nations,
so shall you summon a nation you knew not,
  and nations that knew you not shall run
    to you,

because of the Lord, your God,
  the Holy One of Israel, who has glorified
    you.

Seek the Lord while he may be found,
  call him while he is near.
Let the scoundrel forsake his way,
  and the wicked man his thoughts;
let him turn to the Lord for mercy;
  to our God, who is generous in forgiving.
For my thoughts are not your thoughts,
  nor are your ways my ways, says the Lord.
As high as the heavens are above the earth,
  so high are my ways above your ways
  and my thoughts above your thoughts.

For just as from the heavens
  the rain and snow come down
and do not return there
  till they have watered the earth,
  making it fertile and fruitful,
giving seed to the one who sows
  and bread to the one who eats,
so shall my word be
  that goes forth from my mouth;
my word shall not return to me void,
  but shall do my will,
  achieving the end for which I sent it.

RESPONSORIAL PSALM
Isa 12:2-3, 4, 5-6

R7. (3) You will draw water joyfully from the
  springs of salvation.

God indeed is my savior;
  I am confident and unafraid.
My strength and my courage is the Lord,
  and he has been my savior.
With joy you will draw water
  at the fountain of salvation.

R7. You will draw water joyfully from the
  springs of salvation.

Give thanks to the Lord, acclaim his name;
  among the nations make known his deeds,
  proclaim how exalted is his name.

R7. You will draw water joyfully from the
  springs of salvation.

Sing praise to the Lord for his glorious
    achievement;
  let this be known throughout all the earth.
Shout with exultation, O city of Zion,
  for great in your midst
  is the Holy One of Israel!

R7. You will draw water joyfully from the
  springs of salvation.

SIXTH READING
Bar 3:9-15, 32–4:4

Hear, O Israel, the commandments of life:
  listen, and know prudence!
How is it, Israel,
    that you are in the land of your foes,
    grown old in a foreign land,
defiled with the dead,
    accounted with those destined for the
      netherworld?
You have forsaken the fountain of wisdom!
    Had you walked in the way of God,
    you would have dwelt in enduring peace.
Learn where prudence is,
    where strength, where understanding;
that you may know also
    where are length of days, and life,
    where light of the eyes, and peace.
Who has found the place of wisdom,
    who has entered into her treasuries?

The One who knows all things knows her;
    he has probed her by his knowledge—
the One who established the earth for all time,
    and filled it with four-footed beasts;
he who dismisses the light, and it departs,
    calls it, and it obeys him trembling;
before whom the stars at their posts
    shine and rejoice;
when he calls them, they answer, "Here we are!"
    shining with joy for their Maker.
Such is our God;
    no other is to be compared to him:
he has traced out the whole way of
      understanding,
    and has given her to Jacob, his servant,
    to Israel, his beloved son.

Since then she has appeared on earth,
    and moved among people.
She is the book of the precepts of God,
    the law that endures forever;
all who cling to her will live,
    but those will die who forsake her.
Turn, O Jacob, and receive her:
    walk by her light toward splendor.
Give not your glory to another,
    your privileges to an alien race.
Blessed are we, O Israel;
    for what pleases God is known to us!

RESPONSORIAL PSALM
Ps 19:8, 9, 10, 11

R̂. (John 6:68c) Lord, you have the words of
    everlasting life.

The law of the LORD is perfect,
    refreshing the soul;
the decree of the LORD is trustworthy,
    giving wisdom to the simple.

R̂. Lord, you have the words of everlasting life.

The precepts of the LORD are right,
    rejoicing the heart;
the command of the LORD is clear,
    enlightening the eye.

R̂. Lord, you have the words of everlasting life.

The fear of the LORD is pure,
    enduring forever;
the ordinances of the LORD are true,
    all of them just.

R̂. Lord, you have the words of everlasting life.

They are more precious than gold,
    than a heap of purest gold;
sweeter also than syrup
    or honey from the comb.

R̂. Lord, you have the words of everlasting life.

SEVENTH READING
Ezek 36:16-17a, 18-28

The word of the LORD came to me, saying:
    Son of man, when the house of Israel lived
      in their land,
    they defiled it by their conduct and deeds.
Therefore I poured out my fury upon them
    because of the blood that they poured out
      on the ground,
    and because they defiled it with idols.
I scattered them among the nations,
    dispersing them over foreign lands;
    according to their conduct and deeds I
      judged them.
But when they came among the nations
      wherever they came,
    they served to profane my holy name,
    because it was said of them: "These are the
      people of the LORD,
    yet they had to leave their land."
So I have relented because of my holy name
    which the house of Israel profaned
    among the nations where they came.
Therefore say to the house of Israel: Thus
      says the Lord GOD:
    Not for your sakes do I act, house of Israel,
    but for the sake of my holy name,
    which you profaned among the nations to
      which you came.
I will prove the holiness of my great name,
    profaned among the nations,
    in whose midst you have profaned it.
Thus the nations shall know that I am the
      LORD, says the Lord GOD,
    when in their sight I prove my holiness
      through you.
For I will take you away from among the nations,
    gather you from all the foreign lands,
    and bring you back to your own land.
I will sprinkle clean water upon you
    to cleanse you from all your impurities,
    and from all your idols I will cleanse you.

I will give you a new heart and place a new
      spirit within you,
    taking from your bodies your stony hearts
    and giving you natural hearts.
I will put my spirit within you and make you
      live by my statutes,
    careful to observe my decrees.
You shall live in the land I gave your fathers;
    you shall be my people, and I will be your
      God.

RESPONSORIAL PSALM
Ps 42:3, 5; 43:3, 4

R̂. (42:2) Like a deer that longs for running
    streams, my soul longs for you, my God.

Athirst is my soul for God, the living God.
    When shall I go and behold the face of God?

R̂. Like a deer that longs for running streams,
    my soul longs for you, my God.

I went with the throng
    and led them in procession to the house of God,
amid loud cries of joy and thanksgiving,
    with the multitude keeping festival.

R̂. Like a deer that longs for running streams,
    my soul longs for you, my God.

Send forth your light and your fidelity;
    they shall lead me on
and bring me to your holy mountain,
    to your dwelling-place.

R̂. Like a deer that longs for running streams,
    my soul longs for you, my God.

Then will I go in to the altar of God,
    the God of my gladness and joy;
then will I give you thanks upon the harp,
    O God, my God!

R̂. Like a deer that longs for running streams,
    my soul longs for you, my God.

or

Isa 12:2-3, 4bcd, 5-6

R̂. (3) You will draw water joyfully from the
    springs of salvation.

God indeed is my savior;
    I am confident and unafraid.
My strength and my courage is the LORD,
    and he has been my savior.
With joy you will draw water
    at the fountain of salvation.

R̂. You will draw water joyfully from the
    springs of salvation.

Give thanks to the LORD, acclaim his name;
    among the nations make known his deeds,
    proclaim how exalted is his name.

R̂. You will draw water joyfully from the
    springs of salvation.

Sing praise to the LORD for his glorious
    achievement;
    let this be known throughout all the earth.
Shout with exultation, O city of Zion,
    for great in your midst
    is the Holy One of Israel!

℟. You will draw water joyfully from the
    springs of salvation.

or

Ps 51:12-13, 14-15, 18-19

℟. (12a) Create a clean heart in me, O God.

A clean heart create for me, O God,
    and a steadfast spirit renew within me.
Cast me not out from your presence,
    and your Holy Spirit take not from me.

℟. Create a clean heart in me, O God.

Give me back the joy of your salvation,
    and a willing spirit sustain in me.
I will teach transgressors your ways,
    and sinners shall return to you.

℟. Create a clean heart in me, O God.

For you are not pleased with sacrifices;
    should I offer a holocaust, you would not
    accept it.
My sacrifice, O God, is a contrite spirit;
    a heart contrite and humbled, O God, you
    will not spurn.

℟. Create a clean heart in me, O God.

EPISTLE
Rom 6:3-11

Brothers and sisters:
Are you unaware that we who were baptized
    into Christ Jesus
    were baptized into his death?
We were indeed buried with him through
    baptism into death,
    so that, just as Christ was raised from the
    dead
    by the glory of the Father,
    we too might live in newness of life.

For if we have grown into union with him
    through a death like his,
    we shall also be united with him in the
    resurrection.
We know that our old self was crucified with
    him,
    so that our sinful body might be done away
    with,
    that we might no longer be in slavery to sin.
For a dead person has been absolved from sin.
If, then, we have died with Christ,
    we believe that we shall also live with him.
We know that Christ, raised from the dead,
    dies no more;
    death no longer has power over him.
As to his death, he died to sin once and for all;
    as to his life, he lives for God.
Consequently, you too must think of
    yourselves as being dead to sin
    and living for God in Christ Jesus.

RESPONSORIAL PSALM
Ps 118:1-2, 16-17, 22-23

℟. Alleluia, alleluia, alleluia.

Give thanks to the LORD, for he is good,
    for his mercy endures forever.
Let the house of Israel say,
    "His mercy endures forever."

℟. Alleluia, alleluia, alleluia.

The right hand of the LORD has struck with
    power;
    the right hand of the LORD is exalted.
I shall not die, but live,
    and declare the works of the LORD.

℟. Alleluia, alleluia, alleluia.

The stone which the builders rejected
    has become the cornerstone.
By the LORD has this been done;
    it is wonderful in our eyes.

℟. Alleluia, alleluia, alleluia.

Gospel
Matt 28:1-10; L41ABC

After the sabbath, as the first day of the week was dawning,
  Mary Magdalene and the other Mary came to see the tomb.
And behold, there was a great earthquake;
  for an angel of the Lord descended from heaven,
  approached, rolled back the stone, and sat upon it.
His appearance was like lightning
  and his clothing was white as snow.
The guards were shaken with fear of him
  and became like dead men.
Then the angel said to the women in reply,
  "Do not be afraid!
I know that you are seeking Jesus the crucified.

He is not here, for he has been raised just as he said.
Come and see the place where he lay.
Then go quickly and tell his disciples,
  'He has been raised from the dead,
  and he is going before you to Galilee;
  there you will see him.'
  Behold, I have told you."
Then they went away quickly from the tomb,
  fearful yet overjoyed,
  and ran to announce this to his disciples.
And behold, Jesus met them on their way and greeted them.
They approached, embraced his feet, and did him homage.
Then Jesus said to them, "Do not be afraid.
Go tell my brothers to go to Galilee,
  and there they will see me."

or, at an afternoon or evening Mass

Gospel
Luke 24:13-35; L46A

That very day, the first day of the week,
  two of Jesus' disciples were going
  to a village seven miles from Jerusalem called Emmaus,
  and they were conversing about all the things that had occurred.
And it happened that while they were conversing and debating,
  Jesus himself drew near and walked with them,
  but their eyes were prevented from recognizing him.
He asked them,
  "What are you discussing as you walk along?"
They stopped, looking downcast.
One of them, named Cleopas, said to him in reply,
  "Are you the only visitor to Jerusalem
  who does not know of the things
  that have taken place there in these days?"
And he replied to them, "What sort of things?"
They said to him,
  "The things that happened to Jesus the Nazarene,
  who was a prophet mighty in deed and word
  before God and all the people,
  how our chief priests and rulers both handed him over
  to a sentence of death and crucified him.
But we were hoping that he would be the one to redeem Israel;
  and besides all this,
  it is now the third day since this took place.
Some women from our group, however, have astounded us:
  they were at the tomb early in the morning
  and did not find his body;
  they came back and reported
  that they had indeed seen a vision of angels
  who announced that he was alive.
Then some of those with us went to the tomb
  and found things just as the women had described,
  but him they did not see."

And he said to them, "Oh, how foolish you are!
How slow of heart to believe all that the prophets spoke!
Was it not necessary that the Christ should suffer these things
  and enter into his glory?"
Then beginning with Moses and all the prophets,
  he interpreted to them what referred to him
  in all the Scriptures.
As they approached the village to which they were going,
  he gave the impression that he was going on farther.
But they urged him, "Stay with us,
  for it is nearly evening and the day is almost over."
So he went in to stay with them.
And it happened that, while he was with them at table,
  he took bread, said the blessing,
  broke it, and gave it to them.
With that their eyes were opened and they recognized him,
  but he vanished from their sight.
Then they said to each other,
  "Were not our hearts burning within us
  while he spoke to us on the way and opened the Scriptures to us?"
So they set out at once and returned to Jerusalem
  where they found gathered together
  the eleven and those with them who were saying,
  "The Lord has truly been raised and has appeared to Simon!"
Then the two recounted
  what had taken place on the way
  and how he was made known to them in the breaking of bread.

Easter Sunday, *April 9, 2023*

FIRST READING
Acts 10:34a, 37-43

Peter proceeded to speak and said:
"You know what has happened all over Judea,
beginning in Galilee after the baptism
that John preached,
how God anointed Jesus of Nazareth
with the Holy Spirit and power.
He went about doing good
and healing all those oppressed by the devil,
for God was with him.
We are witnesses of all that he did
both in the country of the Jews and in
Jerusalem.
They put him to death by hanging him on a tree.
This man God raised on the third day and
granted that he be visible,
not to all the people, but to us,
the witnesses chosen by God in advance,
who ate and drank with him after he rose
from the dead.
He commissioned us to preach to the people
and testify that he is the one appointed by God
as judge of the living and the dead.
To him all the prophets bear witness,
that everyone who believes in him
will receive forgiveness of sins through his
name."

RESPONSORIAL PSALM
Ps 118:1-2, 16-17, 22-23

R℣. (24) This is the day the Lord has made; let
us rejoice and be glad.
or:
R℣. Alleluia.

Give thanks to the LORD, for he is good,
for his mercy endures forever.
Let the house of Israel say,
"His mercy endures forever."

R℣. This is the day the Lord has made; let us
rejoice and be glad.
or:
R℣. Alleluia.

"The right hand of the LORD has struck with
power;
the right hand of the LORD is exalted.
I shall not die, but live,
and declare the works of the LORD."

R℣. This is the day the Lord has made; let us
rejoice and be glad.
or:
R℣. Alleluia.

The stone which the builders rejected
has become the cornerstone.
By the LORD has this been done;
it is wonderful in our eyes.

R℣. This is the day the Lord has made; let us
rejoice and be glad.
or:
R℣. Alleluia.

SECOND READING
Col 3:1-4

Brothers and sisters:
If then you were raised with Christ, seek what
is above,
where Christ is seated at the right hand of
God.
Think of what is above, not of what is on
earth.
For you have died, and your life is hidden with
Christ in God.
When Christ your life appears,
then you too will appear with him in glory.

or
1 Cor 5:6b-8

Brothers and sisters:
Do you not know that a little yeast leavens all
the dough?
Clear out the old yeast,
so that you may become a fresh batch of
dough,
inasmuch as you are unleavened.
For our paschal lamb, Christ, has been
sacrificed.
Therefore, let us celebrate the feast,
not with the old yeast, the yeast of malice
and wickedness,
but with the unleavened bread of sincerity
and truth.

SEQUENCE

Victimae paschali laudes
Christians, to the Paschal Victim
Offer your thankful praises!
A Lamb the sheep redeems;
Christ, who only is sinless,
Reconciles sinners to the Father.
Death and life have contended in that combat
stupendous:
The Prince of life, who died, reigns
immortal.
Speak, Mary, declaring
What you saw, wayfaring.
"The tomb of Christ, who is living,
The glory of Jesus' resurrection;
Bright angels attesting,
The shroud and napkin resting.
Yes, Christ my hope is arisen;
To Galilee he goes before you."
Christ indeed from death is risen, our new life
obtaining.
Have mercy, victor King, ever reigning!
Amen. Alleluia.

Second Sunday of Easter (or of Divine Mercy), *April 16, 2023*

Gospel (cont.)
John 20:19-31; L43A

Then he said to Thomas, "Put your finger here and see my hands,
and bring your hand and put it into my side,
and do not be unbelieving, but believe."
Thomas answered and said to him, "My Lord and my God!"
Jesus said to him, "Have you come to believe because you have seen me?
Blessed are those who have not seen and have believed."

Now Jesus did many other signs in the presence of his disciples
that are not written in this book.
But these are written that you may come to believe
that Jesus is the Christ, the Son of God,
and that through this belief you may have life in his name.

Gospel (cont.)
Luke 24:13-35; L46A

But we were hoping that he would be the one to redeem Israel;
and besides all this,
it is now the third day since this took place.
Some women from our group, however, have astounded us:
they were at the tomb early in the morning
and did not find his body;
they came back and reported
that they had indeed seen a vision of angels
who announced that he was alive.
Then some of those with us went to the tomb
and found things just as the women had described,
but him they did not see."
And he said to them, "Oh, how foolish you are!
How slow of heart to believe all that the prophets spoke!
Was it not necessary that the Christ should suffer these things
and enter into his glory?"
Then beginning with Moses and all the prophets,
he interpreted to them what referred to him
in all the Scriptures.
As they approached the village to which they were going,
he gave the impression that he was going on farther.
But they urged him, "Stay with us,
for it is nearly evening and the day is almost over."
So he went in to stay with them.
And it happened that, while he was with them at table,
he took bread, said the blessing,
broke it, and gave it to them.

With that their eyes were opened and they recognized him,
but he vanished from their sight.
Then they said to each other,
"Were not our hearts burning within us
while he spoke to us on the way and opened the Scriptures to us?"
So they set out at once and returned to Jerusalem
where they found gathered together
the eleven and those with them who were saying,
"The Lord has truly been raised and has appeared to Simon!"
Then the two recounted
what had taken place on the way
and how he was made known to them in the breaking of bread.

SECOND READING
1 Pet 1:17-21

Beloved:
If you invoke as Father him who judges impartially
according to each one's works,
conduct yourselves with reverence during the time of your sojourning,
realizing that you were ransomed from your futile conduct,
handed on by your ancestors,
not with perishable things like silver or gold
but with the precious blood of Christ
as of a spotless unblemished lamb.

He was known before the foundation of the world
but revealed in the final time for you,
who through him believe in God
who raised him from the dead and gave him glory,
so that your faith and hope are in God.

Fifth Sunday of Easter, *May 7, 2023*

Gospel (cont.)
John 14:1-12; L52A

The words that I speak to you I do not speak on my own.
The Father who dwells in me is doing his works.
Believe me that I am in the Father and the Father is in me,
or else, believe because of the works themselves.
Amen, amen, I say to you,
whoever believes in me will do the works that I do,
and will do greater ones than these,
because I am going to the Father."

The Ascension of the Lord,
May 18 (Thursday) or May 21, 2023

SECOND READING   Eph 1:17-23

Brothers and sisters:
May the God of our Lord Jesus Christ, the Father of glory,
give you a Spirit of wisdom and revelation
resulting in knowledge of him.
May the eyes of your hearts be enlightened,
that you may know what is the hope that belongs to his call,
what are the riches of glory
in his inheritance among the holy ones,
and what is the surpassing greatness of his power
for us who believe,
in accord with the exercise of his great might,
which he worked in Christ,
raising him from the dead
and seating him at his right hand in the heavens,
far above every principality, authority, power, and dominion,
and every name that is named
not only in this age but also in the one to come.
And he put all things beneath his feet
and gave him as head over all things to the church,
which is his body,
the fullness of the one who fills all things in every way.

SEQUENCE

Veni, Sancte Spiritus

Come, Holy Spirit, come!
And from your celestial home
   Shed a ray of light divine!
Come, Father of the poor!
Come, source of all our store!
   Come, within our bosoms shine.
You, of comforters the best;
You, the soul's most welcome guest;
   Sweet refreshment here below;
In our labor, rest most sweet;
Grateful coolness in the heat;
   Solace in the midst of woe.
O most blessed Light divine,
Shine within these hearts of yours,
   And our inmost being fill!

Where you are not, we have naught,
Nothing good in deed or thought,
   Nothing free from taint of ill.
Heal our wounds, our strength renew;
On our dryness pour your dew;
   Wash the stains of guilt away:
Bend the stubborn heart and will;
Melt the frozen, warm the chill;
   Guide the steps that go astray.
On the faithful, who adore
And confess you, evermore
   In your sevenfold gift descend;
Give them virtue's sure reward;
Give them your salvation, Lord;
   Give them joys that never end. Amen.
   Alleluia.

The Solemnity of the Most Holy Body and Blood of Christ, *June 11, 2023*

OPTIONAL SEQUENCE

Lauda Sion

Laud, O Zion, your salvation,
Laud with hymns of exultation,
   Christ, your king and shepherd true:

Bring him all the praise you know,
He is more than you bestow.
   Never can you reach his due.

Special theme for glad thanksgiving
Is the quick'ning and the living
   Bread today before you set:

From his hands of old partaken,
As we know, by faith unshaken,
   Where the Twelve at supper met.

Full and clear ring out your chanting,
Joy nor sweetest grace be wanting,
   From your heart let praises burst:

For today the feast is holden,
When the institution olden
   Of that supper was rehearsed.

Here the new law's new oblation,
By the new king's revelation,
   Ends the form of ancient rite:

Now the new the old effaces,
Truth away the shadow chases,
   Light dispels the gloom of night.

What he did at supper seated,
Christ ordained to be repeated,
   His memorial ne'er to cease:

And his rule for guidance taking,
Bread and wine we hallow, making
   Thus our sacrifice of peace.

This the truth each Christian learns,
Bread into his flesh he turns,
   To his precious blood the wine:

Sight has fail'd, nor thought conceives,
But a dauntless faith believes,
   Resting on a pow'r divine.

Here beneath these signs are hidden
Priceless things to sense forbidden;
   Signs, not things are all we see:

Blood is poured and flesh is broken,
Yet in either wondrous token
   Christ entire we know to be.

Whoso of this food partakes,
Does not rend the Lord nor breaks;
   Christ is whole to all that taste:

Thousands are, as one, receivers,
One, as thousands of believers,
   Eats of him who cannot waste.

Bad and good the feast are sharing,
Of what divers dooms preparing,
   Endless death, or endless life.

Life to these, to those damnation,
See how like participation
   Is with unlike issues rife.

When the sacrament is broken,
Doubt not, but believe 'tis spoken,

That each sever'd outward token
   doth the very whole contain.

Nought the precious gift divides,
Breaking but the sign betides
   Jesus still the same abides,
   still unbroken does remain.

The shorter form of the sequence begins here.

Lo! the angel's food is given
To the pilgrim who has striven;
   See the children's bread from heaven,
   which on dogs may not be spent.

Truth the ancient types fulfilling,
Isaac bound, a victim willing,
   Paschal lamb, its lifeblood spilling,
   manna to the fathers sent.

Very bread, good shepherd, tend us,
Jesu, of your love befriend us,
   You refresh us, you defend us,
   Your eternal goodness send us
In the land of life to see.

You who all things can and know,
Who on earth such food bestow,
   Grant us with your saints, though lowest,
   Where the heav'nly feast you show,
Fellow heirs and guests to be. Amen. Alleluia.

FIRST READING
Deut 7:6-11

Moses said to the people:
"You are a people sacred to the Lord, your
God;
he has chosen you from all the nations on
the face of the earth
to be a people peculiarly his own.
It was not because you are the largest of all
nations
that the Lord set his heart on you and
chose you,
for you are really the smallest of all
nations.
It was because the Lord loved you
and because of his fidelity to the oath he
had sworn to your fathers,
that he brought you out with his strong
hand
from the place of slavery,
and ransomed you from the hand of
Pharaoh, king of Egypt.
Understand, then, that the Lord, your God, is
God indeed,
the faithful God who keeps his merciful
covenant
down to the thousandth generation
toward those who love him and keep his
commandments,
but who repays with destruction a person
who hates him;
he does not dally with such a one,
but makes them personally pay for it.
You shall therefore carefully observe the
commandments,
the statutes and the decrees that I enjoin on
you today."

RESPONSORIAL PSALM
Ps 103:1-2, 3-4, 6, 8, 10

R̂. (cf. 17) The Lord's kindness is everlasting
to those who fear him.

Bless the Lord, O my soul;
all my being, bless his holy name.
Bless the Lord, O my soul;
and forget not all his benefits.

R̂. The Lord's kindness is everlasting to those
who fear him.

He pardons all your iniquities,
heals all your ills.
He redeems your life from destruction,
crowns you with kindness and compassion.

R̂. The Lord's kindness is everlasting to those
who fear him.

Merciful and gracious is the Lord,
slow to anger and abounding in kindness.
Not according to our sins does he deal with us,
nor does he requite us according to our
crimes.

R̂. The Lord's kindness is everlasting to those
who fear him.

SECOND READING
1 John 4:7-16

Beloved, let us love one another,
because love is of God;
everyone who loves is begotten by God and
knows God.
Whoever is without love does not know God,
for God is love.
In this way the love of God was revealed to
us:
God sent his only Son into the world
so that we might have life through him.
In this is love:
not that we have loved God, but that he
loved us
and sent his Son as expiation for our sins.
Beloved, if God so loved us,
we also must love one another.
No one has ever seen God.
Yet, if we love one another, God remains in us,
and his love is brought to perfection in us.

This is how we know that we remain in him
and he in us,
that he has given us of his Spirit.
Moreover, we have seen and testify
that the Father sent his Son as savior of the
world.
Whoever acknowledges that Jesus is the Son
of God,
God remains in him and he in God.
We have come to know and to believe in the
love God has for us.

God is love, and whoever remains in love
remains in God and God in him.

Gospel (cont.)
Luke 1:57-66, 80; L587

He asked for a tablet and wrote, "John is his name,"
  and all were amazed.
Immediately his mouth was opened, his tongue freed,
  and he spoke blessing God.
Then fear came upon all their neighbors,
  and all these matters were discussed
  throughout the hill country of Judea.
All who heard these things took them to heart, saying,
  "What, then, will this child be?"
For surely the hand of the Lord was with him.

The child grew and became strong in spirit,
  and he was in the desert until the day
  of his manifestation to Israel.

FIRST READING
Isa 49:1-6

Hear me, O coastlands,
  listen, O distant peoples.
The LORD called me from birth,
  from my mother's womb he gave me my
    name.
He made of me a sharp-edged sword
  and concealed me in the shadow of his arm.
He made me a polished arrow,
  in his quiver he hid me.
You are my servant, he said to me,
  Israel, through whom I show my glory.

Though I thought I had toiled in vain,
  and for nothing, uselessly, spent my
    strength,
yet my reward is with the LORD,
  my recompense is with my God.
For now the LORD has spoken
  who formed me as his servant from the
    womb,
that Jacob may be brought back to him
  and Israel gathered to him;
and I am made glorious in the sight of the
    LORD,
  and my God is now my strength!
It is too little, he says, for you to be my
    servant,
  to raise up the tribes of Jacob,
  and restore the survivors of Israel;
I will make you a light to the nations,
  that my salvation may reach to the ends of
    the earth.

RESPONSORIAL PSALM
Ps 139:1b-3, 13-14ab, 14c-15

R̸. (14a) I praise you, for I am wonderfully
    made.

O LORD, you have probed me, you know me;
  you know when I sit and when I stand;
  you understand my thoughts from afar.
My journeys and my rest you scrutinize,
  with all my ways you are familiar.

R̸. I praise you, for I am wonderfully made.

Truly you have formed my inmost being;
  you knit me in my mother's womb.
I give you thanks that I am fearfully,
    wonderfully made;
  wonderful are your works.

R̸. I praise you, for I am wonderfully made.

My soul also you knew full well;
  nor was my frame unknown to you
When I was made in secret,
  when I was fashioned in the depths of the
    earth.

R̸. I praise you, for I am wonderfully made.

SECOND READING
Acts 13:22-26

In those days, Paul said:
"God raised up David as their king;
  of him God testified,
  I have found David, son of Jesse, a man
    after my own heart;
  he will carry out my every wish.
From this man's descendants God, according
    to his promise,
  has brought to Israel a savior, Jesus.
John heralded his coming by proclaiming a
    baptism of repentance
  to all the people of Israel;
  and as John was completing his course, he
    would say,
  'What do you suppose that I am? I am not
    he.
Behold, one is coming after me;
  I am not worthy to unfasten the sandals of
    his feet.'

"My brothers, sons of the family of Abraham,
  and those others among you who are God-
    fearing,
  to us this word of salvation has been sent."

Gospel (cont.)
Matt 16:13-19; L591

And so I say to you, you are Peter,
   and upon this rock I will build my Church,
   and the gates of the netherworld shall not prevail against it.
I will give you the keys to the Kingdom of heaven.
Whatever you bind on earth shall be bound in heaven;
   and whatever you loose on earth shall be loosed in heaven."

FIRST READING
Acts 12:1-11

In those days, King Herod laid hands upon
      some members of the Church to harm
      them.
He had James, the brother of John, killed by
      the sword,
   and when he saw that this was pleasing to
      the Jews
   he proceeded to arrest Peter also.
—It was the feast of Unleavened Bread.—
He had him taken into custody and put in
      prison
   under the guard of four squads of four
      soldiers each.
He intended to bring him before the people
      after Passover.
Peter thus was being kept in prison,
   but prayer by the Church was fervently
      being made
   to God on his behalf.

On the very night before Herod was to bring
      him to trial,
   Peter, secured by double chains,
   was sleeping between two soldiers,
   while outside the door guards kept watch
      on the prison.
Suddenly the angel of the Lord stood by him,
   and a light shone in the cell.
He tapped Peter on the side and awakened
      him, saying,
   "Get up quickly."
The chains fell from his wrists.
The angel said to him, "Put on your belt and
      your sandals."
He did so.
Then he said to him, "Put on your cloak and
      follow me."
So he followed him out,
   not realizing that what was happening
      through the angel was real;
   he thought he was seeing a vision.
They passed the first guard, then the second,
   and came to the iron gate leading out to the
      city,
   which opened for them by itself.

They emerged and made their way down an
      alley,
   and suddenly the angel left him.
Then Peter recovered his senses and said,
   "Now I know for certain
   that the Lord sent his angel
   and rescued me from the hand of Herod
   and from all that the Jewish people had
      been expecting."

RESPONSORIAL PSALM
Ps 34:2-3, 4-5, 6-7, 8-9

R̸. (8) The angel of the Lord will rescue those
      who fear him.

I will bless the LORD at all times;
   his praise shall be ever in my mouth.
Let my soul glory in the LORD;
   the lowly will hear me and be glad.

R̸. The angel of the Lord will rescue those
      who fear him.

Glorify the LORD with me,
   let us together extol his name.
I sought the LORD, and he answered me
   and delivered me from all my fears.

R̸. The angel of the Lord will rescue those
      who fear him.

Look to him that you may be radiant with joy,
   and your faces may not blush with shame.
When the poor one called out, the LORD heard,
   and from all his distress he saved him.

R̸. The angel of the Lord will rescue those
      who fear him.

The angel of the LORD encamps
   around those who fear him, and delivers
      them.
Taste and see how good the LORD is;
   blessed the man who takes refuge in him.

R̸. The angel of the Lord will rescue those
      who fear him.

SECOND READING
2 Tim 4:6-8, 17-18

I, Paul, am already being poured out like a
      libation,
   and the time of my departure is at hand.
I have competed well; I have finished the race;
   I have kept the faith.
From now on the crown of righteousness
      awaits me,
   which the Lord, the just judge,
   will award to me on that day, and not only
      to me,
   but to all who have longed for his
      appearance.

The Lord stood by me and gave me strength,
   so that through me the proclamation might
      be completed
   and all the Gentiles might hear it.
And I was rescued from the lion's mouth.
The Lord will rescue me from every evil threat
   and will bring me safe to his heavenly
      Kingdom.
To him be glory forever and ever. Amen.

Gospel (cont.)

Matt 13:1-23; L103A

This is why I speak to them in parables, because
they look but do not see and hear but do not listen or understand.

Isaiah's prophecy is fulfilled in them, which says:
You shall indeed hear but not understand,
you shall indeed look but never see.
Gross is the heart of this people,
they will hardly hear with their ears,
they have closed their eyes,
lest they see with their eyes
and hear with their ears
and understand with their hearts and be converted,
and I heal them.

"But blessed are your eyes, because they see,
and your ears, because they hear.
Amen, I say to you, many prophets and righteous people
longed to see what you see but did not see it,
and to hear what you hear but did not hear it.

"Hear then the parable of the sower.
The seed sown on the path is the one
who hears the word of the kingdom without understanding it,
and the evil one comes and steals away
what was sown in his heart.
The seed sown on rocky ground
is the one who hears the word and receives it at once with joy.
But he has no root and lasts only for a time.

When some tribulation or persecution comes because of the word,
he immediately falls away.
The seed sown among thorns is the one who hears the word,
but then worldly anxiety and the lure of riches choke the word
and it bears no fruit.
But the seed sown on rich soil
is the one who hears the word and understands it,
who indeed bears fruit and yields a hundred or sixty or thirtyfold."

or Matt 13:1-9

On that day, Jesus went out of the house and sat down by the sea.
Such large crowds gathered around him
that he got into a boat and sat down,
and the whole crowd stood along the shore.
And he spoke to them at length in parables, saying:
"A sower went out to sow.
And as he sowed, some seed fell on the path,
and birds came and ate it up.
Some fell on rocky ground, where it had little soil.
It sprang up at once because the soil was not deep,
and when the sun rose it was scorched,
and it withered for lack of roots.
Some seed fell among thorns, and the thorns grew up and choked it.
But some seed fell on rich soil, and produced fruit,
a hundred or sixty or thirtyfold.
Whoever has ears ought to hear."

Gospel (cont.)
Matt 13:24-43; L106A

It becomes a large bush,
　and the 'birds of the sky come and dwell in its branches.'"

He spoke to them another parable.
"The kingdom of heaven is like yeast
　that a woman took and mixed with three measures of wheat flour
　until the whole batch was leavened."

All these things Jesus spoke to the crowds in parables.
He spoke to them only in parables,
　to fulfill what had been said through the prophet:
　　I will open my mouth in parables,
　　　I will announce what has lain hidden from the foundation
　　　　of the world.

Then, dismissing the crowds, he went into the house.
His disciples approached him and said,
　"Explain to us the parable of the weeds in the field."
He said in reply, "He who sows good seed is the Son of Man,
　the field is the world, the good seed the children of the kingdom.
The weeds are the children of the evil one,
　and the enemy who sows them is the devil.
The harvest is the end of the age, and the harvesters are angels.
Just as weeds are collected and burned up with fire,
　so will it be at the end of the age.
The Son of Man will send his angels,
　and they will collect out of his kingdom
　all who cause others to sin and all evildoers.

They will throw them into the fiery furnace,
　where there will be wailing and grinding of teeth.
Then the righteous will shine like the sun
　in the kingdom of their Father.
Whoever has ears ought to hear."

or Matt 13:24-30

Jesus proposed another parable to the crowds, saying:
"The kingdom of heaven may be likened
　to a man who sowed good seed in his field.
While everyone was asleep his enemy came
　and sowed weeds all through the wheat, and then went off.
When the crop grew and bore fruit, the weeds appeared as well.
The slaves of the householder came to him and said,
　'Master, did you not sow good seed in your field?
Where have the weeds come from?'
He answered, 'An enemy has done this.'
His slaves said to him,
　'Do you want us to go and pull them up?'
He replied, 'No, if you pull up the weeds
　you might uproot the wheat along with them.
Let them grow together until harvest;
　then at harvest time I will say to the harvesters,
　"First collect the weeds and tie them in bundles for burning;
　but gather the wheat into my barn."'"

Gospel
Matt 13:44-46

Jesus said to his disciples:
　"The kingdom of heaven is like a treasure buried in a field,
　which a person finds and hides again,
　and out of joy goes and sells all that he has and buys that field.
Again, the kingdom of heaven is like a merchant
　searching for fine pearls.
When he finds a pearl of great price,
　he goes and sells all that he has and buys it."

Gospel (cont.)
Luke 1:39-56; L622

From this day all generations will call me
blessed:
 the Almighty has done great things for
 me,
 and holy is his Name.
 He has mercy on those who fear him
 in every generation.
He has shown the strength of his arm,
 and has scattered the proud in their
 conceit.
He has cast down the mighty from their
 thrones,
 and has lifted up the lowly.
He has filled the hungry with good things,
 and the rich he has sent away empty.
He has come to the help of his servant
 Israel
 for he has remembered his promise of
 mercy,
 the promise he made to our fathers,
 to Abraham and his children forever."

Mary remained with her about three months
and then returned to her home.

FIRST READING
Rev 11:19a; 12:1-6a, 10ab

God's temple in heaven was opened,
 and the ark of his covenant could be seen
 in the temple.

A great sign appeared in the sky, a woman
 clothed with the sun,
 with the moon under her feet,
 and on her head a crown of twelve stars.
She was with child and wailed aloud in pain
 as she labored to give birth.

Then another sign appeared in the sky;
 it was a huge red dragon, with seven heads
 and ten horns,
 and on its heads were seven diadems.
Its tail swept away a third of the stars in the
 sky
 and hurled them down to the earth.
Then the dragon stood before the woman
 about to give birth,
 to devour her child when she gave birth.
She gave birth to a son, a male child,
 destined to rule all the nations with an iron
 rod.
Her child was caught up to God and his
 throne.
The woman herself fled into the desert
 where she had a place prepared by God.

Then I heard a loud voice in heaven say:
 "Now have salvation and power come,
 and the Kingdom of our God
 and the authority of his Anointed One."

RESPONSORIAL PSALM
Ps 45:10, 11, 12, 16

R̸. (10bc) The queen stands at your right
 hand, arrayed in gold.

The queen takes her place at your right hand
 in gold of Ophir.

R̸. The queen stands at your right hand,
 arrayed in gold.

Hear, O daughter, and see; turn your ear,
 forget your people and your father's house.

R̸. The queen stands at your right hand,
 arrayed in gold.

So shall the king desire your beauty;
 for he is your lord.

R̸. The queen stands at your right hand,
 arrayed in gold.

They are borne in with gladness and joy;
 they enter the palace of the king.

R̸. The queen stands at your right hand,
 arrayed in gold.

SECOND READING
1 Cor 15:20-27

Brothers and sisters:
Christ has been raised from the dead,
 the firstfruits of those who have fallen asleep.
For since death came through man,
 the resurrection of the dead came also
 through man.
For just as in Adam all die,
 so too in Christ shall all be brought to life,
 but each one in proper order:
 Christ the firstfruits;
 then, at his coming, those who belong to
 Christ;
 then comes the end,
 when he hands over the Kingdom to his
 God and Father,
 when he has destroyed every sovereignty
 and every authority and power.
For he must reign until he has put all his
 enemies under his feet.
The last enemy to be destroyed is death,
 for "he subjected everything under his feet."

Gospel (cont.)
Matt 18:21-35; L130A

He seized him and started to choke him, demanding,
 'Pay back what you owe.'
Falling to his knees, his fellow servant begged him,
 'Be patient with me, and I will pay you back.'
But he refused.
Instead, he had the fellow servant put in prison
 until he paid back the debt.
Now when his fellow servants saw what had happened,
 they were deeply disturbed, and went to their master
 and reported the whole affair.

His master summoned him and said to him, 'You wicked servant!
I forgave you your entire debt because you begged me to.
Should you not have had pity on your fellow servant,
 as I had pity on you?'
Then in anger his master handed him over to the torturers
 until he should pay back the whole debt.
So will my heavenly Father do to you,
 unless each of you forgives your brother from your heart."

Twenty-Fifth Sunday in Ordinary Time,
September 24 2023

Gospel (cont.)
Matt 20:1-16a; L133A

And on receiving it they grumbled against the landowner, saying,
 'These last ones worked only one hour,
 and you have made them equal to us,
 who bore the day's burden and the heat.'
He said to one of them in reply,
 'My friend, I am not cheating you.
Did you not agree with me for the usual daily wage?
Take what is yours and go.
What if I wish to give this last one the same as you?
Or am I not free to do as I wish with my own money?
Are you envious because I am generous?'
Thus, the last will be first, and the first will be last."

Twenty-Sixth Sunday in Ordinary Time,
October 1 2023

SECOND READING
Phil 2:1-5

Brothers and sisters:
If there is any encouragement in Christ,
 any solace in love,
 any participation in the Spirit,
 any compassion and mercy,
 complete my joy by being of the same mind, with the same love,
 united in heart, thinking one thing.
Do nothing out of selfishness or out of vainglory;
 rather, humbly regard others as more important than yourselves,
 each looking out not for his own interests,
 but also for those of others.

Have in you the same attitude
 that is also in Christ Jesus.

Twenty-Seventh Sunday in Ordinary Time,
October 8, 2023

Gospel (cont.)
Matt 21:33-43; L139A

Jesus said to them, "Did you never read in the Scriptures:
 The stone that the builders rejected
  has become the cornerstone;
 by the Lord has this been done,
  and it is wonderful in our eyes?
Therefore, I say to you,
 the kingdom of God will be taken away from you
 and given to a people that will produce its fruit."

Gospel (cont.)
Matt 22:1-14; L142A

But when the king came in to meet the guests,
   he saw a man there not dressed in a wedding garment.
The king said to him, 'My friend, how is it
   that you came in here without a wedding garment?'
But he was reduced to silence.
Then the king said to his attendants, 'Bind his hands and feet,
   and cast him into the darkness outside,
   where there will be wailing and grinding of teeth.'
Many are invited, but few are chosen."

or Matt 22:1-10

Jesus again in reply spoke to the chief priests and elders of the people
   in parables, saying,
   "The kingdom of heaven may be likened to a king
   who gave a wedding feast for his son.
He dispatched his servants
to summon the invited guests to the feast,
   but they refused to come.
A second time he sent other servants, saying,
   'Tell those invited: "Behold, I have prepared my banquet,
   my calves and fattened cattle are killed,
   and everything is ready; come to the feast."'
Some ignored the invitation and went away,
   one to his farm, another to his business.
The rest laid hold of his servants,
   mistreated them, and killed them.
The king was enraged and sent his troops,
   destroyed those murderers, and burned their city.
Then he said to his servants, 'The feast is ready,
   but those who were invited were not worthy to come.
Go out, therefore, into the main roads
   and invite to the feast whomever you find.'
The servants went out into the streets
   and gathered all they found, bad and good alike,
   and the hall was filled with guests."

All Saints, *November 1, 2023*

FIRST READING
Rev 7:2-4, 9-14

I, John, saw another angel come up from the East,
   holding the seal of the living God.
He cried out in a loud voice to the four angels
   who were given power to damage the land and the sea,
   "Do not damage the land or the sea or the trees
   until we put the seal on the foreheads of the servants of our God."
I heard the number of those who had been marked with the seal,
   one hundred and forty-four thousand marked
   from every tribe of the children of Israel.

After this I had a vision of a great multitude,
   which no one could count,
   from every nation, race, people, and tongue.
They stood before the throne and before the Lamb,
   wearing white robes and holding palm branches in their hands.
They cried out in a loud voice:

   "Salvation comes from our God,
   who is seated on the throne,
   and from the Lamb."

All the angels stood around the throne
   and around the elders and the four living creatures.
They prostrated themselves before the throne,
   worshiped God, and exclaimed:

   "Amen. Blessing and glory, wisdom and thanksgiving,
   honor, power, and might
   be to our God forever and ever. Amen."

Then one of the elders spoke up and said to me,
   "Who are these wearing white robes, and where did they come from?"
I said to him, "My lord, you are the one who knows."
He said to me,
   "These are the ones who have survived the time of great distress;
   they have washed their robes
   and made them white in the Blood of the Lamb."

RESPONSORIAL PSALM
Ps 24:1bc-2, 3-4ab, 5-6

℟. (cf. 6) Lord, this is the people that longs to see your face.

The Lord's are the earth and its fullness;
   the world and those who dwell in it.
For he founded it upon the seas
   and established it upon the rivers.

℟. Lord, this is the people that longs to see your face.

Who can ascend the mountain of the Lord?
   or who may stand in his holy place?
One whose hands are sinless, whose heart is clean,
   who desires not what is vain.

℟. Lord, this is the people that longs to see your face.

He shall receive a blessing from the Lord,
   a reward from God his savior.
Such is the race that seeks him,
   that seeks the face of the God of Jacob.

℟. Lord, this is the people that longs to see your face.

SECOND READING
1 John 3:1-3

Beloved:
See what love the Father has bestowed on us
   that we may be called the children of God.
Yet so we are.
The reason the world does not know us
   is that it did not know him.
Beloved, we are God's children now;
   what we shall be has not yet been revealed.
We do know that when it is revealed we shall be like him,
   for we shall see him as he is.
Everyone who has this hope based on him
   makes himself pure,
   as he is pure.

All Souls, *November 2, 2023*

FIRST READING

Dan 12:1-3; L1011.7

In those days, I, Daniel, mourned
 and heard this word of the Lord:
At that time there shall arise
 Michael, the great prince,
 guardian of your people;
It shall be a time unsurpassed in distress
 since nations began until that time.
At that time your people shall escape,
 everyone who is found written in the book.

Many of those who sleep in the dust of the
 earth shall awake;
Some shall live forever,
 others shall be an everlasting horror and
 disgrace.
But the wise shall shine brightly
 like the splendor of the firmament,
And those who lead the many to justice
 shall be like the stars forever.

RESPONSORIAL PSALM

Ps 27:1, 4, 7, and 8b, and 9a, 13-14; L1013.3

R̶7. (1a) The Lord is my light and my salvation.
 or:
R̶7. (13) I believe that I shall see the good things
 of the Lord in the land of the living.

The LORD is my light and my salvation;
 whom should I fear?
The LORD is my life's refuge;
 of whom should I be afraid?

R̶7. The Lord is my light and my salvation.
 or:
R̶7. I believe that I shall see the good things of
 the Lord in the land of the living.

One thing I ask of the LORD;
 this I seek:
To dwell in the house of the LORD
 all the days of my life,
That I may gaze on the loveliness of the LORD
 and contemplate his temple.

R̶7. The Lord is my light and my salvation.
 or:
R̶7. I believe that I shall see the good things of
 the Lord in the land of the living.

Hear, O LORD, the sound of my call;
 have pity on me and answer me.
Your presence, O LORD, I seek.
 Hide not your face from me.

R̶7. The Lord is my light and my salvation.
 or:
R̶7. I believe that I shall see the good things of
 the Lord in the land of the living.

I believe that I shall see the bounty of the
 LORD
 in the land of the living.
Wait for the LORD with courage;
 be stouthearted, and wait for the LORD.

R̶7. The Lord is my light and my salvation.
 or:
R̶7. I believe that I shall see the good things of
 the Lord in the land of the living.

SECOND READING

Rom 6:3-9; L1014.3

Brothers and sisters:
Are you unaware that we who were baptized
 into Christ Jesus
 were baptized into his death?
We were indeed buried with him through
 baptism into death,
 so that, just as Christ was raised from the
 dead
 by the glory of the Father,
 we too might live in newness of life.

For if we have grown into union with him
 through a death like his,
 we shall also be united with him in the
 resurrection.
We know that our old self was crucified with
 him,
 so that our sinful body might be done away
 with,
 that we might no longer be in slavery to sin.
For a dead person has been absolved from sin.
If, then, we have died with Christ,
 we believe that we shall also live with him.
We know that Christ, raised from the dead,
 dies no more;
 death no longer has power over him.

Thirty-Second Sunday in Ordinary Time, *November 12, 2023*

SECOND READING

1 Thess 4:13-14

We do not want you to be unaware, brothers and sisters,
 about those who have fallen asleep,
 so that you may not grieve like the rest, who have no hope.
For if we believe that Jesus died and rose,
 so too will God, through Jesus,
 bring with him those who have fallen asleep.

Thirty-Third Sunday in Ordinary Time, *November 19, 2023*

Gospel (cont.)
Matt 25:14-30; L157A

Since you were faithful in small matters,
    I will give you great responsibilities.
Come, share your master's joy.'
Then the one who had received the one talent came forward and said,
    'Master, I knew you were a demanding person,
    harvesting where you did not plant
    and gathering where you did not scatter;
    so out of fear I went off and buried your talent in the ground.
Here it is back.'
His master said to him in reply, 'You wicked, lazy servant!
So you knew that I harvest where I did not plant
    and gather where I did not scatter?
Should you not then have put my money in the bank
    so that I could have got it back with interest on my return?
Now then! Take the talent from him and give it to the one with ten.
For to everyone who has,
    more will be given and he will grow rich;
    but from the one who has not,
    even what he has will be taken away.
And throw this useless servant into the darkness outside,
    where there will be wailing and grinding of teeth.'"

or Matt 25:14-15, 19-21

Jesus told his disciples this parable:
    "A man going on a journey
    called in his servants and entrusted his possessions to them.
To one he gave five talents; to another, two; to a third, one—
    to each according to his ability.
Then he went away.

After a long time
    the master of those servants came back
    and settled accounts with them.
The one who had received five talents came forward
    bringing the additional five.
He said, 'Master, you gave me five talents.
See, I have made five more.'
His master said to him, 'Well done, my good and faithful servant.
Since you were faithful in small matters,
    I will give you great responsibilities.
Come, share your master's joy.'"

Our Lord Jesus Christ, King of the Universe, *November 26, 2023*

Gospel (cont.)
Matt 25:31-46; L160A

Then he will say to those on his left,
    'Depart from me, you accursed,
    into the eternal fire prepared for the devil and his angels.
For I was hungry and you gave me no food,
    I was thirsty and you gave me no drink,
    a stranger and you gave me no welcome,
    naked and you gave me no clothing,
    ill and in prison, and you did not care for me.'
Then they will answer and say,
    'Lord, when did we see you hungry or thirsty
    or a stranger or naked or ill or in prison,
    and not minister to your needs?'
He will answer them, 'Amen, I say to you,
    what you did not do for one of these least ones,
    you did not do for me.'
And these will go off to eternal punishment,
    but the righteous to eternal life."

Lectionary Pronunciation Guide

Lectionary Word	Pronunciation
Aaron	EHR-uhn
Abana	AB-uh-nuh
Abednego	uh-BEHD-nee-go
Abel-Keramin	AY-b'l-KEHR-uh-mihn
Abel-meholah	AY-b'l-mee-HO-lah
Abiathar	uh-BAI-uh-ther
Abiel	AY-bee-ehl
Abiezrite	ay-bai-EHZ-rait
Abijah	uh-BAI-juh
Abilene	ab-uh-LEE-neh
Abishai	uh-BIHSH-ay-ai
Abiud	uh-BAI-uhd
Abner	AHB-ner
Abraham	AY-bruh-ham
Abram	AY-br'm
Achaia	uh-KAY-yuh
Achim	AY-kihm
Aeneas	uh-NEE-uhs
Aenon	AY-nuhn
Agrippa	uh-GRIH-puh
Ahaz	AY-haz
Ahijah	uh-HAI-juh
Ai	AY-ee
Alexandria	al-ehg-ZAN-dree-uh
Alexandrian	al-ehg-ZAN-dree-uhn
Alpha	AHL-fuh
Alphaeus	AL-fee-uhs
Amalek	AM-uh-lehk
Amaziah	am-uh-ZAI-uh
Amminadab	ah-MIHN-uh-dab
Ammonites	AM-uh-naitz
Amorites	AM-uh-raits
Amos	AY-muhs
Amoz	AY-muhz
Ampliatus	am-plee-AY-tuhs
Ananias	an-uh-NAI-uhs
Andronicus	an-draw-NAI-kuhs
Annas	AN-uhs
Antioch	AN-tih-ahk
Antiochus	an-TAI-uh-kuhs
Aphiah	uh-FAI-uh
Apollos	uh-PAH-luhs
Appius	AP-ee-uhs
Aquila	uh-KWIHL-uh
Arabah	EHR-uh-buh
Aram	AY-ram
Arameans	ehr-uh-MEE-uhnz
Areopagus	ehr-ee-AH-puh-guhs
Arimathea	ehr-uh-muh-THEE-uh
Aroer	uh-RO-er

Lectionary Word	Pronunciation
Asaph	AY-saf
Asher	ASH-er
Ashpenaz	ASH-pee-naz
Assyria	a-SIHR-ee-uh
Astarte	as-TAHR-tee
Attalia	at-TAH-lee-uh
Augustus	uh-GUHS-tuhs
Azariah	az-uh-RAI-uh
Azor	AY-sawr
Azotus	uh-ZO-tus
Baal-shalishah	BAY-uhl-shuh-LAI-shuh
Baal-Zephon	BAY-uhl-ZEE-fuhn
Babel	BAY-bl
Babylon	BAB-ih-luhn
Babylonian	bab-ih-LO-nih-uhn
Balaam	BAY-lm
Barabbas	beh-REH-buhs
Barak	BEHR-ak
Barnabas	BAHR-nuh-buhs
Barsabbas	BAHR-suh-buhs
Bartholomew	bar-THAHL-uh-myoo
Bartimaeus	bar-tih-MEE-uhs
Baruch	BEHR-ook
Bashan	BAY-shan
Becorath	bee-KO-rath
Beelzebul	bee-EHL-zee-buhl
Beer-sheba	BEE-er-SHEE-buh
Belshazzar	behl-SHAZ-er
Benjamin	BEHN-juh-mihn
Beor	BEE-awr
Bethany	BEHTH-uh-nee
Bethel	BETH-el
Bethesda	beh-THEHZ-duh
Bethlehem	BEHTH-leh-hehm
Bethphage	BEHTH-fuh-jee
Bethsaida	behth-SAY-ih-duh
Beth-zur	behth-ZER
Bildad	BIHL-dad
Bithynia	bih-THIHN-ih-uh
Boanerges	bo-uh-NER-jeez
Boaz	BO-az
Caesar	SEE-zer
Caesarea	zeh-suh-REE-uh
Caiaphas	KAY-uh-fuhs
Cain	kayn
Cana	KAY-nuh
Canaan	KAY-nuhn
Canaanite	KAY-nuh-nait
Canaanites	KAY-nuh-naits

Lectionary Word	Pronunciation
Candace	kan-DAY-see
Capernaum	kuh-PERR-nay-uhm
Cappadocia	kap-ih-DO-shee-u
Carmel	KAHR-muhl
carnelians	kahr-NEEL-yuhnz
Cenchreae	SEHN-kree-ay
Cephas	SEE-fuhs
Chaldeans	kal-DEE-uhnz
Chemosh	KEE-mahsh
Cherubim	TSHEHR-oo-bihm
Chislev	KIHS-lehv
Chloe	KLO-ee
Chorazin	kor-AY-sihn
Cilicia	sih-LIHSH-ee-uh
Cleopas	KLEE-o-pas
Clopas	KLO-pas
Corinth	KAWR-ihnth
Corinthians	kawr-IHN-thee-uhnz
Cornelius	kawr-NEE-lee-uhs
Crete	kreet
Crispus	KRIHS-puhs
Cushite	CUHSH-ait
Cypriot	SIH-pree-at
Cyrene	sai-REE-nee
Cyreneans	sai-REE-nih-uhnz
Cyrenian	sai-REE-nih-uhn
Cyrenians	sai-REE-nih-uhnz
Cyrus	SAI-ruhs
Damaris	DAM-uh-rihs
Damascus	duh-MAS-kuhs
Danites	DAN-aits
Decapolis	duh-KAP-o-lis
Derbe	DER-bee
Deuteronomy	dyoo-ter-AH-num-mee
Didymus	DID-I-mus
Dionysius	dai-o-NIHSH-ih-uhs
Dioscuri	dai-O-sky-ri
Dorcas	DAWR-kuhs
Dothan	DO-thuhn
dromedaries	DRAH-muh-dher-eez
Ebed-melech	EE-behd-MEE-lehk
Eden	EE-dn
Edom	EE-duhm
Elamites	EE-luh-maitz
Eldad	EHL-dad
Eleazar	ehl-ee-AY-zer
Eli	EE-lai
Eli Eli Lema Sabachthani	AY-lee AY-lee luh-MAH sah-BAHK-tah-nee

Lectionary Word	Pronunciation	Lectionary Word	Pronunciation	Lectionary Word	Pronunciation
Eliab	ee-LAI-ab	Gilead	GIHL-ee-uhd	Joppa	JAH-puh
Eliakim	ee-LAI-uh-kihm	Gilgal	GIHL-gal	Joram	JO-ram
Eliezer	ehl-ih-EE-zer	Golgotha	GAHL-guh-thuh	Jordan	JAWR-dn
Elihu	ee-LAI-hyoo	Gomorrah	guh-MAWR-uh	Joseph	JO-zf
Elijah	ee-LAI-juh	Goshen	GO-shuhn	Joses	JO-seez
Elim	EE-lihm	Habakkuk	huh-BAK-uhk	Joshua	JAH-shou-ah
Elimelech	ee-LIHM-eh-lehk	Hadadrimmon	hay-dad-RIHM-uhn	Josiah	jo-SAI-uh
Elisha	ee-LAI-shuh	Hades	HAY-deez	Jotham	JO-thuhm
Eliud	ee-LAI-uhd	Hagar	HAH-gar	Judah	JOU-duh
Elizabeth	ee-LIHZ-uh-bth	Hananiah	han-uh-NAI-uh	Judas	JOU-duhs
Elkanah	el-KAY-nuh	Hannah	HAN-uh	Judea	jou-DEE-uh
Eloi Eloi Lama	AY-lo-ee AY-lo-ee	Haran	HAY-ruhn	Judean	jou-DEE-uhn
Sabechthani	LAH-mah sah-	Hebron	HEE-bruhn	Junia	jou-nih-uh
	BAHK-tah-nee	Hermes	HER-meez	Justus	JUHS-tuhs
Elymais	ehl-ih-MAY-ihs	Herod	HEHR-uhd	Kephas	KEF-uhs
Emmanuel	eh-MAN-yoo-ehl	Herodians	hehr-O-dee-uhnz	Kidron	KIHD-ruhn
Emmaus	eh-MAY-uhs	Herodias	hehr-O-dee-uhs	Kiriatharba	kihr-ee-ath-AHR-buh
Epaenetus	ee-PEE-nee-tuhs	Hezekiah	heh-zeh-KAI-uh	Kish	kihsh
Epaphras	EH-puh-fras	Hezron	HEHZ-ruhn	Laodicea	lay-o-dih-SEE-uh
ephah	EE-fuh	Hilkiah	hihl-KAI-uh	Lateran	LAT-er-uhn
Ephah	EE-fuh	Hittite	HIH-tait	Lazarus	LAZ-er-uhs
Ephesians	eh-FEE-zhuhnz	Hivites	HAI-vaitz	Leah	LEE-uh
Ephesus	EH-fuh-suhs	Hophni	HAHF-nai	Lebanon	LEH-buh-nuhn
Ephphatha	EHF-uh-thuh	Hor	HAWR	Levi	LEE-vai
Ephraim	EE-fray-ihm	Horeb	HAWR-ehb	Levite	LEE-vait
Ephrathah	EHF-ruh-thuh	Hosea	ho-ZEE-uh	Levites	LEE-vaits
Ephron	EE-frawn	Hur	her	Leviticus	leh-VIH-tih-kous
Epiphanes	eh-PIHF-uh-neez	hyssop	HIH-suhp	Lucius	LOO-shih-uhs
Erastus	ee-RAS-tuhs	Iconium	ai-KO-nih-uhm	Lud	luhd
Esau	EE-saw	Isaac	AI-zuhk	Luke	look
Esther	EHS-ter	Isaiah	ai-ZAY-uh	Luz	luhz
Ethanim	EHTH-uh-nihm	Iscariot	ihs-KEHR-ee-uht	Lycaonian	lihk-ay-O-nih-uhn
Ethiopian	ee-thee-O-pee-uhn	Ishmael	ISH-may-ehl	Lydda	LIH-duh
Euphrates	yoo-FRAY-teez	Ishmaelites	ISH-mayehl-aits	Lydia	LIH-dih-uh
Exodus	EHK-so-duhs	Israel	IHZ-ray-ehl	Lysanias	lai-SAY-nih-uhs
Ezekiel	eh-ZEE-kee-uhl	Ituraea	ih-TSHOOR-ree-uh	Lystra	LIHS-truh
Ezra	EHZ-ruh	Jaar	JAY-ahr	Maccabees	MAK-uh-beez
frankincense	FRANGK-ihn-sehns	Jabbok	JAB-uhk	Macedonia	mas-eh-DO-nih-uh
Gabbatha	GAB-uh-thuh	Jacob	JAY-kuhb	Macedonian	mas-eh-DO-nih-uhn
Gabriel	GAY-bree-ul	Jairus	J-hr-uhs	Machir	MAY-kihr
Gadarenes	GAD-uh-reenz	Javan	JAY-van	Machpelah	mak-PEE-luh
Galatian	guh-LAY-shih-uhn	Jebusites	JEHB-oo-zaits	Magdala	MAG-duh-luh
Galatians	guh-LAY-shih-uhnz	Jechoniah	jehk-o-NAI-uh	Magdalene	MAG-duh-lehn
Galilee	GAL-ih-lee	Jehoiakim	jee-HOI-uh-kihm	magi	MAY-jai
Gallio	GAL-ih-o	Jehoshaphat	jee-HAHSH-uh-fat	Malachi	MAL-uh-kai
Gamaliel	guh-MAY-lih-ehl	Jephthah	JEHF-thuh	Malchiah	mal-KAI-uh
Gaza	GAH-zuh	Jeremiah	jehr-eh-MAI-uh	Malchus	MAL-kuhz
Gehazi	gee-HAY-zai	Jericho	JEHR-ih-ko	Mamre	MAM-ree
Gehenna	geh-HEHN-uh	Jeroham	jehr-RO-ham	Manaen	MAN-uh-ehn
Genesis	JEHN-uh-sihs	Jerusalem	jeh-ROU-suh-lehm	Manasseh	man-AS-eh
Gennesaret	gehn-NEHS-uh-reht	Jesse	JEH-see	Manoah	muh-NO-uh
Gentiles	JEHN-tailz	Jethro	JEHTH-ro	Mark	mahrk
Gerasenes	JEHR-uh-seenz	Joakim	JO-uh-kihm	Mary	MEHR-ee
Gethsemane	gehth-SEHM-uh-ne	Job	JOB	Massah	MAH-suh
Gideon	GIHD-ee-uhn	Jonah	JO-nuh	Mattathias	mat-uh-THAI-uhs

Lectionary Word	Pronunciation	Lectionary Word	Pronunciation	Lectionary Word	Pronunciation
Matthan	MAT-than	Parmenas	PAHR-mee-nas	Sabbath	SAB-uhth
Matthew	MATH-yoo	Parthians	PAHR-thee-uhnz	Sadducees	SAD-joo-seez
Matthias	muh-THAI-uhs	Patmos	PAT-mos	Salem	SAY-lehm
Medad	MEE-dad	Peninnah	pee-NIHN-uh	Salim	SAY-lim
Mede	meed	Pentecost	PEHN-tee-kawst	Salmon	SAL-muhn
Medes	meedz	Penuel	pee-NYOO-ehl	Salome	suh-LO-mee
Megiddo	mee-GIH-do	Perez	PEE-rehz	Salu	SAYL-yoo
Melchizedek	mehl-KIHZ-eh-dehk	Perga	PER-guh	Samaria	suh-MEHR-ih-uh
Mene	MEE-nee	Perizzites	PEHR-ih-zaits	Samaritan	suh-MEHR-ih-tuhn
Meribah	MEHR-ih-bah	Persia	PER-zhuh	Samothrace	SAM-o-thrays
Meshach	MEE-shak	Peter	PEE-ter	Samson	SAM-s'n
Mespotamia	mehs-o-po-TAY-mih-uh	Phanuel	FAN-yoo-ehl	Samuel	SAM-yoo-uhl
		Pharaoh	FEHR-o	Sanhedrin	san-HEE-drihn
Micah	MAI-kuh	Pharisees	FEHR-ih-seez	Sarah	SEHR-uh
Midian	MIH-dih-uhn	Pharpar	FAHR-pahr	Sarai	SAY-rai
Milcom	MIHL-kahm	Philemon	fih-LEE-muhn	saraph	SAY-raf
Miletus	mai-LEE-tuhs	Philippi	fil-LIH-pai	Sardis	SAHR-dihs
Minnith	MIHN-ihth	Philippians	fih-LIHP-ih-uhnz	Saul	sawl
Mishael	MIHSH-ay-ehl	Philistines	fih-LIHS-tihnz	Scythian	SIH-thee-uihn
Mizpah	MIHZ-puh	Phinehas	FEHN-ee-uhs	Seba	SEE-buh
Moreh	MO-reh	Phoenicia	fee-NIHSH-ih-uh	Seth	sehth
Moriah	maw-RAI-uh	Phrygia	FRIH-jih-uh	Shaalim	SHAY-uh-lihm
Mosoch	MAH-sahk	Phrygian	FRIH-jih-uhn	Shadrach	SHAY-drak
myrrh	mer	phylacteries	fih-LAK-ter-eez	Shalishah	shuh-LEE-shuh
Mysia	MIH-shih-uh	Pi-Hahiroth	pai-huh-HAI-rahth	Shaphat	Shay-fat
Naaman	NAY-uh-muhn	Pilate	PAI-luht	Sharon	SHEHR-uhn
Nahshon	NAY-shuhn	Pisidia	pih-SIH-dih-uh	Shealtiel	shee-AL-tih-ehl
Naomi	NAY-o-mai	Pithom	PAI-thahm	Sheba	SHEE-buh
Naphtali	NAF-tuh-lai	Pontius	PAHN-shus	Shebna	SHEB-nuh
Nathan	NAY-thuhn	Pontus	PAHN-tus	Shechem	SHEE-kehm
Nathanael	nuh-THAN-ay-ehl	Praetorium	pray-TAWR-ih-uhm	shekel	SHEHK-uhl
Nazarene	NAZ-awr-een	Priscilla	PRIHS-kill-uh	Shiloh	SHAI-lo
Nazareth	NAZ-uh-rehth	Prochorus	PRAH-kaw-ruhs	Shinar	SHAI-nahr
nazirite	NAZ-uh-rait	Psalm	Sahm	Shittim	sheh-TEEM
Nazorean	naz-aw-REE-uhn	Put	puht	Shuhite	SHOO-ait
Neapolis	nee-AP-o-lihs	Puteoli	pyoo-TEE-o-lai	Shunammite	SHOO-nam-ait
Nebuchadnezzar	neh-byoo-kuhd-NEHZ-er	Qoheleth	ko-HEHL-ehth	Shunem	SHOO-nehm
		qorban	KAWR-bahn	Sidon	SAI-duhn
Negeb	NEH-gehb	Quartus	KWAR-tuhs	Silas	SAI-luhs
Nehemiah	nee-hee-MAI-uh	Quirinius	kwai-RIHN-ih-uhs	Siloam	sih-LO-uhm
Ner	ner	Raamses	ray-AM-seez	Silvanus	sihl-VAY-nuhs
Nicanor	nai-KAY-nawr	Rabbi	RAB-ai	Simeon	SIHM-ee-uhn
Nicodemus	nih-ko-DEE-muhs	Rabbouni	ra-BO-nai	Simon	SAI-muhn
Niger	NAI-jer	Rahab	RAY-hab	Sin (desert)	sihn
Nineveh	NIHN-eh-veh	Ram	ram	Sinai	SAI-nai
Noah	NO-uh	Ramah	RAY-muh	Sirach	SAI-rak
Nun	nuhn	Ramathaim	ray-muh-THAY-ihm	Sodom	SAH-duhm
Obed	O-behd	Raqa	RA-kuh	Solomon	SAH-lo-muhn
Olivet	AH-lih-veht	Rebekah	ree-BEHK-uh	Sosthenes	SAHS-thee-neez
Omega	o-MEE-guh	Rehoboam	ree-ho-BO-am	Stachys	STAY-kihs
Onesimus	o-NEH-sih-muhs	Rephidim	REHF-ih-dihm	Succoth	SUHK-ahth
Ophir	O-fer	Reuben	ROO-b'n	Sychar	SI-kar
Orpah	AWR-puh	Revelation	reh-veh-LAY-shuhn	Syene	sai-EE-nee
Pamphylia	pam-FIHL-ih-uh	Rhegium	REE-jee-uhm	Symeon	SIHM-ee-uhn
Paphos	PAY-fuhs	Rufus	ROO-fuhs	synagogues	SIHN-uh-gahgz

Lectionary Word	Pronunciation	Lectionary Word	Pronunciation	Lectionary Word	Pronunciation
Syrophoenician	SIHR-o fee-NIHSH-ih-uhn	Timon	TAI-muhn	Zebedee	ZEH-beh-dee
Tabitha	TAB-ih-thuh	Titus	TAI-tuhs	Zebulun	ZEH-byoo-luhn
Talitha koum	TAL-ih-thuh-KOOM	Tohu	TO-hyoo	Zechariah	zeh-kuh-RAI-uh
Tamar	TAY-mer	Trachonitis	trak-o-NAI-tis	Zedekiah	zeh-duh-KAI-uh
Tarshish	TAHR-shihsh	Troas	TRO-ahs	Zephaniah	zeh-fuh-NAI-uh
Tarsus	TAHR-suhs	Tubal	TYOO-b'l	Zerah	ZEE-ruh
Tekel	TEH-keel	Tyre	TAI-er	Zeror	ZEE-rawr
Terebinth	TEHR-ee-bihnth	Ur	er	Zerubbabel	zeh-RUH-buh-behl
Thaddeus	THAD-dee-uhs	Urbanus	er-BAY-nuhs	Zeus	zyoos
Theophilus	thee-AH-fih-luhs	Uriah	you-RAI-uh	Zimri	ZIHM-rai
Thessalonians	theh-suh-LO-nih-uhnz	Uzziah	yoo-ZAI-uh	Zion	ZAI-uhn
Theudas	THU-duhs	Wadi	WAH-dee	Ziph	zihf
Thyatira	thai-uh-TAI-ruh	Yahweh-yireh	YAH-weh-yer-AY	Zoar	ZO-er
Tiberias	tai-BIHR-ih-uhs	Zacchaeus	zak-KEE-uhs	Zorah	ZAWR-uh
Timaeus	tai-MEE-uhs	Zadok	ZAY-dahk	Zuphite	ZUHF-ait
		Zarephath	ZEHR-ee-fath		